The
HUMAN BRAIN

For Rebecca

The
HUMAN BRAIN
Essentials of Behavioral Neuroscience

Jackson Beatty

Sage Publications, Inc.
International Educational and Professional Publisher
Thousand Oaks ■ London ■ New Delhi

For information:

Sage Publications, Inc.
2455 Teller Road
Thousand Oaks, California 91320
E-mail: order@sagepub.com

Sage Publications Ltd.
6 Bonhill Street
London EC2A 4PU
United Kingdom

Sage Publications India Pvt. Ltd.
M-32 Market
Greater Kailash I
New Delhi 110 048 India

Printed in the United States of America

Library of Congress Cataloging-in-Publication Data

Beatty, Jackson.
  The human brain: Essentials of behavioral neuroscience / by Jackson Beatty.
    p. cm.
  Includes bibliographical references and index.
  ISBN 0-7619-2061-7 (cloth: alk. paper)
  1. Brain. 2. Neurophysiology. I. Title.
  [DNLM: 1. Brain-physiology. 2. Electrophysiology. 3. Nervous System Disorders.
4. Nervous System Physiology. WL 300 B369h 2000]
QP376.B42 2000
612.8'2—DC21   00-031080

This book is printed on acid-free paper.

03 04 05 06 7 6 5 4 3 2

Acquiring Editor:	Jim Brace-Thompson
Editorial Assistant:	Anna Howland
Production Editor:	Sanford Robinson
Art Coordinator:	MaryAnn Vail
Editorial Assistant:	Cindy Bear
Indexer:	Molly Hall
Cover Designer:	Michelle Lee

Contents

Preface

Brain research has progressed with dramatic speed in the past decade, fueled in part by powerful new methods developed by the physical sciences and information technology. More and more scientists are devoting their careers to the study of the brain, and more and more students are studying the brain at some point in their undergraduate education. *The Human Brain: Essentials of Behavioral Neuroscience* is designed to be be a clearly written, up-to-date, conceptually driven, and rigorous introduction to integrative human neuroscience that will be accessible to a wide and diverse audience.

Finding a proper textbook to teach students about the human brain is a difficult task because as knowledge about the brain has increased, neuroscience textbooks have grown to encyclopedic size. I have found that encyclopedic textbooks complicate both teaching and learning. By attempting to be widely inclusive, they lose a sense of focus. Instead of developing a carefully constructed argument that teaches students the principles by which the nervous system guides the life of an organism, encyclopedic texts treat many things too briefly to be either understood or appreciated.

The approach that I take in writing *The Human Brain: Essentials of Behavioral Neuroscience* comes directly from my experiences in teaching at UCLA. When I have taught my introductory psychobiology course using an "encyclopedic" introductory text, my students became frustrated. They know that far more material is being presented in the book than they could possibly be expected to learn in a single course. I know that they are being given more material than I would wish to give them, a necessary consequence of the "everything but the kitchen sink" school of textbook writing. Thus, my students' reading was driven by one concern: is this something that I need to learn, or is it something that I can skip over? This is a serious problem with a subject as complex as behavioral neuroscience and seems to me to be quite unnecessary. By trying to be too encyclopedic, my earlier book—like others in the field—ended up actually teaching much less to my students than if it had been smaller and more focused.

It is the purpose of *The Human Brain: Essentials of Behavioral Neuroscience* to provide a clearly focused, concise, and coherent introduction to the human brain from the perspective of contemporary integrative neuroscience. It derives from my previous book, *Principles of Behavioral Neuroscience* (Brown & Benchmark, 1995), but the content has been markedly changed. The focus has been narrowed and is truly concerned with the **essentials** of behavioral neuroscience. *The Human Brain: Essentials of Behavioral Neuroscience* is concerned with the functions of nerve cells that permit them to process information, the neurobiology of sensation and perception, movement and behavior, learning, motivation, sleep and waking, and disorders of the human brain. These are all essential issues in both contemporary systems neuroscience as well as the developing interdisciplinary field of cognitive neuroscience.

The Human Brain: Essentials of Behavioral Neuroscience is written in much the same way as I lecture, selecting the most important topics and presenting each in as clear and concise a manner as is possible. Students in my classes respond admirably to this approach, mastering complex concepts and ideas much more easily than if my lectures mirrored standard encyclopedic textbook presentations. Thus, *The Human Brain* is designed to be a *core textbook* of human integrative neuroscience, presenting a carefully selected set of fundamental facts, concepts, and theories with clarity and focus.

Thus, the book would work well as a primary text in lower division undergraduate courses serving a general education requirement, in upper division psychobiology or behavioral neuroscience courses, or in graduate-level courses in need of a core textbook in integrative neuroscience. Of course, in each of these cases the book could (and probably would) be supplemented with additional readings appropriate to the level of the course and the specific interests of the instructor. *The Human Brain* can work at any of these levels because all of these students require a readable, academically sound, first introduction to integrative human neuroscience. I honestly believe that there are certain books—and I hope that *The Human Brain: Essentials of Behavioral Neuroscience* is among them—that can be read with profit by undergraduates and graduate students alike.

However, the book that you have in your hands was written to be more than just a textbook. Individual readers can read and enjoy *The Human Brain: Essentials of Behavioral Neuroscience*, since there is nothing inherently "textbooklike" about this textbook. Because this book is written simply and directly, without any expectation of particular prior knowledge on the part of the reader, it is suitable for individual readers wanting an introduction to the rapidly growing—and frequently news making—field of integrative human neuroscience.

Acknowledgments   There are many people who deserve credit for making this book the beautiful work that it is. First and foremost is Jim Brace-Thompson, Senior Editor at Sage Publications, who had the vision of making this book the cornerstone of his new series of neuroscience textbooks. Anna Howland, Jim's editorial assistant, made sure that everything happened when it needed to and that all the pieces of this project came together on schedule. Sanford Robinson, our production editor, guided this LaTeX typographic project from a prototype on my computer to the finished book that you hold in your hands. This transition from proto-book to real book was accomplished by many people, including Gillian Dickens (copy editing), John Rukkila (proofreading), and Molly Hall (indexing).

Profound thanks are also due to Laura Freberg, who did a magnificent job in constructing a thoughtful and extensive set of test questions that are available to instructors who use my text in their courses.

And finally, there is the art. Barry Burns's insightful anatomical drawings illustrate the human brain and its functions in a way that is truly remarkable. Barry's drawings go to the heart of the concept and make important ideas in behavioral neuroscience easy to understand. Working with Barry—who is both an artist as well as a medical illustrator—has been a true pleasure.

Barry's anatomical drawings are complemented by the fine draftsmanship of Nick Alexander, who created all of the line drawings, charts, and graphs that fill this book. Nick is a talented and gifted young man who is just beginning his career in computer-based graphic arts.

Pulling all the art together to form an integrated and beautiful book was the result of the extraordinary efforts of our gifted and dedicated Art Director, Mary Ann Vail. Many thanks to Barry, Nick, and Mary Ann for creating all the truly magnificent graphics that help make the human brain more comprehensible.

This book was written, edited, and typeset using only open source software. Thanks in particular to all those in the LaTeX and Linux communities who have provided these wonderful tools.

In closing, I would like to thank the reviewers of this book, whose insights helped guide this book in reaching its final form. Thanks to Robert B. Castleberry (University of South Carolina at Sumter), Laura Freberg (California Polytechnic State University), Jon H. Kaas (Vanderbilt University), and Jim Murphy (Purdue School of Science and Indiana University School of Medicine). Your comments were invaluable in making this book work.

Jackson Beatty
Los Angeles

Chapter 1

The Human Brain

The human brain is a complexly organized structure that occupies a volume of about 1,350 cubic centimeters and contains about 100 billion nerve cells, which are called **neurons**. Although 100 billion is an almost unimaginably large number, the estimated number of connections between nerve cells is very much larger: There are from 10 trillion to 100 trillion points of cellular contact or synapses within the human nervous system.

As you might expect, understanding an organ as complex as the brain presents many formidable problems. Nonetheless, brain researchers have learned a great deal in recent years, greatly expanding our understanding of the biological basis of human perception, thought, and action. This book is about what we know about the workings of the neurons of our brains.

1

THINKING ABOUT MIND AND BRAIN

The fascination that the human brain holds is not simply that it is large or complicated or that it is intricately and elegantly organized. Its mystery lies in the fact that it controls our behavior, feelings, and thought. In a very real sense, our brains contain the secrets of our selves. Within this complex organ, the ultimate explanation of both mental life and behavior must be sought. This view reflects the philosophical belief of most, but not all, contemporary brain scientists. The essence of the concept—known as the **psychoneural identity hypothesis**—is that mental and brain processes are one and the same. Thus, the mental events that each of us experiences and each of us believes to be very real are processes of a physical functioning brain. Without a brain, in this view, there can be no mind.

However, scholars have wrestled with the problem of the relation between mind and body since the beginnings of recorded history. Theories of mind and brain can become complicated matters for professional philosophers but are seemingly much simpler to many working neuroscientists. This **mind-brain problem** is considered to be a *philosophical* question because something about it seems problematic and—by and large—the problem arises from the decidedly nonphysical feeling of human conscious experience, although philosophers recognize a number of other equally thorny aspects to the mind-brain problem (Crane, 1999).

Over the years, many theories as to the relation between the brain and the mind have been proposed. Some have heavily influenced philosophical, scientific, and religious thought; others have been mere curiosities in the history of the problem. But despite the diversity of these philosophical theories, most may be classified into three categories: dualisms, pluralisms, and monisms.

Dualisms are theories in which mind and brain are treated as separate and distinct entities. Many different types of dualisms have been suggested over the centuries. Plato's writings provide an ancient example of dualistic philosophy; classical theology presents another, more familiar, example.

Among scientific philosophers, René Descartes's 17th-century formulation of the mind-brain problem is perhaps most well known (Descartes, 1835). Descartes argued that two types of substances must exist: physical substances, like that of the brain, which obey the ordinary laws of nature, and mental substances, like that of the soul, which do not obey natural laws. Decartes's argument was rooted in the belief that the soul is eternal and possesses free will. Thus, the soul could not be material because it both is immortal (because it is eternal) and immune from natural laws (because free will, by definition, cannot be deterministically predicted).

Dualistic theories argue that although mind and brain may interact in some way, neither is reducible to the other. In these theories, mind and brain are fundamentally different.

Pluralisms are theories in which more than two separate and distinct realities are proposed. One recent example of a pluralistic resolution of the mind-brain problem is the three-world theory proposed by John Eccles, a Nobel Prize-winning neurophysiologist, and Karl Popper, a distinguished modern philosopher. They propose that in addition to the subjective world of the mind and the physical world of the brain, there is a third world of objective scientific knowledge. However, this pluralistic proposition has not been widely accepted.

Monisms, in contrast, assert that mind and brain are really the same thing. The psychoneural identity hypothesis is a modern example of a monistic philosophy, which proposes that psychological processes can ultimately be explained in terms of underlying neural events. Today, nearly all brain scientists accept this monistic view as both a philosophical basis for their scientific work and a personal view of the world.

Finally, some philosophers deal with the mind-brain problem by avoiding it. They argue, in one way or another, that the question of the relationship between mental and physical events is a "bad" or poorly formed question. Ludwig Wittgenstein and Bertrand Russell are two influential early 20th-century philosophers who argued that the mind-brain problem should be dismissed rather than resolved. This argument is rarely accepted by scientists who study the brain.

REDUCTIONISM AND SCIENCE

In attempting to understand behavior, all brain science is reductionistic. **Reductionism** is the attempt to explain a phenomenon in terms of the simpler, underlying mechanisms that produce it. To a brain scientist, no attempt to understand the biological basis of behavior is satisfactory unless the neural determinants of that behavior can be specified.

Although it is sometimes argued that reductionism in some way deprives us of our humanness by offering seemingly mechanical explanations of the human brain and human behavior, most scientists think otherwise. In the words of the noted British zoologist J. Z. Young,

> Reductionism provides information about the sources of one's experienced life which could not be known only by introspection. It helps to provide a rational answer to the question: what am I? It tells me how I have come to my present state and...adds greatly to [the] understanding of our possibilities and limitations and hence ability to conduct ourselves wisely, and especially with the fullest respect for other human beings, and indeed for all life.
>
> Reductionism is not only the foundation of biological science, but it also provides us as individuals with a clearer understanding of the mechanisms that govern the world around us, an understanding that is essential to the reasoned conduct of human life. (Young, 1987, p. 215.)

THE ASCENT OF NATURAL SCIENCE

Contemporary **behavioral neuroscience** has roots not only in philosophical reasoning but also in the empirical study of biological and natural phenomena. At the end of the Middle Ages, it was the church that held sway in European thought. Led by its teachings, people viewed life on earth as part of a divine design, with the various well-adapted species of plants and animals individually and elegantly designed by the Creator to fulfill their special roles.

But this conception of earth as a menagerie of divine creations was soon to be seriously challenged. That challenge came not from philosophy but from careful observation of plants, animals, and the geology of the planet itself. Theology was about to give way to observation and reason as the dominant mode of understanding the natural world. The tradition of empiricism, begun in the Renaissance, would soon grow to forever dominate Western thought with the creation of Western science.

Evolutionary Theory

It was Charles Darwin and his 1859 book, *The Origin of Species by Means of Natural Selection, or the Preservation of Favoured Races in the Struggle for Life*, that transformed 19th-century natural science and ushered in 20th-century biology (see Figure 1.1 on the facing page). But it was not Darwin's invention of a theory of evolution itself that was his greatest contribution. Related theories had been suggested previously. Rather, it was Darwin's careful and detailed scientific observations supporting his ideas that made public acceptance of his evolutionary theory inevitable.

Darwin's theory proposed that natural selection molds the evolution of the earth's species, with changes in the environment forcing new adaptations. Thus, evolution brought about both the extinction of old species and the creation of new life forms. This theory rested on a number of new ideas that had been recently introduced to natural science. Particularly important were the modern concepts of species, the vastness of both geological change and geological time, and the nature of population explosions (Hellemans & Bunch, 1988).

In the 17th century, John Ray of Cambridge published his highly regarded *Catalogue of Cambridge Plants*, which contained descriptions of hundreds of diverse plant species found in the local countryside. Ray identified species based on empirical, firsthand knowledge, as opposed to *a priore* or logical classification schemes. Today, Ray's work is considered to be an important first step in the birth of quantitative empirical biology.

Nearly a hundred years later, Carl Linnaeus, in his 1735 treatise *System of Nature*, provided a much larger empirical classification of both plant and animal species. He defined animal species by analyses of both their specific bodily structures and their "natural habits" or behavior. Linnaeus's systematic work forms the basis of our modern classification system for the plant and animal kingdoms. During this same period, natural scientists began to appreciate the wide diversity of characteristics both between different species as well as among members of the same species.

Also in the 18th century, George Leclerc, the Comte de Buffon and the keeper of the King's Garden in Paris, introduced the idea that individual species are defined by reproductive limits. He proposed the modern concept of a species as a set of individuals that can breed freely only with themselves and not with members of other species.

Behavior was becoming increasingly important in biological thought. Scientists such as Baron Georges Cuvier, in his *Leçons d'Anatomie Comparee* (1805), emphasized that anatomists must concern themselves with the functions of bodily parts, as well as their structure, if the relationships between species are to be understood.

Figure 1.1. Charles Darwin. Darwin's clear thinking and careful analysis of naturalistic observations gave force to his arguments that the creation and extinction of species are determined by natural selection pressures operating on populations of genetically diverse organisms. His book, *The Origin of Species* (1859), transformed biology, not only in describing the evolutionary mechanisms of speciation but also by emphasizing the importance of understanding the functions of biological systems. Contemporary behavioral neuroscience retains the functional emphasis of Darwinian evolutionary theory. (Portrait courtesy of the History and Special Collections Division of the Louise M. Darling Biomedical Library, UCLA.)

Finally, geology was teaching the naturalists both that the world was very old and that it had been inhabited by strange plants and animals that no longer exist. The discovery of the fossil record with abundant examples of extinct petrified life forms provided clear evidence that living species are not eternal but rather have changed over time. Furthermore, the discovery of the vastness of geological time—in which one-time mountains had become ocean beds and ocean beds became mountains—provided an appropriate time scale over which evolutionary principles could operate. Both of these intellectual prerequisites for evolutionary theory were provided by the new geologists of the late 18th and early 19th centuries, most notably Charles Lyell, whose *Principles of Geology* was first published in

1830. Lyell later became both a personal friend and a scientific defender of Darwin.

This was the scientific context within which Charles Darwin formulated his theory of evolution. He understood that the change evident in the newly discovered geological record must have resulted in dramatic alterations in the habitats of living creatures. He also knew that each species of animal displayed a wide range of diverse characteristics. It was not hard to imagine that some members of a species would be better adapted to changes in their particular habitat than would others and therefore would be more likely to survive and prosper. As an animal breeder, Darwin understood that systematic selection in mating can produce dramatic transformations in the offspring. But was all this enough to explain the extinction and transformation of species?

Darwin believed that evolution could change species, but what force would drive the evolutionary process itself? The answer came to him not from observations of plants and animals but rather from economic theory. He first read Thomas Malthus's 1826 thesis, *An Essay on the Principle of Population*, in September 1838 (Young, 1992). In that work, Malthus showed that the human population, if unchecked, would double every 25 years, whereas the resources on which human life depends—food, shelter, and so on—could not increase nearly so rapidly. Malthus argued that human or animal populations increase geometrically with time, except as limited by the resources of the environment, which—at best—only grow arithmetically.

Thus, Darwin reasoned that population pressure, coupled with limited supplies of life-sustaining resources, demanded that evolutionary competition must be the shaper of species. Slight advantages in the genetic makeup of some individuals in a species must make enormous differences in determining which individuals will prosper and reproduce and which will not. Population pressure provided the mainspring of power for Darwin's evolutionary machine.

Darwin was right. His ideas rapidly took hold. The ample documentation he provided quickly separated his theory of evolution from other possible hypotheses. Within a decade, Darwin's argument prevailed.

Confirming empirical findings continued to appear. Intermediary life forms with characteristics between those of known species were discovered in the fossil record. Mendel's theory of genetic inheritance provided additional support for the new evolutionary hypothesis. Chromosomes were discovered to be the carriers of genetic information. DNA was established as the carrier molecule. Embryological data revealed homologous structures that support the idea of a common ancestry for extraordinarily diverse modern species. These findings fitted naturally with Darwin's original conception. His theory of evolution has provided a conceptual framework that explains a vast number of facts about life and its history on this planet (Young, 1992).

Today, to say that the theory of evolution is only one theory is of course correct, but it is a theory with such widespread empirically established ramifications and such powerful explanatory power that it truly must be considered to be a natural law of biology. Remember, not all theories are equally well supported or useful.

Empiricism and Functionalism

The theory of evolution produced widespread changes in all of biology and—quite naturally—shaped the subsequent study of brain and behavior. Evolutionary theory created a new scholarly atmosphere within biology stressing **empiricism**, that is, relying on direct observation rather than logical deduction from presumed first principles. Of course, the idea of empiricism transcends evolutionary theory and lies at the base of all modern science.

Furthermore, with humans linked by evolution to other species, questions of *comparative anatomy* and *comparative behavior* gained new and compelling interest. Animal behavior and the brain mechanisms that produce it suddenly acquired a new relevance for understanding the human brain and our own behaviors.

Perhaps as important, evolutionary theory placed questions of behavioral adaptation at the forefront of natural science. It was, after all, the *behavior* of organisms that determined the course of evolution. Thus, the *functions* of behavior became a dominant focus of empirical study. Today, **functionalism**, which—in its broadest sense—is the concern with the activity of an organism in its interactions with its environment, lies at the heart of both psychology and neuroscience more generally.

LEVELS OF ANALYSIS

A biological explanation of behavior requires that the observations made in a psychological laboratory be related to those obtained by other biological sciences. Thus, multiple levels of analysis are required. A successful theory must explain not only what the organism, human or not, is doing but also how that behavior is neurally generated.

This approach was central to the thinking of the early integrative physiologists such as Sir Charles Sherrington, who was awarded a Nobel Prize in 1932 for his research on the function of nerve cells. Sherrington and other early experimental physiologists were concerned about understanding not only the nature of neural connections but also the behavioral functions that they serve. He was well acquainted with the ongoing revolution that evolutionary theory was producing in biology. In fact, his mother had sent him off on summer vacation in 1872 with a copy of the latest edition of Charles Darwin's *The Origin of the Species* to read in his spare time, telling him that Darwin's book "sets the door of the universe ajar" (Young, 1992, p. 138).

In his long and distinguished career, Charles Sherrington carried out an extraordinarily complex and successful program of research examining in detail the neural mechanisms that govern animal behavior. He argued that this research must be carried out at three different levels: at the cellular level, at the level of intercellular communication, and at the integrative or behavioral level. His own words were clear:

> Nerve-cells, like all other cells, lead individual lives—they breathe, they assimilate, they dispense their own stores of energy, they repair their own substantial waste; each is, in short, a living unit, with its nutrition more or less centered in itself.... Secondly, nervous cells

present a feature so characteristically developed in them as to be specially theirs. They have in exceptional measure the power to spatially
transmit (conduct) states of excitement (nerve-impulses) generated
within them.... This field of study may be termed that of nerve-cell
conduction. (Sherrington, 1906, p. 2)

Perhaps most important, Sherrington conceived of the issue of neural
integration in strikingly modern terms:

In the multicellular animal, especially for those higher reactions which
constitute its behavior..., it is nervous reaction which par excellence
integrates it, welds it together from its components, and constitutes it
from a mere collection of organs an animal individual. This integrative action in virtue of which the nervous system unifies from separate
organs an animal possessing solidarity, and individual is the problem
before us.... Though much in need of data derived from the two previously mentioned lines of study, it must in the meantime be carried
forward of itself and for its own sake. (Sherrington, 1906, p. 2)

In his description of neural integration, Charles Sherrington defined
the essence of modern behavioral neuroscience. Throughout his distinguished career, Sherrington made substantial contributions at all three levels.

Unfortunately, in the first half-dozen decades of the 20th century, the
difficult problems of integrative function were slighted in favor of the
more tractable questions of cellular neurobiology. However, in the past
several decades, human neuroscience has again turned studying the integrative behavioral functions of the brain.

One example (among many) of the resurgence of Sherrington's integrative approach to the study of neural function was put forward in the
1970s by David Marr, a brilliant young scientist who died tragically in
1980. Marr argued strongly for the simultaneous analysis of brain and
behavior again at different levels of analysis, but Marr's approach is com-
putationally driven.

Marr observed that in the 1950s and 1960s, a great deal of progress had
been made in understanding the biological basis of behavior by analyz-
ing the activity of single nerve cells. Psychology provided the questions,
a list of phenomena that needed explanation. Anatomy indicated where
within the nervous system solutions were likely to be found. Physiology
provided functional descriptions of the activity of cells in the region of interest. In this way, many of the principles governing the earliest stages of
information processing were discovered.

Despite this progress, a biological understanding of the higher functions of the nervous system remained elusive. Something was wrong.
Marr later wrote,

It gradually became clear that something important was missing that
was not present in either the disciplines of neurophysiology or [psy-
chology]. The key observation is that neurophysiology and [psychol-
ogy] have as their business to describe the behavior of cells or of subjects but not to explain such behavior.... What are the problems in doing it that need explaining, and at what level of description should
such explanations be sought? (Marr, 1982, p. 15)

For Marr, the way to find out what needed explaining was to use computers to solve the same types of problems that the brain solves naturally. Marr was interested in vision, so he concerned himself with the problem of visual object recognition. This approach quickly began to yield fruit.

> The message was plain. There must exist an additional level of understanding at which the character of the information-processing tasks carried out during perception are analyzed and understood that is independent of the particular mechanisms and structures that implement them in our heads. This was what was missing—the analysis of the problem as an information-processing task. Such analysis does not usurp an understanding at the other levels of neurons or of computer programs—but it is a necessary complement to them, since without it there can be no real understanding of the function of all those neurons. (Marr, 1982, p. 19.)

Marr argued, from a computational perspective, that the biological explanation of any intelligent behavior requires multiple levels of analysis. It is first necessary to determine what information-processing task is being done by the nervous system. Next, it is necessary to establish what plan or procedure is to be used in performing the task. There are, after all, a variety of formal procedures for solving any particular information-processing problem.

By knowing what the nervous system is attempting to do, the task, and by discovering the way in which the task is to be carried out, the procedure, it then becomes possible to discover the specific biological mechanisms by which that procedure is physically accomplished, the implementation. All three levels of analysis—task, procedure, and implementation—are needed to yield a satisfactory biological explanation of behavior.

Although Marr's and Sherrington's careers were separated by 80 years, the emphasis that both placed on integrative understanding of neural and behavioral systems at multiple levels of analysis forms the foundation of contemporary human neuroscience at the start of the 21st century.

MODELS AID SCIENTIFIC UNDERSTANDING

Understanding the living human brain is in some sense the ultimate scientific challenge, in essence, asking the human brain to understand itself. This daunting task is made easier by the use of scientific **models**, simplified but analogous representations of the system being studied. Both biological and mathematical models are commonly used in studying the functions of the brain.

Biological models are comparatively simple living organisms or systems that share important properties with more complex biological systems of primary interest. The use of well-chosen biological models has led to many major discoveries. The fundamental properties of nerve cells that permit them to process information electrically were elaborated—in large part—by Alan Hodgkin and Andrew Huxley, who received the 1963 Nobel Prize for their work.

Hodgkin and Huxley would have liked to have studied mammalian, even human, nerve cells, but these cells are much too small to examine with the recording techniques then available. So, at the suggestion of the zoologist J. Z. Young, they turned their attention to the giant axon of the squid as a model of mammalian nerve cells. The squid giant axon differs from mammalian axons in several important respects. It is not a single cell, for example, but rather a structure composed of many separate cells that have fused together. But its large size allowed the necessary recordings to be made. And the squid giant axon proved to be a good model: Its electrical properties turned out to be identical with that of other nerve cells, as later, more refined, methods were established.

Today, other biological models for different mammalian functions are being explored. The simple nervous system of the mollusk *Aplysia* is being studied extensively in the belief—and hope—that the neural mechanisms that it employs in learning are similar to those used in more complex organisms. The hope is that the Aplysia nervous system—like the squid giant axon before it—will prove to be a useful model and a simpler approach to discovering neural mechanisms of plasticity that are widespread in the animal kingdom.

Thus, a biological model is a simple, conveniently studied living system that is analogous to a complex system—such as our own brain—in certain important respects relevant to the issues being investigated.

Other models are mathematical or conceptual. We will see how equations, which are really abstract mathematical models, are useful in describing and predicting the electrical behavior of nerve cells. Mathematical computer network models are being explored to help understand possible biological mechanisms of mammalian learning. Virtually all areas of quantitative neurobiology apply mathematical models to one degree or another.

However, it must be remembered that all models are simplifying analogies. If they are to be useful, they must be similar to the real system in important respects and thus capture these relations in a simplified form.

THE PROCESS OF DISCOVERY

Progress in the sciences, whether physical, biological, or social, has radically changed our view of both our world and ourselves. For example, the electronic, communication, and information technologies that we take for granted today were barely conceivable a few decades ago. Similarly, revolutions in molecular biology and genetics have drastically altered and greatly deepened our understanding of the brain as an organ of behavior. All of these advances can be attributed to the rise of science in the 20th century and the unrelenting use of the scientific method to peel back the shrouds of mystery surrounding the physical universe. The progress of the continuing scientific quest to understand mind and brain is the topic of this book.

Science is sometimes thought of as a dry, methodical process in which boring experiments are performed mechanically and duly reported in obscure journals for other scientists to read. But nothing could be farther from the truth. Far from being mechanical and uncreative, science depends on both curiosity and imagination for its most significant advances. Experimentation only provides the means for choosing between competing ideas, and perhaps—if luck is good—it also suggests new ideas for further testing. Thus, science is both a creative and an empirical enterprise. And nowhere is this more true than in the study of the human brain. For that most mysterious organ, good ideas are of critical importance.

Curiosity is the driving force behind the scientific enterprise. It is natural for humans to wonder about those things that are most human: perception, thought, feeling, and action. How are the ordinary events of our lives accomplished? How do we perceive patterns of light and dark as visual objects, a task that we perform with far more expertise than even the largest of today's computers? How do we think? How do we talk? How do we feel love, hate, fear, or satisfaction? What guides and controls our action? These sorts of questions trigger the curiosity of all people. They are also typical of the questions that motivate the hard work of scientifically investigating the human brain.

Imagination is the key to scientific investigation. Imagination is needed in thinking about new questions, problems, and information and in formulating old ideas in new ways. Sometimes, in science, insights appear suddenly and are quickly confirmed by an experimental test. One such example is provided by Otto Loewi, who conceived of a way to demonstrate the chemical nature of neuronal communication while lying in bed dreaming about the problem. For that leap of the imagination and the experimental test work that followed, Loewi received the Nobel Prize in 1936.

But it is not imagination that separates science from conjecture. That critical role is played by empirical experimentation. Once the question has been artfully posed, once the insight or hunch has been suggested, and once a new approach has been decided, science requires an experimental test. After all, not all imaginative solutions to perplexing problems can be correct; not all "good" ideas are right. Experimentation provides the method for evaluating the correctness of an idea on the basis of empirical data.

THE SCIENTIFIC METHOD

The scientific method lies at the heart of scientific discovery. Textbooks sometimes describe the scientific method as a series of formal and distinct steps, but this view misses the essential point: There is no one scientific method.

Rather, the scientific method is more like a state of mind. It is an approach to problem solving that has been adapted to a wide variety of specific questions in the various fields of inquiry. At the core of the scientific state of mind are a number of common elements.

Objectivity   Objectivity is the attempt to approach experimental questions with an open mind. Although preconceptions and hopes may cloud people's thinking, it is of primary importance to try to minimize such subjective influences.

Observation   One key to the scientific method is observation: the careful and accurate description of the object of study. Observation is sometimes the only method available to a scientist because it is difficult or impossible to experimentally manipulate the phenomena of interest. For example, observation formed the basis of Darwin's theory of evolution because Darwin was in no position to manipulate the forces that regulate evolution. It also is the principal source of information for some contemporary sciences, such as astronomy.

Experimentation   The experimental method couples careful observation with direct manipulation of the object of study and, in so doing, gives the scientific method immense power. By testing the object of study in particular ways, critical reflections of its properties may be observed. Much has been learned about the brain, for example, from the observation of behavior following the destruction of particular brain regions, an approach called lesion analysis. Experimental testing and observation lie at the heart of scientific research.

Proper Controls   Any particular manipulation may have a wide range of effects, only some of which are relevant to the ideas being tested. For example, if damage to a particular brain region disrupts a certain behavior, is it reasonable to conclude that this region is normally necessary for producing the behavior? Such a conclusion may be incorrect. For example, the behavior may have been disrupted as a consequence of the anesthesia used in surgery and not by the tissue destruction itself.

To rule out this and related arguments, sham operations are often employed as an experimental control. The experimental group of animals receives the full surgical procedure, including destruction of the brain region being tested. Another sham-operated group of control animals receives all aspects of the surgery except the actual destruction of brain tissue. By subsequently comparing the behavior of the two groups of animals, any difference between the groups cannot be attributed to the general effects of a surgical operation.

Selection of proper experimental controls is vitally important in framing a good experiment because these controls restrict and clarify the interpretation of experimental results. The selection of useful controls is a matter of careful thinking and good judgment. The choice always depends on the particulars of a given experiment.

Statistical Evaluation   In all experiments, only a limited number of individuals are studied, and only a limited number of observations are obtained. Yet the purpose of any experiment is to learn something about people (or animals) in general. This is done by inferring conclusions about the larger population from the behavior of its members that were actually tested. To accomplish this with the minimum likelihood of error, good statistical procedures must be followed. The sample of individuals to be tested must be drawn from the general population in an unbiased manner. A sufficiently large number of observations must be made so that the experimental results will be stable. Good rules exist in the area of mathematical statistics that enable an empirical scientist to draw conclusions from the experimental data in relative safety.

Independent Verification of Results   All scientists are human and thus are capable of error, albeit unintentional and unknowing error. For this reason, the independent verification of experimental results forms a cornerstone of empirical science. Important and interesting results are usually demonstrated in more than one laboratory by more than one group of scientists before they are fully believed by the scientific community in general. After all, if an experiment is done correctly, it should be able to be repeated again and again with the same results. Replication of research findings provides a powerful error-correcting mechanism in all of the sciences.

The Evolution of Science   Most science, including brain science, is in a process of evolution. For example, ideas often begin as hunches or vague notions. Slowly, these ill-formed concepts are refined, becoming sharper, more insightful, and more powerful. The final result may be a clear and elegant experimental hypothesis.

Similarly, experimental methods and designs also evolve. A research program often begins with a loosely formed "what if we try this" type of experiment. The experimental results may suggest more rigorous and detailed experiments. The final experiment—if luck is good—will be an elegant and beautifully simple experiment that convincingly demonstrates the solution to the problem.

Last—and perhaps most important—scientific concepts and syntheses also evolve. On the basis of clear experimental conclusions and the published findings of other scientists, scientific theories become more powerful and clearer. In this way, understanding grows.

THE TOOLS OF DISCOVERY

Experimentation requires tools, and good tools have historically provided the means by which major scientific advances have occurred. Our current understanding of the human brain would not be possible without the tools of modern neurobiology. Although today we take for granted powerful tools such as scanning electron microscopes and mass spectrometers, these sophisticated instruments are of relatively recent origin.

The fundamental importance of the proper scientific tool may be seen by historical example. In the late 19th century, there was much debate concerning the basic structure of the brain as a tissue. Some, such as the Italian Camillo Golgi, held that the brain was a *reticulum*, a densely interconnected system of continuous tubes through which unknown substances might flow. Others, such as the Spaniard Santiago Ramón y Cajal, believed that the brain was composed of individual and separate cells that could communicate with each other. The resolution of this most basic question was provided by the development of a new scientific tool, a silver stain devised by Golgi, which permitted Ramón y Cajal to selectively stain individual neurons within the brain (see Figure 1.2 on the next page). In this way, he convincingly demonstrated the cellular nature of the brain and established what is now known as the *Neuron Doctrine*. For their individual contributions, Golgi and Ramón y Cajal shared the Nobel Prize in 1906.

Figure 1.2. A Golgi-Stained Cell. This drawing by Ramón y Cajal shows a Golgi stain of a large triangularly shaped pyramidal cell from the human cerebral cortex. (From Santiago Ramón y Cajal, *Histologie du systeme nerveux de l'homme et des vertebres.* Paris: A. Maloine, 1909-1911.)

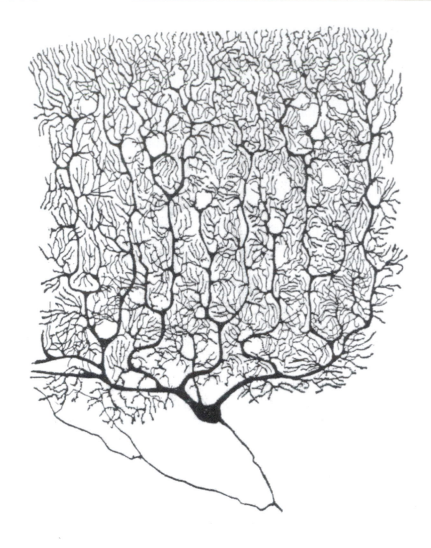

The importance of developing more powerful and more precise tools with which to study the brain cannot be overemphasized. New tools allow even the most pedestrian of scientists to make new discoveries; in the hands of a brilliant scientist, they can bring great advances. Thus, biological science is continually advanced by progress in physics and engineering. For example, the modern understanding of the electrical activity of the nerves was made possible by the development of vacuum tube amplifiers in the early years of the 20th century. As electronic technology improved in the following decades, neurobiologists used its increased power and precision to make ever finer measurements. Today, not only is it possible to record routinely from the interior of neurons, but it is even possible to measure the electrically charged atoms passing through tiny specialized molecular pores within the neuronal membrane.

The methods used to study the brain today are much advanced over those available in Cajal's time, but the use to which these methods are put remains the same: to better understand the biology of behavior and of our selves.

Microscopic Studies

Although glamorous computerized brain-imaging machines are opening a new era in the study of the gross (large-scale) anatomy and function of the human brain, microscopy has contributed for more than a century to the analysis of the cellular structure and—more recently—the cellular function of the nervous system.

The first magnified view of nerve fibers was reported by the Dutch scientist Anton van Leeuwenhoek in 1674, but the early lenses and microscopes were inadequate to the task of a detailed microscopic investigation of the nervous system. It was not until the late 1800s that powerful, low-distortion microscopes were invented, principally by the German firm Carl Zeiss. For this reason, the 1890s began what might be considered the golden era of microscopy and the publication of the pioneering works of Ramón y Cajal, Korbinian Brodmann, and the other founders of cellular neuroanatomy (Williams & Warwick, 1980).

For most kinds of microscopic investigations, the tissue to be imaged must be thin enough for light to pass through it, and portions of it must be of different colors or transparency so that important features are distinguishable. A variety of histological (having to do with the study of the minute structure of tissues) procedures have been devised to meet these objectives (Weiss & Greep, 1977). (**Histology** is the study of microscopic anatomy.)

In most instances, the tissue to be examined must first be prepared by **fixation**, a procedure to stabilize and preserve the fragile neural tissue. After all, neural tissue itself is very watery and soft. Fixation is often accomplished by using an agent—such as formalin—to harden the tissue. Freezing is another useful approach to stabilizing neural tissue.

Once hardened, the tissue is sliced very thinly to render it nearly transparent. One typical procedure is to first embed the tissue in a substance such as paraffin to facilitate holding the specimen. It then can be cut by using a **microtome**, a precise and automatic slicing machine that produces thin, regular sections of the fixed and embedded tissue. The resulting thin sections may then be mounted on glass slides in preparation for viewing.

Such microscopic sections are thin enough for light to pass through them, but—in most cases—they lack sufficient contrast to make different features of the tissue apparent. Staining is a procedure to selectively darken or color particular features of the sectioned tissue. By choosing an appropriate **stain**, different features of the tissue are highlighted.

The first use of staining was probably in the late 1850s. During the subsequent decade, a number of aniline dyes were developed for industrial purposes in Germany. These dyes would also prove to be of considerable help to the fledgling science of histology.

One of the most important basic cell stains was invented by Camillo Golgi at the end of the 19th century. The **Golgi silver stain** has the property of completely darkening only a small number of individual cells in the specimen. Because only a few cells are stained, they stand out with exquisite clarity. The Golgi silver stain is probably the best histological procedure for visualizing single nerve cells. Golgi used his silver stain to describe a wide range of nerve cells, many of which today bear his name. Variants of the Golgi stain remain in wide use.

The usefulness of dyes such as cresyl violet were discovered by the German microscopist Franz Nissl to selectively stain only the cell bodies of individual cells, leaving the long extensions or processes of those cells transparent. His **Nissl stain** is useful for visualizing the distribution of cell bodies in the specimen.

Finally, most nerve cells have axons, which are long, snakelike extensions that make contact with other neurons. These axons form pathways carrying information through the brain. Many of these axons are wrapped in myelin, a lipid sheath that facilitates communication along the axon. **Myelin stains** selectively color this protective coating, a procedure that is useful for mapping connecting pathways in brain tissue.

Other strategies for tracing neural pathways have contributed substantially to our understanding of the neural computations of the brain. Some stains mark neural pathways as they degenerate following brain damage. Other stains can be injected into a specific brain location to map both the cells that send information from that structure to other regions of the brain, as well as determining the locations of cells that send information to the targeted brain structure. **Horseradish peroxidase**, for example, is an enzyme obtained from the horseradish plant that is taken up by the end-feet of a nerve cell and transported within the axon back to the cell body. For this reason, horseradish peroxidase stains are used to track neural pathways from their termination to their source.

These and other methods of quantitatively determining pathways of information exchange within the brain have contributed substantially to understanding the primate and human brain as an information-processing *system*.

Even more specific and specialized stains are now available, thanks to developments in molecular biology and genetic engineering. Monoclonal antibodies are being developed to recognize and mark particular cellular proteins. Recombinant DNA procedures are another tool provided by molecular biology that has proven to be extremely useful in studying special molecular structures within the membrane of the cell.

Finally, microscopic studies may be carried out using electron beams rather than light waves to form the image. Because the electron beam has a wavelength that is thousands of times shorter than visible light, much smaller objects can be resolved. The first **electron microscope** was constructed in Germany in the early 1930s. Today, scanning electron microscopes are routinely used in the biological sciences, producing magnifications of up to one million times.

Brain Imaging

Studies of the human brain and nervous system have become increasingly important in recent years, with the development of advanced brain-imaging techniques. These methods have been used with particular success in studying the so-called higher mental functions, such as human language, for which no appropriate animal model can exist. In this way, the biology of human thought is beginning to be deciphered.

Three technologies form the basis of human brain imaging: computerized tomography, positron-emission tomography, and magnetic resonance imaging. These three methods make possible the study of both brain anatomy and patterns of brain activation in living, healthy human beings. It is not surprising that brain imaging is playing an increasingly large role in the study of the neural basis of human thought and language.

Computerized Tomography   It was **computerized tomography (CT)** that began the brain-imaging revolution, having been commercially introduced in 1973 (Oldendorf, 1980). The first CT scanner was designed by G. N. Hounsfield, using mathematics formalized in 1964 by A. M. Cormack. For these contributions, Hounsfield and Cormack shared the 1979 Nobel Prize in medicine and physiology.

CT is an enhancement of the familiar X-ray procedure. Instead of producing the usual shadow imaging of a conventional X ray, in CT an image of a horizontal slice of tissue is reconstructed. It is as if a slice of brain were surgically removed and placed on a table for inspection. To form this image, a large number of narrow X-ray beams are passed through the head across a single plane at a wide variety of angles. The amount of radiation absorbed along each line is measured. From the measurements associated with each of the many beams passing through the slice, a computer program can determine the density of tissue at each point within the slice. The resulting image is the CT scan.

Positron-Emission Tomography   The second new brain-imaging technology is **positron-emission tomography (PET)**, which has been used for nearly two decades to provide images indicating the *functional* or physiological properties of the living human brain. Thus, PET tells us what the brain is doing rather than what it looks like.

PET involves the injection of a tracer substance labeled with a positron-emitting radionuclide. One common tracer is radioactively labeled oxygen, which is differentially absorbed by active neurons. Thus, metabolically more active portions of the brain will accumulate more radioactivity than will less active regions. By determining where the tracer is accumulating in the brain, patterns of differential brain activation can be mapped.

Tracer distribution is measured by sensing the radioactive decay of the positron-emitting label. At some point in time after injection, the positron is emitted from the radioactive nuclide. After traveling a short distance, the positron interacts with an electron; both are annihilated and are converted to two photons traveling away from each other in opposite directions. The PET scanner detects these photons, and the location of the annihilation (and hence the tracer) is determined in a manner similar to that used in CT scanning.

PET scanning is now widely used to study patterns of brain activity that underlie higher mental functions. By using different tracer substances, a number of types of brain biochemical processing can be mapped by PET. However, many believe that functional MRI will soon replace PET for many uses because MRI has much higher spatial resolution and is noninvasive.

Magnetic Resonance Imaging   The third of the brain-imaging technologies is **magnetic resonance imaging (MRI)**. Like CT, MRI provides images

Figure 1.3. Magnetic Resonance Image (MRI) of a Midsagittal Section Through the Human Head. In this view, a number of major brain regions are clearly visible, including the cerebral cortex (the large folded structure immediately beneath the skull), the corpus callosum (white), the brainstem (the gray structure extending down into the spinal cord), and the cerebellum (the folded tissue to the rear of the brainstem). (Image courtesy of Professor Tyrone Cannon, UCLA.)

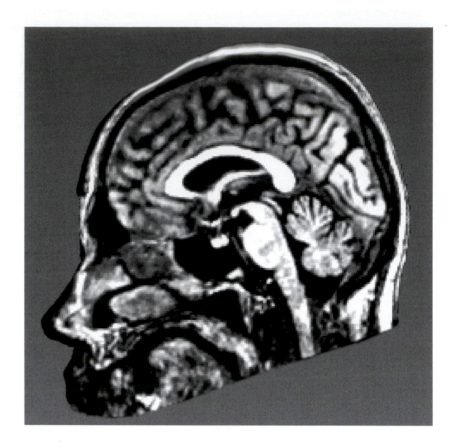

of brain structure using mathematical reconstruction, but it does so by using a very different source of information than the X rays used in CT.

MRI exploits a phenomenon known as *nuclear magnetic resonance*, in which radio frequency energy in a strong magnetic field is used to generate signals from a particular atom—usually hydrogen—contained within the tissue (Kean & Smith, 1986; Oldendorf & Oldendorf, 1988). Incidentally, the word *nuclear* was discarded as MRI became commercial for fear that people would associate the technique with nuclear radiation.

The underlying physics of nuclear magnetic resonance confer a number of advantages to MRI as an imaging technique. First, unlike in CT, no ionizing radiation is employed. Thus, MRI is completely noninvasive and is safe to use over and over again. Second, magnetic resonance images have extremely fine spatial resolution, providing neuroanatomical images of exquisite detail, as shown in Figure 1.3. Third, because of technicalities in the MRI procedure, it is possible to obtain slices at any angle, not just in the horizontal plane, as is the case with CT. Three-dimensional images of the brain also may be generated.

Finally, MRI methods permit the imaging of brain function as well as structure, measuring both brain blood flow and oxidative metabolism. This is possible because of minute changes in the magnetic properties of blood hemoglobin molecules as they release oxygen in the brain. Previously, functional imaging was limited to positron-emission tomography, which uses radioactively labeled oxygen to measure brain blood flow.

Recording Brain Electrical Activity

Nerve cells—like other living cells—maintain an electrical charge across their outer membrane. However, nerve cells are especially adapted to carry and process information by varying that electrical charge (see Chapter 3). For this reason, much can be learned about the functions of the brain by recording the electrical signals that its nerve cells produce. Recording brain electrical activity is the major tool by which brain function has been explored.

Because the electrical signals produced by nerve cells are comparatively small, they must be amplified before they can be measured accurately. Today, this is accomplished by using electronic amplifiers, much like those employed in home audio equipment. The signal itself is sensed by using a pair of **electrodes**, often conductive pieces of metal, connected to the input of the amplifier. The amplified signal is often presented visually, as a trace on a computer screen. In either case, the plot presents the measured voltage (on the ordinate, or y-axis) as a function of time (on the abscissa, or x-axis). It is by examination of the changing electrical potential over time that neural information processing can be analyzed.

The size and placement of the electrodes determine what aspects of neural activity will be recorded. Very large electrodes reflect the activity of large populations of nerve cells; smaller electrodes can record more localized neuroelectric events.

Electroencephalography The **electroencephalogram (EEG)** is the neurologist's term for the electrical activity that may be recorded from electrodes placed on the surface of the scalp (Neidermeyer & Lopes da Silva, 1982). When such a recording is obtained from electrodes placed directly on the surface of the brain—usually during neurosurgery—the measure is called the **electrocorticogram (EcoG)**.

EEG activity was first recorded by Hans Berger, a German psychiatrist, in 1924 and published by him in 1929 (Brazier, 1960). During the intervening 5 years, he protected his discovery with a veil of secrecy. On publication, the existence of "brain waves," as the EEG was called, was viewed with much skepticism until it was replicated in 1934 by Lord Adrian, a distinguished British physiologist and Nobel laureate.

The EEG is generated primarily by the activity of large numbers of nerve cells within the brain. Because the skull, which encloses the brain beneath the scalp, is an electrical insulator, under most circumstances, it is impossible to conclude which portion of the brain is generating any particular part of the EEG signal. The electroencephalogram has proven to be most useful in studying the sleep-waking cycle and in diagnosing epilepsy.

Magnetoencephalography   Just as electrical events in nerve cells generate currents flowing through the body that can be recorded as the EEG, they also produce tiny magnetic fields. To measure such weak fields, one requires the use of a special supercooled sensor called a SQUID (superconducting quantum interference device). This procedure is called **magnetoencephalography (MEG)** (Beatty, Barth, Richer, & Johnson, 1986).

One important difference between MEG and EEG is that the skull is electrically resistant but magnetically transparent. For this reason, magnetic recording may prove to be of value in localizing the source of signals produced by populations of nerve cells within the brain.

Microelectrode Recording   Both the EEG and MEG are measures of brain activity at a very large scale because they are measures of the simultaneous activity of hundreds of thousands of active brain cells. Thus, neither are well suited for the detailed study of the cellular mechanisms that are the ultimate sources of human behavior. For this purpose, a much finer grain of analysis is required.

This level of resolution is provided by **microelectrodes**, which have small enough tips to selectively record the electrical activity of individual nerve cells. Microelectrodes are either metal or glass. The metal electrodes are fashioned from extremely fine wire that is sharpened by etching. The glass electrodes—called **micropipettes**—are made from glass tubing that is heated and stretched to narrow the width of the tube. The micropipette is then filled with a conductive solution such as potassium chloride.

Microelectrodes may be used for either extracellular or intracellular recording. For extracellular recording, the electrode is placed near the nerve cell. In this position, it can measure the currents flowing from the nerve cell into the extracellular fluid that surrounds it. For intracellular recording, the microelectrode is inserted into the interior of the nerve cell itself.

Patch Clamps   Nerve cells regulate their electrical activity by controlling small pores or channels in their outer membrane. One can measure the current flow in individual membrane channels by using a technique called patch clamping. A **patch clamp** is an adaptation of the glass micropipette method in which a small amount of suction is applied to the fluid-filled recording electrode. If the tip of the electrode is placed on the outer surface of the cell membrane, a tight mechanical and electrical seal results. The result is that the electrode measures electrical current only from the portion of the membrane that is clamped to the electrode. In this way, the activity of individual membrane channels can be measured.

Brain Lesion Analysis

A lesion is an abnormal disruption of a tissue, produced by injury or disease. The study of naturally occurring brain lesions in human beings has formed the cornerstone of brain research in the field of neurology. The discovery of the sensory and motor areas of the human brain, for example, was the result of localizing lesions in individuals who suffered a disruption of sensory or motor functions as a result of brain damage. This approach to the study of brain and behavior is called lesion analysis (Damasio & Damasio, 1969).

Lesion analysis is also useful in experimental research using laboratory animals. There, behavior is measured before and after a part of the brain is damaged or removed. The advantage of using laboratory animals for this purpose is that the lesion can be placed precisely within the brain, whereas naturally occurring lesions as seen in the neurological clinic are seldom confined to a particular, distinct brain structure. The use of experimental animals greatly extends the precision—and therefore the usefulness—of the lesion analysis approach.

A number of different procedures may be used to produce brain lesions. One of the simplest, at least for brain areas that are easily accessible, is surgical removal of the targeted tissue. With a surgical knife, the structure of interest is dissected away, and the wound is then closed and surgically dressed. Knife cuts made with direct visual guidance provide a sure method of producing a well-defined and precisely located brain lesion.

Lesions targeted for deeply embedded brain structures are often made by using an electrode through which high-frequency current is passed. Radio frequency current generates heat in the vicinity of the electrode; it is the heat that destroys nerve cells and produces the lesion. The electrode is guided to its target by using a stereotaxic positioning device. A **stereotaxic apparatus** is a mechanism that fastens to the head in a fixed position relative to standard features of the skull. From these skull landmarks, the approximate location of hidden brain structures can be determined. A **stereotaxic atlas**, a map of the typical brain and skull for the species, is used to calculate the coordinates of the tissue to be lesioned. Stereotaxic procedures are also used in human neurosurgery—using radiographic rather than skull landmarks—to produce therapeutic brain lesions in deep regions of the brain that are inaccessible for visually guided dissection.

Finally, temporary lesions can be made by using a refrigerating probe, or **cryoprobe**. A cryoprobe lowers the temperature of nerve cells that it contacts so that they can no longer function. During this time, a functional brain lesion is produced. When the probe is turned off or removed, the nerve cells warm up and function normally again. This procedure allows for very careful comparisons between functioning when the probe is on and off.

No matter how a brain lesion is produced, interpreting the behavioral effects of the lesion can be tricky. First, even experimental brain lesions are not perfectly made. Particularly when the target is a small structure, damage inevitably extends into the surrounding tissue. The extent of such damage must be assessed if the study is to be evaluated accurately. For this reason, histology is necessary after the experiment to verify where the lesion was actually situated and the extent to which nontargeted tissues were damaged.

A second related issue is the inadvertent damage to fibers of passage. **Fibers of passage** are nerve fibers passing through the region of the lesion that neither originate nor terminate in that structure. When such fibers are accidentally damaged, there may be far-reaching behavioral effects that have nothing to do with the function of nerve cells located in the area of

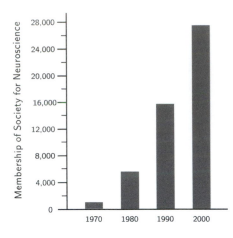

Figure 1.4. Membership in the Society for Neuroscience. The number of members in this interdisciplinary professional society for neuroscientists has grown consistently since its founding in 1970.

the lesion.

A third and perhaps more fundamental problem is that specific functions are often distributed through a number of brain areas. The destruction of a particular part of that circuit may have behavioral consequences that are difficult to understand in isolation. Because interesting behaviors are complex, detailed and sophisticated behavioral procedures are required to identify the exact nature of the deficit produced by any brain lesion.

THE BRAIN SCIENCES

Only a few decades ago, the various brain sciences were viewed as separate research enterprises. Information concerning the physical structure of the nervous system was provided by **neuroanatomy**. Facts concerning the functioning of nerve cells were provided by **neurophysiology**. **Neurochemistry** studied the chemical basis of brain activity. **Psychobiology** (also called **physiological psychology**, or **biological psychology**) concerned itself with the biological basis of behavior.

Such designations persist today but have become increasingly meaningless as each of these once-separate disciplines borrows increasingly from the others. The most striking recent advances in neuroanatomy, for example, depend on neurochemical tracing and labeling methods. Neurochemists are studying membrane currents carried by specific ions passing through specific protein channels on the surface of a nerve cell. Biologically oriented psychologists now employ analysis techniques drawn from all the neural sciences in investigating the biology of behavior. Thus, brain researchers increasingly and appropriately consider themselves as practicing **neuroscience**, a term that reflects the truly interdisciplinary nature of modern brain research. This book is concerned with those aspects of neuroscience that affect behavior, hence the term **behavioral neuroscience**.

It is the multidisciplinary nature of contemporary neuroscience that gives the field its vibrant strength. This new interdisciplinary field has grown dramatically. The Society for Neuroscience—the professional society for all types of neuroscientists—was founded in 1970 with 600 charter members. Today, more than 28,000 scientists are members of that organization (see Figure 1.4). Such rapid growth reflects the extraordinary progress being made in understanding the brain and its control of behavior. Indeed, the 1990s were declared the Decade of the Brain by the U.S. Congress, a title that may be a little grand but—in retrospect—quite appropriate.

ETHICAL ISSUES IN NEUROSCIENCE

Neuroscientists—like all biological scientists—study living beings. In doing so, they adhere to strict ethical principles. Perhaps the primary reason for doing so is that science by its very nature is an ethical and rational pursuit of knowledge and understanding.

Science is also a social enterprise. For that reason, codified statements of these essential ethical standards are put forward by the social institutions of science, the universities, professional societies, and governmental agencies that fund biological research. Ethical guidelines have been established for research involving both human beings and other animal species. Every university has a research review board—composed of a broad range of individuals—that must approve every experiment in which any living being is placed at any degree of risk, either physical or mental. A typical human subjects or animal protection committee will usually include members from the departments involved in such research, faculty members from departments not involved with human or animal research, representatives from the schools of law and medicine whenever possible, and interested nonuniversity members, often clerics. This broad representation of divergent perspectives is encouraged to achieve fairness.

Such committees provide necessary protection if an individual scientist's ethical judgment is compromised by other concerns. Scientists, although attempting to be both ethical and rational, are nonetheless susceptible to human frailties; for this reason, institutional review provides a useful and occasionally necessary safeguard for the rights of experimental subjects.

Experiments With Humans

In studying humans, there are a number of ethical guidelines to be considered by both neuroscientists and their institutional review boards. Some deal with participation in the experiment itself. Participants are to be fully informed as to the nature of the experiment so that they can decide whether they wish to participate on the basis of factual knowledge. People may not be coerced to participate and must be free to withdraw from the experiment at any time without penalty.

Once engaged in an experiment, the subjects must be protected from physical and psychological harm. If harm does occur, it is the experimenter's responsibility to provide an appropriate remedy. Finally, data obtained from the human subjects must remain confidential.

Sometimes, however, the very nature of the research question requires that some of these guidelines be compromised. In AIDS research, for example, state and federal law may require that full confidentiality of data cannot be maintained. Whenever any guideline cannot be fully met, the subject is considered to be at some degree of risk. It is the task of the broadly representative human subjects protection committee to determine whether the potential benefits of the research outweigh the risk involved. It may well be argued that the possible benefits that might be obtained by a relatively unproven treatment would more than justify the risk of possible detrimental side effects of that experimental procedure.

Experiments With Other Species

Ethical issues also arise in the experimental studies of nonhuman species, which form the very heart of neuroscience research. Using laboratory animals as biological models can provide important information that is not obtainable in any other way. Laboratory rats, for example, have been extremely useful in learning about the biology of aging because they have a natural life span of 2 to 3 years. Similar investigations of aging in humans would require a human life span to complete, resulting in experiments lasting about seven decades.

Furthermore, nonhuman species can provide much valuable information about the human brain and human behavior in a number of important areas because—through evolution—their nervous systems are similar to our own. For example, the ways in which nerve cells conduct information are now well understood, thanks to decades of research on species of animals ranging from invertebrates to primates. Virtually everything that has been learned about neural communication in these species can be applied directly and definitively to humans as well. Such knowledge has not only provided us with a deep insight of neural interactions within the human brain but also has given medicine a direct understanding of a wide range of nervous system disorders, such as myesthenia gravis, multiple sclerosis, and muscular dystrophy. In many cases, understanding the basic mechanisms of neural functioning has led physicians to new and better means with which to treat diseases.

Clinical research, as opposed to basic research, is concerned primarily with finding new and more effective treatments for particular disorders. One of the most effective methods to carry out early clinical studies has been to discover an animal model for the human disease. Once developed, an animal model frees further research from dependence on suitable clinical patients, which are often hard to come by. Thus, animal models provide a means for rapidly evaluating a variety of alternative treatments, as well as studying the underlying pathological mechanisms. Without animal models of naturally occurring disorders, both human and veterinary medicine would be greatly impoverished.

The importance of studying living nonhuman animals is made clear in the guidelines for animal research put forward by the Society for Neuroscience:

> Research in the neurosciences contributes to the quality of life by expanding knowledge about living organisms. This improvement in the quality of life stems in part from progress toward ameliorating human disease and disability, in part from advances in animal welfare and veterinary medicine, and in part from the steady increase in knowledge of the abilities and potentialities of human and animal life. Continued progress in many areas of biomedical research requires the use of living animals in order to investigate complex systems and functions because, in such cases, no adequate alternatives exist. Progress in both basic and clinical research in such areas cannot continue without the use of living animals as experimental subjects. The use of living animals in properly designed scientific research is therefore both ethical and appropriate. Nevertheless, our concern for the humane treatment of animals dictates that we weigh carefully the benefits to human knowledge and welfare whenever animal research is undertaken. (Society for Neuroscience, 1993)

All animal research in neuroscience is guided by one overriding principle: that experimental animals must not be subjected to avoidable distress or discomfort. Most animal research, in fact, involves minimal distress and discomfort. However, some degree of discomfort is inherent in studying certain experimental questions; such experiments must be evaluated individually, and the potential benefits must be weighed against the discomfort caused to the animal. Institutional animal research review committees—similar to the human subjects protection committees—must approve any experiment placing an animal in discomfort before the experiment is undertaken. These committees also ensure that the highest standards of veterinary practice and humane care are followed.

Animal Welfare and Animal Rights

Research involving living nonhuman animals has attracted the attention of two quite different segments of the nonscientific public: animal welfare and animal rights or animal liberation groups. Animal welfare groups support research on living animals as long as the animals are given humane care and the potential benefits of the research clearly outweigh any pain caused to the animals. This is, of course, exactly the position of the Society for Neuroscience and other professional groups.

Animal welfare groups are concerned not only about laboratory research involving living animals but also about other aspects of animals' involvement in human society. For example, the American Society for the Prevention of Cruelty to Animals performs a wide variety of services for the community to better the lives of animals, including returning lost pets and finding new homes for abandoned pets. It is interesting to note that for every dog or cat used in a laboratory experiment, 10,000 dogs and cats are abandoned by their owners (Miller, 1985).

In contrast to animal welfare groups, animal rights groups argue that no laboratory research should involve living animals, regardless of the benefits that would result from animal research. Animal rights groups have become very vocal, staging demonstrations and protests, personally attacking research scientists, and even criminally breaking and entering into research laboratories and stealing the animals that they find. Needless to say, such tactics have generated a great deal of media attention. It is important to remember that such groups represent a very small percentage of the members of our society. But because of the attention they have received, professional societies are beginning advertising campaigns to remind us all of the benefits that we and our pets enjoy that have resulted from biomedical research using living animals.

SUMMARY

The human brain is the most complex organ in all of biology; it is also the organ of the mind. As such, it has been both the focus of philosophers' analysis and the object of empirical inquiry. Today, its secrets are being revealed by scientific research at a number of different levels. Increasingly, the study of the brain and behavior has become an interdisciplinary endeavor. Old distinctions, based on divisions between the traditional academic disciplines, are dissolving; today's brain researchers think of themselves as neuroscientists.

SELECTED READINGS

- Finger, S. (1994). *Origins of neuroscience: A history of explorations into brain function.* Oxford, UK: Oxford University Press. A wide-ranging history of the study of human brain functions such as sensation, movement, emotion, sleep, memory, and language, all illustrated with historical photographs.

- Gazzaniga, M. S. (1999). *The new cognitive neurosciences.* Cambridge: MIT Press. An encyclopedic and current survey of the many facets of contemporary cognitive neuroscience in the words of leading researchers.

- Young, D. (1992). *The discovery of evolution.* Cambridge, UK: Cambridge University Press. An extremely readable, insightful, and beautifully illustrated history of the birth of the theory of evolution, which has revolutionized modern biology.

KEY TERMS

behavioral neuroscience The contemporary term for physiological psychology, the study of the biological basis of behavior.

biological psychology See *behavioral neuroscience.*

computerized tomography (CT) A procedure that extracts the image of a two-dimensional slice of tissue from the living organism from data obtained by multiple X-ray measurements.

cryoprobe A probe that can produce a reversible brain lesion by lowering the temperature of brain tissue in its vicinity so that nerve cells are temporarily nonfunctional.

dualism A philosophical theory that considers reality to consist of two irreducible modes, such as mind and brain.

electrocorticogram (ECoG) A record of electrical activity taken directly from the surface of the brain.

electrode A conduction medium (usually metal or conductive fluids) used for electrical recording or stimulation of biological tissues.

electroencephalogram (EEG) The record of electrical activity produced (largely) by the brain that is obtained with electrodes placed on the scalp.

electron microscope A device for viewing very small objects at very high magnification using an electron beam focused by electromagnetic fields instead of visible light focused by lenses, as in conventional microscopy.

empiricism The philosophical theory that all knowledge originates in experience.

fibers of passage Nerve fibers (axons) that pass through a particular brain region and that neither originate nor terminate in that area.

fixation In microscopy, the chemical hardening of tissue in preparing for staining.

functionalism The study of the activity of an organism in its interactions with its environment.

Golgi silver stain A preparation that completely stains very few cells, allowing these cells to be observed in their entirety.

histology The study of the microscopic structure of tissues.

horseradish peroxidase An enzyme obtained from the horseradish plant that is taken up by the end-feet of a nerve cell and transported within the axon back to the cell body; used to track neural pathways from their termination to their source.

lesion analysis The study of the behavioral effects of damage to the nervous system.

magnetic resonance imaging (MRI) A procedure for two- and three-dimensional brain imaging obtained by using radio frequency pulses and signals within a magnetic field, usually imaging the density of hydrogen atoms and their interactions with each other and their macromolecular environment.

magnetoencephalography (MEG) The magnetic counterpart of electroencephalography, in which magnetic fields produced by brain electrical activity are recorded by magnetic sensors placed near the scalp.

microelectrode A very small electrode used to record electrical activity of single cells.

micropipette A fine, fluid-filled tube that may be inserted into living tissue.

microtome A device for making thin, regular sections of embedded and fixed tissue.

mind-brain problem The philosophical problem posed in relating mental processes to the activity of the brain.

model A simplified but appropriate representation of a more complex system to which it is similar or analogous in some important respects.

monism The philosophical view that reality consists of one unified whole.

myelin stain A preparation that selectively stains the myelin, allowing myelinated pathways to be observed.

neuroanatomy The study of the structure of the nervous system.

neurochemistry The study of the chemistry of the nervous system.

neuron An information processing cell of the nervous system, also called a *nerve cell*.

neurophysiology The study of the function of nerve cells.

neuroscience The multidisciplinary study of the nervous system and its function.

neurotoxin A substance that is poisonous or destructive to nerve tissue.

Nissl stain A preparation that selectively stains the cell bodies but not the processes of neurons; it is used to observe the distribution of cell bodies in the tissue.

patch clamp The use of a micropipette to record the electrical activity of a small patch of cell membrane to which it is attached by suction.

physiological psychology See *behavioral neuroscience*.

pluralism The philosophical view that reality consists of more than two separate and irreducible modes.

positron-emission tomography (PET) A method that noninvasively maps brain structure and function by mapping the distribution of radioactively labeled substances, such as 2-deoxyglucose, to measure metabolic activity.

psychobiology See *behavioral neuroscience*.

psychoneural identity hypothesis The view that mental and brain processes are one and the same.

stain A chemical procedure that selectively colors particular features of sectioned tissue.

stereotaxic apparatus A device that guides an electrode to a specific region of the brain, using coordinates relating brain structures to skull landmarks.

stereotaxic atlas A collection of maps of brain structures and coordinates related to the landmarks employed by the stereotaxic apparatus.

Chapter 2

The Nervous System

Man, wrote Santiago Ramón y Cajal, the great 19th-century Spanish neuroanatomist, "reigns over nature through the architectural perfection of his cerebrum. Such is his patent, his indisputable title of nobility and of dominion over the other animals. And if such a lowly mammal as the rodent—the mouse for example—displays a cerebral cortex of delicate and highly complicated construction, what an indescribable structure, what an amazing mechanism must not the convolutions of the human brain present" (Ramón y Cajal, 1937, p. 476).

Never lacking in passion, Cajal (see Figure 2.1 on the following page) dearly loved the brain and its cells, which he examined throughout his life. The development of powerful low-distortion light microscopes in the 19th century permitted the first clear view of the cells of the brain. New histological techniques, such as the silver stain of Camillo Golgi, allowed single cells to be observed in their entirety. With methods such as these, the great microscopists of that period, such as Cajal, were able both to observe a wide variety of different cell types and to begin to piece together the ways in which nerve cells form brain tissues.

Figure 2.1. Santiago Ramón y Cajal, who provided the world with its first detailed microscopic vision of the cells of the brain. For his accomplishments, he received the Nobel Prize for physiology and medicine in 1906. (Portrait courtesy of the History and Special Collections Division of the Louise M. Darling Biomedical Library, UCLA.)

Cajal not only described the principal categories of cells in every major region of the human brain, but he also led the fight to establish—once and forever—that the brain is in fact composed of *individual* and separate cells, called neurons. This concept, a guiding principle of neurobiology, known as the *Neuron Doctrine*, replaced the older idea that the brain consisted of a dense set of interconnecting tubes, or reticulum (Shepherd, 1991). Incidentally, it was Camillo Golgi—the man with whom he shared the Nobel Prize in 1906—who was Cajal's principal opponent in his fight. The cells and structures of the human nervous system are the topics of this chapter.

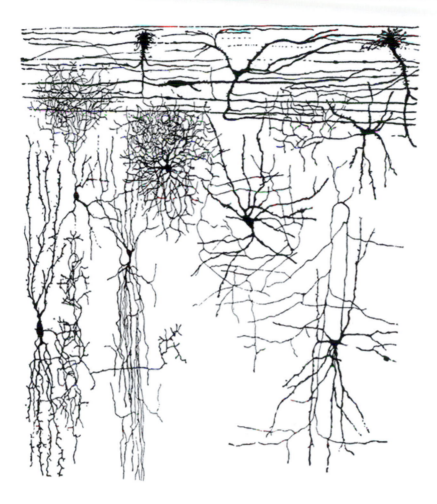

Figure 2.2. The Diversity of Neuronal Forms. These drawings by the Spaniard Santiago Ramón y Cajal beautifully illustrate the wide ranges of cellular forms adopted by neurons in fulfilling specific information-processing functions. They are of cells in the upper layers of the motor cortex of an infant who died at the age of 1 month. (From Santiago Ramón y Cajal, *Histologie du systeme nerveux de l'homme et des vertebres.* Paris: A. Maloine, 1909-1911.)

NEURONS

There are two broad classes of cells in the nervous system: **neurons** and **glia**. Neurons are the nervous system cells that process information and produce behavior. Thus, neurons and their functions are the focus of behavioral neuroscience. Unlike neurons, glia are cells with no known informational functions. Rather, glial cells provide mechanical and metabolic support for neurons, performing a number of apparently mundane but necessary housekeeping functions in the nervous system. Although glial cells are not known to be involved directly in any information-processing activity, some think that they may play a larger role in brain function than is presently realized.

Neurons are structurally diverse, varying widely in both form and size. Figure 2.2, adapted from the century-old ink drawings of Ramón y Cajal, illustrates some of the many varieties of human neurons. As can be seen, some neurons are extraordinarily complicated cells. Neurons also differ from each other in size. In the human nervous system, for example, many cortical neurons are less than 0.1 millimeters in length, whereas others—which descend to the spinal cord—may be nearly as long as a meter. The extreme modifiability of neurons allows the mammalian nervous system to be exquisitely well adapted to the diverse requirements of controlling large, intelligent animals, a conclusion that will be repeatedly illustrated in later chapters.

Despite large differences in neuronal appearance, all neurons share important common characteristics. Each neuron has an outer membrane that regulates electrical signaling in the cell. Every neuron has a form that is dictated by its cytoskeleton. Every neuron has snakelike **processes**—the axons and dendrites that are extensions of the cell body—that funnel information into and out of the cell body. In short, the basic mechanisms by which each neuron carries out its diverse specific functions are strikingly similar, both within a single organism and across animal species.

The Neuronal Membrane

It is the **cell membrane** that defines the limits of the cell, enclosing it and separating it from the surrounding extracellular fluid. It also is responsible for establishing and maintaining the chemical differences between the interior of the cell and its external environment.

The cell membrane of a neuron is a highly complex and specialized molecular machine that performs a wide variety of functions essential for neuronal information processing. All information received by a neuron must pass through the cell membrane, as must all messages that the neurons send to other cells. Much has been learned in the past two decades about the properties of neuronal membranes and the mechanisms by which they operate.

The neural membrane is a very old invention in evolution, one that was so successful that it has remained unchanged in both invertebrate and vertebrate nervous systems. Its major structural components are **phospholipids**, or fatty acids, and **proteins**, complex organic molecules formed from strings of amino acid. Phospholipids are by far the most numerous molecules in the neural membrane, outnumbering protein molecules by more than 150 to 1.

The structure of a phospholipid molecule is shown in Figure 2.3 on the facing page. It has a head that is *hydrophilic*, or "water loving," and two tails that are *hydrophobic*, or "water hating." The tails are composed of fatty acids of differing lengths. Usually, one is unsaturated, with cis-double bonds that bend the tail, and the other is saturated and straight. These properties strongly influence the way in which the phospholipids pack into a membrane (Alberts et al., 1994).

When phospholipids are dissolved in an appropriate agent (such as benzene) and a few drops are placed on a surface of water, a remarkable biochemical self-organizing effect occurs; each molecule orients itself with its hydrophilic head on the water's surface and its hydrophobic tail extended away from the water into the air. Figure 2.4 on page 34 illustrates a number of phospholipid molecules organizing themselves at the water-air boundary.

The cell membrane is constructed of two phospholipid layers, joined at the tips of their hydrophobic tails, with their hydrophilic heads facing the aqueous cytoplasmic and intercellular solutions. The bilayer phospholipid

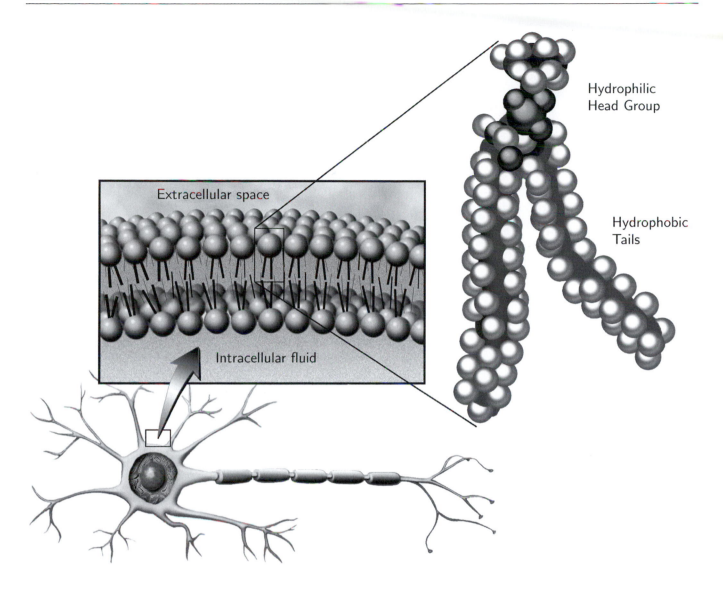

Figure 2.3. The Structure of a Membrane Phospholipid Molecule. Each molecule is composed of a hydrophilic head and two hydrophobic tails.

membrane of the neuron is shown in Figure 2.3. The self-organizing properties of the phospholipid molecules are not only critical to the original construction of the neural membrane but also are responsible for producing speedy repairs whenever the membrane is punctured or torn.

The lipid bilayer membrane is very stable as a molecular structure, but at the molecular level, it is anything except static. Individual phospholipid molecules flow freely along the inner and outer monolayers. Each molecule, for example, exchanges places with its neighbor about 1 million times each second. Thus, a single molecule will transverse the length of a very small cell about once each second. But it is extremely rare that a molecule will leave its monolayer. For this reason, each of the two monolayers of the cell membrane may be considered to behave as a two-dimensional fluid.

Figure 2.4. Self-Organization of Phospholipids. When phospholipids are placed on a surface of water, the molecules orient themselves with their hydrophilic heads on the surface of the water and their hydrophobic tails lifted into the air.

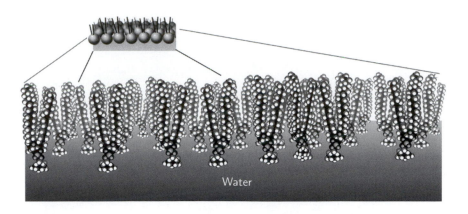

Proteins form the second class of membrane molecules (see Figure 2.5 on the next page). The most important and best understood of these are the **integral proteins**. Integral proteins are embedded within the membrane and extend from it into both the cytoplasm and extracellular fluids. They provide a number of mechanisms that link the interior environment of the cell with its exterior environment.

The integral protein molecules, like the phospholipids that surround them, have hydrophobic and hydrophilic regions. They are configured in the cell membrane with their hydrophilic portions extending into either the cytoplasm or extracellular fluid and—for this reason—are also called **transmembrane proteins**. The hydrophobic regions of the transmembrane proteins are buried within the phospholipid bilayer. Many transmembrane proteins have multiple hydrophobic and hydrophilic segments. These proteins cross the membrane several times, forming elaborate molecular structures, such as membrane channels that are important in electrical signaling. Such molecules are called **multipass transmembrane proteins**. Multipass transmembrane proteins also serve as transport mechanisms for the cell, moving important molecules in and out of the neuron.

Finally, mention should be made of the neuronal glycolipids, sugar-containing lipid molecules that cluster exclusively on the outer surface of the neuronal cell membrane. These glycolipid complexes are common, but the functional roles they might play in the daily activities of nerve cells are a mystery at this time.

The Neuronal Cytoskeleton

It is sometimes useful to think of the cell membrane as the "skin" of a neuron and the cytoskeleton as its "bones." The **cytoskeleton** is a complex structure of fibrillar proteins within the cytoplasm that establishes the shape or overall structure of each individual neuron. Thus, the distinctive and complex form of each nerve cell is determined by the structure of the cytoskeleton within it. The cytoskeleton also anchors special protein structures of the neuronal membrane in their correct positions.

Unlike bone, the cytoskeleton of a neuron is a dynamic structure that

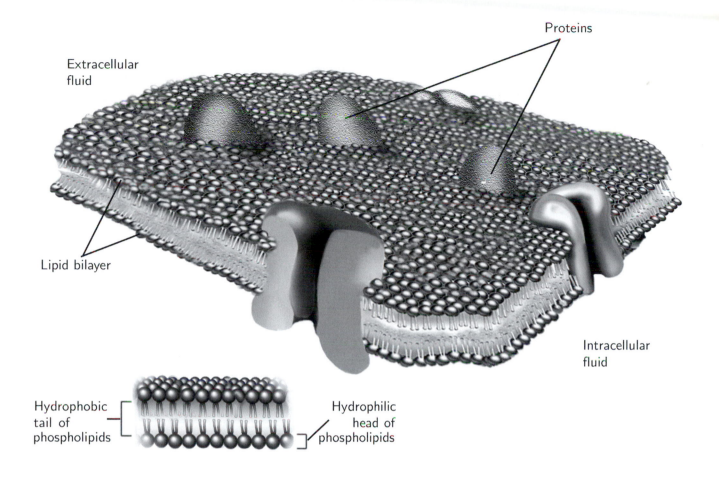

Proteins

Extracellular
fluid

Lipid bilayer

Intracellular
fluid

Hydrophobic
tail of
phospholipids

Hydrophilic
head of
phospholipids

changes its form to meet the continuing demands of its neural environment. Thus, the cytoskeleton is also the "muscle" of the cell, moving organelles from one place in the cell to another. In neurons, the muscular functions of the cytoskeleton play particularly important roles in the movement of substances along the axon.

The cytoskeleton is built from three different types of protein filaments that differ from each other in size (see Figure 2.6 on the following page). The smallest are the **microfilaments**, which are composed of the protein *actin*. Microfilaments are 5 to 9 nanometers (nm; 10^{-9} or one billionth of a meter) in diameter and form complex networks and gels beneath the cell membrane. Next in size are the **intermediate filaments** (10 nm in diameter), which are composed of a variety of similar proteins. Intermediate filaments, among other things, form lattice structures that give mechanical strength to the cell body. The largest of the cytostructural elements are the **microtubules**, which are constructed from the protein *tubulin*. Microtubules are long, cylindrical structures that are the largest (25 nm) of the cytoskeletal components.

The length of even the smallest neural filaments is very much larger

Figure 2.5. A Model of the Membrane Consisting of Two Layers of Phospholipids and Some Intermixed Integral Protein Molecules. Both the intracellular and extracellular fluids consist of water with dissolved salts. Thus, the phospholipid molecules are oriented with their hydrophilic heads facing toward the edges of the membrane. The hydrophobic tails of these molecules are oriented toward the interior of the membrane. This is the basic structure of cell membranes and is shared by all neurons in all animals.

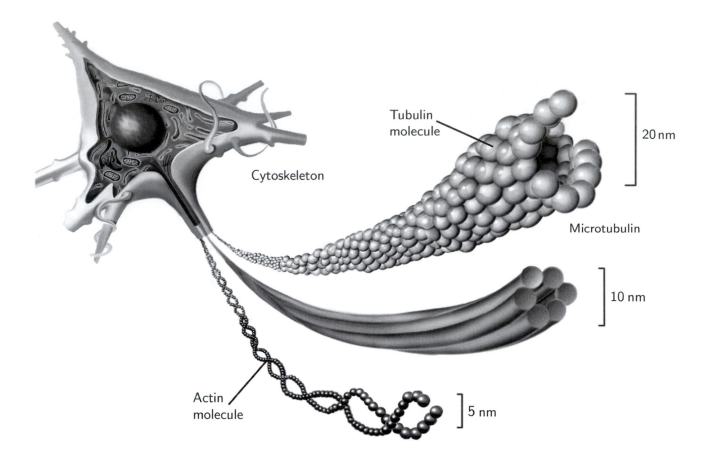

Figure 2.6. Microfilaments, Intermediate Filaments, and Microtubules. The cytoskeleton of a neuron is constructed from molecular components that differ in size. Together, they give neurons the physical shape that they require.

than the size of any of the constituent protein molecules. Each type of filament achieves its length by **polymerization**, the covalent binding of multiple identical molecules (monomers) into a single, elongated molecular structure.

Together, the three types of cytoskeletal filaments perform a number of critical functions for nerve cells. Statically, these filaments establish neuronal form, which dictates many of the functional properties of the cell, particularly the sources of its input and the targets of its output. Dynamically, they transport substances and subcellular organelles along the neurons' spidery processes between the cell body and synaptic regions, performing a variety of functions that are vital to neural information processing.

FUNCTIONAL PARTS OF THE NEURON

A typical neuron may be divided into three distinct regions or parts: its cell body, dendrites, and axon (see Figure 2.7 on the next page). The **cell**

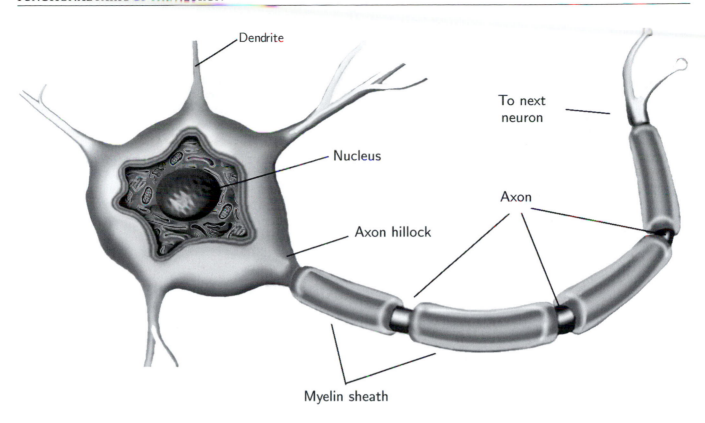

Dendrite

To next neuron

Nucleus

Axon

Axon hillock

Myelin sheath

body, or **soma**, contains the nucleus of the cell and its associated intracellular structures and is similar to that of any other cell in the body. In its processes—specialized extensions of the cell body—neurons are radically different. These processes, called dendrites and axons, are found only in neural cells. A **synapse** is a specialized structure through which cells communicate with each other.

Dendrites are processes that obtain information from other cells and bring that information to the cell body of the neuron. Conversely, axons carry information away from the soma to other neurons or muscle cells. Most neurons have axons, but particularly small neurons may not have true axons. Axons terminate in **axon terminals**, or **terminal boutons** (*boutons* in French means "buttons"), which transmit information to the receiving cell.

The point of communication between one neuron and another is called a **synapse**. Synapses are generally directional in function, with activity at the axon terminal of the sending cell (**presynaptic cell**) affecting the behavior of the receiving cell (**postsynaptic cell**). In most neurons, the postsynaptic membrane is usually on the cell body or dendrites, but synapses between axons also occur.

A primary function of neurons is to process information and to integrate the influences of the cells from which they receive input. In the human brain, a single neuron may receive input at tens of thousands of synapses. Brains are capable of great complexity.

Figure 2.7. The Major Features of a Typical Neuron. Neurons gather information through contacts with other cells on their dendrites and cell body. They communicate with other cells through their axons.

The Cell Body

The cell body integrates synaptic input and determines the message to be transmitted to other cells by the axon, but that is not its only function. The cell body also is responsible for a variety of complex biochemical processes, as it does in every living cell. For example, the cell body contains the metabolic machinery necessary to transform glucose into high-energy compounds that supply the energy needs of other parts of the neuron. Furthermore, the highly active proteins that serve as chemical messengers between cells are manufactured and packaged in the cell body.

The cell body contains a number of smaller, specialized substructures, called **organelles**, or "little organs," which carry out many of the cell's functions. Figure 2.8 on the facing page illustrates the organelles of a typical neuron.

Mitochondria   Supplying metabolic energy to the cell in a form that can be easily used is a primary role of the **mitochondria**. These organelles have their own outer membrane encasing a folded, internal membrane. The major source of energy for the nervous system is the sugar glucose, which is derived from carbohydrate foodstuffs. Mitochondria contain the enzymes needed to transform glucose into high-energy compounds, primarily **adenosine triphosphate (ATP)**. ATP molecules may then be transported to other regions of the cell where their energy is used.

Nucleus   The manufacture of neuronal active compounds and other large protein molecules within the cell body is more complex. The process of protein synthesis begins in the nucleus of the cell. The **nucleus** of a neuron is separated from the intracellular fluid and other organelles by its nuclear membrane. The nucleus is the fundamental organelle of the cell, containing the genetic information that guides cellular function. The genetic template is stored as coded strings of **deoxyribonucleic acid (DNA)**. Each DNA molecule holds the genetic codes for all the cells in the body; only a selected part of this genetic blueprint is used by nerve cells. The nucleus begins the process of building protein molecules by transcribing the relevant portion of DNA code onto a complementary molecule of **ribonucleic acid (RNA)**. RNA molecules then are released by the nucleus into the intracellular fluid surrounding it, where the process of protein synthesis actually takes place.

The **nucleolus** is a separate structure within the nucleus, which also is involved in the process of protein synthesis. However, the nucleolus does not manufacture proteins directly. Instead, it builds molecular complexes, called **ribosomes**, which are involved in protein synthesis. Ribosomes are complexes of RNA and protein that are ejected from the nucleolus and nucleus into the cell body, where they do their work.

Endoplasmic Reticulum and Golgi Apparatus   Two other organelles are primarily responsible for the cellular manufacture of proteins: the endoplasmic reticulum and the Golgi apparatus. Together, they form a minia-

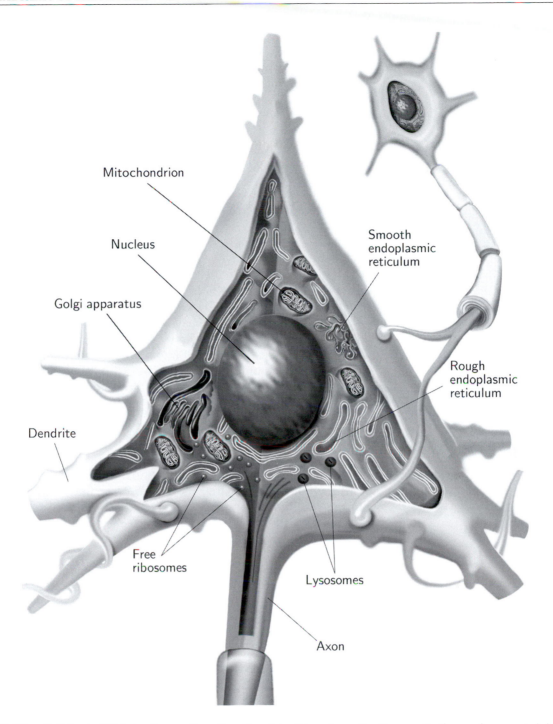

Mitochondrion

Nucleus

Golgi apparatus

Dendrite

Smooth endoplasmic reticulum

Rough endoplasmic reticulum

Free ribosomes

Lysosomes

Axon

Figure 2.8. The Cell Body With Its Organelles. Prominent in this schematic diagram is the nucleus containing a nucleolus within it. Next to the nucleus is the protein-synthesizing machinery of the neuron, a complex of rough endoplasmic reticulum with its adjoining Golgi apparatus. Also illustrated are mitochondria, which provide energy-rich molecules for use elsewhere in the cell.

ture manufacturing and packaging plant. The **endoplasmic reticulum** is a system of tubes, vesicles, and sacs constructed from membranes similar to those surrounding the neuron. The rough endoplasmic reticulum is the initial segment of structure that begins to build protein molecules; it gains its rough appearance from the presence of large numbers of ribosomes bound to its surface. The ribosomes of the rough endoplasmic reticulum construct large segments of protein molecules in the sequence of steps prescribed by the RNA released by the nucleus of the cell. These segments of the protein molecule are moved down the rough endoplasmic reticulum much like a product being assembled on an industrial assembly line. When completed, the segments are released into the smooth endoplasmic reticulum, which lacks ribosomes, and are transported by it to the Golgi apparatus.

The **Golgi apparatus**—named in honor of Camillo Golgi—is a complex of membranes that completes the assembling of the protein and encloses the resulting molecules in their own membrane for release into the cell. It is important that the proteins be packaged in this way because they have strong effects on neural function. When enclosed in a sphere built of membrane, a **vesicle**, the proteins may be moved safely to the portion of the cell in which they will eventually be used. For example, the neurotransmitters that are released by a cell into a synapse are manufactured by the endoplasmic reticulum and Golgi apparatus in the cell body, encased in a vesicle, and then transported down the length of the axon to the synapse where they eventually will be used.

Dendrites

Dendrites may be thought of as continuations of the cell body's membrane, extending that sensitive receptive surface into the surrounding nervous tissue. It is not surprising to find that the pattern of dendritic branching differs widely among cells and reflects the functions that the cell performs. In some cases, the functional properties of a neuron can be completely predicted from its pattern of dendritic spread. The dendrites, with their thin, branching, treelike forms, greatly increase the opportunity for synaptic connections in brain tissue. The dendritic system of a single cell may make as many as 100,000 individual synapses with other neurons.

Electron microscopy confirms the concept of dendrites as extensions of the cell body. The same types of intracellular substructures that characterize the cell body of a neuron are also present in dendrites.

Many types of neurons have dendrites with a special form of synaptic connection, **dendritic spines**. These are small (1-2 mm), thornlike protuberances from the dendrite that form the postsynaptic element of most synapses in the brain (see Figure 2.9 on the next page). The dendritic spines reach out and make contact with nearby axon terminals.

The pattern of the dendritic spines changes over the length of the dendrite. Near the cell body, the spines are usually small and relatively simple enlargements protruding slightly from the side of the dendrite. At greater distances, the spines become larger and more elaborate. Spines emerge from the dendrite and expand, sometimes splitting into a double spine with multiple synapses. At the very least, spines increase the synaptic

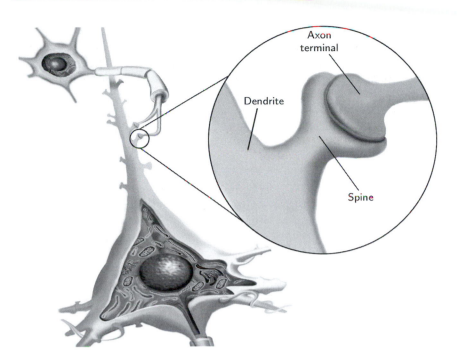

Axon
terminal

Dendrite

Spine

Figure 2.9. Dendritic Spines. These spines are small saclike protuberances, which form the postsynaptic elements in the synapses of that neuron. The formation of these spines appears to be dynamic and provides a mechanism by which synaptic connections can be strengthened significantly.

surface of the dendrite, allowing a maximum of synaptic content with a minimum of dendritic volume.

About 80% of all excitatory synapses (those acting to evoke activity in the postsynaptic cell) are on dendritic spines; the remainder involve other parts of the dendrite. In contrast, less than one third of all inhibitory synapses involve spines, and when they do, they are coupled with an excitatory synapse on the same spine. The specific reasons for this arrangement are a matter of growing interest.

There is now accumulating evidence that dendritic spines are modifiable structures that change with learning and other factors. Whatever their functional role may be, dendritic spines are a major anatomical feature of many classes of neurons in the human nervous system.

The Axon

The **axon** of a neuron arises from the cell body and extends to the region or regions of synaptic contact. Axons are specialized processes that are characterized by having an **excitable membrane**, a membrane that is capable of generating or propagating an action potential (Hille, 1992; Levitan & Kaczmarek, 1991). An action potential is a distinctive electrical response that serves to faithfully carry information along the entire length of the axon.

Usually, cells have only one axon, but it may give off **collaterals**, or branches, to carry the action potential simultaneously to more than one region of the brain.

Axon Hillock   The axon emerges from the cell body in a tapering cone of membrane that forms the **axon hillock**. This structure is very distinct from the rest of the cell body when examined microscopically; it is completely devoid of the ribosomes and endoplasmic reticulum that characterize the rest of the cell body and the neighboring portions of the dendrites. Instead, numerous microtubules and microfilaments form the basis of a transportation system for the axon, aiding in the movement of substances from the cell body to the axon terminal.

Axon Terminal   As an axon approaches its synaptic targets, it will often branch into a number of smaller processes, each of which terminates in an axon terminal. Within each axon terminal are both mitochondria and synaptic vesicles. The synaptic vesicles contain neurotransmitter substances, which are released into the space between the presynaptic membrane of the axon terminal and the postsynaptic membrane of the receiving cell. The space between the presynaptic and postsynaptic membranes is called the **synaptic cleft**.

Flow and Transport in Axons   The axon of a neuron allows signals received by the dendrites and cell body to be communicated to other cells located in other, perhaps distant parts of the nervous system, usually by the release of neurotransmitter substances by the axon terminal. In this respect, neurotransmitter release is similar to secretory discharge in other cells. But for the neuron, the source of the neurotransmitter substance, the cell body, is far removed from the site of discharge, the axon terminal. Special mechanisms are necessary to transport newly formed synaptic vesicles from the cell body to the terminal and to return depleted vesicles to the cell body for repair. In large animals, these distances may be significant, and—for this reason—axons contain specialized transport systems.

The principal mechanism for moving newly formed synaptic vesicles and related material from the cell body to the terminal is **fast axonal transport**. In this system, the motor protein kinesin carries these organelles from the cell body down the axon along the axonal microtubules. Old material is returned to the cell body using the same microtubule system but a different motor protein, dynein. These systems are extremely rapid by biological standards, carrying freshly manufactured molecular cargo from the cell body to the end-foot at rates of up to 0.5 meters per day. Molecular debris is returned to the cell body at about half this speed (Alberts et al., 1994).

In contrast, **slow axoplasmic flow** is unidirectional, proceeding from the cell body to the axon terminal (*axoplasm* is a name for intracellular fluid within an axon). Different components of the axoplasm (axonal cytoplasm) flow at different rates, the fastest being no more than about 5 mm per day, or 1/100th the rate of the fast transport system. Various proteins, including enzymes and replacement components for the filament systems, are carried by slow axoplasmic flow.

TYPES OF NEURONS

There are a number of useful ways in which neurons may be categorized. One is by their appearance, as form often provides clues about function. Most neurons have several dendrites and one axon. Such a neuron is considered to be a **multipolar neuron**. Other neurons have fewer processes: A **bipolar neuron** has one dendrite and one axon, and a **unipolar neuron** has only a single process with which it communicates. Unipolar and bipolar neurons are much less common in vertebrate than in invertebrate nervous systems.

Many types of nerve cells are named for anatomical features that determine their characteristic appearances. Thus, *pyramidal* cells have pyramid-shaped cell bodies, *stellate* cells resemble stars, and *double-bouquet cells* look like, well, two bouquets of flowers. These three types of neurons all are found in the cerebral cortex, but equally descriptive names are used to categorize cells throughout the nervous system.

Perhaps the most important anatomical distinction commonly used to divide nerve cells into general categories contrasts neurons with and neurons without long axons. Long-axoned cells, called **principal neurons**, transmit information over long distances from one brain region to another (Shepherd, 1990). Principal neurons provide the pathways of communication within the nervous system. Principal neurons are also referred to as **projection neurons** or **Golgi Type I neurons**.

In contrast to the principal neurons, **local circuit neurons**, which lack long axons, must exert all their effects in the local region of their cell bodies and dendrites. They are located in brain areas served by the long-axoned principal neurons and act to affect the activity in these pathways. Local circuit neurons—also called **Golgi Type II neurons**—perform integrative and modulating functions in local brain regions.

Principal neurons, with their long axons, usually have large cell bodies. In part, this is because the axon is dependent on the cell body for metabolic energy and for the proteins that it needs to function and maintain itself. Furthermore, cells with large dendritic trees, such as the Purkinje cells of the cerebellum, also tend to have large cell bodies. In contrast, the local circuit neurons, with their short dendrites and small axons (when present), usually have small, compact cell bodies.

Neurons also are classified by the functional roles that they play in the chain of information flow from input to output. **Receptors** are highly specialized neurons that act to encode sensory information. For example, the photoreceptors of the eye transform variations in light intensity into electrical and chemical signals that can be read by other nerve cells. It is the receptor cells that begin the process of sensation and perception. **Interneurons** form the second category of nerve cells. These cells receive signals from and send signals to other neurons. Interneurons serve to process information in many different ways and constitute the bulk of the human nervous system. **Effectors** or **motor neurons** are the final class of neurons in this scheme. Motor neurons send signals directly to the muscles and glands of the body, thereby forming the final step in producing behavior.

A final useful and common set of distinctions group neurons according to the specific neurotransmitter chemicals that they employ.

GLIAL CELLS

Neurons—the prime objects of inquiry in behavioral neuroscience—are not the only cells in the central nervous system. Neurons depend on glial cells, which support them and perform a variety of housekeeping functions in the brain (Fawcett, 1981; Peters, Palay, & Webster, 1991). The term **glia**, by the way, means "glue," a reflection of the fact that glial cells really do help hold the brain together by filling the space between neurons. Glia are usually very small cells, but there are a great many of them. Thus, although a little more than one half of the brain's weight is contributed by glial cells, they outnumber neurons by as much as 50 to 1.

There are three principal types of glial cells: astrocytes, oligodendrocytes, and Schwann cells. The oligodendrocytes and the astrocytes are located within the central nervous system, that is, within the brain and spinal cord. Schwann cells are located outside the central nervous system, where they support peripheral nerve cells.

Oligodendrocytes are small cells that lack the spidery processes of the astroglia. Their cell bodies contain a large number of organelles and many microtubules that are arranged in parallel arrays. Oligodendrocytes may serve a number of functional roles within the central nervous system, but only one is known with certainty. The oligodendrocytes produce **myelin**, which surrounds the axons of many large neurons (see Figure 2.10 on the facing page). This insulating coating is called a **myelin sheath**. Myelination provides both electrical and mechanical insulation for the axon, which greatly increases the speed with which action potentials are transmitted. Each oligodendrocyte may provide myelin wrapping for a dozen or so adjacent neurons within the densely packed central nervous system.

Outside the central nervous system, along the large peripheral nerves that connect the brain and spinal cord with the muscles, glands, and sensory organs of the body, the **Schwann cells** perform myelinating functions. This process of myelination is illustrated in Figure 2.11 on page 46. In the developing nervous system, the Schwann cell first encircles a peripheral nerve axon, then wraps itself around the axon, building a myelin sheath. As it moves, the intracellular fluid is pushed forward, leaving only the membrane of the Schwann cell wrapped around the once-naked axon. Each Schwann cell, unlike the oligodendrocytes, only myelinates a small portion of a single nerve axon. Thus, several hundred Schwann cells are needed to myelinate one large neuron in the peripheral nervous system.

Demyelinating diseases, such as multiple sclerosis and Guillain-Barré syndrome, attack and destroy the myelin sheaths produced by oligodendrocytes and Schwann cells. The results of demyelination are as varied as the functions of the particular neurons affected. Common symptoms include impaired vision, shaking, motor weakness, and impaired speech—dysfunctions that bring home the importance of myelination in the healthy nervous system.

Finally, **astrocytes** are the most numerous type of glial cell. They are named for their star-shaped appearance when Golgi stained. When examined at greater magnification, these small cells show a characteristic lack of organelles within their cell bodies. This indicates that astrocytes are not heavily engaged in synthetic functions, such as building proteins. Astro-

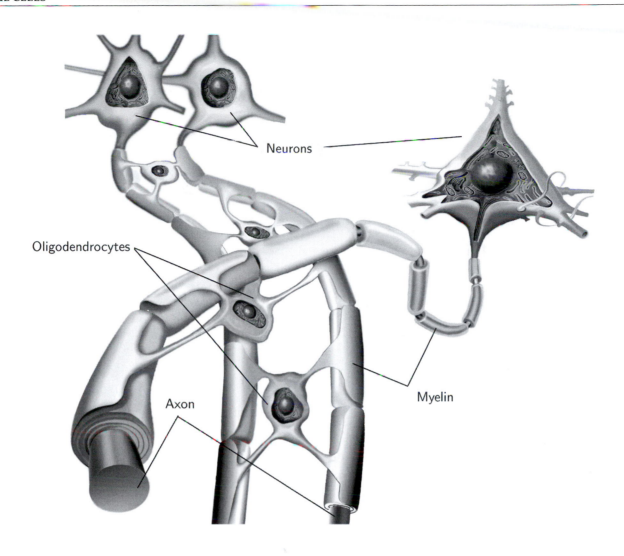

Neurons

Oligodendrocytes

Axon

Myelin

cytes provide structural support for the neurons of the brain and aid in the repair of neurons following damage to the brain. They also regulate the flow of ions and larger molecules in the region of the synapse, a fact of unknown significance. Finally, astrocytes play an important role in the functioning of the blood-brain barrier, protecting the neurons of the brain and spinal cord.

The Blood-Brain Barrier

Neurons are different from other bodily cells. Very ordinary cell membrane properties have been exquisitely adapted to process information by the neurons of the brain. Neurons carry information by electrical signals that are generated by their membranes, as we will see in the following two chapters. These signals depend on differences in the chemical composition of the fluids inside and outside the cell. But when we eat, for example, the

Figure 2.10. Oligodendrocytes and the Myelin Sheath. The myelin sheath is essentially the membrane of the oligodendrocyte, from which all the intracellular fluid has been squeezed. Here, oligodendrocytes can be seen forming multiple elements of the myelin sheaths of several neurons.

Figure 2.11. Construction of the Myelin Sheath. The myelinating glial cell surrounds a length of axon with its membrane and then wraps itself around it a number of times, leaving a sheath of membrane on the axon.

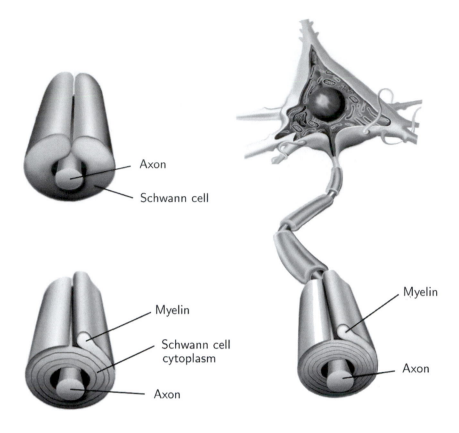

Axon

Schwann cell

Myelin

Schwann cell cytoplasm

Axon

Myelin

Axon

chemical composition of our blood—and therefore of the fluid that bathes cells throughout the body—changes markedly.

For other cells, these changes are of no consequence. But for neurons, the results would be disastrous because even small changes in the composition of the fluids that bathe them would result in false electrical signals, distorting the brain information on which we act. For this and other similar reasons, brain neurons require a very protected, extremely constant molecular environment in which to operate. They are given that protection by the **blood-brain barrier**.

The existence of a barrier between the blood and the brain was discovered nearly a century ago by a pair of simple observations. Potent cellular dyes injected into the bloodstream would stain every cell in the body, except those of the brain and spinal cord. Conversely, dyes inserted into the brain itself completely stained the cells of the central nervous system but no other cells in the body. Something isolated the brain from the general circulation.

The nature of the blood-brain barrier is shown in Figure 2.12 on the facing page. In the brain—as in other regions of the body—endothelial cells surround the capillaries of the vascular system. But unlike in other regions, in the brain and spinal cord, these endothelial cells form tight seals around the vasculature with no gaps through which blood-borne substances can diffuse. Thus, a special adaptation of ordinary endothelial

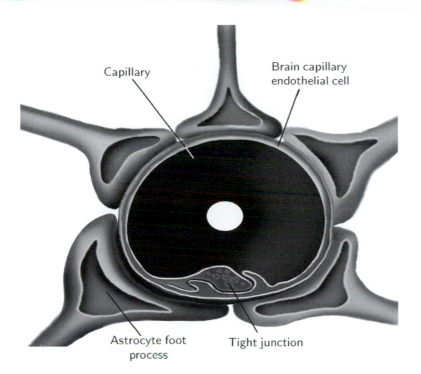

Capillary

Brain capillary
endothelial cell

Astrocyte foot
process

Tight junction

Figure 2.12. The Blood-Brain Barrier. The blood-brain barrier is formed by endothelial cells that prevent the diffusion of blood-borne substances into the brain.

cells forms the physical basis of the blood-brain barrier (Betz, Goldstein, & Katzman, 1994).

Epithelial cell membranes—like membranes of other cells—are composed of phospholipids and proteins. Respiratory gases, such as oxygen and carbon dioxide, are lipid soluble and—for that reason—can pass freely through the endothelial membrane. Most psychoactive drugs are also lipid soluble and can therefore penetrate the blood-brain barrier with ease. This allows compounds such as nicotine, alcohol, heroin, and phenobarbital to enter the brain rapidly by the simple process of diffusion.

All substances that are not lipid soluble must enter the brain through special gates provided by protein molecules embedded in the membrane of the endothelial cell. These proteins—termed **transport carriers**—ensure that the brain receives adequate supplies of glucose, amino acids, proteins, and other essential substances. Ion transporters regulate the ionic content of the extracellular cerebrospinal fluid, providing an active buffer between fluctuating ionic contents of the blood and the carefully regulated cerebrospinal fluid.

Astrocytes appear to play an important role in the blood-brain barrier system. Nearly the entire outer surface of the endothelial cells is covered with specialized synaptic-like astrocyte processes. Moreover, in diseases in which the blood-brain barrier is damaged, these characteristic astrocyte-endothelial contacts are absent. These findings argue for a major role of astrocyte cells in the proper functioning of the blood-brain barrier, but what that contribution may be is—as yet—poorly understood (Betz, Goldstein, & Katzman, 1994).

Finally, there are certain small regions of the brain in which the blood-

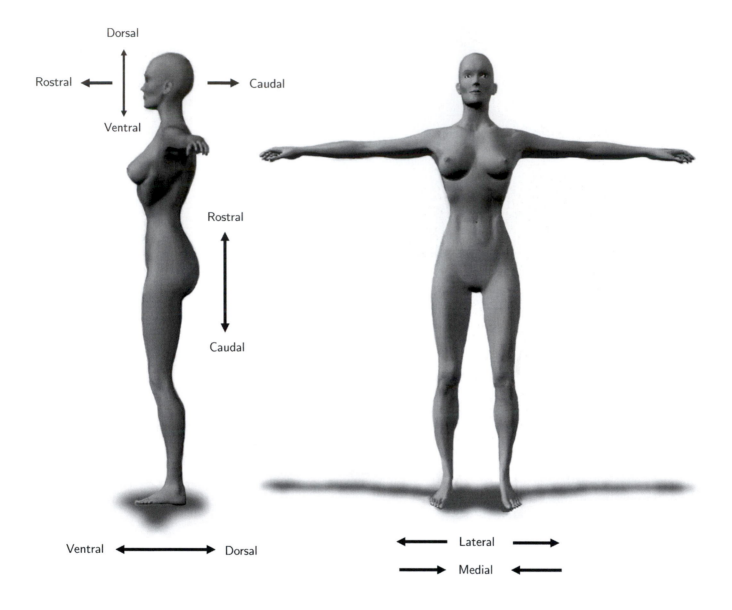

Figure 2.13. Anatomical Directions. A frontal (coronal) and a side (sagittal) view of a person, illustrating the spatial relations among the anatomical directional terms.

brain barrier is incomplete. These include the pituitary and pineal glands, as well as areas believed to monitor various aspects of blood content, as in the regulation of hunger.

THE ANATOMY OF THE NERVOUS SYSTEM

Enormous numbers of individual neurons and glial cells combine to form the diverse structures of the human nervous system. The analysis of these structures is the traditional province of the discipline of neuroanatomy, which—by and large—describes the nervous system at the level of tissues rather than cells.

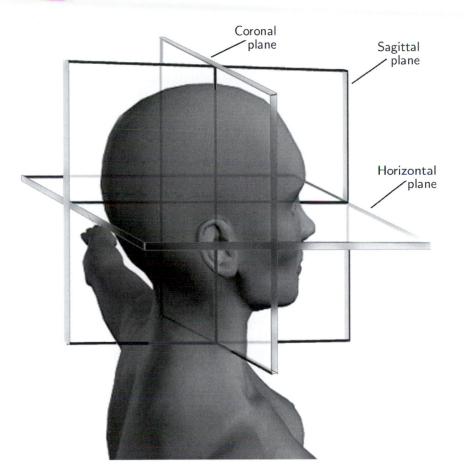

Coronal plane

Sagittal plane

Horizontal plane

Figure 2.14. The Principal Planes of Section Illustrated for a Human Brain. These three planes provide the conventional view of the human nervous system, at both microscopic and macroscopic scales.

In examining the anatomy of the nervous system, it is often necessary to describe the position of one structure in relation to another or with respect to the organism as a whole. Neuroanatomists have adopted a special vocabulary that allows such relations to be expressed precisely and simply. Many anatomical terms are derived from either Greek or—more often—Latin roots, all of which are equally accessible to speakers of any modern European language.

Figure 2.13 on the preceding page illustrates many of these anatomical terms. Consider first the four-footed animal. A structure near the nose is described as **rostral** (from the Latin word *rostrum*, meaning "beak") or **anterior**. Conversely, structures farther back are said to be **caudal** (*cauda* means "tail" in Latin) or **posterior**. The belly, or **inferior**, side of the four-footed animal is its **ventral** side (*ventralis* is Latin for "belly"), whereas its back is its **dorsal** (*dorsum* is Latin for "back") or **superior** side.

In humans, things are a bit different because we stand on two feet rather than on four. In standing, the relation between the brain and the body is turned by 90 degrees. For example, the anterior regions of the four-footed brain now face forward rather than upward. Anatomists want the same words to apply to the same structures in all vertebrate brains; otherwise, unnecessary confusion would result. Therefore, for the standing person, the top of the head is considered to be dorsal, whereas the forehead is rostral.

Finally, structures toward the side are said to be **lateral**, and structures toward the center are considered to be **medial**. These directional terms are applied to the human brain in Figure 2.13 on page 48.

It is often useful to view neuronal structures as a two-dimensional slice, taken through some portion of the brain. Such slices are called *sections*. The term **planes of section** refers to the directions in which the slices may be made. This is also shown in Figure 2.14 on the page before. The plane that would be parallel to the floor when a person is standing is the **horizontal plane**, also termed the **axial plane**. The axis of the body is an imaginary line running through its center from head to toe; the axial plane cuts through this line at right angles.

The plane perpendicular to the floor and parallel to a line between the nose and back of the head is the **sagittal plane**. *Sagitta* is Latin for "arrow." In anatomy, sagittal denotes the anterior-posterior direction, for reasons that William Tell's son might have appreciated.

The third plane of section is also perpendicular to the horizontal but parallel to a line between the ears; this is the **coronal plane**. In Latin, *corona* is the name for a crown or a wreath. All these anatomical terms are employed in describing the orientation of both microscopic cross sections of brain tissue and neuroimages produced by brain scanning.

General Features of the Nervous System

The nervous system is composed of the brain, the spinal cord, and the peripheral nerves, which deliver commands to bring information from the other organs of the body. It is conventionally divided into two sections: the **central nervous system (CNS)**, composed of the brain and spinal cord, and the **peripheral nervous system (PNS)**, made of the nerves that enter and depart the CNS.

The central nervous system develops from a single tubelike piece of embryonic tissue that becomes increasingly differentiated and complex at its forward tip. This tip becomes the brain and is encased within the bony protective cavity of the skull. The remainder becomes the **spinal cord**, which is located within the vertebrae of the spinal column.

The protective cavity of the skull surrounding the delicate tissue of the CNS is filled with **cerebrospinal fluid (CSF)**, a clear liquid with a specific gravity that is slightly greater than that of the brain or spinal cord. Thus, the brain is able to float within the skull; a human brain that weighs 1,500 grams in air weighs only about 50 grams in the CSF. This reduces the strain that otherwise would be placed on the brain by the weight of its own tissues. The brain and spinal cord are separated from the skull and vertebrae by three protective membranes that together form the **meninges** (from the Greek *meninx*, meaning "membrane"). Figure 2.15 on the facing page shows the meninges in cross section.

The outermost meningeal layer is the **dura mater** (in Latin, it means "hard mother"). The dura mater is a tough, dense membrane of connective tissue. It is smooth in appearance and follows the outlines of the skull and spinal canal. In some places, the dura mater folds inward to create

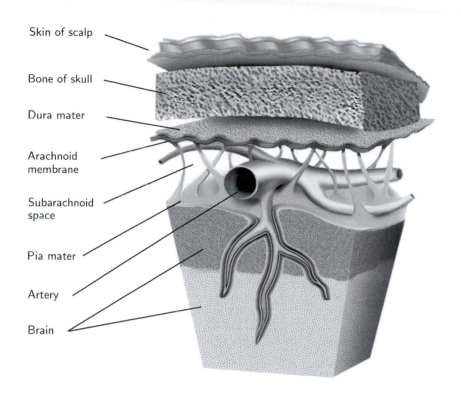

Skin of scalp

Bone of skull

Dura mater

Arachnoid
membrane

Subarachnoid
space

Pia mater

Artery

Brain

Figure 2.15. The Meninges. Three layers of membrane surround the brain and spinal cord. They are the dura mater, the arachnoid, and the pia mater. The subarachnoid space is filled with cerebrospinal fluid and provides space for the arteries that serve the brain.

separate compartments for brain tissue within the cranial cavity. It is this strong membrane that physically isolates the CNS from other bodily structures.

Beneath the dura mater lies the second of the meninges, the **arachnoid**. Its name reflects its appearance, deriving from the Greek *arachne*, or cobweb, and *eidos*, which means "resembling." This thin membrane is next to the dura mater, overlying the **subarachnoid space**. The subarachnoid space contains the cerebrospinal fluid. It varies in thickness according to differences in shape between the skull and brain. The innermost of the meninges is the **pia mater** (Latin, meaning "tender mother"). The pia mater is thin, transparent membrane that follows the contours of the underlying brain tissue exactly. A fine web of **arachnoid trabeculae**, a delicate system of connective fibers, mechanically links the arachnoid with the pia mater. Together, the dura mater, arachnoid, and pia mater encase the CNS and suspend it in its protective cerebrospinal fluid.

Standards for Neuroanatomical Naming

Neuroanatomists have developed international standards for the terms that they use to describe the nervous system and other living structures. Much of the modern work to achieve clear, agreed-on anatomical definitions has been carried out by the International Anatomical Nomenclature Committee in a continually refined set of standards called the *Nomina Anatomica* (1983).

However, the development of computerized three-dimensional neuro-

BRAIN

FOREBRAIN
Diencephalon
Epithalamus
Thalamus
Hypothalamus
Subthalamus

Telencephalon
Cerebral Cortex
Olfactory Bulb
Amygdala
Septal Region
Fornix
Basal Ganglia
Globus Pallidus
Striatum
Putamen
Caudate Nucleus

MIDBRAIN
Tectum
Pretectal Region
Superior Colliculus
Inferior Colliculus

Cerebral Peduncle
Subtantia Nigra
Midbrain Tegmentum
Occulomotor Nucleus
Midbrain RF
Red Nucleus
Central Gray
Raphe Nucleus

HINDBRAIN
Medulla Oblongata
Vestibular Nuclei
Cochlear Nuclei
Medullary RF
Raphe Nuclei
Solitary Nucleus
Olivary Complex
Metencephalon
Pons
Cerebellum

Figure 2.16. Major Anatomical Divisions of the Central Nervous System. These names provide the international standard for anatomical research on the brain.

anatomical atlases has intensified the need for organized naming standards that assign each individual point in the three-dimensional brain space to a single neuroanatomical structure, no matter what the scale of analysis. Such a classification system is of necessity hierarchical, first dividing the nervous system into broad regions, and then subdividing each of these regions into smaller and smaller subregions. The most recent standard is the *NeuroNames Brain Hierarchy* (Bowden & Martin, 1995), which identifies 783 separate structures at nine hierarchical levels of analysis. The broadest of the *NeuroNames* divisions are shown in Figure 2.16. This hierarchy serves as a useful tool in understanding the relations between various brain regions.

BRAIN AND SPINAL CORD

In its appearance, the brain of the adult human appears very complicated. It is marked by the large, convoluted (or folded) cerebral hemispheres that overlie the stalklike brain stem. However, to the anatomist, there is much order in this apparent complexity. One way of appreciating that order is to look at the brain as it develops in the embryo. In this simpler form, the anatomical plan of the CNS can be readily observed (Noback, Strominger, & Demarest, 1996).

The CNS develops from a tube of primitive tissue, as shown in Figure 2.17 on the facing page. The rostral end of this tube, the tissue that will become the **brain**, develops more rapidly than the caudal section, which will become the spinal cord. Initially, three enlargements in the tube may be discerned; they correspond to the three principal divisions of the brain: the **forebrain**, the **midbrain**, and the **hindbrain**. At later stages, the forebrain divides into two parts.

The **telencephalon** is the most rostral portion of the forebrain and derives its name for the Greek *telos*, or "end," and *enkephalos*, or "brain." The telencephalon is composed of the **cerebral hemispheres** and their ancillary structures. It is the cerebral hemispheres that dominate the human CNS and contain much of the neural machinery responsible for human thought.

The **diencephalon** is the second, interior region of the forebrain; it lies beneath the telencephalon. All information entering or leaving the telencephalon must pass through the diencephalon, as reflected in its name (*dia* means "through" in Greek). Portions of the diencephalon maintain close connections with telencephalic structures. The diencephalon lies on top of the **brain stem**, which is composed of the midbrain and the hindbrain.

The midbrain is interposed between the forebrain and the hindbrain. In anatomy, it is called the **mesencephalon**, deriving its name from the Greek word *mesos*, meaning "middle."

The hindbrain—like the forebrain—also divides into two distinct regions during development. The more rostral of the two is the **metencephalon** (*meta* is from Greek, meaning "between"), which includes the **pons** and **cerebellum**. The most caudal region of the brain is the **medulla oblongata** (*medulla* is "marrow," and *oblongata* refers to its elongated shape; both terms are Latin). The medulla oblongata (often just the medulla) is also called the **myelencephalon**, in reference to the many myelinated

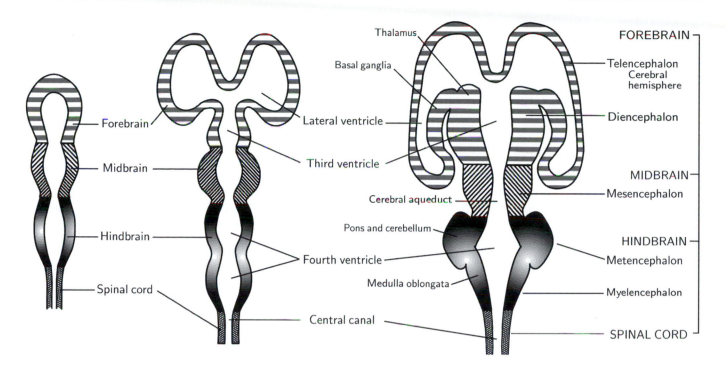

Figure 2.17. The Plan of the Developing Central Nervous System. The drawing in the lower center shows the outline of the neural tube early in development; three divisions may be seen in the area that will become the brain. In the upper left and upper right drawings, increased differentiation is apparent. Here, the major divisions of the central nervous system may be distinguished. This general organization persists in the adult human brain.

tracts that pass through this upper extension of the spinal cord. Figure 2.17 illustrates these five basic regions in the adult human brain.

Notice that the tubelike structure of the developing brain is preserved in the adult, although in a highly altered form. The hollow interior of the tube becomes filled with cerebrospinal fluid in development. At maturity, the interior of the primitive tube has become a series of interconnected **ventricles**, or cavities. The lateral ventricles lie within the left and right cerebral hemispheres of the forebrain. These two forebrain ventricles are joined with the midline third ventricle at the level of the diencephalon and midbrain. The fourth ventricle is located in the hindbrain and is linked to the third ventricle above and the **central canal** of the spinal cord below. Thus, despite a profound rearrangement during the growth of the brain, the tubelike structure of the embryonic brain is preserved in the adult.

The developing neural tube provides a useful model for studying the neuroanatomy of the CNS. We shall now examine more closely each of its divisions in the adult brain, beginning with the spinal cord and working our way toward the telencephalon. (For a more detailed treatment, see Brodal, 1981, or Noback, Strominger, & Demarest, 1996.)

The Spinal Cord The spinal cord is a long column of nervous tissue located within the vertebrae of the spine. Although it forms only 2% of the human central nervous system, the spinal cord is of extreme importance. First, it provides a conduit through which sensory information from the body reaches the brain. Second, the cord also contains pathways for voluntary control of the skeletal muscles; for this reason, lesions of the cord often produce profound and unrecoverable paralysis. Third, neural systems of the spinal cord provide the physiological basis for the integrated and coordinated movement of the limbs through the spinal reflexes. Finally, the neural systems that regulate much of the functioning of the internal organs also are located within the spinal cord. Thus, in the human nervous system, the fiber pathways of the cord provide the vital linkage of brain and body, and neural systems within the cord control primitive but essential internal and skeletal motor functions.

Like the brain above it, the spinal cord is covered by the three-layered system of meninges. Figure 2.18 on the facing page shows a section of the spinal cord and its meningeal coverings. The tubelike structure of the developing brain is retained, however. The central canal, running the length of the cord through its center, is filled with cerebrospinal fluid.

The cord itself, viewed in cross section, appears divided into regions, a butterfly-shaped central core of gray matter and a surrounding region of white matter. The **gray matter** is an area of cell bodies and synaptic connections. Two principal zones of gray matter are conventionally distinguished: the dorsal and ventral horns, as seen in Figure 2.18 on the next page. These regions received their names from their anatomical appearance. Within the gray matter are neurons serving a wide variety of functions, including low-level processing of sensory and motor information.

Unlike the gray matter, the **white matter** contains axons of fibers traveling up and down the spinal cord. The white matter receives its characteristic coloration from the shiny white myelin sheaths covering many of these axons. Not surprisingly, the relative amount of white matter increases at higher levels of the cord. This is because the highest levels of the cord contain nerve fibers coming from and going to all lower regions; at lower levels, many of these fibers have terminated, reducing the proportion of white matter.

Although the interior of the spinal cord is not divided into sections, or segmented, the entrance and exit of the **spinal nerves** between the vertebrae give the cord a segmented appearance. There are 31 pairs of spinal nerves that connect with the spinal cord over the length of the spinal column.

Each pair of spinal nerves—one on the left, the other on the right—is composed of fibers from the dorsal and ventral **spinal roots**. The dorsal and ventral roots are named for their relative positions and communicate with the dorsal and ventral horns, respectively. This distinction is functional as well as neuroanatomical. The dorsal roots are composed of sensory fibers, bringing information into the spinal cord from sensory receptors in the body. The sensory region served by a single dorsal root is called a **dermatome**. Conversely, the ventral roots are composed of motor neurons, carrying commands from the spinal cord to the muscles and internal organs.

Within the gray matter of the spinal cord, a number of distinct groups of cell bodies, or **nuclei**, may be differentiated. Similarly, the white matter is composed of a number of separate fiber pathways, each defined by its own origin and destination.

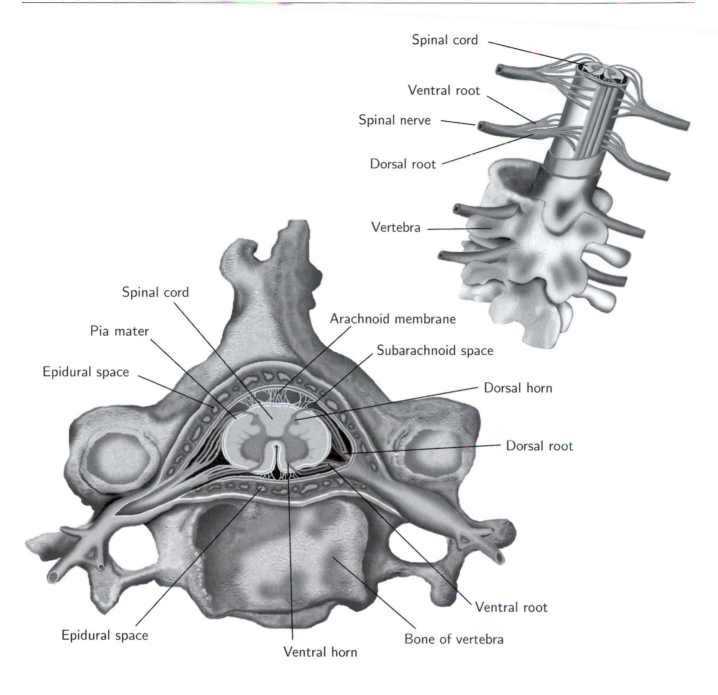

Figure 2.18. The Structure of the Spinal Cord. Shown are the gray and white matter, the dorsal and ventral roots, and their filaments that join together to form the spinal nerves. The cord, like the brain, is covered by three layers of meninges.

The Medulla Oblongata   Immediately above the spinal cord is the brain stem, which may be seen in Figure 2.19 on the following page. The myelencephalon is composed of a single structure, the **medulla oblongata**. The medulla is the most caudal portion of the brain stem, fusing with the spinal cord at the boundary between the skull and spinal column. Figure 2.20 on page 57 shows the major structures of the brain stem. The medulla widens as it leaves the spinal junction and loses the characteristic butterfly ap-

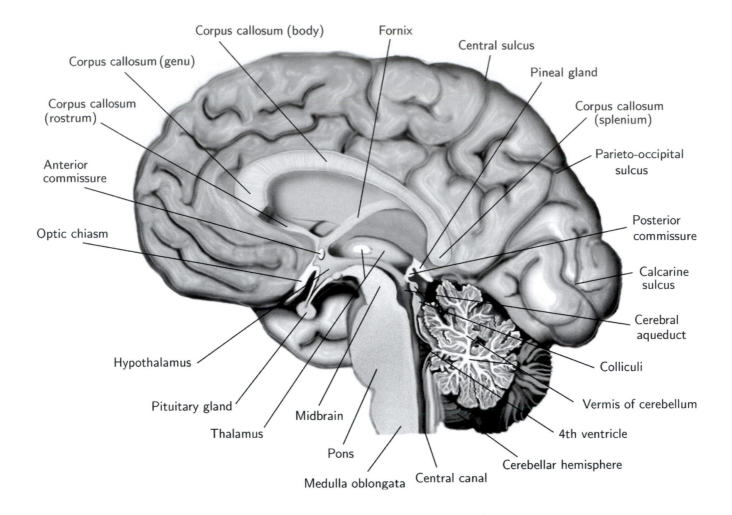

Corpus callosum (body)   Fornix
Corpus callosum (genu)   Central sulcus
                                                      Pineal gland
Corpus callosum
(rostrum)   Corpus callosum
                                                      (splenium)
Anterior   Parieto-occipital
commissure   sulcus
                                                      Posterior
Optic chiasm   commissure
                                                      Calcarine
                                                      sulcus
                                                      Cerebral
                                                      aqueduct
Hypothalamus   Colliculi
                                                      Vermis of cerebellum
Pituitary gland   4th ventricle
        Thalamus   Midbrain
                                                      Cerebellar hemisphere
                          Pons
            Medulla oblongata   Central canal

Figure 2.19. A Midsagittal View of the Human Brain. Here, major midline structures may be seen from the level of the hindbrain through the forebrain.

pearance of the cord. The central canal also widens, forming the fourth ventricle of the brain.

Although less differentiated than more rostral regions of the human nervous system, the medulla contains a number of distinct substructures, including nuclei serving sensory and motor systems. Many visceral functions, such as the regulation of heart rate and blood pressure, take place within the medulla. Several cranial nerves also terminate in this region. Also present in most medial regions of the medulla are several nuclei belonging to the brain stem **reticular formation**. These reticular nuclei form a system that is involved in the integration of information from the senses, attention, arousal, and the control of sleep and wakefulness.

The medulla is also characterized by a number of ascending and descending tracts of fibers. Such pathways are prominent, as the medulla is the only structure linking higher regions of the brain with the spinal cord.

The Metencephalon The metencephalon consists of two principal structures, the **pons** and the **cerebellum**. The pons receives its name from the

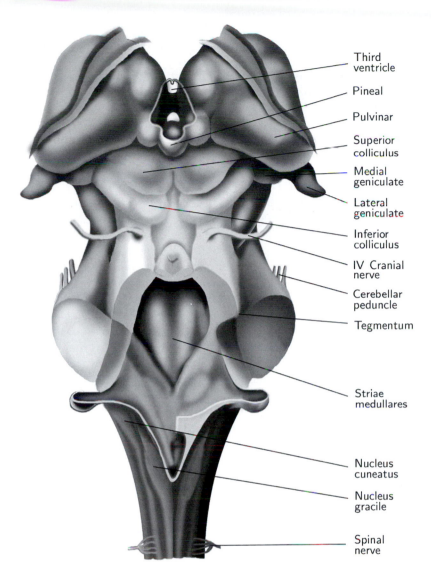

Third
ventricle

Pineal

Pulvinar

Superior
colliculus

Medial
geniculate

Lateral
geniculate

Inferior
colliculus

IV Cranial
nerve

Cerebellar
peduncle

Tegmentum

Striae
medullares

Nucleus
cuneatus

Nucleus
gracile

Spinal
nerve

Figure 2.20. The Human Brain Stem. Here, the major structures of the brain stem may be seen.

Latin word for "bridge," a reference to the lateral pathway formed by many of its most superficial fibers. The dorsal portion of the pons, the **pontine tegmentum** (*tegmentum* is Latin for "cover"), forms the roof of the pons for a quadruped and represents the rostral extension of the reticular formation of the medulla.

The reticular nuclei are more elaborated at this level of the brain stem, being divided into several major substructures. The tegmentum is also the home of several nuclei that project to wide regions of the nervous system and thus may regulate general aspects of brain function. These nuclei include the serotonergic *raphe nuclei*, the noradrenergic *locus ceruleus*, and the cholinergic *pedunculopontine nuclei*. These nuclei play major roles in regulating the function of the nervous system as a whole.

In addition to such modulatory systems, certain cranial nerves have their nuclei in the pontine tegmentum. The dorsal pons, for example, contains the *cochlear nucleus*, the entry point of the auditory system into the brain. *Vestibular nuclei*—responsible for the sense of balance—are located in this region.

The ventral portion of the pons is formed by an enlargement of the brain stem and contains an orderly arrangement of ascending and descending fiber pathways that link higher brain structures with the medulla and the spinal cord.

The second principal structure of the metencephalon is the **cerebellum** (Latin, meaning "little brain"), which is located on the dorsal surface of the pons. The large and convoluted cerebellum. The cerebellum is composed of three parts: the cerebellar cortex, its underlying white matter, and the embedded deep nuclei. Like the cerebral cortex of the forebrain, the cerebellar cortex (**cortex** means "rind" or "bark") is composed of a thin surface of gray matter that is folded into a pattern of hills and valleys. Axons connecting the gray matter of the surface with other neurons form the white matter of the cerebellum. The deep, or intrinsic, nuclei of the cerebellum receive projections from all parts of the cerebellar cortex.

The cerebellum developed rather early in the evolution of the brain. It is a complex structure that functions to control and guide the movements, as well as maintain muscle tone. Damage of the cortex of the cerebellum in humans results in characteristic disorders of movement. There are gross errors in the strength and directions of coordinated movements. What should be delicate movements may be executed violently, and forceful movements may be weak. Complex movements seem to be decomposed into a series of independent simpler movements, which—as one might suspect—are ineffective in achieving the object of the intended action. Speech disturbances are also common. Finally, there is tremor—or shaking—that occurs only when a voluntary movement is intended. This tremor has been attributed to a failure of feedback processes to control the movement as it progresses.

The Mesencephalon The mesencephalon, or midbrain, is the smallest portion of the brain stem. It is arranged in a manner similar to that of the pons. At the central core of the midbrain is the **mesencephalic tegmentum**, the rostral continuation of the pontine tegmentum. The tegmentum surrounds the **cerebral aqueduct**, a thin canal that links the third and fourth ventricles and is a direct extension of the central canal of the spinal cord.

The nuclei of the midbrain reticular formation are among the specialized cell groups of the tegmentum. Cells of the midbrain reticular formation have long branching axons that bifurcate or split, one branch ascending as far as the diencephalon and the other descending to the base of the medulla. This system plays a critical role in attention and alerting.

Another prominent nucleus of the midbrain is the **red nucleus**, with its characteristic pinkish coloration. The red nucleus plays a major role in the control of movement.

Ventral to the tegmentum is the **crus cerebri**, a massive system of descending fibers that link the forebrain to the lower hindbrain and to the spinal cord. Its name derives from Latin: *crus* means "leg" and is often used to describe anatomical structures forming diverging bands that somewhat resemble a pair of spreading legs. The fibers of the crus cerebri pass through the midbrain without synapsing.

Between the tegmentum and the crus cerebri lies the **substantia nigra** (Latin for "black substance"). The substantia nigra contains many neurons that are rich in the neurotransmitter dopamine. A loss of dopamine produced by damage to the substantia nigra results in a rigidity of the muscles. Tension is chronically increased in the opposing muscles of the arms and legs. What should be free movements result in a series of jerks because of the increased tension opposing the intended movement. The result is known as the cogwheel phenomenon.

The remaining portion of the midbrain is its **tectum** ("roof" in Latin). Located on the dorsal surface of the brain stem, the tectum is composed of four enlargements, or prominences. These are the **colliculi** (literally "little hills" in Latin). The more caudal pair of colliculi, the inferior colliculi, forms a part of the auditory system, relaying information from lower brain stem nuclei to the diencephalon above. The more rostral superior colliculi are a part of the visual system of the brain stem that is concerned with visually guided movements.

The Diencephalon   The diencephalon is situated at the head of the brain stem, linking the cerebral cortex above the lower CNS structures. But the diencephalon is not formed by a system of fiber pathways; rather, it is composed primarily of gray matter and must be responsible for a wide range of CNS functions. As a part of the forebrain, the evolution of much of the diencephalon parallels that of the cerebral cortex above it. The diencephalon consists of two large structures—the thalamus and the hypothalamus— and two smaller areas, the epithalamus and the subthalamus. All these structures are composed of individual specialized nuclei, dense concentrations of gray matter that perform different functional roles.

The **hypothalamus** is located in the walls of the third ventricle and represents an extension and specialization of the central gray matter present in the midbrain and hindbrain. Within this tissue, a number of distinct nuclei may be distinguished.

The hypothalamus is the portion of the forebrain that specializes in the control of the internal organs, the autonomic nervous system, and the endocrine system. Hypothalamic nuclei are critically involved in the regulation of emotion, hunger, thirst, body temperature, and sexual functions.

In contrast, the **thalamus** is composed of a number of nuclei that interconnect extensively with different regions of the cerebral cortex. It receives its name from the Greek word *thalamos*, or "bed," as it forms the seat on which the cerebral hemispheres lie. Most of the input that the cortex receives originates in thalamic nuclei. Thus, cortical and thalamic functions must be substantially interrelated.

The thalamic nuclei are often classified in terms of their major functions. The *relay nuclei* function to carry information to and from the cortex. Sensory areas of relay nuclei form the diencephalic way stations for the ascending sensory system. They project or send axons to the specific sensory areas of the cortex.

The *specific association nuclei* of the thalamus make many connections with other diencephalic structures and project to the regions of the cere-

Cerebral Cortex

Frontal Lobe

Parietal Lobe

Insula

Temporal Lobe

Occipital Lobe

Parahippocampal Gyrus

Archicortex

Hippocampal Formation

Supracallosal Gyrus

Figure 2.21. Anatomical Divisions of the Cerebral Cortex.

bral cortex that are neither exclusively sensory nor motor areas. Finally, the *nonspecific thalamic nuclei* project to widespread regions of the cerebral cortex. They receive input from other thalamic nuclei, from the cerebral cortex, and from the reticular formation of the brain stem, among other areas. The nonspecific nuclei are thought to play a major role in arousing and regulating the level of activity in wide regions of the cerebral cortex.

The Telencephalon   The human nervous system is dominated by the telencephalon, particularly by its **cerebral hemispheres**, which form the **cerebrum** ("brain" in Latin). This massive structure at the most rostral portion of the nervous system has grown impressively in evolution.

The cerebral hemispheres are composed of an outer cortex of gray matter and an inner bulk of white matter. As elsewhere in the nervous system, the gray matter is a dense collection of cell bodies, whereas the white matter is formed of myelinated and unmyelinated axons that link neurons in the cortex with other neurons.

Neocortex   About 90% of the human cerebrum is composed of the recently evolved **neocortex**, or **cerebral cortex**. Remember that in Latin, *cortex* means "bark," reflecting the fact that the cerebral cortex covers the cerebral hemispheres much as bark covers the body of a tree.

The neocortex is distinguished by six separable layers of cells, yet it is extremely thin. In humans, the thickness of the neocortex ranges between a mere 1.5 mm in the primary visual area to a little over 4 mm in the primary motor area. The human cerebral cortex is folded into a series of hills (or **gyri**) and valleys (or **sulci**). The deeper divisions between sulci form the **fissures** of the cortex.

Geometrically, the cerebral cortex may be viewed as a vast sheet of neurons in which many types of interconnections and interactions are possible. The extent of this "rind" of the cerebrum is hard to overstate. If the gray matter of the cortex were unfolded, it would cover about 2.5 feet of surface area. It contains between 10 billion and 15 billion neurons. Figure 2.21 shows the components of the cerebral cortex as defined by both the *Nomina Anatomica* (International Anatomical Nomenclature Committee, 1983) and the *NeuroNames* brain hierarchy (Bowden & Martin, 1995).

Anatomists conventionally divide the cortex into four general regions, or **lobes**. Most anterior is the **frontal lobe**, which is separated from the remainder of the cerebral cortex by the **central fissure**. This fissure is also called the **Rolandic fissure**, in honor of Luigi Rolando, the prolific Italian anatomist (1773-1831).

Immediately posterior to the frontal lobe is the **parietal lobe**. Inferior to both of these lobes is the **lateral fissure**, also called the **Sylvian fissure**. (The designation "Sylvian" honors the German anatomist Professor Franz De le Boë of Leiden, who first described the lateral fissure in 1641. In all his writings, De le Boë used the Latin name Franciscus Sylvius.) The temporal lobe of the neocortex lies immediately beneath the lateral fissure.

Finally, the most posterior tip of the cortex, unmarked by any of the major cortical fissures, is the **occipital lobe**. These four lobes of the neocortex are not only anatomically distinct, but they are also functionally

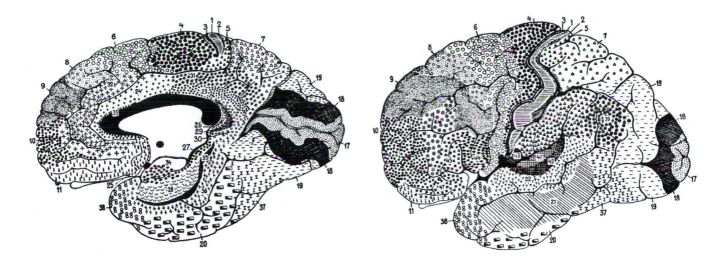

specialized; very different types of operations are performed by neurons of the four lobes of the cerebral cortex.

Anatomists have proposed further, more refined mappings of the cortex that have proved to be quite useful. These finer divisions are based on cytoarchitectonic variations in the structure of the cortex. The term **cytoarchitecture** refers to patterns of cellular construction or arrangement; in the cerebral cortex, cytoarchitectural maps primarily reflect differences in the patterning of six cortical layers. Although as many as 200 separate regions have been proposed by some neuroanatomists, the most generally accepted cytoarchitectural maps are those published by Korbinian Brodmann in 1908. The 47 cytoarchitectonic regions that he proposed have proved to form the basis of a useful and widely accepted system for specifying smaller, anatomically distinct regions of the cerebral cortex, even though a number of important modifications in his mapping are now known. Figure 2.22 shows Brodmann's classical mapping of the human cerebral hemispheres.

Other schemes for dividing the cerebral cortex into smaller regions are based on purely functional criteria. Primary sensory areas are those that receive the direct input from the subcortical sensory systems. Conversely, the primary motor area projects directly to the subcortical motor systems. Those areas of the cortex that are neither sensory nor motor have traditionally been considered to form the association cortex, in the belief that these regions of the brain somehow link sensation with action. Over the past decade, much has been learned about the functions of the so-called association cortex.

The white matter of the cerebral hemispheres contains the axons of neurons carrying information to and from the cortical surface. These pathways are highly organized and may be classified by their origins and destinations. The **association fibers** link one portion of the cortex with another in the same hemisphere. Some association pathways are very short, joining adjacent cortical regions, whereas others are much longer, connecting

Figure 2.22. Brodmann's Cytoarchitectonic Mapping of the Human Cerebral Cortex. Brodmann numbered each cortical area in the order that he studied them. Even today, his numbering scheme persists as a standard method of designating various cortical regions.

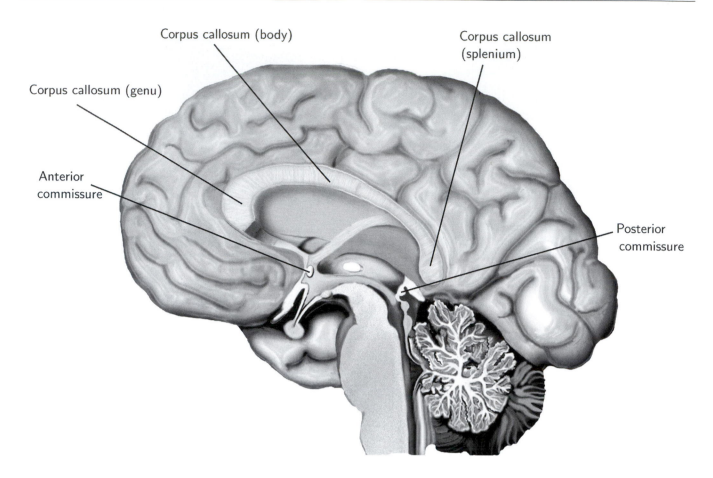

Figure 2.23. The Commissures of the Neocortex. Two commissures connect the neocortical tissue of the right and left cerebral hemispheres. Of these, the corpus callosum is by far the largest; the anterior commissure contains many fewer fibers. In addition, other commissures connect nonneocortical structures, such as the hippocampal commissure linking the right and left hippocampus.

cells in different cortical lobes.

Fibers that link the two cerebral hemispheres are termed **commissural fibers**. The most massive system of commissural fibers is the **corpus callosum**, which is shown in Figure 2.23. In humans, the **anterior commissure** forms a second, much smaller pathway between the right and left cerebral hemispheres.

The remaining portion of the white matter connects the cortex with the brain stem. These are the **projection fibers** and may be either ascending or descending. Many of the projection fibers link the thalamus and the cortex. Other projection fibers connect the cortex with more caudal regions of the brain stem and the spinal cord. Particularly impressive in large mammals are the corticospinal projection cells connecting the cortex and the spinal cord. In humans, these cells may have axons that are nearly a meter in length; in even larger animals, such as the giraffe, such cells are several meters long.

Other Telencephalic Structures   Several other telencephalic structures are located at the base of the cerebrum adjacent to the brain stem. Many of them participate in what is called the **limbic system**.

The first of these is the **hippocampal formation** or **hippocampus**. The hippocampus forms the floor of the lateral ventricle of the temporal lobe. Other important limbic structures are the **amygdala** (amygdaloid nuclear complex), the **fornix**, the **septal nuclei**, the **parahippocampal gyrus**, and the **cingulate gyrus**. The limbic structures interact in a highly interconnected system, which has been implicated in the cortical control of emotion, motivation, and memory.

The final structures of the telencephalon are its deep telencephalic nuclei, dense collections of cells located beneath the cerebrum and near the brain stem. Some of these nuclei form part of the basal ganglia. The **basal ganglia** include the **globus pallidus**, the **caudate nucleus**, and the **putamen**. The caudate nucleus and putamen together form the **striatum**. Some functional definitions of the basal ganglia also incorporate two brain stem nuclei as well, the **subthalamic nucleus** and the **substantia nigra**. The basal ganglia function as a motor system, regulating the movements of the skeletal musculature in conjunction with the motor cortex and the cerebellum.

PERIPHERAL NERVOUS SYSTEM

The peripheral nervous system links the brain with the world. The **peripheral nervous system (PNS)** is the set of neurons and fibers that links the brain and spinal cord with the other organs and tissues of the body. The **efferent**, or motor, nerve fibers carry commands from the CNS to the muscles, glands, and visceral organs. The **afferent**, or sensory, fibers carry signals in the other direction, bringing information from the sensory receptors to the central sensory systems. Most of the **nerves**, or bundles of nerve fibers, are mixed. Mixed nerves contain axons from both afferent and efferent neurons.

Cranial and Spinal Nerves Both the brain and the spinal cord send and receive information through the peripheral nerves. The **cranial nerves** are the portion of the PNS that directly serves the brain. There are 12 numbered pairs of cranial nerves. The first 2 primarily serve the cerebrum; the remaining 10 pairs provide input to and receive output from the brain stem systems.

The rest of the peripheral nervous system is connected to the spinal cord. Thirty-one pairs of **spinal nerves** enter and exit the spinal cord through spaces between the vertebrae.

All spinal nerves are mixed nerves, containing both afferent fibers, which form the dorsal root filaments once within the spinal column, and efferent fibers, which originate in the ventral roots. (See Figure 2.18 on page 55 for a view of the internal structure of the spinal cord and its roots.) Each pair of spinal nerves (one on the left and the other on the right) is named for the vertebra over which it exits. Thus, there are 8 cervical spinal nerves (CI through C8), 12 thoracic nerves (TI through T12), 5 lumbar nerves (L1 through L5), and 5 sacral nerves (S1 through S5). The last of the spinal nerves is the small coccygeal nerve at the base of the spine. On exiting from the spinal column, some of the spinal nerves merge together and then divide again to form the large peripheral nerves of the body.

Somatic and Autonomic PNS Both the cranial and the spinal nerves may be classified according to the functions they perform and the structures they innervate. Thus, it is conventional to distinguish between the two great divisions of the peripheral nervous system: the somatic and autonomic divisions. The **somatic nervous system** transmits commands to the voluntary skeletal musculature and receives sensory information from the muscles and the skin. The somatic division is responsible for movement, touch, the sense of position, and the perception of temperature and pain.

The **autonomic nervous system** innervates the glands and the visceral organs of the body. The term *autonomic* means self-controlling; most of the functions of the autonomic nervous system are involuntary and not amenable to conscious regulation. Because of this independence, the autonomic nervous system can perform the housekeeping chores of the body without conscious decision making. Functions such as heart rate, dilation of the arteries, pupillary movements, and the activity of the gastrointestinal system are all routinely regulated by the autonomic nervous system.

Some functions of the autonomic nervous system are obvious and well known, such as the fact that heart rate increases during vigorous exercise and decreases during inactivity. However, other aspects of autonomic adaptation are less obvious. When one arises from bed, for example, a complicated series of cardiovascular adjustments takes place under the control of the autonomic nervous system: Blood pressure and heart rate increase, blood flow to much of the body is reduced, but blood flow to the head increases. These compensatory changes prevent the draining of blood from the head, which would deprive the brain of oxygen. Without this complex adaptive response of the autonomic nervous system, arising from sleep would be fatal.

The autonomic nervous system is composed of two opposing branches. The **sympathetic branch** arouses the organism, increasing heart rate, activating the release of epinephrine into the blood by the adrenal glands, and suppressing activity in the digestive system. Sympathetic activation appears to ready the organism for action, the so-called fight-or-flight response. In contrast, the **parasympathetic branch** slows the heart, quiets the organism, and promotes activity in the digestive tract. For this reason, the parasympathetic branch is viewed as the vegetative portion of the autonomic system, promoting digestion and reducing the expenditure of energy by other organs.

In neither branch of the autonomic nervous system do the spinal nerves directly innervate their target organs. Instead, they synapse on collections of cell bodies in the periphery, called **ganglia**. It is the axons of the ganglionic neurons that proceed to innervate the visceral organs and glands. The positions of these ganglia differ in the two branches of the autonomic nervous system. In the sympathetic branch, the ganglia are located near the spinal column; in the parasympathetic branch, the ganglia are typically located in the vicinity of the target organ. Figure 2.24 on the facing page illustrates this arrangement.

In both branches, preganglionic fibers of the spinal nerves use acetylcholine as a neurotransmitter. But in the postganglionic fibers that innervate the target organs, two different neurotransmitters are employed.

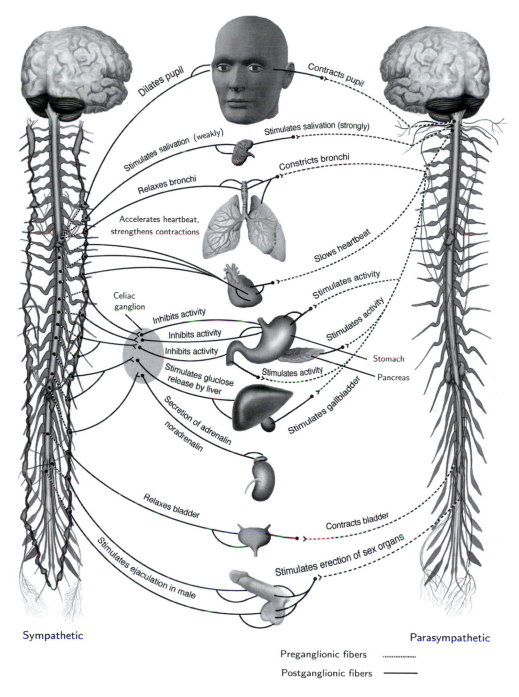

Sympathetic

Parasympathetic

Preganglionic fibers ....
Postganglionic fibers ——————

Figure 2.24. The Peripheral Pathways of the Autonomic Nervous System. The sympathetic and parasympathetic branches of the autonomic nervous system often exert opposing effects on the organs that they innervate. All autonomic nerves synapse once at a collection of nerve cells called a ganglion before reaching bodily organs. The sympathetic ganglia are located close to the central nervous system, whereas the parasympathetic ganglia are found near the target organs.

Parasympathetic postganglionic neurons use acetylcholine, whereas sympathetic postganglionic neurons use norepinephrine as the transmitter by which they affect the viscera and glands. Thus, the antagonistic nature of the two autonomic branches is reflected in the ultimate neurotransmitter substances that each employs.

SUMMARY

Information processing in the nervous system is carried out by neurons. A neuron may be divided into three specialized regions. The dendrites of a neuron provide an extended receptive surface for the cell, increasing greatly the number of synaptic inputs. The cell body integrates information from the dendrites and other synaptic inputs in determining the messages to be transmitted to other cells through its axon. Finally, the neuron's axon carries messages in the form of action potentials from the cell body to the axon terminals, which synapse on other neurons or effector organs. Glial cells support these neurons in a number of different ways.

Large numbers of these cells combine to form the nervous system, which is composed of the brain, the spinal cord, and the peripheral nerves that innervate the other tissues of the body. Although the human brain is an extraordinarily complex structure, its basic organization follows a simple embryological plan that is shared among many species.

SELECTED READINGS

- Alberts, B., Bray, D., Lewis, J., Raff, M., Roberts, K., & Watson, J. D. (1994). *Molecular biology of the cell* (3rd ed.). New York: Garland. An extensive, clearly written, and up-to-date text on cellular microbiology.

- Bowden, D. M., & Martin, R. F. (1995). NeuroNames brain hierarchy. *Neuroimage, 2,* 63-83. Hardly interesting reading, but this article, which is really a long table, can be extraordinarily useful. It presents the English names and preferred abbreviations of 783 human neuroanatomical structures in a hierarchical organized list. Designed for use with computerized neuroanatomical databases, the terms presented in *NeuroNames* are used throughout this textbook as the current scientific standard for human neuroanatomy.

- Brodal, A. (1981). *Neurological anatomy in relation to clinical medicine.* New York: Oxford University Press. This is the final edition of Alf Brodal's magnificent synthesis of human neuroanatomy, which first appeared in 1948. Unlike other texts, Brodal's book is really about anatomy as a basis of function and behavior. It is a unique book, filled with insights and—in the words of one of its reviewers—just plain "fun to read" (Scheibel, 1988).

KEY TERMS

adenosine triphosphate (ATP) A high-energy molecule that is the primary energy source for many cellular functions.

afferent Refers to pathways bringing information to more central nervous system structures, as in sensory pathways.

amygdala An almond-shaped collection of nuclei deep in the temporal lobe that forms a part of the limbic system.

anterior Rostral; toward the snout of a four-legged animal along the head-to-tail axis.

anterior commissure A small bundle of fibers connecting portions of the right and left anterior cerebral cortex.

arachnoid The second meningeal layer, resembling a spider's web.

arachnoid trabeculae A delicate system of connective fibers that mechanically links the arachnoid with the pia mater.

association fibers Pathways in the white matter of the cerebrum linking cortical structures of the same hemisphere.

astrocyte A common type of small glial cell in the central nervous system.

autonomic nervous system In vertebrates, that portion of the peripheral nervous system controlling internal organs and glands.

axial plane A section through the brain of a standing human that is parallel to the floor.

axon A process of a neuron, composed of excitable membrane, that normally transmits action potentials from the cell body to its axon terminal.

axon hillock The transition regions between the cell body and its axon, where action potentials are usually initiated.

axon terminal The terminal enlargement of an axon, containing neurotransmitter and forming the axonal portion of a synapse.

basal ganglia A collection of forebrain structures, usually including the amygdala, globus pallidus, caudate nucleus, and putamen.

bipolar neuron A neuron with two processes, usually a dendrite and an axon.

blood-brain barrier The system of endothelial cells that line the vasculature of the brain and spinal cord regulating the transfer of substances between the blood and the cerebrospinal fluid.

brain The rostral portion of the central nervous system.

brain stem The midbrain and the hindbrain.

caudal Toward the tail of a four-legged animal along the nose-to-tail axis.

caudate nucleus A telencephalic nucleus forming a part of the basal ganglia.

cell body The region of the cell containing the nucleus.

cell membrane The thin structure surrounding each neuron and composing some of its organelles, consisting of a phospholipid bilayer with its associated protein molecules.

central canal The central tubelike opening of the spinal cord, which is filled with cerebrospinal fluid.

central fissure The fissure separating the frontal and parietal lobes of the cerebrum; also called the Rolandic fissure.

central nervous system (CNS) The brain and spinal cord.

cerebellum The large, bilaterally symmetric, cortical structure on the dorsal aspect of the metencephalon, which plays a role in motor coordination.

cerebral aqueduct The narrow canal of the mesencephalon connecting the third ventricle of the diencephalon with the fourth ventricle of the metencephalon.

cerebral cortex See *neocortex*.

cerebral hemispheres See *cerebrum*.

cerebrospinal fluid (CSF) The heavy, clear fluid filling the ventricles, subarachnoid space, and central canal.

cerebrum The cerebral cortex and its underlying white matter.

cingulate gyrus A cortical structure overlying the corpus callosurn that is part of the limbic system.

collateral A secondary branch of an axon.

colliculi The inferior and superior colliculi form the tecturn of the midbrain.

commissural fibers Fibers connecting the left and right cerebral hemispheres: the corpus callosurn and the anterior commissure.

coronal plane The plane of section that is perpendicular to the axial plane and parallel to a line between the ears.

corpus callosum The massive bundle of fibers connecting the right and left cerebral hemispheres.

cortex The outer layer of some tissues; usually either the cerebral cortex or the cerebellar cortex.

cranial nerve One of 12 pairs of nerves that enter the brain rather than the spinal cord.

crus cerebri A large structure formed of descending cortical fibers in the ventral midbrain.

cytoarchitecture The pattern or organization of cells within a structure.

cytoskeleton The complex structure of fibrillar proteins within the cytoplasm that establishes the shape or overall structure of each individual neuron.

dendrite The branched processes of a neuron that receive input from other neurons and transmit that information toward the cell body.

dendritic spine A small outgrowth of a dendrite that serves as a postsynaptic element.

deoxyribonucleic acid (DNA) A long, complex nucleic acid that carries all genetic information for the cell, consisting of a sugar backbone along which four bases (cytosine, adenine, guanine, and thymine) are arranged in sequences of three that provide the physical basis for the genetic code.

dermatome The region of the body serviced by a single spinal dorsal root.

diencephalon The region of the forebrain between the telencephalon and the mesencephalon.

dorsal Toward the back of a four-legged animal; superior.

dura mater The outermost of the meninges.

effector A cell in a muscle or gland that produces (effects) action.

efferent Refers to pathways carrying information away from central structures, as in motor pathways.

endoplasmic reticulum An organelle within the cell body formed of folded membrane. The rough endoplasmic reticulum contains ribosomes and manufactures segments of proteins. The smooth endoplasmic reticulum is involved in transporting molecules between organelles.

excitable membrane The membrane of a process that is capable of sustaining an action potential.

fast axonal transport The active movement of organelles and related subcellular structures along the microtubular system from the cell body to the axon terminal and vice versa.

fissure A deep groove, particularly in the surface of the cortex.

forebrain The telencephalon and diencephalon.

fornix A fiber bundle that serves as an output pathway for the hippocampus.

frontal lobe The most rostral lobe of the cerebral cortex.

ganglion In gross anatomy, a group of cell bodies in the peripheral nervous system (plural, *ganglia*).

glia Nonneural cells in the central nervous system that serve supporting and nutritive roles for the neurons.

globus pallidus One of the basal ganglia of the telencephalon.

Golgi apparatus An organelle within the cell body where protein molecules are assembled and/or packaged in vesicles.

Golgi Type I neurons See *principal neurons*.

Golgi Type II neurons See *local circuit neurons*.

gray matter Neural tissue that is rich in cell bodies.

gyri The raised portions of the folded surface of the cortex.

hindbrain The myelencephalon and metencephalon.

hippocampal formation See *hippocampus*.

hippocampus An allocortical structure on the floor of the third ventricle that is a part of the limbic system.

horizontal plane See *axial plane*.

hypothalamus A collection of caudal diencephalic nuclei that are involved in the regulation of functions such as feeding, drinking, and emotion.

inferior See *ventral*.

integral protein A protein molecule embedded in the cell membrane.

intermediate filaments Midsized protein filaments (10 nm in diameter) that form part of the neuronal cytoskeleton.

interneuron A neuron that connects a receptor, effector, or neuron to other neurons.

lateral Away from the midline on the horizontal plane.

lateral fissure See *Sylvian fissure*.

limbic system A collection of structures, usually including the hippocampus, dentate gyrus, cingulate gyrus, septal nuclei, hypothalamus, and amygdala. Opinions differ as to the exact composition of this physiological system, which is thought to be involved in emotion and other functions.

lobe Of the cerebral cortex, one of four great anatomical regions: the frontal, temporal, parietal, and occipital areas.

local circuit neurons Short-axoned or axonless neurons that exert their influence in their immediate neural environment.

medial Toward the midline on the horizontal plane.

medulla oblongata The structure composing the myelencephalon that joins the spinal cord with higher structures of the brain stem.

meninges The protective membranes covering the brain and spinal cord: the dura mater, arachnoid, and pia mater.

mesencephalic tegmentum The region of the midbrain immediately beneath the tecturn and above the substantia nigra.

mesencephalon The midbrain, located between the forebrain and the hindbrain.

metencephalon The hindbrain region containing the pons and the cerebellum.

microfilaments Submicroscopic filaments found in the cell body that are believed to aid the cell in maintaining its form.

microtubules Slender, tubular submicroscopic structures that aid in maintaining cell shape and in the intracellular transport of substances.

midbrain The region of the brain stem between the forebrain and the hindbrain.

mitochondria Small organelles that are actively involved in metabolism, producing adenosine triphosphate from glucose.

motor neurons Neurons that innervate muscle tissue.

multipass transmembrane proteins Proteins that cross the membrane many times and in so doing form elaborate molecular structures such as ion channels and ion pumps.

multipolar neuron A neuron with multiple processes, often many dendrites and a single axon.

myelin A white, fatty substance produced by oligodendrocytes and Schwann cells surrounding portions of axons, which provides insulation.

myelencephalon The medulla.

myelin sheath The insulating coating surrounding some axons.

neocortex The evolutionarily advanced portions of the cerebral cortex characterized by a six-layered structure.

nerve In the peripheral nervous system, a collection of axons traveling together.

neuron Nerve cells; the conducting cells of the nervous system.

nucleolus An organelle within the nucleus that manufactures ribosomes.

nucleus In cell biology, a spherical structure enclosed by a membrane within the cell body containing the genetic material and a nucleolus. In gross anatomy, a group of cell bodies in the central nervous system.

occipital lobe The most posterior lobe of the cerebral cortex.

oligodendrocytes A type of glial cell that produces myelin.

organelle Any of several membrane-bound substructures within a cell, including mitochondria, ribosomes, Golgi apparatus, and other similar substructures.

parahippocampal gyrus The convolution on the inferior surface of each cerebral hemisphere that is adjacent to the hippocampus; a part of the limbic system.

parasympathetic branch The division of the autonomic nervous system serving vegetative functions, such as digestion.

parietal lobe The lobe of the cerebral cortex immediately posterior to the frontal lobe, anterior to the occipital lobe, and superior to the temporal lobe.

peripheral nervous system (PNS) The portion of the nervous system outside the brain and spinal cord.

phospholipids The major constituent of the cell membrane, having a hydrophilic (water-loving) head and a hydrophobic (water-hating) tail.

pia mater The innermost of the meninges.

planes of section Orientations of cross sections taken through the nervous system: horizontal, sagittal, and transverse or coronal.

polymerization The covalent binding of multiple identical molecules (monomers) into a single, elongated molecular structure.

pons A major structure of the metencephalon.

pontine tegmentum The extension of the midbrain tegmentum at the level of the pons.

posterior See *caudal*.

postsynaptic cell The cell that receives information across a synapse from the presynaptic cell.

presynaptic cell The cell that transmits information across a synapse to the postsynaptic cell.

principal neuron A long-axoned neuron that links different regions of the nervous system.

processes The processes of a neuron are its dendrites and axon.

projection fibers The efferent connections from one region of the brain to another.

projection neurons See *principal neurons*.

protein A complex organic molecule constructed from amino acids that may function as a structural element of a cell or serve as an enzyme.

putamen One of the basal ganglia.

receptor A type of cell in the peripheral nervous system that recodes information from a physical stimulus into a neuronal representation.

red nucleus A motor nucleus, pinkish in color, located in the midbrain.

reticular formation A diffuse collection of medial nuclei in the midbrain and hindbrain that is important in the regulation of sleep, motor activity, and other integrative functions.

ribonucleic acid (RNA) A large molecule that is similar in construction to deoxyribonucleic acid, except that it replaces thymine with uracil. RNA functions to carry genetic information out of the nucleus and to control protein synthesis.

ribosome An organelle that serves in protein synthesis.

Rolandic fissure See *central fissure*.

rostral Toward the nose.

sagittal plane The plane that is perpendicular to the axial plane and parallel to a line from the nose to the back of the head.

Schwann cell The myelinating cell in the peripheral nervous system, analogous to the oligodendrocytes of the central nervous system.

septal nuclei A part of the limbic system.

slow axoplasmic flow The movement of axonal proteins suspended in the cytoplasm from the cell body to the axon terminals.

soma See *cell body*.

somatic nervous system The division of the peripheral nervous system that innervates the skin and muscles.

spinal cord The most caudal portion of the central nervous system, which is encased within the spinal column.

spinal nerves The nerves entering and exiting the spinal cord.

spinal roots The fibers within the spinal column that join to form the spinal nerves; the dorsal roots are sensory, and the ventral roots are motor in function.

spine See *dendritic spine* or *spinal cord*.

striatum The caudate nucleus and putamen.

subarachnoid space The area between the arachnoid and pia mater, which is filled with cerebrospinal fluid.

substantia nigra A pair of mesencephalic nuclei that form a part of the basal ganglia.

subthalamic nucleus The portion of the subthalamus immediately rostral to the substantia nigra.

sulci The indentations of the folded cortical surface that separate gyri.

superior See *dorsal*.

Sylvian fissure The fissure separating the frontal and temporal lobes; also called the lateral fissure.

sympathetic branch The division of the autonomic nervous system that serves to prepare the organism for action.

synapse The junction between an axon terminal and a postsynaptic membrane.

synaptic cleft The small gap between the presynaptic and postsynaptic membranes.

tectum The superior and inferior colliculi of the midbrain.

telencephalon The most recently evolved division of the forebrain.

terminal bouton See *axon terminal*.

thalamus A large group of rostral diencephalic nuclei that are closely interconnected with the cortex.

transmembrane proteins Integral proteins that cross the cell membrane, extending into both the cytoplasm and extracellular fluid.

transport carriers Specialized proteins that move specific types of molecules across the cell membrane.

unipolar neuron A neuron with a single process, which may serve a variety of functions.

ventral Toward the belly of a four-footed animal.

ventricles Any of four cavities in the brain filled with cerebrospinal fluid; the two lateral ventricles of the cerebrum and the third and fourth ventricles of the brain stem.

vesicle A small container composed of a membrane separating its contents from the surrounding fluids.

white matter Areas of the central nervous system that are composed almost entirely of axons.

Chapter 3

Electrical Signaling

Our neurons *are* our minds. They are the cells that sense the world around us, make decisions about it, and evoke our behavior. As diverse and complex as our mental functions of our brains may seem, they are all nonetheless the results of relatively simple cellular processes occurring in groups of individual nerve cells.

Here we take stock of these processes. We will see that nerve cells use the electrical potentials that all living cells possess to signal and process information. At the root of all these signals are simple, electrically charged atoms of sodium, potassium, and other elements. Electrical signals are produced by the action of large protein molecules that regulate the flow of these charged atoms in and out of the nerve cell.

Together, these simple processes can form neural systems of sufficient complexity to provide each of us with all the subtleties and nuances of our most complicated behavior, thoughts, hopes, and dreams. But in this chapter, we concern ourselves with understanding the most basic elements of neuronal electrical activity: the resting potential, which characterizes the electrical state of an inactive neuron, and the propagated action potential, a special type of signal used for internal communication in large nerve cells. Communication *between* neurons is examined in the following chapter.

IONS AND THE CELL MEMBRANE

Both resting and action potentials arise from similar biophysical processes (Fain, 1999). Each results from molecular events occurring on the outer membrane of the nerve cell. Each is carried by the movement of charged particles through specialized molecular channels.

Ions

Electrical signals within living organisms are carried by the movements of ions across the membranes of cells. **Ions** are atoms that have either gained or lost electrons, resulting in an imbalance of protons and electrons in the atom and therefore carrying charge. Atoms with extra electrons are called **anions**; they are negatively charged. Atoms that have lost electrons are called **cations** and are positively charged. Anions and cations are of opposite charge and electrically attract each other.

Thus, when anions and cations are separated, a force pulls them together. If there is a barrier between the charges, the force exists nonetheless. That force, the amount of work required to move the charges together, is **voltage**. If the barrier is removed, the charges move toward each other. That movement is **current**. Current is the rate at which charges move.

Both the **intracellular fluid** (also called **cytoplasm**) and **extracellular fluid** are rich in ions. But the concentrations of ions in these two fluids differ in important ways. Figure 3.1 on the next page shows the relative concentrations of the most important ions in the intracellular fluid and extracellular fluids, as well as seawater.

Notice that the ionic composition of the blood, extracellular fluid, and seawater is very much the same. Thus, the neurons live in an environment that is similar to the seas from which life evolved. The extracellular fluid is rich in both sodium and chloride ions. Like seawater, extracellular fluid is dominated by the presence of dissolved common salt. When a salt molecule is dissolved in water, two hydrated ions, Na^+ and Cl^-, are formed. A **hydrated ion** is simply an ion, here a Na^+ or Cl^- ion, and the water molecules to which it is momentarily bonded. These hydrated ions differ in size. Size is important because it is a major factor controlling the movement of ions across the cell membrane.

The cell membrane presents a solid barrier that prevents many molecules from diffusing into the cell. Small, oil-soluble (hydrophobic) molecules can cross the bilipid cell membrane with ease. Blood gases—such as oxygen and carbon dioxide—diffuse freely in and out of the cell, as does water and ethanol. However, the membrane effectively blocks ions from diffusing into or out of the cell: The permeability of the bilipid membrane to ions is about one billionth (10^{-9}) of the membrane's permeability to water.

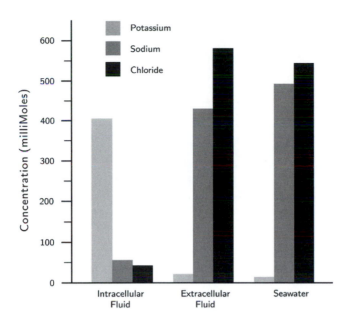

Figure 3.1. Concentrations of Ions Inside and Outside the Squid Giant Axon. The concentrations of sodium, potassium, and chloride differ markedly inside and outside the cell. The ionic composition of the extracellular fluid is remarkably like that of seawater, from which life is presumed to have evolved.

Ions use specialized **membrane transport proteins** to enter or exit the cell. Membrane transport proteins are proteins embedded in the neural membrane that serve as entry and departure points for ions and other biologically important molecules.

There are two types of membrane transport proteins: **membrane channels** and **membrane carriers**. Membrane channels are **pores** within transmembrane protein molecules through which selected ions can pass. The protein molecules forming the channel do not interact with the molecules being transported. In contrast, membrane carriers are transmembrane proteins that *do* interact with the molecules that they carry to and from the cytoplasm. Thanks to many recent striking advances in electrophysiology and molecular biology, a great deal is now known about both the channel and carrier proteins of the neural membrane.

In this chapter, four different membrane protein transport proteins are introduced. Two of them, potassium-leak channels and sodium-potassium pumps, establish the resting potential of the neuron. The other two are the voltage-gated sodium channels and the voltage-gated potassium channels that together are responsible for producing action potentials in the axons of larger neurons. Together, these four types of membrane transport proteins provide the basis of all intracellular signaling within a neuron. Communication between neurons is the responsibility of other types of membrane channels and carriers, which are introduced in the next chapter.

Ion Channels

Ion channels are the simplest types of mechanisms by which ions can cross the neural membrane. Ion channel proteins are ion-selective gates through which the selected ions species can enter or exit the cell. In entering or exiting the cell through these pores, the ion does not interact with the mem-

Figure 3.2. A Model Ion Channel. Ion channels are relatively simple transmembrane proteins that permit the passage of a selected ion species when opened. In this conceptual model, the selectivity mechanism is indicated by the constriction of the transmembrane pore.

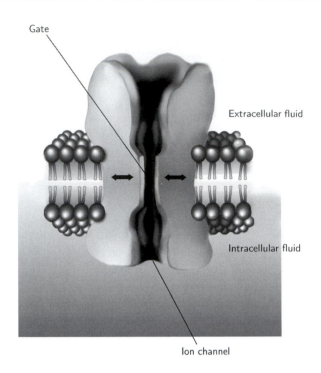

brane; rather, it travels through an open connecting channel like a boat through a canal. Figure 3.2 illustrates the essential features of an ion channel.

Well over a hundred different types of ion channels are now known to exist in various types of living cells, all of which share two important properties. First, they are *selective* as to the species of ions that may pass through the channel. For nerve cells, potassium-, sodium-, chloride-, and calcium-selective channels are of particular importance in neural signaling and communication. These ion channel proteins achieve their selectivity by configuring their passageways so that only molecules of a specific size and electrical charge may successfully pass completely through their pore and thereby cross the membrane.

The second property of many ion channels is that they are *gated*. Gating means that the channel may be switched open and shut. When closed, no ions of any type may transverse the channel. When open, the selected ion species may cross the membrane freely.

Channels can transport selected ions across the membrane at very high rates when open. More than one million ions can cross the membrane in a second through a single open ion channel. This high rate of net ion flow is possible in part because membrane channel proteins do not bind with the transported substance. For the same reason, ion channels consume no metabolic energy in the ion transfer process.

There are three general mechanisms by which a channel gate may be controlled. Some gates respond to a specific change in voltage across the membrane in the vicinity of the gate. These are called **voltage-gated ion channels**. Voltage-gated ion channels play a number of critical roles in neural signaling, including regulating the generation of action potentials in the nerve axon.

Other gates respond to mechanical stress, that is, stretching and distorting the shape of the cell membrane. These **mechanically gated ion channels** form the basis of the senses of touch and limb position, as described in Chapter 6.

The third class of membrane channels responds to chemical ligands. A **ligand** is a molecule that binds to a specific site on protein or other biologically active molecules, and the gates that respond to them are called **ligand-gated channels**.

Three types of ligand gates are important in neural functioning. The first are the gates that respond to molecules *outside* the nerve cell, specifically, extracellular neurotransmitter molecules released by other neurons. These are the **neurotransmitter-gated channels**. The remaining types of ligand gates are controlled by *intracellular* substances, which may be either ions (**ion-gated channels**) or nucleotides (**nucleotide-gated channels**). Together, these three types of ligand-gated channels—in conjunction with various voltage-gated channels—are used in nerve cells to construct very powerful systems for neural computation and cellular information processing.

Ion Carriers

Unlike ion channels, membrane carrier proteins are integral protein molecules that *do* bind with specific ions on one side of the membrane and transfer those ions to the other side of the membrane through a series of conformational changes. **Carrier transport** is needed for a variety of reasons (Hall, 1992). For example, cells need sugars to provide energy, but the large sugar molecules cannot cross the cell membrane without some special help. Some form of carrier molecule within the membrane is required. Carrier transport is also necessary for establishing and maintaining the resting potential.

Two general types of carrier transport are important in nerve cells. The first is **facilitated transport**. In facilitated transport, the molecule to be moved is recognized by the membrane carrier molecule and incorporated by it, forming a new molecular complex. It is then moved across the membrane in a process called **translocation**, which is accomplished in different ways by different carriers. Finally, the molecule, once transported across the membrane, is then released, completing the process of facilitated molecular transport. In facilitated transport, the carrier molecule aids the movement but contributes no energy to the transport process.

The second type of carrier transport is **active transport**, which differs from facilitated transport in that the carrier uses energy and performs work in moving the target molecule across the membrane of the neuron. Ion pumps, like the sodium-potassium pumps that play a crucial role in generating the resting potential of a nerve cell, are prime examples of active transport systems.

THE RESTING POTENTIAL

The **resting potential** of a nerve cell is its membrane potential in the absence of electrical signaling. (The **membrane potential** of a cell is the electrical potential or voltage difference between the interior and exterior of the cell at a given moment.) The resting potential is generated by three factors:

1. differences in ion concentrations inside and outside the nerve cell,

2. simple potassium-leak channels that permit the ungated movement of potassium ions across the cell membrane,

3. the sodium-potassium pump that actively maintains the ionic concentrations of the intracellular and extracellular fluids over long periods of time.

Perhaps the easiest way to understand the relation between the resting potential and the ion differences in the intracellular and extracellular fluids is to begin with the hypothesis proposed by Julius Bernstein a century ago in 1902. Bernstein suggested that the membrane of the neuron at rest could be considered a semipermeable membrane (Bernstein, 1979).

The idea of a **semipermeable membrane** is simple: A semipermeable membrane allows only selected molecules to pass through it, serving as a barrier to all others. Bernstein proposed that if the neural membrane allowed *only* potassium ions to pass through it, an electrical potential would be created between the interior and exterior of the cell that would be equivalent to the actual potential observed when a nerve cell is at rest. It is now known that Bernstein's century-old conjecture is substantially correct, although matters are somewhat more complicated than he had foreseen.

As Bernstein suggested, the membrane of a neuron is semipermeable to potassium, having small pores that permit only potassium ions to transverse the membrane. These pores are the **potassium-leak channels**, which are two-way streets that permit potassium traffic only; potassium ions alone can pass freely through the channel from inside to outside and from outside to inside.

Potassium ions, moving randomly in both the intracellular and extracellular fluids, will pass through any open potassium-leak channel if they approach the channel with the proper direction and energy. Many collide against the membrane where there are no channels; these ions do not cross the membrane. Others are driven toward the membrane at the location of a potassium channel; these ions cross the membrane and enter or exit the cell.

Ionic Diffusion and Ionic Concentration Gradients

Because there are many more potassium ions in the intracellular fluid than in the extracellular fluid, it is much more likely that potassium ions from the potassium-rich intracellular fluid will leave the cell than that potassium ions will enter the cell from the potassium-poor extracellular fluid.

Diffusion is the name given to the process of random movement of molecules and ions in solution. Diffusion always tends to make the distribution of such particles uniform within the solution. Because there are

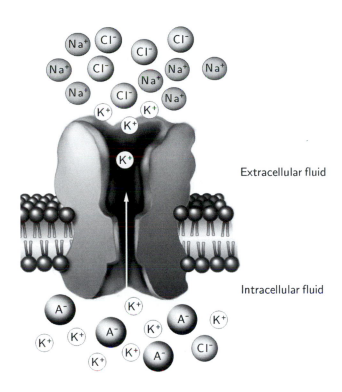

Extracellular fluid

Intracellular fluid

Figure 3.3. The Potassium Membrane. If only potassium ions can pass through the open pores of the membrane, there is a net outward movement of potassium along its concentration gradient. This creates a loss of positive ions on the inside of the cell and a surplus of positive ions on the outside. Because no other positively charged ions, such as sodium, can enter the cell to counteract the outward flow of potassium, a membrane potential must develop in which the intracellular fluid becomes negative with respect to the extracellular fluid.

about 20 times more potassium ions inside than outside the cell, the odds that an intracellular potassium ion will leave the cell are about 20 times higher than the odds that an extracellular potassium ion will enter the cell.

For this reason, potassium ions diffuse across the membrane from the inside, where they are highly concentrated, to the outside, where they are weakly concentrated. This difference in the concentration of potassium ions creates a **concentration gradient** across the membrane. If ions are allowed to cross the membrane and if they are not impeded by other forces, there will be a net flow of ions down the concentration gradient from the region of high concentration toward the region of low concentration.

But because potassium ions are charged particles and are presumed to be the only type of ion that can cross the membrane, the movement of positively charged potassium ions (from the inside to the outside of the membrane along the concentration gradient) creates an electrical imbalance, or a charge, across the membrane. Thus, *the outward diffusion of potassium ions results in a net loss of positive ions on the inside and a surplus of positive ions on the outside*, generating a membrane potential: The interior of the cell becomes negatively charged with respect to the outside. Figure 3.3 illustrates this process.

The development of a potassium-based membrane potential necessarily slows the further movement of potassium ions. Because positively charged particles repel other positive charges and are attracted to negative charges, as the membrane potential grows, it creates an electrical force that tends to counteract the further outward migration of potassium ions.

Eventually, a point will be reached at which the membrane potential is sufficiently strong to balance the concentration gradient. At that point, for every ion driven out of the cell by the process of diffusion, another is attracted back into the cell by electrical charge across the membrane. When this occurs, an electrochemical equilibrium is reached, in which there is no net flow of potassium ions in either direction.

It is the strength of the concentration gradient that determines the **equilibrium potential** across the membrane. The greater the difference in concentration of potassium across the membrane, the larger the electrical force required to stem the tide of exiting potassium ions. This relation is expressed by the **Nernst equation**, which gives the membrane equilibrium potential of a cell membrane permeable to one species of ion as a function of that ion's concentration gradient:

$$Voltage = k \log \frac{Concentration_{out}}{Concentration_{in}}$$

In this equation, the membrane potential is determined completely by the ratio of the potassium concentrations inside and outside the cell. The constant **k** reflects several factors; at 20 degrees C (room temperature), its value is about +58 for positively charged ions, such as potassium. (For negatively charged ions, the constant is −58 rather than +58.) The equation itself is taken from classical thermodynamic theory in physics. When applied to the concentration difference across the membrane for potassium ions (about 1 to 20), the Nernst equation predicts that the equilibrium potential for potassium is approximately −75 millivolts (mV). This is quite close to the actual resting potential of about −70 mV. Bernstein's conjecture was substantially but not completely correct. In all fairness to Bernstein, it should be noted that in 1902, it was not possible to measure the actual membrane potential with the required degree of exactness.

Precise Measurement of the Resting Potential

Precise recording of the membrane potential was not realized until some 40 years later. The development of electronic amplifiers made an important contribution to the recording of electrical events within single cells, but the largest barrier to the accurate measurement of the membrane potential arises from the small size of neurons in mammalian nervous systems. To electrically measure the electrical potential across the membrane, one must place electrodes on both sides of that membrane. It was simply too difficult to place recording electrodes inside these tiny neurons without damaging the cells.

An elegant solution to this problem was proposed in 1936 by J. Z. Young, a noted British zoologist. Young suggested that neurobiologists use an unusual cellular structure, the giant axon of the squid, in investigating the properties of neural membranes (Young, 1936). This axon, which controls the contraction of the squid's mantle to propel the animal through the water, is distinguished by its size; the axon may be as large as 0.5 millimeters (mm) in diameter. (If that seems small, remember that axons in the human nervous system range from less than 0.001 mm to a *maximum* of about 0.02 mm in diameter.)

Young made a fortunate suggestion. The membrane of the giant squid axon proved to be like those of mammalian neurons but was far easier to work with. This biological model permitted the detailed study of membrane function and established the physical basis of the action potential, work that won Alan Lloyd Hodgkin and Andrew F. Huxley a Nobel Prize in 1963.

Using the giant squid axon, Hodgkin and Huxley were able to confirm that Bernstein had been nearly correct; potassium diffusion is the primary determinant of the resting potential. However, Hodgkin and Huxley demonstrated that an additional ion—sodium—plays a minor role in determining the actual resting potential of a nerve cell.

Recall that the measured resting potential of the squid axon is about −70 mV, but the equilibrium potential of a purely potassium-permeable membrane is −75 mV. Something must account for this 5-mV discrepancy, and that something is a tiny trickle of sodium ions moving into the cell at rest. Because sodium is a positively charged ion that is concentrated on the outside of the cell at a ratio of about 9 to 1 (see Figure 3.1 on page 77), the Nernst equation gives its equilibrium potential as +55 mV, the inside of the cell being positive. Thus, any inward movement of Na^+ ions—however small—could move the membrane potential from the K^+ equilibrium potential toward the experimentally measured resting potential of −70 mV.

Hodgkin and Huxley showed that manipulating the concentration ratio of sodium across the membrane does have a small but systematic effect on the measured resting potential of the squid axon. By carefully measuring these tiny changes, they were able to demonstrate that the resting membrane, although primarily permeable to potassium, is slightly permeable to sodium. In fact, sodium permeability is about 1/100 that of potassium when the membrane is at rest.

This extremely small inward trickle of sodium ions is driven by two forces. First, the sodium concentration gradient produces a net sodium flow from extracellular to the intracellular fluids. Second, the electrical gradient established by potassium attracts the positively charged extracellular sodium ions to the negatively charged intracellular fluid. The resulting small influx of sodium ions accounts for the slight difference between the measured resting potential of real neurons and the predicted equilibrium potential for potassium alone.

THE SODIUM-POTASSIUM PUMP

Not only is there a small inward movement of sodium ions when the cell is at rest, because the actual resting potential of the neuron is not exactly equal to K^+ equilibrium potential, but a small amount of potassium also trickles outward from the cell. Although neither of these ion flows is large, both are steady. Given enough time, the interior concentration of sodium would continue to grow, and the interior concentration of potassium would continue to shrink. Thus, something must be counteracting these ion movements, and that something is the **sodium-potassium pump**, a metabolic system within the membrane that forces sodium out of the cell and returns escaped potassium ions back into the neuron.

To maintain the resting potential, both sodium and potassium must be transported by the pump against their own substantial concentration gradients, an undertaking that requires work and consumes energy. Most animal cells devote about 30% of their energy usage to the sodium-potassium pump to osmotically maintain cell volume. But in nerve cells, electrical signaling is carried out by the movement of ions across the cell membrane, which increases the demands on the pump to maintain the resting potential in the face of such additional ionic movements. In neurons, the sodium-potassium pump accounts for about two thirds of the cell's energy use (Alberts et al., 1994; Hall, 1992). In this very real sense, thinking is work.

The sodium-potassium pump consists of a large transmembrane protein and a smaller glycoprotein of unknown function. The large protein contains sodium-binding sites on its intracellular surface and potassium-binding sites on its extracellular surface. The interior surface also contains binding sites for the energy-rich molecule, adenosine triphosphate (ATP), which powers the pump. Figure 3.4 on the next page illustrates this arrangement.

The details by which the sodium-potassium pump operates at a molecular level are now fairly well understood (Alberts et al., 1994). At the onset of each pumping cycle, two potassium ions are bound to the exterior of the pump, and three sodium ions are bound to the interior. The pump then exchanges the positions of the sodium and potassium ions, using energy supplied by hydrolyzing ATP to adenosine diphosphate (ADP). The ATP is obtained from its cytoplasmic binding site. The entire pumping cycle is so tightly coupled that if the ATP molecule or any of the two potassium ions or the three sodium ions is missing, the pump will not operate. Because the sodium-potassium pump transfers three positively charged sodium ions out of the cell for every two positively charged potassium ions that it brings into the cell, the pump is **electrogenic**; that is, it creates an electrical potential across the membrane when it is active.

A small neuron has on the order of a million sodium-potassium pumping molecules embedded in its membrane; large neurons have many, many more. When operating at full capacity, a single pumping molecule carries 200 sodium ions and 133 potassium ions across the membrane in a second; in fact, such a rate is rarely achieved. Instead, the pump works only when needed. Because sodium ions enter the cell when it is active, these ions must be removed by the sodium-potassium pump. For this reason, the pump becomes more active when the neuron is transmitting information.

Finally, it should be mentioned that the sodium-potassium pump not only maintains the special ionic composition of the cytoplasm but also is probably responsible for creating the ionic properties of the intracellular fluid in the first place. By exchanging sodium and potassium molecules across a membrane that is relatively impermeable to one ion and not the other, a membrane potential is developed. Sodium is pumped out of the interior of the cell and, in the main, prevented from returning. Because the membrane is permeable to the negatively charged chloride ion, chloride follows the sodium out of the cell into the positively charged extracellular fluid. Thus, the pump is also responsible for removing chloride ions from the cytoplasm, although this effect is indirect. The sodium-potassium pump, therefore, removes common salt (NaCl) from the cyto-

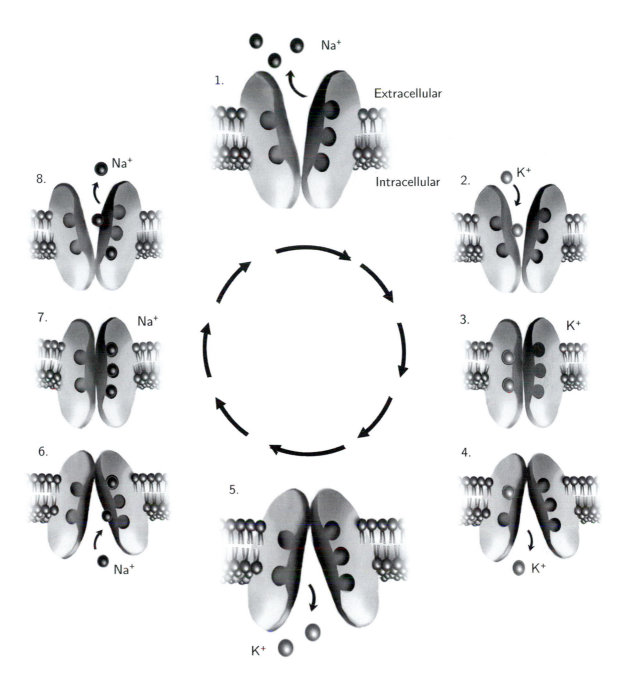

Figure 3.4. Model of the Sodium-Potassium Pump. The sodium-potassium pump is an active membrane carrier protein that first binds with two extracellular potassium ions, returns them to the cytoplasm, and then binds three intracellular sodium ions and returns them to the extracellular fluid. Exchanging the positions of the two ions species—moving sodium out and potassium into the neuron—requires energy, which is supplied by ATP.

plasm while building the interior concentration of potassium. This process is not unique to neurons, but it is exploited by neurons to provide the molecular basis for electrical signaling in the nervous system.

NEURONAL COMMUNICATION

To help us understand the relationship between the resting potential and action potentials, consider the simple example of sensing light touch by a finger. When our fingertips touch an object, special sensory receptors cells beneath the skin are mechanically stretched, which opens sodium pores in the membrane of the cell and permits extracellular Na^+ to enter. Because Na^+ is a positively charged ion, the membrane potential of the cell becomes less negative, a signal that the receptor has been stimulated. In this way, the mechanical act of touching is encoded as an electrical signal in a touch receptor cell.

However, if the nervous system is to make use of that information, it must be relayed to other neurons by synaptic activity at the receptor's axon terminal. In a very small cell, such signals are spread throughout the neuron by passive electrotonic conduction. The term **electrotonic conduction** refers to the passive flow of current within a neuron.

The processes of a neuron—be they dendrites or axons—are relatively slender, fluid-filled tubes. Current is carried within these processes by the movement of ions, but—because the processes are thin—ions frequently collide with other molecules as they move along the electrical gradients of the cell. Such collisions constitute *electrical resistance*, which increases with distance because there are more opportunities for collisions the further an ion travels.

Because current takes the path of least resistance, the amount of current decreases (exponentially) with distance from the source. This means that the electrical currents produced by sodium influx in our touch receptor dissipate rapidly with distance from the sodium pore. Increasing the diameter of an axon decreases its electrical resistance to some extent, as does insulating it with myelin, but neither is sufficient to carry an electrical signal from the fingertip to the spinal cord. Some other signal that is much more robust is required: That signal is the action potential.

THE ACTION POTENTIAL

The **action potential** is the standard signal used to transmit information between distant points within the nervous system (Hille, 1992; Katz, 1966). It is also referred to as a **nerve impulse** or **spike** because of its sharp, almost explosive, character. Usually, an action potential is triggered in the **axon hillock** at the junction between the cell body and axon; from there it spreads down the axon. However, recent studies using voltage-sensitive dyes have provided strong evidence that multiple-spike initiation sites exist within the nerve cell (Zecevic, 1996). The implication of this finding is that the signal-processing capacity of single neurons may be greater than is conventionally thought.

An action potential has a number of unusual properties. First, it is an all-or-none event; either it occurs or it does not.

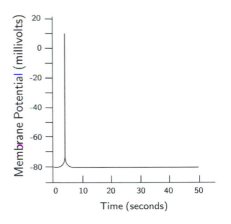
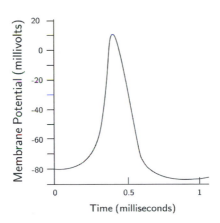

Figure 3.5. The Action Potential. The left panel shows a single action potential recorded from an axon. On this time scale, the impulselike nature of the action potential may be seen. It is not surprising that action potentials are also called "spikes" by neurophysiologists. The right panel shows the same action potential, drawn on a greatly expanded time scale; the entire episode of spike production and return to the resting potential takes place very quickly.

Second, all action potentials are of about the same size; this is a consequence of the manner in which they are generated at the membrane of the cell. Within a single neuron, the similarity between potentials is even closer. Thus, action potentials must carry information by their occurrence, not by changes in size or shape.

Third, action potentials undergo **propagation** by the axon; that is, the signal is continuously regenerated by the membrane of the axon as the signal passes from the initial segment of the axon to its end terminals. It is this feature that gives action potentials remarkable reliability in carrying information from one place to another.

One example of an action potential is shown in Figure 3.5. It is a short, violent movement of the resting membrane potential. The membrane potential, which at rest is about −70 mV, suddenly shifts: In less than 1 millisecond (1 msec equals 1/1,000 second), the membrane potential changes from negative to positive and then returns to its negative resting level. The effect is to produce a voltage spike on the surface of the membrane. This impulse travels down the axon carrying its message. The fact that the impulse is so large and brief contributes significantly to its usefulness as a communication signal. An action potential is difficult to confuse with any other event in the nervous system.

Neurons transmit different messages from the cell body to the end terminals by varying the pattern of action potentials that they produce. Figure 3.6 on the next page presents some examples of different patterns of action potentials. In the human brain, patterns of firing can be quite complex, but despite this complexity, the principle is straightforward: Neurons transmit information from the cell body to the end terminal by changing the rate and pattern of spike activity. The form of the action potential itself remains the same.

Recording the Action Potential

Recordings from the giant axon of the squid first revealed many of the secrets of the action potential. Figure 3.7 on page 89 shows the way in which recordings of action potentials are made.

Figure 3.6. Different Patterns of Action Potentials. (A) Suppressed firing. (B) Clocklike regular discharges, characteristic of neurons that perform timing functions. (C) Repetitive burst firing. (D) A complex discharge pattern.

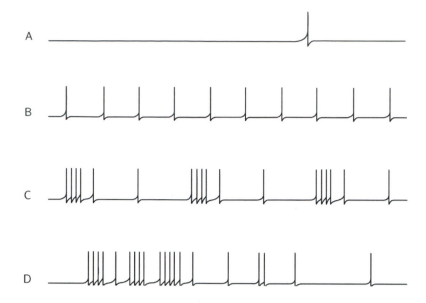

In response to a weak stimulating current, the axon becomes slightly less negative. This partial breakdown of the resting potential is termed **depolarization** because the membrane becomes less polarized (i.e., less charged). With respect to neurons, depolarization always means reducing the size of the membrane potential—that is, moving it closer to zero voltage. Conversely, **hyperpolarization** means increasing the membrane potential.

With stronger stimulating currents, a larger depolarization occurs that may be sufficient to trigger an action potential. Neurons have a characteristic **threshold** for eliciting an action potential. If the stimulus-induced depolarization does not reach this threshold, no action potential is produced. If the depolarization crosses the threshold, a nerve impulse results. The threshold for an action potential is usually 5 to 10 mV less than the resting potential for the cell (e.g., if the resting potential is about −70 mV, the threshold will be about −65 or −60 mV).

Another feature of the nerve impulse is that the membrane potential briefly reverses itself, the inside of the membrane becoming momentarily positive with respect to the outside. At its maximum, the interior of the squid axon has a potential value of about +40 mV.

Finally, at the end of the nerve impulse, the membrane potential not only returns to the resting level but also actually undershoots it; for a short period after the passing of the spike, the membrane of the axon is slightly hyperpolarized.

The most important feature of the action potential is that it is propagated along the axon. The action potential can be thought of as a profound distrubance of the resting potential that is regenerated over and over again as it is carried along the membrane of the axon from the cell body to the end terminal. Action potentials commonly originate at the initial segment of the axon adjacent to the cell body and continue to be propagated along the length of the axon to its end terminals.

Ionic Basis of the Action Potential

The action potential represents a rapid fluctuation of the membrane potential in the axon. It, like the resting potential, is produced by the movement of ions across the membrane. For this reason, action potentials must be the result of momentary changes in the membrane's permeability to various ions. The permeability of a membrane is a measure of the ease with which a specific ion may cross from one side to the other.

A detailed ionic theory of the nerve impulse was offered in 1952 by Hodgkin and Huxley, who based their hypothesis on a large body of carefully collected cell recordings (Fain, 1999; Hille, 1992; Hodgkin, 1964). Hodgkin and Huxley were able to show that the action potential resulted from separate changes in the sodium and potassium permeabilities of the membrane. Furthermore, they demonstrated that these permeabilities vary with the membrane potential itself, with the flow of current across the membrane and, finally, with time. They were able to construct a series of equations based on experimental data that could be used to explain not only the action potential but also a number of other related properties of the nerve axon. This was one of the most significant advances in modern neuroscience.

Hodgkin and Huxley proposed that changing the relative permeabilities of the membrane for sodium and potassium ions would explain the reversal of the membrane potential observed at the height of the nerve impulse. By using the squid axon as a representative neuron, the equilibrium potentials for each ion may be calculated from the concentrations of the ions inside and outside the cell using the Nernst equation. For potassium, the equilibrium potential is about −75 mV, but for sodium it is +55 mV. Thus, the neuron, in principle, may attain any membrane potential between −75 and +55 mV by varying the ratio of sodium and potassium

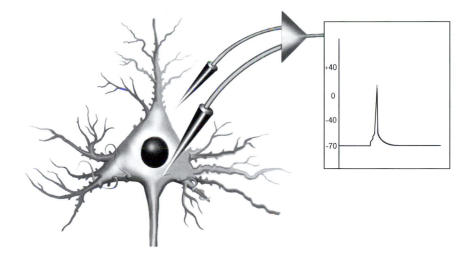

Figure 3.7. Electrical Recording. Recordings are made by placing one electrode within the cell and the other in the fluid surrounding the cell. This illustration shows how one would record from cortical neurons. Hodgkin and Huxley used a similar method to record the action potential nearly half a century ago in their Nobel Prize–winning investigations.

permeabilities of the membrane. This is one key to understanding the nerve impulse.

The overshoot, or polarization reversal, at the peak of the nerve impulse varies as a function of the equilibrium potential of sodium. In a classic experiment, Hodgkin and Bernard Katz (1949) examined the effects of changing the *extracellular* concentration of sodium on the size of the nerve impulse. With a squid axon bathed in normal seawater, which is similar in composition to extracellular fluid, the action potential produces an overshoot to about −40 mV. However, when the sodium concentration is reduced by one half or one third, the size of the overshoot is correspondingly smaller. In all cases, the amount of overshoot may be predicted by the Nernst equation for sodium. Thus, the height of the action potential is controlled by the equilibrium potential for sodium, which—in turn—is determined by the interior and exterior Na^+ concentrations.

Triggering an Action Potential   Depolarization of the membrane is the trigger that begins the action potential. One effect of depolarization is to momentarily open sodium channels on the nerve membrane. The greater the depolarization, the more channels are initially opened. Because sodium is a positively charged ion concentrated outside the neuron, the opening of sodium channels allows more sodium to enter the cell and thereby depolarizes the membrane still further. This is an example of positive feedback.

For a very small depolarization that does not trigger an action potential, only a few sodium channels are opened. If the resulting inward flow of sodium is less than the normal outward movements of potassium that characterize the neuron at rest, the depolarization subsides, and the cell returns to its resting potential. If, however, the triggering depolarization is larger, so that more sodium ions enter the neuron than potassium ions leave, a threshold is effectively crossed, and the membrane becomes—at least for the moment—a sodium membrane, and the membrane potential reverses as the nerve impulse is produced. Hodgkin and Huxley were able to explain the threshold properties of the action potential in terms of the movement of sodium and potassium ions across the membrane.

Terminating the Action Potential

Two factors act to terminate the action potential and return the membrane to its resting value. The first is that the opening of the sodium channels is a transient process; once they are opened, they close quickly and undergo **inactivation**; that is, they are unable to be opened again for several milliseconds. For this reason, high sodium influx across the membrane cannot be maintained.

The second factor returning the membrane potential to its resting level is an opening of voltage-gated potassium channels, which begins after the opening of the sodium channels but continues much longer. Increasing the permeability of the membrane to potassium hastens the return to the resting potential. Figure 3.8 on the next page graphs these changes in the membrane potential, sodium conductance, and potassium conductance across the membrane. It can be seen that the rising portion of the nerve

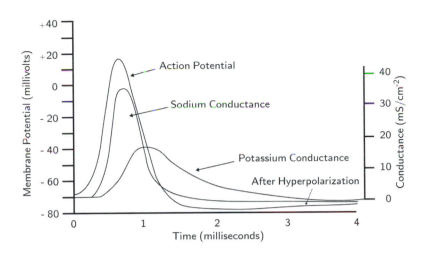

Figure 3.8. Changes in Membrane Permeability During the Action Potential. As the action potential begins, there is a marked increase in sodium conductance, g_{Na+}, that rapidly subsides as sodium channels are inactivated. The increase in potassium conductance, g_{K+}, begins more slowly and is longer lasting.

impulse is dominated by ion flow through the sodium channels, whereas the falling portion is controlled by the reverse ion flow in potassium channels.

Both these factors, the inactivation of sodium channels and the increased permeability of the membrane to potassium, result in an inability of the membrane to produce two nerve impulses in rapid succession. In most neurons, for about a millisecond after initiating a spike, no other action potentials may be produced; this is the **absolute refractory period** of the neuron. For a somewhat longer period, there is a continued increase in potassium permeability. This has the effect of temporarily hyperpolarizing the neuron and raising its spike threshold because sodium inflow must exceed potassium outflow to cross the threshold and trigger a nerve impulse. This period of heightened threshold following the absolute refractory period is called the **relative refractory period**. In the relative refractory period, a stronger than usual input is required to trigger another action potential.

One of the most remarkable aspects of the nerve impulse is how much can be accomplished by the axon with the movement of relatively few ions across its membrane. To produce a spike in the squid axon, only about 1 potassium ion in 10 million must trade places with a sodium ion. Although, over the long run, the production of action potentials would lead to an alteration of the intracellular and extracellular concentrations of sodium and potassium (were it not for the sodium-potassium pump described later), in the short run, these effects are not large.

Hodgkin and Huxley's work on ionic flows in the action potential was based on electrophysiological measurements—careful analyses of the relations between current and voltage in the squid axon. Through these methods, many of the most important properties of the voltage-sensitive sodium and potassium gates were discovered. Today, other methods are available to study the sodium and potassium gates; this newer work has confirmed and extended Hodgkin and Huxley's original conclusions.

Figure 3.9. Propagation of the Nerve Impulse. The electrochemical events involved in generating an action potential—the initial depolarization, the inward rush of sodium making the spike, and the outward flow of potassium terminating the spike—progress millisecond by millisecond from the axon hillock (left) toward the axon terminal.

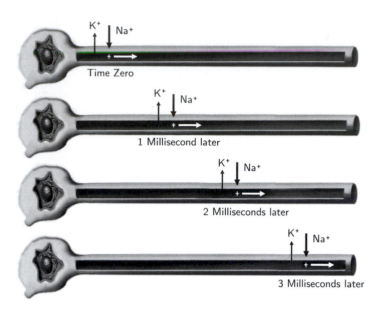

Propagating the Action Potential

Action potentials are produced by changes in the voltage-gated sodium and potassium channels of the axonal membrane, but it is the flow of current resulting from these changes that allows an action potential to be propagated along the axon (Hille, 1992; Katz, 1966). This occurs because the electrical currents produced by ionic movements spread along the axon and act to depolarize adjacent regions of the membrane. It is apparent that the depolarizing effects of an action potential extend a considerable distance along the axon. This spreading depolarization normally acts to trigger other action potentials, thereby propagating the disturbance along the axon from the cell body to the end terminal. In this manner, the action potential passes down the axon as a wave of electrochemical energy.

Figure 3.9 illustrates the propagation of an action potential. Notice that the depolarizing current spreads out around the momentary site of the action potential in both directions, but the action potential propagates only in the forward direction. This directional property of spike propagation results from the inactivation of sodium channels and the increased activity of potassium channels following production of an action potential. The impulse cannot spread backward because the membrane that just produced an action potential is in its absolute refractory period. Therefore, impulse propagation proceeds in one direction, even though depolarizing currents spread in both directions around the active site, because the portions of the axon from which the action potential arrived are not yet ready to produce another nerve impulse.

Incidentally, if a piece of axon is artificially stimulated halfway between the cell body and the end terminals, two spikes are produced: one traveling toward the cell body and the other toward the end terminals. Thus, the axon itself can transmit a spike in either direction, but a nerve impulse can never reverse itself and travel back over the axon on which it has just arrived.

The speed at which the nerve impulse travels—its **conduction velocity**—becomes important, particularly in the evolution of large animals. If conduction is too slow, then the organism's ability to react appropriately to the environment may be compromised. Conduction velocity is not related to the time needed to generate the spike; for all axonal membranes, the time required to produce an action potential is approximately 1 msec.

Instead, the speed of propagation of the nerve impulse depends on the spatial extent of the passive spread of depolarization around the action potential. If the spread is very narrow, then the action potential will affect only the immediately surrounding membrane, and the progress of the spike along the axon will be slow. Conversely, if the depolarizing effects of the spike are wider, the spike will be propagated down the membrane with greater speed. The velocity of the nerve impulse depends on distance ahead of the action potential at which suprathreshold depolarization is produced. Conduction velocity increases with increasing passive spread of the depolarizing current.

But what governs the spread of current about an action potential along the axon? The lengthwise electrical resistance of small nerve fibers is very high; therefore, the spread of current about the action potential is very limited. However, the lengthwise resistance of an axon decreases as its diameter increases. For this reason, larger fibers have higher conduction speed because the electrical depolarizing effects of the action potential reach farther down the axon. Some invertebrates have capitalized on this relation and developed a few very large, faster neurons to control high-speed responses. The giant axon of the squid, which triggers the animal's escape response, is one such example. But the problem with using size to gain speed is that large axons take up a great deal of space; there is not room enough for many large axons within the nervous system. This may be one reason why large invertebrates have not evolved.

Propagation in Myelinated Fibers

Vertebrates have taken another approach to the problem of rapid conduction in neurons. Instead of decreasing the electrical resistance of the axon by increasing its diameter, the effectiveness of the propagated action potential is increased by insulating the axon, much as rubber or plastic is used to insulate wire in electrical systems. That insulation is myelin, and **myelinated fibers** are used in vertebrates to allow rapid communication over long distances within the nervous system. Myelination speeds the action potential by confining all current flow across the membrane to the gaps between the myelin segments. In this way, the current flowing around the action potential is concentrated at the next site of propagation.

The importance of myelination in the evolution of large, intelligent vertebrates is hard to overestimate. Consider the problem of impulse conduction in coordinating the behavior of the animal. In the crab, a typical invertebrate, a large (30 microns in diameter) unmyelinated axon has a maximum conduction speed of 5 meters per second. The extremely large (500 microns) giant axon of the squid propagates impulses at the speed

Figure 3.10. The Nodes of Ranvier. Action potentials can only be generated at the nodes of Ranvier, where the axon membrane makes contact with the extracellular fluid.

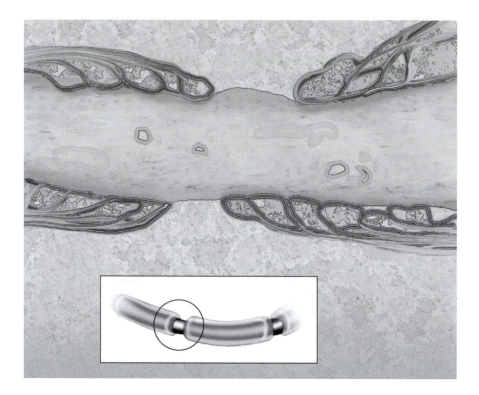

of 20 meters per second. Conversely, a 20-micron myelinated axon in the human has a conduction velocity that is about six times faster (120 meters per second). A large amount of information may be rapidly processed in a myelinated nervous system. Virtually all major pathways within the human central nervous system are myelinated, as are the major connections between the sensory organs, the brain, and the muscles. Myelination allows complex communications to occur rapidly between different regions of the nervous system. Myelination also permits a greater number of such connections to be maintained because the size of myelinated axons is relatively small.

One major effect of myelination on impulse propagation is that it prevents contact between the axon membrane and the extracellular fluid, thus eliminating the flow of current across the membrane in the myelinated region. For this reason, action potentials cannot be generated beneath the myelin sheath. Action potentials occur only at the exposed gaps between segments of the myelin cover. These gaps, the **nodes of Ranvier**, are shown in Figure 3.10. The depolarization from the action potential generated at the node of Ranvier at one end of the myelinated segment spreads down the axon to the next node, where another action potential is produced. At each node, the action potential is generated anew; between nodes, there are no action potentials but only the spread of depolarizing current from one node to the next. This effect is termed **saltatory conduction**, from the Latin verb meaning "to leap." Figure 3.11 on the facing page illustrates the difference in propagation between myelinated and unmyelinated fibers.

Figure 3.11. Propagation Is Speeded by Myelination. Here, the process of saltatory conduction can be seen by examining the progress of the action potential in three moments in time, shown here from left to right. In myelinated fibers, the action potential is propagated only at the nodes of Ranvier, where the extracellular fluid has contact with the cell membrane. The myelin sheath, which separates the nodes, greatly extends the distance that the electrical effects of the action potential can spread down the axon. Thus, myelination increases conduction time for the action potential by both maximizing the distance that it travels using passive current spread and minimizing the number of times that the action potential needs to be regenerated as it speeds from the cell body to the axon terminals of a cell.

Because action potentials are generated only at the nodes of Ranvier and not beneath the myelin sheath, one might expect some specialization of the axon membrane at the nodes of Ranvier. This, in fact, is the case; the membrane at the node is exceptionally rich in both sodium and potassium channels. These ionic channels are about 10 times denser at a node of Ranvier of a myelinated fiber than at any position along the membrane of an unmyelinated neuron. This may be an example of an evolutionary specialization that ensures the reliability of the conduction of the nerve impulse in myelinated fibers.

Finally, it appears that myelination, in addition to increasing the speed of nervous conduction, also reduces the metabolic cost of impulse transmission. The production of action potentials, being restricted to the nodes of Ranvier, affects only about 1% of the membrane surface of the axon. For this reason, the total movement of ions associated with a nerve impulse is greatly reduced. And with many fewer ions moving, the demand placed on the energy-consuming sodium-potassium pump is correspondingly smaller. This is an interesting example of a biological invention that not only increased the speed and efficiency of neuronal communication but also did so with a substantial reduction of metabolic cost.

The functional importance of the myelin sheath is shown in diseases that damage myelin, such as multiple sclerosis (MS). MS produces diverse symptoms, depending on the particular region of the brain in which the lesions occur. Muscular weakness and visual disorders are common.

Drugs That Affect the Action Potential

Because the action potential is controlled by the activity of membrane proteins, drugs that affect these proteins can and do alter neuronal activity. For example, local anesthetics are very basic tools of every physician. These agents achieve their effects by temporarily blocking the voltage-gated sodium channels of neuronal axons. Cocaine was the first such substance to be used as a local anesthetic, being introduced to medical practice in 1884 by a Viennese surgeon, Carl Koller, who successfully used a cocaine solution to anesthetize the cornea of his patients (Lema, 1995). Today, cocaine has been replaced by related safer and more effective synthetic compounds, such as lidocaine and procaine.

All of these local anesthetics are small, lipid-soluble molecules. They act by binding with hydrophobic sites of the voltage-gated transmembrane protein molecule, which inactivates the sodium pore (Hille & Catterall, 1994). This both decreases the inward conductance of sodium in response to any stimulus and reduces the amplitude of the action potential itself.

By reducing the response of somatosensory receptors cells to noxious stimuli, both pain and other sensations arising in the anesthetized area are reduced.

SUMMARY

Neurons communicate with each other using electrical signals, which appear as variations of the membrane potential from its resting value. The resting potential arises because the membrane allows only potassium and not sodium to pass freely through it. The strength of the outward current produced by the movement of potassium and the resulting equilibrium potential is a function of the concentration gradient for potassium across the membrane and is given by the Nernst equation.

Action potentials are the signals used to carry information along the axons of neurons. These nerve impulses do not vary in size or duration; they carry information by their presence or absence. Action potentials are triggered by suprathreshold depolarization and are propagated down the axon. In this way, individual nerve cells can carry information over long distances, allowing the evolution of large organisms, such as human beings.

SELECTED READING

- Fain, G. L. (1999). *Molecular and cellular physiology of neurons*. Cambridge, MA: Harvard University Press. A high-level but very readable treatment of the electrophysiology of nerve cells by one of the world's leading authorities. Destined to become the definitive reference in this field.

KEY TERMS

absolute refractory period The period of time (about 1 msec) after an action potential is produced by an axon during which another action potential cannot be elicited.

action potential A stereotyped sequence of membrane potential and permeability changes that is propagated along the axon of a neuron; the electrochemical signal that carries information from the cell body to the end terminals of most neurons.

active transport The action of transmembrane carriers that do require the expenditure of metabolic energy.

anions Negatively charged ions.

axon hillock The area of transition between the cell body and its axon, where action potentials are usually initiated.

carrier transport The transfer of a specific molecule across the membrane effected by binding of the molecule with a membrane molecule.

cations Positively charged ions.

concentration gradient The difference in concentration of a substance in solution, particularly between the cytoplasm and the extracellular solution across the membrane.

conduction velocity The speed at which an action potential is propagated along an axon.

current The rate at which a charge moves.

cytoplasm See *intracellular fluid*.

depolarization A change in membrane potential that reduces the voltage difference across the membrane; in neurons, it usually refers to a reduction of the negative resting potential, which tends to elicit an action potential.

diffusion The movement of molecules from regions of high concentration to areas of lower concentration, accomplished by the probabilistic movement of molecules driven by thermal energy.

electrogenic Relating to the production of electrical potentials in biological tissue.

electrotonic conduction The passive flow of current within a nerve cell, as distinguished from the propagated action potential.

equilibrium potential The voltage across the cell membrane at which no net movement of ions across the membrane occurs.

extracellular fluid The fluid surrounding the cells of the body.

facilitated transport Carrier transport that does not require energy.

hydrated ions Ions in solution that are bound to water molecules.

hyperpolarization An increase in the voltage difference across the membrane; in neurons, it often refers to an increase in the negative resting potential, which tends to prevent the triggering of an action potential.

inactivation With reference to action potentials, the closing of sodium channels that establishes a temporary increase in sodium permeability of the membrane.

intracellular fluid The fluid contained within the cell membrane.

ion An atom that has either lost or gained one or more electrons and hence has a net electrical charge.

ion-gated channel A membrane channel that opens in response to binding with a specific ion.

mechanically gated channels Membrane channels that open in response to mechanical stimulation.

membrane channel A pore within a transmembrane protein molecule through which selected ions or other substances can pass.

membrane transport protein A specialized membrane protein that allows specific molecules to cross the cell membrane.

membrane potential The electrical potential (voltage) difference between the inside and outside of a cell membrane, stated with reference to the inside of the cell.

myelinated fibers Neurons with myelinated axons.

Nernst equation The equation that gives the equilibrium potential for one type of ion as a function of the intracellular and extracellular concentrations of that ion and of a temperature-dependent constant:
$$Voltage = k \log \frac{Concentration(outside)}{Concentration(inside)}.$$

neurotransmitter-gated channels Membrane ion gates that respond to molecules outside the nerve cell, specifically, extracellular neurotransmitter molecules released by other neurons.

nerve impulse An action potential.

nodes of Ranvier Gaps in the myelin sheath of an axon that allow for saltatory conduction of action potentials.

nucleotide-gated ion channel A membrane channel that opens in response to binding with a specific nucleotide.

pores Protein channels in the membrane through which hydrated ions may pass.

potassium-leak channels Ungated protein pores in the membrane that allow the passage of hydrated potassium ions.

propagation The active process by which an action potential is passed along the length of the axon.

relative refractory period The period following the absolute refractory period of an action potential in which a second action potential may be elicited only by a stronger-than-normal stimulus.

resting potential The membrane potential of a neuron in the absence of electrical signaling.

saltatory conduction The jumping of an action potential from one node of Ranvier to the next along the length of a myelinated axon.

semipermeable membrane A membrane that allows only certain substances to pass through it.

sodium-potassium pump An active transport system that moves sodium out of and potassium into the cell.

spike An action potential.

threshold With reference to neurons, the level of membrane depolarization in the axon hillock or axon at which an action potential is triggered.

translocation In carrier transport, the process of moving the transported molecule across the membrane.

voltage The amount of work necessary to move a charge from one point to another.

voltage-gated ion channels Membrane channels that are opened by specific changes in local membrane potential.

Chapter 4

Synapses

Synapses are points of connection between the axon terminal of one neuron and the membrane of another. The word is derived from the Greek word *synapsis*, meaning "connection." It is at a synapse that one cell influences the activity of another.

Nearly all synapses in the human nervous system operate chemically. At chemical synapses, one cell communicates with another by releasing molecules of a special signaling chemical, called a **neurotransmitter**.

However, a few neurons—particularly in invertebrates—communicate with each other electrically, by allowing current to flow directly between the cytoplasm of two cells. Such a connection is called a **gap junction**, but it is also referred to as an *electrical synapse*. In this book—as is common in contemporary neuroscience—the word *synapse* always will refer to the chemical type of intercellular connection because chemical synapses are by far the predominant and most important type of functional connection between nerve cells.

GAP JUNCTIONS

Gap junctions—the electrical type of synapses—are specialized membrane structures that electrically link the interiors of two adjacent cells, as shown in Figure 4.1 on the next page. At a gap junction, ionic currents carry information from one cell to another by providing electrical continuity of current flow between the two cells.

A gap junction is formed by the outer membranes of the two communicating cells. In the region of the junction, there is no extracellular fluid between the two cellular membranes. Each of the membranes contains a regularly spaced matrix of transmembrane protein channels, similar in many ways to the ion channels that mediate the resting and action potentials. These protein channels are precisely aligned, as Figure 4.1 on the facing page illustrates. Gap junction protein channels are composed of a ring of six subunits giving the channel sufficiently wide pores to allow both inorganic ions and small organic molecules to cross freely.

The ion channels of a gap junction are not wide enough to permit the passage of macromolecules, such as cytoplasmic proteins or nucleic acids. The result of this arrangement is that the membrane potential of one cell directly affects the membrane potential of the other, much as the membrane potential at two different regions of a single neuron interacts.

The channel proteins of the gap junction matrix may be gated, permitting the two cells to be coupled and uncoupled by as yet unknown cellular controls. However, it appears at this time that gap junctions play a rather small role in the functioning of the human nervous system.

SYNAPSES

Synapses—that is, *chemical* synapses—are the primary mechanisms for intercellular communication and computation in the mammalian nervous system. Synapses are far more powerful than gap junctions as a means of linking single nerve cells into computational circuits. Unlike gap junctions, which can only act to spread electrical events from one cell to another, chemical synapses can induce a wide variety of short- and long-term changes in the cell receiving synaptic input. Activity at chemical synapses not only can affect the membrane potential of a cell, but cellular structure can be altered as well.

The **synapse** is composed of three primary elements: (a) the synaptic terminal of the sending neuron, (b) the membrane and related structures of the receiving neuron, and (c) the space between them. Figure 4.2 on page 104 presents an idealized synapse, illustrating many of its most important features. The transmission of information at the idealized chemical synapse is one-directional, from the axon terminal of the **presynaptic** or sending neuron, across the synaptic cleft, to the membrane of the **postsynaptic** or receiving neuron. Thus, unlike gap junctions in which ions flow in either direction, chemical synapses are **polarized**, meaning that information usually flows in one direction only, from the presynaptic to the postsynaptic cell.

Perhaps the most striking anatomical feature of the presynaptic axon terminal at a synapse is the presence of **vesicles**, tiny spheres of mem-

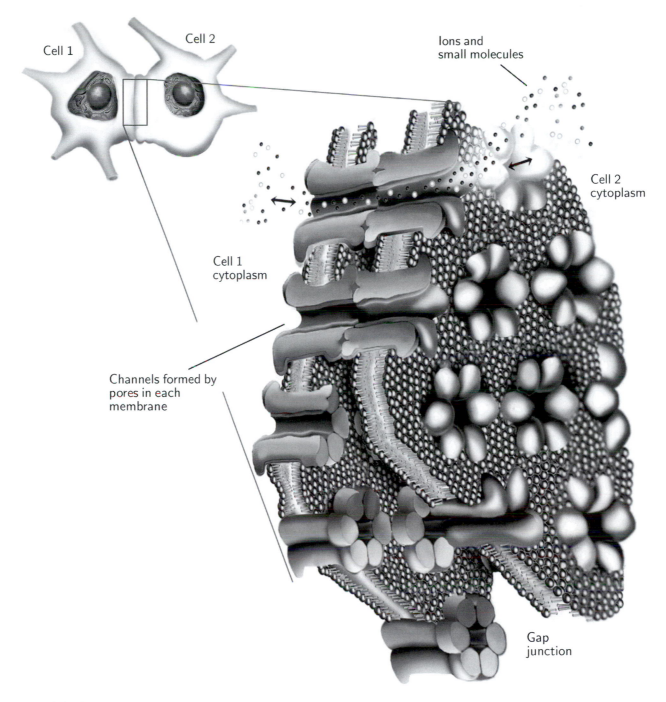

Figure 4.1. Gap Junction Channels. Some cells communicate electrically using specialized structures called gap junctions. Gap junctions are formed by aligned pairs of transmembrane proteins that form contiguous pores. Many such protein pairs may be involved in forming a functional junction. At gap junctions, the membranes of the two nerve cells are in tight apposition, with no extracellular fluid separating them.

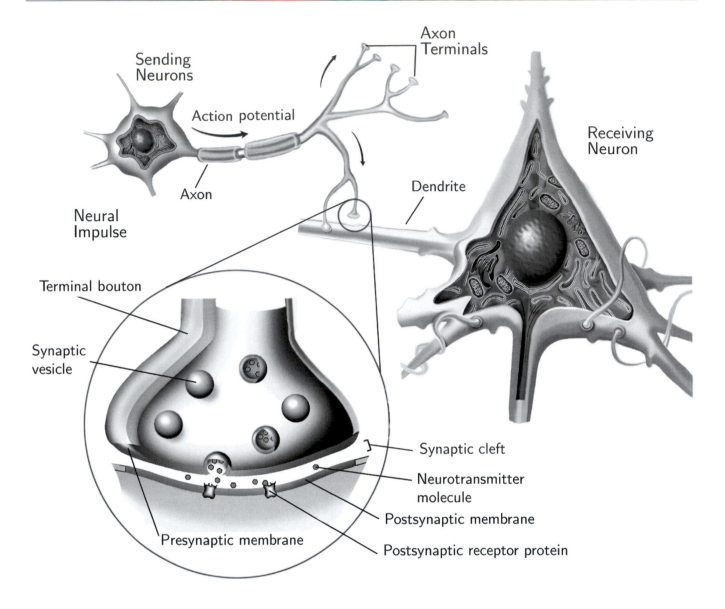

Figure 4.2. The Basic Structure of a Chemical Synapse. In this illustration, the major features of a chemical synapse are shown: a) the axon terminal of the presynaptic ("sending") neuron, b) the postsynaptic membrane of the "receiving" neuron, and the space between them, which is called the *synaptic cleft*. Molecules of neurotransmitter substances communicate between the presynaptic and postsynaptic cells at the synapse.

brane that contain neurotransmitter substances. A **neurotransmitter** is a chemical substance that is released by an axon terminal that affects the activity of the postsynaptic cell. When safely packaged within a vesicle, the highly active neurotransmitter substance may be transported to and stored within the axon terminal.

Axon terminals are also rich in mitochondria. This is an anatomical indication that the biochemical machinery of the axon terminal requires an abundant supply of high-energy materials. In fact, a number of complex energy-using biochemical processes are carried out within the presynaptic element of the synapse.

The space between the presynaptic and postsynaptic membranes is the **synaptic cleft**. This gap is about 20 to 30 nanometers wide and contains a large, chemically complex fluid component. The synaptic cleft also contains strands, or filaments, that act to hold the presynaptic and postsynaptic membranes in close proximity to each other. This binding, called the *synaptic web*, may be exceedingly strong; when brain tissue is broken up for chemical analyses, for example, the presynaptic and postsynaptic elements tend to remain together. The entire detached complex—the axon terminal, the synaptic web, and the postsynaptic membrane—is called a *synaptosome*.

The postsynaptic membrane is the third part of the synapse. This portion of the outer membrane of the receiving neuron contains specialized subsynaptic structures, which may be quite complex.

Classifying Synapses by Microscopic Appearance

Different types of synapses have different appearances, a fact that provided an early clue to understanding the different functions of synapses in the nervous system. Several methods of anatomically classifying synapses within the central nervous system are commonly employed.

Synaptic Location   One basic method divides synapses according to the location of the synapse on the postsynaptic neuron. If the synapse is on a dendrite, it is said to be **axodendritic synapse** (from an axon to a dendrite). If the synapse is found on the cell body, it is an **axosomatic synapse**. If the postsynaptic element is another axon terminal or an axon, the synapse is termed an **axoaxonic synapse**. But the presynaptic element is not always an axon terminal. Synapse also may occur between dendrites of two neurons. Illustrations of synapses in various locations are shown in Figure 4.3 on the following page.

In addition to these four common synaptic arrangements, dendrosomatic and dendroaxonal synapses also have been described. It now appears that virtually any conceivable combination of microanatomical connection is possible, as are more complex synaptic arrangements, such as reciprocal synapses in which both cells affect each other.

Finally, the presynaptic axon terminal sometimes has membrane receptors for its own neurotransmitter. Thus, a single structure, an axon terminal, serves as one postsynaptic element for the neurotransmitter that it releases. Such **autoreceptors**, as they are called, provide a mechanism for regulating the activity of an axon terminal on the basis of its previous secretory activity.

Symmetry and Vesicular Form   Synapses also may be classified according to the distribution of dense material on the presynaptic and postsynaptic membranes, as seen by electron microscopy with conventional staining methods. This classification is useful in examining synapses on the large, principal neurons of cerebral cortex. One type is termed an **asymmetrical synapse**, as the dense material accumulated on the postsynaptic membrane is substantially larger than that on the presynaptic membrane. In these synapses, the vesicles have a characteristic spherical shape; these are called **round vesicles**. In a **symmetrical synapse**, these two densities are more equal. Here vesicles are elongated rather than spherical. These are

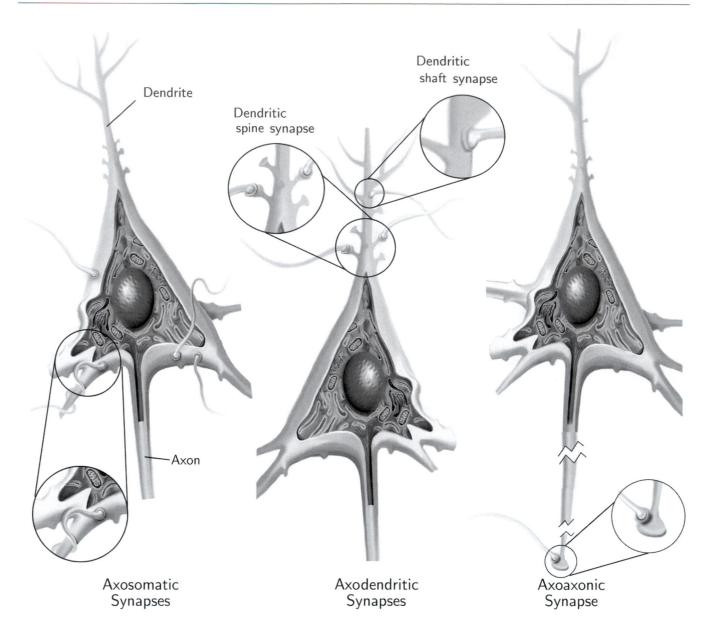

Figure 4.3. Three Types of Synapses, Classified by Postsynaptic Location. Left: Axosomatic synapses are located on the soma of the postsynaptic cell. Center: Axodendritic synapses have a dendrite as the postsynaptic element. Right: Axoaxonic synapses terminate on an axon, usually an axon terminal.

called **flattened vesicles**. Both types are illustrated in Figure 4.4 on the next page.

These differences in the microscopic structure of synapses within the central nervous system are more than anatomical curiosities. They also have fundamental functional significance. It is now clear that the round vesicles of asymmetrical synapses excite postsynaptic cells, moving their membrane potential toward the threshold for firing. Conversely, input from symmetrical synapses with flattened vesicles acts to inhibit postsynaptic cells. Thus, it is possible to learn about the functional properties of synaptic communications by microscopic inspection.

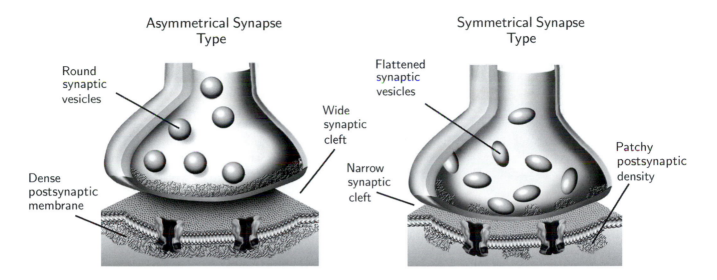

Figure 4.4. Symmetrical and Asymmetrical Synapses. Symmetrical synapses have flattened vesicles and are believed to be inhibitory in function, whereas asymmetrical synapses have rounded vesicles and are thought to be excitatory.

Asymmetric and symmetric synapses also differ from their postsynaptic distributions on the large principal neurons such as the pyramidal cells of the cerebral cortex. The dendrites of cortical pyramidal cells tend to receive input from asymmetrical synapses with rounded vesicles, whereas the synapses on their cell bodies tend to be symmetrical, with flattened vesicles. Findings such as these suggest that the cell bodies of these large neurons may function as a gate that balances the excitatory input of the dendrites with the inhibitory input to the soma to determine whether an action potential will be produced in the initial segment of the axon.

Neurotransmitter Release

The release of neurotransmitter substance by the axon terminal is instigated by the arrival of an action potential from the axon. Depolarization of the terminal triggers the *voltage-gated calcium channels* to open momentarily. Calcium is concentrated in the extracellular fluid; the cytoplasm has very low levels of calcium. Thus, when calcium ion channels are opened, there is an inrush of that ion, briefly increasing calcium concentrations in the interior of the axon terminal in the region of its membrane.

It is this sudden increase in intracellular calcium that triggers the opening of synaptic vesicles into the synaptic cleft and the release of neurotransmitter substance. The molecular mechanisms by which entering calcium ions facilitate transmitter release are not known in detail, but something such as the following occurs: A neurotransmitter is packaged in small vesicles of membrane, each containing equivalent amounts of the transmitter substance. Each synaptic vesicle contains something on the order of 1,000 to 5,000 molecules of neurotransmitter. These packages are manufactured long before they are actually used, so cytoplasmic calcium levels cannot affect the amount of neurotransmitter within the vesicles.

Rather, the influx of calcium during depolarization of the axon terminal appears to activate a system of microtubules within the axon terminal. The

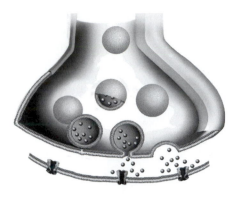

Figure 4.5. The Stages of Neurotransmitter Release. Vesicles congregate near the synaptic membrane. Triggered by an influx of calcium ions, the vesicle fuses with the synaptic membrane, and the vesicular membrane is broken open, spilling its contents into the synaptic cleft. The emptied synaptic vesicle is then reclaimed and returned to the interior of the axon terminal for refilling with neurotransmitter substance.

microtubules exert mechanical force and induce the movement of vesicles toward the presynaptic membrane.

Exocytosis   As calcium levels rise within the axon terminal, some synaptic vesicles in the vicinity of the cell membrane fuse with that membrane and release their contents into the synaptic cleft. This process is called **exocytosis**. There are probably specific neurotransmitter release sites along the presynaptic membrane of the axon terminal. The influx of calcium ions in some way activates these sites, causing the membrane of a vesicle to fuse with the presynaptic membrane, opening the vesicle and spilling its contents into the synaptic cleft. Figure 4.5 illustrates this process.

The cycle of exocytosis is as follows: First, a vesicle approaches the membrane, on its way to an active site. Second, the vesicle begins to fuse with the membrane at such a site. Third, the vesicle joins the outer membrane of the axon terminal and, in so doing, releases its contents into the synaptic cleft. Finally, the vesicle, devoid of most of its neurotransmitter, is reclaimed and returns to the interior of the axon terminal for return to the cell body for refilling.

Reuse of Synaptic Vesicles   The process of using and reusing synaptic vesicles is a fascinating one. Vesicles are manufactured in the cell body, not in the axon terminal. Fresh vesicles, filled with neurotransmitter substance and various complexes of enzymes, are shipped from the cell body down the axon to the axon terminals of the neuron. This process of **axoplasmic transport** (*axoplasm* is a term for the cytoplasm or intracellular fluid of an axon) may be demonstrated by tying off the axon between the cell body and axon terminal. After some time has passed, a number of vesicles will collect on the cell body side of the obstruction. These are vesicles whose transport to the axon terminals was interrupted.

Once emptied by exocytosis, vesicles that contained large molecule neurotransmitters, such as the catecholamines discussed below, are returned to the cell body for refilling by the process of **reversed axoplasmic transport**. This is especially remarkable in long-axoned neurons, in which vesicles may be carried over distances of a meter or more in their movement from the cell body to axon terminal and, perhaps, back again. In contrast, small molecule neurotransmitters, such as glutamate or acetylcholine, may be refilled within the axon terminal itself. These vesicles are much smaller (about 50 nanometers in diameter) and are locally maintained.

Neurotransmitter Binding   Many hundreds of identical neurotransmitter molecules are released into the synaptic cleft by the exocytosis of a single presynaptic terminal vesicle. These molecules rapidly diffuse through the synaptic web, and many make contact with specialized postsynaptic transmembrane protein molecules with which they selectively bind. These postsynaptic transmembrane proteins are called receptors. A **receptor** is a membrane protein that binds with a specific extracellular signaling molecule (called a **ligand**) and triggers a response in the cell, produced by an **effector** molecule.

When a molecule of neurotransmitter substance binds with its post-synaptic receptor, any of a range of molecular consequences may occur in the postsynaptic cell. What the cell does depends only on the molecular properties of the receptor molecule, not on the characteristics of the neurotransmitter substance itself. It is important to remember that the direct effects of a neurotransmitter on the postsynaptic cell are *permissive*, not *instructive*. Neurotransmitter binding permits postsynaptic molecular machinery to act; it does not instruct the postsynaptic cell what actions to undertake. Thus, the same neurotransmitter may have very different effects and different synapses, depending on the particular receptor molecules employed by the different postsynaptic neurons.

Thus, receptors are matched to ligands as locks are matched to keys. However, as good as these molecular lock-and-key arrangements may be, they are not perfect. Many psychoactive drugs exert their effects by mimicking natural neurotransmitters sufficiently well that brain synaptic receptors are inappropriately activated. Natural selection has taken advantage of this fact in the selection of neurotoxins that alter the relation between prey and predator, a fact that provides neurochemists with a powerful set of tools for studying the synapse.

Thus, one of the most important methods of studying neurotransmitters and receptors is to examine the effects of different drugs or compounds on synaptic function. Some drugs are capable of binding with a receptor and trigger the response of the effector complex; these drugs, termed **agonists**, function in the same manner as the naturally occurring neurotransmitter. Heroin, for example, is an agonist of the brain neurotransmitter endorphin.

Other drugs, called **antagonists**, reduce or block the response of the receptor to either the neurotransmitter or its agonist. One way that antagonists produce their effects is to occupy the receptor site without triggering the effector. In this way, action of the neurotransmitter is blocked.

Still other compounds act at the synapse to **potentiate** the effects of either neurotransmitter or agonist. One common type of potentiator blocks enzymes that normally inactivate the neurotransmitter substance; this results in an increase in the number of active neurotransmitter molecules that remain capable of binding with receptors. By determining the types of compounds that act as agonists, antagonists, and potentiators at a particular synapse, the biochemical properties of both neurotransmitter and receptor molecules may be established.

Postsynaptic Functions

Once a neurotransmitter substance has been bound to a receptor molecule in the postsynaptic membrane, it is up to that receptor molecule to effect a change in the activity of the postsynaptic cell. The postsynaptic response may occur either directly or indirectly. Some receptors are directly linked to an ion channel, whereas others use a second messenger to control ion channels elsewhere on the membrane.

Transmitter-Gated Ion Channels   A **transmitter-gated ion channel** incorporates both the controlling extracellular neurotransmitter binding site

Figure 4.6. Model of a Transmitter-Gated Ion Channel, the Nicotinic Acetylcholine (ACh) Receptor and Ion Channel. The nicotinic receptor molecule has two binding sites for ACh on its outer surface. When these sites are occupied by ACh or its agonists, the transmembrane channel opens, permitting the inward movement of sodium ions and the outward movement of potassium ions. These movements act to depolarize the postsynaptic membrane; hence, its effect is excitatory. This channel remains open for about a millisecond, before the ACh molecules are released from the receptor and inactivated by the enzyme acetylcholinesterase.

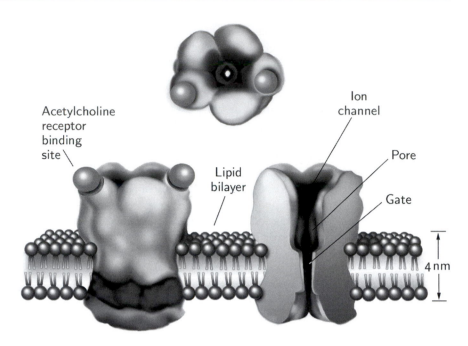

and the responding ion channel in a single transmembrane protein molecule. Such receptors respond to the binding of a neurotransmitter in its extracellular receptor by rapidly reconfiguring its transmembrane ion channel to alter the membrane's permeability to that particular ion species.

Transmitter-gated ion channels are always closed, unless their binding site is occupied by a neurotransmitter or its agonist. Binding opens the ion channel, as shown in Figure 4.6. By opening a closed ion channel, these receptors produce rapid changes in the membrane potential of the postsynaptic neuron. Transmitter-gated ion channels are also called **iontrophic channels**, meaning that the direct effect of synaptic binding is to open an ion channel. Such channels are responsible for a great deal of the rapid signaling in which neurons are engaged.

G-Proteins Systems   Other receptors do not incorporate a membrane ion channel into their molecular structure. Rather, they instigate a response elsewhere in the postsynaptic cell by releasing a special molecule, called *guanosine triphosphate (GTP)-binding protein*, or, more simply, a *G-protein* (Duman & Nestler, 1995). These systems are called *G-protein-linked receptors* and are illustrated in Figure 4.7 on the facing page. G-protein-linked receptors are all composed of seven subunits, but these subunits do not themselves form an ion pore of any kind.

The binding of a molecule of neurotransmitter with a G-protein-linked receptor activates the associated G-protein molecule. The G-protein molecule is composed of three subunits, termed *alpha, beta,* and *gamma*. At rest, G-protein molecules, which are present in the vicinity of membrane receptors, are bound with guanosine diphosphate (GDP) at the alpha subunit. When such a G-protein molecule contacts a membrane receptor that is bound to a neurotransmitter molecule, the G-protein is activated. The

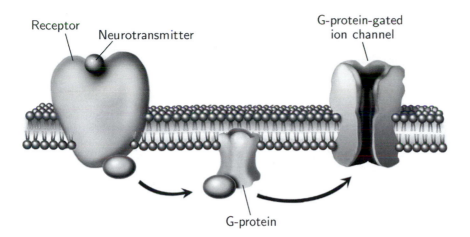

Receptor
Neurotransmitter
G-protein-gated ion channel
G-protein

Figure 4.7. Model of G-Protein-Linked Synaptic Receptor, the Muscarinic Acetylcholine Receptor. At a muscarinic synapse, when ACh binds with the receptor, the G-protein to which the receptor is coupled is activated. The subunits are unbound, and the α-subunit bound to cytoplasmic cyclic guanosine triphosphate is released into the intracellular fluid where it can interact with an effector molecule, opening an ion channel.

activated G-protein exchanges its GDP molecule for a GTP molecule (from the cytoplasm), and the alpha subunit (with the GTP) splits apart from the beta and gamma subunits of the G-protein. At this point, the alpha subunit with its GTP can activate other proteins within the postsynaptic cell. Eventually, the activated alpha subunit is recombined with beta and gamma components, restoring the G-protein for further use.

Activated G-proteins trigger other transmembrane proteins to produce one of two types of changes in the postsynaptic neuron. If the target transmembrane protein is itself an ion channel, that channel is opened. For such systems, the synaptic action is like that of a transmitter-gated ion channel, except that the receptor function (neurotransmitter binding) and the effector function (opening a closed ion channel) are performed by two separate transmembrane proteins. Furthermore, such cellular responses are somewhat slower than the direct iontropic response because an intermediate step—G-protein activation—is required.

The second effect that an activated G-protein may produce is to activate a *membrane-bound enzyme*. By enabling an enzyme, a wide variety of cellular effects may be achieved. These include altering the concentration of other intracellular signaling molecules or initiating the synthesis of proteins and other substances. Such effects can be wide-ranging and produce significant alterations within the postsynaptic cell. Enzyme-produced, G-protein-triggered postsynaptic changes are called metatrobic responses, reflecting the metabolic rather than the simply ionic nature of these effects. Neurotransmitters are called neuromodulators when they elicit slow metatrobic responses. Metatrobic responses are of necessity much slower than the rapid electrical effects achieved by transmitter-gated ion channels.

The enzyme system and related molecules released when a G-protein interacts with a membrane-bound enzyme is called a **second messenger**. Second messengers are intracellular signaling molecules that broadcast the message originally brought to a G-protein-linked receptor on the postsynaptic cell by the neurotransmitter (the first messenger). These intracellular carriers may affect many widespread target regions of the postsynaptic

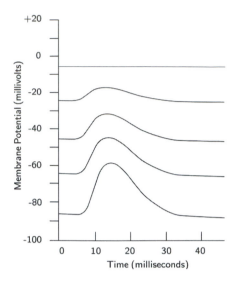

Figure 4.8. Excitatory Postsynaptic Potentials (EPSPs). An EPSP is a graded potential that drives the cell membrane in a depolarizing direction. Notice that the size of these potentials depends on the preexisting membrane potential, being zero at the equilibrium potential for sodium and potassium combined.

neuron. Thus, second-messenger systems allow synaptic input to be amplified and to achieve large-scale postsynaptic effects. Cyclic adenosine monophosphate (AMP) and cyclic guanosine monophosphate (GMP) are two major second messengers in human brain neurons.

Excitatory Synapses   When neurotransmitter substance is released at an excitatory synapse, the response is to depolarize the postsynaptic neuron, sometimes with sufficient strength to induce an action potential in that neuron. The depolarization produced by a single excitatory synapse is usually insufficient to actually trigger a nerve impulse, but its effect is to excite the postsynaptic neuron (Hille, 1992).

This depolarizing response is called an **excitatory postsynaptic potential (EPSP)**. Figure 4.8 presents examples of typical EPSPs. Although the amplitudes and durations of EPSPs may differ, all responses share certain essential features.

1. EPSPs are depolarizing postsynaptic potentials, moving the membrane potential temporarily toward the cell's threshold for producing a nerve impulse.

2. All EPSPs are rather long lasting, at least when compared with action potentials; EPSPs typically continue for 5 to 10 msec before their depolarizing effects are completely dissipated, in contrast to the 1-msec duration of a nerve impulse.

3. The size of the EPSP produced by a given amount of neurotransmitter increases with the size of the membrane potential of the postsynaptic cell. EPSPs are larger when the postsynaptic membrane is highly polarized than when it is relatively depolarized.

4. Finally, all EPSPs show a synaptic delay of approximately 1 msec, the time elapsing between the arrival of an action potential at the presynaptic element and the first appearance of electrical activity at the postsynaptic element of the synapse. The presence of synaptic delay indicates conclusively that the EPSP cannot be the result of a spread of current from the presynaptic to the postsynaptic element; current spread is instantaneous. The synaptic delay, instead, reflects the time taken to release packets of neurotransmitter and for the molecules of neurotransmitter to diffuse across the synaptic cleft.

The ionic basis of the EPSP is now well established. The arrival of excitatory transmitter substance at specialized sites on the postsynaptic membrane increases membrane permeability to both sodium and potassium by opening a nonselective cation channel.

In an EPSP, there is a breakdown in the selective permeability of the membrane for potassium and sodium. This is demonstrated by measuring the **equilibrium potential** for the excitatory synapse by observing the effects of transmitter release while artificially varying the resting membrane potential (see Figure 4.8). Such experiments indicate that the equilibrium potential of the EPSP is approximately -10 mV, the "compromise" potential predicted by the Nernst equation for a membrane that is permeable to both potassium and sodium (Hille, 1992).

During an EPSP, postsynaptic cation channels are continuously opening and closing; a single sodium-potassium channel remains open for only 1 msec. But during that time, it is estimated that something like 20,000 sodium ions enter the neuron, driven by both the electrical gradient and their own concentration gradient. A much smaller number of potassium ions leave the neuron at the same time. Potassium is driven out by its concentration gradient but not its electrical gradient, which acts to impede the outward movement of potassium ions. The net dominance of sodium movement produces the depolarizing effect of the EPSP, driving the cell closer to its threshold. In this way, excitatory postsynaptic potentials act to trigger action potentials within the postsynaptic neuron.

There are two important differences between the ion channels opened by a neurotransmitter at an excitatory synapse and the sodium and potassium channels involved in propagating an action potential that were described in the previous chapter. First, in an EPSP, the increase in both sodium and potassium permeability occurs at the same time; this reflects the fact that both ions are using the same channels to cross the membrane. In the action potential, the change in permeabilities occurs in sequence; initially, sodium permeability increases as the sodium channels are opened, and only later does potassium permeability change, reflecting the opening of the potassium channels to restore the membrane potential. Second, the channels opened by an excitatory neurotransmitter are not voltage sensitive; for this reason, there is no explosive increase in sodium permeability like that characteristic of the nerve impulse.

Inhibitory Synapses At an inhibitory chemical synapse, the effect of neurotransmitter release is to hyperpolarize the postsynaptic neuron and thereby decrease the probability that the neuron will fire. Like excitation, inhibition plays a critical role in the control of behavior by the brain. Excitatory and inhibitory synapses have opposing effects on the activity of the postsynaptic neuron, the resulting neural activity often depending on the balance between excitatory and inhibitory influences. Figure 4.9 illustrates **inhibitory postsynaptic potentials (IPSP)**. IPSPs share a number of features with EPSPs. Both are **graded potentials**; they increase in size as a function of the amount of neurotransmitter released. Both have similar durations, and both show synaptic delay. But one acts to increase and the other to decrease the excitability of the postsynaptic neuron. IPSPs and EPSPs are partners in regulating the activity of neurons.

Inhibitory postsynaptic ion channels produce IPSPs by opening chloride channels. Recall that the negatively charged chloride anion is concentrated outside the neuron. When synaptic chloride gates are opened, the anion is driven into the neuron by its concentration gradient, thereby making the membrane potential of the neuron more negative. Thus, IPSPs act to hyperpolarize the postsynaptic cell, reducing the probability that an action potential will be generated.

However, for many neurons, the resting potential is already very close to the equilibrium potential for chloride ions. For these cells, opening synaptic chloride gates will not make the membrane potential more negative. Nonetheless, the opened chloride gates will still make it more difficult for other influences to depolarize the cell, thereby producing a net

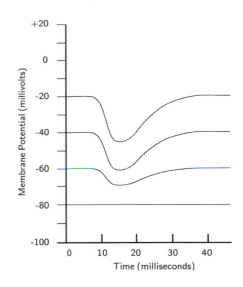

Figure 4.9. Inhibitory Postsynaptic Potentials (IPSPs). Like EPSPs, the amplitude of an IPSP depends on the preexisting membrane potential. The equilibrium potential for IPSPs is about −80 mV, the equilibrium potential for potassium. IPSPs and EPSPs act together in decision making.

Figure 4.10. Three Neurons Are Involved in Presynaptic Inhibition. Here, neuron A makes a conventional excitatory synapse on B. Neuron C synapses on the axon terminal of A and can suppress the effectiveness of the A to B synapse by presynaptically inhibiting the axon terminal of A.

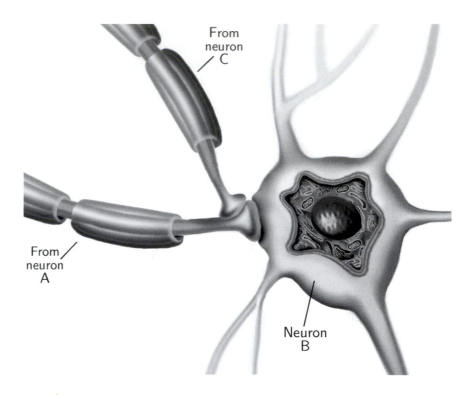

inhibitory effect.

Inhibitory postsynaptic potentials play varying roles in different parts of the nervous system. In addition to participating in neuronal decision making, inhibition serves as a stabilizing influence, preventing neurons from mutually exciting each other and producing a convulsive seizure of electrical firing, such as occurs in epilepsy.

Presynaptic Inhibition   In addition to directly affecting ion channels on the postsynaptic membrane, there is yet another synaptic mechanism by which neurons may affect the activity of other neurons. In **presynaptic inhibition**, three neurons are involved. The first neuron (A) synapses on a second neuron (B) in the conventional manner. But a third neuron (C) can control the effectiveness of the synapse from A to B by its own synapse on the axon terminal of A. Thus, C is an axoaxonic synapse that modulates the primary connection between A and B. Figure 4.10 illustrates these relationships.

Paradoxically, if C has an excitatory effect on the axon terminal of A, presynaptic inhibition will occur between A and B. Activation of C acts to reduce the efficiency of the voltage-sensitive calcium channels in the axon terminal of A. Remember, it is the influx of calcium that triggers the release of neurotransmitter in an axon terminal. Thus, by partial blocking of the calcium channels at the axon terminal, less transmitter is released by A when it is activated by an action potential. It is in this special sense that the axoaxonic synapse on A reduces the effect of A on B's postsynaptic membrane.

It is particularly important that presynaptic inhibition not be confused with postsynaptic inhibition. Presynaptic inhibition always involves a complex of three cells. It modulates the efficiency of a primary synapse between two neurons. No IPSPs are produced; instead, the effectiveness of a normal excitatory synapse is reduced by presynaptic inhibitory input. Presynaptic inhibition is an example of the inventiveness of evolution in producing a method of selectively regulating some informational pathways while leaving others unaffected.

Disposal of Neurotransmitter Substance

The neurotransmitters that elicit either EPSPs or IPSPs produce profound effects at the postsynaptic membrane. If these effects were to persist, the synapse would quickly become unresponsive to further synaptic input. Something must be done at the synapse to remove old neurotransmitter molecules and ready the synapse for further input. There are two principal mechanisms by which transmitter substance is disposed of: **enzymatic degradation** and **reuptake**.

Enzymatic degradation involves the use of specific molecules at the postsynaptic membrane that break down the active transmitter into molecules that do not affect membrane permeability. These inactivated compounds can then be reprocessed by the neuron and used for other purposes. The enzymes involved in inactivating neurotransmitter substance play a critical role in the cycle of synaptic activity and, as we will see later, may be involved in mental illness and its treatment.

Reuptake is the mechanism by which neurotransmitter substance is removed from the synaptic cleft. Special high-affinity binding sites for the neurotransmitter are present on the membrane of the presynaptic cell, capturing diffusing molecules of neurotransmitter and returning them safely for repackaging and reuse at the chemical synapse. Both enzymatic degradation and reuptake appear to be needed to maintain chemical synapses in the required state of readiness for further use.

TEMPORAL AND SPATIAL SUMMATION

In most neurons, a single synapse cannot force the cell to produce an action potential. To trigger a nerve impulse, many synaptic influences must be combined. Synaptic potentials summate; that is, they add with each other in moving the membrane potential closer to or farther from the threshold of the nerve impulse in the process of summation.

It is useful to distinguish between **spatial summation** and **temporal summation** of synaptic potentials. Spatial summation refers to the adding together of polarizing and depolarizing effects of different simultaneously active synapses. Temporal summation emphasizes that synaptic potentials linger and therefore can add together over time. Figure 4.11 on the next page illustrates the summation of synaptic potentials.

Spatial summation is particularly important in considering the ways in which neurons are interconnected. Most neurons receive converging information from many other neurons; **convergence** of information is a major feature of the organization of the nervous system. A large neuron

Figure 4.11. Spatial and Temporal Summation. In spatial summation, simultaneous inputs from more than one axon terminal produce a larger response in the postsynaptic cell. In temporal summation, a rapid sequence of action potentials in a single axon terminal produces an enhanced response in the postsynaptic cell.

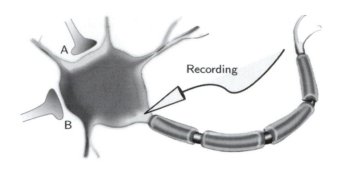

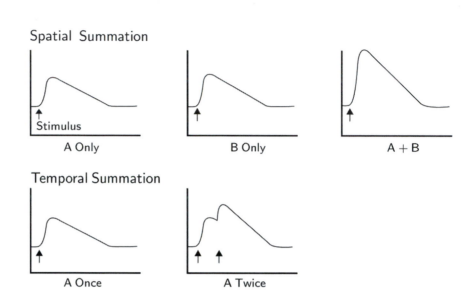

within the human brain may be covered by many tens of thousands of synapses. Spatial summation must be the rule in such cells.

Temporal summation is an important mechanism by which the rate of firing in one cell affects the size of the postsynaptic response of another.

If one nerve impulse arrives at a synapse before the effects of a previous postsynaptic potential have disappeared, the two postsynaptic potentials summate in time, producing a larger change in the membrane potential of the receiving cell. In this way, the synapse converts information coded at the axon by the rate of firing into information coded at the postsynaptic membrane by the size of the summated postsynaptic potential.

Spatial summation and temporal summation provide a means of integrating information within the postsynaptic neuron. Many influences may be felt, but the neuron must act with one voice; it has but a single axon with which to communicate its decisions.

In this way, the effects of the stream of neurochemicals released at the many synapses of a cell are integrated.

BIOCHEMISTRY OF NEUROTRANSMISSION

The biochemical processes involved in neurotransmission share several general features, even though the neurons and the effects of synaptic activity may differ markedly in different regions of the nervous system (Cooper, Bloom, & Roth, 1996). For every chemical synapse, neurotransmitter substance must be synthesized and stored for future use. The neurotransmitter must be released into the synaptic cleft in response to the arrival of an action potential at the presynaptic element, or axon terminal. The neurotransmitter then must bind with a receptor molecule on the outer surface of the postsynaptic membrane to produce its characteristic effect within the receiving neuron. Finally, the neurotransmitter substance must be removed from the synapse, either by returning the molecule to the presynaptic element or by inactivating the molecule through a biochemical transformation. All chemical synapses share these essential features, but the specific mechanisms and molecules vary from synapse to synapse. It is this variation that permits different types of synapses to exert different physiological effects.

Enzymes and Substrates   All neurotransmitter function depends on a precise sequence of molecular transformations. First, the substance is synthesized within the presynaptic neuron. On release, a subset of these molecules successfully crosses the synaptic cleft and binds with a receptor molecule on the postsynaptic membrane, resulting in a second molecular transformation. A third transformation occurs when the neurotransmitter molecule is inactivated. Finally, inactivated molecules are reprocessed and recycled to enter again into the molecular metabolism of the neuron. Each of these steps involves a biochemical transformation that is guided and controlled by special molecules called enzymes. For each neurotransmitter, the details of these transformations differ, but the same general principles apply.

An **enzyme** is a specialized molecule that speeds and facilitates biochemical reactions without entering into that reaction. Enzymes function as biochemical catalysts that act on a very limited set of very specific molecules. The molecules on which they act are the **substrates** of the enzyme and are the **precursors** that the enzyme chemically transforms. (It is easy to recognize an enzyme when reading about it; the names of most enzymes end in –ase).

Enzymes are large protein molecules that are folded into complicated, irregular shapes with grooves, or pockets, into which molecules of the substrate may fit. These pockets form the active sites of the enzyme. They are matched to the conformation of the molecules of the substrate: Where the substrate has a hill, there is a valley in the active site; where the substrate carries a positive charge, there is a negative charge at the active site; and where the substrate is hydrophilic or hydrophobic, the active site is also. The enzyme, by precisely positioning the substrate molecules entering into a reaction, can facilitate the reaction enormously. The active site functions as a complicated molecular lock, with the substrate providing the key. This is the reason that enzymes perform in a highly specific manner.

Identifying Specific Neurotransmitters

One of the most fundamental problems in synaptic neurochemistry is to identify the neurotransmitters used in different regions of the brain. Most would agree that any neurotransmitter should pass the following tests (Cooper, Bloom, & Roth, 1996):

1. The substance should be present within the nervous system in quantities typical of transmitter agents. Thus, esoteric chemicals that may be produced in the laboratory or extracted from other species may have powerful synaptic effects, but if they are not detectable in the nervous system, they are not likely to be neurotransmitters.

2. The substance must be present in the axon terminals of neurons. Neurotransmitters are stored in vesicles within the terminal boutons; therefore, it is in these terminals that the substance should be concentrated.

3. The substance must be synthesized within the neuron. Thus, the specific enzymes responsible for synthesizing the substance from its precursors must be present.

4. There must be evidence of enzymes that inactivate or destroy the substance in the vicinity of the synapse.

5. The substance must act on receptor sites. When applied to the postsynaptic surface as a drug, it should have exactly the same effect as the natural activation of the synapse.

In practice, no compound has completely fulfilled all of these criteria for a neurotransmitter within the human brain. Instead, neuroscientists have adopted an attitude of justifiable caution toward this subject. If a reasonable number of these criteria are met, the compound is regarded as a neurotransmitter.

Many compounds are generally agreed to serve as neurotransmitters in the human brain, including the amino acids (gamma-aminobutyric acid [GABA], glutamate, and glycine), biological amines (acetylcholine, dopamine, epinephrine, norepinephrine, serotonin, and histamine), and various neuropeptides.

It was once believed that each and every neuron may be characterized by the one specific neurotransmitter that it uses at its synapses, an idea enshrined as **Dale's law**, after Sir Henry Dale, who shared the 1936 Nobel Prize with Otto Loewi. The idea that each neuron has its own specific neurotransmitter formed the basis of much of Dale's work. (Of course, neurons may receive information from other neurons that use a variety of neurotransmitters; otherwise, it would not be possible to record EPSPs and IPSPs from a single cell.)

However, many exceptions to the "one-neuron, one-transmitter" rule have proliferated in recent years (Cooper, Bloom, & Roth, 1996). Many developing neurons are now known to synthesize and release more than one transmitter substance. Furthermore, it is clear that some neurons— including neurons in the human brain—may contain as many as half a dozen different chemical agents, which they release into the synaptic cleft.

It is not known whether all axon terminals of these multitransmitter neurons use the same set or subsets of transmitter agents. Thus, it seems a good bet that Dale's law certainly does not hold for all neurons. Nonetheless, it is still important to know which neurotransmitters are used in a given set of neural connections.

Families of Receptor Molecules

The various postsynaptic receptor molecules of the human nervous system are molecularly related to each other, forming molecular families that share many similarities. Furthermore, many transmitters are not associated with a single postsynaptic receptor molecule but rather with a family of different but related receptors, which operate both in different portions of the nervous system and in different species of organisms (Watson & Girdlestone, 1995).

Thus, each neurotransmitter substance is a key to a family of related locks, or postsynaptic membrane receptor molecules. The members of these receptor families differ from their siblings in a number of ways, including having different channel speeds and ionic preferences and having different receptor binding affinities for other drugs and neurotoxins. This diversity of binding and functional properties within a family of receptor molecules presents a marvelous opportunity for designing extremely specific neuroactive drugs to precisely control specific neurological dysfunctions.

The systematic differences among related receptor molecules also provide evidence of their evolutionary history. By comparing the protein amino acid sequences of known receptor molecules and assuming a constancy in the rate of amino acid substitutions over evolutionary time (the so-called molecular clock) (for an introduction, see Li & Graur, 1991), it is possible to describe both the relationships among members of a single receptor family and the evolution of superfamilies of mammalian neuronal receptors.

Several familial traits of the transmitter-gated ion channel molecules are apparent in such analyses (Ortells & Lunt, 1995). The first and most ancient division in the family was the divergence of the inhibitory anion channels from the excitatory cation channels. The next split was among the receptors having cation channels, which split into serotonin- and acetylcholine-binding molecules. Similar divisions may be seen on the anion side of the superfamily, in which glycine receptors broke away from the GABA family receptors at a comparatively more recent date. It is important to recognize that among today's diverse crop of receptor molecules, there is an orderly pattern of precise molecular structure.

Although the variety of individual neurotransmitter receptor molecules is large, the number of substances known to serve as neurotransmitters is much more limited. These compounds range in size from small molecules to amino acids to molecules as large as neuropeptides. These molecules are listed in Figure 4.12 on the following page and are described briefly below.

Figure 4.12. Substances Functioning as Neurotransmitters Within the Human Brain.

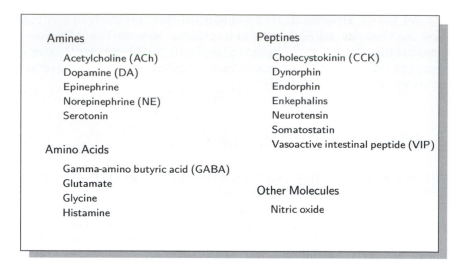

Amines

    Acetylcholine (ACh)
    Dopamine (DA)
    Epinephrine
    Norepinephrine (NE)
    Serotonin

Amino Acids

    Gamma-amino butyric acid (GABA)
    Glutamate
    Glycine
    Histamine

Peptines

    Cholecystokinin (CCK)
    Dynorphin
    Endorphin
    Enkephalins
    Neurotensin
    Somatostatin
    Vasoactive intestinal peptide (VIP)

Other Molecules

    Nitric oxide

ACETYLCHOLINE

The neurotransmitter **acetylcholine (ACh)** was first identified by Sir Henry Dale nearly 80 years ago, who coined the term **cholinergic** to refer to any neuron that releases acetylcholine at its axon terminals (Dale, 1953). Acetylcholine will be discussed at some length, not only because it is well understood but because it illustrated many important properties of other neurotransmitters as well.

Acetylcholine is widely used as a neurotransmitter within the peripheral nervous system. For example, ACh is the transmitter released by the vagus nerve to the heart as well as the transmitter used to control all of the voluntary skeletal muscles of the body. As such, the cholinergic system provides the most direct linkage between nervous system activity and behavior.

Some diseases result from dysfunction of the peripheral acetylcholinergic system. Myasthenia gravis is a disorder of the neuromuscular junction, a synapselike arrangement between the motor nerves and the muscles themselves (Penn & Rowland, 1984). The disease results in a progressive weakness that may terminate in death. Electrophysiological studies show that the effect of the release of ACh onto the muscle becomes increasingly diminished as the disease progresses. Either less ACh is released or there are fewer ACh receptors on the muscle fibers. The latter is in fact the case: Myasthenia gravis is an autoimmune disease in which the immune system forms antibodies that attack the ACh receptors on the muscles. As time goes on, the skeletal muscles become increasingly denervated.

Furthermore, certain species exploit the chemical vulnerability of the cholinergic neuromuscular junction for their own competitive advantage. Both the cobra and the krait (*genus Bungarus*) are two poisonous hooded snakes that kill their victims by paralysis. The venom of these snakes contains a neurotoxin that blocks the neuromuscular junction, so that the release of ACh by a motor neuron will not result in muscular contraction. The snake's victim suffocates as all breathing stops.

The neurotoxins produced by cobras and kraits differ in their exact amino acid sequences. Both the neurotoxin of the cobra (*cobra α-neurotoxin*) and the krait (*α-bungarotoxin*) have been used successfully by neurochemists to characterize the molecular structure of the acetycholine receptor at the neuromuscular junction.

Incidentally, the effects of natural selection on the evolution of species, even at the molecular level, are often marvelously subtle. Both the krait and the cobra have had to evolve variations in the acetylcholine receptors of their own neuromuscular junctions so that they would not fall prey to their own lethal neurotoxins. This can be accomplished because binding properties of the neurotoxins are similar to, but not identical with, the binding properties of acetylcholine. Thus, all of the snakes' ACh receptors will bind with acetylcholine but not venom molecules.

Cobras and kraits would have no natural enemies, because they can kill any potential predator, were it not for the mongoose. The Indian gray mongoose is a fierce hunter that is known for its ability as a cobra killer. It has earned its ecological niche by evolving a variant ACh receptor at its own neuromuscular junctions, just as the cobras and kraits had done. For the mongoose, neither cobra α-neurotoxin nor α-bungarotoxin pose the slightest of threats (Kachalsky, Jensen, Barchan, & Fuchs, 1995). In addition to its peripheral uses, acetylcholine also serves as an important neurotransmitter within the central nervous system (Taylor & Brown, 1994).

ACh Synthesis   The synthesis of ACh is a straightforward chemical reaction involving a single step. Acetyl-coenzyme A and choline are the substrates; choline acetyltransferase (CAT) is the enzyme mediating the reaction:

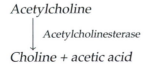

$$\textit{Choline + acetyl-coenzyme A}$$

Choline acetyltransferase

$$\textit{Acetylcholine + acetyl-coenzyme A}$$

In the synthesis of ACh, the coenzyme is used to bring an acetyl group into the reaction. CAT acts to transfer the acetyl group to the choline molecule, hence the enzyme's name. Neither the enzyme nor the coenzyme is altered in the reaction.

Similarly, an ACh molecule is inactivated in a single step by the enzyme **acetylcholinesterase (AChE)**, a reaction that yields choline and acetate:

$$\textit{Acetylcholine}$$

Acetylcholinesterase

$$\textit{Choline + acetic acid}$$

Incidentally, acetylcholinesterase is an exceptionally active and powerful enzyme; 1 mg of purified AChE is capable of inactivating up to 150 g of ACh per hour, or 150,000 times its own weight in ACh.

The distribution of ACh and its related enzymes within the cholinergic neuron and synapse conforms to the pattern required of a neurotransmitter. ACh is found within the axon terminals of cholinergic cells, where it is present in a form indicative of vesicular storage. CAT is also found within the synaptosome. In contrast, AChE—the inactivating enzyme—is more widely distributed and tends to be associated with fragments of cell membrane. That, of course, is the site at which AChE acts.

Acetyl-coenzyme A is produced in the mitochondria and made available for the synthesis of ACh. Apparently, the availability of choline determines the rate of ACh production in the cholinergic neuron; the enzyme CAT is able to rapidly convert any substrate molecules present into free ACh. Once synthesized, ACh is bound into synaptic vesicles and thereby protected from inactivation by AChE. The release of packets of ACh into the synapse is triggered by the arrival of the nerve impulse and accomplished by exocytosis. ACh released into the synaptic cleft may then find its way to a receptor on the postsynaptic membrane, with which it binds.

Two broad categories of cholinergic receptors differ in their primary agonists (Cooper, Bloom, & Roth, 1996). For one type of cholinergic receptor, nicotine mimics the action of ACh; for the other, the agonist is muscarine, a compound that is derived from the fungus *Amanita muscaria*. Nicotinic and muscarinic cholinergic receptors have very different properties and mechanisms of action. The nicotinic receptor for acetylcholine is a classical neurotransmitter-gated ion channel. In contrast, the muscarinic receptor is a G-protein-mediated second-messenger system.

The Nicotinic Receptor

The **nicotinic receptor** is a fast-responding, transmitter-gated ion channel, producing its effect within milliseconds following binding. A number of different subtypes of nicotinic receptors have been identified, with different subtypes appearing in different parts of the nervous system and in different species. Figure 4.6 on page 110 illustrates one model of a typical nicotinic receptor.

The action of ACh at the nicotinic receptor site may be described statistically. Approximately 10,000 molecules of ACh are released from a single vesicle into the synapse. Within about 1/10 msec, these molecules cross the synaptic cleft and reach a receptor site at the postsynaptic membrane. Because both of the active sites on the receptor molecule must be occupied by neurotransmitter molecules to open the channel, and reuptake removes many ACh molecules from the cleft, only about 2,000 receptors are opened by the ACh contained within a single synaptic vesicle. These channels remain open only briefly; ACh molecules are quickly dissociated from the receptor's binding sites and inactivated by the enzyme AChE. But during the time that the channels are opened, something on the order of 20,000 sodium ions enter the postsynaptic neuron. When more than one vesicle of neurotransmitter is released, more receptor channels are opened, and the magnitude of the resulting excitatory depolarization is increased. The nicotinic receptor is a classic transmitter-gated ion channel (Cooper, Bloom, & Roth, 1996).

The Muscarinic Receptor

The **muscarinic receptor** is more complex than the nicotinic receptor, and its physiological effects are more varied. At least five different types have been identified at present. The postsynaptic responses to activation of a muscarinic receptor by ACh develop more slowly and are longer lasting than those of the nicotinic receptor, as is typical of the neuromodulating functions of metatrobic synapses.

Although some muscarinic receptors are present in the periphery, in the central nervous system, they are truly the dominant cholinergic receptor; more than 99% of all cholinergic synapses within the brain are muscarinic.

Activation of a muscarinic receptor is accomplished in the following manner (Cooper, Bloom, & Roth, 1996). As shown in Figure 4.7 on page 111, the muscarinic transmembrane receptor protein first binds with acetylcholine in the extracellular fluid of the synapse. This activates a coupled G-protein located on the interior surface of the cell membrane. When ACh binds with the receptor, the α-subunit binds with cytoplasmic cyclic guanosine triphosphate. In so doing, the GTP-alpha complex is released into the intercellular fluid, where it can interact with effector proteins. The effector proteins available in a particular cell will then produce their own characteristic responses. The muscarinic receptor provides a clear example of a G-protein-coupled receptor chained to a second-messenger system.

THE CATECHOLAMINES

The **catecholamines—dopamine**, **norepinephrine**, and **epinephrine**—are a set of biochemically related, biologically active compounds that play a variety of roles within the nervous system (Cooper, Bloom, & Roth, 1996; Weiner & Molinoff, 1994). They derive their family name from their chemical structures; all are formed by a catechol ring with a tail of amines.

Both dopamine and norepinephrine are known to act as neurotransmitters within the central nervous system. The case for epinephrine as a central neurotransmitter is much weaker.

But outside the brain and spinal cord, epinephrine is the sympathetic transmitter substance. Neurons releasing epinephrine are said to be **adrenergic** because the older name for epinephrine was adrenalin.

Although the proportion of catecholaminergic neurons within the human brain is very small, the influence of these cells on brain function may be disproportionately large because many of these cells have large, widely synapsing axons. For example, one dopaminergic neuron in a small area of the rat's brain (the substantia nigra) sends as many as 500,000 synaptic terminals into its forebrain. In humans, with our large forebrains, the number may be more like 5 million.

Catecholaminergic neurons play an important modulating role in human brain function. Their widespread divergence permits them to regulate activity in large regions of the brain. Furthermore, the postsynaptic response to catecholaminergic transmitters is very slow, suggesting the involvement of a second-messenger system.

All the catecholamines are synthesized from tyrosine, a common dietary amino acid, in the following sequence:

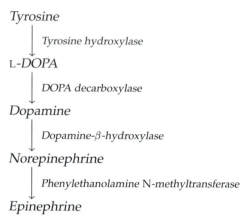

The steps involved are the following:

1. The first step is the formation of a precursor for all catecholamine neurotransmitters, L-dihydroxyphenylalanine (L-DOPA), by the enzyme tyrosine hydroxylase.

2. Next, L-DOPAis converted to dopamine (DA) by the enzyme DOPA decarboxylase.

3. Then, norepinephrine (NE) is synthesized from dopamine by the enzyme dopamine-β-hydroxylase.

4. Finally, epinephrine is synthesized from norepinephrine by the enzyme phynlethanolamine N-methyltransferase.

This common pathway is used by the different catecholamine neurotransmitters to the extent necessary for each given transmitter substance.

In the dopaminergic neuron, tyrosine is first transformed to L-DOPAand then to free dopamine. Free dopamine is then bound into vesicles, where it is stored for synaptic release, or it is destroyed by the intracellular inactivating agent **monoamine oxidase (MAO)**. The arrival of a nerve impulse produces the release of bound dopamine by exocytosis into the synaptic cleft. There, it either binds with a dopaminergic receptor or is inactivated by the synaptic enzyme catechol-O-methyl transferase (COMT).

The biochemical steps involved at the noradrenergic synapse are exactly those present at the dopaminergic synapse, with the addition of the extra step involved in the synthesis of norepinephrine from dopamine.

Both dopamine and norepinephrine induce the G-protein system to release second messengers within the postsynaptic neuron.

SEROTONIN

The neurotransmitter **serotonin** is another central nervous system neurotransmitter of major importance; it is synthesized and inactivated within the brain, it is present at the axon terminals of serotonergic neurons, and it meets other tests required of brain neurotransmitters as well (Frazer & Hensler, 1994). It has been suggested that a disorder of brain serotonin systems is responsible for a number of mental disorders.

Serotonin is synthesized from the dietary amino acid tryptophan. The enzyme tryptophan hydroxylase converts tryptophan to the 5-hydroxytryptophan (5-HTP), the immediate precursor of serotonin:

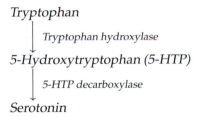

Tryptophan

| *Tryptophan hydroxylase*

5-Hydroxytryptophan (5-HTP)

| *5-HTP decarboxylase*

Serotonin

5-HTP is then converted to serotonin by the enzyme 5-HTP decarboxylase: Notice that the synthesis of serotonin very closely parallels the biochemical pathway involved in manufacturing dopamine.

Chemically, serotonin is an **indoleamine**, meaning that it is composed of an indole ring with an amine tail. This structure is like that of the catecholamines; thus, the indoleamines and catecholamines together are termed **monoamines**. It is not surprising, therefore, that the similarities between serotonin and catecholamine metabolism also extend to their inactivating enzyme; like dopamine and noradrenalin, serotonin is inactivated by MAO. MAO is used to inactivate serotonin within both the presynaptic and postsynaptic elements.

AMINO ACIDS AND NEUROPEPTIDES

The **amino acids** are small molecules, each containing an amino group (NH_2) and a carboxyl group (COOH). There are 20 amino acids that form building blocks from which proteins are constructed. The idea that amino acids may also serve as neurotransmitters is not particularly new, but for many years it was difficult to gather strong evidence on this point. The problem is to distinguish between amino acids functioning as neurotransmitters and those same acids playing other roles in the metabolism of the cell. In contrast, the fact that acetylcholine and the monoamines function only as transmitter substances has made the investigation of these transmitter systems much easier.

It is now clear that amino acids are used as transmitters at chemical synapses; in fact, they appear to be the most common neurotransmitters by far within the mammalian brain (DeLorey & Olsen, 1994; Dingledine & McBain, 1994).

Glutamate The amino acid **glutamate** and the closely related amino **aspartate** are used at most excitatory synapses in the human nervous system (Dingledine & McBain, 1994). Many glutamate receptors are transmitter-gated ion channels and so directly affect the flow of cations into the postsynaptic cell. Three different subtypes of glutamate receptors have been identified, based on the particular agonists that bond to these postsynaptic receptors. These are the molecules **NMDA (N-methyl-D-aspartate)**, AMPA (α-amino-3-hydroxy-5-methyl-4-isoxazxolepropionic acid), and KA (kainate).

Of the glutamate receptor subtypes, the NMDA receptor has received the most intense study. There are at least five separate molecular binding sites on the outer surface of the NMDA receptor molecule. Binding at these sites selectively affects the state of its ion channel. Some sites act to open the channel, whereas others act to close it. NMDA receptors have been implicated in long-term potentiation, a plastic modification of synaptic activity that may form the basis of some types of learning.

GABA and Glycine Two amino acids that function as major inhibitory neurotransmitters within the human nervous system are **GABA (gamma-aminobutyric acid)** and **glycine**. There are two subtypes of GABA receptors, termed $GABA_A$ and $GABA_B$ receptors. A great deal is known about the $GABA_A$ subtype of receptors. This is a GABA-controlled Cl^- anion channel that, when open, acts to keep the membrane from reaching its threshold firing level. Much less is known about the $GABA_B$ receptors, which produce inhibition using a G-protein system. Like $GABA_A$ receptors, glycine receptors inhibit by opening chloride anion channels.

Neuropeptides Peptides are molecules formed by short chains of amino acids; **neuropeptides** are peptides that are found in brain tissue. These substances are found at synaptic terminals, indicating that they may serve as neurotransmitters. Others are known to act as neurohormones, biologically active compounds that may be released into the circulation, for example, to affect the functioning of other cells located at some distance.

A large number of peptides may be involved in neuronal transmission and regulation (Brownstein, 1994). Most coexist with other neurotransmitters in the axon terminal of the cell. Perhaps most attention has been paid to the subclass called the **opioid peptides**, a term that refers to substances that are produced by neurons that mimic the effects of the opiate morphine. There are somewhat more than a handful of substances that meet this criterion. These include β-endorphin, dymorphin, met-enkephalin, and leu-enkephalin. All of these opioid peptides produce strong analgesic, or painkilling, effects and may hold an important key to the understanding of pain.

The study of neuropeptides is one of the most exciting and active research areas in contemporary neuroscience. These comparatively small molecules seem to play important roles in the control of complex central nervous system processes, roles that are now only beginning to be appreciated.

NITRIC OXIDE

The gas nitric oxide has come to the attention of neuroscientists as an example of an important but very unconventional neuronal signaling molecule. Like conventional neurotransmitters, nitric oxide appears to be a chemical signal that is released by one neuron to affect the activity of other neurons in the immediate vicinity. Classical neurotransmitter substances are hydrophillic molecules that bind to extracellular receptor proteins on the postsynaptic cell. In contrast, nitric oxide (NO) is a small, hydrophobic gaseous molecule that can pass directly through the plasma membrane of both the sending and receiving neurons to bind with specific intracellular proteins. Its signaling roles are varied within the nervous system. Penile erection, for example, is directly produced by NO that is released by autonomic nerves in the penis, causing the dilation of nearby blood vessels. The effects of NO release are rapid, local, and short-lived, in large part because NO is rapidly degraded in the extracellular space (Snyder & Dawson, 1995). Nitric oxide gas represents a novel mechanism by which neurons can exert control of other cells.

DRUGS AND SYNAPSES

Chemical synapses represent the major point of chemical vulnerability. Most drugs that are therapeutically useful or commonly abused act on chemical synapses. Both substances of abuse (e.g., opiates, amphetamines, and LSD) and therapeutic drugs, such as tranquilizers and antipsychotic agents, exert their effects at chemical synapses. Thus, much of modern psychopharmacology is in fact the investigation of the synaptic effects of psychoactive agents.

Addictive Drugs Activate the Dopamine System   Addiction and drug abuse are increasingly common problems in contemporary society. But the roots of addiction are not in human society, as one might think, but instead are contained within the mammalian brain. Although societal conventions might further or retard the spread of addictive drug use, the principal reason that drugs are abused is that they exert powerful effects on the dopaminergic pathways common to all mammalian brains. It is in this sense that drug addiction is a problem of neurobiology, not human culture.

All drugs of addiction for humans also affect brain stem dopaminergic neurons. These include opiates, cocaine, amphetamine, PCP, marijuana, nicotine, and alcohol. All of these drugs with one exception—alcohol— exert their effect by binding with a specific neuronal receptor type.

The compounds that we abuse are chemically and physiologically diverse, belonging to very different chemical families and binding to physiologically distinct neuronal receptor proteins. Perhaps even more striking is the fact that this list corresponds exactly to the list of substances for which laboratory animals will perform self-stimulation tasks, that is, tasks in which they do work to receive small amounts of a substance. The physiological action that all these compounds share is that they effectively stimulate a widespread set of dopaminergic pathways within the brain (London, Grant, Morgan, & Zukin, 1996).

It was half a century ago that James Olds and Peter Milner discovered that animals would work very hard to receive electrical stimulation in the septum and other brain regions (Olds & Milner, 1954). The finding that only a certain small number of sites produced this behavior suggested that

Figure 4.13. The Dopamine System of the Human Brain. Dopamine neurons in the substantia nigra and related brain stem regions project to widespread regions of the human brain.

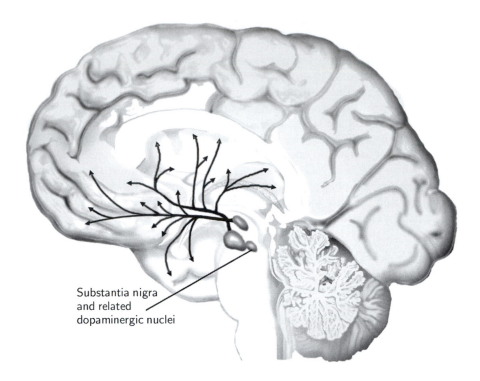

Substantia nigra and related dopaminergic nuclei

the brain's reward system was anatomically discrete. Furthermore, these same regions were involved in naturally occurring rewarding behaviors. Finally, all substances of human addictive abuse alter activity within this same system of neurons. It is for these reasons that brain reward systems are central to human drug addiction (London, Grant, Morgan, & Zukin, 1996).

The core of the reward system is the dopamine system of the midbrain and limbic regions, shown in Figure 4.13. The system originates in the ventral tegmental area and projects rostrally to the nucleus accumbens, the amygdala, and the prefrontal cortex. It is this system that supports lever pressing in laboratory animals to receive addicting substances, such as opiates and cocaine.

Opiates   Opiates, a class of chemical substances originally derived from the juicy resin of the opium poppy, were known to the ancient Greeks and Sumerians. (The word *opium* derives from the Greek word meaning "juice.") The term *opioid* is now used to refer to opiatelike substances, whether derived from the opium poppy, naturally produced by the nervous system, or chemically manufactured.

Arab traders and their physicians were familiar with opium and introduced the substance to the Orient, where it was used as a treatment for dysentery. Opium was reintroduced into Europe in the 16th century by the Swiss alchemist and physician Paracelsus (Philippus Aureolus, 1493–1541). Opium use had declined markedly in Europe because of problems with toxicity. Within two centuries, opium smoking for pleasure had become popular in the Orient, and opium eating for the same reason was relatively widespread in Europe (Hardman & Limbird, 1996).

Opium is extracted from the milky juice of the seed capsules of the opium poppy, which is dried to form a brown gum. This is further dried and powdered. Originally grown only in the Middle East, opium is now produced, legally or illegally, in many regions of the world.

The dried opium powder contains some two dozen alkaloids of varying psychopharmacological potency. In 1806, Frederich Sertrner extracted the principal active component of powdered opium, which he named morphine after Morpheus, the Greek god of dreaming. Codeine is a second opiate contained in the opium poppy but at only about one twentieth the concentration of morphine. Pharmacologically, codeine is much weaker in its central nervous system effects.

Historically, the opiates have played a major medical role in the relief of severe pain. Morphine indeed served as a "miracle drug" in the earliest days of medicine, when the ability to block pain—especially in the absence of the ability to effect a cure—was a blessed relief for both patient and physician. Interestingly, opiates given for the relief of intense pain are not addictive.

Heroin is an opiate alkaloid derived from morphine. It is the strongest of the all substances produced from poppy resin. Heroin was first created by a German chemist named Dreser, who was employed by the Bayer Drug Company. Dreser added two acetyl groups to morphine, which allowed the compound to cross the blood-brain barrier much more easily. This accounts for the rapid effects of heroin and its enhanced potency (Snyder, 1980).

Although opium poppy opioids are mildly addictive in the form of morphine when ingested, heroin taken intravenously is extremely addictive. The injection of an opiate, such as heroin, results in an intense physiological and psychological reaction, often termed a *rush* or *kick*. There is a warm flushing of the skin and abdominal sensations lasting less than a minute that opiate addicts describe as being similar to sexual orgasm. A prolonged state of dreamy indifference that follows is referred to as the opium "high."

In addition to these emotionally laden changes of mood, opiates exert wide-ranging effects on the functions of the central nervous system and the bowel. These include analgesia, drowsiness, mood changes, mental clouding, reduced movement and secretion in the gastrointestinal system (often with nausea and vomiting), and other alterations of autonomic function. From a medical perspective, the most important use of the opiates is that of producing analgesia, the relief from pain.

Ingested or injected opiates appear to exert powerful effects within the brain on the dopaminergic neurons of the CNS reward system, effects that go a long way in explaining the addictive properties of these drugs. Animals will press a lever—self-stimulate—to receive injections of opiates directly into either the ventral tegmental area or the nucleus accumbens, to which the tegmental neurons project (Wise & Bozarth, 1987). Furthermore, prior injection of an opiate receptor-blocking agent into either of these areas greatly reduces opiate-motivated self-stimulation. Animals will not work to receive opiates if the dopaminergic neurons of the reward system are inactivated.

Additional evidence supports the idea that opiate addiction depends on the effects of the drug on the reward system. Chemical lesions of those dopaminergic neurons, for example, reduce intravenous self-administration of heroin in laboratory animals (Bozarth & Wise, 1986), as do lesions of the nucleus accumbens (Zito, Vickers, & Roberts, 1985). Moreover, intravenous administration of opiates is known to trigger the release of dopamine in the nucleus accumbens and related brain regions (DiChiara & Imperato, 1987). Such findings point compellingly to the conclusion that opiates are addictive precisely because they selectively activate the powerful reward and reinforcement systems of the brain stem.

Cocaine and Amphetamine   Cocaine and amphetamine are central nervous system stimulants that, although chemically different, have very similar psychopharmacological properties. Cocaine first became known to the European world following the Spanish conquest of the Inca Empire. The Spanish explorers discovered that the Indians of South America chewed the leaves of the coca plant. Taken in this form, coca leaves produce a mild elevation of mood, increased energy, heightened alertness, and a suppression of appetite. Coca extracts having similar effects were used in a number of tonics and commercial remedies—including the drink Coca-Cola— in the 1800s. By the beginning of the 20th century, the soft drink was made with decocainized coca leaves.

Amphetamine, in contrast, was first synthesized in the 1920s by Gordon Alles and Chauncey Leake at the University of California San Francisco Medical Center, who were studying the pharmacology of a Chinese desert plant, mahuang or *Ephedra vulgaris*, which was used as a treatment for asthma in Chinese folk medicine. Of the various related phenylalkylamines, dextroamphetamine (dexedrine) appeared to be the most effective and least toxic. In clinical trials, dexedrine was shown to increase alertness, combat fatigue and boredom, and suppress appetite.

Amphetamines were widely used by all sides in World War II to maintain alertness. Following the war, large supplies of the drug were placed on the open market in Japan, resulting in many cases of amphetamine abuse and amphetamine psychosis. In the decades that followed, amphetamine abuse became prevalent in both Europe and the United States, where it remains a serious social problem today.

The relatively mild physiological and psychological consequences of ingesting coca leaves contrast sharply with the effects obtained by the injection or intranasal administration of purified cocaine. (When purified cocaine is inhaled, it rapidly passes through the nasal mucosa and enters the bloodstream.) At low oral doses, the effect of either stimulant depends largely on the environment and the psychological makeup of the user. At higher, rapidly administered dosages, the effects of both the environment and the individual experiences become less important; a characteristic stimulant syndrome begins to unfold. It matters little which drug is administered. Experienced cocaine users, for example, cannot distinguish between the subjective effects of pharmacologically equivalent doses of cocaine and dexedrine administered intravenously (Fischman, 1984).

In the early stages of intravenous stimulant addiction, an injection results in euphoria, a sensation of enhanced physical and mental capacity, and the loss of the subjective need for either sleep or food. Both men and women report that orgasm is both delayed and intensified during stimulant intoxication. Moreover, there is a "rush" following amphetamine or cocaine injections (but not oral or nasal cocaine use) that is extremely pleasurable and of a sexual nature, although quite distinct from the "rush" following opiate injection.

With continued use, larger and larger dosages are required to achieve the same level of euphoria. Toxic symptoms begin to appear. Paranoia becomes increasingly common and extreme. Perceptual abnormalities develop, including the sensation that the skin is covered with tiny bugs as well as visual hallucinations. The user may become occupied with his or her own thinking processes and the "nature of meaning" or become inclined to disassemble mechanical objects and, although equally inclined to reassemble the object, usually be incapable of doing so. Users become hyperactive and may respond to their own paranoid delusions. They may also begin to mix concoctions containing multiple drugs, such as opiates, to counteract some of the toxic side effects of the stimulants.

As with the opiates, cocaine and amphetamines exert their addicting effects by altering the activity of the dopaminergic brain reward systems. Specifically, cocaine increases the effectiveness of dopaminergic synapses by blocking the reuptake of the neurotransmitter. Amphetamine both blocks dopamine reuptake and increases dopamine release. Although similar effects occur at noradrenergic synapses, it appears that the dopaminergic synapses are actually responsible for both the euphoric and addictive properties of these stimulants (Wise & Bozarth, 1987). For example, dopamine—but not norepinephrine—blocking agents eliminate the rewarding effects of intravenously injected stimulants (Risner & Jones, 1980). Further evidence of the dependence of stimulant addiction on the dopaminergic reward systems is the finding that a single dosage of amphetamine in "addicted" rats selectively increases the release of dopamine in the nucleus accumbens, as well as eliciting behavioral evidence of increased toxic side effects (Sato, 1986). These and similar findings provide strong support for the belief that opiates, cocaine, and amphetamines, which are addictive precisely because they produce such profound, emotionally compelling sensations, act principally by modifying the activity of the dopaminergic brain reward systems.

SUMMARY

Chemical synapses—the functional connections between most neurons—are composed of a presynaptic element (usually an axon terminal), the synaptic cleft, and a postsynaptic element (a dendrite, a cell body, or another axon terminal). Neurotransmitter substance is released by the arrival of a nerve impulse, producing membrane depolarization that opens calcium channels in the membrane. This allows the entry of calcium, which mediates the release of transmitter substance by exocytosis.

The neurotransmitter substance affects the postsynaptic neuron when it binds to special membrane proteins called receptors. Receptors can either activate an ion channel located within the same protein molecule or activate a G-protein system, which will open ion pores elsewhere on the membrane or produce other cellular effects.

A number of molecules serve as neurotransmitters within the human nervous system, all of which activate specific members of the family of postsynaptic receptor proteins. Acetylcholine was one of the first neurotransmitters to be isolated. Other neurotransmitters include the catecholamines, serotonin, and certain amino acids and neuropeptides. Recent studies also have shown that small molecules such as nitric oxide are important local signaling substances in some neuronal systems. The biochemical diversity of chemical communication between the neurons of the nervous system is only now beginning to be fully appreciated.

SELECTED READING

- Cooper, J. R., Bloom, F. E., & Roth, R. H. (1996). *The biochemical basis of neuropharmacology* (7th ed.). New York: Oxford University Press. The seventh edition of this classical and approachable book is a must-read for anyone interested in the pharmacology of synapses.

- Bloom, F. E., & Kuffer, D. J. (Eds.). (1995). *Pharmacology: The fourth generation of progress.* New York: Raven. This is a monster of a volume (nearly 2,000 pages) that represents the latest findings concerning neurochemistry, drugs, and behavior. Many chapters are directly concerned with clinical problems, such as psychiatric and neurological disorders. An official publication of the American College of Neuropharmacology, this volume is both definitive and current.

KEY TERMS

acetylcholine (ACh) A neurotransmitter synthesized from choline and acetyl-coenzyme A by the enzyme choline acetyltransferase within the cell body of the neuron.

acetylcholinesterase (AChE) An enzyme that hydrolyzes acetylcholine.

adrenergic Any neuron that releases either epinephrine or norepinephrine at its synapses.

agonist A compound that mimics the action of a neurotransmitter at a synaptic receptor site.

amino acid One of about 20 small molecules, each containing an amino and a carboxyl group, that are chained together to form peptides and protein molecules.

antagonist With respect to synapses, a compound that blocks the action of a neurotransmitter or its agonist.

aspartate An amino acid that functions as a neurotransmitter at many excitatory synapses in mammalian nervous systems.

asymmetrical synapse A synapse with dense material substantially more prominent on the postsynaptic membrane; believed to be an excitatory synapse.

autoreceptor A receptor molecule located in the membrane of the presynaptic neuron that binds with the neurotransmitter that the presynaptic cell itself releases.

axoaxonic synapse A synapse in which the postsynaptic element is an axon or an axon terminal.

axodendritic synapse A synapse in which the postsynaptic element is a dendrite.

axoplasmic transport A system for moving material, such as synaptic vesicles, from the cell body through the axoplasm of the axon to an axon terminal.

axosomatic synapse A synapse in which the postsynaptic element is a cell body (soma).

catecholamines A group of chemicals made from the amino acid tyrosine, distinguished by a catechol ring and an amine tail (e.g., dopamine, norepinephrine, and epinephrine).

cholinergic Any neuron that releases acetylcholine at its synapses.

convergence In a neuronal system, the channeling of information from several sources or neurons to one location or neuron.

Dale's law The proposition that any single neuron makes use of the same neurotransmitter substance at all of its synapses.

depolarization A change in membrane potential that reduces the voltage difference across the membrane; in neurons, this usually refers to a reduction of the negative resting potential, which tends to elicit an action potential.

dopamine A catecholaminergic neurotransmitter produced from L-DOPA by the enzyme DOPA decarboxylase.

effector At a receptor-effector complex of a synapse, the molecule or molecules that produce a physiological response in the postsynaptic cell.

enzymatic degradation At the synapse, a process converting neurotransmitter substance into other, less active compounds.

enzyme A specialized protein that catalyzes or facilitates a chemical reaction without entering into that reaction itself.

epinephrine A catecholinergic neurotransmitter that is a potent stimulator of the sympathetic nervous system. It raises blood pressure and increases heart rate.

equilibrium potential The voltage across the cell membrane at which no net movement of ions across the membrane occurs.

excitatory postsynaptic potential (EPSP) A temporary and partial depolarization in a postsynaptic neuron, resulting from synaptic activity.

exocytosis The process by which a synaptic vesicle fuses with the membrane, opening the vesicle and releasing neurotransmitter into the synaptic cleft.

flattened vesicles Elliptical-appearing synaptic vesicles that are believed to contain inhibitory neurotransmitter substance.

gamma-aminobutyric acid (GABA) A central nervous system neurotransmitter that is synthesized from glutamate in a single step that is catalyzed by the enzyme glutamic acid decarboxylase. It is thought to have a strong inhibitory action.

gap junction An electrical synapse at which current flows directly between the cytoplasm of two cells.

glutamate An amino acid that functions as a neurotransmitter at many excitatory synapses in mammalian nervous systems.

glycine An amino acid that is generally regarded as a central nervous system neurotransmitter.

graded potentials Potentials that may vary in size, such as EPSPs and IPSPs.

hyperpolarization An increase in the voltage difference across the membrane; in neurons, this often refers to an increase in the negative resting potential, which tends to prevent the triggering of an action potential.

indoleamine A monoamine composed of an indole ring and an amine tail.

inhibitory postsynaptic potential (IPSP) A temporary hyperpolarization in a postsynaptic neuron resulting from synaptic activity.

ionotropic channel A postsynaptic receptor that is directly linked to an ion channel.

ligand Any molecule that binds to a specific site on a protein or other biologically active molecule.

monoamine An amine molecule with one amino group (e.g., dopamine, noradrenalin, or serotonin).

monoamine oxidase (MAO) An intracellular-inactivating agent that attacks monoamines.

muscarinic receptor An acetylcholine receptor that is also affected by muscarine.

neuropeptide Small molecules composed of strings of amino acids that are found in brain tissue.

neurotransmitter A chemical substance, released into the synaptic cleft by a presynaptic neuron, that acts to alter the behavior of the postsynaptic cell, often by excitation or inhibition.

nicotinic receptor An acetylcholine receptor that is also affected by nicotine.

norepinephrine A neurotransmitter substance that is synthesized from dopamine by the enzyme dopamine-β-hydroxylase.

nucleotide-gated channels Membrane channels that change their state in response to a specific intracellularly released nucleotide.

opioid peptides Neuropeptides that mimic the effects of the opiate morphine.

polarized With respect to the synapse, having a definite direction of information flow from the presynaptic to the postsynaptic cell.

postsynaptic The cell that receives information at a synapse.

potentiate At the synapse, to pharmacologically accentuate the effects of a neurotransmitter or its agonist.

precursor A substance from which another is formed.

presynaptic The cell that transmits information at a synapse.

presynaptic inhibition At an axoaxonic synapse, the process by which one neuron regulates the effectiveness of excitatory synaptic transmission between two other neurons.

receptor At the synapse, a protein molecule within the postsynaptic membrane to which a neurotransmitter binds in effecting synaptic activity and triggers a response in the cell.

reuptake The process of returning neurotransmitter substance to the cell that released it.

reversed axoplasmic transport The process of carrying substances toward the cell body in an axon.

round vesicles Spherical vesicles that are believed to contain excitatory neurotransmitters.

second-messenger system An intracellular signaling system by which the binding of a neurotransmitter at a G-protein-linked receptor releases another substance that in turn has widespread physiological effects within the postsynaptic cell.

serotonin A central nervous system neurotransmitter made from the tryptophan intermediate 5-HTP by 5-HTP decarboxylase.

spatial summation The adding together of postsynaptic potentials produced at two or more synapses within a single postsynaptic cell.

substrate A substance on which an enzyme acts.

summation The adding together of postsynaptic potentials.

symmetrical synapse A synapse at which the densities of the presynaptic and postsynaptic membranes are similar; believed to indicate an inhibitory synapse.

synapse The place at which two neurons make functional connection.

synaptic cleft The gap between the presynaptic and postsynaptic elements of a synapse.

temporal summation The adding together of postsynaptic potentials produced at a single synapse when action potentials arrive in quick succession.

transmitter-gated channels Membrane channels that open in response to an extracellularly released neurotransmitter substance.

vesicle A small sphere of membrane that contains neurotransmitter substance.

Chapter 5

Vision

We humans—like other primates—have visual brains. We have vastly more cortical tissue devoted to processing visual information than for any of the other senses. This is one reason why the study of vision is so important in understanding human brain function. Vision research has been the source of major advances in both physiological psychology and neuroscience more generally.

Anatomically, the vertebrate visual system is organized in a way that makes it comparatively easy to study. For this reason, many general features of nervous system function were first discovered in studies of the visual system. The visual system is, in many ways, a model of all sensory systems. In learning about vision, one learns something about perception more generally. And perception is our only source of knowledge about the world outside of our selves.

VISION

To understand any of the bodily senses—be it vision, hearing, taste, smell, or touch—we need to find answers to at least three questions. The first is the question of sensory transduction: How is nonneural sensory information—such as a pattern of reflected light—translated into electrical cellular responses, which form the language of nerve cells? After all, light really has nothing in common with the cellular events that it evokes within the human visual system. Rather, it is the function of special cells, called receptors, to convert light energy into another form that can be understood by the neurons of the brain.

This process of converting sensory information into neural signals is called **sensory transduction** (from the Latin *transducere*, meaning "to lead across" or "to transfer"). Each sensory system must solve this problem in a somewhat different way because the forms of external information to be encoded differ among the various human senses.

The second question that must be addressed is that of **sensory coding**. This is the issue of representing sensory events as neural signals, by extracting important properties of the physical stimulus and discarding other, less relevant sensory information. Notice the use of the word *events*, which are meaningful happenings in the real world. One must always remember that sensory systems have evolved to tell nervous systems about external events of significance. Thus, the information contained in changing patterns of the light that enter the eye must be coded and recoded by the visual system to produce an internal representation of selected aspects of the world around us.

Sensory coding is the process of neurally extracting selected types of information from the raw transduced sensory signals provided by the sensory receptors. For vision, the neural chain of sensory coding and recoding begins in the retina of the eye and continues through large portions of the primate cerebral cortex.

The final question raised in understanding any sensory system is the issue of perceptual representation. By **perceptual representation** is meant the high-level internal image that, in the case of human vision, we see as the world. Unlike the retinal visual image, which consists of a mosaic of photoreceptors excited to various degrees by the momentary visual stimulus, the internal visual representation is actively constructed by our brains and is composed of objects and scenes, which change in time to form visual events.

Thus, although the eye might be like a camera, the visual system of the brain is very much different. It does not merely copy and store a particular pattern of reflected light; rather, it *sees*, thereby constructing a model of visual reality on which we, as human beings, base our actions. The internal sensory image is carefully crafted by our sensory systems as an aid to the survival of our species.

With this in mind, we begin our examination of visual perception by examining reflected light, which is the physical stimulus for vision and the sensory source of all visual information. We next consider the issue of sensory coding at a number of levels, both in the retina and in the brain. We complete our treatment of the visual system with some thoughts about perceptual representation and conscious visual experience.

Light Is the Visual Stimulus

Light is electromagnetic energy. Although physicists use the term very generally, the word *light* is more commonly employed in a restricted way to mean visible light. One way of representing light is as a continuously moving wave. Wave theory is useful in describing the reflection and refraction of light and, for that reason, has formed the basis of the optical sciences. Furthermore, wave theory is appropriate for understanding color vision because the color of visible light is specified by its wavelength.

For other purposes, however, physicists consider light to be electromagnetic energy that is contained in discrete packets, or quanta, rather than flowing as a continuous wave. The quantum aspect of light is important to the biologist in treating the absorption of light by photoreceptors in the eye.

Vision provides us with information about the objects that surround us as patterns of reflected light. Objects differ in the proportions of light that they absorb and reflect; light-colored objects reflect a great deal of light, whereas dark-colored objects reflect very little of the light that illuminates them. Thus, this page appears white because it is highly reflective. The ink appears dark because it is highly absorbent of light energy in the visible wavelengths.

Colored objects selectively absorb certain wavelengths of light while reflecting others. The characteristic colors of objects are given by the wavelengths of light that they reflect. Blue objects, for example, reflect shortwave and absorb long-wave light. Thus, visual information about the objects depends very much on the patterns of light, darkness, and color reflected from their surfaces. The visual system is adapted to transform patterns of reflected light as viewed by the eye into a mental image of the world.

Structure of the Eye

The human eye is a relatively simple but exquisitely constructed sensory organ. Figure 5.1 on the following page illustrates its principal features. The outermost surface of the eye, covering both the iris and the pupil, is the **cornea**. This thin, tough, transparent layer forms the eye's first optical element. The cornea itself is supplied with small sensory nerves that carry information about touch and pain. Although the cornea is composed of living tissue, it has no blood supply. Instead, it obtains oxygen by diffusion with the air and obtains glucose and other nutrients by diffusion with adjacent structures of the eye, particularly the **aqueous humor** that lies beneath it in the **anterior chamber**. The aqueous humor is similar to protein-free blood plasma.

The major optical work of the eye is performed by its crystalline **lens**. Like the cornea, the lens has no blood supply but receives both oxygen and glucose by diffusion from the aqueous humor. If a cataract is formed, the lens loses its transparency, and vision is impaired.

The principal cavity of the eye is its **vitreous chamber**, which is filled with a transparent gel, the **vitreous humor**. Along its rear wall lies the nervous tissue that performs the first analyses of visual information, the

Figure 5.1. The Mechanical Structure of the Eye as an Imaging Device. The lens of the eye acts in a manner similar to that of a camera. The face is imaged in inverted and reversed form on the retina. If the curvature of the lens is properly suited to the shape of the eye and the distance of the object, the projected image on the retinal surface is sharply focused. When the shape of the lens and the eye are not properly matched, corrective lenses—glasses—are required to achieve proper focus.

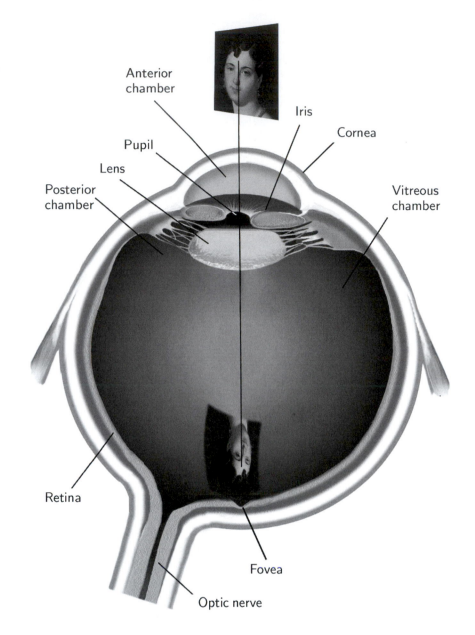

retina. The retina contains both the **photoreceptors**, which transform patterns of light into patterns of membrane potential, and the retinal interneurons, which process the visual information provided by the photoreceptors. The retina develops from embryonic brain tissue during the growth of the organism and, for that reason, may be considered to be a visual brain that has migrated to the back of the eye.

The way in which the lens projects an image of objects in the visual environment on the retina is also shown in Figure 5.1. The lens of the eye, like that of a camera, projects onto the retina a focused, inverted, and reversed image of the environment. Objects in the world that are to the left of the line of gaze are imaged on the right side of the retina; conversely, objects on the right in the world are imaged on the left side of the retina. In a similar fashion, objects above the line of gaze are projected on the lower portion of the retina, and objects below the line are projected on the upper portion of the retina.

It is the function of the lens to provide a precisely focused visual image to the retina, but sometimes this is not possible. Many people, particularly as they grow older, show differences between the shape of the eye and the focal properties of the lens; the visual image may be projected onto a plane that lies either in front of or behind the retina. Eyeglasses or contact lenses are used to correct such optical deficiencies.

Even in the healthy young eye, not all objects can be brought into proper focus by the lens without some special adaptation. The **ciliary muscles** that surround the lens perform this function; by contracting, the ciliary muscles allow the lens to assume a more rounded shape that increases its optical power. This process of **accommodation** permits one to focus on near objects more clearly.

Between the lens and the cornea lies the ring-shaped musculature of the **iris**. The **pupil**, in the center of the iris, provides the pathway by which light enters the eye. There are two types of muscles in the iris: The **dilator pupillae** are arranged in a radial fashion and are innervated by fibers from the sympathetic nervous system; opposing them are the parasympathetically innervated **sphincter pupillae**. Pupillary dilation results from either the contraction of the dilator pupillae or the relaxation of the sphincter pupillae. Pupillary movements are important in regulating both the amount of light entering the eye and the sharpness of the visual image in much the same way as the iris of a camera affects both exposure and depth of field.

The final set of muscles important in vision are the **extraocular muscles**. These opposing muscles move the eyes within their orbits, thereby selecting the portion of the world that is projected on the retina by the lens.

THE RETINA

The retina is a thin (0.25 mm), highly organized sheet of neural tissue lying on the rear inner surface of each eye (Dowling, 1987). But when viewed as a tissue, a distinct series of layers may be seen (see Figure 5.2 on the following page). Notice (and this may seem surprising) that the photoreceptors are not located at the inner surface of the retina facing the vitreous chamber but instead are buried beneath the other retinal layers. Thus, the light entering the eye must travel through several layers of neural tissue before reaching the photoreceptors to begin the process of visual perception. However, this presents no real problem because the retina itself, with the exception of the blood vessels, is so thin and nearly transparent that light passes through it easily.

Vision begins with the excitation of the photoreceptors by light energy and continues with the synaptic transmission of information between cells in the various retinal layers, which are shown in Figure 5.2 on the next page. The cell bodies of the photoreceptors are located in the **outer nuclear layer**, but the highly specialized portions of these cells that are actually

Figure 5.2. The Human Retina. The retina is constructed in a layered fashion, with the outer segments of the photoreceptors furthest from the lens. This arrangement has little optical effect because the retina is very thin and its cells are nearly transparent.

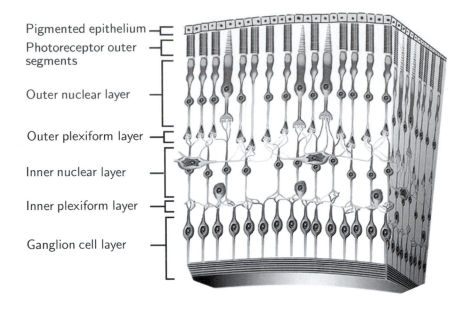

Pigmented epithelium

Photoreceptor outer segments

Outer nuclear layer

Outer plexiform layer

Inner nuclear layer

Inner plexiform layer

Ganglion cell layer

light sensitive form the region of the **outer segments** (see 5.3 on the facing page). Beneath the photoreceptors is the **outer plexiform layer**, which derives its name from the Latin *plexus*, meaning "tangle." The outer plexiform layer is, in fact, a web of dense synaptic connections that contains few cell bodies.

The **inner nuclear layer**, like the outer nuclear layer, is rich in cell bodies. The bodies of the **horizontal cells** are located in the inner nuclear layer; these cells extend their dendrites and axons into the outer plexiform layer, where they make extensive synaptic connections. The horizontal cells are anatomically well suited for integrating information across the surface of the retina and, for that reason, are said to provide a **lateral signal pathway**.

The second type of neuron located within the inner nuclear layer is the bipolar cell. As the name implies, **bipolar cells** have two distinct sets of processes that extend in opposite directions. The dendrites of the bipolar cells reach into the outer plexiform layer, where they receive input. The axons of the bipolar cells carry information from the rods and cones to more central neurons of the visual system. Bipolar cells form a part of the **straight signal pathway** of the retina.

The **amacrine cells** are the third type of neurons with cell bodies in the inner nuclear layer. These neurons are located in the lower portion of that layer and extend both dendrites and axons into the **inner plexiform layer**, a second zone of synaptic connection. Like the horizontal cells at the outer plexiform layer, the amacrine cells serve as the lateral signal pathway for the inner plexiform layer and play an important role in determining temporal adaptation of the retina to visual input.

The final elements of the straight signal pathway of the retina are the **ganglion cells**. The bodies of these neurons are located in the **ganglion cell layer**. They receive synaptic input from their dendrites, which extend into the inner plexiform layer. Each ganglion cell has but a single axon,

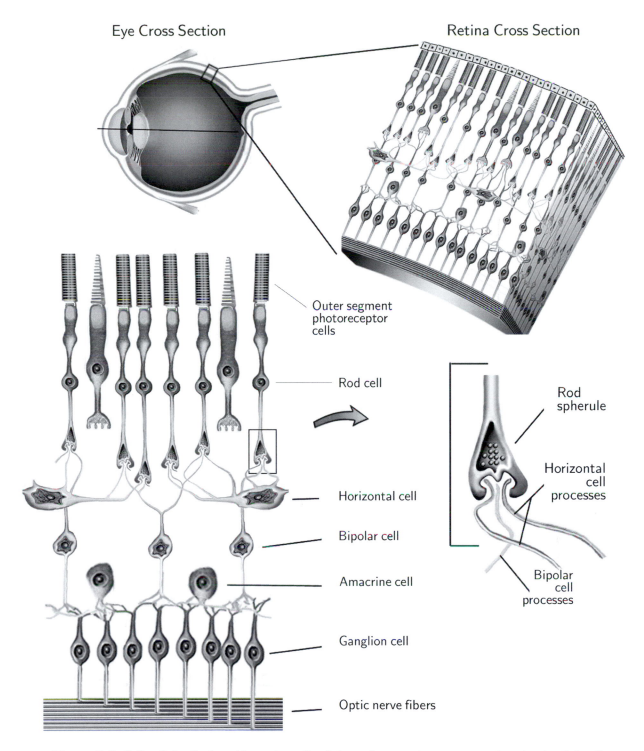

Eye Cross Section

Retina Cross Section

Outer segment photoreceptor cells

Rod cell

Rod spherule

Horizontal cell

Horizontal cell processes

Bipolar cell

Amacrine cell

Bipolar cell processes

Ganglion cell

Optic nerve fibers

Figure 5.3. Cells of the Retina. Here, the cells of the retina may be seen at various levels of detail.

Figure 5.5. The Distribution of Rods and Cones in the Human Eye. Cones, which are responsible for high-acuity color vision, are concentrated in the fovea, whereas rods are much more widely distributed.

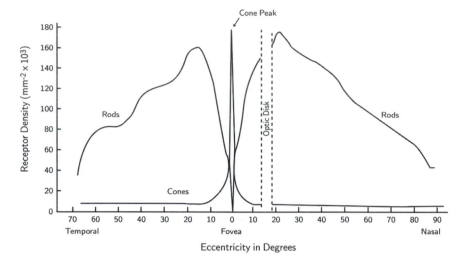

which enters the layer of nerve fibers and leaves the retina to form the **optic nerve**.

Phototransduction

Vision begins when light passes through the lens of the eye and alters the activity of photoreceptor cells in the retina. There are two major classes of photoreceptor cells, the **rods** and the **cones**, which differ in both their microscopic shape and the exact uses to which they are put in visual perception. Both types have highly specialized outer segments that contain light-sensitive photochemicals. In the rods, these processes are long and tubular; in cones, the processes are conical in form, as shown in Figure 5.4.

The distribution of rods and cones differs across the retina. The central area of the retina, called the **macula** (Latin for a "spot"), is about 6 mm in diameter and lies at the optical center of the eye. Within the macula is the **fovea**, which appears as a small depression in the thickness of the retina that is only 1.8 mm in diameter. The fovea is responsible for highly detailed color vision; it contains about 34,000 cones in its most central region but no rods whatsoever.

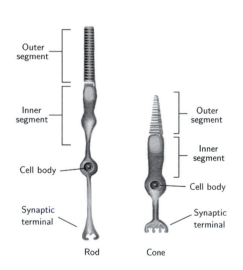

Figure 5.4. The Structure of the Rods and Cones. The outer segments of the rods are cylindrical in shape and enclose a large number of photochemical-containing disks. In contrast, the cones have a pointed appearance and contain their photochemicals in the outer membrane of the cone itself.

The proportion of rods to cones increases in the outer regions of the central area and in the periphery that surrounds it, as is shown in Figure 5.5. The central fovea is rich in cones, but the periphery is not. Altogether, there are approximately 120 million rods and 6 million cones in the human eye (Schwartz, 1994).

Rods and cones serve differing and complementary visual functions, as shown in Figure 5.6 on the next page. The rods form the basis of **scotopic vision** (from the Greek *skotos*, meaning "darkness," and *ope*, meaning "sight"), which provides us with visual information in near-total darkness, as on a starlit night.

Scotopic vision is extraordinarily sensitive, with single rods capable of responding to single photons of light under optimal conditions. This exquisite sensitivity is important in providing us with at least a sketch of

	Scotopic System	Photopic System
Receptors	Rods	Cones
Photopigments	Rhodopsin(507nm)	Erythrolabe (565 nm or long) Chlorolabe (535 nm or medium) Cyanolabe (430 nm or short)
Color Vision	Color Blind	Color Sensitive
Absolute Sensitivity	Excellent	Poor
Spatial Acuity	Poor (20/200)	Excellent (20/20)
Temporal Acuity	Poor (20Hz)	Excellent (70Hz)
Region of Peak Density	20° From Fovea	Fovea

Figure 5.6. Scotopic and Photopic Vision. Scotopic vision, which operates at illumination levels like that of starlight, is responsible for detecting weak visual signals in near darkness, whereas photopic vision operates at daylight levels of illumination with high acuity. (Adapted from Schwartz, S. H. [1994], *Visual perception: A clinical orientation.* Norwalk, CT: Appleton and Lange.)

our environment under very dim lighting conditions. The price to be paid for absolute sensitivity to light, however, is relatively poor acuity or spatial resolution and a complete absence of color selectivity. Compared with daylight photopic vision, starlight scotopic vision is about 20/200. This means that the smallest object that can be resolved at a viewing distance of 20 feet under scotopic conditions can be resolved at 200 feet photopically.

Cones, not rods, are the receptors for **photopic vision** (from the Greek *photos* for "light"), which functions at higher levels of illumination, such as bright moonlight or sunlight. With strong illumination, high absolute sensitivity to light energy is not needed. Instead, under improved lighting, the photopic cone system provides high visual resolution and spatial acuity. The photopic spatial resolution of the human visual system is very good but certainly not the best in the animal kingdom. In comparison to the scotopic rod system, the photopic cone system is also vastly superior in detecting rapid temporal changes in a visual stimulus.

Finally, the photopic cone system is capable of distinguishing between objects that differ in color, whereas the scotopic rod system is color-blind. This results from the fact that the cone system uses three different photochemicals, each with different spectral properties, whereas the rod system employs a single photochemical, rhodopsin.

Photoreceptor Structure   Photoreceptors are among the most remarkably specialized of all living cells; they are neurons that have become adapted to respond to visible light by producing variations in their membrane potentials. To accomplish this task, photoreceptors have evolved a unique anatomical structure and molecular biochemistry.

Each photoreceptor is composed of two segments. The **inner segment** is much like the cell body of any neuron; it contains the cell nucleus, a very large number of mitochondria, and other usual subcellular structures. It is the outer segment of the photoreceptor that contains the specialized structures that make sensory transduction possible.

In rods, the outer segment contains a tall stack of microscopic disks.

Each disk contains the photochemical **rhodopsin**, which is used in the initial step of sensory transduction. (The name *rhodopsin* is derived from the Greek work *rhodon* meaning "rose" or "red" and *opsis*, or "vision"; the chemical rhodopsin is in fact purplish in color.)

Disks containing rhodopsin are manufactured continuously at the base of the outer segment and migrate upward over time. The disks at the top of the stack are in the process of degenerating and are removed from the outer segment of the rod by specialized glial cells. The inner and outer segments of the rods are joined by a small **connecting cilium**, a hairlike bridge through which all molecules moving between the inner and outer segments must pass.

The structure of the outer segments of the cones is similar to that of the rods in many respects; however, there are also some differences between them of unknown importance. Whereas in the rods the photochemical is contained in separate disks in the outer segment, in cones the photochemical is contained in the folded outer membrane of the cell. These folds decrease in size at the outer portions of the segment, giving the cones their characteristically pointed appearance. The outer segments of the cones are much smaller than the outer segments of the rods. As in the rods, there appears to be a mechanism in the cones by which the photosensitive folded sheet of the outer segment is rejuvenated; however, less is known about the replacement of the photochemical membrane in the cones than about the replacement of the disks in the rods.

Finally, unlike the rod system, the cone system uses three different photochemicals that differentially absorb different wavelengths of light. The first is **erythrolabe** (from the Greek *erythros*, meaning "red," and *lambanein*, meaning "to take or absorb"), and it is most effective in absorbing long wavelength or red light. The second is **chlorolabe** (from *chloros*, meaning "green"), and it is best stimulated by middle wavelength or greenish light. The third photochemical is **cyanolabe** (from *kyanos* or "blue"), which is selective for short-wavelength light.

Each cone contains one—and only one—of these photochemicals. For this reason, each class of cone will respond differentially to light of any given wavelength or color. The presence of multiple photochemicals with different spectral absorption characteristics in different classes permits the cone system to distinguish color from intensity. The rod system, having only a single photochemical, rhodopsin, is of necessity color-blind.

Despite these differences, the mechanism of sensory transduction appears to be very much the same in the rods and in the cones; however, the rods have been most extensively studied, primarily because of the difficulty of extracting the photochemicals contained in the outer segments of the cones.

Biochemistry of Phototransduction   Photoreception in rods begins with the absorption of a quantum of light energy by a single molecule of the photochemical rhodopsin, which is located in a disk of the outer segment. There are approximately 3 billion rhodopsin molecules in each disk and between 1,000 and 2,000 individual disks in the outer segment of a single rod. Rhodopsin, like the photochemicals of the cones, is composed of two parts: a large transmembrane protein molecule, **opsin**, and the chromophore 11-cis **retinal**, which is an aldehyde of Vitamin A1. (The term *chromophore* refers to "a color-giving chemical group.") Retinal is a long, thin molecule that normally is arranged in a straightened all-trans configuration. But to form rhodopsin, the retinal molecule must be bent into its 11-cis configuration, in which it can bind with the opsin molecule.

When a quantum of light is absorbed by the retinal chromophore of a rhodopsin molecule, it reverts to its chemically more stable straightened, all-trans form, which cannot bond with the protein opsin. Therefore, the rhodopsin molecule is split into its two components, retinal and opsin. (It was for this, among other discoveries, that George Wald received his Nobel Prize in 1967.)

The breakup of rhodopsin by light begins the process of visual perception by initiating a catalytic cascade that amplifies the light-induced response of a single photochemical molecule and alters the membrane potential of the entire cell. This occurs in the following manner.

The cell membrane of the outer segment contains a large number of transmembrane protein channels that are gated by cyclic GMP. In the absence of light, these channels are kept open by cyclic GMP molecules that are bound to the individual channels. Because these channels are open, positively charged sodium ions enter the cell with ease, driven both by their concentration gradient (sodium is concentrated outside the cell) and the electrical gradient (the interior of the rod is negative with respect to the extracellular fluid). The movement of sodium ions into the rod's outer segment through open cyclic-GMP-gated Na^+ channels is called the **dark current**. Thus, in darkness, cyclic-GMP-gated sodium channels are open, and the cell membrane is actively depolarized by the influx of sodium ions. Membrane potentials of mammalian rods in darkness have been measured at about −35 mv, reflecting the depolarizing effect of the dark current (Schneeweis & Schnapf, 1995).

The breakup of a rhodopsin molecule begins an amplified biochemical process that closes many of these gates, with the ultimate consequence reducing the depolarization of the photoreceptor by the dark current (Baylor, 1996; Kaupp & Koch, 1992; Simon, Strathmann, & Gautam, 1991). The excitation of a single molecule of rhodopsin activates about 500 molecules of the GTP-binding protein **transducin**, as shown in Figures 5.7 on the following page and 5.8 on page 149.

The transducin molecules in turn activate a similar number of molecules of cGMP phosphodiesterase. The cyclic GMP (cGMP) phosphodiesterase hydrolyzes more than 100,000 molecules of cGMP forming GMP molecules, which are incapable of keeping the receptor's sodium channels open. As a consequence, about 250 of these channels close, blocking the entrance of 1 to 10 million sodium ions each second. The result is that some of the depolarizing dark current is blocked, and the membrane potential shifts about 1 millivolt in the negative direction, toward the normal resting potential of a neuron (about −70 mv). Through this remarkable catalytic cascade, the light-induced alteration of the form of one rhodopsin molecule produces a shift in the membrane potential of a photoreceptor cell. This is the molecular basis of sensory transduction in the visual system.

Rods and cones affect the activity of other retinal cells by the thoroughly conventional release of neurotransmitter substances at chemical

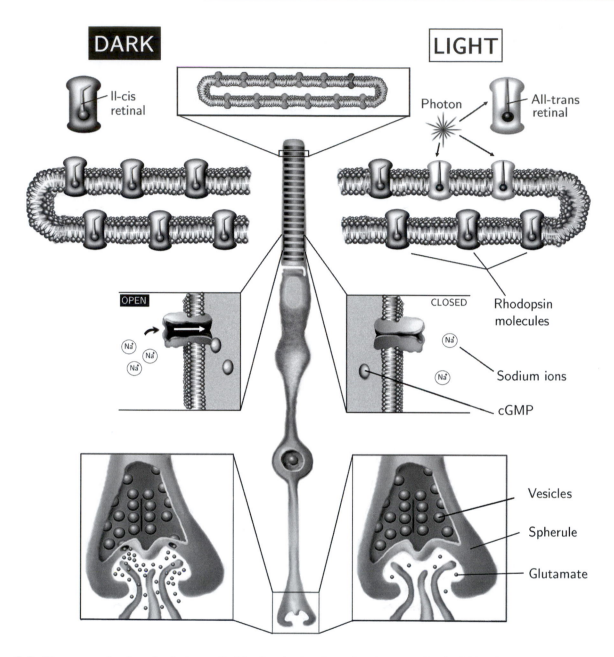

Figure 5.7. Phototransduction. In darkness (left), the rhodopsin molecules contained within the disks are inactivated, and sodium pores in the outer segment are open. This results in a large influx of positively charged sodium ions (the dark current), which depolarize the cell. This causes the release of the neurotransmitter glutamate at the rod synapse. In light (right), the absorption of a photon of light by a molecule of rhodopsin in the disks of a rod reduces the dark current and hyperpolarizes the cell. The absorption of a photon of light by rhodopsin activates a G-protein that—in turn—activates the enzyme phosphodiesterase (PDE). PDE converts cyclic GMP (cGMP) to GMP. Because cGMP keeps the sodium channels of the outer membrane open in the dark, any reduction of cGMP levels within the rod acts to close some of the sodium channels. This makes the cell less depolarized and reduces the rate of neurotransmitter release.

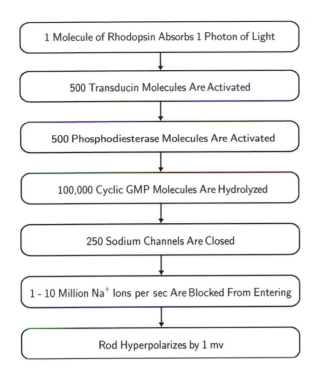

Figure 5.8. The Molecular Cascade in Phototransduction. The absorption of a photon of light by a molecule of rhodopsin is amplified to produce a biologically significant change in the membrane potential of the cell. In the dark, sodium pores in the outer membrane of the rod are kept open by the presence of intracellular cyclic GMP, depolarizing the cell. The breakup of rhodopsin activates the G-protein, transducin, which then activates cGMP phosphodiesterase. Phosphodiesterase molecules hydrolyze cyclic GMP (cGMP), forming GMP, which closes the open sodium channels. In this way, the rod is hyperpolarized by a millivolt, reducing its output of neurotransmitter to other retinal cells and signaling the presence of light. Multiple arrows indicate the stages in this molecular cascade where amplification takes place.

synapses. As is the case elsewhere in the nervous system, the presynaptic terminal releases neurotransmitter substance to the extent that it is depolarized. This means—and it seems counterintuitive—that the highest rate of transmitter release occurs in darkness. Light falling on the receptor (a) reduces the depolarizing dark current, (b) allows the membrane potential to become more negative or hyperpolarized, and (c) reduces the amount of neurotransmitter substance that is released by the photoreceptor on the other retinal cells that it contacts. In this strange way, the visual system transforms information contained in a single light quantum into a conventional membrane potential change that affects synaptic activity.

Receptive Fields of Retinal Neurons

The photoreceptors—the rods and cones of the eye—are the only cells possessing the molecular machinery necessary to transform the patterns of light that are focused on the retina into neural signals. Every other cell in the nervous system that processes visual information must be processing signals that originated in a photoreceptor, either directly or indirectly. Such cells are called **sensory interneurons**, as opposed to sensory receptors. Sensory interneurons (or often, just "sensory neurons" as opposed to "sensory receptors") are neurons that respond to the output of the receptor cells and not to the stimulus itself. Sensory interneurons are always indirectly activated by the sensory stimulus.

One very important idea in understanding sensory processing in the

Figure 5.9. The Idea of a Receptive Field. The receptive field of a nerve cell in a sensory system is defined ultimately by the specific receptors that provide it with input, either directly or indirectly. Here, the receptive field of the visual bipolar cell is shown. The receptors from which it receives direct input are darkened; those from which it receives indirect input via the horizontal cells are lightly shaded. The other receptors from which it receives no information and are not a part of its receptive field are shown in gray.

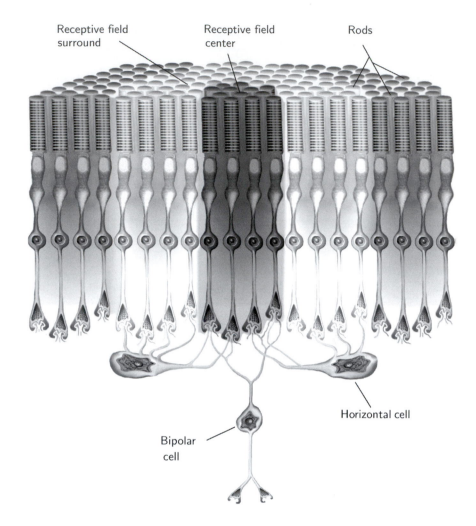

brain is the concept of **receptive field**, illustrated in Figure 5.9. In the visual system, receptor cells are arranged in an orderly two-dimensional array on the retina. They provide output to the sensory interneurons of the retina, but any given sensory interneuron receives input from only a restricted region of the total array of photoreceptor cells. The region of receptor array providing input to any particular visual interneuron is said to be the receptive field of that interneuron. The receptive field of a sensory interneuron is the particular set of sensory receptors from which it receives input, either directly or indirectly.

The receptive field of a visual system cell may be mapped by recording the electrical response of the cell while stimulating various parts of the retina with light; only when light falls within the receptive field of the neuron will the electrical activity of that neuron be altered. Although the neuron being studied may be located anywhere within the visual system, the receptive field of a visual interneuron is always a map of the photoreceptor layer of the retina, showing where light may affect the electrical activity of the cell in question. The receptive field of any visual system interneuron may in principle be determined by tracing all connections between that neuron and the photoreceptors of the retina.

Horizontal Cells   The horizontal cells spread their processes across the synaptic field of the outer plexiform layer, where they receive input from the photoreceptors. Their characteristic branching pattern is shown in Figure 5.2 on page 142. Because of their shape and location, horizontal cells might be expected to integrate information over the region of the retina that they innervate; this, in fact, is the case.

As with the photoreceptors, the membrane potential of the horizontal cells in the absence of visual stimulation is low compared with typical neurons. Furthermore, also like the photoreceptors, the response of the horizontal cell to illumination of receptors within its receptive field is hyperpolarization. This results from the fact that the synapse between a photoreceptor and a horizontal cell is chemical and excitatory in nature. Because the rods and the cones release the maximum amount of excitatory neurotransmitter in the dark, activating the photoreceptors by light hyperpolarizes them and reduces the amount of excitatory neurotransmitter that they release onto the horizontal cells. By reducing the release of excitatory neurotransmitter onto the horizontal cells, the horizontal cells become less depolarized (hence, hyperpolarized).

It is important to distinguish between the reduction of depolarization that occurs at the photoreceptor-horizontal synapse and the hyperpolarization occurring at inhibitory synapses elsewhere in the nervous system. At an inhibitory synapse, the release of an inhibitory neurotransmitter actively opens channels for particular ions that act to hyperpolarize the postsynaptic membrane. At the photoreceptor-horizontal cell synapse, it is the release of an excitatory neurotransmitter that is being suppressed as illumination of the photoreceptor is increased. The horizontal cell is not being hyperpolarized; rather, a profound depolarizing influence is being removed.

Electrophysiological evidence indicates that the horizontal cells integrate visual information within the region of the retina that they innervate. The response of the cell increases as more photoreceptors in its receptive field are illuminated. Furthermore, its response increases as the intensity of stimulation within its receptive field is increased. Thus, the response of the horizontal cell is a function of the average intensity of illumination of the photoreceptors within its receptive field. Through its widely branching processes, the horizontal cell integrates visual information across adjacent regions of the retina.

Bipolar Cells   The bipolar cells are a part of the straight signal system of the retina, carrying visual information from the photoreceptors to the ganglion cells that form the optic nerve. There are two principal types of bipolar cells, differing from each other in size. The larger bipolar type innervates the rods, whereas the smaller (midget) bipolars service the cones. Both types of bipolar cells, like photoreceptors and horizontal cells, produce no action potentials; rather, their response to visual input appears as a slow-graded shift from a membrane potential in response to synaptic input from the photoreceptors and horizontal cells.

Figure 5.10. The Response of Hyperpolarizing and Depolarizing Bipolar Cells to Light. The left-hand column shows the effect of light falling on a depolarizing-center bipolar cell; the right-hand column shows the effect of stimulating a hyperpolarizing-center bipolar cell.

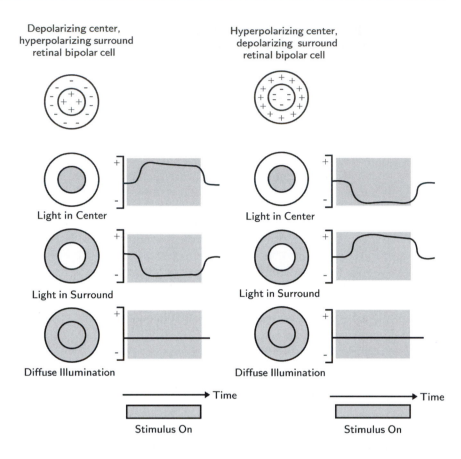

The receptive field of most bipolar cells is complex, divided into a small circular central region and a larger, doughnutlike surround. Stimulation of photoreceptors within the central area may produce either depolarization or hyperpolarization of the bipolar cell, the polarity of the response being a fixed characteristic of individual bipolar cells. The number of cells of each type is approximately the same.

Illuminating photoreceptors in the surround or outer portion of the bipolar's receptive field has the effect of reducing the response to central stimulation. Because stimulation of the surround counteracts the effect of stimulation of the center of the receptive field, these regions are said to exhibit **antagonism**. Thus, a bipolar cell may be driven to its maximal positive or negative response when the central and surround portions of its receptive field differ markedly in illumination. Figure 5.10 shows the electrical response of the bipolar cells to central and diffuse stimulation.

This center-surround organization of the bipolar's receptive field provides a striking and important example of visual feature extraction by a neuronal circuit. The bipolar cell, unlike either the photoreceptors or the horizontal cells, does not function as a simple detector of light energy; instead, it acts to extract a pattern from the visual image—namely, a bright region or spot surrounded by darkness or the converse, depending on the characteristics of the cell in question. In testing for differences in the illumination of the center and the surround, bipolar cells begin a process of pattern analysis that continues at higher levels in the visual system.

The center-surround organization of the receptive field of the bipolar cells may be traced to the structure of the synaptic connections within the outer plexiform layer. Figure 5.3 on page 143 shows the characteristic complex synapse between a bipolar cell, a rod, and two horizontal cells. In this arrangement, the horizontal cells are in a position to modulate or regulate the direct synaptic pathway between photoreceptors and bipolar cells.

In the central portion of the fovea, the smallest of the bipolar cells may receive input from only one cone, giving rise to an extremely small central area of the receptive field. However, in the periphery, a rod bipolar cell may make direct synaptic connections with a large number of peripheral photoreceptors. Thus, the size of the central area of a bipolar cell's receptive field depends on the functions that the cell is to perform and is determined by the pattern of connection between the photoreceptors and the bipolar cell.

The neurotransmitter released by the photoreceptors to all bipolar cells is glutamate. Some bipolar cells respond to glutamate in an excitatory manner and others in an inhibitory manner, depending on the type of molecular effector complex on the postsynaptic membrane of the individual bipolar cells.

If these photoreceptor-bipolar cell glutamate-gated synapses have an excitatory effect (which is the normal response to glutamate elsewhere in the nervous system), then the response of the bipolar cell will be to hyperpolarize when the center of its receptive field is illuminated. Because the photoreceptors emit the maximum amount of neurotransmitter in the dark, illumination reduces the secretion of transmitter at the photoreceptor-bipolar cell synapse. A bipolar cell, receiving less excitatory neurotransmitter, becomes more polarized. These bipolar cells, which respond to light in the center of their receptive fields by hyperpolarizing, are called **off-center bipolar cells**.

In the depolarizing type of bipolar cell, the situation is just reversed; these cells respond to glutamate in an inhibitory manner. Although the molecular mechanism of their response is not known, it is likely to involve a G-protein inhibitory system. In these bipolars, light in the central region of the receptive field reduces the output of the inhibitory glutamate and moves the membrane potential of the bipolar cell in the depolarizing direction. These bipolar cells are called **on-center bipolar cells**.

Thus, the character of a bipolar cell's response to light stimulation of the central area of its receptive field depends on the type of postsynaptic response evoked by glutamate at the bipolar/photoreceptor synapse.

For both on-center bipolar cells and off-center bipolar cells, the effect of stimulation on the surround portion of the receptive field is to negate the direct effect of the photoreceptor-bipolar cell synapse. However, some bipolar cells lack an antagonistic surround altogether; these cells appear to function as brightness, not contrast, detectors.

Amacrine Cells   Amacrine cells respond to the light in their receptive field by a graded depolarizing potential on which one or two action potentials may be superimposed (Dowling, 1987). Amacrine cells are axonless neurons and synapse with the ganglion cells, the bipolar cells, and other amacrine cells.

Amacrine cells seem to function to detect changes in visual stimuli. Many of these cells respond only to stimulus onset or stimulus offset; when a stimulus is prolonged, amacrine cells cease to fire. Through their input to the ganglion cells, the amacrine cells convey this information to higher centers of the visual system. These cells play an important role in processing the dynamic aspects of the visual stimulus. The amacrine cells, together with the horizontal and bipolar cells, provide the first steps of signal processing in the visual system. These retinal interneurons form the basis for the perception of spatial and temporal pattern vision.

Ganglion Cells   The ganglion cells are the output neurons of the retina. They receive input from the bipolar and amacrine cells and translate this information into patterns of action potentials. The axons of the ganglion cells leave the retina to form the optic nerve. Figure 5.11 on the facing page illustrates two major types of ganglion cells: the **on-center ganglion cells** with on-centers and off-surrounds and the **off-center ganglion cells** with off-centers and on-surrounds (Kuffler, 1953).

An on-center, off-surround ganglion cell shows an increase in firing when the central portion of its receptive field is differentially illuminated. These cells probably are driven by the center-depolarizing type of bipolar cell. Conversely, off-center ganglion cells reduce their firing rate with central illumination and probably receive input from the center-hyperpolarizing type of bipolar cell.

It is important to note that no significant changes in receptive field organization occur at the level of the ganglion cells. Ganglion cells preserve the pattern of receptive field organization established in the outer plexiform layer by the bipolar cells. Thus, on-center ganglion cells receive input from on-center bipolar cells. Conversely, off-center ganglion cells receive input from off-center bipolar cells.

Recent discoveries suggest that sensory coding in the ganglion cells may be more sophisticated than had been previously supposed. Meister and his colleagues (Meister, Lagnado, & Baylor, 1995; Meister, 1996) simultaneously measured the visual responses of between 30 and 50 retinal ganglion cells of the salamander using an innovative large array of recording microelectrodes. This procedure permitted—really for the first time—the analysis of the temporal relations between individual ganglion cells as they fire to specific stimuli. They found that many adjacent ganglion cells fired in synchrony with each other. That is, many cells responded in pairs. When this occurs, the receptive field signaled by the pair of simultaneous discharging cells was smaller than when either cell of the pair fired alone. This means that the pattern of paired firing of retinal ganglion cells carries additional information to the brain concerning the precise location of the retinal stimulus. This striking finding opens an entirely new aspect to sensory coding of location within the visual system.

Retinal Coding of Color

Human vision not only is specialized for detecting spatial patterns of light and darkness but is also capable of resolving the colors of objects, given

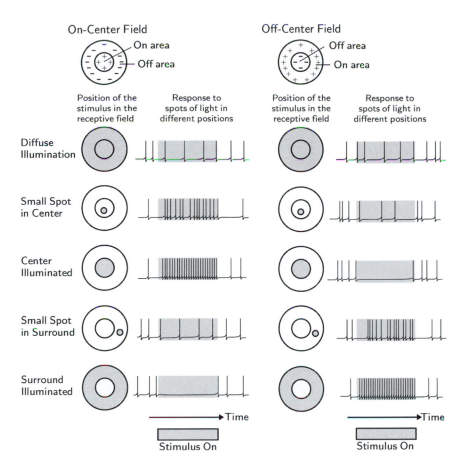

Figure 5.11. Response of an On-Center and an Off-Center Ganglion Cell to Light. As shown at left, an on-center cell responds most vigorously to light in the center of its receptive field and is inhibited by light in its surround. The reverse is true of the off-center cell, as shown on the right. Compare these responses with those of the bipolar cells shown in Figure 5.10 on page 152.

adequate illumination. Color vision permits us to distinguish between objects on the basis of the wavelengths of light that they reflect, contributing much richness to visual perception.

Trichromacy Students of human color vision have long known that it is fundamentally trichromatic. From a behavioral point of view, **trichromacy** means that any perceptible hue may be exactly matched in human vision by mixing together lights of three different wavelengths. (Any three wavelengths of light may be used, provided that none of them may be matched by a mixture of the other two.) In the 1700s, the trichromatic nature of perceived color was used to reproduce paintings by three-color printing processes, in which three well-chosen inks were used to produce the whole spectrum of colors. Trichromacy was widely believed to be a fact of physics rather than a consequence of physiology. Thomas Young, an English physicist and physician, was the first to suggest otherwise.

To Young, it seemed obvious that color was a sensation, rather than a physical phenomenon. The fact of color matching suggested to Young that there were three different physiological mechanisms in the retina. Light of different wavelengths excited these separate mechanisms in differing proportions. Color matching could be accomplished by manipulating these

Figure 5.12. Spectral Absorption Curves for Cones. Because the three types of cones differ in spectral absorption, they will respond in different ways to lights of different color. This makes it possible for the cone system to distinguish between color and brightness. The rod system, having only one type of receptor, is of necessity color-blind.

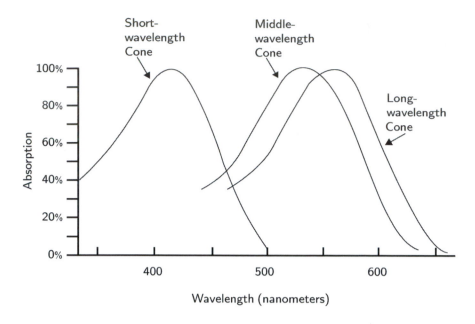

three different retinal mechanisms more or less independently until the exact pattern produced by a specific light is duplicated. Young's conjecture, however, was largely ignored for nearly half a century until it was revived by Herman von Helmholtz, a professor of physics at the University of Berlin. Helmholtz extended Young's ideas, resulting in the modern concept of retinal trichromacy.

Today, trichromacy is recognized as a consequence of the fact that humans have three types of cones, each containing a different photosensitive pigment. These three photochemicals differ from each other in the wavelengths of light that they most readily absorb, as shown in Figure 5.12. These three types of receptors are usually called short (S), medium (M), and long (L) wavelength cones. They differ in **spectral absorption**, the relative probability that a molecule of photochemical will absorb a photon of light as a function of wavelength (Wandell, 1995). The differing spectral absorption of the three types of cones provides the initial physical basis for human color perception.

The three cone photochemicals, such as rhodopsin, consist of opsin molecules bound to 11-cis retinal. The retinal molecule is common to all photochemicals, but its absorption characteristics change as a function of the type of opsin to which it is bound. Peak absorption is at about 420 nm (violet) for the S cones, 530 nm (green) for the M cones, and 560 nm (yellow green) for the L cones. (These cones are sometimes referred to as the blue, green, and red cones, respectively, but many dislike this practice.)

The photochemicals of the cones, like the photochemical rhodopsin in the rods, are said to obey the **principle of univariance**. Univariance refers to the fact that the input to a cone varies in two dimensions (intensity and wavelength), but its output varies only in one dimension (strength of hyperpolarization). For this reason, no single type of photoreceptor can distinguish in its response between changes in stimulus intensity and stimulus color. Increasing hyperpolarization, for example, will result if either the intensity of the stimulus is increased or the wavelength of the stimulus is changed to one of more efficient absorption. Thus, each individual class of cones by itself is as color-blind as the rods. Color vision must therefore depend on the three classes of cones as a system, rather than the independent functioning of any single class of cones.

Opponent Processes   In contrast to Young's and Helmholtz's trichromatic color theories, an alternative type of theory was formulated to account for other behavioral facts about color vision. Many students of vision, including the Italian artist Leonardo da Vinci and the German poet Johann von Goethe, have argued that there "naturally" seem to be four truly primary colors: red, yellow, green, and blue. This idea is based on a number of observations. For example, although red and green light mix to produce yellow, no one would ever describe yellow as a "reddish green"; in contrast, terms such as "reddish-yellow" or "bluish-green" seem perfectly acceptable; there is something subjectively primary about yellow, even as a mixture, that does not seem to be true of other mixed colors. Furthermore, pairs of these "fundamental" colors appear to be opposites of each other; a number of perceptual illusions indicate that red and green are opposite colors, as are blue and yellow. Therefore, there appear to be perceptual phenomena in color vision that are not accounted for by trichromacy theory.

On the basis of such data, Ewald Hering, a professor of physiology at the Universities of Prague and Leipzig, proposed in 1874 that color vision is mediated by a system of **opponent processes** within the retina. One process encodes the dimension of red versus green, a second encodes blue versus yellow, and a third—not related to color vision—signals black versus white. At first appearance, such a color opposition arrangement would appear to be incompatible with the idea of trichromacy.

In fact, in the human retina, about 60% of all ganglion cells are color sensitive. These cells appear to receive excitatory and inhibitory input from different classes of cones. Most common are cells contrasting input from the M cones and inhibitory input from the L cones or the reverse pattern. Most of these cells also have the familiar concentric center-surround receptive field organization. Thus, a typical cell might receive excitatory input from the L cones located in the central portion of its receptive field and inhibitory input from M cones located in the surround.

Cells receiving opposing input from the M and L wavelength cones show a spectral response pattern that corresponds to the difference between the spectral absorption curves of the two types of cells; the largest differences between these curves occur at both shorter and longer wavelengths of the individual contributing cones. Such cells respond maximally to red light and are inhibited by light in the green range. These ganglion cells are often referred to as red-green cells. They function to magnify the rather small differences in spectral absorption that characterize the M and L wavelength cones. In this way, color discrimination is enhanced.

The short-wavelength cones constitute a small fraction of the primate retina. These cones also contribute to an opponent process but one that contrasts their output to the mixed output of M and L wavelength recep-

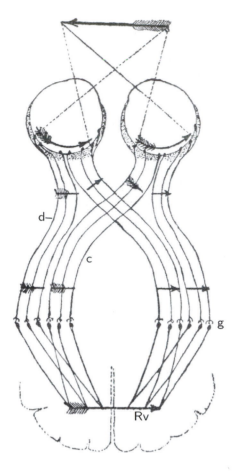

Figure 5.13. Cajal's View of the Visual Pathway. Here, the visual scene is represented by a feathered arrow. In Ramón y Cajal's notation: (c) the nasal portion of the optic nerve, (d) the temporal portion of the optic nerve, (g) the lateral geniculate nucleus, and (Rv) the right primary visual cortex. (From Santiago Ramón y Cajal, *Histologie du systeme nerveux de l'homme et des vertebres.* Paris: A. Maloine, 1909-1911.)

tors. Because both M and L cones contribute equally to this opponent system, they effectively produce a spectral absorption curve that peaks in the yellow region of the spectrum. Ganglion cells that are sensitive to input from the relatively rare S cones appear to always have an on-center with S cone input and an off-surround with mixed M and L cone input. Such ganglion cells are commonly referred to as blue-yellow cells and constitute about 6% of the ganglion cells in the primate retina.

Because most ganglion cells encode both spatial features of the stimulus (center-surround receptive field organization) and color information (differential input from the S, M, and L cones), both types of information are relayed to the central nervous system for further analysis. It is the neurons of the central nervous system that must ultimately be responsible for disentangling the complex spatial and chromatic messages by the retinal ganglion cells.

Color Blindness   Color blindness is an abnormality or deficit of normal color vision that usually results from abnormalities of the cones themselves. The most common type of color blindness is **dichromacy**, in which the observer behaves as if one type of cone is missing. Dichromatic individuals can match any color with a mixture of only two wavelengths of light, rather than the three required by color-normal individuals, the observation for which the disorder was named. The condition is genetically determined, affecting about 4% of males but only 0.5% of females. In these individuals, either the M or the L wavelength photochemical is missing. Cases of congenital absence of the S photochemical are extremely rare and are not sex linked.

Other types of genetic color blindness also occur, with differing degrees of rarity. In **anomalous trichromacy**, all three types of cones are present, but the absorption spectra of the photochemicals are altered. In **monochromacy**, only a single type of cone is present; other types of monochromacy involve a complete absence of cones and a total dependence on the rod system for vision. Monochromatism in any form is rare.

Color blindness also can be acquired during life. Infections of the retina, diabetes mellitus, and chronic alcoholism are all known to produce acquired color deficiencies. These disorders do not resemble genetic color blindness and frequently involve a deterioration of the already rare short-wavelength cones.

THE VISUAL PATHWAY

The bundles of ganglion cell axons that leave each eye form the two optic nerves (see Figure 5.14 on the facing page). Within each of these nerves, a **retinotopic organization** is maintained; that is, axons from ganglion cells near each other in the retina remain near each other in the optic nerve. In this way, important spatial aspects of the visual stimulus are retained in transmission to the central nervous system. A century-old drawing by Santiago Ramón y Cajal showing this relationship more schematically is shown in Figure 5.13.

On the way to the brain, each optic nerve divides into two branches, one proceeding centrally on the ipsilateral (same) side of the brain and the

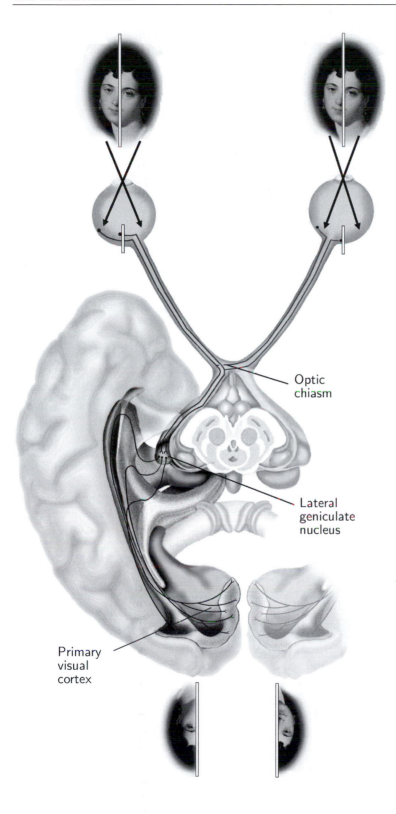

Optic chiasm

Lateral geniculate nucleus

Primary visual cortex

Figure 5.14. The Visual Pathway. Retinotopically organized visual information leaves the retina by the optic nerve, which is composed of the axons of retinal ganglion cells. At the optic chiasm, each nerve splits so that all fibers originating in the nasal hemiretina (the half of the retina nearest the nose) cross the midline and continue to the opposite side of the brain. Fibers originating in the temporal hemiretina (the half nearest the temples) continue on to the same side of the brain. This arrangement permits information from corresponding parts of the retina of the two eyes to be processed together in the brain. The optic nerve fibers synapse at the lateral geniculate nucleus (LGN) of the thalamus. The LGN, in turn, sends information to the primary visual cortex (Brodmann's area 17).

other crossing the midline to synapse on the contralateral (opposite) side. The point at which the optic nerve divides is called the **optic chiasm**; as the axons of the retinal ganglion cells depart the optic chiasm, they form the **optic tracts**.

The division of the human optic nerves is orderly. In development, each retina is divided in half along a vertical line passing through the fovea. The medial **hemiretina** (the half of each retina), nearer the nose, is termed the *nasal hemiretina*; similarly, the lateral half of each retina, being nearer the temples, is the *temporal hemiretina*. At the optic chiasm, fibers from ganglion cells in the nasal hemiretina cross the midline, whereas fibers originating in the lateral hemiretina do not. However, there is some overlap of visual information from the midline being represented in both the nasal and temporal pathways. The crossing of fibers from the nasal hemiretina has the effect of routing information from the same portions of the retina, and therefore the same portions of the visual world, to the same regions of the central visual system.

Some fibers of the optic nerve send secondary collateral branches to visual areas of the brain stem, primarily to the superior colliculus. The **superior colliculus** is a primitive visual center located on the dorsal surface of the midbrain. The superior colliculus sends its own output to a variety of other brain structures. Of particular importance is the projection to deeper layers of the colliculus, which are involved in the control of eye, head, and body movements. These neurons initiate and regulate **saccadic eye movements**, the rapid direct movements of the eyes that shift the line of gaze from one portion of the visual field to another. The collicular system functions to integrate the visual world with the world of the body. It controls visual orientation, moving the eyes, head, and body to focus objects of interest within the central retina . Thus, the superior colliculus regulates visual orientation and, in so doing, provides the basis for more complex analysis of visual information by the evolutionarily more recent visual systems of the forebrain.

Collateral branches of the optic tract also innervate the **pretectal area** of the brain stem. Neurons in the pretectal area of the midbrain project to the **Edinger-Westphal nucleus**, a portion of the nucleus of the third cranial nerve. One major function of the Edinger-Westphal nucleus is the regulation of the parasympathetic innervation of the muscles of the iris. It is the pathway from retina to pretectal area to the Edinger-Westphal nucleus that controls the pupillary response to light. The pretectal region participates in a number of other visual reflexes.

The Lateral Geniculate Nucleus The principal target of the optic nerve is the lateral geniculate nucleus of the thalamus. The **lateral geniculate nucleus (LGN)** is the thalamic relay nucleus for the visual system. Incoming fibers from the retina synapse directly on the principal neurons of the LGN, which, in turn, send their own axons to the cerebral cortex. Axons of LGN neurons pass through the white matter of the cortex as a widening sheet of fibers that together form the **optic radiations**. The LGN is considered a relay nucleus because little synaptic processing takes place there; the function of the LGN appears to be the reliable transmission of visual information from the eye to the cortex.

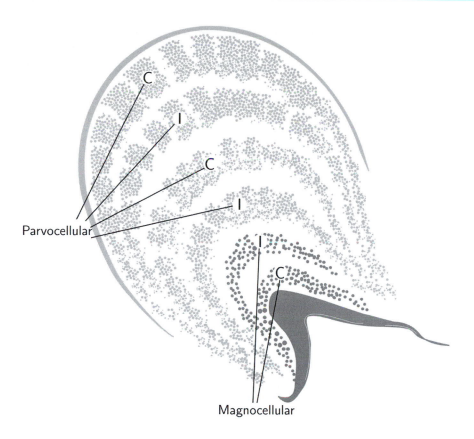

Parvocellular

Magnocellular

Figure 5.15. Lateral Geniculate Nucleus (LGN). The primate LGN has six layers. The two most ventral layers are composed of large cells and constitute the *magnocellular system.* The remaining four layers are composed of small cells and form the *parvocellular system.* It is the parvocellular system that is responsible for high-acuity vision. All cells in the LGN are strictly monocular; that is, they receive input from only one of the two eyes. The arrangement of the ipsilateral (I) and contralaterally (C) driven layers is indicated.

The lateral geniculate nucleus in primates is composed of six distinct layers, as shown in Figure 5.15. The two ventral layers differ both anatomically and functionally from the four dorsal layers. Anatomically, the two ventral layers, containing primarily large cells, form the **magnocellular subdivision** of the LGN. In contrast, the cells of the four dorsal layers making up the **parvocellular subdivision** are much smaller. Each eye projects to one of the magnocellular layers and two of the parvocellular layers. All layers contain a complete representation of the hemiretina, and all six representations are in precise alignment (Hubel & Wiesel, 1961).

In both systems, cells have circular receptive fields, and about 90% have an antagonistic center-surround organization. About half of these respond to center stimulation by increasing their rate of firing; the other half show the opposite pattern. The remaining 10% of the cells exhibit no center-surround antagonism. Despite these similarities, there are major differences in receptive field properties of neurons in the parvocellular and magnocellular systems (see Figure 5.16 on the next page).

One major difference is in acuity. As in the retina, the size of the receptive fields in both divisions of the LGN varies with retinotopic position; receptive fields in the central fovea are very small, whereas more peripheral fields become increasingly large. This is to be expected because the central fovea mediates the most detailed pattern vision.

The parvocellular system seems to be designed for high spatial acuity.

At any position on the retina, the receptive fields of magnocellular neurons are two to three times larger than are the corresponding receptive fields in the parvocellular system. Thus, the parvocellular system is capable of detecting much finer features in the visual image.

A second difference between these two divisions of the LGN is in their response to color. About 90% of the parvocellular neurons are color sensitive, whereas magnocellular neurons are not. In the parvocellular system, the antagonistic receptive fields are arranged to subtract and compare input from different cone systems. For example, a parvocellular neuron may receive excitatory input from red cones in the center of its receptive field and inhibitory input from green cones in the surround. Not only will such a neuron carry contrast information (it will be excited by a spot of white light in its center and inhibited by a similar spot in its surround), but it will also encode color information as well. It will be excited by diffuse red light (because its center will be differentially stimulated) and inhibited by diffuse green light (which selectively stimulates the surround). In contrast, cells in the magnocellular system sum input from all types of cones in both the center and the surround. For this reason, they are contrast sensitive and color insensitive. Magnocellular neurons are also more sensitive to moving stimuli and to very low levels of contrast between center and surround in their receptive fields.

Thus, neurons of the parvocellular and magnocellular division of the lateral geniculate nucleus have very different functional properties. They differ in spatial acuity, color sensitivity, motion sensitivity, and contrast detection. These two subdivisions represent specialized functional streams of information that are kept separated in the LGN and remain separated as they project to the cerebral cortex (Hubel & Livingston, 1987; Livingstone & Hubel, 1987a, 1987b, 1988; Wandell, 1995).

Figure 5.16. Deficits Following Destruction of the Magnocellular and Parvocellular Divisions of the Lateral Geniculate Nucleus (LGN). The parvocellular division of the LGN is responsible for high-acuity vision, whereas the magnocellular division specializes in motion detection. (Adapted from Schiller, P. H., & Logothetis, N. K. [1990], The color-opponent and broadband channels of the primate visual system. *Trends in Neuroscience, 13*, 392-398.)

Function	Parvocellular Lesion	Magnocellular Lesion
Color Vision	Severe	None
Texture Perception	Severe	None
Pattern Perception	Severe	None
Fine Shape Perception	Severe	None
Coarse Shape Perception	Mild	None
3D Vision	Severe	None
Motion Perception	None	Moderate
Flicker Perception	None	Severe

STRIATE CORTEX

The LGN projects directly to the **primary visual cortex**, the first of the many cortical areas to process visual information. The primary visual cortex is also known by several other names. Early anatomists called it the **striate cortex**, from the striped or banded appearance given to it by the optic radiations as they synapse in this region. It is also referred to both as **area 17**, a designation taken from classical cytoarchitectural maps drawn by Korbinian Brodmann at the beginning of this century, and as **V1**, or the first visual area.

The striate cortex is located at the posterior tip and the adjacent medial surface of the occipital lobe in humans. The pathway from the retina from the LGN to the striate cortex constitutes the **geniculostriate pathway**. In turn, the striate cortex sends information to other cortical regions involved in visual information processing.

The striate cortex of the human brain appears as a sheet of neuronal tissues about 1.5 mm in thickness. This thin sheet is composed of six distinct layers, which differ in prominence in different cortical areas.

Each of these layers is distinguished by features of the cells that it contains. For example, the outermost layer of the cortex, Layer 1, contains virtually no cell bodies; instead, it is a region of synaptic connection between axons and dendrites of neurons located in the deeper laminae. Layers 2 and 4 form the outer and inner granular layers, respectively; they are so named because they contain large numbers of granule cells; these tiny cells look like grains of sand when viewed microscopically.

Granule cells are local circuit neurons, lacking long axons. The granular layers are much expanded in the visual cortex, as compared to other regions of the cerebral hemispheres, perhaps indicating that the small granular cells play a particularly important role in processing sensory information. Layer 4 also serves as the primary region of input to area 17; projections from the LGN synapse in Layer 4.

The larger, long-axoned pyramidal cells are concentrated in Layers 3 and 5. However, these layers are much reduced in size in the visual cortex as compared with other brain areas. Large pyramidal cells function as output fibers for the cerebral cortex, sending their axons to other regions of cortex and to deeper structures of the brain. Layer 6 also contains other large efferent neurons that are similar to the pyramidal cells in many ways.

Thus, in its laminar structure, the visual cortex is characterized by a dense accumulation of the small granular cells and a relative lack of pyramidal or other large efferent cells. Exactly the opposite pattern may be seen in the motor regions of the cerebral cortex.

Receptive Field Properties

Most cells in the striate cortex respond most vigorously to lines or edges, rather than to spots or rings of light. Hubel and Wiesel—who received the Nobel Prize for their work in 1981—identified two principal types of these orientation-sensitive neurons, which they termed simple and complex cortical cells (see Hubel, 1982).

Simple Cortical Cells   A **simple cortical cell** is characterized by receptive fields with clearly defined antagonistic regions in the form of bars or edges; the receptive field of a simple cortical cell is defined both by its retinal position and angle of orientation (Hubel, 1982). Figure 5.17 on the facing page illustrates the receptive field of a representative simple cortical cell. Each receptive field has distinct excitatory and inhibitory regions. But because these receptive fields are long and thin, spots of light are rather ineffective stimuli for simple cortical cells. Far more effective is a bar or line of light that falls only in the excitatory region of the cell's receptive field and not at all in the inhibitory region. For this reason, simple cortical cells function as line or edge detectors. These neurons are well suited for defining contours or boundaries separating objects from the background.

Simple cortical cells show both position and orientation specificity in response to stimulation by a bar of light. It can be seen that this cell responds only to a particular pattern of light and dark. When the bar of light is positioned exactly on its excitatory region, the simple cortical cell responds vigorously; as the bar is rotated, the cell's response declines rapidly. The simple cortical cell responds selectively to a particular visual feature, a line of light at a specific location and orientation on the retina.

Complex Cortical Cells   A **complex cortical cell** has a somewhat larger receptive field than does a simple cortical cell and—like a simple cell—is specific with respect to the angle of orientation of its preferred stimulus input (Hubel, 1982).

However, complex cortical cells are not position specific; a line in the correct orientation anywhere within its receptive field will act to excite the complex cortical cell. These receptive fields cannot be mapped by using small spots of light because they are not divided into fixed excitatory and inhibitory regions. Figure 5.18 on page 166 illustrates the response of a complex cortical cell to various visual stimuli. In a sense, a complex cell responds to visual features of a higher order than does a simple cortical cell; the complex cell abstracts information about the orientation of lines within a general region of the retina and discards specific information concerning exact position. For this reason, a complex cell will not be sensitive to small eye movements and other factors that affect the exact positioning of features of the visual stimulus on the retina.

End-Stopped Cells   Hubel and Wiesel originally described a number of cells with even more complicated receptive field patterns. Some were like the complex cells, responding vigorously to a line of light at a particular orientation anywhere within their receptive fields. However, unlike the complex cells, the strength of their response diminished if the line extended outside the measured receptive field area on one or both ends. These cells would not, therefore, respond well to an extended line or edge but could respond optimally if the stimulus terminated in the vicinity of the cell's receptive field. Such neurons would be well suited for detecting corners of objects and other boundaries.

Hubel and Wiesel initially called these neurons "hypercomplex cells," but today the term *end-stopped* is more widely used. An **end-stopped cell** responds best to a line of light at the preferred orientation that falls within

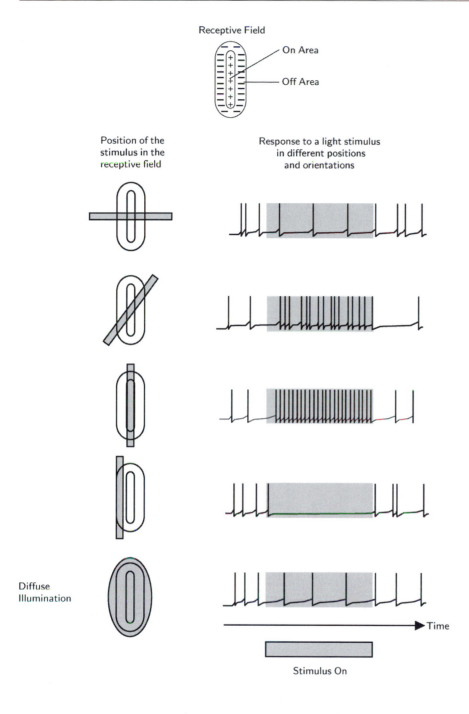

Receptive Field

On Area

Off Area

Position of the
stimulus in the
receptive field

Response to a light stimulus
in different positions
and orientations

Diffuse
Illumination

Time

Stimulus On

Figure 5.17. The Response of a Simple Cortical Cell to a Bar of Light in Various Orientations. Top: the map of the receptive field of the cell. Bottom: the response of the cell to a bar of light as it is rotated through 180 degrees and the response of the cell to spots of light in both the center and the surround.

the excitatory region of its receptive field and does not extend beyond that region. Thus, the receptive field of an end-stopped cell includes a hidden, inhibitory area that abuts the excitatory receptive field. Both simple and complex cells may be end-stopped (Hubel & Wiesel, 1962; Hubel, 1982).

One way of understanding the transformation in receptive field properties between lateral geniculate, simple cortical, and complex cortical cells and beyond is provided by a simple serial model. This idea suggests that

Figure 5.18. The Response of a Complex Cortical Cell to a Bar of Light. This cell responds vigorously to a vertical bar of light anywhere within its receptive field. It gives no response to lines of somewhat different orientation.

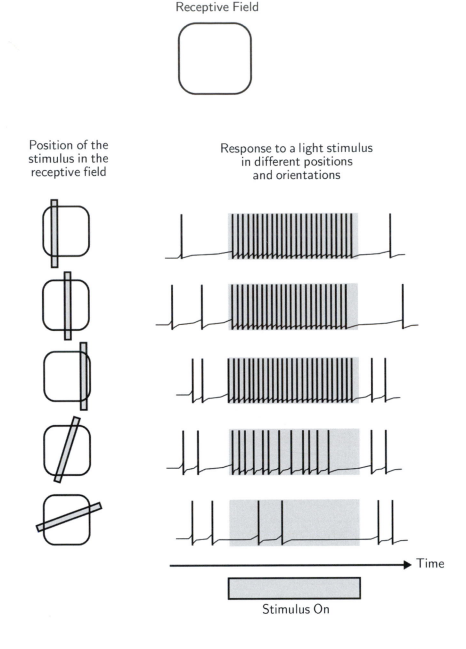

Receptive Field

Position of the stimulus in the receptive field

Response to a light stimulus in different positions and orientations

Time

Stimulus On

each level of cells in the visual system provides input to the next. Thus, the elongated pattern that is characteristic of simple cortical cells could result from the selective excitatory input from a number of LGN cells, the receptive fields of which are arranged in a line on the retina.

Similarly, complex cortical cells might receive input from a number of simple cortical cells, all sharing the same angle of orientation but differing in the exact retinal position of their receptive fields. If these connections were excitatory, then the complex cortical cell would be expected to fire whenever any of the simple cortical cells that drive it are activated. In this way, angle of orientation, but not positional information, would be preserved.

One of the strengths of the serial model is its ability to account for the orderly extraction of progressively more complex visual features by successive stages of neurons within the striate cortex. Direct confirmation of the hypothesis would require a detailed analysis of the synaptic connections between a number of cortical neurons as well as identification of the functional characteristics of each cell; such a definitive analysis seems technically impossible at this time.

Finally, and more optimistically, recent neural simulation analyses suggest that these orientation- and localization-specific simple cortical cells could easily have evolved if the visual system were under selective pressure to develop highly efficient neural codes for complex, naturally occurring scenes. Olshausen and Field (1996) tested this hypothesis by using *encoding sparseness* or the efficiency of representations in real-world stimuli as a criterion in training a mathematical neural net model to process visual stimuli. They discovered that by rewarding efficient encoding alone, simulated cortical neurons developed coding properties that are very similar to real simple cortical cells in the primate visual system. This suggests that the primate visual system may be specifically adapted to the features of the real world that all real visual systems must encode.

Retinotopic Organization

The flow of information from the retina, through the lateral geniculate nucleus, to the cortex maintains spatial order. This retinotopic organization ensures that objects that are adjacent to each other in the visual world are processed by adjacent sets of neurons at higher levels of the visual system; in this way, the spatial pattern of light and dark arriving at the retina is preserved at the cortical level.

Not all areas of the retina receive equal space in the striate cortex. Rather, equal distances in the visual field are expanded logarithmically in the striate cortex as a function of their proximity to the central fovea. In this way, more brain space is given to the detailed processing of stimuli that fall on the fovea. Thus, the retinotopic organization of area 17 maintains the spatial arrangement of the visual input but selectively magnifies that portion of the input falling on the more foveal regions of retina. This arrangement is shown in Figure 5.19 on the following page.

There are patterns of organization within the retinotopic organization of the primary visual cortex that reflect the physiological or functional properties of cortical neurons. The columnar organization of the visual cortex, first discovered by Hubel and Wiesel in their investigations of cortical receptive field patterns, represents a fundamental advance in unlocking the riddles of cerebral function (Hubel, 1982; Wandell, 1995).

The receptive fields of neurons in striate cortex may be mapped by systematically moving a microelectrode through the cortex of a restrained and anesthetized animal. As the electrode approaches a cortical neuron, the neuron's firing can be recorded. In this way, an active cortical neuron is located; its receptive field is mapped by systematically changing the visual

Figure 5.19. The Retinotopic Organization of Striate Cortex. Top: a map of the visual field divided into sectors. Bottom: the left and right posterior medial cortex, showing the mapping of the sectors onto the primary visual cortex.

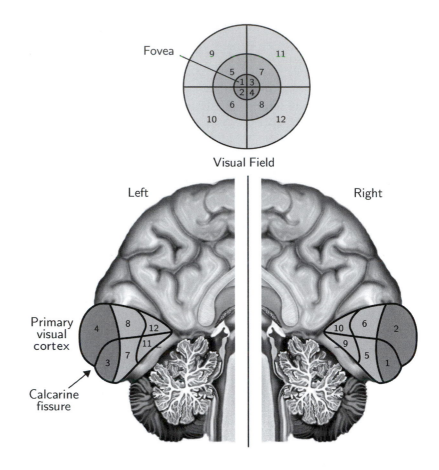

input while recording the firing of the cell. When the electrode pathway is perfectly perpendicular to the cortical surface, all cells encountered share three properties: Their receptive fields are in the same small region of the retina, the angle of orientation for the best response is identical, and all cells respond most effectively to stimuli presented to the same eye. However, if the electrode is moved just a few millimeters before insertion, one or more aspects of the cells' response are changed.

This finding provides evidence of cortical columns. A **cortical column** is a functional arrangement of neurons in the cortex in which there is intense vertical communication between neurons within the same column but rather little lateral communication between neurons of adjacent columns. This pattern of columnar organization is now known to be a fundamental property of neural interconnection in many regions of the cerebral cortex.

Two systems of functional columns in the visual cortex appear to operate independently of each other. The **ocular dominance columns** are slabs of cerebral cortex about 1 mm in width that are preferentially excited by input from the right or left eye. Right- and left-eye ocular dominance columns alternate across the visual cortex.

In contrast, **orientation columns** are much thinner, about 50 microns in width. Within each orientation column, all simple and complex cortical cells show the same angle of orientation. As the recording electrode passes from one orientation column into its neighbor, a shift of preferred orientation of about 10 degrees may be seen. This kind of step-by-step rotation between adjacent columns proceeds in an orderly manner; a complex rotation of 180 degrees occurs over a space of about 1 mm. Such a set of adjacent orientation columns covering all possible angles of orientation is termed a **hypercolumn**.

Cytochrome Oxidase Blobs   The organization of the color vision system in area 17 has long been puzzling. Although color-sensitive cells had been reported in the earliest microelectrode studies, their occurrence appeared to be sporadic. However, a major advance in understanding the representation of color in the striate cortex has resulted from an apparently unrelated development: the discovery of **cytochrome oxidase blobs**.

Cytochrome oxidase is a mitochondrial enzyme that plays an important role in the oxidative metabolism. This enzyme is not evenly distributed throughout the striate cortex but rather is concentrated in tiny patches, now known as cytochrome oxidase blobs. The cytochrome oxidase blobs are organized in parallel rows that are exactly aligned with the ocular dominance columns. The correspondence between the blobs and the ocular dominance columns is demonstrated by the fact that removal of one eye leads to the disappearance of alternate rows of blobs.

Cells located within the blob are very different from the other neurons of striate cortex. These cells lack orientation specificity but instead are color coded in a manner similar to those seen in the lateral geniculate nucleus. Both anatomical and physiological evidence suggests that the cytochrome oxidase blobs contain a neuronal system that imparts color to the spatial image of the world created by the orientation-specific cells of the hypercolumns of the primary visual cortex.

Cortical Modules   The discovery of cytochrome oxidase blobs and their association with ocular dominance columns has provided additional support to the powerful concept of cortical function, the idea of modular small-scale cortical organization. Each **module** of striate cortex is composed of two hypercolumns and two cytochrome oxidase blobs, one pair driven by the right eye and the other by the left eye (see Figure 5.20 on the next page). All cells within this module share a common **aggregate receptive field**; that is, they process visual information from the same region of the retina. Adjacent modules have nonoverlapping aggregate receptive fields. Other possible arrangements of the interior details of a module also have been suggested by Blasdel and Salama (1986) and Blasdel, Obermayer, and Kiorpes (1995).

Each module of the striate cortex contains all the necessary neuronal machinery to completely process visual input from the part of the retina that it serves. Contour or orientation information coming from either eye is processed by the hypercolumn associated with that eye. Color information is analyzed by the appropriate cytochrome oxidase blob. Once these analyses have been completed, the results are transmitted to other regions of the cortex.

Figure 5.20. One View of a Module in Striate Cortex. In the ice cube model—named for its rectilinear structure—each module is composed of two hypercolumns, one with right and the other with left ocular dominance. Each hypercolumn, in turn, consists of a full set of columns with a full 180° of preferred angle of orientation. Each hypercolumn also contains a pair of cytochrome oxidase blobs. All cells in the module share the same aggregate receptive field.

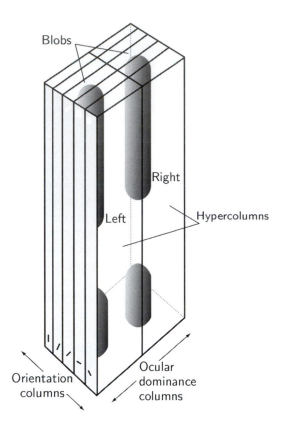

Thus, the striate cortex may be thought of as a series of a few thousand cortical modules, each serving a different region of the retina. Each module is identical in its cellular structure, inputs, outputs, and the computations that it performs. In understanding one module, the workings of the entire striate cortex may be known.

EXTRASTRIATE VISUAL AREAS

Although the striate cortex is the only area of the primate cerebrum to receive visual information from the lateral geniculate nucleus, it is not the only region of the cortex to process visual information. At least 32 separate areas of the cortex are responsive to visual stimuli. Some of these lie within Brodmann's areas 18 and 19, adjacent to the primary visual cortex. Others are located within the temporal and parietal lobes, forming a dorsal and a ventral chain that rejoin each other in visual association areas of the frontal cortex (Maunsell & Newsome, 1987; Essen, Anderson, & Felleman, 1992).

Each extrastriate visual area is unique in several ways. The extrastriate visual cortical areas differ in **cytoarchitecture**, or characteristic patterns of cellular organization. Each visual area is now known to have its own unique structural arrangements of cells in the cortical lamina. These areas also differ in their patterns of connectivity. **Connectivity** refers to the pattern of projections that cells in an area send and receive. Every cortical area has a unique pattern of incoming and outgoing pathways. Finally—

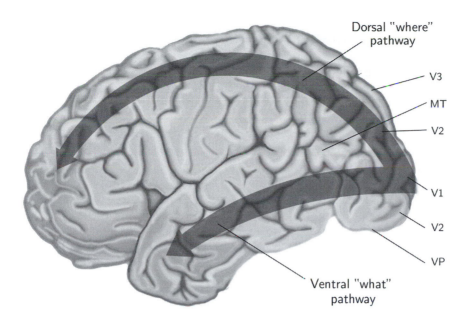

Dorsal "where" pathway

V3

MT

V2

V1

V2

VP

Ventral "what" pathway

Figure 5.21. Visual Areas of the Human Brain. In humans, many of the early visual areas are located on the medial surface of the cortex. Here, portions of V1, V2, and V3 may be seen, along with area MT. These areas form two major streams that carry "where" information dorsally through the parietal lobes and "what" information ventrally through the temporal lobes. These streams converge in the frontal cortex.

to the extent that they are understood—the 32 extrastriate visual areas also differ in *function*. Each area appears to process a different aspect of visual information.

Many visual areas, such as the striate cortex, are retinotopically organized, containing a single representation of a visual hemifield. Mapping of the hemifield is one way of defining the visual area. No visual area contains more than one retinotopic map. However, some cortical areas seem to have only partial maps, processing information from either the upper or the lower quadrant of the visual field, rather than from the entire hemifield. Other areas appear to have no real retinotopic organization; these areas are probably involved in higher aspects of visual information processing. Despite such exceptions, the presence of retinotopic organization has been an extraordinarily useful method of establishing the boundaries of extrastriate visual areas.

In studying primates, such as the owl monkey, a system of naming cortical regions that was originally devised by physiologists, rather than anatomists, is often employed. In this terminology, V1 corresponds to the striate cortex; V2, V3, V4, and similar designations constitute additional visual areas, as shown in Figure 5.21.

The functional properties of such extrastriate visual areas are now beginning to be understood. In V2, for example, many cells are sensitive to the disparity of images between the two eyes. Often, these cells require binocular input to yield a response. Such cells would be well suited for processing depth information on the basis of the differential projections of images on the retinae of the two eyes. Cells in V2 may also be involved in processing higher-order features of visual stimuli, such as the recognition of visual textures.

In V3, cells tend to have larger receptive fields than in the striate cortex, some of which show color selectivity. Similarly, many cells in V4 are also color sensitive as well.

In contrast, in V5 or MT (midtemporal cortex), few neurons show color selectivity, but many are movement sensitive. These cells are tuned for sensing a wide range of velocities and directions of movement. About half the cells are also disparity selective. By processing both retinal disparity and velocity of movement, area MT is well suited for the analysis of objects moving in three-dimensional space.

This analysis of the functions of the extrastriate visual areas leads to the conclusion that each visual area is a unique information-processing structure. Each has its own individual cellular structure for cytoarchitecture. Each area has a characteristic pattern of input and output pathways, linking it to other functional areas of the cortex. Each area has a unique set of computations that it performs on its input. By understanding the nature of these visual areas and their interconnections, an understanding of visual perception itself becomes a realistic possibility.

Hierarchy of Visual Areas   The multiple visual areas of the primate cerebral cortex appear to be organized in a hierarchical manner. *Hierarchical organization* means that they are grouped into interconnected ascending tiers of complexity. Evidence for this idea comes from the analysis of the patterns of interconnection between the visual areas of the cortex, provided by van Essen and his collaborators (Felleman & Essen, 1991). By using recently developed neuronal staining techniques, at least 300 pathways connecting the visual areas have been identified. In all known cases, these pathways occur in reciprocal pairs: If Area A projects to Area B, B also invariably projects to A. Thus, all connections between cortical visual areas are bidirectional.

Although these reciprocal connections are bidirectional, most are not symmetric. The *ascending pathway* bringing visual information from the lateral geniculate nucleus to the striate cortex (V1 in monkeys) terminates in Layer 4, as do all projections from V1 to other visual areas. Thus, it is reasonable to infer that ascending pathways elsewhere in the cortical visual system are also marked anatomically by their termination in the fourth cortical layer. Therefore, the reciprocal pathway, which does not synapse in Layer 4, must be a descending pathway.

Working from these assumptions, it is possible to construct a hierarchical flowchart for the 32 known and suspected visual areas of the macaque monkey, which is shown in simplified form in Figure 5.22 on the next page. There are 300 known reciprocal pathways connecting these areas (Essen, Anderson, & Felleman, 1992). Most interconnections are of the asymmetric ascending- and descending-type pairings. They permit the cortical regions to be arranged into a hierarchical structure with only about a dozen distinct levels. There are also some reciprocal pathways that do not show the usual ascending-descending asymmetry. These symmetric pathways link areas located at the same level of the visual hierarchy.

Such an arrangement leads to a view of the visual cortex that is very elegant in its organization. Each visual area appears to serve as a specialized visual processor. Each area performs a particular set of computations on the information that it receives and then transmits its results to the other visual areas with which it is connected.

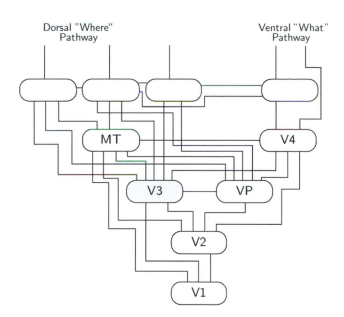

Figure 5.22. The Hierarchical Pattern of Connections of the Primate Visual Areas. The visual areas of the occipital, temporal, and parietal cortex form a pair of divergent, hierarchical streams of functional information in the primate brain. V1 is the cortical origin of visual sensory information. V2, V3, and VP are extrastriate areas that further process visual information. At higher levels, visual information splits into two separate pathways, a parietal or "where" pathway and a temporal or "what" pathway. These pathways rejoin each other in regions of the frontal cortex.

Motion Processing in Area MT   The idea that visual perception might be linked very directly to the activity of single cells in the higher visual areas has received support in a series of elegant experiments by William Newsome and his collaborators (Newsome, Britten, & Movshon, 1989; Salzman, Britten, & Newsome, 1990). Newsome studied the behavior of cells in area MT of the rhesus monkey, a fifth-level visual area concerned almost exclusively with the detection of motion. Like many visual areas, MT is retinotopically organized.

Newsome trained the monkeys to discriminate patterns of randomly moving dots presented to a small portion of the visual field while recording from single cells in area MT. In the one experiment, a restricted chemical lesion was made in a region of MT that corresponded to the retinotopic position of the visual stimulus. Following the lesion, motion detection performance dropped dramatically for that portion of the visual field but remained normal in other areas. Furthermore, another type of visual discrimination task—contrast judgment—was unaffected in this region. These results indicate that area MT is necessary for high-quality performance of the motion detection task.

In another experiment, detailed single-cell recordings were made in area MT of other rhesus monkeys as they performed the motion discrimination task. Newsome examined these recordings and attempted to predict whether a moving target had been presented on each experimental trial. In fact, the predictions corresponded almost exactly with the animal's actual performance. These results demonstrate that single cells in area MT have sufficient information to account for perception and performance of the motion discrimination task.

Knowing that MT was necessary for correct motion discrimination and that cells in that area had sufficient information to account for the behavior of the animal, Newsome then attempted to show that these cells in fact played a causal role in monkey motion perception. That was done by electrically stimulating small numbers of MT cells that had particular directional preferences for the moving dots. Newsome and his collaborators found that electrical stimulation of cells with a particular directional preference increased the tendency of the animals to report that the stimulus was moving in the direction favored by the stimulated cells, regardless of the direction in which the dots actually moved. This provides evidence that small groups of cells in area MT may actually play a causal role in determining the monkey's perception of visual motion.

PERCEPTUAL REPRESENTATION

At the outset of this chapter, three issues were raised. The first was the question of sensory transduction. How does the nervous system transform information contained in patterns of reflected light into the neural signals of changing cellular membrane potentials? The answer is that specialized visual receptor cells, the rods and cones of the eye, contain the unique biochemical machinery necessary to convert the absorption of light quanta into highly amplified membrane events.

The second issue was that of sensory coding. How does the nervous system extract significant and meaningful visual features from the patterns of activation occurring within the photoreceptor mosaic? Here, answers are less clear, but much has been learned in recent years concerning the receptive field properties of visual interneurons at different levels of the visual system from the retina to extrastriate cortex.

The third and most mysterious question is that of perceptual representation. How does our visual system create the perceptual world that each of us "sees" so convincingly? The answer to this question is fragmentary at best, but one thing seems clear. The visual world that we perceive is not always derived in a straightforward manner from the signals that the retina transmits to the brain. Some examples make that fact clear.

First is the issue of grain or resolution across the perceptual scene. We know about differences in grain from experiences with printed pictures. The coarse grain of black-and-white pictures printed in a cheap newspaper is obvious to us all. We can see the individual dots of varying density that make up the printed image. In contrast, the glossy photographic reproductions that appear in an expensive art book appear to be without grain, so fine are the individual elements that comprise the picture. Nonetheless, if we reexamine glossy photography with a magnifying lens, the grain of the photographic emulsion becomes apparent. It is impossible for us to confuse the representations provided by newspaper and art book photographs; they look so strikingly different.

Yet the grain of the information that our retina provides to our brain differs even more dramatically between the periphery of our visual field and the center of our line of gaze, a fact of which we are normally unaware. In fact, the receptive fields of retinal ganglion cells increase by a factor of 10 in diameter from the central fovea to the far periphery, producing similar differences in psychometrically measured visual acuity (Olzak & Thomas, 1986).

But more convincing evidence that our perceptual representation is not strictly dependent on sensory input comes from perceptual phenomena

arising from transient scotomas, as may occur in the period preceding the onset of migraine headache.

Figure 5.23. Karl Lashley's Scotoma. For a complete description, see the text.

Migraine is a headache of vascular origin, the headache itself resulting from a weakening and swelling of the blood vessels in the scalp (Dalessio & Silberstein, 1993). A pounding headache occurs as the force of each heartbeat stretches the walls of the blood vessels and produces pain. But in migraine headaches of the so-called classical type, the headache is preceded by a period in which the cerebral arteries, particularly the artery supplying the primary visual cortex, are constricted, temporarily reducing the supply of oxygen and glucose to regions of the striate cortex. The result is that portions of the striate cortex temporarily cease to function, producing a cortical blind spot in the affected area of the visual field. The blind spot is called a **scotoma**.

Karl Lashley, the great American neuropsychologist, was a chronic migraine sufferer who used his training in brain science to study the visual effects of his own migraine-induced scotomas. He was the first to report the curious phenomenon of visual completion within the scotoma in migraine, a finding that provides striking insight into the nature of perceptual representation (see Figure 5.23 on the preceding page). He described his observations in a 1941 report. He wrote,

> A scotoma may completely escape observation... unless it obscures some object to which attention is directed. Talking with a friend, I glanced just to the right of his face, whereon his head disappeared. His shoulders and necktie were still visible, but the vertical stripes in the wallpaper behind him seemed to extend right down to the necktie. Quick mapping revealed an area of total blindness covering about 30 degrees [in central vision]. It was quite impossible to see this as a blank area when projected on the striped wall or other uniformly patterned surface, although any intervening object failed to be seen.... [Filling in the blind spot must] represent some intrinsic organizing function of the cortex. The figures completed are reduplicated patterns or very simple symmetric figures. (Lashley, 1941, pp. 338-339)

Something similar but certainly less dramatic can be observed in our own nonpathological blind spots, the point at which the ganglion cell axons of each eye join together to exit the retina. There are no photoreceptors in this region, nor are their columns within the striate cortex awaiting such input. However, we do not notice the blind spots, in part because they are located in the peripheral rather than central retina and in part because of the cortical completion phenomenon. However, by looking at Figure 5.23 on the page before, you can experience something similar to what Lashley reported in his migrainous scotomas. Regular patterns appearing on either side of the blind spot are perceptually completed within it, even though there is no sensory input that supports such an erroneous perception.

Thus, we are left with the view that our visual brains create for each of us our visual worlds, based on evidence supplied by the photoreceptors but not limited to that input. The resulting perceptual representation serves each of us very well in doing the task for which the visual system was evolved, allowing us to respond adaptively to real objects sensed by the rods and cones of our eyes.

SUMMARY

The eye performs like an optical instrument, projecting a focused image of the external world onto the photoreceptors of the retina. There, photoreceptors are responsible for sensory transduction of visual information. The interneurons of the retina, particularly the horizontal and bipolar cells, extract information about contrast from the output of the photoreceptors and thereby begin the processing of visual objects.

Color vision is accomplished through the cone system of the central retina. This system exhibits trichromacy, a consequence of the fact that the cone system employs three types of photoreceptors with different spectral absorption characteristics. The trichromacy of the photoreceptors is transformed into a spectrally opponent system by the retinal interneurons.

The lateral geniculate is the thalamic nucleus that projects to primary visual cortex. The receptive fields of lateral geniculate neurons typically are circular with antagonistic center and surround regions. In primary visual cortex, receptive field organization changes from coding dots of contrast to the definition of line segments. This appears to be an essential step in defining visual objects.

The striate cortex shows several types of organization. Like other cortical regions, it has a laminar structure defined by a unique distribution of cell types. It also has a lateral retinotopic organization, in which information from the retina is represented once and only once in a topography-preserving pattern. Finally, there is vertical organization of columns, hypercolumns, modules, and cytochrome oxidase blobs.

The extrastriate visual cortex in primates is composed of three dozen or so separate cortical regions. Each has a unique cytoarchitecture, connectivity pattern, and functional properties. Many but not all of these regions are retinotopically organized. Each area appears to be functionally specialized and performs a unique set of computations in contributing to visual perception.

The visual system, then, extends from the photoreceptors of the retina through the extrastriate visual regions of the cerebral cortex. It is this neuronal system that creates for each of us our own visual worlds, the perceptual representation of the objects that surround us.

SELECTED READINGS

- Hubel, D. H. (1995). *Eye, brain, and vision* (2nd ed.). New York: Scientific American Library. A beautifully illustrated introduction to the functions of the visual system by a man who earned his Nobel Prize for its study. The book is clear, concise, and highly recommended.

- Rodieck, R. W. (1998). *The first steps in seeing*. Sunderland, MA: Sinauer. A marvelous and beautiful treatise on vision, from retina to cortex, that is quite unlike any other and highly recommended.

- Palmer, S. E. (1999). *Vision science: Photons to phenomenology*. Cambridge: MIT Press. A comprehensive and extremely readable introduction to vision from the perspective of cognitive science.

- Wandell, B. A. (1995). *Foundations of vision*. Sunderland, MA: Sinauer. An examination of the state of knowledge about the human visual system that emphasizes visual representation and the interpretation of visual information. An excellent introduction to computational aspects of contemporary visual science.

KEY TERMS

accommodation In vision, the focusing of the lens of the eye.

aggregate receptive field The receptive field common to all cells within a cortical column.

amacrine cell A neuron in the retina, the processes of which laterally synapse with bipolar and ganglion cells.

anomalous trichromacy A form of color blindness resulting from an abnormal distribution of the three types of cones.

antagonism Opposition between similar things; with respect to vision, the opposing effects of stimulation in the center and the surround of differentiated receptive fields.

anterior chamber The space between the lens and the cornea of the eye.

aqueous humor The watery fluid filling the anterior chamber of the eye.

area 17 See *striate cortex*.

bipolar cell In the retina, a cell forming a portion of the straight signal pathway that receives input from photoreceptors and horizontal cells and projects to amacrine and ganglion cells.

chlorolabe The cone photochemical that is most responsive to medium wavelength (green) light.

ciliary muscle A small muscle that controls the shape of the lens of the eye in accommodation.

complex cortical cell A type of cell in the visual cortex that responds most strongly to such stimuli as lines of light of specific orientation anywhere within the receptive field of the cell.

cones The cone-shaped photoreceptor cells of the central retina that mediate high-acuity color vision.

connecting cilium In photoreceptors, the threadlike tube of membrane connecting the inner and outer segments of the cell.

connectivity The pattern of projections that cells in a cortical region send and receive.

cornea The transparent structure covering the anterior of the eye.

cortical column A vertical grouping of cortical neurons, perpendicular to and extending throughout the six cortical laminae, that share common functional properties, such as orientation, ocular dominance, or spectral sensitivity.

cyanolabe The cone photochemical most responsive to short-wavelength (blue) light.

cytoarchitecture The characteristic laminar pattern of cellular organization.

cytochrome oxidase blobs An orderly array of patches in the striate cortex, staining intensely for the enzyme cytochrome oxidase, that contain cells that are color sensitive but not orientation specific.

dark current In photoreceptors, a depolarizing current flowing between the inner and outer segments that is greatest in darkness.

dichromacy The most common type of color blindness, in which one of the three types of cones is missing.

dilator pupillae Sympathetically innervated muscles within the iris that act to expand the pupil as they contract.

Edinger-Westphal nucleus The portion of the third nerve nucleus of the midbrain that mediates the pupillary light reflex, among other functions.

end-stopped cell A simple or complex cell that responds best to a line of light at a preferred orientation that does not extend beyond the measured receptive field of the cell.

erythrolabe The cone photochemical most responsive to long-wavelength (red) light.

extraocular muscle A muscle attached to the exterior of the eye that governs its position with respect to the head.

fovea The small depression in the central retina that is composed primarily of cones and is responsible for highest-acuity vision.

ganglion cell In the retina, visual interneurons that form the optic nerve.

ganglion cell layer The retinal layer containing the bodies of the ganglion cells.

geniculostriate pathway The visual system of the forebrain, including the lateral geniculate and the visual cortex.

hemiretina One half of the retina, divided by a vertical line through the fovea. The *nasal hemiretina* is the medial half, nearer the nose; the *temporal hemiretina* is the lateral half, nearer the temple.

horizontal cells In the retina, visual interneurons providing a lateral pathway for the outer plexiform layer.

hypercolumn An adjacent series of orientation columns in the visual cortex that span a full 180 degrees of receptive field angle.

inner nuclear layer The layer of the retina containing the cell bodies of horizontal, bipolar, and amacrine cells that is juxtaposed between the two plexiform layers.

inner plexiform layer The region of synaptic interaction between the inner nuclear and ganglion cell layers of the retina.

inner segment The cell body of a photoreceptor.

iris The circular pigmented membrane behind the cornea and surrounding the pupil that contains the dilator and sphincter pupillae.

lateral geniculate nucleus (LGN) The thalamic relay nucleus of the visual system.

lateral signal pathway In the retina, a pathway for the flow of information across the retina in the outer and inner plexiform layers that is provided by the horizontal and amacrine cells, respectively.

lens In the eye, the double-convex transparent body between the anterior and vitreous chambers that acts to focus images of the visual world on the retina.

macula The area of the retina, about 6 mm in diameter, that lies at the optical center of the eye.

magnocellular subdivision The two ventral layers of the lateral geniculate nucleus containing large cells.

module In the striate cortex, a pair of hypercolumns and cytochrome oxidase blobs of differing ocular dominance sharing the same aggregate receptive field.

monochromacy A type of color blindness in which only a single type of cone is present or in which only the rod system is functional.

ocular dominance column A slab of primary visual cortex about 1 mm in width that is preferentially excited by input from the right or left eye.

off-center bipolar cell A retinal bipolar cell that hyperpolarizes when the central region of its receptive field is illuminated.

off-center ganglion cell A retinal ganglion cell that is inhibited when the central region of its receptive field is illuminated.

on-center bipolar cell A retinal bipolar cell that depolarizes when the central region of its receptive field is illuminated.

on-center ganglion cell A retinal ganglion cell that is excited when the central region of its receptive field is illuminated.

opponent process In color vision, a neuron that responds vigorously to one but is suppressed by another wavelength of light in its receptive field.

opsin A class of complex proteins that combines with retinal to form a photochemical.

optic chiasm The place at which the medial portions of the optic nerves cross the midline.

optic nerves The cranial nerves formed by the axons of the retinal ganglion cells as they leave the eye.

optic radiations The spreading fiber tract formed by the axons of the lateral geniculate cells that project to the visual cortex.

optic tract The fiber tract formed by the axons of the retinal ganglion cells as they pass through the optic chiasm and proceed to the lateral geniculate nucleus.

orientation column A small slab of primary visual cortex about 50 microns in width, within which all simple and complex cortical cells show the same preferred angle of orientation.

outer nuclear layer The layer in the retina containing the cell bodies of the photoreceptors.

outer plexiform layer The region of synaptic interaction between outer and inner nuclear layers of the retina.

outer segment The specialized layered structure of a photoreceptor in which the absorption of a quantum of light energy by a molecule of photochemical begins the process of visual perception.

parvocellular subdivision The four dorsal layers of the lateral geniculate nucleus containing small cells.

perceptual representation In vision, the high-level internal image that we see as the world.

photopic vision The cone-based system that provides visual information at moderate to high levels of illumination, as in sunlight.

photoreceptor A receptor cell that responds efficiently to light; a rod or a cone.

pretectal area A collection of cell bodies in the midbrain that receives input from the optic tract and, in part, projects to the Edinger-Westphal nucleus, mediating the pupillary light reflex.

primary visual cortex See *striate cortex*.

principle of univariance Although visual stimuli may vary in both intensity and wavelength, the response of a photoreceptor is one-dimensional, varying only in the strength of its hyperpolarizing response.

pupil The circular opening of the iris of the eye.

receptive field The area of a receptor surface to which a sensory neuron responds; in vision, the area of the retina in which light stimuli influence the activity of the sensory neuron in question.

retina The layered sheet of neural tissue on the inner posterior surface of the eye containing photoreceptors and visual interneurons.

retinal An aldehyde of Vitamin A1 that, in its 11-cis form, may be combined with an opsin to form a photochemical.

retinotopic organization The orderly representation of visual information in visual system structures that preserves that relative location of retinal stimuli.

rhodopsin The photochemical of the rod system.

rods The rod-shaped photoreceptor cells of the peripheral retina.

saccadic eye movement A rapid movement of the eyes from one point of fixation to another.

scotoma A region of the visual field in which vision is absent or suppressed.

scotopic vision The rod-based system that provides visual information in near-total darkness, as on a starlit night.

sensory coding The transformation of sensory information by neural processing.

sensory interneurons All neurons of a sensory system that are not photoreceptors.

sensory transduction At receptor cells, a process of changing patterns of environmental energy into neuronal signals.

simple cortical cell A class of cell in the visual cortex that responds most vigorously to stimuli such as lines of light in a particular orientation and particular position in the visual field.

spectral absorption The function giving the probability that a particular substance will absorb light quanta as the wavelength of light is varied.

sphincter pupillae The parasympathetically innervated muscles of the iris that close the pupil as they contract.

straight signal pathway In the retina, the direct pathway formed by the bipolar and ganglion cells that act to carry information from the photoreceptors to more central structures.

striate cortex The sensory area of the cortex that receives input from the lateral geniculate nucleus. Also referred to as the primary visual cortex and Brodmann's area 17.

superior colliculus One of a bilateral pair of nuclei that protrude from the dorsal surface of the midbrain and are involved in visual orienting. The excitation of rhodopsin activates about 500 molecules of the GTP-binding protein.

transducin The GTP-binding protein triggered by rhodopsin.

trichromacy The fact that any perceptible color may be matched exactly by a mixture of three other lights of different wavelengths, provided that none of the three wavelengths may be matched by a mixture of the remaining two; a consequence of the three types of cones in the human visual system.

V1 See *striate cortex*.

vitreous chamber The spherical space within the eye between the lens and the retina.

vitreous humor The thick fluid filling the vitreous chamber of the eye.

Chapter 6

Auditory, Bodily, and Chemical Senses

In addition to seeing, we sense our bodies and our environments in many other, very different ways. In this chapter, we examine the auditory, vestibular, chemical, and bodily senses and find that many of the principles governing information processing in the visual system also apply to the other senses as well.

Like the visual system, the auditory system acts to obtain information about the environment by sensing vibrations of the air and transforming them into neural signals that we interpret as sound. Closely related to the auditory system is the vestibular system, which provides information concerning the position and movement of the head in space.

Smell and taste are chemical senses. Our olfactory systems are capable of detecting minute amounts of odorant molecules carried in the air that we breathe. The sense of taste provides information about the food that we are about to eat. These two primordial senses, on which the survival of many organisms depends, are less elaborately organized than the more complex sensory systems serving vision, audition, and tactile sensation.

Touch, pressure, and position are three aspects of bodily or somatic sensation. Together, they provide information concerning the environment as it contacts the body and the position of the body within the environment. Pain and temperature sensation—two primitive body senses—inform the brain about the well-being of the body. Although seeing, hearing, and dexterous touch created civilization, pain, thermal sense, smell, and taste have permitted the survival of the species.

HEARING

The sounds that we hear are vibrations of air molecules produced by moving objects, much like the ripples in a pond produced by a falling stone. The rumble of traffic, the music of an orchestra, the barking of a dog, the conversation of a friend—all result in fluctuations of air pressure that we hear as sound.

Consider the way in which a violin produces sound. As the rosin-covered bow is drawn across a string, vibrations are set up and transmitted to the soundboard, which amplifies the sound and sets its tonal quality. As the soundboard moves upward, it compresses the air, forcing air molecules closer together for an instant. When the soundboard moves downward, it momentarily draws air particles away from each other. It is the pattern of compression and rarefaction of air particles that we hear as sound.

It is important to note that the vibrating soundboard does not propel individual particles of air from its surface to the ear of the listener. Rather, air is an elastic medium that can be compressed. Individual particles simply move back and forth over very small distances, toward a momentary location of compression and away from a momentary location of rarefaction. It is the pressure wave that travels forward, not the gas molecules of the air. The pressure wave is like a ripple on a pond that travels away from a fallen stone; a speck of dust on the surface of the water does not follow the ripple—it only moves up and down as the wave passes by.

Sound waves may be characterized by their frequency and intensity. The **frequency** of a wave is measured by the number of cycles it completes in 1 second, which defines the unit **hertz (Hz)**. The pure tone produced by a tuning fork has but a single frequency. The sounds of musical instruments are more complex, being a mixture of related frequencies, or harmonics. Harmonics are multiples of the fundamental frequency being played; different musical instruments generate different patterns of harmonic tones, giving each instrument its characteristic sound.

Other sounds may not be described so easily. The rustle of leaves, the roar of an aircraft, and the speech of a person have unique and complicated frequency patterns. Natural phenomena produce sound energy over an extremely wide spectrum; however, the human auditory system responds only to sound waves between about 20 and 20,000 Hz. It is most sensitive to sounds in the 1,000 to 3,000 Hz range.

A sound is also characterized by its intensity. The **intensity** of a sound wave is usually measured in units of pressure because it is the pressure difference between the peak and the trough of the sound wave that is related most directly to perceived loudness. The range of intensities over which we can hear is very large. For this reason, a logarithmic measure, originally proposed by Alexander Graham Bell, is commonly used to express the intensity of a given sound with respect to the faintest sound that can be heard. This measure, the **decibel (dB)**, is defined as

$$SPL_{dB} = 20 \log_{10} \frac{P}{P_{ref}}$$

where SPL is sound pressure level, P is the pressure of the sound being measured, and P_{ref} is the reference pressure. Thus, a sound 10 times as intense as a reference has an SPL of 20 dB. Because the log of 10 = 1, the log of 100 = 2, the log of 1,000 = 3, and so on, it follows that each tenfold change in sound pressure level is represented by a 20-dB change in auditory intensity.

By convention, the reference pressure for the human auditory system is taken to be 0.0002 dyne/cm^2, which is approximately the intensity of the threshold for hearing a pure tone of 1,000 Hz. When this value is used as a reference for the decibel, the resulting numbers can be taken as a standard measure of SPL. The loudest sound that can be heard without pain is 1 million times (120 dB) greater in pressure than is the threshold reference. The decibel scale, to which the inventor of the telephone gave his name, is widely used in the study of hearing because it can represent a large range of stimulus intensities and relations between intensities in a convenient and meaningful manner.

Transduction in Hearing

For variations in air pressure to be perceived as sound requires a sensory receptor system to transform the mechanical stimulus into the language of neurons, variations in membrane potential. The **ear** is the organ that contains the sensory receptors for audition. It is a complex structure that is well adapted for the efficient sensing and encoding of auditory information. The ear is divided into three adjacent structures, each performing different but related functions in the process of auditory perception. Figure 6.1 on the following page illustrates its principal features.

The **outer ear** channels sound energy into the deeper structures of the ear. It is composed of two elements: the **pinna**, an external, funnel-shaped organ that protrudes from the side of the head, and the **external auditory meatus**, a tube that penetrates the skull and connects with the middle ear.

The pinna is particularly important in auditory localization because it more effectively captures sound energy arising from sources to the side and the front than from those in the rear. Humans capitalize on this property of the pinna by turning their heads when attempting to localize the unseen source of an interesting sound. Other animals, such as the cat and the horse, have highly developed muscular control of the pinna. Ear movements make an important contribution to sound localization in such animals.

The external auditory meatus serves as a passageway for sound energy to the middle ear. However, its physical properties are also of functional importance. Because of its shape and size, it selectively enhances the transmission of acoustic signals between 2,000 and 4,000 Hz, the region of the frequency spectrum that is used in human speech.

The **middle ear** provides the linkage between the airborne vibrations that are sound and the auditory receptor cells of the fluid-filled inner ear.

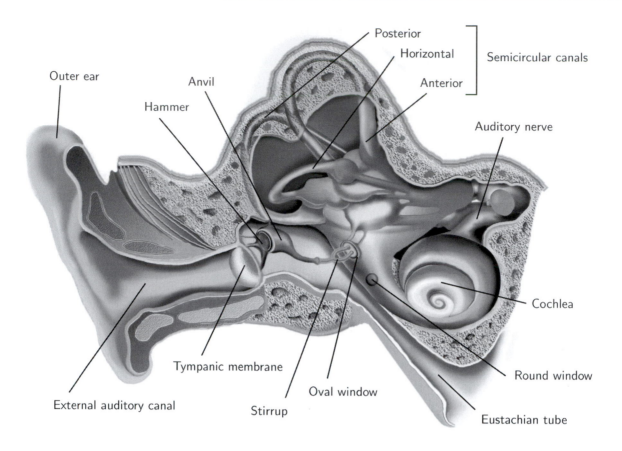

Figure 6.1. The Ear. The principal structures of the outer, middle, and inner ear may be seen in relation to each other in this illustration.

Because the physical characteristics of air and watery fluid are extremely different, there is a problem in effectively transforming pressure waves in air to pressure waves in fluid. For example, a sound wave crossing from air to water passes on only 0.1% of its original energy; 99.9% of its energy is lost at the air-water boundary. This accounts for the fact that we cannot hear poolside conversation when swimming underwater.

The middle ear solves this problem by using a system of membranes and bones to transfer sound energy from the outer to the inner ear. The boundary between the outer and the middle ear is covered by the **tympanic membrane**; the **oval window** connects the middle and inner ears. Movements of the tympanic membrane are transferred to the oval window by a system of three bones—the **malleus** (hammer), the **incus** (anvil), and the **stapes** (stirrup)—which together are called the **ossicles**.

The middle ear transmits sound energy effectively for several reasons. First, the ossicles function as a lever, transforming the larger excursions of the tympanic membrane into smaller but more forceful movements at the oval window. Second, a mechanical advantage is also gained by transferring energy from the larger area of the tympanic membrane to the smaller area of the stapes at the oval window. Finally, the curved shape of the tympanic membrane itself improves the mechanical transfer of energy through the middle ear, an idea first put forth by Hermann von Helmholtz in the

1860s but only recently confirmed by modern laser measurement techniques.

It is in the **inner ear**, or **cochlea**, that the neural encoding of auditory information begins. The cochlea, named for the Greek word for "snail," is a small coiled tube of hard bone that is divided lengthwise into three chambers. It is contained within a system of tunnels called the bony labyrinth, which also houses the receptors of the vestibular system.

Figure 6.2 on the next page shows the anatomy of the inner ear. The **cochlear duct**, also known as the **scala media**, is by far the smallest of the cochlear chambers, accounting for less than 10% of the volume of the cochlea. But it is the cochlear duct that contains the neural structures that accomplish the sensory transduction of acoustic signals.

The floor of the cochlear duct is formed by the **basilar membrane**, which separates the scala media from the **scala tympani** below it. **Reissner's membrane** forms the roof of the cochlear duct, separating it from the **scala vestibuli** above. Resting on the basilar membrane is an elegant structure composed of the **hair cells** and the **tectorial membrane**. The delicate contact between the hair cells and the tectorial membrane is shown in the lower left-hand panel of Figure 6.2 on the following page. The hair cells are organized into one inner and three outer rows that extend through the length of cochlea. At the top of each of these cells are between 50 and 100 **cilia**, or fine hairs, that extend upward and make contact with the tectorial membrane.

These hair cells are arranged in bundles of unequal length that are linked at their tips. This mechanical arrangement is such that an upward movement of the basilar membrane bends the hair cells toward the tallest hair cell, whereas a downward movement bends the hair cells in the opposite direction. At rest, the membrane potential of the hair cell is about -60 mV. An upward movement of the membrane causes special K^+ pores to open. K^+ is concentrated outside the cell in the **endolymph** of the cochlea. Therefore, the *influx* of K^+ *depolarizes* the hair cell. (Keep in mind that this situation is very different from that in most neurons, in which K^+ is concentrated *inside*, not outside, the cell body.) Conversely, a downward movement of the basilar membrane acts to close the K^+ channels and hyperpolarizes the hair cell. In this unique way, sound-induced movements of the basilar membrane are transformed into fluctuations of the membrane potential of the hair cells.

As is the case with the photoreceptors of the retina, depolarization of the hair cells increases the release of a neurotransmitter by these receptors. The hair cells synapse directly with the bipolar neurons of the auditory nerve.

Frequency Coding in the Cochlea   From a mechanical point of view, the inner structure of the cochlea may be thought of as an elongated tube divided in half lengthwise by a single flexible membrane, the basilar membrane with the associated structures of the cochlear duct. Sound energy enters the cochlea at its base through the movement of the stapes at the oval window. At the far, or apical, end of the cochlea, fluid may flow between the scala vestibuli and the scala tympani through a small opening in the basilar membrane, the **helicotrema**. The **round window** is a flexible

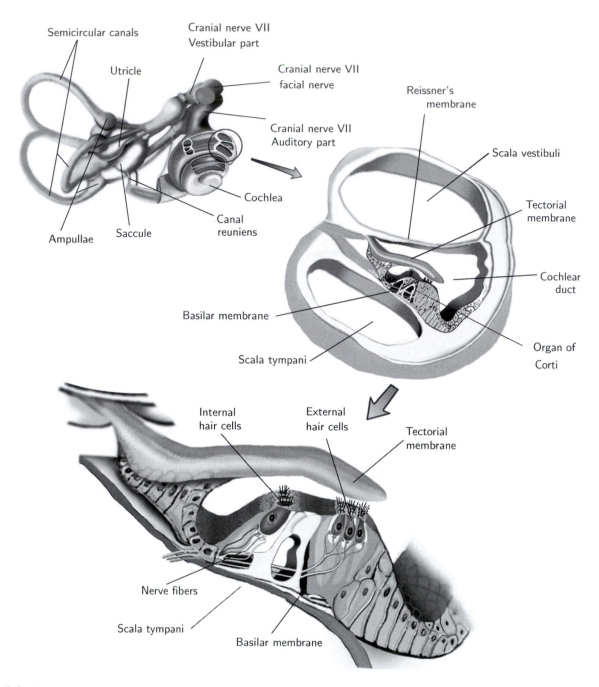

Figure 6.2. The Cochlea and Related Structures. Above left: The cochlea may be seen in relation to the structures of the vestibular system and the cranial nerves. Middle right: The cochlea is shown in cross section, showing the position of the organ of Corti with respect to the basilar and tectorial membranes. Lower left: The organ of Corti is shown in detail. Notice the way in which the cilia of the hair cells are mechanically positioned to be pulled and pushed with movements of the basilar membrane. Acoustic vibrations flex the basilar membrane, producing a change in the electrical potential of the hair cells. This provides the physical basis for sensory transduction in the auditory system.

membrane at the basal end of the scala tympani.

The plungerlike movements of the stapes disturb the fluids of the inner ear in such a way as to produce vertical displacements of the basilar membrane. The manner in which the basilar membrane moves is now reasonably well understood, thanks in large part to a series of experiments by Georg von Békésy (1956, 1960). Békésy was awarded a Nobel Prize in 1961 "for his discoveries concerning the physical mechanisms of stimulation within cochlea."

The physical properties of the basilar membrane change markedly over its length. The basilar membrane is supported on each side by the bony structure of the cochlea. Near the oval window, the basilar membrane is quite narrow (100 microns), but at the apex, it is considerably wider (500 microns). In addition, the basilar membrane is taut at its base and much more loosely suspended at the apex. These two factors combine to alter the response of different portions of the basilar membrane to sounds of different frequencies.

Von Békésy was able to show that sound enters the cochlea as a traveling wave. The traveling wave begins at the base of the cochlea and moves down toward the apex very rapidly. In this way, it is like the wave produced by shaking one end of a rope with the other end tied to a fence post; the wave moves smoothly from one end of the rope to the other. In the cochlea, the traveling wave is completely dissipated by the time it reaches the helicotrema and therefore is not reflected back from the end of the cochlea.

Because the basilar membrane varies in stiffness and width, different frequencies of sound produce the greatest displacement of the membrane at different regions of the membrane. High frequencies affect the basilar membrane where it is narrow and taut near the oval window, whereas lower frequencies have their greatest effects closer to the apex of the cochlea. Figure 6.3 on the next page illustrates the cochlear traveling wave and the point of maximum deflection of the basilar membrane as a function of stimulus frequency.

Thus, the human cochlea functions as a frequency analyzer. Acoustic stimuli of different frequencies displace the basilar membrane most strongly at different distances from its base. Because the hair cells respond more vigorously to more severe displacements of the basilar membrane, different hair cells respond most actively to signals of different frequencies. The pattern of activity in the hair cells, extending from the base of the cochlea to its apex, reflect the pattern of movement of the basilar membrane; in this way, different hair cells encode different frequencies of auditory stimulation.

Sensory Coding in Audition

The Ascending Auditory Pathway   The **ascending auditory pathway** is the route by which auditory information from the ear reaches the cerebral cortex. It begins at the **auditory nerve** (the eighth cranial nerve). The neurons of the auditory nerve are **bipolar neurons**. The cell bodies of these neurons form the **spiral ganglia**, located in the bony structure surrounding the cochlea. In this type of bipolar cell, the cell body is located along

Figure 6.3. Traveling Waves. Left: A wave traveling along the basilar membrane is shown at a number of sequential instants. The dashed line shows the envelope of the traveling wave, the maximum excursion of the membrane for a 200 Hz tone. Right: The envelope of the movement of the basilar membrane for tones of different frequency. These measurements were made by von Békésy (1960).

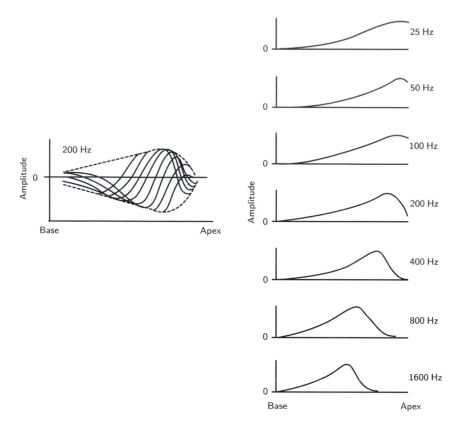

the axon and does not participate in the information-processing functions of the cell; instead, it serves only to fulfill the usual metabolic functions that any neuron requires. Each bipolar cell gives off two processes, both of which are axons. One proceeds into the cochlea, where it makes synaptic contact with the hair cells; the other proceeds toward the brain as a part of the auditory nerve. Action potentials originate at the hair cell synapse and pass down both axons of the bipolar cell into the central nervous system.

There are about 30,000 cells in the human spiral ganglion. Of these, about 95% innervate the row of inner hair cells. Each of these fibers makes synaptic connections with a single hair cell; each hair cell synapses with between 10 and 20 auditory nerve fibers. Thus, the inner hair cells are heavily innervated by the auditory nerve. In sharp contrast, only about 5% of the fibers in the auditory nerve make contact with the more numerous outer hair cells of the cochlea. Each of these fibers synapses with about 10 different outer hair cells. By comparison with the inner hair cells, the outer hair cells are poorly represented in the auditory nerve.

The ascending auditory system within the brain stem consists of a number of discrete nuclei and pathways. Figure 6.4 on the facing page illustrates the anatomical relations between the nuclei and pathways of the central auditory system, showing the major and minor routes by which auditory information may reach the cerebral cortex.

All fibers of the auditory nerve enter the brain stem, where they branch before synapsing in the dorsal or ventral portions of the **cochlear nucleus**.

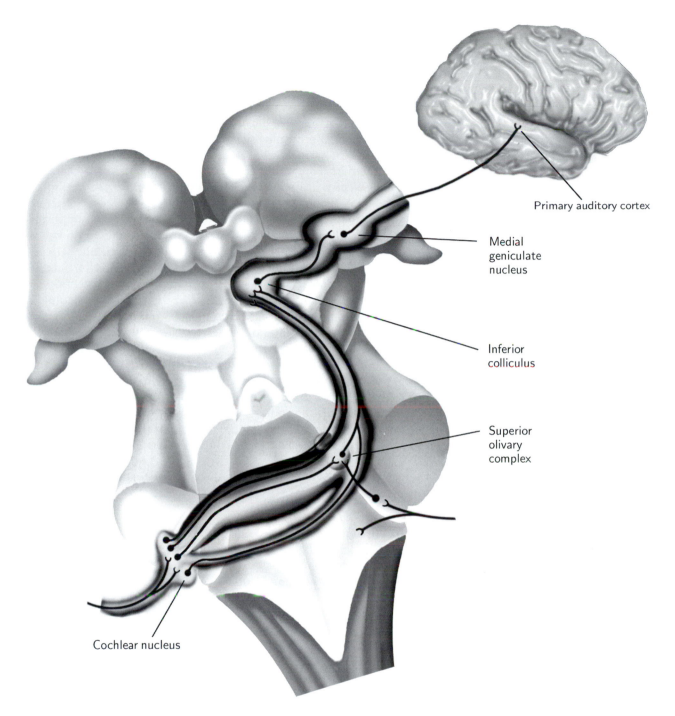

Primary auditory cortex

Medial
geniculate
nucleus

Inferior
colliculus

Superior
olivary
complex

Cochlear nucleus

Figure 6.4. The Central Auditory System. Auditory information from the cochlea enters the brain through the auditory nerve, which synapses at the cochlear nucleus of the brain stem. This information is relayed through the superior olivary complex and the inferior colliculus to the medial geniculate nucleus (MGN) of the thalamus. The MGN sends its fibers to the primary auditory cortex of the temporal lobe.

From the cochlear nucleus, fibers may take a variety of routes in reaching the auditory areas of the forebrain. Some of these pathways are direct projections to the central auditory nuclei, whereas other fibers take a more complex course, synapsing at several intermediate nuclei before reaching the forebrain.

The principal auditory nuclei of the brain stem, in addition to the cochlear nuclei, are the nuclei of the **superior olivary complex** and the **inferior colliculus**. The superior olivary complex is a collection of nuclei located in the brain stem at the level of the medulla. The inferior colliculus is located on the dorsal surface of the midbrain, immediately posterior to the superior colliculus. The inferior colliculus projects to the auditory relay nucleus of the thalamus, the **medial geniculate nucleus**, which in turn sends fibers to the primary auditory cortex of the superior temporal lobe.

A number of major pathways link the nuclei of the auditory system. The **trapezoid body** is formed by fibers that communicate between the cochlear nuclei on the right and left halves of the medulla. The **lateral lemniscus** is the major fiber tract that carries information from the cochlear nucleus and superior olivary nuclei to the inferior colliculus. Contained within the lateral lemniscus is a small collection of cell bodies that form the **nucleus of the lateral lemniscus**. The pathway from the inferior colliculus to the medial geniculate nucleus is called the **brachium of the inferior colliculus**. The fibers connecting the medial geniculate and the primary auditory cortex are called the **auditory radiations**.

Thus, the central auditory nuclei and their projections form a complex interrelated system for auditory information processing. Within each of its components, there is a **tonotopic organization**, which means that signals originating in adjacent regions of the cochlea remain together as they travel through the auditory system. In this way, the frequency information originally extracted by the hair cells of the cochlea is maintained within the central nervous system.

Localizing Sounds in Space   One of the major functions of the auditory system is to determine the source of sounds in space. The cells of the superior olivary complex appear to be particularly important in this regard. The superior olivary complex not only receives direct input from the cochlear nucleus on its own side of the brain, but it also receives a massive input from the contralateral side, by way of the trapezoid body. Lesions of either the trapezoid body or the superior olivary complex result in severe deficits in localizing the source of sounds. Damage at higher levels of the auditory system does not produce this effect.

Cells in the superior olivary complex perform their localizing functions in two ways. In the medial portion of the superior olive, populations of cells may be found that have two major systems of dendrites extending in opposite directions. One branch makes contact with fibers originating in the ipsilateral cochlear nucleus, the other with fibers from the contralateral cochlear nucleus. These cells are tuned primarily for low-frequency sounds and are extremely sensitive to small differences in arrival time between the ipsilateral and contralateral input. By comparing the arrival times, these cells of the medial superior olivary nucleus determine which ear was closer to the source of the sound. These cells project to the inferior colliculus on the same side of the brain.

The second method by which localizing information is extracted in the superior olivary complex is by intensity comparisons. Cells in the lateral superior olive are tuned to a wide range of frequencies and receive input from both cochlear nuclei. These neurons are extremely sensitive to intensity differences between stimuli presented to the two ears. They transmit this information bilaterally to both inferior colliculi.

In these two ways, the comparison of arrival times and relative intensities, the neurons of the superior olivary complex provide the higher stations of the central auditory system with information concerning the probable locations of the sound sources in the environment.

The Auditory Cortex The **primary auditory cortex** of the human brain lies on the bank of the temporal lobe beneath the Sylvian fissure and is often referred to as **Heschl's gyrus**. The primary auditory cortex receives projections from the medial geniculate nucleus of the thalamus.

Electrical stimulation of the auditory cortex during neurosurgery results in simple auditory sensations, such as ringing, humming, or buzzing. These sensations are nearly always experienced as arising from the opposite ear. More complex phenomena, such as auditory hallucinations, have been reported when electrical stimulation is applied to tissue surrounding the primary auditory area.

The auditory cortex is tonotopically organized, as are the auditory nuclei of the brain stem. This has been established quite clearly in many species, including primates, from recordings made directly from cortical tissue. Evidence from patients with small lesions in the temporal lobe also suggests that the same is true in the human brain, with higher frequencies represented more medially and lower frequencies more laterally.

The auditory cortex, like other regions of the cerebrum, is functionally organized into columns. One characteristic of the auditory cortical columns is frequency specificity; all sharply tuned cells within a column are tuned to nearly identical frequencies.

The columns of the auditory cortex also differ in both **aural dominance** (the ear in which stimulation most effectively excites auditory neurons) and in **binaural interaction** (the way in which auditory stimuli presented to the two ears affect each other). In some columns, auditory input to both ears produces a more vigorous cellular response than input to either ear alone. Such columns are called **binaural summation columns**. Conversely, in **binaural suppression columns**, the response to simulation of the two ears together is weaker than the same stimulation presented to one ear alone.

The secondary auditory cortex lies adjacent to the primary auditory cortex, from which it receives projections. Less is known concerning the functional properties of neurons in these higher auditory areas because they respond weakly, if at all, to pure tone stimuli. The problem is analogous to trying to stimulate complex cells in the primary visual cortex with small spots of light; both are simple stimuli that are inappropriate for activating higher-order neurons that encode more complex stimulus features.

Recently, a set of interesting findings has been reported by Rauschecker, Tian, and Hauser (1995), who mapped responses in the higher auditory areas of the macaque cortex using bursts of band pass noise (BPN) of variable bandwidth around a given center frequency. These stimuli are much more complex than simple tones but contain more structure than wide-band white noise (similar to the sound of radio static) and somewhat analogous to the uses of lines or edges to stimulate higher-order cells in the visual system.

Rauschecker et al. (1995) found that more than 90% of the cells in the secondary auditory cortex responded vigorously to BPN stimuli but were only weakly responsive to pure tones. Using this method, Rauschecker et al. were able to identify three separate tonotopic representations of the cochlea in the secondary auditory cortex, just as multiple retinotopic maps characterize the various known extrastriate cortical areas of the visual system.

Finally, a number of the cells in each of these three tonotopic regions preferred natural monkey calls as stimuli to either pure tones or BPN, as indicated by the vigor of their stimulus-elicited responses. Interestingly, these areas of the macaque secondary auditory cortex correspond to regions of the human brain in which damage results in impairments of speech perception.

The Descending Auditory Pathway   Complementing the ascending auditory system, which brings information from the cochlea to the cortex, is a system of descending fibers that carries information in the opposite direction. The brain stem **descending auditory pathway** begins at the auditory cortex. There, efferent fibers project back to the medial geniculate nuclei and the inferior colliculi. Lower descending projections connect these diencephalic and mesencephalic structures with the olivary and cochlear nuclei. The final pathways of this system link both the superior olivary complex and the cochlear nuclei with the hair cells of the cochlea, by way of efferent fibers in the auditory nerve.

The descending and ascending auditory systems run in parallel. This provides the opportunity for extensive feedback and interaction between the several nuclei of the auditory system.

VESTIBULAR SENSATION

The **vestibular system**, which senses movement and gravity, is closely related to the auditory system and operates in much the same way. Both systems evolved from a more primitive sensory system in fish that is used to sense vibration in water (Bergeijk, 1967). Information from the vestibular system is critical for coordinating motor movements, maintaining balance, and controlling posture.

Unlike other sensory systems, we are seldom aware of vestibular sensation. But if the vestibular system malfunctions, powerful sensations of dizziness and nausea result.

The receptors of the vestibular system—like the cochlea of the auditory system—are housed within the bony labyrinth, a system of hard bone and fluid-filled canals, shown in Figure 6.2 on page 188. It is composed of three **semicircular ducts** and two **otoliths**—the **utricle** and the **saccule**, as shown in Figure 6.2 on page 188 (Howard, 1986).

The three fluid-filled semicircular ducts are arranged perpendicularly to each other, one in the horizontal plane, a second in the sagittal plane, and a third in the coronal plane. Thus, any movement of the head in three-dimensional space will affect the fluid in at least one of the three ducts. A special structure, called the **ampulla**, is located at the junction of the ducts and the utricle. The ampulla contains **vestibular hair cell bundles**, which are the receptor cells for the vestibular system.

The hair cell bundles themselves are covered with a gelatinous mass, the **cupula**. When the head moves, the fluid in the semicircular ducts presses on the cupula, which in turn displaces the outer portion of the vestibular hair cells.

Each hair cell bundle consists of tens or hundreds of **stereocilia**, which are similar in many respects to the hair cells of the cochlea, and a single **kinocilium**, which serves as a mechanical anchor for the bundle. Each stereocilium is linked to its neighbor at both its tips and its base. When displaced by the movement of fluid in the semicircular canals, the hair cell bundle leans either toward or away from the supporting kinocilium.

When the bundle is displaced toward the kinocilium, the individual hair cells become depolarized; when it is bent away from the kinocilium, hyperpolarization results. When hair cells are depolarized, they release a neurotransmitter that depolarizes afferent fibers of the eighth cranial nerve on which they synapse. Thus, hair cell depolarization increases the firing of these afferent fibers, whereas hyperpolarization decreases their firing.

In contrast to the semicircular ducts, which signal accelerated movement, the otoliths sense the position of the head with respect to gravity as well as sustained movements of the head in space. Yet they operate by the same basic principles. The otoliths contain hair cell bundles, which are covered by a gelatinous mass containing crystals of calcium carbonate. When these crystals are displaced by gravity as the head is moved, they bend the hair cells either toward or away from the kinocilia, changing the membrane potential of the hair cells and therefore the activity of the eighth nerve fibers on which they synapse.

The difference between the two otoliths is their orientation in space when the head is in the normal standing position. The hair cell bundles of the utricle are horizontally positioned, whereas those of the saccule are vertically oriented. Combined output from the two otoliths can therefore specify the position of the head in space with respect to gravity.

Central Connections of the Vestibular System   The vestibular portion of the eighth cranial nerve consists of about 20,000 fibers for the vestibular apparatus on each side of the head. These fibers enter the brain stem at the level of the pons, where they synapse.

Unlike the fibers of the auditory nerve, the vestibular fibers do not contribute to an ascending sensory system that eventually reaches the cerebral cortex. Rather, the vestibular nerve contributes to a number of brain stem reflex centers, where its information contributes to the modulation of motor movements. These include the regulation of posture and eye movements. Signals originating in the vestibular system do not contribute to conscious awareness.

TASTE

Taste is a chemical sense. It originates in the taste receptors of the mouth, which are activated selectively by certain types of molecules. However, the experience of taste is also determined by nonchemical factors such as the temperature and the consistency of a substance. Both chemical and physical properties combine to produce the complex sensations of taste that we routinely experience in daily life. Part of the function of taste is to provide guidance and warning to the gastrointestinal tract. Guidance is illustrated by food preferences, which helped our ancestors select the most nutritious foods from a number of more or less appetizing alternatives. Warnings come from unusual tastes that have been associated with illness in the past (Garcia & Rusiniak, 1977). In these and other ways, the chemical sense of taste has profound effects on behavior.

The Dimensions of Taste   Knowledge of the neural basis of taste is relatively scant in comparison with our knowledge of other sensory systems; however, recent developments in molecular biology, brain imaging, and genetics have provided new insights into the mammalian taste system.

The sense of taste is known to have four fundamental dimensions: salty, sour, sweet, and bitter. These four primitive tastes combine smell and tactile sensations to produce the distinctive flavors that we associate with different foods.

Each type of taste corresponds to a different type of chemical compound. Salty tastes are produced primarily by inorganic compounds that ionize in solution, such as sodium chloride, or common table salt. Sour tastes are associated with acidic substances such as acetic acid. Sweet tastes are produced primarily by organic compounds such as the sugars and some alcohols. Bitter tastes are characteristic of other organic compounds such as the alkaloids. In nature, sweet tastes usually signify carbohydrate nutrients, whereas bitter tastes are characteristic of many of the poisonous vegetable alkaloids. Because different tastes are elicited by different classes of molecules, the sense of taste may provide the brain with a rudimentary chemical analysis of substances as they are being ingested.

Taste Buds   The receptors for taste are located within the **taste buds**, which are concentrated on the tongue but are also found elsewhere in the mouth (Roper, 1992). The number of taste buds is variable; most people have between 2,000 and 5,000 taste buds, but numbers up to 20,000 have been reported.

Taste buds themselves are multicellular structures clustered in small elevations on the surface of the tongue and elsewhere (Roper, 1992). Figure 6.5 on the next page illustrates a human taste bud. There are two principal types of cells within a taste bud: the **taste receptor cells** and the nonneural supporting cells. The taste bud itself is covered by epithelial (skin) cells, except for a small opening at the very top of the structure, the **outer taste pore**. This pore provides the channel by which substances within the mouth can affect the receptor cells. The receptor cells themselves have a very short life span, only a few days in most species. They are continually being replaced by new cells, produced by the division of the supporting

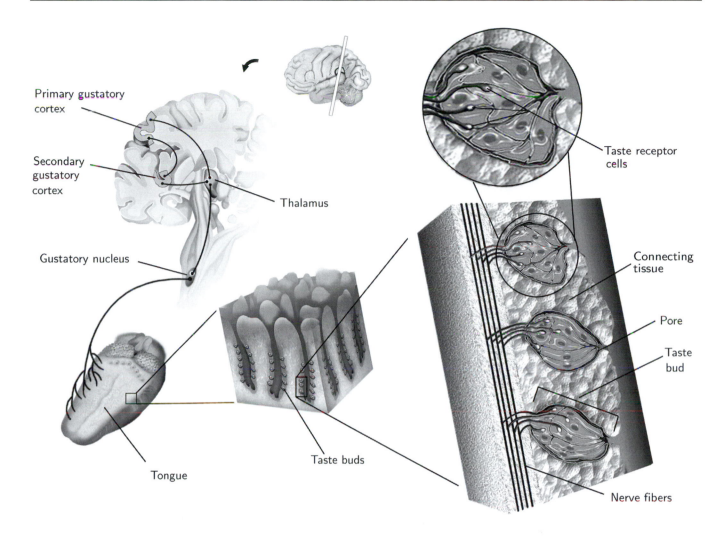

Figure 6.5. The Human Taste System. Human taste originates from sensory receptors within the tongue and mouth (lower left). The structure of the taste bud is shown in the right-hand panels. The neural pathway for taste sensation is indicated in the upper left-hand panels.

cells of the taste bud. New receptors are formed at the edge of the taste bud and migrate toward its center during their brief lives.

Sensory transduction in taste receptor cells is accomplished by a variety of mechanisms. In all taste receptors, there are voltage-gated potassium channels at the tips of the cells near the outer taste pore. These channels are open at rest, hyperpolarizing the cell. Sour and bitter substances act to close these channels, depolarizing the receptor. Salt receptors appear to depolarize in response to the passive influx of sodium through nongated sodium channels. Sugar receptors operate using a second-messenger system. A number of other ionic mechanisms of sensory transduction also may be used. In all cases, however, the response of the receptor is to depolarize when activated by the appropriate chemical stimulus.

Bitterness receptors appear to use a particular G-protein, **gustducin**, to induce an amplified biochemical cascade to close voltage-gated potassium channels (Kinnamon & Cummings, 1992). Gustducin, by the way, is very closely related to transducin, which performs a similar function in the rods of the visual system. Recent evidence suggests that this same protein may mediate the transduction of sweet, as well as bitter, tastes. Wong, Gannon, and Margolskee (1996) used newly developed gene replacement techniques to produce a strain of mice that were specifically deficient in the alpha-subunit of the gastducin protein, rendering it inoperative. These mice, as expected, were both behaviorally and electrophysiologically deficient in their response to bitter stimuli. Lacking an appropriate taste receptor for bitter substances, the mice were unresponsive to the bitter compound. Also, as expected, the genetically gustducin-deficient mice responded completely normally to both salty and sour compounds. But it was not expected that the genetically engineered strain would also be unresponsive to sweet stimuli as well, but that was what Kinnamon and Cummings's data clearly indicate. It thus appears that gustducin is the principal mediator of both bitter and sweet signal transduction in the mammalian taste system, a fact that would have been very difficult to establish without the benefit of genetic engineering technology.

Sensory Pathways for Taste   The receptor cells of the taste buds of the tongue make synaptic contact with nerve cells from the facial (7th) and the glossopharyngeal (9th) cranial nerves. Chemical neurotransmitters are employed. The facial nerve carries information from taste buds in the anterior two thirds of the tongue, and the glossopharyngeal nerve supplies the posterior region. The vagus (10th) nerve relays information from taste buds located elsewhere within the mouth. Taste fibers in all three of these cranial nerves respond to synaptic activation by producing action potentials. Some taste fibers have no real taste specificity, responding to a wide range of substances with equal vigor. However, others are more selective, responding to only certain classes of chemicals. How these fibers extract information from the continually migrating receptor cells of the taste bud is another of the unsolved problems in understanding the perception of taste.

Axons of taste fibers in the facial, glossopharyngeal, and vagus nerves project to the ipsilateral **solitary nucleus** of the medulla. Cells in this medullary nucleus in turn project to a pontine taste area (Davis, 1991). Cells in this recently discovered region in turn project to the thalamus, probably to the thalamic area that receives somatosensory information from the tongue. There are undoubtedly other projections of the taste system to nuclei in other regions of the brain stem, but the available evidence on the organization of the brain stem taste system is sparse.

The cortical representation of taste is in the region of the frontal operculum and the adjoining anterior **insula**. The frontal operculum is in the vicinity of the tongue area of the motor strip; the insula is involved with visceral sensation. Irritation of this region results in widespread visceral effects.

About 5% of individual neurons in this region respond preferentially to one of the four basic tastes: sweet, salty, sour, or bitter. Of the nontaste responsive cells, about a third respond to tongue movements. The functions of the remaining 60% of the cells in this region are unknown.

The largest responses of the taste-sensitive cells were obtained with either salty or sweet stimulation, a finding that is similar to human psychophysical data. The strength of these cell responses increases with the intensity of the taste stimulus. Individual taste-sensitive neurons appear to be randomly intermingled in this region. Thus, unlike the retinotopic organization of visual cortex and the tonotopic organization of auditory cortex, there is no evidence of chemotopic organization of the taste cortex (Plata-Salaman & Scott, 1992).

SMELL

Sensations of odor—like those of taste–are also the result of chemical interactions with the environment. Although the sense of smell is more developed in many other species, the sensitivity of the human olfactory system is still remarkable. The perception of odor is a response to chemical substances suspended in the air; certain odors may be detected in concentrations as low as one in several billion parts. When compared with taste, the sensitivity of the olfactory system is even more striking; a substance such as ethyl alcohol may be detected by its odor at 1/25,000 the concentration required for detection by taste. It is little wonder that **olfaction**, the sense of smell, is so important in guiding specific behaviors in many species. In a wide range of mammals, smell plays a major role in feeding, mating, and social behavior. In humans, the sense of smell is often considered a "digestive sensation," but—in the words of the 19th-century British neurologist John Hughlings Jackson—it is also the most suggestive of all senses (Critchley, 1986). Smells have the extraordinary ability to remind us of things past. A single odor can bring forth a cascade of memories quite involuntarily.

Olfactory Receptors   The fact that the human olfactory system can discriminate something like 10,000 individual odors places a serious burden on the olfactory receptor system. The olfactory receptors are protein molecules embedded in the membrane of the olfactory receptor cell. This system is shown in Figure 6.6 on the following page.

When an odorant—usually small, volatile, lipid-soluble molecules— binds to the protein receptor, it triggers a special guanosine triphosphate–binding protein. That, in turn, releases an intracellular messenger, cyclic AMP, which opens ion channels specific for sodium on the membrane of the olfactory receptor cell. These channels are very much like those regulating the dark current in photoreceptors. The influx of sodium depolarizes the receptor and may produce action potentials. The most vigorous responses are evoked by fruity and floral odors. Recent studies indicate that there may be a large family of olfactory receptor proteins, but it is not clear that each is associated with a separate receptor cell. Current evidence indicates that each receptor cell responds to a variety of odorant molecules. Either the receptor molecules are responsive to a range of odorants, or the receptor cell has a variety of receptor molecules on its membrane (Anholt, 1993).

The receptor cells for olfaction are found in the **nasal mucosa**, the watery mucous membrane of the nose. In humans, the olfactory receptor cells are confined to only a few square centimeters of mucous membrane; in other vertebrates with greater olfactory sensitivity, this region is much

Figure 6.6. Molecular Mechanism of Olfactory Transduction. The odorant molecule binds with an odor receptor protein embedded in the membrane of the cilia of the odor receptor neuron. This activates the enzyme adenylate cyclase by way of a special molecular G-protein pathway. Adenylate cyclase in turn converts adenosine triphosphate (ATP) into cyclic adenosine monophosphate (cyclic AMP). Cyclic AMP opens a cation channel in the membrane, allowing the influx of both sodium (Na^+) and calcium (Ca^+), depolarizing the cilia.

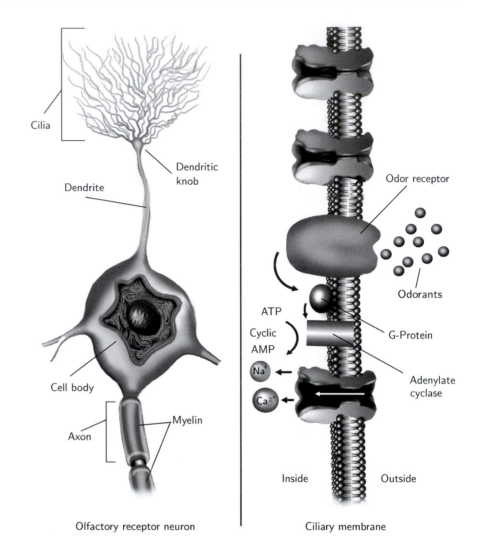

Olfactory receptor neuron   Ciliary membrane

larger. The receptors for olfaction are especially adapted **bipolar neurons**. The dendrite of the olfactory bipolar cell extends from its oval-shaped cell body to the surface of the mucosa, where the dendrite enlarges to form an **olfactory knob**. Extending from the olfactory knob in all directions are tiny, threadlike cilia. These cilia are numerous and reach into the surface of the mucous membrane, where they form a densely interwoven web. Apparently, it is this web that traps odorous particles and serves as the site of sensory transduction for the sense of smell.

The depolarization produced by the absorption of odorants in the cilia is transmitted along the dendrite of the olfactory receptor to its cell body. Each dendrite is effectively isolated from every other by the supporting cells that surround it. Thus, there appears to be no opportunity for electrical interaction between receptor cells outside the ciliary layer.

Axons of the olfactory bipolar cells, among the smallest and slowest in the nervous system, leave the cell body and extend to join with other axons and become wrapped by Schwann cells. These small bundles of shielded

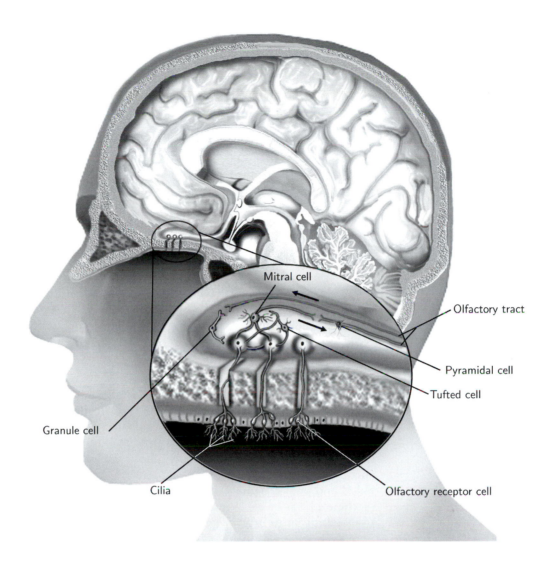

Mitral cell

Olfactory tract

Pyramidal cell

Tufted cell

Granule cell

Cilia

Olfactory receptor cell

afferent fibers leave the nasal mucosa and penetrate the bony base of the cranial cavity to enter the olfactory bulb of the brain. The central olfactory system is shown in Figure 6.7.

Figure 6.7. The Central Olfactory System. Olfactory receptors send signals to the olfactory bulb, which project to the basal forebrain.

Olfactory Bulb   The **olfactory bulb** contains the initial neuronal machinery for processing olfactory information (Shepherd & Greer, 1994). In many ways, the synaptic organization of the olfactory bulb is like that of the retina, with two levels of lateral interaction interrupting the straight signal pathway.

The most striking and important structures of the olfactory bulb are its glomeruli. Each **glomerulus** is a large, dense, interwoven synaptic ball in which the fine axons of the olfactory receptor cells synapse with the dendrites of mitral and other cells of the olfactory bulb, carrying information from a receptor cell to a number of mitral cells. The **mitral cells** are the principal neurons of the olfactory bulb. Mitral cells receive input from a very large number of olfactory receptors. The overlapping mitral dendrites provide a second lateral pathway within the bulb. A third lateral pathway is provided by the **granule cells**, which carry signals between different mitral cells. Although the physiological patterns of interconnection within the olfactory bulb are becoming increasingly clear, the functional significance of these connections remains unknown.

The mitral cells project either directly or through interneurons to four brain structures: the primary olfactory cortex, the amygdala, the **olfactory tubercle** (an olfactory area at the base of the forebrain), and the septal area. The **primary olfactory cortex** is located within the most primitive regions of the forebrain; it includes both the piriform and entorhinal cortex. In turn, the entorhinal cortex projects to the hippocampus, a region that has long been implicated in the formation of memory. The central olfactory system also sends information to the hypothalamus, the reticular formation, and a variety of limbic structures. Thus, the central representation of smell is intimately related to the older visceral and motivational regions of the human brain.

SOMATOSENSATION

Somatosensation refers to the many mechanical sensations arising from the body. The tactile sensations of touch and pressure provide information about the environment as it comes into contact with the surface of the body. Proprioceptive sensations produced by movements of the muscles and joints allow us to perceive the position of the body within the surrounding environment. These aspects of somatic sensation provide detailed and precise signals that serve as the mechanical foundation for the biological basis of behavior. They are represented at the highest levels of the cerebral cortex in an elegantly and complexly organized neural system.

Touch

The sense of touch provides information about the contact of the skin with objects in the environment. Touch sensation originates in **mechanoreceptors**, cells that respond to pressure changes by producing neural signals. Mechanoreceptors are specialized neurons, consisting of a pressure-sensitive tip, a cell body, and an axon. It is at the tip of the neuron that mechanical force is transduced, generating the sensory signal. The effect of pressure there is to induce depolarization at the nerve ending. When the depolarization exceeds the threshold of the receptor, an action potential results. More intense pressure results in greater depolarization of the pressure-sensitive region of the mechanoreceptor; the axon of the receptor responds by producing action potentials at a faster rate. Individual mechanoreceptors signal the intensity by increasing the number of action potentials that they produce in response to the stimulus.

Intensity information is also conveyed by the number of mechanoreceptors responding to a particular stimulus. If the pressure applied to the body surface is weak, only the most sensitive mechanoreceptors will respond. But a more intense stimulus not only will elicit a more vigorous response from these receptor cells, but it will also trigger responses from other, less sensitive mechanoreceptors. Stronger stimuli recruit responses from a larger population of touch receptors. By knowing the relative sensitivity of individual receptor cells, the central nervous system obtains additional information about the strength of a mechanical stimulus.

Sensory Transduction in Touch   The process of sensory transduction is both simple and elegant. In most mechanoreceptor cells, the pressure-sensitive region of the cell membrane contains a number of pores, each of which is normally smaller than a hydrated sodium ion. However, mechanical force stretches this pressure-sensitive region, enlarging the pores so that sodium ions may enter the cell. Sodium ions are concentrated in the extracellular fluid and so are driven into the cell by their concentration gradient, as well as being electrically attracted to the cell's negative interior.

Thus, stretching open the ion pores results in a net influx of sodium, depolarizing the pressure-sensitive region of the mechanoreceptor cell. If the depolarization is of sufficient magnitude, an action potential is generated by the axon of the receptor. In these respects, sensory transduction of mechanical displacement in mechanoreceptor cells is similar to the ordinary, chemically induced excitatory postsynaptic potentials found elsewhere in the nervous system.

Types of Mechanoreceptors   There are two principal types of receptors mediating the sensation of touch and pressure: free nerve endings and encapsulated nerve endings. In free nerve endings, the pressure-sensitive region is not covered by any other cellular structure. Encapsulated nerve endings are encased in more complicated mechanical arrangements. Examples of both types of endings are shown in Figure 6.8 on the following page.

The **free nerve endings** appear much as their name suggests; they are naked tips of axons that innervate the skin and related structures. Free nerve endings are found throughout the body. Many arise from unmyelinated axons, but others do not; the latter shed their myelin sheaths as they terminate in the skin. Some bodily structures, such as the cornea of the eye, contain only free nerve endings; there, all somatic sensation, including touch, temperature, and pain, must be sensed by this single type of receptor.

The **encapsulated nerve endings** are similar to free nerve endings but are encased in complicated structures formed of connective tissue. Perhaps the most complex and best studied of the encapsulated nerve endings is the **pacinian corpuscle**. Pacinian corpuscles are large in comparison with other mechanoreceptors, ranging between 1 and 4 mm in length. Each pacinian corpuscle is formed by a series of concentric fluid-filled capsules covering the centrally located nerve ending (see Figure 6.9 on page 205). The nerve innervating the corpuscle is myelinated, but it loses its myelin sheath within the protective structure of the corpuscle.

Figure 6.8. Somatosensory Receptors. Several distinctive types of receptor cells process different types of somatosensory information.

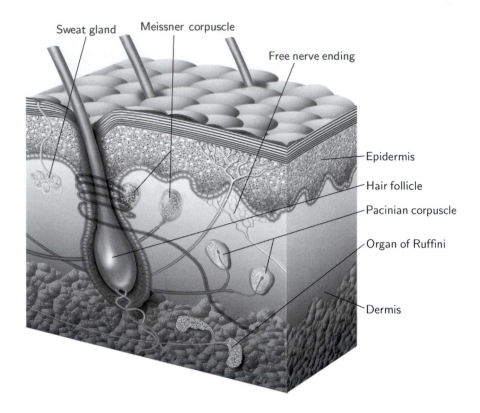

When pressure is applied to a pacinian corpuscle, fluid shifts within the compartments in such a way as to remove pressure from the tip of the nerve fiber. When the stimulus is taken away, fluids flow back to their original state, reexciting the nerve ending in the process. The effect of this mechanical arrangement is to disturb the nerve ending whenever pressure is either applied or removed. During periods of sustained pressure, no external forces act on the nerve ending. For this reason, the pacinian corpuscle responds only to changes in pressure; it gives no response in the absence of change. The pacinian corpuscle provides an excellent example of a rapidly adapting mechanoreceptor.

Two other types of encapsulated endings are generally believed to be of importance. The **Meissner corpuscles** are elongated oval structures that are positioned on a plane parallel to the surface of the skin. Each Meissner corpuscle is innervated by up to six myelinated fibers. Meissner corpuscles are especially predominant in the sensitive hairless skin of the fingers. **Ruffini end bulbs** are large, elongated structures that are found in hairy skin. Each Ruffini end bulb is innervated by a single myelinated fiber.

Mechanoreceptors differ from each other in a number of respects, including receptive field size, sensitivity, and rate of adaptation. Thus, different types of mechanoreceptors are capable of encoding different aspects of somatic stimuli. Cells with small receptive fields that respond to weak stimuli are important in mediating high-acuity tactile discrimination, for example. Rapidly adapting cells emphasize changes in the pattern of somatosensory stimulation. Such differences represent simple forms of stimulus feature extraction.

Finally, it is possible to study the responses of individual mechanoreceptors in unanesthetized human beings and thus compare neuronal and perceptual responses. This is accomplished by using extremely fine electrodes to record from single axons within the large nerve tracts of the human arm and leg. These cells differ both in the size of their receptive fields and in their rate of adaptation. It is interesting to note that the threshold for conscious verbal report of pressure stimuli in humans is similar to the threshold for eliciting a single action potential in a single nerve fiber (Jarvilehto, Hamalainen, & Soininen, 1981).

Segmental Innervation of Somatic Receptors   The axons from most somatosensory receptors enter the central nervous system through the spinal cord; the remainder enter through the cranial nerves. Although the spinal cord itself is a continuous structure filling most of the length of the spinal column, a **segmental organization** is imposed on it by the fact that afferent fibers have access to the spinal cord only through the 31 pairs (right and left) of dorsal roots that enter the spinal column in the spaces between the vertebrae.

Each dorsal root innervates and serves a particular region of the body called a **dermatome**. Although adjacent dermatomes overlap to a considerable extent, they nonetheless provide a clear segmental organization for the peripheral portion of the somatic sensory system.

Within each dorsal root, fibers serving all somatic sensory modalities or qualities are mixed. However, on entering the spinal column, the somatic afferent fibers sort themselves out and proceed upward in an orderly manner, with fibers serving different functional roles following separate anatomical routes.

It is the dorsal column–medial lemniscal pathway that carries the precise information required for the sense of touch from the skin to the brain. The structure of this system is shown in Figure 6.10 on the following page. The cell bodies of the peripheral mechanoreceptor cells are located near the spinal cord in groups called the **dorsal root ganglia**. As in the spiral ganglia of the auditory system, the cell bodies of these neurons perform metabolic functions and are not part of the information pathway that links the receptor ending with the central nervous system. These fibers are both large and myelinated, capable of carrying messages swiftly along their length. They enter the spinal cord in one of the dorsal roots and turn upward, forming the **dorsal column**. They synapse on the **dorsal column nuclei** within the medulla.

The dorsal column is a major pathway through the spinal cord. As it progresses upward, dorsal root fibers from each successive segment of the cord join the column on its lateral surface. Thus, the dorsal columns grow wider as they ascend, with information from more anterior structures represented laterally and information from more posterior structures represented medially. In this way, the dorsal columns maintain a somatotopic organization, in which fibers originating in the same part of the body remain together in the dorsal columns.

The importance of the dorsal column system for conveying precise information about touch cannot be overstated. In primates, damage to these

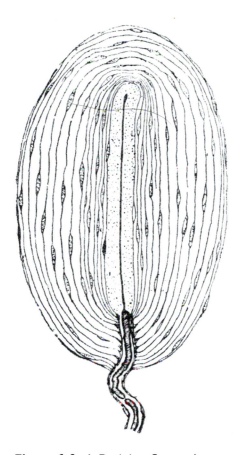

Figure 6.9. A Pacinian Corpuscle. This century-old drawing by Santiago Ramón y Cajal shows the important structure of the pacinian corpuscle. It is a free nerve ending surrounded by a series of fluid-filled membranes that act as a rapidly adapting shock absorber for the nerve cell. Thus, pacinian corpuscles respond to changes in pressure applied to the body of the corpuscle itself. (From Santiago Ramón y Cajal, *Histologie du systeme nerveux de l'homme et des vertebres.* Paris: A. Maloine, 1909-1911.)

Figure 6.10. The Dorsal Column–Medial Lemniscal System. This system is responsible for carrying information for the precise bodily sensations, such as touch and limb position, from the spinal cord to the cerebral cortex.

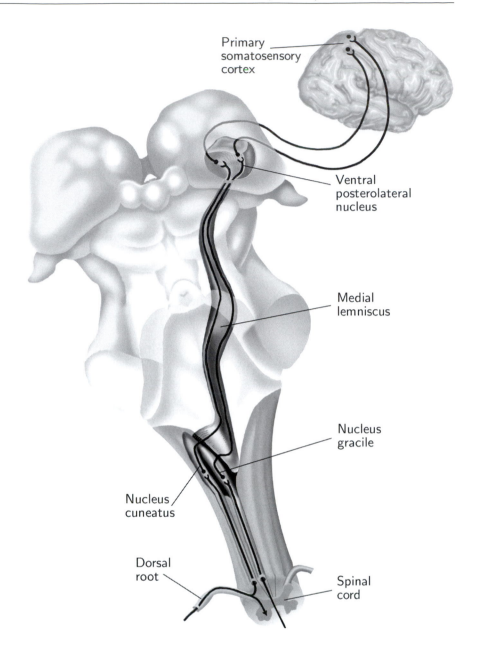

Primary somatosensory cortex

Ventral posterolateral nucleus

Medial lemniscus

Nucleus gracile

Nucleus cuneatus

Dorsal root

Spinal cord

pathways causes severe disruption of tactile discrimination; given dorsal column damage, monkeys cannot successfully select between objects by touch, as can normal animals.

Similar to the retinotopic organization of the visual system, there is **somatotopic organization** in the dorsal column nuclei of the medulla, in which various parts of the body are represented in an orderly fashion. There are two dorsal column nuclei: the **nucleus gracilis**, which receives input from the lower body, and the **nucleus cuneatus**, which is the target of somatosensory projections from the upper body.

Fibers from both of the dorsal column nuclei cross the midline and as-

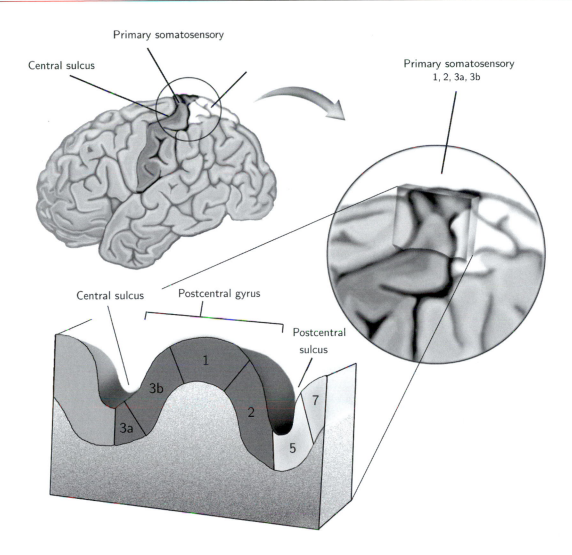

Figure 6.11. Primary Somatosensory Cortex. A view of the left cerebral hemisphere showing the postcentral gyrus in relation to other cortical regions, illustrating the positions of Brodmann's areas 1, 2, 3a, and 3b.

cend as a group to the thalamus, forming the **medial lemniscus**. Most of the fibers of the medial lemniscus synapse within the **ventral posterior lateral nucleus (VPL)** of the thalamus. The VPL constitutes the major portion of the larger region of the thalamus serving somatosensation, which is called the **ventrobasal complex**. In addition to the VPL, the ventrobasal complex includes the **ventral posterior medial nucleus (VPM)**. The VPM is similar to the VPL, but the VPM receives its input from the trigeminal nerve, which serves the lip and mouth area.

The VPL and VPM serve as thalamic relay nuclei for the somatosensory system, functioning in much the same way as the lateral geniculate nucleus does for vision or the medial geniculate nucleus for hearing. Cells of the ventrobasal complex project to the primary somatosensory cortex.

The **primary somatosensory cortex** is located on the postcentral gyrus of the parietal lobe, as shown in Figure 6.11. The postcentral gyrus corresponds to Brodmann's areas 1, 2, 3a, and 3b.

Somatosensory Receptive Fields   The pathway from periphery to cortex formed by the dorsal column nuclei, ventrobasal complex, and primary somatosensory cortex is a highly organized system that is capable of rapidly processing discriminative information from the sense of touch. This is reflected in the physiological properties of its cells and in the organization of their **receptive fields**, the region of the body where appropriate stimulation produces a change in the firing of the cell.

Throughout the central touch system, cells have well-defined receptive fields. The sizes of these fields differ dramatically, however, depending on the region of the skin on which they are located. Cells that process information from the densely innervated regions where tactile acuity or resolution is greatest, such as the tips of the fingers and the tongue, have very small receptive fields. In contrast, large receptive fields are found for sparsely innervated regions where sensory acuity is low.

The receptive fields of many touch cells are complex, with inhibitory as well as excitatory regions. This arrangement has the effect of increasing the acuity of the touch system; it allows well-defined spatial properties of tactile stimuli to be transmitted to higher levels of the nervous system. Such inhibitory effects are observed at the dorsal column nuclei and at all succeeding stations within the touch system.

Throughout the pathway from the dorsal columns to the somatosensory cortex, individual neurons are highly specific with respect to the types of stimuli to which they respond. Cells that respond vigorously to superficial touch do not respond to deep pressure. Cells that signal the movement of a hair do not discharge to skin indentation. At each level of the ascending somatosensory system, these different aspects of touch sensation are transmitted separately. Thus, different types of sensation are independently transmitted by sets of somatosensory neurons. For this reason, tactile quality is said to be encoded by *labeled lines*; within the central nervous system, the qualitative features of the sensory stimulus may be extracted by determining which fibers in the afferent pathway are activated.

Somatosensory Cortex   The primary somatosensory cortex is the neocortical area receiving direct projects from the ventrobasal complex. Situated on the postcentral gyrus of the parietal lobe, this region of the cortex is a complex of four distinct and separate regions. These regions are known as areas 1, 2, 3a, and 3b, on the basis of a labeling system originally proposed by Korbinian Brodmann.

Each area not only has a distinct and characteristic cellular architecture but is functionally specialized as well. Each area has its own unique pattern of inputs. Area 3a receives information from mechanoreceptors located within muscle tissues, whereas areas 3b and 1 receive input from receptors located in the skin. However, area 1 also has input from pacinian corpuscles, but area 3b does not. Mechanoreceptors located in the joints and other deep tissues project to area 2.

Each area also maintains its own separate and unique map of the body surface, in which each part of the body is represented once and only once. An example of these detailed somatotopic maps is shown in Figure 6.12. Notice that the maps for adjacent areas are mirror images of each other horizontally but are in parallel with each other vertically.

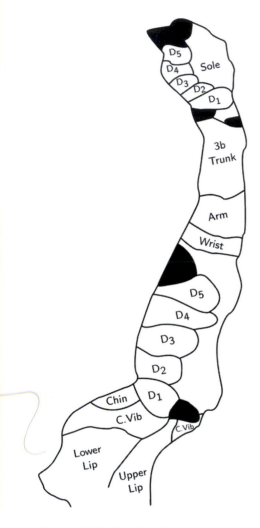

Figure 6.12. Detailed Somatotopic Mapping of Primary Somatosensory Area 3b. Notice that there is an orderly representation of the bodily parts in which the size of the representation is proportional to the density of sensory innervation of each area.

All along this pathway, a strict somatotopic mapping is maintained. However, differing amounts of neural space are devoted to different regions of the body; a great deal of neural tissue is allocated to sensitive regions of the body, whereas rather less is given to the insensitive regions, as shown in Figure 6.12 on the preceding page.

The amount of cerebral cortex devoted to processing somatosensory information from different parts of the body differs among species. Humans, for example, have a disproportionately large representation of two small bodily areas of particular importance to us: the muscular tongue that we use in speech and the opposable thumb that we use to grasp and manipulate objects.

The primary somatosensory cortex, like many other cortical regions, is functionally organized into a matrix of columns, each extending throughout the six layers of the cortex. Within a column, all neurons share two essential features: They respond to the same quality or aspect of somatosensory stimuli, and their receptive fields are extremely similar. Thus, the columns of the somatosensory cortex appear to serve as independent functional units, each processing a particular type of somatosensory information from a particular small region of the body surface.

Proprioception

Proprioception is the sense of bodily position and movement. Like tactile sensation, proprioceptive sensation is exact and precise. It is, after all, exceptionally important for a behaving organism to detect even small movements of the limbs or slight changes of position to function safely and effectively. Furthermore, there is little adaptation of proprioceptive sensations; we always know the position of a limb, for example, even when it has not been recently moved. It is proprioceptive sensation that allows skilled and dexterous movement. Proprioception has its origins in somatosensory receptors located in both the joints of the skeleton and the skeletal muscles.

Joint receptors are specialized mechanoreceptors that are positioned within the joints of the body in such a way as to signal the angle of that joint. Four types of joint receptors have been described.

Type I receptors are positioned in the fibrous joint capsule and maintain a continuous discharge that varies with limb position. Each Type I receptor has a characteristic best position, at which it responds maximally; as the limb is moved away from that position in either direction, the firing rate of the receptor is reduced.

Type II receptors resemble pacinian corpuscles. They too are located within the fibrous joint capsule. The Type II receptors adapt very rapidly; they are maximally activated by rapid movements and, for that reason, may function as detectors of acceleration.

Type III receptors are the largest of the joint receptors and are positioned along the ligaments of the joint. These fibers have a very high threshold and adapt quite slowly. The function of the Type III receptors is unknown; it has been suggested that they may serve some role in mediating protective reflexes.

Type IV receptors are complexes of fine, unmyelinated nerve fibers and may play a role in the perception of pain. These joint receptors appear to be best suited for signaling movements of the limb at the extremes of flexion and extension.

However, joint receptors cannot be entirely responsible for sensing limb position and movement. In patients with artificial hips, for example, a strong sense of proprioception for the limb remains, even in the absence of joint receptors. These individuals can sense both active and passive limb movements, although not quite as accurately as before replacement surgery.

An additional and important source of proprioception information is provided by specially adapted mechanoreceptors located within the skeletal muscles. These receptors form a critical part of the muscle spindles, which signal length and tension in many muscles and thus contribute to the sense of proprioception. (Muscle spindles are treated in detail in the following chapter.)

Central Mechanisms in Proprioception Like the sense of touch, proprioceptive information from the joint receptors and the muscle spindles of the limbs enters the brain through the dorsal column–medial lemniscal pathway.

At the level of the cortex, tactile and proprioceptive information is processed in different regions. Signals originating from muscle afferents project primarily to area 3a. Information from the joint receptors is preferentially treated in area 2. (Tactile data coming from the mechanoreceptors of the skin are processed in areas 3b and 1.)

However, the cortical processing of tactile and proprioceptive signals is probably not completely independent. Portions of each of these four areas serving a particular part of the body lie in close proximity to each other along the postcentral gyrus. Furthermore, all of these somatosensory areas send projections to and receive projection from each of the other areas. Higher-level processing of both tactile and proprioceptive information occurs in more posterior regions of the parietal lobe; it is in these regions that tactile and positional information from the limbs is integrated.

PAIN

Unlike the senses of vision, audition, and touch, the sense of pain not only informs, but it also motivates. One dictionary defines pain as *a more or less localized sensation of discomfort, distress, or agony*, all words that are reflective of pain's motivational and emotional aspects.

It is often said that pain serves a protective function. After all, does not the searing pain of a burn impel the withdrawal of one's hand from a flame? Does not the presence of pain motivate a visit to one's physician so that the source of the discomfort may be identified and repaired? Pain does provide evidence of bodily harm and thus has significant adaptive value.

But there is a darker side to pain as well. Pain is not a perfect sentinel of health. Progressive and fatal diseases proceed relentlessly without ever

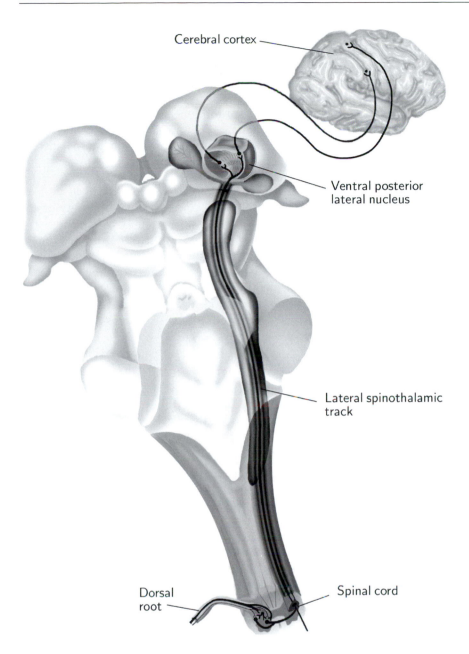

Cerebral cortex

Ventral posterior
lateral nucleus

Lateral spinothalamic
track

Dorsal
root

Spinal cord

Figure 6.13. The Anterolateral
System. This primitive neural system
carries temperature and pain
information from the spinal cord to the
brain. This drawing of the
anterolateral system shows the
ascending pathways involved in the
perception of pain.

a telltale warning of discomfort. Conversely, other disorders produce intense pain that has no adaptive value whatsoever. The pain that is often
perceived as originating in an amputated limb provides a clear example of
nonadaptive painful sensation.

The experience of pain—particularly prolonged, intense pain—can in
itself be destructive. It is exhausting, depriving both body and mind of
strength and vigor. The ordinary acts of one's life become arduous. Health
may deteriorate solely as a consequence of pain. In the words of Albert
Schweitzer, "Pain is a more terrible lord of mankind than even death itself."

That the pain system is not infallibly adaptive should not be surprising, considering that its evolutionary roots go deep into the past. The system is very old and in some ways a primitive neuronal structure, sharing many similarities across a wide range of species. However, pain is not a simple response to tissue damage; rather, it is the product of a sensory stimulus interacting with central influences that govern the experience and meaning of painful sensations. The same objective stimulus may produce a wide range of subjective responses in different circumstances.

Pain Receptors   The perception of pain occurs in a wide variety of circumstances involving stimuli that are at least potentially damaging to tissues of the body. Pain receptors, or **nociceptors** (from Latin *nocere*, "to injure"), are widely dispersed throughout the body; however, much more is known about the nociceptors located in the skin and in the superficial muscles than about those located in the deeper internal organs. In all instances, however, the cells that function as nociceptors have proved to be free nerve endings. No special microanatomical structures are associated with pain receptors.

Although all nociceptors are anatomically similar, they differ in the type of physical stimuli to which they most readily respond. Mechanical nociceptors respond primarily to intense mechanical stimulation, such as pressure from a sharp object. Heat nociceptors respond primarily to strong heat—heat that is capable of rapidly burning the tissue in which they are embedded. Other pain receptors function as mixed nociceptors, responding to both types of painful stimuli.

Furthermore, many nociceptors are chemically sensitive. Such cells respond to a range of pain-producing substances, including potassium, histamine, acetylcholine, bradykinin, and substance P. Potassium is particularly interesting because in many types of cellular damage, potassium is spilled into the extracellular fluid from cytoplasm of the damaged cells. Thus, if a receptor signals a rise in extracellular K^+, it could be signaling tissue damage as well. However, there is little agreement on which, if any, of these substances are actually involved in signaling pain. Although substantial progress has been made in recent years, detailed knowledge of the receptor mechanism or mechanisms that operate in nociceptors remains elusive.

Nociceptors communicate with the spinal cord by two types of fibers that differ in conduction velocity: **A-delta fibers** are small, thinly myelinated fibers that propagate action potentials at rates between 5 and 30 meters per second. Activation of the A-delta fibers is perceived as "fast pain," the kind that is abrupt in onset and has a sharp, pricking quality. The smaller, unmyelinated **C fibers** are responsible for "slow pain." C fibers are slower (0.5 to 2 meters per second) and bring forth a characteristic dull, burning, sickening sensation. Although not all A-delta and C fibers are involved in pain perception, no other categories of peripheral nerve fibers participate in the pain system; A-delta and C fibers are the only types of peripheral neurons that carry information from the nociceptors to the central nervous system.

Central Nervous System Pain Pathways   Both the A-delta and C nociceptive fibers enter the spinal cord through the dorsal roots and branch upward through several segments synapsing within the dorsal horn of the spinal cord. The **dorsal horn** is the portion of the butterfly-shaped gray matter of the spinal cord nearest the dorsal root. Neurochemical evidence indicates that **substance P**, a polypeptide, serves as the transmitter for the unmyelinated C fibers at these synapses. Unfortunately, rather little else is known about the local processing of pain information within the spinal cord except that such processing does occur and is rather extensive. Because of these complicated synaptic interactions within the dorsal horn, it is difficult to trace directly the flow of information from the nociceptors to the spinal pathways that carry pain signals to the brain.

Pain signals from the dorsal horn are relayed to the brain by pathways of the **anterolateral system**, shown in Figure 6.13 on page 211. In humans, these projections originate almost entirely within the contralateral dorsal horn, although a small ipsilateral contribution is probably also present. The importance of the anterolateral projection system for pain is suggested by three findings.

1. Surgical transection of the anterolateral quadrant of the spinal cord (cordotomy) in patients with intractable pain results in a marked decrease in pain sensitivity for the opposite side of the body. This decrease begins a few segments below the point of the lesion. This shift in segments reflects the upward branching of the A-delta and C fibers while synapsing in the dorsal horn. Unfortunately, the reduction in pain sensitivity produced by anterolateral cordotomy is not always permanent, perhaps because ipsilateral projections acquire a new importance after the loss of the major contralateral pathways.

2. Furthermore, electrical stimulation of the anterolateral pathways results in the experience of pain and produces sensations of warmth and cold as well.

3. Finally, lesions of no other region of the spinal cord relieve pain, which is further evidence that the ascending pathways of the anterolateral system are essential for the perception of pain.

Pain Is a Subcortical Sense   Pain differs from vision, hearing, and tactile somatosensation in another important respect: The cerebral cortex appears to be almost unnecessary for the experience of pain. There is no cortical area that, when surgically removed, either relieves chronic pain or produces a significant change in pain thresholds. This includes removal of the somatosensory cortex and related areas.

However, some recent evidence (Coghill et al., 1994) using positron-emission tomography suggests that cortical responses to painful thermal stimuli are present in the primary and secondary somatosensory cortices of the contralateral cerebral hemisphere, regions that are also activated by innocuous somatosensory stimuli. Thermal pain also activates regions of the anterior insula. The insula is a cortical area that has close connections with both the somatosensory system and the emotion-laden limbic system. These findings are in accord with the general view that pain represents an older, largely nonencephalized sensory system that has served a wide variety of species well in protecting them from bodily damage as that damage is taking place.

TEMPERATURE

The sensations of warmth and cold that we experience when grasping a cup of hot coffee or a glass of iced tea originate in the activity of **thermoreceptors**. Thermoreceptors are specialized neurons that alter their rate of firing as a function of their temperature.

Thermoreceptors are distributed across the bodily surface in a spotty fashion. Temperature-sensitive spots can be demonstrated by warming or cooling small patches of skin and testing for the perception of thermal change. In the course of such experiments more than a century ago, it was discovered that most skin is not temperature sensitive. Instead, discrete patches about 1 mm in diameter respond to thermal change. These areas are called warm and cold spots. As their names suggest, increasing the temperature of a warm spot produces the sensation of skin warming; conversely, lowering the temperature of a cold spot results in the sensation of coldness. With one interesting exception, the opposite pattern of stimulation (i.e., cooling a warm spot or gently warming a cool spot) results in no thermal sensation.

When a stimulus at a physiologically extreme temperature (e.g., 115° F, or about 45° C) is applied to a large area of skin containing both warm and cold spots, the resulting sensation is one of painful heat. But if a small, quite hot stimulus is applied selectively to a single cold spot, the subjective sensation is one of cold instead. This paradoxical effect of heat producing the sensation of coldness apparently results from the cold receptor being excited by a physical stimulus outside the normal physiological range of skin temperatures. The heightened response by a single cold receptor is always interpreted by the brain as an indication of skin coldness. When a larger area of skin is stimulated, however, both warm and cold spots are stimulated; from this more extensive range of sensory signals, the brain makes a more accurate determination of skin temperature.

Since the discovery of warm and cold spots, it has been presumed that each contains a single thermoreceptor. For a number of years, the identity of these specialized cells remained a topic of lively debate among sensory neuroanatomists. Today, however, most agree that thermoreceptors constitute a specialized class of free nerve endings.

Temperature-sensitive free nerve endings, like those in the pain system, are found on neurons with small A-delta and C fibers as axons. Sensations of warmth are encoded almost exclusively by the unmyelinated C fibers. Discharge rates in these cells increase with temperature throughout the range that people describe as "warm." At higher temperatures (above about 45° C), sensations of warmth give rise to the perception of painful heat. In this range, the relation between perceived skin temperature and the discharge rate of C fiber thermoreceptors becomes weak. Instead, a second system of heat nociceptors comes into play. These higher-temperature thermoreceptors, with their thinly myelinated A-delta fibers, fire in proportion to the intensity of painfully hot stimuli.

Cold receptors carry information about the cooling of the skin below a physiological and psychological neutral point at which the skin is perceived as being neither warm nor cool. Cold receptors use both A-delta and C fibers.

Spatial Acuity of Thermal Sensation   Although the warm and cold spots containing the thermoreceptors are small and discrete, the sensation of temperature is spatially very indistinct and general. Unlike the sense of touch, in which very fine mechanical features of a stimulus may be resolved, the localizing ability of people for purely thermal information is exceedingly poor.

For temperature, matters are quite different. Consider three pennies placed in a row, the outer pennies being cooled to freezing ($0°$ C) and the center coin at skin temperature (about $35°$ C). If the middle finger is placed on the center (neutral temperature) coin, that penny feels very much warmer than it does when the index and ring fingers are simultaneously touching the freezing pennies. This psychophysical observation suggests that the receptive fields in the temperature system are very broad, integrating thermal information across at least three fingers to give a very general indication of skin temperature in the hand.

Brain Mechanisms in Thermal Sensation   The central nervous system mechanisms mediating thermal sensitivity—to the extent that they are known—are similar to those of the pain system. For both, the afferent receptor fibers are of the small A-delta and C types. Within the spinal cord, both use the anterolateral system of projections to the brain stem and thalamic nuclei. Finally, for temperature, like pain, no cortical representation has yet been discovered. Although many subtle differences exist between the pain and temperature systems in terms of their overall structure and organization, significant similarities are apparent.

SUMMARY

Auditory perception begins as sound energy displaces the basilar membrane, introducing mechanical forces on the cilia that generate receptor potentials within the hair cells and action potentials in the auditory nerve. The fibers of the auditory nerve synapse in both the dorsal and the ventral regions of the cochlear nucleus. Auditory information is relayed through a series of brain stem nuclei to the medial geniculate, which projects to the primary auditory cortex. Within all the auditory nuclei and pathways, a tonotopic organization of fibers and synapses is maintained.

The vestibular system is closely related to the auditory system, sharing the bony labyrinth of the skull as the site of sensory transduction. A system of three orthogonally positioned semicircular canals signals accelerated movement of the head in any arbitrary plane. The two otoliths provide information about both linear acceleration of the head and the static position of the head with respect to gravity.

Taste receptors respond to substances by depolarizing. Taste information is relayed by cranial nerve fibers to the solitary nucleus of the medulla, which in turn projects to the ventral posterior medial nucleus of the thalamus and elsewhere. Similarly, olfactory receptors are specialized bipolar neurons located in the nasal mucosa. The axons of the olfactory receptors enter the brain, where they synapse within the olfactory bulb. Olfactory information is relayed to limbic regions, particularly the hypothalamus and the amygdala, and to the cerebral cortex by way of the posterior medial nucleus of the thalamus.

The somatosensory system mediates the sensations of touch, limb position, temperature, and pain. Mechanoreceptors transform variations in mechanical pressure on the skin into action potentials. The primary somatosensory cortex has a columnar organization; within a column, all cells respond to the same type of somatosensory stimuli and have similar receptive fields.

Pain and thermosensation are primitive senses concerned with the well-being and protection of the body. The perception of pain originates in the free nerve endings that serve as nociceptors. Pain information is transmitted to the brain by fibers of the anterolateral system. Similarly, thermoreceptors are also free nerve endings and are distributed over the body surface in a spotty fashion. The central organization of the temperature system is very much like that of the pain system. There is no known cortical representation for thermal sensation.

SELECTED READINGS

- Axel, R. (1995). The molecular logic of smell. *Scientific American, 273*(4), 154-159. Axel provides a clear and thoroughly up-to-date review of the molecular basis of olfaction, a research area that has generated a number of substantial new findings in recent years.

- Coren, S., Ward, L. M., & Enns, J. T. (1994). *Sensation and perception* (4th ed.). New York: Harcourt Brace. Coren and his collaborators provide an excellent account of the roles that sensory mechanisms play in human perception.

KEY TERMS

A-delta fibers Small, thinly myelinated peripheral nerve fibers with conduction velocities between 5 and 30 meters per second; in nociception, A-delta fibers mediate fast, sharp pain.

ampulla The structure of the system of semicircular canals containing the hair cell bundles.

anterolateral system The spinal pathways carrying pain and temperature information from the spinal cord to the brain.

ascending auditory pathway The afferent component of the auditory system that carries information from the ear to the cortex.

auditory nerve The eighth cranial nerve, which innervates the cochlea.

auditory radiations The ascending and descending fibers linking the medial geniculate nucleus with the primary auditory cortex.

aural dominance In a column of the primary auditory cortex, the tendency of cells to be driven preferentially by acoustic input to one ear.

basilar membrane The membrane that forms the floor of the cochlear duct and performs the initial stage of frequency analysis in the auditory system.

binaural interaction The way in which auditory information presented to one ear affects the processing of other auditory information presented to the other ear.

binaural summation columns Columns of cells in the primary auditory cortex in which cells respond to binaural stimulation more strongly than to monaural stimulation of either ear alone.

binaural suppression columns Columns of cells in the primary auditory cortex in which cells respond to binaural stimulation more weakly than to monaural stimulation.

bipolar neuron A neuron having a single dendrite and a single axon located at opposing ends of the cell body; in olfaction, the receptor cells. In the auditory system, the cells of the spiral ganglion, the processes of which innervate the hair cells of the cochlea and the cochlear nucleus.

brachium of the inferior colliculus The fiber pathway linking the inferior colliculus and the medial geniculate nucleus.

C fiber Small, unmyelinated peripheral nerve fibers with conduction velocities between 0.5 and 2 meters per second; in nociception, C fibers mediate slow, burning pain.

cilia Minute, hairlike processes that extend from the surface of a cell; in olfaction, the portion of the receptor cell in which sensory transduction occurs.

cochlea The spiral-shaped organ of the inner ear containing the sensory receptors for the auditory system.

cochlear duct The portion of the cochlea between the basilar and Reissner's membranes that contains the hair cells; also known as the scala media.

cochlear nucleus The first relay nucleus of the auditory pathway, located in the medulla.

cupula A gelatinous mass overlaying the hair cell bundles in the ampulla.

decibel (dB) A unit for measuring the ratio between two quantities; or acoustic pressures, equal to 20 times the common logarithm of the pressure ratio.

dermatome The region of the body serviced by a single spinal dorsal root.

descending auditory pathway The efferent component of the auditory system that originates in the auditory cortex, parallels the afferent (ascending) auditory system, and terminates at the hair cells of the cochlea.

dorsal column The afferent somatosensory pathway composed of axons of dorsal root ganglia cells that synapse on the medullary dorsal column nuclei.

dorsal column nuclei The nucleus cuneatus and the nucleus gracilis, on which the fibers of the dorsal column synapse.

dorsal horn The region of gray matter within the spinal column nearest the dorsal roots.

dorsal root ganglia The collections of cell bodies from dorsal afferent fibers.

ear The receptor structure of audition, divided into its outer, middle, and inner sections.

encapsulated nerve ending A somatosensory afferent with one of several specialized structures encasing the receptor.

endolymph The potassium-rich fluid surrounding the hair cell bundles within the ampulla of the vestibular system.

external auditory meatus The canal linking the pinna with the middle ear.

free nerve endings Unencapsulated somatosensory receptors, including those mediating pain.

frequency In audition, the number of waves of condensation and rarefaction produced by an acoustic stimulus each second.

glomerulus In the olfactory system, one of the small spherical masses of dense synaptic connections within the olfactory bulb that forms the first synapse in the olfactory pathway.

granule cell In the olfactory bulb, a cell providing lateral communication between mitral cells.

gustducin A G-protein used in sensory transduction of bitter and sweet tastes.

hair cells In the auditory system, the sensory receptors of the cochlea.

helicotrema The opening in the basilar membrane at the apical end of the cochlea.

hertz (Hz) Cycles per second.

Heschl's gyrus See *primary auditory cortex*.

incus The anvillike bone in the middle ear that serves to transmit air-driven vibrations from the outer ear to the inner ear.

inferior colliculus A nucleus of the brain stem auditory system located on the dorsal surface of the midbrain.

inner ear See *cochlea*.

insula The portion of the lateral surface of the cerebral hemisphere that is covered by portions of the frontal and temporal lobes.

intensity In audition, the strength of an acoustic stimulus.

joint receptor The somatosensory receptors at the joints of the body. Type I joint receptors resemble Ruffini endings; Type II are similar to pacinian corpuscles; Type III are large receptors with a high threshold; Type IV are complexes of fine, unmyelinated nerve fibers.

kinocilium The single supporting cell in each hair cell bundle of the vestibular hair cell bundles.

lateral lemniscus The system of fibers linking the medullary auditory nuclei and the inferior colliculus of the midbrain.

malleus The hammerlike bone in the middle ear that serves to transmit air-driven vibrations from the outer ear to the inner ear.

mechanoreceptor Sensory receptors that respond to physical displacement, as in touch.

medial geniculate nucleus The thalamic relay nucleus for audition.

medial lemniscus The projection from the medullary dorsal column nuclei to the ventral posterior lateral nucleus of the thalamus.

Meissner corpuscle A type of encapsulated somatosensory receptor.

middle ear The mechanical system that transfers acoustic signals from the outer ear to the inner ear.

mitral cells The principal neurons of the olfactory bulb.

nasal mucosa The mucous membrane of the nose.

nociceptors Sensory receptors for pain that are classified as mechanical, heat, or mixed in type.

nucleus cuneatus One of two dorsal column nuclei in the somatosensory system.

nucleus gracilis One of two dorsal column nuclei in the somatosensory system.

nucleus of the lateral lemniscus A small auditory nucleus located within the lateral lemniscus.

olfaction The sense of smell.

olfactory bulb The bulblike expansion of the olfactory tract on the undersurface of the frontal lobe; the site of the first synaptic interactions within the olfactory system.

olfactory knob The terminal enlargement of the dendrite of a bipolar cell from which emerge the olfactory cilia.

olfactory tubercle An olfactory area at the base of the forebrain.

ossicles The three small bones in the middle ear that serve to transmit air-driven vibrations from the outer ear to the inner ear.

otoliths The utricle and the saccule, two specialized structures of the vestibular system that sense linear acceleration and the position of the head relative to gravity.

outer ear The pinna and the external auditory meatus.

outer taste pore The outer opening of a taste bud.

oval window The membrane-covered, oval-shaped opening separating the middle ear and the inner ear, through which the vibrational energy of the stapes is transmitted to the fluid-filled cochlea.

pacinian corpuscle A specialized encapsulated somatosensory receptor that responds to changing but not sustained pressure.

pinna The portion of the outer ear that extends away from the head.

primary auditory cortex The first cortical area to receive information from the lower auditory system, Brodmann's areas 41 and 42, also known as Heschl's gyrus.

primary olfactory cortex The uncus and nearby cortical areas.

primary somatosensory cortex The region of the cerebral cortex receiving input from the somatosensory relay nuclei of the thalamus, forming the postcentral gyrus; Brodmann's areas 1, 2, 3a, and 3b, the postcentral gyrus.

proprioception The sensations of bodily position and movement.

receptive field In somatosensation, that region of the body where appropriate stimulation produces a change in the activity of a somatosensory neuron.

Reissner's membrane The membrane of the inner ear that forms the roof of the cochlear duct.

round window The membrane-covered opening of the scala tympani.

Ruffini end bulb An encapsulated somatosensory receptor.

saccule See *otolith*.

scala media See *cochlear duct*.

scala tympani The portion of the cochlea below the basilar membrane.

scala vestibuli The portion of the cochlea above Reissner's membrane.

segmental organization The pattern imposed on the spinal cord by its dorsal and ventral roots.

semicircular ducts The three circular tubes of the vestibular system that sense acceleration and deceleration of the head in each of the three approximately orthogonal planes.

solitary nucleus The brain stem nucleus receiving afferent input from the cranial nerves serving taste.

somatosensation The bodily senses of touch or pressure, limb position and movement, temperature, and pain.

somatotopic organization An arrangement by which somatosensory information originating in neighboring regions of the body is processed by adjacent regions within the brain.

spiral ganglia A collection of cell bodies, the processes of which form the auditory nerve.

stapes The stirruplike bone in the middle ear that serves to transmit air-driven vibrations from the outer ear to the inner ear.

stereocilia The specialized hair cells of the vestibular and auditory systems that encode information concerning their movement as changes in membrane potential.

substance P A polypeptide known to serve as the neurotransmitter within the dorsal horn for C fiber nociceptors.

superior olivary complex A collection of auditory nuclei within the medulla, portions of which are involved in auditory localization.

taste buds The multicellular organs containing sensory receptors for the taste system.

taste receptor cells The cells of the taste bud in which sensory transduction takes place.

tectorial membrane A thick membrane of the cochlea against which the cilia of the hair cells are displaced by movements of the basilar membrane.

thermoreceptor A somatosensory receptor specialized for sensing temperature information; either a warm receptor or a cold receptor.

tonotopic organization An arrangement in which similar frequencies are processed in adjacent regions of the nucleus or fiber tract.

trapezoid body A mass of transverse fibers forming an auditory pathway at the level of the pons.

tympanic membrane The thin membrane separating the outer ear and the middle ear, commonly referred to as the eardrum.

utricle See *otoliths*.

ventral posterior lateral nucleus (VPL) The thalamic somatosensory relay nucleus for fibers from the medial lemniscus.

ventral posterior medial nucleus (VPM) The thalamic somatosensory relay nucleus serving fibers from the trigeminal nerve.

ventrobasal complex The region of the thalamus that serves as a relay for touch and kinesthetic information, composed of the ventral posterior lateral nucleus and the ventral posterior medial nucleus.

vestibular hair cell bundles The groups of stereocilia and kinocilia of the otoliths and semicircular canals that transduce information in the vestibular system.

vestibular system The sensory system that encodes information about the position of the head with respect to gravity, its linear movement, and its acceleration.

Chapter 7

Movement

Humans—like other species—make their way through the world by their actions. Actions are movements, and movements are produced only by muscles. In this real—but limited—sense, the control of muscles *is* the ultimate source of behavior and action.

Much of our basic understanding of human movement and its neuronal basis was discovered nearly a century ago by Charles Sherrington, a British neurophysiologist who both received the Nobel Prize and was knighted for his work (see Figure 7.1 on the next page). Sherrington's approach to understanding movement is reflected in this reminescence of one of his students, John Eccles:

> One morning Sir Charles arrived with an inspired look on his face. He recounted vividly how he had seen a cat walking solemnly on a stone wall that was interrupted by an open gate. The cat paused, inspected the gap, then leaped exactly to the right distance, landed with ease

Figure 7.1. Sir Charles Sherrington. Sherrington won the Nobel Prize in 1932 for his work on spinal reflexes and the integrative activity of the nervous system. (Portrait courtesy of the History and Special Collections Division of the Louise M. Darling Biomedical Library, UCLA.)

and grace and resumed its solemn progression. A very ordinary happening, yet to Sherrington on that morning it was replete with problems for future research. How had the visual image of the gap been transmuted by "judgment" into the exactly organized motor mechanism of the leap? How had the strength of the muscle contractions been calculated so that the leap was exactly right for the gap? How after the landing was it arranged that the stately walk was resumed? Of course these questions were largely for the future, but some...could be answered in part. (Eccles & Gibson, 1979, p. 57)

Many of the answers to Sherrington's questions were discovered by Sir Charles himself. Sherrington is regarded as the founder of modern neurophysiology. His laboratory at Oxford in the earlier years of the 20th century became the training ground for later generations of distinguished neuroscientists. Sherrington concentrated his investigations on the mechanisms by which the spinal cord controls the movements of the body and, through those physiological investigations, developed a deeper understanding of the integrative activity of the nervous system.

MUSCLES

Sherrington's cat's leap was the result of a complex series of events occurring within its nervous system, but the movement itself was accomplished by the coordinated contractions of its muscles, in particular the **skeletal muscles** (Guyton, 1991). These are the muscles that are attached to the bones of the skeleton; by contracting, they produce bodily movements. In this limited sense, the skeletal muscles provide the most immediate biological basis of behavior.

In addition to the skeletal muscles, there are two other types of muscle tissue in the body: **cardiac muscle** and **smooth muscle**. Cardiac muscle is the muscle tissue of the heart; smooth muscle supplies mechanical power for the visceral system. Smooth muscle, for example, provides the force necessary to move food through the gastrointestinal tract in the process of digestion. Although smooth and cardiac muscle perform involuntary functions, they operate by principles very similar to those governing the voluntary movement of skeletal muscles.

Skeletal muscle is a highly organized tissue composed of specialized cells, the **muscle fibers**. Muscle fibers are long, thin structures that span the length of the muscle or a substantial portion of that distance. Muscle fibers are formed by the fusion of a number of separate muscle cells during growth; for this reason, muscle fibers may have many cell nuclei. But the bulk of a muscle fiber is composed of narrow (one- to two-micron) elements, the **myofibrils**, which extend through the entire length of the cell. These myofibrils provide the contractile strength of muscle cells. The myofibrils themselves are composed of two types of even smaller ultrastructural elements, the thick and thin **myofilaments**, often referred to simply as **filaments**. The thin filaments are composed primarily of the protein **actin**, whereas the thick filaments are composed of the protein **myosin**.

Muscle fibers contract as the thin and thick filaments move past each other (see Figure 7.2 on the facing page). To understand how this remarkable feat is accomplished, it is necessary to examine the arrangement of

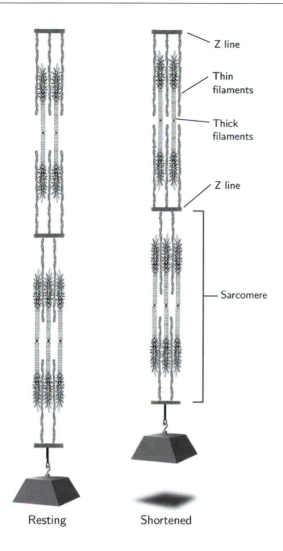

Figure 7.2. The Sliding Filament Theory of Muscular Contraction. As the muscle contracts, the overlap between thin and thick filaments within each of the sarcomeres of the muscle increases, shortening the length of the entire muscle.

thin and thick filaments as they lie beside each other within the muscle fiber. These filaments are organized into repeating assemblies that give the muscle tissue its characteristically banded appearance.

Each assembly of striped muscle is called a **sarcomere**, which appears microscopically as a series of light and dark bands across the myofibrils. The large dark stripe is the **A band**; the large light stripe is the **I band**. In the center of the I band is a thin, dark stripe, the **Z line**, as shown in Figure 7.2.

As sarcomere, bounded at each end by a Z line, contracts, the muscle fiber itself is necessarily shortened. This is accomplished by a shrinking of the I band, which is composed only of thin filaments. The thin filaments are fastened at one end to the Z line separating the sarcomeres; the other end of the thin filaments extends into the region of the A band. The contraction of a sarcomere is accomplished by increasing the *overlap* of thin and thick filaments within the A band, which shrinks the I band and therefore the overall length of the sarcomere. This is the sliding filament

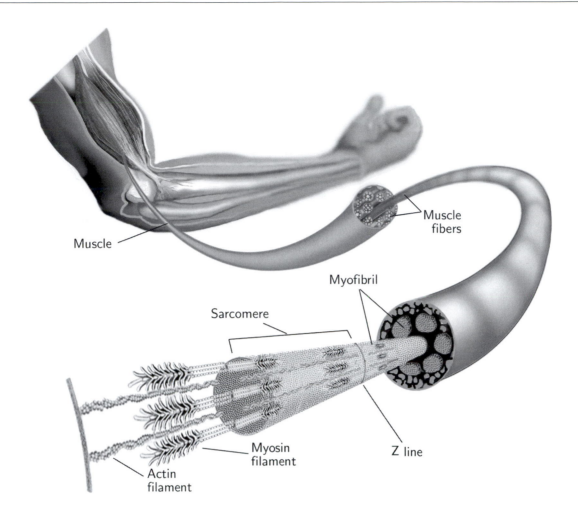

Muscle

Muscle fibers

Myofibril

Sarcomere

Z line

Myosin filament

Actin filament

Figure 7.3. The Structure of a Muscle Fiber. The fiber itself is formed by the fusion of many individual cells during growth. Myofibrils are the next smaller anatomical unit within the muscle fiber. These cells, which contain the filaments, extend the length of the muscle fiber. Cross-bridges link the actin and myosin filaments.

hypothesis of muscular contraction.

But what generates the force of muscular contraction, pulling the thin filaments into the region of the thick filaments? A part of the answer is shown in Figure 7.3. Between the thin and thick filaments are a series of tiny arms, called **cross-bridges**, that link the filaments together. In contraction, these cross-bridges function much like the oars on a long rowing boat and provide the force necessary to slide the thin filaments past the thick filaments. Thus, the cross-bridges of the thin filaments seem to walk along the thick filaments to produce contraction of the muscle.

Muscles derive the energy needed for contraction by converting adenosine triphosphate to adenosine diphosphate in a very thrifty manner; the efficiency of the conversion of chemical energy to mechanical energy may be as high as 70%. Thus, the skeletal musculature is well adapted to serve the mechanical needs of the body.

Muscles generate force as they *contract*; thus, muscles pull rather than push. But because the limbs of the body must exert force in more than one direction, muscles are often arranged in opposing pairs at bodily joints,

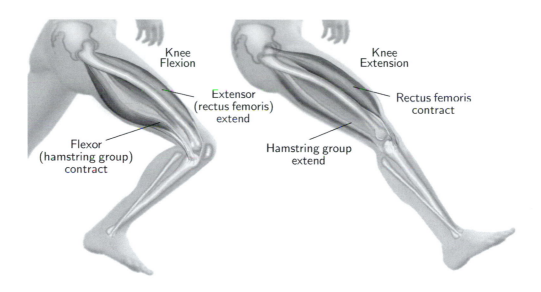

Knee
Flexion

Extensor
(rectus femoris)
extend

Flexor
(hamstring group)
contract

Knee
Extension

Rectus femoris
contract

Hamstring group
extend

as illustrated in Figure 7.4. Anatomists consider the **extensor** muscle to be the member of the pair that acts to straighten the joint as it contracts. The **flexor**, in contrast, serves to bend the joint. This opposition, or **antagonism**, of extensor and flexor is a characteristic pattern in the mechanical arrangement of skeletal muscles. However, the muscular attachments of some joints are more complicated, with additional muscles serving to permit rotation of the joint and other complex movements.

Figure 7.4. Opposition of Antagonistic Muscles at a Joint. The antagonistic extensor and flexor muscles are arranged in such a way that when the extensor contracts, the joint is straightened; when the flexor contracts, the joint is bent.

NEURAL CONTROL OF MUSCLE CONTRACTION

The contraction of skeletal muscle fibers is controlled completely by the motor neurons innervating muscle tissue. A **motor neuron** is a neuron—with its cell body either in the spinal cord or in one of the cranial nerve nuclei—that synapses on muscle tissue. Because *all* commands that regulate muscle activity and therefore behavior must pass through a motor neuron just before reaching the muscle, Sherrington (1906) considered the motor neurons to constitute the **final common pathway** for neuronal control of behavior. We do only what our motor neurons dictate.

The motor neurons that innervate most of the skeletal muscles are large cells with rapidly propagating action potentials; they are the **alpha motor neurons**, an anatomical classification of peripheral nervous system cells based on fiber diameter. Alpha motor neurons communicate with muscle fibers at a complex and extremely efficient synaptic-like arrangement, the **neuromuscular junction**. Figure 7.5 on the following page illustrates the essential features of this neurochemical connection between nerve and muscle.

The neuromuscular junction, with its complex folding and extensive area of contact between neuron and muscle fiber, must be viewed as a connection designed for extremely reliable and faithful communication from

Figure 7.5. Principal Features of the Neuromuscular Junction. The neuromuscular junction is designed to produce a reliable activation of the muscle fiber in response to each action potential. Here an extensive region of contact between the end-foot of the motor neuron and the muscle fiber is visible.

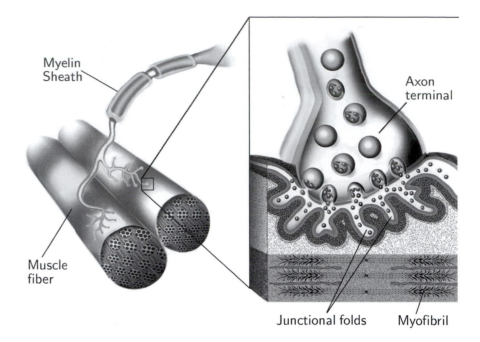

neuron to muscle fiber. Its action is not subject to probability because the neuromuscular junction is constructed in such a manner as to ensure that an action potential arriving in the motor neuron will be effectively translated into a motor action.

The neurotransmitter at the neuromuscular junction is **acetylcholine (ACh)**. ACh is bound in synaptic vesicles within the axon terminal element of the junction. With the arrival of an action potential, the contents of a few hundred of these vesicles are spilled into the gap between presynaptic and postsynaptic elements. There, some ACh molecules make contact with ACh receptors embedded within the membrane of the muscle fiber, to which they bind.

The ACh receptor of the muscle fiber responds to binding by briefly (about 1 msec) opening an ion channel and thus permitting the passage of small, positively charged ions—namely, sodium, potassium, and calcium. Of these, only sodium enters the muscle fiber in quantity, driven by both its concentration gradient and its electrical gradient. Thus, the neuromuscular junction is like a typical excitatory synapse within the central nervous system. At the neuromuscular junction, the release of ACh causes a depolarization of the membrane of the muscle fiber that is mediated by sodium ions.

The membrane of the muscle fiber shares a unique property with the axons of nerve cells; both are excitable membranes. An **excitable membrane** is capable of producing an action potential when depolarized. When depolarized to its threshold, the muscle fiber produces an action potential at the neuromuscular junction, which spreads out from that point in both directions, traveling both up and down the muscle fiber. The action potential, traveling the length of the muscle fiber, directly induces a wave of contraction in the muscle cell.

It appears that the depolarizing action potential in the muscle fiber triggers the release of calcium into the cytoplasm from intracellular storage sites near the myofibrils. This occurs very rapidly; within milliseconds of the initiation of the action potential, calcium is released throughout the length of the muscle fiber. For this reason, every sarcomere of the muscle fiber contracts simultaneously.

Each action potential arriving at the neuromuscular junction produces a single wave of contraction in the muscle fiber. This wave is not sustained but passes rapidly, a response that is naturally called a **muscle twitch**. The fact that movements seem to take place smoothly and in a graded fashion reflects the fact that a large number of twitches in the many fibers of the muscle blend together to construct a smooth and sustained contraction from the many brief contractions of the individual muscle cells.

The Motor Unit

Because the neuromuscular junction is so effective in producing a single twitch of the postsynaptic muscle fiber for each action potential arriving on the motor nerve, it makes sense to think of a motor neuron and its muscle fibers as forming a single functional entity (Burke, 1978)). This arrangement makes sure that every action potential conducted by the motor neuron's axon produces a simultaneous twitch in all the fibers connected to that axon. Sir Charles Sherrington coined the term **motor unit** to describe an individual motor neuron and all of the muscle fibers that it innervates. Motor units are the smallest functional unit in the control of muscle tissue, as shown in Figure 7.6 on the next page.

Motor units differ from each other in several respects, one of the most important being size. The axon of a motor neuron branches as it enters the muscle and may synapse with a number of muscle fibers. In some muscles, particularly those used for delicate movements, the motor units are small, with each motor neuron innervating only a few muscle fibers. In contrast, motor units in the large muscles of the back and leg, which must provide a great deal of force but are not required to exhibit precise control, have very large motor units. There, a single axon may branch and form neuromuscular junctions with as many as 1,000 individual muscle fibers. The size of a motor unit is determined in large part by the types of movement required of the muscle.

The characteristics of the muscle fibers themselves are also adapted to the functions required of the muscle. One fundamental difference between muscles is contraction speed. Fast muscles, such as the small internal rectus muscle that helps position the eye in its orbit, differ in a number of important respects from slow muscles, such the large soleus muscle of the leg. The **fast muscles** are adapted for rapid, intense, short-duration movements. Thus, the fast muscles have metabolic processes that enable them to use rapidly adenosine triphosphate in the absence of oxygen. This speedy anaerobic metabolic pathway is directly responsible for the rapid contraction of the fast muscles. Fast muscles are also known as white muscles because of their pale appearance.

In contrast to the fast muscles, the **slow muscles** are adapted for maintaining contractile force for prolonged periods of time. Thus, slow muscles

Figure 7.6. Motor Unit. A motor unit is composed of all the muscle fibers that are innervated by a single motor neuron.

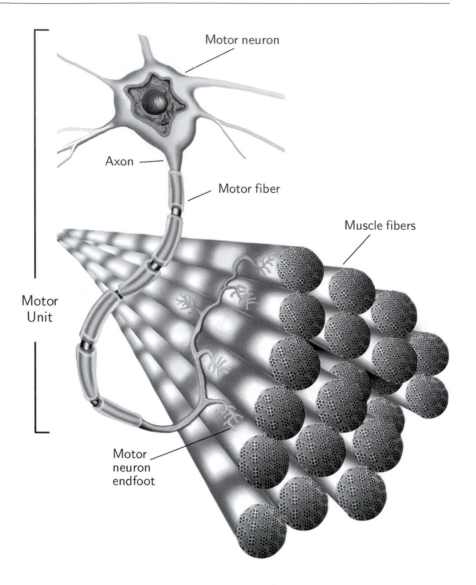

are used for maintaining posture and other similar functions. Slow muscle tissue is deep red in color, rich in mitochondria, and amply supplied with blood. These fibers employ oxidative metabolism in fulfilling their energy requirements, an important factor in understanding the high resistance to fatigue that characterizes slow muscle tissue.

However, many of the bodily muscles are neither purely white nor red but instead show mixed properties that reflect the unique set of requirements placed on them. Muscle tissue appears to be continually adapting to the tasks placed before it, always striking a balance between speed of movement, resistance to fatigue, and the efficient use of energy.

In many muscles, a mix of muscle fiber types may be found. But within a motor unit, that is not the case (Burke, 1978). Each motor neuron appears to innervate only one type of muscle fiber, as determined by histological techniques. Thus, even in a muscle containing differing types of muscle fibers, the composition of individual motor units remains pure. This probably reflects the capacity of motor fibers to adapt to the messages transmitted at the neuromuscular junction; because all muscle fibers in a motor unit are the recipients of exactly the same sequence of action potentials, all have exactly the same physiological characteristics.

The precise level of force exerted by a muscle is controlled in two ways (Guyton, 1991). The first is by raising the firing rate of a motor neuron. This increases the contribution made by that motor unit to the total output of the muscle. The second way of increasing the force of contraction is by increasing the number of motor units discharging within the muscle tissue, a process known as recruitment. When more motor units are recruited into responding, the resulting contractile force of the muscle is greater.

The **recruitment** of individual motor units of a muscle in the process of contraction takes place in an exquisitely orderly fashion, determined principally by the size of the motor neurons. Neurons with the smallest cell bodies have the smallest axons and innervate the fewest muscle fibers; thus, the size of the motor unit is a direct function of the size of the motor neuron. However, small motor neurons are also most easily excited by synaptic input. The increased sensitivity of small cell bodies to synaptic input results, at least in part, from the increased likelihood that a synaptic input can effectively reach the axon hillock of the neuron. These facts together suggest that weak synaptic input to the pool of motor neurons serving a particular muscle will excite only the smallest motor neurons, producing a weak contraction of the muscle. But as synaptic input increases, increasingly larger and more powerful motor units will be brought into play. Thus, there is an **order of recruitment** of motor units, beginning with the smallest and weakest and ending with the final activation of the largest and most powerful.

One effect of this arrangement is to maintain effective control of muscular force over a wide range of contraction strengths. As each new motor unit is activated, increasingly large increments of force are added. But at any level, all smaller motor units continue to discharge. In many muscles, these two factors balance each other to produce a constant increment in the percentage of contraction force as each new motor unit is included in the pool of discharging fibers. By successively recruiting progressively more powerful motor units as the demands for contractile strength increase, precise proportional control of force is retained.

Disorders of the Neuromuscular Junction   Two disorders of chemical transmission at the neuromuscular junctions of the motor unit are of particular importance. They are curare poisoning and the disease myasthenia gravis.

Curare is the name of a family of South American arrow poisons that produce death by paralyzing the skeletal muscles. It was used for hunting wild animals by native Indians from the upper Amazon to Ecuador (Koelle, 1965). These substances were prepared in secrecy by tribal witch doctors in elaborate rituals with demonstrations of magic. A diverse variety of procedures were employed. Central to all the poisons was a black, gummy, water-soluble resin. Several sources for the resins were probably employed. When the 16th-century European explorers brought samples back from South America for analysis, they were stored in three different ways: Pot curare was kept in clay jars, calabash curare was transported in dried gourds, and tube curare was stored in bamboo tubes. The contemporary scientific name for the most common form of curare is D-tubocurarine, a reference to its original shipping container.

Curare and related compounds act by binding with nicotinic cholinergic receptors on the muscle fiber at the neuromuscular junction (Gilman, Goodman, Rall, & Murad, 1985). They prevent ACh from binding with that receptor and depolarizing the muscle fiber. In this way, blocking the nicotinic receptor paralyzes the muscle. Muscle weakness rapidly gives way to complete flaccid paralysis, with the muscles exerting no tension whatsoever. Small muscles are the first to be affected, but soon even the largest muscles are affected. Breathing then stops, and, barring intervention, death ensues. If the dose is nonlethal, the muscles return to normal function in the reverse order, from large to small. Curare exerts virtually no effects on the brain or spinal cord.

Mimicking the effects of curare is **myasthenia gravis** (the name means "muscle weakness"), an autoimmune disorder in which the immune system produces antibodies that attack the nicotinic cholinergic receptors at neuromuscular synapses. By shrinking the normal supply of ACh receptors on the muscle fibers, it becomes increasingly difficult to maintain normal contraction of the musculature. Normally, the arrival of an action potential at the neuromuscular junction releases as much as four times the ACh required to elicit a contraction of the muscle. If the number of receptors available for binding is sufficiently reduced, action potentials will begin to fail to evoke a muscle twitch.

Myasthenia gravis often affects the muscles innervated by the cranial nerves; severely drooping eyelids are a common symptom, as is weakness of the arms and legs. The extent of the weakness varies considerably, both from day to day and from hour to hour. That it is an autoimmune disease was first suggested by the finding that it tends to co-occur with other autoimmune disorders, such as rheumatoid arthritis. Today, the actual antibodies that attack the nicotinic receptor have been identified.

Sensory Feedback From Muscles

The coordination of movements in many muscles depends not only on the carefully regulated recruitment of individual motor units but also on sensory feedback from the muscles themselves. **Feedback** in this case means that the muscles supply the central nervous system with information about the length and tension of individual muscles. The central nervous system can use such afferent information in many ways, including the making of fine adjustments to ensure that movements are properly completed.

The best understood source of sensory feedback from muscles comes from the **muscle spindles**. Muscle spindles derive their name from their shape, which is reminiscent of the slender rods with tapered ends that once were used with spinning wheels. Each spindle is attached at its ends to the muscle fibers that provide the contractile force of the muscle. As

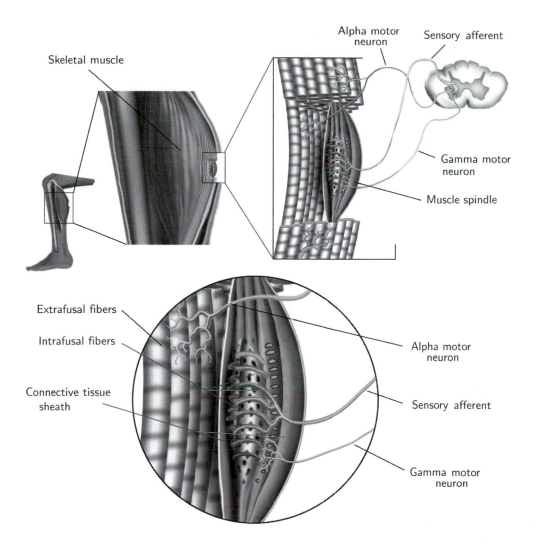

Figure 7.7. The Muscle Spindle. Sensory information originating in the spindle is relayed to the central nervous system by the sensory afferent fibers, which control the extrafusal fibers of the muscle.

might be expected, muscle spindles are more numerous in muscles used for delicate movements than in the large, powerful muscles that do not require precise adjustments.

Muscle spindles contain both sensory and motor elements. Figure 7.7 illustrates the structure of a muscle spindle. The bulk of the muscle spindle is formed by the **intrafusal muscle fibers**. Intrafusal muscle fibers are thin, pale muscle fibers that are specialized for the roles they play in the muscle spindle (*fusal* means "spindle-shaped"). The ordinary muscle fibers that actually move the body are called **extrafusal muscle fibers** to distinguish them from the intrafusal fibers of the muscle spindle.

Each muscle spindle contains no more than a dozen intrafusal fibers. Many of the intrafusal fibers have an enlarged central region called the **nuclear bag**. The intrafusal fibers of the muscle spindle are innervated by the **gamma motor neurons**, a class of very small-diameter and relatively slow motor neurons.

The sensory component of the muscle spindle is supplied by small afferent fibers that terminate within the nuclear bag and on other regions of the muscle spindle. These sensory fibers are wrapped around the intrafusal fibers and function as mechanoreceptors; they discharge when their endings are placed under tension.

These two elements, the weak intrafusal muscle fibers and the mechanoreceptive sensory fibers, provide the central nervous system with information concerning the length of the whole muscle. When a muscle is stretched, the muscle spindle, attached to extrafusal fibers, is placed under tension, and its afferent fibers discharge. The more tension is placed on the intrafusal fibers of the muscle spindle, the greater is the response of the spindle afferents.

One role of the intrafusal fibers is to determine the length of the muscle spindle at which the spindle will begin to be stretched. Because the intrafusal fibers are very weak, their contraction has no effect on the length of the whole muscle. But by contracting the intrafusal fibers, the gamma motor system can place the muscle spindle itself under tension. Thus, each level of gamma efferent input to the muscle spindle is associated with a particular length of the spindle, above which the muscle spindle will discharge and below which it will be quiescent. In this way, the muscle spindle informs the central nervous system about the length of the muscle. Such a system can and does participate in the feedback control of muscular contraction.

REFLEXIVE MOVEMENTS

The importance of muscle spindles in the regulation of bodily movement is most clearly seen in the stretch reflex (Sherrington, 1906). A **reflex** is an automatic, involuntary response to a particular stimulus, which literally "reflects" a sensory event into a motor action. The **stretch reflex**, an example of which is the well-known knee jerk, appears as a brief, strong contraction of a muscle that is momentarily lengthened. The neuronal pathways that mediate the stretch reflex were discovered by Sherrington and formed a firm foundation for the study of motor systems of the spinal cord.

Reflex Arcs   That the contraction produced by stretching a muscle was reflexive in nature and not the result of mechanical properties of the muscle itself was demonstrated by Sherrington in a convincing and straightforward manner; he showed that the contraction could be abolished by cutting either the motor nerve entering the muscle or the sensory nerve leaving it (Sherrington, 1906). For the stretch reflex to occur, the neuronal pathways from muscle to spinal cord and back again must remain intact. This set of connections forms a **reflex arc**.

Sherrington established a number of facts concerning this fundamental spinal reflex. In a long series of experiments, he and his colleagues were able to show that lengthening itself is the most effective stimulus for eliciting the reflex and that the response is specific to the muscle being stretched. The response is rapid in its onset and does not outlast the duration of the stimulus. Finally, Sherrington demonstrated that the stretch

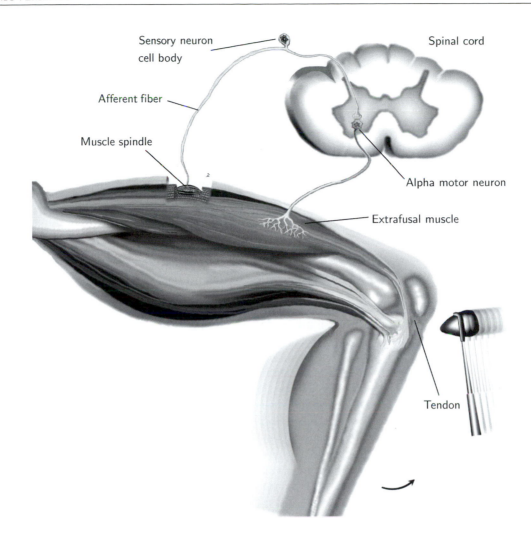

Sensory neuron cell body

Spinal cord

Afferent fiber

Muscle spindle

Alpha motor neuron

Extrafusal muscle

Tendon

reflex is a **spinal reflex**, meaning that it is mediated solely by neurons within the spinal cord. Thus, the stretch reflex remains when the spinal cord is surgically disconnected from the brain above it.

Neural Basis of the Stretch Reflex

The neural mechanisms mediating the stretch reflex are simple and elegant, as Figure 7.8 shows. Sensory fibers from the muscle spindles enter the spinal cord through its dorsal roots. There, the afferent axons branch and send branches of its axon directly to the alpha motor neurons that innervate the same muscle. This synapse between the sensory afferent fiber and the alpha motor neuron is excitatory, causing the alpha motor neurons to discharge, contracting the powerful extrafusal fibers of the muscle. The reflex arc is **monosynaptic** because only a single synapse is involved, accounting for the short latency of the stretch reflex.

The way in which this arrangement operates may be illustrated with

Figure 7.8. A Monosynaptic Spinal Reflex. The knee jerk reflex is a classic example of a monosynaptic stretch reflex in which a tap to the knee stretches the muscle spindle, activating its sensory afferents, which in turn excite the alpha motor neurons that control that muscle.

the knee jerk reflex. Here, the tendon serving the extensor muscles of the leg is tapped sharply with a hammer where it is exposed on the shin just below the kneecap. Tapping the tendon briefly lengthens the extensor muscle, putting its muscle spindles under tension. The muscle spindles respond by discharging, sending a volley of impulses along its afferents into the spinal cord. There, they excite the alpha motor neurons that supply the extrafusal fibers of the muscle, producing the characteristic knee jerk response.

The reflex arc accounting for the stretch reflex is of major importance in the ordinary spinal control and coordination of limb movements; it is not a neuronal adaptation to ensure knee jerks to tendon taps. The stretch reflex circuitry allows precise feedback control of muscle length by the gamma efferent system, which innervates the muscle spindles. By increasing input to the muscle spindles, the spinal cord may place the spindle under tension. This produces afferent discharge from the spindles that in turn reflexively activates the alpha motor neurons serving the same muscle. It is the alpha motor neuron input to the extrafusal fibers that provides the force for muscular contraction, shortening the muscle until the muscle spindles are no longer under tension. At this point, muscle spindle input to the spinal cord is diminished, causing a reduction in alpha motor neuron discharge. The muscle begins to relax, but relaxation of the whole muscle places the muscle spindles under tension again, increasing afferent input to the spinal cord and consequently alpha motor neuron discharge. The contractile force of the muscle again increases.

This reflex system of feedback ensures that the muscle will remain at the length dictated by the gamma efferent input to the muscle spindles. Thus, the gamma system may set the desired length of a muscle, but the alpha motor neuron–extrafusal fiber system provides the force necessary for contraction under the control of a monosynaptic reflex pathway.

Polysynaptic Spinal Reflexes

Other reflex arcs within the spinal cord act to coordinate the activity of different muscles. Unlike the monosynaptic pathway of the stretch reflex, these reflex pathways are **polysynaptic**—that is, they cross two or more synapses within the spinal cord. One of the simplest of the polysynaptic reflexes governs the activation of opposing muscle groups, such as extensors and flexors.

This pathway serves as an elaboration of the stretch reflex to control the contraction of opposing muscles. The afferent fibers from the muscle spindles within one muscle group excite a group of inhibitory interneurons within the spinal cord, in addition to exciting the returning alpha motor neurons. These inhibitory spinal interneurons project to the alpha motor neurons innervating the opposing muscle group. Thus, as the extensor contracts, the flexor is inhibited and relaxes; conversely, contraction of the flexor elicits relaxation of the extensor by way of a similar set of interneurons arranged in the opposite manner. Reflexive antagonist inhibition is one way in which the spinal cord simplifies the problem of motor coordination for the motor systems of the brain. In this respect, the motor system is hierarchically organized.

Another type of simple polysynaptic reflex is the **flexion reflex**. The flexion reflexes produce the withdrawal of a limb by contraction of a flexor and relaxation of the corresponding extensor muscle. Flexion reflexes can be produced by gentle mechanical stimulation of the skin, but a much more powerful response is elicited by intense, painful stimuli. The involuntary withdrawal movements produced by spinal interneurons of the flexion reflex are of obvious survival value, acting quickly to protect the organism from harm.

There are also more complicated and extensive spinal reflex pathways within the spinal cord. These **cross-spinal reflexes** coordinate the movement of muscles in the right and left limbs. These reflexes act to produce the opposite pattern of extension and flexion in a pair of limbs. When one leg is extended, the other is reflexively flexed. This bilateral response, which can be overridden by other commands to the spinal motor neurons, provides useful spinal assistance to the acts of walking and running.

The **suprasegmental reflexes**, also called the **long spinal reflexes**, coordinate the flexion and extension of the forelimbs and hindlimbs, which is of particular importance in four-footed animals. Suprasegmental pathways, which carry information between segments of the spinal cord, act to produce opposing patterns of extension and flexion in the two sets of limbs. This reflexive action is useful not only in locomotion but also in supporting the reflexive withdrawal of a limb from a painful stimulus (the flexion reflex). By ensuring that the left hindlimb remains extended when the left forelimb is reflexively withdrawn, the long spinal reflexes permit the four-footed animal to remain standing.

Thus, there are a number of spinal reflexes, each of which depends on a specific set of pathways and synaptic connections within the spinal cord. These reflexes are sufficient to produce a considerable range of motor responses in animals in which the spinal cord has been surgically separated from the brain. But the importance of the spinal reflexes is in the roles that they normally play in the control of movement. The spinal reflexes serve as an aid to the motor systems of the brain in coordinating the movements of the body. In a wide variety of ways, the spinal reflexes simplify the demands placed on the brain in controlling behavior.

BRAIN MOTOR SYSTEMS

The riddle of the brain motor systems must be solved in three general regions (Brodal, 1981). The first is the cerebral cortex. Three regions here are of particular importance. One is the **primary motor cortex**, the most posterior strip of the frontal cortex that forms the precentral gyrus, also known as Brodmann's area 4. The primary motor cortex was once thought to represent the highest level of the brain motor system; now that view is changing. The second cortical region is the **supplementary motor area (SMA)**, which lies immediately adjacent to portions of the primary motor cortex on the medial surface of the frontal lobe (the medial portion of Brodmann's area 6). The third is the **premotor area**, which is the lateral portion of area 6. The roles played by the supplementary motor area and premotor cortex in movement and cognition are at present a lively research area in cognitive neuroscience.

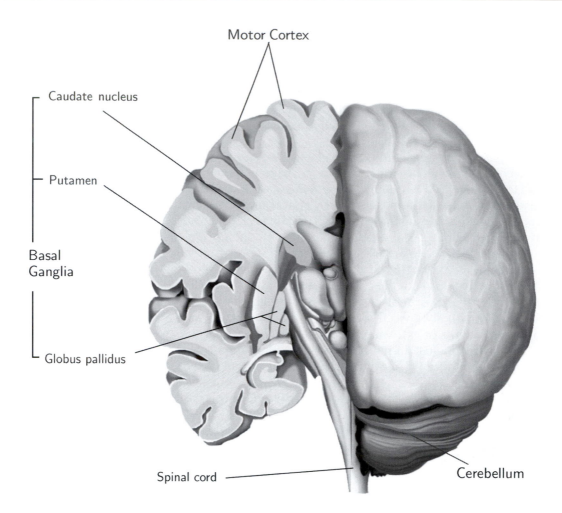

Figure 7.9. Motor System of the Brain. The three major components of the motor system—the motor cortex, basal ganglia, and cerebellum—may be seen.

The second brain motor region is a group of subcortical nuclei, the **basal ganglia**. The definition of the basal ganglia has been somewhat controversial. There is now general agreement that the basal ganglia consist of the caudate, the putamen, and the globus pallidus (Bowden & Martin, 1995). Closely related to the basal ganglia in its motor functions is the substantia nigra of the mesencephalon. The basal ganglia and related nuclei form the second key to the riddle of motor control.

The final key motor region of the brain is its **cerebellum**. The cerebellum is a primitive cortical structure—with a gray rind of neurons covering a white core of connecting fibers—that is attached to the brain stem at the level of the pons. Figure 7.9 illustrates the motor cortex, the basal ganglia, and the cerebellum.

These three regions of the brain motor system are connected to the motor neurons of the spinal cord by a number of anatomically distinct pathways; historical usage classifies these fiber tracts into two general groups: the pyramidal and the extrapyramidal motor systems. These are shown in Figures 7.10 on the next page and 7.11 on page 240.

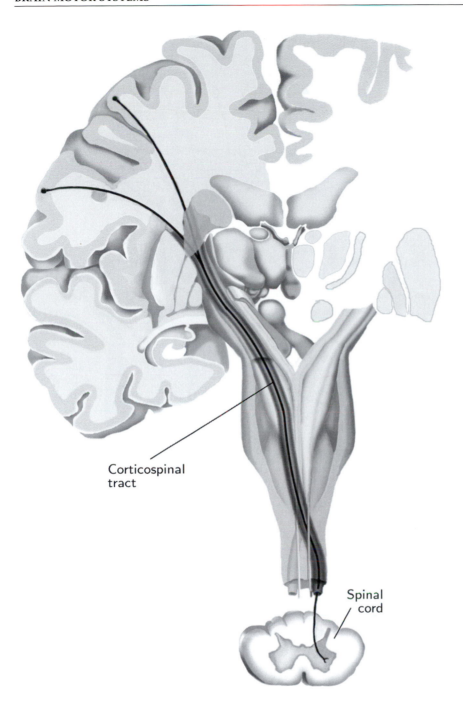

Figure 7.10. The Pyramidal Pathway. The pyramidal pathway provides a direct linkage between the cerebral cortex and the spinal cord.

Corticospinal tract

Spinal cord

The Pyramidal Motor System

The **pyramidal motor system** is composed of the pathways that originate in the cerebral cortex and project directly to the spinal cord. The pyramidal tract receives its name from the pyramidlike shape that this bundle of fibers assumes as it passes through the medulla of the brain stem on the way to the spinal cord.

Figure 7.11. The Extrapyramidal Pathway. Unlike the pyramidal pathway, the extrapyramidal system makes complex synaptic connections between the forebrain and the spinal cord. Although it is traditional to distinguish between the pyramidal and extrapyramidal pathways, these systems are not functionally independent. Instead, they act together in the regulation of movement.

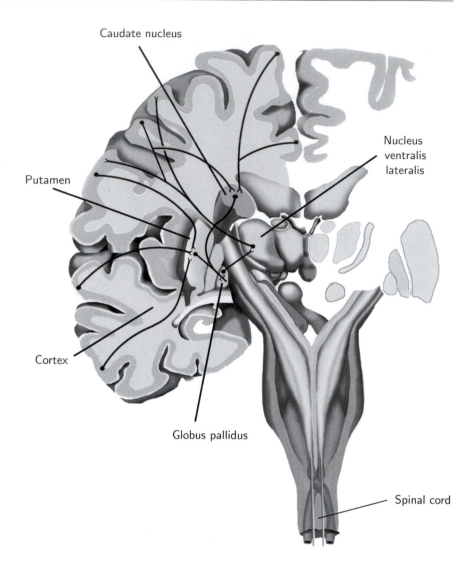

The neurons of the pyramidal system are the longest in the nervous system. Consider the giraffe, in which individual pyramidal neurons extend from the roof of its brain to the tail of its spine—indeed, remarkable cells. But even though all neurons of the pyramidal tract do synapse within the spinal cord, often directly on the motor neurons, they also project to other motor regions of the brain; the axons of pyramidal tract neurons give off many collaterals, or branches, on their way from the cortex to the cord. In this way, the cells of the pyramidal system may perform a variety of roles.

The Extrapyramidal Motor System

The **extrapyramidal motor system** consists of the pathways from noncortical areas that lead ultimately to the motor systems of the spinal cord. The extrapyramidal motor system includes not only the major noncortical descending pathways but also those central pathways that link the basal ganglia, cerebellum, and similar structures. It was once thought that the extrapyramidal motor system controlled only the lower, automatic, involuntary forms of movement, but this conjecture has proved to be incorrect. The extrapyramidal system plays important roles in the initiation and guidance of voluntary movements.

MOTOR REGIONS OF THE CEREBRAL CORTEX

More is known about the primary motor cortex than about any other portion of the brain motor system, perhaps because it is easily accessible and uniformly organized (Parent, 1996). The primary motor cortex, located on the precentral gyrus, is defined anatomically as area 4 of Brodmann, who distinguished it from adjacent cortical tissue on the basis of its cellular architecture.

The primary motor cortex differs from other parts of the cortex in two respects. First, Layer IV, with its small granular cells, is virtually absent. For this reason, the motor cortex is also referred to as the **agranular cortex**.

Second, the pyramidal cell Layers III and V are correspondingly enlarged. Because the primary motor cortex is populated with large neurons, it is not surprising to find that this region is the thickest of all cortical tissue, on the order of 3.5 to 4.0 mm in humans (compared to 1.5–2.0 mm for the human visual cortex). The large pyramidal cells are the output, or efferent, neurons of the cortex, with their pyramid-shaped cell bodies located in the deeper cortical layers, their single apical dendrites extending into the more superficial layers, and their axons usually leaving the cortex and entering the white matter. The primary motor cortex contains a variety of pyramidal cells, including the giant pyramidal **Betz cells**. The axons of primary motor cortex pyramidal cells constitute about 60% of all fibers in the human pyramidal tract.

Immediately anterior to the primary motor cortex are the premotor and supplementary areas of the frontal cortex, which corresponds to Brodmann's area 6. These areas are thought to perform more general motor functions, as indicated by the more generalized effects of electrical stimulation in this region. Area 6 also contributes a substantial number of fibers to the pyramidal tract.

Posterior to the primary motor cortex is the primary somatosensory cortex, located on the postcentral gyrus of the parietal lobe. Although the somatosensory cortex processes afferent information originating in the skin, joints, and muscles, its functions may be more than sensory in nature; axons of pyramidal cells in the precentral gyrus are the third major component of the pyramidal tract. The roles played by these fibers remain a puzzle. Thus, the pyramidal tract, although dominated by axons from the primary motor cortex, also carries information from the premotor and somatosensory cortex as well.

Mapping the Motor Cortex   As has been known for more than a century, stimulation of different portions of the motor cortex produces different motor actions. This is true of the human brain as well as that of nonhuman mammals.

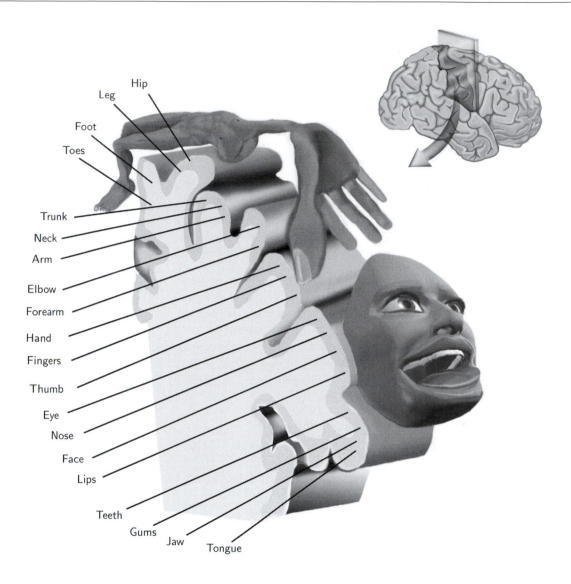

Figure 7.12. Penfield's Motor Map of the Human Brain. Penfield's map looks distorted, but it characterizes the motor cortex with great accuracy. The area of the cortex that regulates a particular muscle is shown in proportion to the number of motor neurons that innervate it.

In a series of detailed clinical investigations in the 1940s and 1950s, Wilder Penfield and his colleagues at the Montreal Neurological Institute mapped the motor cortex of patients during neurosurgery (Penfield & Rasmussen, 1950). Such mappings not only provide scientific information about the organization of the human motor cortex but, more important for the patients involved, also are used to establish the functional anatomy of each individual's cortex as a guide for surgery. An adaptation of Penfield's mapping of the human motor cortex is shown in Figure 7.12.

Two features of Penfield's map are of special importance. First, there is a strict somatotopic organization to the primary motor cortex. Cortical cells serving similar regions of the body are—to the extent possible—located near to each other in the motor cortex. Thus, the same principle of bodily representation that is observed in the somatosensory cortex on the postcentral gyrus is present in the motor cortex of the precentral gyrus. Second, not all bodily regions are equally represented on the motor cortex. A great deal of cortical tissue is devoted to the muscles of the hand, tongue, and face; this is not surprising because these are the muscles involved in the precise voluntary movements of speech and finger manipulation. The representation of muscles in the precentral gyrus increases with the delicacy of control required of those muscles.

One important modification of Penfield's map needs to be made, however. In the past two decades, convincing evidence has accumulated indicating that the primary motor cortex of the primate brain does not contain just one representation of the body's musculature but that it instead has multiple, independent somatotopic mappings (Zeffiro, 1990). More recently, evidence of multiple primary motor areas in humans has been obtained using functional neuroimaging methods.

Sanes and his collaborators (Sanes, Donoghue, Thangaraj, Edelman, & Warach, 1995) used functional magnetic resonance imaging to map the cortical response to finger and wrist movements in normal human volunteers. They found clear indications of a distributed and overlapping pattern of response to these movements across the posterior portion of the precentral gyrus.

In addition, Geyer showed microscopically that the primary motor cortex in humans may divided into an anterior and posterior strip that differ quantitatively in aspects of their cytoarchitecture, such as the size and packing of Layer III pyramidal cells. These same boundaries were apparent in synaptic receptor autoradiography. Finally, functional data obtained using positron-emission tomography reveal dual representation of the digits of the hand, one in the anterior region and the other in the posterior region of the human precentral gyrus. Thus, it appears that at least two separate areas may be identified within the human primary motor cortex that differ from each other in cytoarchitecture, histochemistry, and functional activation (Geyer et al., 1996).

Columnar Organization of the Motor Cortex The primary motor cortex, like the primary sensory cortex, is organized into functional columns. Using microelectrodes capable of selectively exciting individual or small groups of pyramidal cells in the motor cortex, Hiroshi Asanuma found that points at which electrical stimulation gives a common motor response are organized as columns within the cortex. These columns are perpendicular to the cortical surface and extend throughout the depth of the cortical gray matter. Asanuma termed these columnlike functional structures **cortical efferent zones**. Within each zone, several hundred pyramidal cells are present, each performing similar tasks of muscle control (Asanuma, 1989).

The activation of pyramidal cells within an efferent zone also has been shown to inhibit simultaneously the discharge of pyramidal cells in adjacent zones. The inhibitory pathways that are presumed to exist between zones may serve to reduce competition of incompatible motor responses and ensure that the output commands from cortex to spinal cord are free of conflict.

Many of the larger pyramidal cells within an efferent zone that form the pyramidal tract project directly to alpha motor neurons within the spinal cord. Smaller and slower pyramidal fibers synapse on the gamma motor neurons that innervate the muscle spindles. In voluntary movements, both alpha and gamma motor neurons are monosynaptically excited, a phenomenon referred to as **coactivation**.

This coactivation of the alpha and gamma system does not occur simultaneously, however, because the smaller pyramidal cells that supply the gamma system are very slow. Thus, a discharge in the pyramidal system results first in the excitation of alpha motor neurons and the resulting contraction of the extrafusal fibers of the muscle. Only later, when the movement is under way, does the gamma efferent system put the muscle fibers under tension and begin the process of feedback regulation of muscle length. This is one way in which the pyramidal system participates directly in the regulation of movement using feedback from the muscle spindles.

Patterned Cortical Activation in Movement

There are many indications that premotor and supplementary motor areas are involved in different aspects of motor control. One of the most elegant demonstrations of their specialized functions comes from the study of local cerebral energy use during motor activity.

Per Roland and his colleagues at the Karolinska Hospital in Stockholm have used a noninvasive method of measuring regional cerebral blood flow (rCBF) in human volunteers performing a variety of information-processing tasks (Roland, 1985). These studies are based on the fact that the local rate of blood flow through any region of the cortex is determined primarily by the momentary level of activation of that tissue. Thus, rCBF can provide an index of the involvement of different cortical regions mediating particular behaviors. Roland and his colleagues have taken this approach to study the functional properties of the premotor and supplementary motor areas in the production and control of human movement.

The production of any movement always results in increased neuronal activity and thus increased regional cerebral blood flow within the primary motor cortex. Activation of the primary motor cortex appears to be a necessary accompaniment of overt behavior of any sort.

In contrast, activation of either the premotor area or the supplemental motor area occurs only when more complex control or planning of movements is required. For example, voluntary behavior that requires the production of a complex sequence of movements results in a large increase in rCBF within the supplementary motor area. The SMA, for example, is activated in tasks such as solving pencil mazes and producing complicated patterns of finger movements.

The SMA is also activated in planning complex movements for execution at some future time, as in mentally rehearsing a skilled movement pattern. In this case, rCBF increases are seen in the SMA alone; there is no elevation of activity within the primary motor cortex because no overt movement takes place.

Voluntary complex movements of the fingers, hands, or feet increase blood flow in the SMA, premotor, and primary motor cortex. The premotor cortex appears to be particularly involved in voluntary movements requiring sensory guidance. However, not all voluntary movements require such sensory guidance, in which case the premotor cortex is not needed to produce the behavior in question. For example, in normal adult speech, only the SMA and the primary motor cortex—not the premotor area—participate in controlling language output. However, there are increases of rCBF in cortical language areas.

Motor Effects of Cortical Damage

Two types of movement disorders are known to result from damage to the cerebral cortex. The first is **hemiplegia**, which is characterized by a loss of voluntary movement on one side of the body. The second is **apraxia**, which is marked by a selective loss of skilled movements.

Hemiplegia is the result of damage to the primary motor cortex, although in many clinical cases, the exact site of injury is never established (Adams, Victor, & Ropper, 1997). Perhaps the most frequent cause of hemiplegia is a dysfunction of the middle cerebral artery, which supplies the primary motor cortex and adjacent cortical regions with oxygen and nutrients. A failure of a part of this arterial system quickly results in cell death in the affected region of the cortex. Hemiplegia always affects the side of the body that is contralateral to the damaged cortex.

In addition to the inability to move the affected muscles in producing voluntary movements, there are also characteristic changes in the tone or tenseness of these muscles and in the properties of certain involuntary reflexes.

Immediately following damage to the motor cortex, the contralateral muscles are paralyzed and flaccid; both voluntary and reflex movements are absent. However, after some days or weeks, the limp, unresponsive muscles change their tone and become exceptionally tense (neurologists say "hypertonic" or "spastic"). At this time, many of the reflexes that normally serve to support the body against the force of gravity reappear in an exaggerated form. The antigravity reflexes become unusually excitable or hyperreflexive.

The effect of the hypertonic musculatures gives the body a characteristic appearance. The arm is flexed, the fingers are curled, and the general posture of the upper body presents an exaggerated image of a normal individual running. However, the legs are fully extended and are moved only as a whole, without individual control of the muscles that move the joints of the knee and ankle.

One characteristic reflex indication of hemiplegia is Babinski's sign. **Babinski's sign** is the downward flexion of the toes evoked by gently rubbing the sole of the foot. In hemiplegia, Babinski's sign is absent. This test is one of the simplest and most reliable clinical indications that the contralateral motor cortex has been damaged.

Hemiplegia also produces a weakness in controlling the muscles of the contralateral lips, jaw, and face. (Unlike the hands and feet, there is both contralateral and ipsilateral innervation of the muscles along the midline of the body.) Thus, the use of the facial muscles to produce voluntary movements, such as smiling on command, is often impaired. However, the natural use of these same muscles in the facial expression of genuine emotion is completely unaffected. This suggests that emotional expression does not require the participation of the motor cortex.

In contrast to hemiplegia, apraxia refers to a specific loss of skilled voluntary movements in the absence of any obvious sensory or motor defect (Adams, Victor, & Ropper, 1997). An apraxic individual is capable of moving any muscle of the body with appropriate force, direction, and speed but cannot do so when such movements should be integrated into a complex voluntary sequence. Apraxic errors are most common when the behavior occurs outside a natural context. For example, a patient may wave goodbye quite normally in the context of leaving a friend but fail to produce the same sequence of movements when asked. This is the primary deficit in most apraxic patients.

Unlike hemiplegia, in which the disorder is confined to the muscles of the body that are contralateral to the cortical lesion, apraxia disrupts both sides of the body. This deficit is not linked to any specific set of muscles or their cerebral representation but instead is more general.

In virtually all right-handed individuals, apraxia results from damage to the left cerebral cortex; right hemispheric damage rarely interferes with skilled movement. In this respect, apraxia is similar to aphasia (the disruption of language), which also typically results from left, rather than right, hemispheric lesions. This similarity between the two disorders raises the possibility that the apraxic deficit is really one of language comprehension, but such is not the case. Although some individuals with larger left-hemisphere lesions are both apraxic and aphasic, most apraxic individuals show no evidence of any linguistic impairment whatsoever. Furthermore, surgical removal of the language areas of the left hemisphere produces a profound aphasia but only minimally affects the production of skilled movements. Thus, apraxia appears not to arise from any failure of the language system.

Further evidence of the importance of the left cerebral hemisphere in the production of complex movement was provided by Brenda Milner at the Montreal Neurological Institute (Milner, 1976). Milner trained people to make a complex sequence of arm movements and tested their ability to execute the sequence when either the right or the left hemisphere was selectively anesthetized by amobarbital, a barbiturate. Only anesthesia of the left hemisphere disrupted the trained motor behavior; anesthesia of the right hemisphere had no effect.

THE BASAL GANGLIA

The term *ganglion* (*ganglia* in the plural) usually refers to a collection of nerve cell bodies outside the brain and spinal cord; within the central nervous system, such collections are called *nuclei*. But there is one exception to this rule: a special set of nuclei at the base of the forebrain that is historically called the **basal ganglia**.

The basal ganglia consist of the **caudate nucleus**, the **putamen**, and the **globus pallidus**. The caudate nucleus and the putamen together form the **neostriatum** (Brodal, 1981). These neostriatal nuclei are similar in cellular structure and develop from telencephalic tissue, as does the cerebral

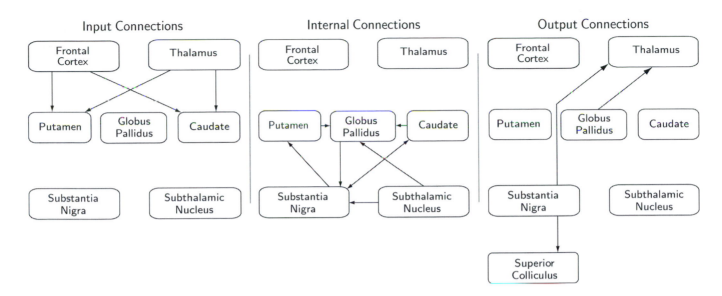

Figure 7.13. Connections of the Basal Ganglia. To make this complex system more understandable, its connections are divided into three groups: input connections (left), internal connections (center), and output connections (right).

cortex. In contrast, the globus pallidus is the **paleostriatum** ("old striatum"), which develops from the diencephalon and is very different from the neostriatum in its cellular structure.

Closely related to the basal ganglia is the **substantia nigra**, which functions with basal ganglia nuclei in the control of movement. Similarly, the **subthalamic nucleus** of the diencephalon also shares some motor functions with the nuclei of the basal ganglia.

The basal ganglia do not receive inputs from the spinal cord, nor do they project directly to the spinal cord. Instead, they communicate upward with the motor regions of the cerebral cortex.

The major afferent input to the basal ganglia comes from the forebrain. The putamen receives input from many regions of the cerebral cortex, including motor, sensory, and association areas. The caudate nucleus receives input from both the cerebral cortex and certain nuclei of the thalamus. These are shown in Figure 7.13 (left).

The interconnections of the basal ganglia and input from important neighboring nuclei are illustrated in Figure 7.13 (middle). Processed input from both the putamen and the caudate is received by both the globus pallidus and the substantia nigra. In turn, the substantia nigra sends out to both the putamen and the caudate nucleus. Finally, the nearby subthalamic nucleus sends information to both the globus pallidus and the substantia nigra.

The principal output from the basal ganglia is from the globus pallidus to the thalamus, which is relayed to the premotor and supplementary motor cortices, shown in Figure 7.13 (right). The substantia nigra projects to both the thalamus and the superior colliculus of the brain stem. Thus, the basal ganglia and related nuclei receive input from and provide output to the cortex and thalamus. These input and output projections are topographically arranged so that the orderly cortical representation of the body is maintained as information passes through the basal ganglia.

It appears that much of the function of the basal ganglia is directed to the higher-order control of movement. Other circuits within the basal ganglia participate in the control of eye movements and the position of movements in space. In addition to their motor functions, the basal ganglia also are involved in aspects of cognition or memory.

The importance of the basal ganglia in cognition is illustrated in two disorders of these nuclei: Parkinson's disease and Huntington's chorea. Patients with these disorders show a progressive decline of cognitive function, which neurologists call **dementia**.

Parkinson's Disease

Parkinson's disease provided the first clue in unraveling the motor functions of the basal ganglia (Adams, Victor, & Ropper, 1997). James Parkinson was an English physician of the early 19th century. In his 1817 book, *An Essay on the Shaking Palsy*, Parkinson described the disorder that now bears his name. It is characterized by "involuntary tremulous motion, with lessened muscular power, in parts not in action and even when supported; with a propensity to bend the trunk forwards, and to pass from a walking to a running pace; the senses and intellects being uninjured."

The constant shaking that marks the patient with Parkinson's disease at rest is the least of the patient's problems. A more profound trouble is a difficulty in initiating voluntary movements. Getting up from bed or rising from a chair takes immense effort and concentration. Patients must plan their movements carefully, trying to accomplish their most important objectives with a tolerable amount of mental effort. To complicate matters further, reflexive movements are also impaired and slowed in parkinsonism; thus, when thrown off balance, the parkinsonian patient will fall to the ground long before the normal compensatory reflexes are brought into play.

The biochemical basis of Parkinson's disease was clarified in the early 1960s (Cooper, Bloom, & Roth, 1996). First came the finding that a disorder much like Parkinson's disease occurred in psychiatric patients who were given the antipsychotic compound reserpine.

Next, Avid Carlsson, a Swedish neurochemist, showed that the neostriatum normally contains very high concentrations of dopamine and that reserpine depletes dopamine in these nuclei.

The final clue was provided by a large-scale study of monoamine concentrations in postmortem examination; in reviewing the medical histories of the patients, all patients showing severely reduced brain dopamine had suffered from Parkinson's disease. This was the first time that a specific clinical disorder had been linked to a deficiency of a specifiable central nervous system neurotransmitter. Today, Parkinson's disease is believed to result from damage to the dopaminergic projection from the substantia nigra to the basal ganglia. This results in an insufficiency of dopamine within the basal ganglia. Consequently, temporary relief from the symptoms of Parkinson's disease may be obtained by administering the dopamine precursor L-DOPA.

A disorder very much like Parkinson's disease may be chemically induced. In California, a number of young heroin users developed a severe Parkinson's-like syndrome after using a particular type of synthetic heroin. This homemade product was shown to contain a neurally toxic substance, 1-methyl-4-phenyl, 1,2,3,6-tetrahydropyridine, or MPTP. This neurotoxin destroys dopaminergic neurons in the substantia nigra. As tragic as this event may have been, isolating the neurotoxin provided the basis for developing an animal model of the disorder, which is an important step in developing drug therapies for Parkinson's disease itself.

Huntington's Chorea

Another clinical clue to the motor functions of the basal ganglia is found in **Huntington's chorea** (the term **chorea** refers to complex involuntary jerky movements). George Huntington was an American physician who practiced medicine with his father in East Hampton, Long Island (see Figure 7.14). In the community were patients with a hereditary chorea, a disorder characterized by a wide variety of rapid, complicated, jerky movements that appear coordinated but occur involuntarily. Virtually all of these patients were descendants of a few early settlers who immigrated in 1630 to New York from a small town in Suffolk, England. Both the hereditary nature of the chorea and its devastating motor effects were evident to Huntington, who wrote the following of these patients:

Figure 7.14. George Huntington. Huntington was the American physician who described the chorea that affected a number of people in East Hampton, Long Island, where he practiced medicine. (Portrait courtesy of the History and Special Collections Division of the Louise M. Darling Biomedical Library, UCLA.)

> The hereditary chorea, as I shall call it, is confined to certain and fortunately few families, and has been transmitted to them, an heirloom from generations away back in the dim past. It is spoken of by those in whose veins the seeds of the disease are known to exist, with a kind of horror and not all alluded to except through dire necessity, when it is mentioned as "that disorder." It is attended generally by all the symptoms of common chorea, only in an aggravated degree, hardly ever manifesting itself until adult or middle life, and then coming on gradually, but surely, increasing by degrees, and often occupying years in its development until the hapless sufferer is but a quivering wreck of his former self. (McHenry, 1969, pp. 410-411)

The motor aspects of Huntington's chorea are now known to arise from a disorder of neurotransmitters within the basal ganglia. In Huntington's chorea, there is a marked loss of small cholinergic neurons that synapse within the basal ganglia as well as GABA-containing neurons that project to the substantia nigra. This neuronal loss is thought to result in a disinhibition of the dopaminergic neurons of the substantia nigra, which in turn produces excessive inhibition of the projection from the globus pallidus to the thalamus and motor cortex.

Although such a theory is in large portion presumptive, there is biochemical evidence that a balance of neurotransmitters within the basal ganglia is required for normal motor function. In Huntington's chorea, there is a marked decrease in the neostriatum of both choline acetyltransferase, the enzyme required for producing acetylcholine (ACh), and of GABA and its biosynthetic enzyme, glutamic acid decarboxylase. Thus, Huntington's chorea is characterized by an excess of dopamine and a lack of ACh and GABA within the basal ganglia. Interestingly, the symptoms of Huntington's chorea worsen when L-DOPA is administered, a treatment that should further upset the balance of neurotransmitters. Completing the picture, parkinsonian patients may develop Huntington-like symptoms if too much L-DOPA is given in treatment, converting their dopamine deficiency into a dopamine excess.

THE CEREBELLUM

The cerebellum is the third of the major motor structures of the human brain. Located on the dorsal surface of the brain stem at the level of the pons, the cerebellum acts cooperatively with the cerebral cortex to provide for the coordination of finely executed complex movements, including speech (Parent, 1996; Brodal, 1981).

The structure of the cerebellum is relatively straightforward. The cerebellum consists of an outer surface of gray matter, the **cerebellar cortex**, which overlies the internal white matter of fibers passing to and from the cortical surface. Beneath the white matter are three pairs of **deep cerebellar nuclei**: the **fastigial nuclei**, the **interposed nuclei**, and the **dentate nuclei**. The deep nuclei of the cerebellum are the origin of efferent fibers that leave the cerebellum and project to the motor regions of the cerebral cortex and the brain stem.

The cerebellum receives afferent input from the cerebral cortex, the basal ganglia, and the spinal cord; through these connections, the cerebellum is informed of activity elsewhere within the motor system. The cerebellum also receives sensory input, by both direct and indirect pathways, from all regions of the body.

Effects of Cerebellar Damage   The importance of the cerebellum in the control of movement is indicated by the motor disturbances that result from cerebellar lesions (Roland, 1984). Cerebellar damage is marked by a loss of motor coordination. The coordinated contraction of antagonistic muscle groups is often absent during voluntary action. The smooth sequencing of contractions that characterizes complex movements disappears; the patient is forced to execute a series of simple movements, each one under voluntary control, to complete the complex movement that a normal individual would execute "without thinking."

The role of the cerebellum as a coordinating and correcting computer for complex movement is most apparent in cases of **intention tremor** following cerebellar damage. Intention tremor is a shaking disorder that begins as a voluntary movement is initiated and becomes increasingly more pronounced as the movement proceeds. This pattern of increasingly disregulated voluntary movements suggests that the cerebellum normally provides a continuous source of error-correcting information and commands to other parts of the motor system. When the cerebellum itself is disordered, its commands do not act to smooth and coordinate naturally occurring errors in movement but rather serve to worsen the problem. Intention tremor occurs only during voluntary movements.

Cerebellar disease also results frequently in changes of muscular tone. Typically, the level of tension in opposing muscle groups at rest is diminished, so that the limb is flaccid and presents little resistance to movement or manipulation.

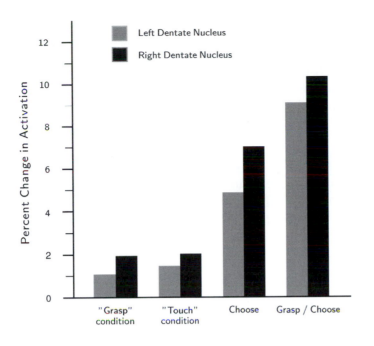

Figure 7.15. Cerebellar Activation in Sensory and Motor Tasks. Changes in cerebral blood flow in the dentate nuclei of the cerebellum occur during cognitive processing. Notice that much larger increases in cerebellar activity are evoked when sensory discriminations are required (in the "Choose" conditions) than either in the simple sensory stimulation ("Touch" condition) or the coordinated movement ("Grasp" condition). Such a result suggests that the cerebellum may play important roles in higher cognitive functions in addition to the motor purposes that it serves.

Finally, speech may be disturbed by cerebellar damage. This disorder is called **dysarthria**, a dysfunction of the fine articulatory movements of the vocal system. In such cases, speech is slurred and often slowed, indicative of the difficulty in executing speech movements exactly. However, there is no disruption of the symbolic or linguistic aspects of language. Cerebellar dysarthria is purely a motor disorder.

Thus, the cerebellum appears to serve a variety of coordinating and error-correcting roles within the motor system of the brain. It has continued to evolve with the cerebral cortex of the forebrain, to which it is intimately connected. The cerebellum, once regarded as a brain stem system for producing automatic movements, is now recognized as an essential part of the brain systems that mediate voluntary movements as well.

Other Roles for the Cerebellum   But even this expanded view of the cerebellum as a high-level motor system has been questioned in the past few years, in the face of mounting evidence of apparent cerebellar involvement in nonmotor, high-level cognitive processes. Consider the experiment reported by Goa et al. (1996), who measured brain activation using positron-emission tomography under four experimental conditions: (a) grasping, in which they repeatedly grasped, raised, and then dropped an object; (b) touching, in which the fingers of each hand were stimulated by gently rubbing with sandpaper; (c) choosing, in which they judged the comparative coarseness of different sandpaper stimuli; and (d) grasping/choosing, in which they grasped two different objects with their two hands and judged if the shapes of the objects were the same. If the cerebellum is a motor structure, then it should be the grasping tasks that activate it, but that was not what the positron-emission tomography (PET) scans indicated, as may be seen in Figure 7.15 (Goa et al., 1996).

Activation was observed in both the right and the left dentate nuclei of the cerebellum, as indicated by PET blood flow imaging, but the motoric grasping task itself resulted in only a small, statistically insignificant increase in cerebellar activity. A somewhat stronger activation accompanied the simple sensory stimulation condition.

In contrast, a large increase in cerebellar activity occurred when a sensory discrimination was required, whether movement was involved (as in the grasping/choosing condition) or not (as in the simple choosing task). Such results make no sense whatsoever if the cerebellum's functions are limited to the domain of motor processing but are congruent with the growing body of evidence that the cerebellum contributes to human cognitive function in a higher-level, more general manner. But what these higher cerebellar functions may be is not at all clear at present.

SUMMARY

The skeletal musculature is the only tissue capable of producing bodily movements. Sensory feedback from muscle tissue is supplied by the muscle spindles. The spinal reflexes provide a complex spinal system for motor control through which the higher motor centers of the brain can exert their effects.

The three major regions of the central nervous system concerned with the control of movement are the cortical motor areas, the basal ganglia, and the cerebellum. The primary motor, premotor, and supplementary motor cortex regulate movement at the cortical level. The premotor and supplementary motor areas appear to play important roles during complex movements requiring sensory guidance. The roles played by the basal ganglia in voluntary movement are beginning to be understood through the study of patients with disorders in this region, particularly patients with Parkinson's disease and Huntington's chorea. Finally, damage to the cerebellum results in disorders of coordinated movement. Intention tremor and a loss of muscle tone also mark cerebellar damage.

SELECTED READING

- Bizzi, E. (2000). Motor systems. In M. Gazzaniga (Ed.), *The new cognitive neurosciences*. Cambridge: MIT Press. This set of nine individual chapters provides an overview of the neural basis of motor behavior from the perspectives of leading researchers in this field.

KEY TERMS

A band The region of the sarcomere containing thick filaments.

acetylcholine (ACh) The transmitter substance of the neuromuscular junction.

actin A protein in muscle that is the principal component of the thin filaments.

agranular cortex The primary motor cortex, which has relatively few small granular cells.

alpha motor neuron A large motor neuron innervating extrafusal fibers.

antagonism In opposition; antagonist muscles are arranged to move a limb in opposite directions.

apraxia The selective loss of skilled movements in the absence of simple sensory or motor defects.

Babinski's sign The downward flexion of the toes evoked by gently rubbing the sole of the foot.

basal ganglia The collection of nuclei located at the base of the cerebral hemispheres that includes the caudate nucleus, putamen, globus pallidus, and amygdala.

Betz cells The large pyramidal cells of the motor cortex.

cardiac muscle The muscle tissue of the heart.

caudate nucleus One of the basal ganglia and a part of the extrapyramidal motor system.

cerebellar cortex The gray matter on the outer surface of the cerebellum.

cerebellum The large cortical structure of the metencephalon, important in the coordination of voluntary movements.

chorea A neurological disorder marked by an unending sequence of a wide variety of rapid, complex, jerky, well-coordinated, involuntary movements (from the Greek word for "dancing").

coactivation With respect to motor systems, the simultaneous involvement of alpha and gamma motor neurons in producing voluntary movement.

cortical efferent zone A functional column of the motor cortex.

cross-bridges The molecular attachments by which thin filaments are pulled along thick filaments.

cross-spinal reflex A reflex affecting muscles on the opposite side of the body.

curare A compound that paralyzes the skeletal muscles by binding to nicotinic cholinergic receptors at the neuromuscular junction.

deep cerebellar nuclei The nuclear masses at the base of the cerebellum.

dementia The loss of intellectual function produced by brain damage or disease.

dentate nucleus One of the deep nuclei of the cerebellum.

dysarthria A dysfunction of the fine articulatory movements of the vocal system.

excitable membrane A cell membrane that is capable of sustaining an action potential; axons and muscle fibers.

extensor A muscle that acts to extend a joint.

extrafusal muscle fiber All skeletal muscle fibers except those of muscle spindles.

extrapyramidal motor system All brain structures involved in the control of movement, except the pyramidal system.

fast muscle A muscle fiber that is capable of rapid contraction; white muscle.

fastigial nucleus One of the deep cerebellar nuclei.

feedback The flow of information from the output to the input of a controlled system, from which the future behavior of the system can be adjusted.

filament See *myofilament*.

final common pathway Sherrington's concept of the motor neuron as the ultimate determinant of muscle activity and therefore the last segment of the circuit through which all motor commands must travel.

flexion reflex A polysynaptic reflex acting to withdraw a limb from a stimulus.

flexor A muscle that acts to flex a joint.

gamma motor neuron A small motor neuron innervating the muscle spindles.

globus pallidus One of the basal ganglia and a part of the extrapyramidal motor system.

hemiplegia The loss of voluntary movement on one side of the body as a result of cortical damage.

Huntington's chorea A particularly violent form of hereditary chorea.

I band The region of a sarcomere containing only thin filaments.

intention tremor A tremor or shaking that occurs only during the performance of voluntary movements, often the result of cerebellar damage.

interposed nucleus One of the deep cerebellar nuclei.

intrafusal muscle fiber The muscle fibers of the muscle spindles.

long spinal reflex See *suprasegmental reflex*.

monosynaptic Pertaining to a pathway interrupted by only one synapse.

motor neuron A central nervous system neuron that terminates in muscle tissue and acts to control its contraction.

motor unit A single motor neuron and all the muscle fibers that it innervates.

muscle fibers The elongated contractile cells of muscle tissue.

muscle spindles Complex organs found in muscle tissue composed of both intrafusal muscle fibers and mechanoreceptors; they provide information concerning the length of the muscle.

muscle twitch The movement of a muscle fiber induced by a single action potential arriving at the neuromuscular junction.

myasthenia gravis An autoimmune disorder in which antibodies attach to nicotinic cholinergic receptors at the neuromuscular junction, producing muscular weakness.

myofibrils A unit of the muscle fiber that is composed of myofilaments.

myofilaments The thick and thin filaments that move in relation to each other, providing the molecular basis for muscular contraction.

myosin A protein that is the principal component of the thick filaments.

neostriatum The putamen and caudate nucleus.

neuromuscular junction The synaptic-like arrangement in which a motor neuron makes contact with a muscle fiber.

nuclear bag The enlarged central region of a muscle spindle.

order of recruitment The sequence in which individual motor units are activated by increasing excitatory input to the population of motor neurons innervating a muscle.

paleostriatum See *globus pallidus*.

Parkinson's disease A neurological disorder marked by tremor, rigidity, and an inability to initiate voluntary movement.

polysynaptic Pertaining to a pathway interrupted by two or more synapses.

premotor area The higher cortical motor area located on the lateral surface of the frontal lobe, adjacent to the central portion of the primary motor cortex.

primary motor cortex The precentral gyrus of the frontal lobe, Brodmann's area 4.

putamen One of the basal ganglia and a part of the extrapyramidal motor system.

pyramidal motor system The motor system of the brain originating in the cerebral cortex and projecting to the spinal cord by way of the pyramidal tract.

recruitment The activation of an individual motor unit.

reflex An automatic, involuntary response to a stimulus.

reflex arc The neural pathway mediating a reflexive action.

sarcomere A single contractile segment of a muscle fiber that is bounded at each end by a Z line.

skeletal muscle Striated muscle that is attached to the bones.

slow muscle A muscle fiber that contracts relatively slowly; red muscle.

smooth muscle In humans, the muscle tissue of all visceral organs, except the heart.

spinal reflex A reflex involving no central nervous system structures above the spinal cord.

stretch reflex The monosynaptic spinal reflex that produces a contraction of a muscle when that muscle is stretched.

substantia nigra A mesencephalic nucleus forming a part of the extrapyramidal motor system.

subthalamic nucleus An oval-shaped nucleus of the basal diencephalon that is immediately ventral to and contiguous with the substantia nigra.

supplementary motor area (SMA) The higher cortical motor area anterior to the primary motor cortex on the medial surface of the cerebral hemisphere.

suprasegmental reflex A reflex mediated by a pathway crossing segments of the spinal cord; also called the long spinal reflex.

Z line The dark stripe marking the end of a sarcomere.

Chapter 8

Sleep and Waking

Wakefulness and sleep are naturally occurring, alternating states of the brain and body. In **wakefulness**, the brain is in close contact with the environment. All the senses are active. Perceptions are remembered so that they may later be recalled. The nervous system is capable of complex thought, of manipulating abstract ideas, and of forming new concepts. Language is used to communicate with other individuals. Mental activity is often complex, and behavior may be voluntary and highly skilled. When awake, we are conscious of our perceptions, thoughts, words, and actions.

In **sleep**, all of this changes. The individual no longer interacts closely with the environment. Behavior ceases, and the quality of thought and consciousness undergoes profound alterations. The state of the brain is very different in sleep and wakefulness.

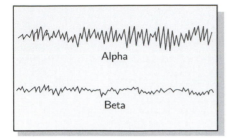

Figure 8.1. The Waking Electroencephalogram. Two electroencephalographic patterns characterize the EEG of the waking human. These patterns are alpha activity (top) and beta activity (bottom).

SLEEP AND WAKING

Over the past several decades, a great deal has been learned about the nature of both sleep and waking. This progress has been made possible in large part by the study of brain electrical activity recorded from electrodes placed on the human scalp. A recording of brain activity obtained from surface electrodes is called an **electroencephalogram (EEG)**.

The Waking State

In the waking state, the human brain displays two characteristic patterns of electrical activity (see Figure 8.1). The most prominent periodic pattern of the waking EEG, the **alpha rhythm**, was first described by a German psychiatrist, Hans Berger, in 1929 (Gloor, 1969). The alpha rhythm may be recorded from electrodes placed over the posterior portion of the skull, in the region of the occipital lobe. Alpha activity appears as a rhythmic oscillation of the EEG at a frequency of almost exactly 10 Hz (cycles per second). The amplitude of the alpha rhythm is enhanced when the eyes are closed and may be reduced or blocked when the eyes are open. The alpha rhythm is often said to reflect a brain state of relaxed wakefulness, but there is little actual evidence to support this conjecture. In fact, no one knows what the functional significance of the alpha rhythm may be or even whether it is of functional importance at all. Some individuals show large amounts of alpha activity; others exhibit virtually none. Nonetheless, the alpha rhythm is one characteristic electroencephalographic sign of the waking brain; it is not present during sleep.

A second EEG pattern that is observed in waking was termed the **beta rhythm** by Berger. In contrast to the rhythmic sinusoidal nature of alpha activity, beta activity consists of low-voltage, rapid, irregular oscillations. Beta activity may be recorded from all regions of the brain, including the occipital region when the alpha rhythm is blocked. The EEG in normal wakefulness consists of an alternation between alpha and beta activity in most individuals.

All EEG activity, including the alpha and beta rhythms, is believed to result from the summation of postsynaptic potentials originating in large populations of brain cells (Nunez, 1995). The idea is that the voltage of the EEG will increase when the synaptic activity of many neurons is synchronized. Conversely, if the neurons of the brain are acting independently of each other, the EEG will be rather flat because the cells that give rise to the EEG are doing different things at different times.

It is much like listening to the footsteps of musicians in a marching band. When they march in synchrony, their footsteps are loud, and the period between steps is quiet. But when the parade is over and the musicians depart, only the gentle constant sound of many people walking may be heard. Similarly, the alpha rhythm provides an example of synchronous neuronal activity, whereas the beta rhythm reflects desynchronized neural activity.

However, it is not clear which neurons contribute to the scalp voltages that are recorded as EEG. A number of theoretical arguments suggest that the EEG primarily reflects synaptic activity of large neurons that are arranged in a parallel fashion. The pyramidal cells of the cerebral cortex are a major class of central nervous system neurons that meet this requirement (Brodal, 1981).

It is not in the study of the waking brain but rather in the study of sleep that the electroencephalogram has made its major contribution. Recording the electrical activity of the brain during entire nights of sleep has made it apparent that sleep is not simply the lack of wakefulness, a kind of natural coma that occurs when the nervous system is no longer aroused by sensory stimuli. Instead, sleep is marked by a regular alternation of **sleep stages**, each with its own characteristic electroencephalographic and physiological patterns. These states are now designated as the four stages of slow-wave sleep and one type of rapid eye movement sleep. The discovery of these quite different types of sleep led to the modern view that the sleep states, like waking, are actively produced states of central nervous system organization.

Slow-Wave Sleep

Slow-wave sleep (SWS), as its name suggests, is characterized by the presence of slower activity in the EEG. Four stages of slow-wave sleep are usually distinguished, primarily on the basis of characteristics of the EEG record (see Figure 8.2).

- **Stage I sleep** is the first and lightest of the four stages. The EEG resembles that of wakefulness. The most distinctive electroencephalographic feature of Stage I sleep is the presence of short periods of **theta activity** (4-7 Hz). Theta activity is an indication of drowsiness when observed in the waking EEG. Thus, Stage I sleep may be considered to represent a transition between waking and sleep.

- **Stage II sleep** is marked by the appearance of **sleep spindles**. Sleep spindles are rhythmic bursts of 12- to 15-Hz EEG activity that slowly increase and then decrease in amplitude, giving the EEG tracing a spindlelike appearance.

- **Stage III sleep** differs from Stage II sleep in the addition of some very low-frequency (1-4 Hz) **delta waves** to the spindling pattern. These delta waves may be quite large in amplitude.

- **Stage IV sleep** is similar to Stage III sleep but is characterized by more extensive delta wave activity, which dominates at least one half of the recording. Stage IV is the deepest stage of slow-wave sleep, from which arousal is most difficult.

Slow-wave sleep differs from wakefulness in several respects. When awake, perception is vivid and is generated by stimuli that are present in the environment. In slow-wave sleep, perception is minimal or altogether absent. The sleeper is perceptually disconnected from the environment. When awake, thought is logical and progressive, allowing one to build rapidly on previous ideas, as in problem solving. In contrast, thought in slow-wave sleep tends to be preservative in nature, although still logical. The same idea may recur over and over again.

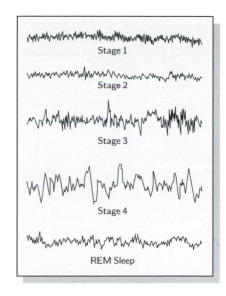

Figure 8.2. The EEG in Slow-Wave Sleep. Here, EEG tracings for slow-wave sleep Stages I to IV are illustrated.

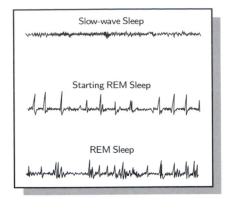

Figure 8.3. PGO Spikes. Originally observed in the pons, the lateral geniculate, and occipital cortex, PGO spikes not only mark periods of rapid eye movement sleep, but they also actually precede the onset of REM sleep. Similar spikes also can be recorded in other brain structures.

With respect to movement, the waking individual is always active, and the resulting behavior expresses the intentions of the person (Hobson, 1995). In SWS, however, the sleeper is usually inactive, with only occasional bursts of involuntary movement. Muscle tone or tension is reduced. Most individuals change their position every 10 or 20 minutes during SWS but are otherwise still. In the autonomic nervous system, slow-wave sleep represents a period of parasympathetic dominance. The cardiovascular system becomes less active, with decreases in both blood pressure and heart rate. Respiration also slows. Conversely, activity of the gastrointestinal system increases, and movements of the gastrointestinal tract become more frequent. From every point of view, slow-wave sleep appears to provide a period of rest for the skeletal muscles and increased activity for the housekeeping systems of the body that maintain the internal environment.

Neural Activity in Slow-Wave Sleep   Slow-wave sleep, particularly in its deeper stages, is marked by a decrease in cellular firing in most regions of the brain when compared with waking levels (Steriade, 1992). Firing rates are reduced throughout wide regions of the forebrain, including the association and motor cortex. Activity in thalamic nuclei such as the lateral geniculate nucleus is also reduced. Decreased firing in SWS characterizes many regions of the brain stem, including the reticular formation, the dorsal raphe nucleus, and the locus coeruleus (Steriade, 1992). The cerebellar cortex shows little change in its activity between SWS and waking, whereas increasing firing may be observed in portions of the amygdala and the hypothalamus. SWS produces a pattern of decreased activity in the thalamocortical system, increased activity in portions of the limbic system, and either decreased or unchanged activity within the brain stem.

Rapid Eye Movement Sleep

Against this background of SWS, periods of **rapid eye movement sleep (REM sleep)** stand out in sharp contrast (Dement, 1974; Hobson, 1995). Periods of REM sleep begin with a series of PGO waves. **PGO waves** are sharp electrical spikes beginning in the pons, continuing to the lateral geniculate nucleus, and finally reaching the occipital cortex, hence the abbreviation (see Figure 8.3). Each PGO wave is accompanied by an eye movement. PGO waves continue sporadically through the period of REM sleep.

In REM sleep, the EEG is flat and desynchronized, very similar to the waking EEG activity. In some people, the REM EEG is punctuated with bursts of 3-Hz sawtooth waves, but usually the REM and waking EEG recordings are indistinguishable. However, unlike in the waking state, in REM sleep, there is a profound inhibition of the great postural muscles of the body, such as those of the back, legs, and neck. Electrical recordings obtained from the postural muscles become silent, indicating that there is no activity within these muscles during REM sleep. In humans, REM sleep is marked by an absence of postural adjustments and a slackening of the lower jaw. In cats, the onset of REM sleep may be even more obvious; as the postural muscles are inhibited, the animal is no longer able to sleep upright but instead rolls over on its side.

In contrast to the massive tonic or steady inhibition of the postural muscles in REM sleep, there are also phasic movements—really twitches—that occur in the extraocular muscles, the facial muscles, and the flexor muscles of the fingers and toes. It is the abrupt movement of the extraocular muscles that gives rapid eye movement sleep its name. Rapid movements of the tips of the paws in the family cat mark REM sleep in that species, reflecting phasic muscular activity in the distal flexor muscles of its limbs.

Similar bursts of phasic activity also occur within the autonomic nervous system during REM sleep. There are periods of cardiac acceleration and increased blood pressure. Breathing may increase and become more variable. In males, REM sleep also is marked by penile erection; in females, there is increased vaginal blood flow. There are abundant signs of substantial visceral activity in REM sleep.

Dreams Occur in REM Sleep   Dreaming is associated primarily with REM sleep, although SWS is not devoid of dreams by any measure. The differences between dreams in the two sleep states are several. When awakened from REM sleep, people are more likely to report that they had been dreaming than when awakened from SWS; thus, dreaming is more frequent during periods of REM sleep. Furthermore, dreams reported during REM sleep are usually more elaborate and detailed than those in SWS.

Consider a typical dream report given by a young adult awakened from SWS:

> I had been dreaming about getting ready to take some kind of an exam. It had been a very short dream. That's just about all that it contained. I don't think I was worried about it.

When the same person was awakened later that night during a REM period, the reported dream was as follows:

> I was dreaming about exams. In the early part of the dream, I was dreaming that I had just finished taking an exam and it was a very sunny day outside. I was walking with a boy who was in some of my classes with me. There was a sort of a...break, and someone mentioned a grade they had gotten in a social science exam, and I asked them if the social science marks had come in. They said yes. I didn't get mine because I had been away for a day. (Dement, 1974, p. 44)

Dreams reported from REM sleep are also more vivid and intense than dreams reported from SWS. Unlike the logical preservative thought of slow-wave sleep, the dreams of REM are often illogical and bizarre. Disorientation in either time or space occurs frequently. The dreamer may experience illogical or impossible situations. The contents of the dream itself may shift suddenly and dramatically. Past and present may be woven together to form a mental state that is logically impossible. But all memories of the dream, as vivid as it might have been, begin to fade on awakening. Usually, there is complete amnesia for the contents of the dream; indeed, nearly all dreams are immediately forgotten.

Thus, the dreams that occur during REM sleep provide evidence of a highly activated brain that is prevented from actually carrying out its bizarre fantasies by a massive blockade of the skeletal motor system. REM

Figure 8.4. REM Sleep is Necessary for Consolidating a Visual Skill. Here, students were given practice on a visual perceptual learning task. When tested the following day, they showed substantial improvement when either they had enjoyed a normal night of sleep or when only slow-wave sleep was selectively disrupted. But if they had been REM deprived, there was no evidence of perceptual learning.

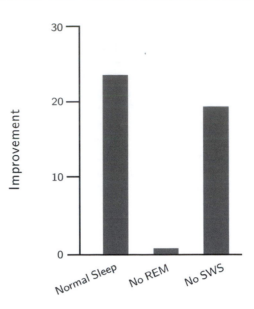

periods may be important in the mental life of advanced species in which REM is prevalent. Slow-wave sleep, for example, is commonly seen in reptiles, but REM sleep is not. Only the mammals show clear evidence of REM.

REM sleep is most pronounced in more intelligent mammalian species. Birds, for example, are evolutionarily primitive animals and exhibit only brief periods of REM following birth; adult birds do not display REM. All higher mammalian species have well-developed patterns of REM sleep. Thus, REM abundance and the appearance of complex brain functions are closely linked in the evolution of the higher animals.

Memory Consolidation and REM Sleep   REM sleep in humans appears to play an important role in establishing permanent memory for certain types of learning in both humans and other mammals. Perceptual skill learning, such as learning to rapidly recognize particular visual patterns, is one example of learning that depends on REM sleep in this way. Perceptual learning is thought to result from changes in neural activity at very early stages in visual information processing. The process of making these changes permanent is called consolidation.

Karni and his colleagues (Karni, Tanne, Rubenstein, Askenasy, & Sagi, 1994) examined the role of REM sleep making permanent learned improvements in detecting certain types of visual stimuli. The targets were small groups of lines presented against a background of otherwise identical lines that differed from the targets only in their orientation. Such a stimulus is shown in Figure 8.4.

In this task, training produces large improvements in detection speed that appear over consecutive days of practice. Interestingly, the effects of learning are restricted to the particular regions of the visual field in which the targets are presented in practice. Thus, detection can be trained in different portions of the visual field on different days, providing a means to test various manipulations of the learning process in the same individuals, which is exactly what Karni and his colleagues did. Subjects received practice with the targets in one portion of their visual field and were tested on the following day after either an uninterrupted night's sleep or a night of selective awakening, depriving the learner of either REM or SWS.

Their results were striking. When the subjects had a normal night's sleep between training and testing—or when they were selectively deprived of slow-wave sleep—they showed substantial improvement in detecting targets in the newly trained portion of the visual field. But if they were REM deprived between training and test, no improvement was observed (see Figure 8.4 on the preceding page). Their failure to show learning was not because they were tired or had trouble processing visual information after REM deprivation because performance for previously learned targets (in other regions of the visual field) remained enhanced. Thus, the experience of REM sleep between training and testing is necessary to permanently establish this kind of long-term perceptual learning. Karni et al.'s (1994) results strongly suggest that the consolidation or solid establishment of certain types of memories depends on brain processes that occur during REM sleep.

Neural Activity in REM Sleep   Most brain regions show an increase in activity during REM sleep when compared with SWS (Steriade, 1992). The REM pattern is much more similar to that of the waking brain. High rates of firing are found in the visual cortex and the lateral geniculate nucleus, but no changes of activity occur in the fibers of the optic nerve. This indicates that the increased firing in the central visual system is produced by intrinsic sources of activation during REM sleep, not in response to actual sensory stimulation.

With the motor systems, particularly dramatic increases in firing are observed during REM. Increased activity is seen in the motor cortex, the pyramidal tract, and the cerebellum. However, most motor neurons—the final connection between brain and muscle—are profoundly inhibited during REM. In short, periods of REM sleep are characterized by central sensory and motor activation that is completely dependent on intrinsic generators.

Such findings obtained from recordings made with intracranial electrodes have been confirmed and extended by noninvasive measurements of cerebral blood flow (CBF) in humans using positron-emission tomography (PET). CBF is a function of neural activity and provides an excellent index of brain activation. In light SWS (Stage II), there is a small global reduction in CBF. But in deep SWS (Stages III and IV), CBF is nearly halved. Global levels of CBF return to waking levels during REM sleep. These data indicate that in humans—as in nonhuman species—cortical activity is markedly suppressed in SWS but not in REM sleep (Madsen & Vorstrup, 1991).

Manquet and his colleagues (Manquet et al., 1996) measured cerebral blood flow using PET in seven volunteers during waking, slow-wave sleep and REM sleep. On awakening from REM sleep, all reported complex dreams. During REM sleep, significant increases in oxygen consumption and blood flow were observed in the anterior cingulate cortex, amygdala,

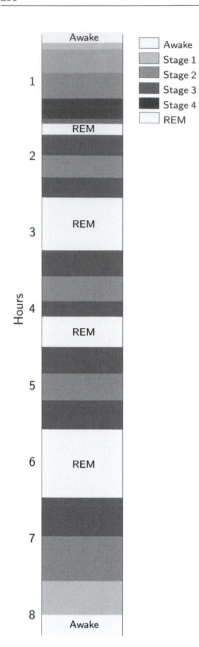

Figure 8.5. The Sequence of States and Stages of Sleep in a Healthy Young Adult. There is an ultradian rhythm of about 90 minutes between slow-wave and REM sleep. As the night progresses, the amount of Stage III and Stage IV sleep decreases, and the amount of REM sleep increases.

entorhinal cortex, and right opercular area. These are all regions of the deep forebrain that are involved in limbic system function and in the experience of emotion. These findings are physiological evidence of the highly charged emotional content that frequently characterizes our dreams. Some subcortical regions also were activated in REM. These include thalamic nuclei, the dorsal midbrain, and the pontine tegmentum. These latter brain stem structures form a part of the brain stem reticular formation, which is responsible for activating the forebrain during REM sleep.

REM sleep is also distinguished by the cortical areas that are inactivated. Most striking are vast regions of the dorsolateral prefrontal cortex of both the right and left cerebral hemispheres. These regions are known to play important roles in short-term or working memory in both primates and humans (see Chapter 12). There, inactivation during REM sleep may very well be related to our notorious inability to remember our dreams even minutes after waking. Other inactivated regions include parts of the parietal cortex and posterior cingulate gyrus.

SLEEP CYCLES

The transitions from wakefulness to sleep and from sleep to wakefulness are part of the daily rhythm of life (Moore-Ede, Sulzman, & Fuller, 1982). Most people establish a fixed sleep-waking cycle, retiring at about the same time every night and awakening at about the same time every morning. The sleep-waking cycle, with its 24-hour period, is an example of a **circadian rhythm** (*circa* in Latin means "about," and *dies* means "day"). In humans, circadian rhythms exert major effects on bodily functions.

There are also much shorter cycles that govern the transitions between the stages of sleep during the night. Figure 8.5 illustrates the sequence of stages of sleep occurring in a young adult. There is a definite rhythm to the night's sleep that cycles between SWS and REM sleep over a period of about 90 minutes. This is an example of an **ultradian rhythm**, a biological rhythm having a period that is much less than 24 hours.

There are consistent differences, however, between the pattern of sleeping early and late in the night. Sleep nearly always begins with slow-wave sleep. Most people reach Stage IV sleep during the first sleep cycle. As the first cycle of SWS draws to an end, the sleeper usually experiences a short period of REM sleep. As the night progresses, the periods of SWS become both shorter and lighter; people are less likely to reach Stage IV sleep in the later sleep cycles. Furthermore, the periods of REM sleep become more pronounced. Finally, the whole sleep cycle is extended. The initial sleep cycle is often only 70 to 80 minutes in duration, whereas the second and third cycles may be as long as 110 minutes. Toward morning, sleep cycles again become shorter. Interspersed in the night's sleep are very brief periods of awakening that, for many people, pass unnoticed and unremembered. Such awakenings occur in both slow-wave and REM sleep.

Slow-wave and REM sleep respond in different ways to commonly used psychoactive compounds. Alcohol and the barbiturates, for example, selectively suppress REM sleep while having little effect on SWS. Conversely, the benzodiazepines, which include commonly prescribed tran-

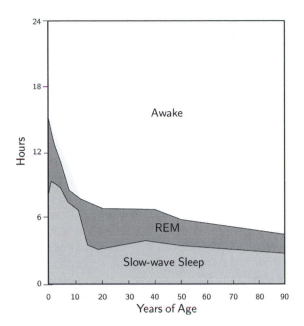

Figure 8.6. Total Amount of Wakefulness, REM Sleep, and Slow-Wave Sleep From Infancy to Old Age.

quilizers Librium and Valium, selectively reduce the amount of Stage IV sleep while leaving REM sleep relatively unaffected. This is one type of evidence indicating that SWS and REM sleep are mediated by different brain mechanisms.

THE DEVELOPMENT OF SLEEP

Sleep patterns change rather dramatically over the human life span. Figure 8.6 shows the proportion of each day spent in REM sleep, SWS, and wakefulness from birth to old age. The human newborn sleeps two thirds of each day, and one half of that sleep is REM sleep. An even more striking abundance of REM sleep is seen in infants born prematurely. Fully 80% of the sleep of 10-week premature infants is REM sleep, a figure that drops to 60% in infants born 2 to 4 weeks prematurely. Data such as these give rise to speculations that REM sleep may serve an important role in the development of the nervous system, but what that role may be is unknown.

The infant's sleep differs from adult sleep in another important respect, as any parent can testify. The sleep of the newborn is not controlled strongly by a circadian rhythm but rather is distributed throughout both day and night. The 90-minute ultradian rhythm seen in adults dominates the sleep-waking cycle of infants. As the child matures, sleeping periods are consolidated into the night as the normal circadian rhythm of adulthood is established.

Aging also produces changes of sleep patterns, but they are not nearly as dramatic as the alteration of sleep patterns observed in the growing infant. Compared to the young adult, the older individual sleeps less soundly. The total period of sleeping is reduced, and there is a reduction of deep Stage IV sleep. In other respects, however, the sleep of the aged is like that of the young adult.

SLEEP LOSS

The effects of sleep loss are diverse, affecting many aspects of behavior (Coleman, 1986). A number of careful investigations have led to the conclusion that normal healthy young adults can tolerate up to 10 days of sleep deprivation without medical impairment. (However, individuals with a history of psychiatric disturbance may report passing atypical episodes, such as visual hallucinations.) Sleep loss may increase the frequency of seizures in some epileptic patients. In all individuals, sleep deprivation upsets a number of biological rhythms that are normally linked to the circadian sleep-waking cycle.

Performance of brief simple tasks, such as adding numbers or tracking a moving target, shows no deterioration with increasing sleep loss. However, when experimental tasks are made longer or more complex or when speed is emphasized, decrements in performance often occur. In many situations, both electrophysiological and behavioral data indicate that the waking sleep-deprived person engages in short (several second) periods of sleep. During these microsleeps, the person simply fails to respond to the demands of the task. Sleep loss can have severe social ramifications, including increased accident rates in sleep-deprived physicians, drivers, pilots, and operators of other complex systems, including nuclear power plants.

The effects of selective loss of REM sleep also have been tested, as we have seen, by monitoring the EEG and waking the sleeper at the onset of each REM episode. Early experiments suggested that REM deprivation results in psychological deterioration bordering on mental illness; however, later and more careful investigations have failed to confirm these early reports. Nonetheless, there is undoubtedly a need for REM sleep. As REM deprivation is prolonged, for example, sleepers attempt to enter REM periods with increasing frequency. Moreover, supernormal amounts of REM sleep appear when REM deprivation is ended. This suggests that the person is making up for the REM sleep periods that were lost on previous nights.

FUNCTIONS OF SLEEP

Although a great deal is known about the nature of sleep and the brain mechanism responsible for the production of sleep, no one really understands why we sleep in the first place (Hobson, 1987). A number of theories concerning functions of sleep have been proposed.

One of the most common theories is that sleep is restorative, allowing recovery from the stress of active life. It has been suggested that the two kinds of sleep serve different restorative functions, SWS providing rest for the body and REM sleep giving rest to the brain. As sensible as these propositions may seem, particularly in view of the fact that we feel tired before we sleep and rested afterward, there is little direct biological evidence indicating how such restorative functions are affected.

A related idea is that sleep serves to conserve energy and protect the organism from eventual exhaustion. In support of this type of theory is the fact that total sleep time correlates highly (+0.65) with metabolic rate in a wide range of species; those species that expend more energy spend more of their time asleep, presumably to conserve scarce biological resources.

A third possibility is that sleep serves an adaptive ethological role to enhance the survival of the species. In this view, species evolve sleep habits that remove them from danger during periods of vulnerability, such as the night for nonnocturnal animals. These ethological theories suggest that sleep serves as a protective mechanism to keep organisms, including humans, away from predators and therefore out of trouble.

All of these are interesting ideas, and each may contain an element of truth. However, at present, there is no evidence that convincingly and exclusively supports any of these hypothesized functions of sleep, but perhaps that is not so surprising. Science is always much better at answering how questions than why questions.

BRAIN MECHANISMS CONTROLLING SLEEP

The classical approach to searching for the regions of the brain that regulate sleep and wakefulness involves surgically destroying brain tissue and examining the effects of the resulting brain lesion on sleep and waking. However, the results of such experiments are always difficult to interpret, particularly if the effect of the lesion is to disrupt either sleep or waking. The reason for cautious interpretation is that any brain lesion produces multiple effects, including swelling, disruption of circulation, and incidental damage to the surrounding brain tissue. Such problems are particularly troublesome in the brain stem, the home of the evolutionarily old neural structures that are responsible for controlling the basic life-sustaining functions of the body. Thus, a complex state such as REM sleep may be disrupted not by any direct effect of the lesion but rather by an incidental side effect of the operation. Cautious interpretation of lesion data is always wise.

Studies of Brain Stem Lesions

Much of what is known about the localization of the neural control of sleep and wakefulness was discovered by examining the effects of complete **transection** (cutting) of the brain stem. When the brain stem is completely severed, all higher influence on the motor neurons controlled by the spinal cord is lost. Therefore, most bodily signs cannot be used to study the wakefulness of the forebrain. However, the state of wakefulness of the forebrain can still be assessed by recording the electroencephalogram and by studying eye movements and changes in pupillary diameter, which are mediated by the third central nerve. The results of these investigations suggest that neuronal mechanisms located in different regions of the brain stem make different contributions in regulating sleep and wakefulness.

The lowest of these transections is the **encéphale isolé**, a lesion named by a Belgian neurophysiologist, Frederic Bremer (Bremer, 1977). In the encéphale isolé preparation, the brain stem is cut at its base, below the medulla and above the spinal cord. This lesion does not prevent the normal alternation between sleep and waking. In cats with an encéphale isolé lesion, both SWS and REM sleep appear to be normal. This finding, first reported by Bremer in the late 1930s, indicates that neither sleep nor waking is critically dependent on the spinal cord. The mechanisms governing sleep and waking must be located within the brain.

In contrast, transection of the brain stem made at the level of the pons, just anterior to the root of the fifth (trigeminal) nerve, produces a forebrain that is nearly always awake. This **midpontine pretrigeminal lesion** shows EEG characteristics of a waking brain, with only short periods of synchronous activity that differ in quality from the EEG patterns observed during SWS. These findings indicate that neural centers needed for producing SWS are located below the level of the mid-pons.

A still higher lesion of the brain stem, at the level of the midbrain behind the root of the third (oculomotor) nerve, is the **cerveau isolé**, another phrase of Bremer's. Immediately after a cerveau isolé lesion, the forebrain enters a continuous state of SWS. However, if the animal is carefully nursed, after several weeks the forebrain shows signs of an alternation between sleep and waking. This indicates that there is a region within the upper brain stem that facilitates waking in the normal animal. The presence of SWS with a cerveau isolé lesion usually is attributed to the massive loss of the sensory input to the forebrain.

These findings formed the basis for modern work on the neuroanatomical basis of sleep and waking. But the picture given by such data is not simple. It is difficult to escape the conclusion that both wakefulness and the sleep states are not unitary phenomena produced by unitary "waking" or "sleeping" centers but rather reflect complexly organized brain states produced by a number of brain mechanisms. Several brain regions seem to be of particular importance in governing these states. The current understanding of these systems follows.

The Reticular Activating System

The **reticular formation** is a diverse collection of cells located in the medial portion of the brain stem that extends from the spinal cord through the midbrain (Brodal, 1981; Steriade, 1996). It was originally believed that the reticular formation lacked an internal structure and instead formed a dense interconnecting network of nerve cells, or a "reticulum." Today, however, this anatomical view is known to be incorrect; the tissue that was originally classified as the unitary reticular formation is now known to contain a number of discrete nuclei and fiber tracts, which serve very different physiological functions.

The idea of a **reticular activating system** originated in the pioneering work of Giuseppi Moruzzi and Horace Magoun. In 1949, Moruzzi and Magoun first reported that electrical stimulation in the region of the midbrain reticular formation awakens the sleeping animal and alerts the awake animal. Moruzzi and Magoun took this as evidence that the cells of the reticular formation function as an activating system. Furthermore, other investigations demonstrated that lesions of the medial midbrain in the region of the reticular formation resulted in continuous SWS. Similar lesions placed more laterally at the same level disrupted the classical sensory pathways but had no effect on sleep or wakefulness. This further

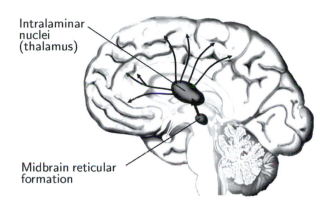

Intralaminar
nuclei
(thalamus)

Midbrain reticular
formation

Figure 8.7. Reticular Activation. Nuclei of the midbrain reticular activation system project to a variety of brain structures to produce coordinated activation of the organism.

suggested that the reticular formation plays a critical role in the regulation of conscious wakefulness. The reports of Moruzzi and Magoun began an intensive series of investigations of the role that brain stem neurons play in the regulation of sleep, waking, and attention.

The idea that human attention involves the activation of the midbrain reticular formation has recently received strong empirical support. Kinomura, Larsson, Gulyas, and Roland (1996) measured regional cerebral blood flow in a group of 10 volunteers under three conditions: (a) awake and relaxed, (b) performing an attention-demanding visual reaction-time task, and (c) performing a similar somatosensory task. Performance of either attention-demanding task increased neural activity in both the midbrain tegmentum of the reticular activating system and the intralaminar nuclei of the thalamus to which the midbrain tegmentum projects. The intralaminar nuclei are considered to be "nonspecific" nuclei that project to widespread regions of the cerebral cortex. Activation of the intralaminar nuclei is known to result in increased cortical activity and cerebral blood flow.

The pathway from the midbrain reticular formation, through the intralaminar thalamic nuclei, to the cerebral cortex is shown in Figure 8.7. This brain stem system is not only responsible for activating the forebrain in waking attention but also activates the forebrain in REM sleep as well. Moreover, stimulating the base of the midbrain reticular formation (near the junction with the pons) in waking animals produces sharp, spikelike responses that are similar to the PGO waves that occur naturally in mammals during REM sleep (Steriade, 1996). Thus, the reticular activating system plays a number of critical and active roles in the regulation of REM sleep, waking, and human attention.

Brain Stem Cholinergic and Monoaminergic Systems

Today, much is known about both the anatomy and the pharmacology of the brain stem systems that regulate the thalamus and cerebral cortex (Cooper, Bloom, & Roth, 1996). One important system is a cholinergic set of projections originating from a set of nuclei at the border of the pons and midbrain (mesopontine nuclei) and terminating in the thalamus. These cholinergic cells act to initiate and maintain activation of the forebrain.

During both waking and REM sleep, the cells of the mesopontine nuclei are active; during SWS, they are quiet. But perhaps most interesting is the fact that in the transition from SWS to either REM sleep or waking, these cells start firing up to a minute before any sign of activation can be detected in the EEG. Furthermore, stimulation of the mesopontine system elicits PGO spikes, whereas lesioning the nucleus abolishes them (Steriade, 1992).

Brain stem monoamine neurons also change their activity dramatically between waking, REM, and SWS (Jones, 1991). Both noradrenergic cells in the locus ceruleus and serotonergic neurons in the dorsal raphe nucleus are active when awake, slow during SWS, and completely silent during REM. Thus, these monoamine systems together with the mesopontine cholinergic system may act to produce wakefulness. But it appears to be the cholinergic system alone that generates cortical activation in REM sleep.

Nucleus of the Solitary Tract

The **nucleus of the solitary tract**, located within the medulla, also has been implicated in the regulation of SWS (Kelly, 1991c). Low-frequency electrical stimulation of the nucleus produces synchronized slow-wave activity in the EEG and, when continued, results in behavioral sleep as well. The nucleus of the solitary tract is an autonomic center of the brain stem that receives visceral input from the vagus nerve. Interestingly, rhythmic electrical stimulation of the vagus also promotes SWS. However, the role of the nucleus of the solitary tract appears to be limited to the modulation of sleep, rather than being necessary for producing sleep, because damage to the nucleus does not produce insomnia.

The Suprachiasmatic Nuclei

Although brain stem structures are involved in the production of wakefulness, SWS, and REM sleep, the coordination of these states into the normal adult circadian rhythm depends on a tiny pair of nuclei located within the hypothalamus (Klein, Moore, & Reppert, 1992). This was first suspected nearly 40 years ago in the work of Curt Richter (1965). Richter began his search for the "circadian clock" by showing that removal of any of the major endocrine and exocrine organs, including the pituitary, adrenals, thyroid, pineal, pancreas, and gonads, had no effect on the circadian activity rhythm of laboratory rats. Richter then tested the effects of lesions placed at hundreds of different locations within the central nervous system, but the only area in which lesions affected the daily activity rhythm was the ventral hypothalamus.

This finding was in accord with human clinical data. Brain tumors in the region of the ventral hypothalamus have long been known to produce excessive sleepiness and disruption of the normal circadian sleep-waking cycle. This is particularly true for tumors along the walls of the third ventricle in the vicinity of the optic chiasm.

In recent years, the region of the hypothalamus that controls the sleep-waking cycle has been localized even more exactly. The circadian rhythm

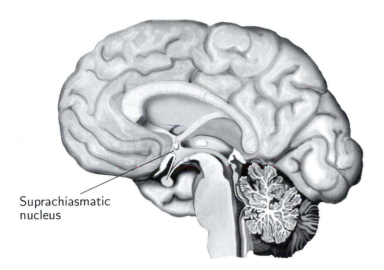

Figure 8.8. The Location of the Suprachiasmatic Nucleus.

Suprachiasmatic
nucleus

of sleep and waking is upset only when the suprachiasmatic nuclei are damaged; lesions elsewhere within the hypothalamus have no effect on the circadian sleep-waking rhythms. The **suprachiasmatic nuclei (SCN)** are a pair of small clusters of nerve cells within the anterior ventral hypothalamus, sitting immediately above the optic chiasm. (The optic chiasm is the place where the optic nerves from the right and left eye meet as they proceed to the brain.) The position of the SCN is shown in Figure 8.8.

These nuclei are extremely small. In the rat, each suprachiasmatic nucleus is composed of approximately 10,000 small neurons occupying a volume of about 0.05 mm in diameter; in humans, the SCN are not much larger (Klein, Moore, & Reppert, 1992; Moore-Ede, Sulzman, & Fuller, 1982). Each of the SCN receives direct input from the retinae of the eyes by way of the **retinohypothalamic tract**. Direct projections from the retina to the SCN can be demonstrated by injecting radioactively labeled amino acids into the vitreous humor of the eye. This technique is useful for mapping functional pathways because some of the radioactive label crosses successive synapses and thereby radioactively marks the series of synaptically connected cells. The retinohypothalamic pathway provides a mechanism by which the circadian sleep-waking rhythm may be entrained by the light-dark cycle of the natural environment. Glutamate is the neurotransmitter released by the axon terminals of retinohypothalamic cells (Vries, Cardozo, Want, Wolf, & Meijer, 1993).

Furthermore, the SCN projects to a wide variety of brain areas, as is required for a primary pacemaker for the sleep-waking cycle (Klein, Moore, & Reppert, 1992). These projections include other regions of the hypothalamus, the brain stem, the pineal gland, and the pituitary. Thus, the SCN are in an anatomical position to orchestrate both directly and indirectly the activity of the sleep and waking systems of the brain stem.

Much has been learned recently about the physiology and pharmacology of the SCN clock from studies of both intact animals, usually rodents, and rodent brain slices. In rodents and other species, a single, brief exposure of light during the subjective night can reset the circadian clock of the animal. If the light comes early in the night, the daily rhythm shifts forward, with the new night both beginning and ending later in real time, as if the animals' bedtime had been moved ahead. However, if the light comes nearer to subjective morning, the cycle is shifted backward, with the animal both going to sleep and awakening earlier in real time. Light has a powerful effect in entraining the rodent's sleep-waking cycle.

The pharmacology of this system has been uncovered in an elegant set of experiments by Ding and coworkers, who studied the circadian clock in brain slices taken from the SCN of the rat (Ding et al., 1994). Rat SCN tissue was prepared and maintained as a brain slice for 3 days. Continuous electrical recordings were made of the firing of SCN neurons in the slice. The average firing rate of these cells formed a smooth sinusoidal curve with a period of 24 hours. Without intervention, peak SCN activity occurred at circadian hour 7, mirroring the sleep-waking cycle of the living rat. (The circadian day is often used by the sleep researcher for convenience. It begins with hour 0 as daybreak and awakening. Thus, hour 7 corresponds to midday in the intact animal.)

The normal rhythm of the brain slice can be reset by a microinjection of glutamate, the neurotransmitter used by the retinohypothalamic cells that innervate the SCN. If the glutamate injection is given early in the night's sleep, the circadian rhythm of the cells in the brain slice is delayed by about 3 hours, and that delay is maintained at least over the subsequent 24-hour period. If the injection is given nearer to awakening, the rhythm is advanced instead by about over 3 hours. But when glutamate is injected during the normal "daytime" of the brain slice, the circadian rhythm of the slice is unaffected. Thus, it appears that microinjections of glutamate in an SCN brain slice mimic the natural effect of light in controlling the circadian rhythm of the SCN in the living rodent.

Further analysis revealed more about the pharmacology of the mammalian circadian clock. Glutamate from the retinohypothalamic pathway cells appears to activate NMDA-type glutamate receptors that in turn trigger the production of nitric oxide, which serves as a local neuroactivating agent. It appears that the actual daily clock in the rat lies somewhere beyond the SCN cells that are directly activated by glutamate. Studies such as these have greatly advanced our understanding of the pharmacology and physiology of the regulation of circadian rhythms in the living nervous system.

SLEEP DISORDERS

Everyone has difficulty sleeping or staying awake from time to time, but in some individuals, such problems are more pronounced. Sleep disturbances result from a number of quite different causes and may profoundly affect the quality of an individual's life.

Insomnia   Insomnia is the most common of all sleep disorders. As we all know, **insomnia** is the inability to sleep or to obtain sufficient sleep to function adequately during the waking hours (Mendelson, 1993). However, the perception of sleep loss in the insomniac may be more apparent than real. Many insomniacs will sleep normally when tested in a sleep laboratory, showing typical latencies of sleep onset (about 15 minutes) and normal sleep durations (about 7 hours). Furthermore, these insomniacs often show the normal ultradian cycling between SWS and REM sleep. Yet, on waking in the morning, they will report that they barely slept through the night. However, other insomniacs exhibit profound physiological disruptions of both SWS and REM sleep. Thus, insomnia is not a single disorder of sleep but a symptom that may result from many causes. Insomnia becomes increasingly prevalent with advancing age.

Insomnia is often related to psychological disturbances. Anxious individuals frequently experience difficulty in falling asleep. Conversely, depressed people often are troubled by early awakenings. The solution to the problem of insomnia in such cases is not to be found in the treatment of the sleep disturbance but rather in dealing with the psychological problem that is giving rise to the insomnia.

Insomnia also may be produced by pharmacological agents. Alcohol abuse, for example, is one cause of drug-induced insomnia. Alcohol acts as a depressant and may force the onset of sleep. Later in the night, however, sleep becomes agitated, and periods of wakefulness are common. But throughout the night, alcohol and its metabolites selectively suppress REM sleep. Alcohol is one of the most frequently used psychoactive chemicals that disrupts normal sleep.

There are also physiological causes of insomnia, such as nocturnal myoclonus, the occasional contraction of muscles, most frequently in the legs. Typically, the individual is unaware of these contractions that do objectively disrupt normal sleep. Similar restless movements, again of the legs, may prevent the onset of sleep in other individuals.

Somnambulism   A more dramatic type of sleep disorder is **somnambulism**, or sleepwalking (Dement, 1974). In a sleepwalking episode, the individual will slowly rise from the bed and begin to move about. Gradually, the movements become more coordinated and more complex. The sleepwalker may perform complicated automatic actions and successfully avoid tripping over or bumping into household objects. Nonetheless, it is very difficult to attract the attention of the sleepwalker, who seems unaware of other people. Sleepwalking episodes usually end quite naturally, with the sleepwalker returning to bed and pulling up the covers. In the morning, the sleepwalker usually has no memory of the previous night's ramblings.

Although one might think that a sleepwalker is acting out a dream, this is clearly not the case. Sleepwalking nearly always occurs in Stage III or IV SWS and virtually never includes periods of REM sleep. Sleepwalking frequently begins just as the individual enters deep SWS. Such episodes are most common in the first third of the night, when REM sleep is less frequent and SWS dominates.

Closely related to somnambulism is **nocturnal enuresis**, or nighttime bed-wetting. Like sleepwalking, nocturnal enuresis, a disorder usually found in children, generally occurs in SWS and not in REM sleep. Preceding the episode, the child, while sleeping soundly, begins to toss and turn, and then movement ceases. Bed-wetting soon follows, and the child wakes, surprised to find the bedclothes soaked. The child has no memory of dreaming and is often confused. Nocturnal enuresis is more frequent in psychologically disturbed or institutionalized children. It may be exacerbated by disorders of the urinary tract and other physical difficulties.

Both somnambulism and nocturnal enuresis tend to run in families. Children who experience bed-wetting often have relatives who sleepwalk and vice versa.

Night Terrors and Incubus   Children also may experience **night terrors**, which, like nocturnal enuresis, begin in Stage III or IV SWS (Kelly, 1991a). An attack of night terrors generally occurs within the first sleep cycle. The child suddenly bolts upright, screaming, with eyes fixed on some invisible object. The term *terror* is fully justified in describing these attacks; the child's breathing is difficult and irregular, and the face and body are dripping with perspiration, classic autonomic signs of fear. Like the sleepwalker, the child does not respond to the environment; parental comforting has little effect. Within a few minutes, the attack passes, and the child returns to sleep. In the morning, there is little recollection of the previous night's trauma.

Adults also may show nighttime fear attacks that, like the child's night terrors, occur during SWS. These attacks usually involve respiratory suppression, partial paralysis, and intense fear. Such attacks are called **incubus**, a reference to the sensation of pressure on the chest. (The term *incubus* refers to a mythological evil spirit that lies on a sleeping person, particularly a male spirit that has sexual intercourse with a sleeping female; in contrast, the mythological *succubus* is a devil in female form that has intercourse with a sleeping male.)

Attacks of night terrors in children and incubus in adults must be distinguished from the bad dreams that everyone experiences from time to time. Unpleasant and disturbing dreams are usually REM sleep phenomena and are therefore physiologically quite different from the attacks of fear that arise abruptly from slow-wave sleep.

REM Behavior Disorder   **REM behavior disorder** is a bizarre and often violent syndrome in which the sleeper literally acts out a dream (Mahowald & Schenck, 1992). Dreams, of course, are seldom logical and often fantastic in their content. The defect in REM behavior disorder is that the inhibition of the motor system that normally accompanies REM sleep is missing, so the sleeper's muscles are following the imagined actions of the dream. The result is a violent episode that frequently harms both the dreamer and the dreamer's bed partner. For example, Kelly (1991a) describes a 67-year-old grocer who, while dreaming he was playing football, got up wearing only his pajamas and tackled his dresser. Approximately half of the individuals who exhibit REM behavior disorder also show evidence of neurological damage in the waking state.

Lucid Dreaming   The phenomenon of **lucid dreaming** is another aberration of the sleep-waking cycle, in which wakefulness intrudes into REM sleep (Mahowald & Schenck, 1992). The sleeper is in the REM state and therefore is dreaming. But being also wakeful, the person is aware that he or she is dreaming and is able to control both the content and the outcome of the dream. This state convinces some people that they are having an "out-of-body" experience.

Sleep Apnea   Respiration is controlled by two major neural systems. The first, located in the medulla, is responsible for continued, nonvoluntary breathing. The second is a forebrain system that accomplishes the voluntary regulation of the respiratory muscles necessary for speech. In sleep, not only is the role of the voluntary system altered, but changes in the activity of the automatic brain stem system also occur.

For this reason, large changes in respiration accompany normal sleep. In slow-wave sleep, breathing becomes both deeper and slower. However, with the onset of a REM period, the respiratory system is activated; breathing is faster, shallower, and far less regular. These changes reflect alterations in the activity of both forebrain and brain stem respiratory centers.

However, in some individuals, pathological respiratory disorders occur during sleep. In **sleep apnea** (*apnea* refers to the cessation of respiration), there are repeated periods without breathing (Hobson, 1985). Although short periods of apnea are common in normal individuals during REM sleep, in affected people, such episodes are more frequent and prolonged. It is common to record more than 30 periods of respiratory cessation of at least 10 seconds' duration within an hour (Chase & Weitzman, 1983).

Sleep apnea is much more common in men than in women. The disorder may be at least partially genetically determined, a family history being common. Particularly prone to sleep apnea are obese middle-aged men who snore loudly.

Apnic episodes may end with a sudden awakening, as the result of an internal warning signal alerting the sleeper to a dangerous change in blood gases. These frequent awakenings account in part for the daytime sleepiness that is common to patients with sleep apnea.

Sudden Infant Death Syndrome   Perhaps related to sleep apnea is the **sudden infant death syndrome**, although there is considerable controversy concerning this suggestion. The sudden infant death syndrome is marked by the unexpected death of a sleeping infant. Although little is known with certainty about the cause of this fatal disorder, an important contribution by sleep apnea has been proposed. The brain of the infant is not yet fully mature and thus may exhibit periods of relative instability. Moreover, infants spend a disproportionate amount of their sleeping time in REM, the state in which episodes of apnea are most likely in adults. As with sleep apnea, the sudden infant death syndrome is primarily a disease of males.

Hypersomnia   In many ways, the opposite of insomnia, **hypersomnia** is a family of disorders marked by inadvertent or excessive sleep (Parkes, 1993). The most common cause of hypersomnia is depression, a pathological dejection of mood. Many depressed individuals tend to sleep long hours. Such people often exhibit an enhancement of REM sleep: The onset of REM is more rapid, the duration of REM is increased, and the density of the rapid eye movements themselves is intensified. Daytime napping is also common in depressed individuals.

Against this background of hypersomnia is a characteristic pattern of early morning waking. This arousal from a REM period that often occurs in the dead of night leaves the depressed individual worried and dejected. Thus, clinical depression may be associated with both hypersomnia and disruptions of normal sleep. Interestingly, many normal individuals who characteristically sleep for long periods also show minor signs of mental depression.

Narcolepsy Far more dramatic than the hypersomnia of depression is the abrupt and unexpected sleep of the narcoleptic. This disorder of **narcolepsy** is a hypersomnia characterized by sudden, inappropriate intrusions of sleep into the waking day (Aldrich, 1992). Such attacks may occur under what would seem to be arousing circumstances, such as when working intensely, during a medical examination, or—as in the case of Monsieur G—when dealt an exceptionally good hand of cards. Nearly half of all narcoleptic patients report having fallen asleep while driving at least once in the past. Something like .5% to 1% of the population is narcoleptic.

The first medical description of narcolepsy was written in 1879 by Jean Baptiste Èdouard Gélineau, a French physician. Gelineau coined the term *narcolepsy* in describing the unusual case of Monsieur G, a middle-aged Parisian cask merchant:

> When playing cards, if he was dealt a good hand he would succumb to a fit of weakness and be unable to move his arms; his head would droop, and he would fall asleep, only to awaken a moment later....This urgent need to sleep became increasingly troublesome. At table his meals were interrupted four or five times by the desire to sleep: his lids would droop; his fork, knife, or glass would fall from his hand; he would finish with difficulty—stammering in a whisper—the sentence which he had begun in a loud voice; his head would nod, and he would sleep....If he was standing in the street when the urge to sleep overtook him, he would totter and stumble about like a drunkard; people would accuse him of being intoxicated and jeer at him. He would be unable to answer them. Their mockeries would bear him down, and he would fall, instinctively avoiding the horses and carriages that were passing by.
>
> Asked to give a detailed account of the onset of a sleep attack, G replied that he feels no pain at the moment of being stricken; he described a profound heaviness, a mental blankness, a sort of whirling around inside his head and a heavy weight on his forehead and behind his eyes. His thoughts grow dim and fade away, his lids droop. Hearing is unaffected; he remains conscious. Finally, his lids close completely, and he sleeps. All this occurs very rapidly so that the preliminary stage of physiologic sleep, which normally lasts five, ten, or twenty minutes, lasts barely a few seconds in G's case. (Gelineau, 1880/1977)[pp. 283-285]

This unusual affliction, marked—in the words of Gelineau—by "the recurrence, at more or less frequent intervals, of a sudden, transient but irresistible urge to sleep" represents a dramatic breakdown in the neural systems that control sleep, wakefulness, and conscious experience.

Narcoleptic attacks are often accompanied by **cataplexy**, an abrupt loss of muscle tone causing a loss of use of the affected limb or limbs. If the legs are affected, the patient will instantly fall to the ground. However, a loss of consciousness need not occur. Narcolepsy, with or without cataplexy, causes severe disruptions in the quality of life.

Narcoleptic people also frequently experience sleep paralysis, episodes in which the spinal motor system is paralyzed (as it is in REM) while the person is partially awake and partially asleep. The individual is unable to move, although he or she is awake and usually experiences shallowness of breath.

Narcoleptic attacks are thought to represent intrusions of REM sleep into wakefulness. The catalepsy results from the inhibition of the lower motor system that characterizes normal REM sleep. The fact that narcoleptic individuals display periods of REM during wakefulness also explains the tendency of these patients to experience hallucinations preceding sleep; such hallucinations are nothing more or less than an illogical and unreal dream beginning before sleep onset. Consequently, narcolepsy has been considered to be the result of either hyperactivation of the REM system or the lack of normal control of that system's operations. Amphetamines are useful in suppressing narcoleptic attacks.

SUMMARY

Wakefulness and sleep are naturally occurring states of the central nervous system. Wakefulness is marked by consciousness, and the electroencephalogram shows both the alpha and beta rhythms. In the four stages of slow-wave sleep, the EEG is marked by increasingly lower-frequency and higher-voltage EEG activity. In rapid eye movement sleep, the EEG is flat and desynchronized, and PGO waves are present. Also in REM sleep, the postural muscles are inhibited, and there are phasic movements of the extrocular muscles, the facial muscles, and the distal flexors. When awakened from REM sleep, people are much more likely to report complex, detailed dreams than when awakened from SWS. In a normal night's sleep, there is an ultradian cycle of about 90 minutes in which SWS and REM sleep periods alternate.

Evidence from transection studies indicates that the mechanisms responsible for SWS are located within the brain stem, between the region of the mid-pons and the spinal cord. Wakefulness requires the support of brain tissue between the mid-pons and the upper midbrain. Portions of the reticular activating system are necessary for maintaining wakefulness. The regulation of the basic circadian sleep-waking cycle is mediated by the suprachiasmatic nucleus of the hypothalamus.

The normal pattern of sleep and waking may be disturbed in a number of ways, including insomnia (the reported inability to fall asleep), somnambulism, nocturnal enuresis, night terrors, incubus, REM behavior disorders, and narcolepsy.

SELECTED READINGS

- Hobson, J. A. (1995). *Sleep*. New York: Scientific American Library. This highly readable and beautifully illustrated book provides an introduction to the biology of sleep by one of the world's leading researchers in the area. It provides the reader with ample food for thought.

- The function of sleep. (1995). *Proceedings of an International Symposium: Behavioural Brain Research, 69*(1-2), 1-217. Various possible functions of sleep are discussed in this collection of papers, which was originally presented in Ravello, Italy, in May 1994. A good source of information and ideas for anyone interested in the why of sleeping.

- Klein, D. C., Moore, R. Y., & Reppert, S. M. (1992). *Suprachiasmatic nucleus: The mind's clock*. New York: Oxford University Press. A scholarly and wide-ranging treatment of the suprachiasmatic nucleus and circadian timing.

KEY TERMS

alpha rhythm Rhythmic activity between 8 and 12 Hz observed during wakefulness in the posterior electroencephalogram that may be blocked by visual input.

beta rhythm Low-voltage, fast activity observed in the electroencephalogram during wakefulness.

cataplexy A sudden loss of motor tone, producing muscular weakness and paralysis, often associated with narcolepsy.

cerveau isolé A lesion transecting the brain stem at the midbrain behind the root of the oculomotor nerve, separating the forebrain from most of the brain stem and the spinal cord.

circadian rhythm A rhythm or cycle having a period of about 24 hours.

delta waves These 1- to 4-Hz waves appear in the electroencephalogram.

electroencephalogram (EEG) Recording of brain electrical activity from electrodes placed on the surface of the scalp.

encéphale isolé A lesion transecting the brain stem at its base below the medulla separating the brain from the spinal cord.

hypersomnia A family of disorders marked by inadvertent or excessive sleep.

incubus A period of terror arising from slow-wave sleep in adults that is marked by respiratory suppression, partial paralysis, and intense fear.

insomnia The perceived inability to sleep or to obtain sufficient sleep to function adequately during waking.

midpontine pretrigeminal lesion A complete transection of the brain stem immediately anterior to the root of the trigeminal nerve.

narcolepsy A disorder marked by sudden, uncontrollable attacks of sleep during wakefulness, often with accompanying cataplexy.

night terrors A period of terror during slow-wave sleep in children that is marked by autonomic arousal, screaming, and unresponsiveness to the environment.

nocturnal enuresis Nighttime bed-wetting in children that often occurs during slow-wave sleep.

nucleus of the solitary tract The nucleus at which the visceral afferent fibers of the facial, glossopharyngeal, and vagus nerves terminate within the brain stem.

PGO waves Sharp electrical spikes originating in the pons, continuing to the lateral geniculate nucleus, and finally reaching the occipital cortex that occur in REM sleep.

rapid eye movement (REM) sleep A stage of sleep characterized by a desynchronized electroencephalogram, inhibition of the postural muscles, and twitches of the extraocular and distal flexor muscles.

REM behavior disorder Violent periods of activity during REM sleep, resulting from the lack of inhibition of the motor system while dreaming.

reticular activating system A functional system of the brain stem, originally but no longer associated with the entire reticular formation, that plays a major role in the production and maintenance of wakefulness.

reticular formation The central core of brain tissue that extends throughout the brain stem.

retinohypothalamic tract The pathway linking the retinae of the eyes with the suprachiasmatic nuclei of the hypothalamus.

sleep Naturally occurring periods of nonwakefulness, inactivity, and relative unconsciousness that normally follow a circadian rhythm.

sleep apnea A sleep disorder characterized by frequent cessation of respiration.

sleep spindles Rhythmic bursts of 12- to 15-Hz activity in the electroencephalogram.

sleep stage One of four categories of slow-wave (non-REM) sleep that differ in the amplitude and frequency of the electroencephalogram.

slow-wave sleep (SWS) One of four stages of sleep marked by relaxation but not total inhibition of the postural muscles, parasympathetic dominance, and varying degrees of synchronous electroencephalographic activity.

somnambulism Sleepwalking.

Stage I sleep The lightest stage of slow-wave sleep, marked by short periods of theta frequency EEG activity.

Stage II sleep Slow-wave sleep characterized by the presence of sleep spindles.

Stage III sleep Slow-wave sleep marked by the appearance of some delta waves in addition to sleep spindles.

Stage IV sleep Slow-wave sleep in which at least half of the EEG shows evidence of delta waves.

sudden infant death syndrome A syndrome marked by the unexpected death of a sleeping infant, perhaps due to sleep apnea.

suprachiasmatic nuclei (SCN) Two small clusters of neurons within the hypothalamus in the immediate vicinity of the optic chiasm that mediate the circadian sleep-waking rhythm.

theta activity Short periods of 4- to 7-Hz waves in the electroencephalogram.

transection A lesion that completely severs a structure such as the brain stem.

ultradian rhythm A rhythm or cycle having a period that is substantially less than 24 hours.

wakefulness The absence of sleep, characterized by alert, coordinated behavior.

Chapter 9

Emotion and Stress

Emotion, according to one dictionary, is filled with energy and bodily activity, "a state of mental excitement characterized by alteration of feeling tone and by physiological behavioral changes"[1]; to another, it is more refined, the "affective aspect of consciousness."[2] In fact, **emotion** is a concept that is extremely difficult to define with satisfactory precision. The term is used by some biologists to refer to certain observable complex behaviors, such as feeding, predation, or copulation. Others use the term to refer to expressive reactions, such as the cowering behavior of a fearful dog. In human biology, emotion often refers to a range of internal feelings that are partially expressed through the physiology of the body.

Some indication of the range of human emotion is provided by analysis of the interrelations among emotional adjectives, the words that we use to describe our emotional states (Shaver, Schwartz, Kirson, & O'Connor, 1987). Shaver presented 200 such words to a group of volunteers, who sorted these adjectives on the basis of their perceived similarities. These judgments were then analyzed by a clustering procedure that grouped the

---

[1] *Dorland's Illustrated Medical Dictionary*, 26th edition, 1981, p. 434.
[2] *Webster's New Collegiate Dictionary*, 1981, p. 369.

emotion-laden adjectives into a "family tree." The English adjectives that we use to describe our feelings cluster into a handful of major groupings, which he labeled *love, joy, surprise, anger, sadness,* and *fear.* As we will see, at least some of these emotions are served by specific, identifiable neural structures within the human brain.

It is important to distinguish between emotional expression, emotional experience, and the viseral activity that accompanies emotion. **Emotional expression** refers to outward signs of emotional activation that may be perceived by others. **Emotional experience** is the inward aspect of emotional activation that we describe in terms of feelings. Finally, visceral activity is simply the activation of the various organ systems involved in emotion.

These different aspects of emotion serve a range of functions for the organism. The outward behavioral expression of emotion serves important roles in social communication. These outward signs of internal states are important in a wide range of complex societal communications, including the social control of aggression, social dominance, courting, and other emotionally driven behaviors.

In contrast, the internal visceral or autonomic expression of emotion—emotional arousal or quiescence—prepares the organism for emotionally driven behavior, including fighting or fleeing a perceived threat. Emotional experience also colors and gives a motivating richness to cognition and subjective experience.

Finally, there is a major neuroendocrine response to stressful emotions that unleashes a wide range of hormonal changes throughout the body, preparing us for short-term responses to perceived or real threat. Thus, our emotional responses to external (or internal) stimuli are expressed in three major bodily systems or axes, as they are called: the autonomic axis, the endocrine axis, and the behavioral or skeletal motor axis.

Emotion in its various facets—expressive reactions, inner feelings, hormonal responses, or the complex behaviors that are driven by emotional activation—is central to the life of higher organisms.

FACIAL EXPRESSION OF EMOTION

Charles Darwin, in his book *The Expression of Emotion in Man and Animals* (1872), argues that the physical expression of emotion plays an extraordinarily important role in social communication and social regulation in humans and other primates (Allman & Brothers, 1994). Some animals, such as cats and dogs, communicate feelings through the use of distinctive and stereotyped postures or displays that involve the entire body. In humans, however, emotional expression is most successfully and powerfully produced by movements of the facial musculature (Rinn, 1984). Figure 9.1 on the facing page is taken from Darwin's book and illustrates an extreme of facially expressed emotion.

The human face is the focal point for human communications, both linguistic and emotional. In everyday life, it is not difficult to determine the emotional state of the individuals that we encounter simply from "the way they look."

Emotional expression results from the stereotyped movements of the

Figure 9.1. The Facial Expression of Emotion. This illustration, taken from Darwin's 1872 book *The Expression of Emotion in Man and Animals*, illustrates "horror and agony," in Darwin's words.

facial muscles, which create folding in the skin and movements of facial features, such as the mouth and eyebrows. Thus, from a physiological perspective, facial expression is most accurately and profitably described in terms of the state of activation of the individual facial muscles. In fact, electrical recordings obtained from these muscles may permit the detection of subtle differences in emotional state that are invisible to the naked eye.

One rarely realizes the abundance of facial expressions and gestures that occur in ordinary conversation. The muscles of the face and head are in constant activity, producing a wide variety of expressions, some long lasting and others fleeting. These expressions punctuate normal speech and give it richness and emotional depth. Under some circumstances, however, expressive movements are minimized as we may seek to suppress the emotions that we experience in social situations.

Innervation of the Facial Muscles   There are two very different types of facial muscles. The first is used for mastication (chewing) and for speech; the second is involved in facial emotional expression. These two sets of muscles are shown in Figure 9.2 on the next page. The **mastication muscles** attach to bone and move the jaw in eating and speaking. They are innervated by the trigeminal (fifth) cranial nerve, which carries the com-

Figure 9.2. The Muscles of the Human Face. The masseter, temporalis, and internal and external pterygoid muscles (which are not shown in this view) are used for chewing and speech, not emotional expression. Emotions are conveyed by the remainder of the facial muscles, which are referred to as the expressive muscles.

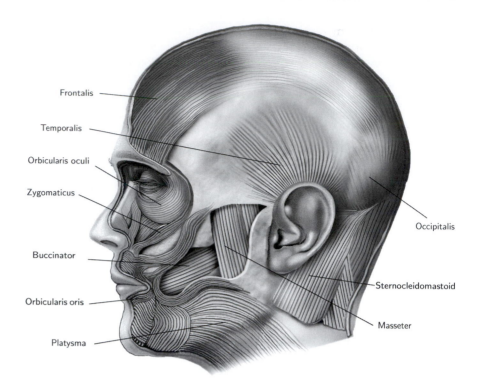

Frontalis

Temporalis

Orbicularis oculi

Zygomaticus

Buccinator

Orbicularis oris

Platysma

Occipitalis

Sternocleidomastoid

Masseter

mands governing speech to the muscles of the face. However, the mastication muscles play only a minimal role in emotional expression.

All the remaining muscles of the face are **expressive muscles**. They attach to the skin and serve to move the skin and facial features to form stereotypic facial expressions. It is the facial (seventh) cranial nerve that is specialized for nonlinguistic expression of emotion.

The human facial nerve is composed of five major branches. Each branch serves a distinctive region of the face involved in emotional expression. The facial nerve has its origins in the **facial nerve nucleus**, which is located within the brain stem at the level of the pons. Each branch of the nerve is regulated by a separate subnucleus within the facial nerve nucleus.

Both the left and right facial nerves and their associated facial nerve nuclei are completely independent of each other; the fact that facial expressions are bilaterally coordinated reflects similar input to the facial nerve nuclei from higher levels of the brain.

Facial Nerve Nucleus   The facial nerve nucleus receives input from the cerebral cortex by two routes, one direct and the other indirect. The direct projections originate in the face region of the motor cortex (precentral gyrus). This input is somatotopically organized.

For the lower half of the face, the direct projections are strictly contralateral. For the upper face, there are ipsilateral projections as well; the cortical projections for the eyebrows and forehead, for example, are about equally divided between the two hemispheres. For this reason, it is easy to produce unilateral movements of the muscles of the lower face but much harder to execute unilateral movements of the upper facial muscles; many individuals have difficulty winking just one eye. Because of this difference in cortical input to the facial nuclei, unilateral damage to the facial motor area of one cerebral hemisphere produces contralateral paralysis of the lower face, and the upper face is virtually unaffected.

The contralaterally innervated muscles of the lower face differ from the bilaterally innervated muscles of the upper face in two other respects: the degree to which they may be controlled voluntarily and the amount of cerebral cortex devoted to each muscle.

The contralaterally innervated muscles are generously represented on the cortical motor strip and are easily controlled voluntarily. These muscles are involved in learned behavior, such as speaking, and are capable of finely regulated movements. In contrast, the bilaterally innervated muscles of the upper face are difficult to control voluntarily, are capable of only coarse voluntary movements, and are more sparingly represented in the somatotopic representation of the motor cortex.

Extrapyramidal Contributions   Voluntary facial movements result from the direct cortical activation of the facial nerve nuclei by cells of the pyramidal tract. Emotional facial expressions, however, are produced by an evolutionarily older, more complex route through the extrapyramidal motor system. This system is really a complex of interacting nuclei, distributed throughout the brain but concentrated within the brain stem.

There is much clinical evidence that emotional expression depends on the extrapyramidal system, not the pyramidal system.

- First, patients with cortical damage that paralyzes the lower face cannot voluntarily move their lips on the side opposite the lesion; however, such patients can spontaneously smile bilaterally when appropriate. Because the smile uses the same muscles that appear to be paralyzed in voluntary movement, different central pathways to the facial nuclei must be involved.

- Second, disorders of the extrapyramidal system, such as Parkinson's disease, result in an absence of spontaneous facial emotional expression while retaining voluntary control of the facial muscles.

- Third, there are large differences between spontaneously produced facial expressions and posed or voluntarily constructed attempts to achieve a desired appearance. Any photographer knows that it is much better to trigger a smile with a little joke than to simply request a smiling countenance. A posed expression must be executed consciously through the pyramidal system of voluntary motor control, whereas genuine expressions of emotion involve entirely different central nervous system pathways.

VISCERAL EXPRESSION OF EMOTION

Emotion not only serves a social or communicative function, but it also provides much of the force or drive behind behavior. In this respect, emo-

Figure 9.3. The James-Lange Theory of Emotion. The James-Lange hypothesis maintains that emotional experience is the result of the perception of autonomic activation, which results from the perception of an emotion-eliciting stimulus.

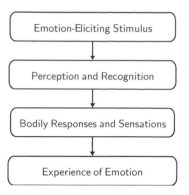

tion is the source of internal feelings. Fear, hate, love, and happiness are all commonly felt emotions. When aroused, any of these emotions has powerful effects on bodily physiology. This well-known truth led some to conclude that emotion is not a central nervous system phenomenon but rather the perception of the peripheral physiological changes accompanying emotional arousal. In the words of William James, the 19th-century psychologist, "Common sense says, we lose our fortune, are sorry and weep; we meet a bear, are frightened and run.... The more rational statement is that we feel sorry because we cry, afraid because we tremble" (James, 1890, pp. 449-450). James's argument is that the perception of peripheral changes *is* the emotion, purely and simply.

This view of emotion, outlined in Figure 9.3, is called the **James-Lange theory**. (Carl Lange was a Danish physiologist who had previously put forward a similar analysis of the emotions.) But for a number of years, the James-Lange hypothesis was effectively discarded, following a detailed critique by Walter Cannon, the distinguished U.S. physiologist.

Cannon put forth three arguments against the James-Lange theory: (a) that the sensory receptors of the viscera were too insensitive to mediate the delicate emotions, (b) that similar visceral changes accompany a variety of subjectively very different emotions, and (c) that these visceral changes are much too slow to result in the rapid fluctuations of feeling that we all experience. Such criticisms are indeed important, but they are not wholly correct; the quality of emotional experience is affected by visceral function.

Cannon and his colleague Philip Bard proposed instead that the neural centers regulating emotion affect not only the peripheral nervous system but also higher brain regions that produce the cognitive component of emotion, as shown in Figure 9.4 on the next page. The **Cannon-Bard theory** argued that emotion is perceived only when both the peripheral nervous system and the forebrain are activated. The sympathetic branch of the autonomic nervous system provides the arousal of emotion, and the forebrain system determines its cognitive content.

Although the Cannon-Bard theory held sway for a number of years, an accumulation of findings has blunted Cannon's critique of the James-Lange hypothesis. Evidence that the perception of visceral events does play a role in the normal experience of emotion comes from a number of sources, but none is more striking than the study of patients who have

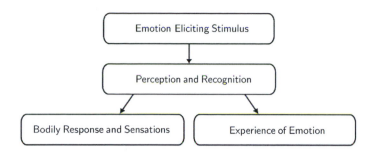

Figure 9.4. The Cannon-Bard Theory of Emotion. The Cannon-Bard hypothesis argues that both emotional experiences and autonomic responses are the direct results of such perceptions.

had their spinal cords completely transected, usually as the result of an accident. Because much of the communication between the viscera and the brain is accomplished by the spinal nerves, patients with spinal cord injury are more or less deprived of visceral input. This is particularly true of patients with high spinal injuries, as shown in Figure 9.5 on the following page. Patients with high spinal transection have very little sensory input from the viscera, whereas those with low spinal injuries have nearly normal autonomic input.

Following spinal injury, emotion loses some of its intensity. Injured individuals still experience emotion, but it is described as colder and weaker than before the injury. For example, one patient remarked that when he becomes angry, "It's a mental sort of anger." The raw, visceral component of emotion is missing. Most interesting is the fact that this change in emotion is greatest in people with high, rather than low, spinal transection. The visceral component of emotion varies with the extent of visceral input from the gut to the brain.

Furthermore, there is evidence that different emotions produce different patterns of activation within the peripheral autonomic nervous system, a finding that contradicts the Cannon-Bard hypothesis (LeDoux & Hirst, 1986; Levinson, 1992). This can be demonstrated by recording peripheral nervous system activity while people are mentally reliving different emotion-laden experiences (Schwartz, 1986). However, it is unlikely that these autonomic patterns are sufficiently unique to support the James-Lange hypothesis in its original simplicity. As is the case in other motivational systems, such as the control of hunger, both central and peripheral nervous system mechanisms appear to play important roles.

NEUROANATOMY OF EMOTION

The search for central mechanisms that control the experience and expression of emotion has centered in the region between the brain stem and the neocortex, particularly in a set of structures called the limbic system. Three areas are of particular importance: the hypothalamus, the amygdala, and the septal area (see Figure 9.6 on page 289), all parts of a collection of basal forebrain structures that form the limbic system.

The term **limbic system** originated with Paul Broca, the distinguished 19th-century French neurologist. Broca first used the phrase *le grand lobe limbique* (the great limbic lobe) to describe a set of neural structures at the

Figure 9.5. Visceral Aspects of Emotion. Spinal injury reduces the raw, visceral aspect of emotion. The extent of emotional loss is greatest for high spinal transections.

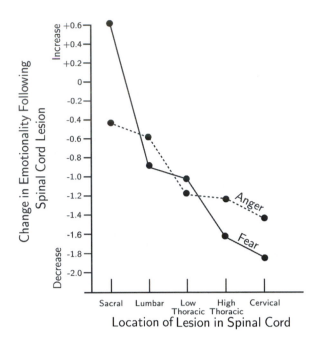

central base of the forebrain. The word *limbic* derives from the Latin *limbus*, meaning "fringe" or "border." In Broca's conception, the **limbic lobe** included the hippocampal formation, the parahippocampal gyrus, the cingulate gyrus, and the subcallosal gyrus. For Broca, the limbic system was a strictly anatomical concept.

However, in the century since Broca published his seminal observations, new ideas have emerged concerning the function of the limbic structures. In the 1930s, James Papez and others began to stress the role of that region of the brain as providing the neural basis of emotion. Papez proposed that these limbic structures provided a pathway by which emotion can reach consciousness, therefore involving the cerebral cortex (Papez, 1937).

To accommodate these changing views, Paul MacLean suggested that the term *limbic system* be used to designate an expanded collection of structures that appears to participate in the perception and expression of emotion. The contemporary definition of the limbic system includes the structures of Broca's original limbic lobe, portions of the hypothalamus, the septal area, the **nucleus accumbens** (a nuclear region that is lateral to the septal area), and the amygdala (Van Hoesen, Morecraft, & Semendeferi, 1996).

Limbic System Lesions Alter Emotion   Emotion and emotion-laden behavior may be altered in specific ways by lesions of the limbic system of the brain (Heilman & Satz, 1983). Consistent effects have been observed in a wide range of nonhuman species, including rats, cats, and some monkeys.

Similar findings hold true for the human brain as well: Emotional changes are a frequent consequence of brain damage. Limbic structures

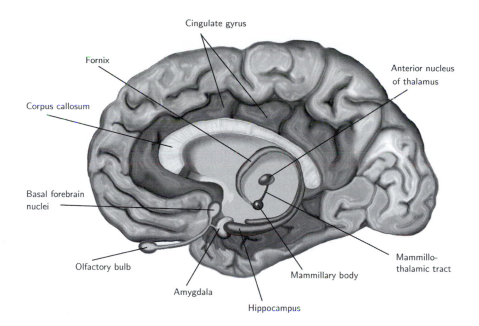

Cingulate gyrus

Fornix

Corpus callosum

Anterior nucleus of thalamus

Basal forebrain nuclei

Olfactory bulb

Amygdala

Mammillary body

Hippocampus

Mammillo-thalamic tract

Figure 9.6. Principal Midline Brain Structures Involved in Emotions.

also are particularly susceptible to inflammatory disorders, for reasons that are currently unknown. Herpes simplex encephalitis, a viral infection of the brain, selectively destroys the basal portions of the frontal lobe and the anterior regions of the temporal lobes, together with the associated limbic structures (Adams, Victor, & Ropper, 1997). Such infections often result in an increase in impulsive, uncontrolled behavior; agitation with or without depression; and memory loss. Rabies also selectively strikes the limbic structures and produces profound anxiety and agitation.

Brain Stimulation Also Affects Emotion Much of what is known about the functions of limbic system structures has been learned from the study of the effects of brain lesions on behavior. Another approach, however, involves the use of electrical stimulation of the brain. This procedure involves the surgical implantation of wire-stimulating electrodes. Often, an array of electrodes is used, so that more than one brain region may be stimulated. After recovery from the surgery, the effects of passing electrical currents through selected electrodes can be measured. In laboratory animals, a number of specific behavioral tests may be employed. In neurological patients, direct verbal report is possible.

Although stimulation procedures seem straightforward, there are difficulties in interpreting experimental results. First, electrical stimulation is very coarse when compared with the delicate patterns of synaptic potentials that characterize normal neuronal activity. Thus, electrical stimulation may not only "activate" a brain area but also may disrupt its normal pattern of functioning. The question of current spread also must be considered. How far away from the stimulating electrodes do the injected currents exert their effects? Finally, there is the difficult issue of *fibers of passage*. The limbic region contains not only nuclear groups of neurons but also a large number of fibers, the origins and destinations of which are widely distributed throughout the brain. Electrical stimulation may affect such fibers and thereby produce unknown consequences throughout the brain. Despite these and other problems, experiments involving electrical stimulation of limbic system structures have been tantalizing and informative.

Functional Brain Imaging Can Map Emotion   The newest method of studying the anatomy of emotion is that of functional brain imaging. By comparing measurements of brain activation in different emotional states, naturally occurring patterns of neural activity underlying emotional perception and expression may be identified (Posner & Raichle, 1994). Each of these methods—lesion analysis, brain stimulation, and brain imaging—has helped to identify the functional anatomy of emotion in the human central nervous system.

Cerebral Cortex

Frontal Lobes   The control of human emotion differs from that of many other species because of the presence of the massive cerebral hemispheres, which act, in part, to regulate the functions of many lower brain systems. The importance of the cerebral hemispheres for emotion, particularly the frontal lobes, was made strikingly clear more than a century ago by the case of Phineas Gage, the foreman of a railroad crew who suffered a remarkable injury (Damasio, Grabowski, Frank, Galaburda, & Damasio, 1994; Stuss & Benson, 1983). An accidental explosion drove an iron rod into Gage's cheek and out through the top of his skull (see Figure 9.7 on the facing page). Miraculously, he survived the injury but suffered a massive lesion of the frontal lobes. Before the accident, Gage was a model citizen and employee, but the frontal damage transformed his very character. Gage's physician described the change as follows:

> The equilibrium or balance, so to speak, between his intellectual faculty and animal propensities, seems to have been destroyed. He is fitful, irreverent, indulging at times in the grossest profanity (which was not previously his custom), manifesting but little deference for his fellows, impatient of restraint or advice when it conflicts with his desires, at times pertinaciously obstinate, yet capricious and vacillating, devising many plans of future operation, which are no sooner arranged that they are abandoned in turn for others... His mind was radically changed, so decidedly that his friends and acquaintances said that he was "no longer Gage." (Quoted in Stuss & Benson, 1983, pp. 111-112.)

The case of Phineas Gage is very dramatic. Similar cases, although less spectacular, continue to be reported. They occur following extensive frontal lobe surgery. Such patients usually remain well oriented, alert, with memory intact. Intellectual capacity seems undiminished, at least on the surface. However, as with Gage, there is a loss of sustained attention. The ability to plan and order daily activities is also markedly reduced.

With respect to emotion, there are also marked changes. Often, the patient seems to cease to experience strong emotion. Feelings become transitory and superficial. To Egas Moniz, a Portuguese professor of neurology, the remarkable thing about such patients was that fear and anxiety

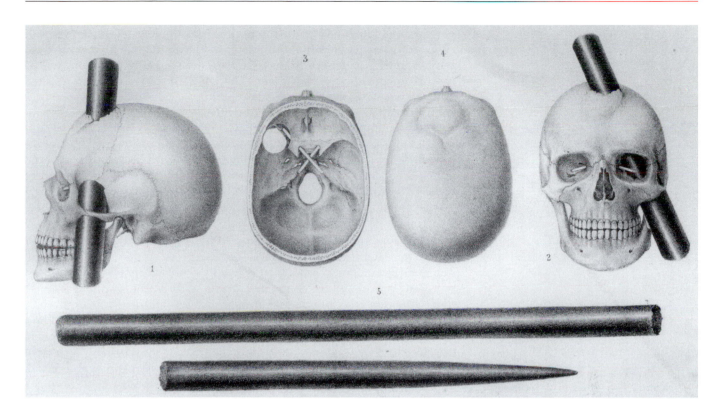

had been reduced, but the obvious cognitive functions were spared. The disruptions in the patients' lives introduced by frontal lobe damage impressed Moniz much less. This perspective, coupled with observations of frontal lobe damage to experimental animals, led Moniz in the mid-1930s to propose the surgical lesioning of the anterior frontal lobes as a treatment for anxiety. The procedure, called **frontal leukotomy**, in which the fiber tracks of the frontal lobe are severed, enjoyed a decade of intermittent popularity and eventually won Moniz a Nobel Prize posthumously in 1949. More than 10,000 leukotomies or similar operations were carried out in the period between the mid-1940s and the early 1950s.

Today, the operation is no longer performed. In part, this reflects the availability of effective drugs for the treatment of anxiety. But it is almost universally recognized that a frontal leukotomy produces more harm than good. Frontal leukotomy seems to be an unfortunate episode in the history of medicine. Nonetheless, this operation gave birth to psychosurgery, the surgical treatment of behavioral or psychiatric disorders.

The medical experience of intentionally damaging the frontal cortex did in fact alter human emotionality. That conclusion, drawn from the history of an unfortunate human experience, emphasizes the importance of the frontal lobes in the control and expression of human emotion.

Right Posterior Cortex   There is also evidence that some regions of the posterior cortex of the right hemisphere may play a specialized role in the

Figure 9.7. Gage's Wound. Drawings 1, 2, and 3: Gage's skull. 4: A cast of Gage's scalp, in which the area of the wound may be faintly discerned. 5: The iron tamping bar, which entered Gage's skull through his cheek and exited through the top of his skull, severely damaging one of his frontal lobes. Remarkably, he survived this injury, but his personality was forever altered. (Illustration courtesy of the History and Special Collections Division of the Louise M. Darling Biomedical Library, UCLA.)

perception and expression of emotion, just as the left hemisphere is specialized for language. One example of evidence for this idea came from the report of a patient with massive left-hemisphere damage but whose right hemisphere remained intact. The left-hemisphere damage resulted in a characteristic loss of language function (Kenneth Heilman, personal communication). This patient could neither follow simple commands nor respond to simple yes-or-no questions. Yet, when given a choice of four faces expressing happiness, sadness, anger, and indifference and when read a neutral sentence with different affective tones, the patient could match the face to the tone without error. Patients with right-hemisphere damage perform poorly on this test, a finding suggesting that the perception of emotional tone may be selectively processed by right-hemisphere structures.

Other types of evidence lend support to this view. Patients with right-hemisphere damage can use language to express emotion, but their language lacks emotional tone; they speak in a neutral monotone that does not convey emotion. In contrast, patients with left-hemisphere damage have difficulty with language, but their meager linguistic output may be peppered with emotional inflection. Despite these findings, it would be a mistake to conclude that the emotional functions of the right hemisphere are close to being understood. Such data are only tantalizing glimpses of the neocortical mechanisms involved in the expression and experience of emotion.

Hypothalamus

Because visceral feelings make a major contribution to the experience of emotion, it is not surprising that hypothalamic nuclei participate in emotional behaviors. The **hypothalamus** is often considered to form the highest brain region controlling autonomic function. The most ventral structure in the diencephalon, the hypothalamus is composed of a number of discrete nuclei with their interconnecting fiber tracts. It is a bilaterally symmetrical structure located on the walls of the third ventricle.

The autonomic functions of the hypothalamus are somewhat better understood than its emotional functions. There is a general tendency for the anterior regions of the hypothalamus to participate in the control of parasympathetic functions and for the posterior regions to mediate sympathetic activities. This generalization has been useful historically but does not capture the richness of hypothalamic organization. Very specific autonomic responses can be elicited by discrete activation of specific hypothalamic nuclei, for example. Lesions of the hypothalamus result in a variety of emotional consequences.

Electrical stimulation of the hypothalamus can have striking emotional consequences in animals. In some regions, stimulation elicits intense rage and aggressive behavior. In other areas, stimulation is intensely rewarding and may produce sexual arousal. Direct autonomic responses also occur, with sympathetic effects generally resulting from stimulation in the posterior hypothalamus and parasympathetic effects occurring with anterior stimulation. The cells of the hypothalamus probably form the highest level of direct autonomic integration in the mammalian nervous system.

In humans, hypothalamic stimulation has emotional consequences. In the rostral areas of the hypothalamus, electrical stimulation produces sensations of discomfort associated with intense autonomic imbalance; abdominal upset, flushing, feelings of warmth, and pounding of the heart are all commonly reported. Stimulation of the medial hypothalamus may result in fear and anxiety. However, stimulation of the lateral regions has quite the opposite effect. Patients frequently report that lateral hypothalamic stimulation is pleasurable and "feels good" (Heath, 1964).

Amygdala

The **amygdala** is formed by a group of nuclei located beneath the anterior portion of the temporal lobe at the tip of the lateral ventricles. They are clustered in an almond-shaped formation, giving rise to its name (*amygdala* means "almond" in Greek). Experts differ in their estimates of the number of distinct nuclei comprising the amygdala, but most divide the structure into four areas: the lateral, central, basolateral, and basomedial regions. Of these, the lateral amygdala is the largest.

The various amygdalar nuclei maintain a number of major connecting pathways to the cerebral cortex, brain stem, and surrounding diencephalic structures. The basolateral region has reciprocal connections with both the frontal and temporal lobes. It also projects to the basal ganglia. The basomedial amygdala connects with the olfactory bulb and olfactory cortex.

The amygdala is connected to the medial hypothalamus through a major projection termed the *stria terminalis*; connection with the lateral hypothalamus is by way of the ventral amygdalar pathway. There are additional pathways leading to and from various regions of the brain stem, including the locus ceruleus, the mesencephalic central gray, and the nucleus accumbens.

Lesions of amygdala have profound effects on emotional behavior, but these effects are far from simple. In dogs, for example, a lesion confined to the medial region produces fear and depression with occasional outbursts of aggression. A second lesion of the lateral area reverses these effects. In a wide range of species, including the monkey, amygdalar damage produces a reduction in social dominance. In a natural environment, lesions of the amygdala change a primate into a social isolate, living alone and not responding to social signals from its troopmates.

In humans, bilateral destruction of the amygdala has been reported to reduce rage in chronically aggressive patients (Saver, Salloway, Devinsky, & Bear, 1996). Larger lesions involving the temporal lobes also have been claimed to have a tranquilizing effect. It must be remembered, however, that the amygdalar nuclei and the surrounding tissue form a complexly organized system: The emotional and behavioral effects of large lesions in this region are consequently very difficult to interpret.

Electrical stimulation of the amygdala also produces profound visceral effects. Changes in both heart rate and respiration are common. Stimulation in some regions of the amygdala results in cardiac acceleration. This effect is produced by activation of the sympathetic branch of the autonomic nervous system. In other regions, cardiac slowing occurs. A deceleration is mediated by the vagus nerve. Atropine, a compound that blocks

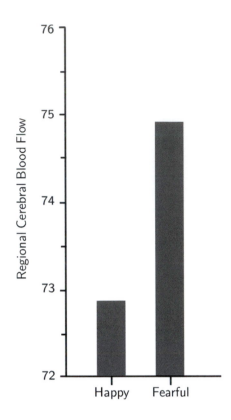

Figure 9.8. Activation of the Amygdala by Facial Expression. Viewing pictures of fearful faces produces activation of the normal human amygdala, as indicated by increased amygdalar blood flow (Morris et al., 1996).

the action of acetylcholine, abolishes this effect. There appears to be no simple scheme to explain where stimulation will produce acceleration and where deceleration will result (Reis & LeDoux, 1987).

Emotional changes also occur following stimulation of the amygdala. In animals, stimulation of the amygdala in the lateral and central regions often produces evidence of fear. Defensive and aggressive responses are elicited by stimulation in the general area of the basomedial region.

Electrical stimulation of the human amygdala is distinctly unpleasant. Extremely uncomfortable emotional reactions, such as fear and anxiety, frequently occur. These results are in reasonable accord with the data from electrical stimulation of the amygdala in lower species (Heath, 1964). Fear is the normal consequence of amygdalar stimulation.

Some pharmacological agents that evoke fear in humans also produce activation of the amygdala. For example, Ketter et al. (1996) used intravenous procaine to activate limbic structures in human volunteers. Intravenous procaine results in strong emotional activation, but the kind of emotion it arouses varies widely among people. Many individuals experience intense fear, but others react with euphoria. Ketter used positron-emission tomography to access the patterns of procaine-induced limbic activation. Intravenously injected procaine induced increased neural activity within the left amygdala of subjects who responded fearfully. Furthermore, the amount of amygdalar arousal was directly related to the intensity of the fear these people experienced (Ketter, Andreason, George, & Lee, 1996).

The amygdala also appears to be directly involved in the processing of fearful facial expressions in humans. Facial expressions, as Darwin suggested, are used in social species such as humans to convey internal emotional states to other members of the group (Ekman, 1982). Morris measured regional cerebral blood flow using positron-emission tomography as volunteers observed pictures of emotionally expressive faces (Morris et al., 1996). These faces reflected either happiness or fear, with varying levels of emotional intensity. Subjects were simply required to indicate the gender of the face; explicit judgments of the expressed emotions were not required.

Viewing the fearful faces—as opposed to happy faces—selectively activated the left amygdala in these normal volunteers, as shown in Figure 9.8. Furthermore, left amygdala activation was directly related to the intensity of fear expressed in the photographed faces. Because the amygdala is closely connected with higher-order visual areas of the temporal lobe, it has direct access to the cortical systems that process face perception. Because the amygdala also provides a major input to the autonomic nervous system, it is well positioned to process the emotional information revealed in facial expressions and thus plays a major role in the emotional regulation of human social behavior.

The idea that the amygdala plays a special role in the perception of fear finds further support in the report of an unusual patient with bilateral calcification and atrophy of the amygdala (Adolphs, Tranel, Damasio, & Damasio, 1994, 1995). The patient, S. M., was a 30-year-old woman of normal intelligence but with a personal history marked by very poor personal and social decisions. She suffered from Urbach-Wiethe disease, a

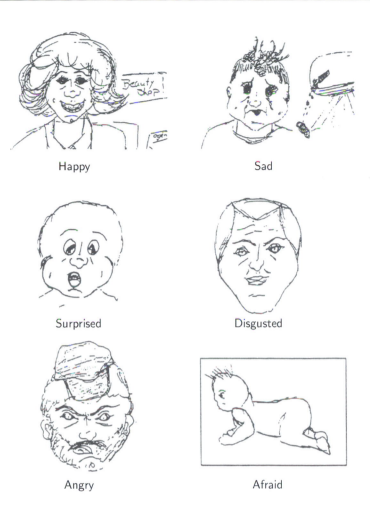

Happy

Sad

Surprised

Disgusted

Angry

Afraid

Figure 9.9. S. M.'s Drawings of Facial Expressions. S. M., whose amygdalae were bilaterally lesioned, drew these facial expressions illustrating different emotions from memory. She emphatically stated that she did not know how to draw a fearful face and was dissatisfied with the drawing that she did make after much prodding. (From the *Journal of Neuroscience,* 1995, 15(9), p. 5888.)

rare disorder that had ravaged both amygdalae but had left the surrounding limbic structures unimpaired.

S. M. was shown a series of photographs of faces that were either emotionally neutral or expressed one of six basic emotions (happiness, surprise, fear, anger, disgust, or sadness). She was asked to rate each face using several emotional adjectives. The same test was given to 12 brain-damaged control patients and to a group of 7 normal volunteers. S. M.'s ratings indicated that she perceived less fear, anger, and surprise than did any of the control subjects. Her ratings of other emotions were perfectly normal.

It was the judgment of fear that was most aberrant for this unusual patient. Her ratings of the various faces on all categories except fear corresponded with those of non-brain-damaged controls. She could correctly sense happiness, anger, or any of the other emotions as reflected in facial expressions. But her judgments of fear in the faces were virtually unrelated with the same judgments made by the normal subjects. It was as if she could not see fear in the photographs that she was shown.

Perhaps the most revealing indication of the importance of the amygdala in the perception of fear appeared when S. M. was asked to draw facial expressions reflecting various emotions. Her drawings are shown in Figure 9.9 on the preceding page. For the other emotions, her depictions were more than passable. She clearly grasped the facial expressions of happiness, sadness, surprise, disgust, and anger. But as for fear, she explained that "she did not know what an afraid face would look like and therefore could not draw the expression" (Adolphs, Tranel, Damasio, & Damasio, 1995, p. 5887). Her drawing confirmed that she simply had no idea of what a fearful face might look like. From these and similar data, it is clear that the amygdala plays a critical role in the human perception of fear.

Septal Area

The **septal area** is positioned beneath the anterior corpus callosum in the medial forebrain. This area may be divided into two principal regions: the lateral and medial divisions of the septum.

The lateral region is by far the larger of the two and includes many fibers of passage, which extend through the region without synapsing. The cells of the lateral septal area project heavily to the medial septal area and the adjacent band of Broca. The lateral septal nuclei also make connections with the mammillary bodies, the midbrain tegmentum, and certain hypothalamic nuclei.

The medial division of the septal area is situated on the midline and is composed of larger-sized cells. The medial septal area makes extensive connections with cells of the habenulae (a pair of structures located near the dorsal thalamus), the hypothalamus, and the hippocampus.

Lesions in the septal area result in a period of hyperemotionality in many species. In humans, a tumor in this region may produce ragelike attacks with increased excitability. Septally damaged animals often show aggressive responses that appear to be the result of heightened defensive reactions. Exaggerated motor responses to sensory stimuli also are common.

Electrical stimulation of the septal area appears to be appealing to animals, which choose electrical stimulation in this region in preference to electrical stimulation in other regions. Electrical stimulation in this region also has autonomic effects. For example, stimulation of the lateral division of the septum decreases heart rate, whereas medial stimulation produces cardiac acceleration. Other autonomic changes also have been reported.

In humans, electrical stimulation of the septum results in pleasurable emotion. This effect is very consistent. Patients who are depressed exhibit a marked elevation in mood following septal stimulation. Robert Heath, who has made extensive studies using brain electrical stimulant, reports the following:

> Changes in content of thought were often striking, the most dramatic shifts occurring when prestimulation associations were pervaded with depressive affect. Expressions of anguish, self-condemnation, and despair changed precipitously to expressions of optimism and elaborations of pleasant experiences, past and anticipated. (Heath, 1964)

Heath's patients were unaware as to when electrical stimulation was applied. Although they did not directly sense the stimulation, its effects were nonetheless profound:

> When questioned concerning changes in mental content, they were generally at a loss to explain them. For example, one patient on the verge of tears described his father's near fatal illness and condemned himself as somehow responsible, but when the septal region was stimulated, he immediately terminated this conversation within 15 seconds and exhibited a broad grin as he discussed plans to date and seduce a girl friend. When asked why he had changed the conversation so abruptly, he replied that the plans concerning the girl suddenly came to him. This phenomenon was repeated several times in the patient. (Heath, 1964)

Although pleasurable thoughts of a sexual nature are often induced by septal stimulation, overt sexual responses are infrequent. Nonetheless, they may occur. For example, Heath reports an instance of orgasm in a female following chemical stimulation of the septal region (Heath, 1964). In this patient, acetylcholine was introduced into the septum though a cannula, or small tube. Acetylcholine produced repeated high-voltage discharges within the septum during the period of sexual arousal.

Reward Systems of the Brain

If electrical stimulation of the human brain can evoke feelings of pleasure, could not the desire to receive such stimulation provide a goal that motivates behavior? Will people or animals perform work to receive electrical brain stimulation as a reward? Such appears to be the case.

The discovery that electrical stimulation of the brain can be rewarding was first made by James Olds and Peter Milner (1954). In the process of conducting an experiment involving electrical stimulation of the brain, Olds observed that some animals seemed to be behaving in a manner that increased the amount of intracranial stimulation that they received. This observation was quickly confirmed; laboratory animals in fact will perform work to obtain electrical stimulation in certain areas of the brain. These effects may be profound. Rats will press a lever as rapidly as 2,000 times each hour to obtain electrical brain stimulation. They will continue responding at this rate for 24 hours or longer. They will ignore other rewards, such as food and water, to continue working for electrical stimulation. The apparent potency of electrical stimulation in motivating behavior initiated a vigorous attempt by investigators to learn more about the reward systems of the brain.

Self-produced electrical stimulation of the brain, called **intracranial self-stimulation (ICSS)**, may be obtained from a wide variety of brain areas. Many years ago, neuroscientists hoped that the anatomical basis for positive reward could be determined by mapping the frequency at which animals will press a lever to obtain electrical stimulation in different regions of the brain. Perhaps the most extensive mapping effort was made by Olds and his collaborators in the late 1950s. Olds and Olds (1963) reported that the highest rates of ICSS were obtained for the septal area, the

Figure 9.10. The Midbrain Dopamine System.

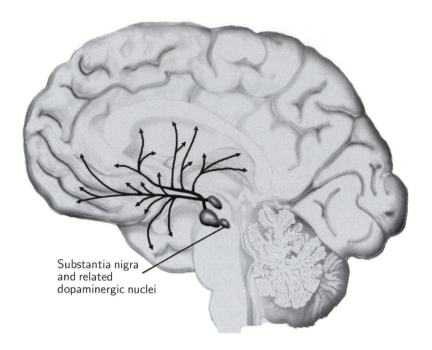

Substantia nigra
and related
dopaminergic nuclei

amygdala, and the anterior hypothalamus. More moderate but still substantial rates of ICSS were observed in related limbic structures, particularly the hippocampus, cingulate gyrus, anterior thalamus, and posterior hypothalamus. However, ICSS is not confined to the region of the limbic system; ICSS may be obtained from selected structures ranging from portions of the medulla to the prefrontal cerebral cortex.

Of all brain sites giving rise to ICSS, none is more powerful than the region of the medial forebrain bundle in the lateral hypothalamus. The **medial forebrain bundle (MFB)** is a diffuse system of fibers that connects structures in the limbic region with various areas of the brain stem. The MFB contains a mixture of both ascending and descending fibers. It begins in the region of the anterior commissure of the basal forebrain and proceeds into the lateral hypothalamus. From there, fibers continue medially and posteriorly into the brain stem. However, most of the fibers of the MFB are short and serve to connect the septum with the lateral hypothalamus. It is in this region of the MFB that the highest rates of ICSS are observed. The particular potency of MFB stimulation requires an explanation. It now appears that MFB stimulation exerts its effects by activating dopaminergic systems of the brain stem (Phillips & Fibiger, 1989; Wise & Bozarth, 1987).

The Midbrain Dopamine System   Two closely related midbrain nuclei—the **substantia nigra** and the **ventral tegmental area**—are composed of dopamine-containing neurons that project rostrally to a number of forebrain sites. These include regions of the lateral hypothalamus, the preoptic area, and the nucleus accumbens located near the septal area, as well as other limbic and cortical regions. Figure 9.10 illustrates these pathways.

These pathways linking the substantia nigra and the ventral tegmental area with forebrain structures all pass through the medial forebrain bundle. Electrical stimulation of the MFB could directly activate these fibers. However, there is considerable evidence that MFB stimulation exerts its rewarding effects by stimulating descending, nondopaminergic fibers that in turn activate cells in the substantia nigra and the ventral tegmental area (Shizgaal & Murray, 1989).

A number of lines of experimental evidence indicate that dopaminergic neurons play a particularly important role in the ICSS phenomena. First, electrical stimulation is more rewarding in those regions of the substantia nigra and the ventral tegmental area that contain the highest concentrations of dopaminergic neurons (Corbett & Wise, 1980). This is a good indication that these fibers actually mediate ICSS.

Second, the release of dopamine by cells of the ventral tegmental area is increased following stimulation of that structure. Moreover, when the dopaminergic neurons of the ventral tegmental area on one side of the brain are selectively destroyed by injections of 6-hydroxydopamine, the strength of the self-stimulation effect is reduced for electrodes in the lesioned side of the brain but not for contralateral electrodes (Fibiger, Le Piane, Jakubovic, & Phillips, 1987). Thus, the ICSS effect depends on the presence of dopaminergic target cells.

Third, injection of a dopamine-blocking agent in the nucleus accumbens, the forebrain target of the dopamine system, reduces the effectiveness of MFB stimulation; the strength of the MFB stimulus had to be increased to maintain high levels of self-stimulation (Stellar, Kelley, & Corbett, 1983).

If a rat will press a lever 2,000 times each hour to receive electrical stimulation of the MFB, one might say that MFB stimulation is addictive. Perhaps, therefore, it is not surprising to find that many drugs of addiction for humans also affect brain stem dopaminergic neurons. These include opiates, cocaine, amphetamine, nicotine, and alcohol. Such drugs subvert the normal role of the brain's reward system, the reinforcement of useful behaviors.

STRESS

Unless we are addicted, it is not the pursuit of pleasure that disrupts our well-being. Rather, it is the worry, anxiety, and agitation produced by unpleasant and worrisome events and concerns that upset us. Such aversive stimuli—whether internal or external—trigger continuing long-term activation of our emotional systems, upsetting us, causing stress, diminishing our happiness, and ultimately compromising our health.

The word **stress** has many meanings. Here, we follow the lead of Walter Cannon (1929) in using stress to refer to what he called the physiological **stress response**, the physiological reaction of the nervous system and body to perceived threat. **Stressors** are the stimuli that evoke the stress response.

All sorts of stimuli can be stressors. Some stressors are simple physiological stimuli, such as extreme heat or cold. Others are situational, such as a major examination, a bad accident, or—for us Californians—an earthquake. Such stressors are a real if unwelcomed part of the world in which

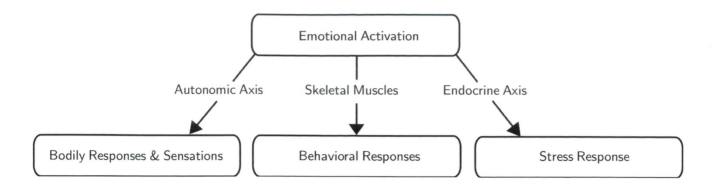

Figure 9.11. Parallel Endocrine and Autonomic Outputs of the Stress Response.

we live. But stressors need not be "real" to produce stress. Imagined threats, supposed difficulties, and potential disasters can all evoke very real and sometimes debilitating physiological stress responses.

The stress response can be adaptive and useful in coping with short-term stressors. The stress response engages autonomic, behavioral, and endocrine changes that support what Cannon (1929) called the **fight-or-flight response**, an orchestrated configuration of bodily adjustments that mobilize the body's resources and facilitate immediate coping with short-term crises. But as adaptive as the stress response is on a short-term basis, when prolonged, it produces a wide range of detrimental consequences. The body cannot sustain a state of high physiological preparedness for extended periods of time.

The Stress Response

Evolution has provided humans, like all other organisms from the simple to the complex, with a number of mechanisms by which they deal with significant changes in their external or internal environment (Akil & Morano, 1996). Three major categories of responses are mobilized. One is *behavioral*, which directs the activity of a person in the face of a perceived stressor. A second is *autonomic*, resulting in sympathetic activation and parasympathetic inactivation. The third is *endocrinological*, mobilizing a variety of hormonally mediated changes in bodily function. Together, these three classes or axes of activation constitute the human stress response.

Behavioral responses can vary widely in their nature. Sometimes, we take decisive and effective action to deal with a stressor and restore bodily and psychological equilibrium. However, we can also engage in inappropriate, maladaptive, self-defeating activities that—in the long run—are injurious to our own well-being.

In contrast to the variability of behavioral stress reactions, the autonomic and endocrine responses are usually stereotypic and widespread bodily expressions of the primal fight-or-flight response. The pathways involved in both autonomic and neuroendocrine axes of the stress response are shown in Figure 9.11.

For both systems, activation occurs as the result of the perception of a real—or imaginary—stressor by forebrain cognitive systems. In the autonomic nervous system, this results in a profound shift to sympathetic dominance, with the expected increases in heart rate and other typical sympathetic signs of activation.

Sympathetic Activation   In addition to specific neural activation of target organs, such as the heart, sympathetic arousal also induces the release of both epinephrine and norepinephrine into the general circulation by the adrenal medulla, a part of the adrenal gland.

The adrenal glands are located just above the kidneys. The inner portion of the adrenal gland is the adrenal medulla, which is a part of the sympathetic nervous system. The outer portion of the adrenal gland is the adrenal cortex, a part of the endocrine system. The adrenal cortex secretes a variety of steroid hormones in response to neuroendocrine activation. But it is the adrenal medulla—not the adrenal cortex—that secretes the catecholamines epinephrine and norepinephrine during sympathetic activation.

The stress-induced excretion of catecholamines by the adrenal medulla and the sympathetic neural activation of the heart are regulated by a single set of central sympathetic command neurons within the brain stem and hypothalamus. Jansen and his colleagues (Jansen, Nguyen, Karpitskiy, Mettenleiter, & Loewy, 1995) injected two different genetically engineered forms of a pseudorabis virus into the stellate ganglia (which provide sympathetic control of the heart) and the adrenal medulla (which excretes catecholamines in response to stress). These distinctive viruses serve as antigen tracers that travel up the neuronal synaptic chains from the locus of injection, labeling the cells that they encounter along the way.

Jansen et al. (1995) found groups of neurons within the ventromedial and ventrolateral rostral medulla and the caudal raphe nuclei that carried the labels from both the stellate ganglionic and adrenal medullary injections, indicating that these brain stem neurons sent projections directly to both the adrenal medulla and heart. In addition, double-labeled neurons were found in the paraventricular nucleus of the hypothalamus and related hypothalamic structures. Such central command neurons act to produce a coordinated response within the varied organ systems controlled by the sympathetic nervous system. Thus, stress-induced catecholamine excretion by the adrenal medulla, like cardiac acceleration, should be considered a direct result of sympathetic autonomic activation.

These sympathetic responses are the first wave of the body's stress response (McEwen & Sapolsky, 1995). They occur within seconds and elicit a series of second-messenger cascades throughout the organism. Autonomic activation is fast.

Endocrine Activation   The second wave of the stress response is generated by the endocrine system. This slower and longer-lasting response to a stressor activates what is called the **hypothalamic-pituitary-adrenocortical axis (HPA)**. The HPA is a descending system of endocrinological activation that begins in the hypothalamus, a structure well positioned to receive emotion-laden and stress-related information. Several hypothalamic nuclei are involved in regulating anterior pituitary activity, but the

paraventricular nucleus (PVN), located on the sides of the third ventricle, produces the endocrinological stress response.

The PVN is the first stage in the HPA chain. It is linked to the pituitary gland, the second structure in the endocrinological response to stress, by a special circulatory system through which substances released by PVN neurons are transported to cells in the anterior portion of the pituitary gland.

The **pituitary** (also called the *hypophysis*) is a small rounded gland that is attached to the base of the hypothalamus by the pituitary stalk. It is divided into three functionally distinct regions (its anterior, posterior, and intermediate lobes). The HPA stress axis involves the **anterior pituitary**. (The intermediate pituitary is vestigial in the human adult, and the posterior pituitary regulates other bodily functions.) The anterior pituitary (or adenohypophysis) is controlled by regulatory peptides secreted by hypothalamic cells into the portal system, chemically linking the hypothalamus and anterior pituitary. Some of these hypothalamic regulatory peptides are involved in controlling feeding and sexual activity. But one is the principal endocrine component of the stress response.

Stressors trigger the paraventricular nucleus to secrete **corticotropin-releasing hormone (CRH)**, which is also called *corticotropin-releasing factor*, into the pituitary's portal system, which, in turn, activates excretory cells in the anterior pituitary (Ur & Grossman, 1994).

But the paraventricular nucleus and CRH also act to coordinate other aspects of the stress response as well by exerting a primary influence on both the sympathetic nervous system and the immune system (Tsagarakis & Grossman, 1995). The paraventricular nucleus receives major neural input from a variety of other hypothalamic nuclei, as well as from the limbic system and the brain stem's somatic and motor centers. Thus, the PVN has access to a variety of emotional and somatic inputs and is well positioned to play a pivotal role in coordinating the stress response of the body.

The corticotropin-releasing hormone excreted by the PVN is the primary integrating peptide for the stress response, affecting not only the brain's endocrinological response to stress but also the sympathetic and immune responses. CRH release increases norepinephrine turnover within the forebrain. Similarly, the release of norepinephrine by central sympathetic neurons increases CRH release by the PVN. Thus, the endocrine CRH and sympathetic norepinephrine systems are mutually interrelated and facilitatory (Southwick, Bremner, Krystal, & Charney, 1994).

However, the most direct effect of CRH secretion is endocrinological. In response to CRH produced by the paraventricular nuclei, the anterior pituitary releases **adrenocorticotropic hormone (ACTH)** into the general circulation as its component of the stress response (DeMoranville & Jackson, 1996). ACTH secretion is the direct endocrine response to CRH secretion by the paraventricular nucleus.

ACTH travels through the general circulation to the adrenal cortex, where it stimulates endocrine cells to secrete the steroid hormone **cortisol**, which is also called *hydrocortisone* (Akil & Morano, 1996). Cortisol is a glucocorticoid, the class of steroids that affects glucose metabolism. (Cortisol is the glucocorticoid hormone released by the primate adrenal cortex. However, in rodents things are somewhat different. In these animals, the glucocorticoid corticosterone is released by the adrenal cortex.)

The glucocorticoids cortisol and corticosterone are highly catabolic, vigorously promoting the breakdown of lipids, sugars, and proteins to increase the bodily levels of free fatty acids, glucose, and amino acids, all important energy sources needed to support strenuous bodily action (De-Moranville & Jackson, 1996).

Glucocorticoids also suppress immune functions, which may act to increase an organism's mobility during physiological stress but also, unfortunately, increases the chances of infection following injury (DeMoranville & Jackson, 1996). Even though cortisol excretion begins within minutes following the onset of stress, the bodily effects produced by cortisol are only fully felt some hours later (McEwen & Sapolsky, 1995).

Thus, the HPA cortisol response to acute stress results in a series of bodily changes that can be immediately beneficial to an animal facing immediate physical danger. But when these same endocrinologically mediated stress reactions—proven so useful in dealing with short-term physical danger—are evoked in humans by prolonged psychological stress, the results may be devastating. Long-term stress responses, either real or imagined, can be dangerous to one's health.

Stress and Health

The physiological effects produced by ACTH in a number of organ systems are profound, which makes the HPA axis so effective in supporting short periods of activity under stressful conditions. ACTH has a broad range of activity, affecting the expression and regulation of genes in tissues throughout the body (Akil & Morano, 1996).

It is precisely because ACTH is so powerful that its excretion is so carefully regulated. A number of biochemical negative feedback loops within the endocrine system operate under normal conditions to ensure that ACTH secretion is abruptly terminated when the stressor is no longer present. These feedback loops are interrelated and have evolved to protect the bodily tissues from unnecessary catabolic activity. However, prolonged, sustained stress activation can override these endocrinological controls and, in so doing, transform the stress response from the body's protector to its attacker.

One of the best-known relations between prolonged stress and health is that found with certain cardiovascular diseases. Chronic stress induces chronic sympathetic activation, with the concomitant increases in blood pressure and heart rate. In turn, long-term hypertension increases the possibilities of stroke (cerebrovascular accident), heart attack, and atherosclerosis (Van De Graaff & Fox, 1992).

Acute periods of stress also affect bodily health and well-being. For example, it has long been recognized that bereavement among the elderly produces an increase in the incidence of major medical problems for the widower. Parkes, Benjamin, and Fitzgerald (1969) reported a 40% increase in mortality within the first 6 months following spousal loss, a finding that remains generally accepted (Krantz, Kop, Santiago, & Gottdiener, 1996).

Similar findings have been observed in general populations that have been subjected to an acute, fear-producing stressor. For example, at the onset of the 1991 Gulf War, admissions to the intensive care unit of a Tel Aviv medical center were substantially increased during the first days of the Iraqi missile bombardment of that city (Krantz, Kop, Santiago, & Gottdiener, 1996). The number of fatal and nonfatal cardiac events was elevated, as compared with either the week prior to the bombardment or to the same week of the previous year.

Similar effects of societal threats on heart attacks have been reported for a number of different natural disasters. For example, in Athens, the number of cardiac deaths was nearly twice the normal rate in the 5 days following the 1981 Athens earthquake (Trichopoulos, Katsouyanni, & Zavitsanos, 1983). Similarly, the incidence of acute myocardial infarctions was nearly twice the normal rate in the week following the 1994 Los Angeles earthquake in the 15 miles surrounding the Northridge epicenter of that disaster (Krantz, Kop, Santiago, & Gottdiener, 1996; Leor & Kloner, 1995).

Posttraumatic Stress Disorder

Those experiencing a natural disaster, such as the Los Angeles earthquake, do not soon forget the impact of the event on their lives. But for many people, the effects of such a stressor reach much further and are far more devastating. Intense reactions are increasingly common for longer-lasting and more violent life disruptions. Neurologists and psychiatrists use the term *posttraumatic stress disorder* to describe this response syndrome. Not surprisingly, the symptoms of posttraumatic stress disorder were first described in battlefield soldiers, in reports dating back to the early Greeks and Romans. In the American Civil War, battlefield physicians spoke of cases of *soldier's heart*. In World War I, the term was *shell shock* (Tomb, 1994). Soldiers with shell shock were tormented by continuing fear, exhaustion, and anxiety, an extreme toll taken by extreme life stress.

The modern concept of posttraumatic stress disorder in neuropsychiatry has changed in the half century since World War II (Tomb, 1994). It was first described as a gross stress reaction that may, in some people, progress into a personality disturbance of some sort. But the widespread psychological disruptions produced by the Vietnam War in its veterans—as well as increased experience with civilian catastrophes—caused a rethinking of the nature of posttraumatic stress responses.

Today, **posttraumatic stress disorder (PTSD)** is defined as a persistent disorder a) in persons exposed to a traumatic, life-threatening event; b) that is reexperienced often, as in recurring recollections, reenactments, or dreams; c) with persistent avoidance of stimuli related to the traumatic event; d) involving persistent symptoms of increased arousal; e) of long duration; and f) causing significant distress or impairment of functioning (American Psychiatric Association (APA), 1994). In the past several years, the range of situations in which the diagnosis of PTSD is being applied has broadened considerably. No longer limited to the traumas of war, violent rape, and torture, more ordinary life experiences such as accidents and illnesses are being viewed as sources of stress that result in major functional disorders (Tomb, 1994).

Neuropsychiatric evidence has indicated that the incidence of PTSD varies dramatically with the nature of the trauma experienced. Nearly every prisoner of war (Sutker, Winstead, & Galina, 1991) or person who has suffered prolonged, intense torture (Kuch & Cox, 1992) will show strong signs of posttraumatic stress disorder. These effects, at least in the young, may be persistent. A recent study by Sack et al. (1993) reported that the prevalence of PTSD in profoundly traumatized Cambodian refugee children had fallen from 50% at release to 38% 6 years later. Despite the lingering effects of truly inhumane torture and abuse, these young men and women have done surprisingly well in creating stable and productive social and occupational lives for themselves. They have learned to cope with the chilling aftereffects of extreme and brutal stress.

The enhanced stressor-induced arousal characteristic of posttraumatic stress disorder has been demonstrated repeatedly over the years. For example, in 1918, Meakins and Wilson showed that shell-shocked World War I soldiers reacted with exaggerated respiratory and heart rate responses to gunfire and sulfuric flames. In the same year, Fraser and Wilson found that shell-shocked soldiers responded to intravenous injections of epinephrine with similarly exaggerated autonomic responses and increased subjective anxiety. It is now known that uncontrollable stress results in an enhanced activation of the locus coeruleus, which contains most of the noradrenergic neurons within the human brain (Southwick, Bremner, Krystal, & Charney, 1994).

Psychoneuroimmunology

Both the sympathetic and neuroendocrine components of the stress response were clearly identified many years ago, but the discovery of the final component of the body's stress response—the suppression of immune system activity—is by comparison a recent discovery. It is now becoming clear that changes in immunoprotection are a characteristic and widespread consequence of stress on bodily function. The study of behavioral and neural factors on the body's immune system has emerged as a new and extremely important branch of neuroscientific and clinical investigation, which is called **psychoneuroimmunology**.

Our bodies defend themselves against invading biological microorganisms with a general-purpose nonspecific attack on foreign biological material by two general ways. First, certain white blood cells, the macrophages and neutrophils, destroy foreign cells by ingesting them. (Macrophages also play an important role in removing dead bodily cells, again by swallowing them.) This type of nonspecific destruction of foreign biological substances is shared with invertebrates and provides our bodies with their first defense against infectious agents.

In all vertebrates, the **immune system** provides a second level of protection that is absolutely essential to our existence. Our immune system is a system of white blood cells that protects us from specific sources of infection by learning to recognize particular foreign molecules. Without an immune system, any vertebrate animal would soon die from massive bacterial, viral, or fungal infections.

We all know that after people have recovered from many types of infections, those infections rarely recur. This is because the initial infection triggered a disease-specific immunity against the specific infecting agent.

That protection, or immunity, is produced by our immune systems.

The immune system can be triggered by any macromolecule that is foreign to the individual. Such substances are called **antigens** (antibody generators). The problem faced by the vertebrate immune system is to distinguish between foreign and self molecules, which is a remarkably complex task considering both the diversity and relatedness of biological molecules across individuals and over species. Yet, it is a task that the immune system performs with high accuracy. It can distinguish between proteins that differ by as little as a single amino acid in their entire structure (Alberts et al., 1994). This distinction is learned by the immune system, based on its experience in the initial infection.

The immune system employs two types of responses to foreign molecules. First, it produces **antibodies**, which are proteins that circulate throughout the body and attack any cells displaying one particular antigen molecule. Antibodies inactivate both viruses and bacterial toxins by binding to them and thereby preventing them from infecting other host cells. Antibodies also mark foreign cells for destruction by other systems by binding to them. The immune system also initiates **cell-mediated immune responses**, in which specialized cells are produced that react to specific antigens. These specialized immune cells can kill infected cells directly or trigger their destruction by macrophages.

Both responses are the product of lymphocytes, a special category of white blood cells. **B cells** are lymphocytes produced in the bone marrow (hence their name). It is the B cells that make antibodies. **T cells** are lymphocytes produced in the thymus. It is the T cells that execute cell-mediated immune responses. There are two different types of T cells, called cytotoxic and helper T cells. The **cytotoxic T cells** attack and kill infected cells directly. The **helper T cells** both aid other white blood cells in destroying foreign cells and contribute to the production of antibodies as well. Together, the T and B cells produce remarkable effective and lethal attacks on any cell bearing the antigens to which they respond.

There is also a third type of white blood cell that is similar to the lymphocytes that are involved in bodily protection. These are the **natural killer cells** or NK cells. Like T cells, natural killer cells kill virus-infected cells and also attack some types of tumor cells. NK cells make a major contribution to the elimination of infectious foreign biological agents.

Autoimmune diseases result when either antibodies or cell-mediated responses are triggered by proteins manufactured by the body of the organism. The immune response is no less effective when triggered by the body's own protein than when activated by foreign biological molecules. The resulting error, however, can be devastating, with the power of the immune system unleashed against the body's own tissues. In myasthenia gravis, for example, the acetylcholine receptor of the neuromuscular junction is the target of the immune response. As these peripheral cholinergic receptors are destroyed, muscle tissue becomes less and less responsive to neuronal control, and progressive weakening and paralysis result.

There is ample evidence that many forms of stress impair immune function. Herbert and Cohen (1993) conducted a meta-analysis of the effects of depression on immunity. Depression is a major clinical sign of prolonged stress and is often accompanied by persistent high levels of circulating glucocorticoids (Akil & Morano, 1996). Herbert and Cohen found strong agreement among the published reports that clinical depression is associated with marked reductions in many aspects of cellular immunity, including lowering natural killer cell activity and altering the numbers of several other types of white blood cells. Interestingly, the degree of immune system suppression increased with the clinical intensity of depression.

One significant mechanism by which the HPA axis affects the immune system is by the production of glucocorticoids (Ader, Madden, Felten, Bellinger, & Schiffer, 1996). Glucocorticoids in high concentrations are often used in clinical medicine as immunosuppressive agents. However, naturally circulating glucocorticoids suppress and regulate immune function as well, by binding with both B and T lymphocytes, as well as macrophages. After binding, glucocorticoids penetrate the cell membrane, bind with cellular DNA, and modify gene expression in the immune system cells. Through this mechanism, glucocorticoid excretion, under stress or otherwise, can affect many aspects of immune system function.

However, there is now increasing evidence that the central nervous system also affects immune system activity by other mechanisms in addition to the ACTH-glucocorticoid pathway because some immunosuppression has been observed in the absence of the adrenal gland.

Stress and the Brain

Prolonged stress, marked by chronically high levels of circulating glucocorticoids, has long been known to exert damaging effects on various bodily systems, but only recently have its neurotoxic effects become clear. The hippocampus, which is critically involved in memory function, is a brain structure that is now known to be damaged by high levels of stress-produced glucocorticoids. In rodents, Stein-Behrens et al. (1994) have shown that both stress-induced glucocorticoids in normal rats and high physiological levels of glucocorticoids in adrenalectomized rats produced hippocampal cell death in animals challenged with the cytotoxin kainic acid. These and similar results indicate that stress-induced glucocorticoids can have pathological effects on critical neuronal structures of the mammalian forebrain.

A series of recent reports has extended this conclusion to humans (Sapolsky, 1996). Sapolsky reports that hippocampal atrophy is produced by high levels of circulating the glucocorticoid cortisol in humans as a result of three different types of stress. Furthermore, these effects become increasingly severe as the levels of stress-induced cortisol increase.

One piece of evidence supporting this conclusion is a report by Sheline showing that the hippocampus is smaller in size in patients with a history of major depression than in nondepressed individuals (Sheline, Wang, Gado, Csernansky, & Vannier, 1996). Furthermore, the reduction in hippocampal volume is positively correlated with the total duration of major depression experienced by each individual. Such findings are congruent with the idea that the heightened levels of circulating cortisol associated with depressive illness have produced cytotoxic effects in the human hippocampus similar to that observed previously in rodents.

A second finding making a similar argument was reported by Bremner in a study of hippocampal volume in patients with combat-related posttraumatic stress disorder (Bremner et al., 1995). Bremner used high-resolution magnetic resonance images to compare the volumes of the hippocampus in 26 Vietnam combat veterans with posttraumatic stress disorder with hippocampal volumes in 22 matched control subjects. The veterans showed reductions of hippocampal volume that were directly correlated with the number of months of combat exposure experienced by these traumatized soldiers.

Finally, Starkman reports a similar relation between hippocampal volume and circulating cortisol levels in 12 patients with Cushing's syndrome (Starkman, Gebarski, Berent, & Schteingart, 1992). These people were not subject to either depression or posttraumatic stress disorder. Rather, they suffered from an endocrinological disorder characterized by an increased adrenocortical secretion of cortisol. They reported a significant correlation between plasma cortisol levels and MRI-measured hippocampal volume, such that patients with higher cortisol levels had greater hippocampal atrophy. Furthermore, the cortisol-induced hippocampal shrinkage seemed to have a cognitive impact because hippocampal size correlated for three different measures of learning in these patients.

Thus, there seems to be growing evidence that leads to one somewhat chilling conclusion, that indeed stress—which is all too common—is in fact bad for your brain (Sapolsky, 1996).

SUMMARY

Emotion refers to the internal feeling states that are expressed through the physiology of the body, including the muscles of the face. These movements are not strictly voluntary and result from activity within the extrapyramidal motor system.

The peripheral nervous system plays a prominent role in the experience of emotion, providing the raw, visceral component of felt emotion. Centrally, the cerebral cortex mediates human emotion at its highest levels. Frontal lobe damage often has the effect of reducing the intensity of emotional feelings, and portions of the posterior cortex of the right hemisphere are involved in the perception and expression of emotion. However, the limbic system, a collection of nuclei and pathways located in the basal forebrain, is most directly involved in human and animal emotion. These structures provide connections between the neocortex and the hypothalamic and brain stem systems that regulate visceral function, forming a system known as the **Papez circuit**.

Environmental stress also activates the brain structures involved in emotion. The stress response supports the organism's emergency behaviors of *fight or flight*, not only by activating the sympathetic nervous system but also by stimulating the hypothalamic-pituitary-adrenocortical axis of the endocrine system. These two system are coordinated with overt behavior during short-term crises, but when stress is prolonged, the same pattern of neuronal and endocrine response that was initially adaptive begins to compromise health and well-being.

SELECTED READINGS

- Damasio, A. (1994). *Descarte's error: Emotion, reason, and the human brain*. New York: Putman. Damasio, who is widely renowned in the field of cognitive neurology, provides a new outlook on the importance of emotion in human cognition, which opens with the best existing account of the strange and influential case of Phineas Gage. Well worth reading.

- LeDoux, J. (1996). *The emotional brain: The mysterious underpinnings of emotional life*. New York: Simon & Schuster. An extremely readable and accurate overview of the neurobiology of human emotion, written by a leading researcher in contemporary neuroscience. An excellent choice for further study of this very human question.

- Toates, F. (1995). *Stress: Conceptual and biological aspects*. Chichester, England: Wiley. A comprehensive study of the stress response in relation to psychological theory. Provides a contemporary overview and analysis of this literature.

KEY TERMS

adrenocorticotropic hormone (ACTH) A hormone released by the anterior pituitary that regulates the activity of the adrenal cortex.

amygdala A structure composed of the group of nuclei located beneath the anterior portion of the temporal lobe that forms a principal part of the limbic system.

anterior pituitary The anterior portion of the pituitary gland, which is controlled by substances excreted by hypothalamic cells and in turn releases a variety of trophic

antibody A protective immune system protein that is evoked by an antigen.

antigen Any foreign macromolecule that can trigger an immune system response. An antibody generator. hormones into the general circulation. Also called the *adenohypophysis*.

B cells Lymphocytes produced by bone marrow that make antibodies.

Cannon-Bard theory The proposal that the experience of emotion requires both autonomic arousal and cortical activation, which interprets the autonomic arousal.

cell-mediated immune response A response of the immune system involving the production of special cells that react with an antigen.

corticotropin-releasing hormone (CRH) The hormone release by the hypothalamus that stimulates the anterior pituitary to secrete adrenocorticotropic hormone into the general circulation.

cortisol A glucocorticoid hormone produced by the adrenal cortex, also called *hydrocortisone*.

cytotoxic T cells T cells that attack and kill infected cells.

emotion A mental state marked by changes in both feeling tone and physiological activation.

emotional experience The inward aspect of emotional activation that we describe in terms of feelings and arousal.

emotional expression The outward signs of emotional activation that may be perceived by others.

expressive muscles All facial muscles other than those used in mastication.

facial nerve nucleus A nucleus of the pontine brain stem that gives rise to the facial nerve, which innervates the expressive facial muscles.

fight-or-flight response An orchestrated configuration of bodily adjustments that mobilizes the body's resources and facilitates immediate coping with short-term crises.

frontal leukotomy An operation that severs fiber tracts within the white matter of the frontal lobe.

helper T cells Immune system T cells that both aid other white blood cells in destroying foreign cells and also contribute to the production of antibodies.

hypothalamic-pituitary-adrenocortical axis (HPA) A descending neuroendocrinological system responsible for aspects of the stress response.

hypothalamus A collection of nuclei that form the most ventral portion of the diencephalon and play important roles in the regulation of visceral function and emotion.

immune system The system of white blood cells that protects vertebrates from infection.

intracranial self-stimulation (ICSS) Electrical stimulation of specific brain structures that is controlled by the subject.

James-Lange theory The view that emotion is solely the perception of changes in the autonomic and skeletal nervous system that accompany emotional arousal.

limbic lobe An anatomical term referring to the hippocampus, the parahippocampal gyrus, the cingulate gyrus, and the subcallosal gyrus.

limbic system A collection of structures located in the region of the basal forebrain, usually including the cingulate gyrus, the hippocampus, the parahippocampal gyrus, the septum, the amygdala, and a few other neighboring structures.

mastication muscles The masseter, temporalis, and internal and external pterygoid muscles of the face that are used in chewing and speech.

medial forebrain bundle (MFB) A pathway made of ascending and descending small neurons extending from the region of the anterior commissure, through the lateral hypothalamus, into the brain stem; a potent site for intracranial self-stimulation.

natural killer (NK) cells White blood cells that are similar to the lymphocytes and can kill virus-infected cells and some types of tumor cells.

nucleus accumbens A basal forebrain area in the vicinity of the septal area that receives dopaminergic projections from the ventral tegmental area and plays a critical role in the brain reward system.

Papez circuit A hypothetical set of pathways linking the neocortex with the hypothalamus, proposed to be involved in the cortical regulation of emotion.

paraventricular nucleus (PVA) A pair of hypothalamic nuclei on the sides of the third ventricle that form a part of the HPA.

pituitary (hypophysis) A compound glandular structure suspended from the base of the hypothalamus by the pituitary stalk, consisting of an anterior and posterior lobe in the adult human.

posttraumatic stress disorder (PTSD) A persistent, distressing disorder in persons exposed to a traumatic event that is marked by recurrent recollections or dreams, avoidance of stimuli related to the event, and persistent symptoms of increased arousal.

psychoneuroimmunology A branch of neuroscience that studies the immune system in relation to the nervous system and behavior.

septal area A group of nuclei of the medial forebrain, situated beneath the anterior portion of the corpus callosum, that forms a part of the limbic system.

stress See *stress response*.

stress response The reaction of the nervous system to perceived threat.

stressors Stimuli that evoke the stress response.

substantia nigra The region of the midbrain tegmentum that is darkly pigmented in humans and some other primates.

T cell A lymphocyte produced by the thymus that is involved in direct cell-mediated immune responses.

ventral tegmental area A nucleus in the ventral midbrain tegmentum containing dopaminergic neurons that project to regions of the forebrain, including the nucleus accumbens.

Chapter 10

Thirst, Hunger, and Sex

In our more rational moments, we believe that we think with our brains and that our actions are governed by our rational decisions, which—in turn—are the product of reasoned considerations. Yet, at other times, none of this seems true. Instead, our actions and our thoughts are impelled not by reason but by bodily urges, which psychologists call *drives*.

Most drives motivate behavior that is essential to the individual organism. Thus, water-deprived animals seek liquids with which to quench their thirst, and starving animals seek food to satisfy their hunger. Because thirst and hunger are both powerful driving forces for behavior and easily induced in experimental animals, they have been the focus of experimental research attempting to discover the biological basis of animal—and human—motivation.

In contrast, other drives—in particular sex—are not necessary for individual survival but are essential for the survival of the species as a whole.

In humans, as in other species, sex drives human behavior, sometimes in subtle but occasionally in dramatic ways. This chapter explores some of the ways in which thirst, hunger, and sex—so-called "bodily instincts"—can occupy our minds and determine our behavior.

THIRST

Seafarers have always understood the significance of clear water and the meaning of thirst. Samuel Taylor Coleridge, the British Romantic poet, described in *The Rime of the Ancient Mariner* (see Figure 10.1 on the next page) the hellish circumstances of an ill-fated sailing ship becalmed and left to perish under the "bloody sun" of the equatorial Pacific Ocean. "Water, water, every where, Nor any drop to drink," the most quoted line of this mysterious and romantic poem, points to the paradox of the need for fresh water in a species that evolved from the sea. It is fresh water, not salt water, that quenches thirst, but it is salt that is required to retain fresh water within the body. Understanding this paradox provides the key to the problem of water regulation and the nature of thirst.

Water, so common and abundant, is essential for human life. Its simple molecules, each composed of one oxygen atom and two hydrogen atoms, form the bulk of the fluids of the body. Claude Bernard, the 19th-century French physician who is widely regarded as the father of experimental medicine, estimated that 90% of the body is composed of water. He based this conclusion on a comparison of the weights of living persons and that of carefully preserved Egyptian mummies, whose bodies had dried completely during the centuries of their entombment. Modern estimates of the water content of the human body are only somewhat less striking; about 70% of the weight of lean tissue is contributed by water. The watery fluids that surround the cells of the body are vestiges of the sea in which life originated.

Physiology of Water Regulation

Physiologists distinguish between the **intracellular fluid**, which is contained within the cells of the body, and the **extracellular fluid**, which surrounds the cells of the brain and other structures (the *interstitial fluid*). **Blood plasma**, found within the arteries, capillaries, and veins, is the extracellular fluid in which the living cells of the blood are suspended.

The intracellular fluid of the body is by far the most voluminous, constituting about 40% of the body's weight. The extracellular interstitial fluid and blood plasma account for about 16% and 4% of body weight, respectively.

The intracellular and extracellular fluids have very different chemical compositions. In particular, both types of extracellular fluids are rich in sodium and chloride, as is seawater. There is no significant boundary between the blood plasma and interstitial fluid, so their chemical compositions are virtually identical.

In contrast, intracellular fluid has very little sodium or chloride but instead contains large quantities of potassium. Furthermore, there are many large, negatively charged protein molecules in intracellular fluid.

Figure 10.1. "Water, water, every where, Nor any drop to drink." This illustration for Samuel Coleridge's *Rime of the Ancient Mariner* is by Gustave Doré, a 19th-century French illustrator and painter. It is fresh water—not salt water—that is necessary for human life, but it is salt that permits the retention of fresh water by the body.

This imbalance of sodium and potassium between the intracellular and interstitial fluids forms the basis of electrical signaling of nerve cells, a topic that occupied the initial chapters of this book. But it is sodium alone that plays the critical ionic role in the control of water intake as the body attempts to regulate both the ionic concentrations and the relative volumes of the intracellular and extracellular body fluids. It is sodium that governs the movement of water between the extracellular fluid and the intracellular fluid by the process of osmosis.

Figure 10.2. The Osmotic Movement of Water Across a Semipermeable Membrane. In this example, the membrane is permeable to water but not sodium and chloride ions. To equalize the concentration of water on the two sides of the membrane, there is a net movement of water molecules from the pure water to the salt solution.

● Water Molecule
○ Solute Molecule

Nonpermeable Membrane

Semipermeable Membrane

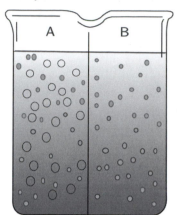
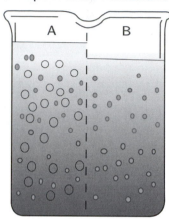

Osmosis   The processes of **osmosis** and **diffusion** govern the movement of solvents and solutes, respectively, as a function of their concentration ratios. You may recall that diffusion is the net movement of dissolved particles from a region of high concentration to a region of lower concentration. If the cell membrane is permeable to such particles, diffusion may take place across the cell membrane.

But dissolved substances are not the only molecules that can cross a cell membrane; cell membranes are also permeable to water, the solvent. Osmosis is the net movement of water across a semipermeable membrane from a region of low water concentration to a region of higher water concentration. The same principles that govern the movement of solutes as diffusion also control the movement of the solvent as osmosis.

The cell membrane is exceptionally permeable to water; the permeability of the cell membrane to water molecules is more than 1 million times greater than the permeability of sodium. Thus, water molecules move freely across the cell membrane; in some small cells, there can be a complete exchange of water molecules within the cell in less than 1 second. Despite all this movement, the volume of the cell remains constant because the forces driving water into the cell are exactly equal to those driving water out of the cell. Thus, the net movement of water across the membrane is zero. But if the composition of either the extracellular fluid or the intracellular fluid is altered, a net osmotic flow of water does occur across the cell membrane, and the volume of the cell will change.

Osmotic movement of water is governed by the total number of nondiffusible molecules in the intracellular and extracellular solutions. Why this occurs may be seen in the following example. Figure 10.2 illustrates a beaker, divided by a semipermeable membrane. This membrane is similar to the membrane of living cells in that it is permeable to water but impermeable to both sodium and chloride ions. If pure water is poured into one half of the beaker and saltwater into the other, the conditions for osmotic movement will be present. The salty solution is relatively poor in water molecules because it is a mixture of water, sodium, and chloride. For this reason, there will be a net movement of water molecules from the pure side to the saltwater side; this movement acts to equalize the concentration of water on the two sides of the membrane. Because the membrane was constructed to be impermeable to both sodium and chloride ions, these ions cannot cross from the salt solution to the pure water.

The net movement of water into the salt solution increases its volume, and its level rises while the level of the pure water falls. This creates an **osmotic pressure** that tends to reduce the further influx of water molecules into the salt solution. The strength of the pressure needed to produce an osmotic equilibrium, in which the movement of water molecules is equal in both directions, depends only on the number of nondiffusible solute particles on the two sides of the membrane. The greater the discrepancy, the larger will be the resulting osmotic pressure at equilibrium.

In living tissue, the cellular membrane is permeable to chloride ions but relatively impermeable to sodium. This means that chloride ions can enter and exit the cell freely and therefore do not contribute to any osmotic effect. In contrast, sodium is the major extracellular ion that governs the osmotic movement of water across the cell membrane, accounting for more than 90% of the osmotically relevant solutes in the blood plasma.

Thus, it should not be surprising that the adjustment of sodium levels in the extracellular fluids is an important feature of body fluid regulation. Most people ingest more than 10 grams of salt each day, but only about 0.5 grams is needed to maintain appropriate sodium levels in the blood plasma. Sodium balance is maintained by the control of sodium excretion. It is the kidneys that regulate the excretion of sodium from the body.

Kidneys   The **kidneys** are among the most elegantly organized structures of the body; they provide a nearly perfect biological solution to a fundamental problem, the regulation of the amounts of body fluids. These two large brown organs, located at the back of the abdominal cavity, bear the primary responsibility for regulating both water and sodium balance. The kidneys filter blood plasma and remove excess water, sodium, and other substances, including waste products, which are excreted as urine.

Each kidney is composed of more than 1 million functional units, called **nephrons**. The nephron is the key to understanding the kidneys because each nephron is capable of performing all the functions of the kidney as a whole.

The function of every nephron is to clean the blood plasma of unwanted substances, which are excreted in the urine. Each nephron consists of two principal parts: a glomerulus, through which unfiltered plasma enters the nephron, and a long **tubule**, which carries unwanted substances from the nephron to the urinary system and returns wanted substances to the blood.

The **glomerulus** is a collection of several dozen parallel capillaries. Blood enters the glomerulus through its **afferent arteriole** and exits by its **efferent arteriole**. (An arteriole is a very small artery.) The fine capillaries of the glomerulus are extremely permeable. Because the hydrostatic pressure within these capillaries is about three times that of the surrounding fluids, blood plasma together with many impurities filters out of the capillaries and enters the tubular system of the nephron.

The process of returning substances from the tubules of the nephrons to the circulation occurs in a variety of ways: Some are passive, requiring no metabolic energy; in other instances, active transport occurs. Moreover, the processes of reabsorption are not constant but are under hormonal and neuronal control to permit appropriate responses to the needs of the body.

Sodium and Water Regulation

Sodium is one substance that can return to the circulation only by way of an active transport mechanism, and it is sodium that provides the key to water regulation. As sodium ions are actively returned to the circulation from the fluid in the tubules, the relative sodium concentration of the two fluids is altered and regulated. Thus, an osmotic pressure gradient is created that returns water molecules from the tubular filtrate to the blood. This is the only mechanism by which the water concentration of the blood plasma is regulated.

In performing these roles of salt and water regulation and in cleansing the blood of the end products of metabolism, the kidneys are exceedingly active. The kidneys receive about 20% of the total output of the heart. Furthermore, about 20% of the blood plasma entering the kidneys is transferred into the tubular system at the glomeruli of the nephrons. It is not surprising, therefore, that more than 99% of all sodium, chloride, and water entering the tubule system is returned to the bloodstream within the nephron. Were that not the case, the body would rapidly be depleted of both salt and water. The processes of sodium and water regulation take place on a longer time scale, produced by tiny variations in reabsorption rates. Thus, over periods of minutes or hours, plasma concentrations of sodium and water remain properly balanced.

Control of Kidney Function   Kidney function is regulated by mechanical, neuronal, and hormonal factors. The major mechanical factor affecting the kidneys is blood pressure. As blood pressure increases, the rate at which blood plasma drains into the tubular system also grows because the hydrostatic pressure difference between the blood and the tubule is increased. However, unless the reabsorption of sodium—and therefore of water—is also altered, a general loss in blood plasma volume results, which acts to lower blood pressure. This is one mechanism by which blood pressure is maintained at normal levels.

The kidneys are also under the control of the sympathetic nervous system. One known function of the sympathetic innervation is to regulate the diameter of the capillaries within the glomerulus, thereby controlling the rate at which blood plasma passes into the tubular system. The sympathetic nervous system also affects the release of hormones that act to alter kidney function.

Hormones are particularly important in the control of kidney function. One such hormone is **aldosterone**, which is produced by the **adrenal glands** located above each kidney. Aldosterone increases the reabsorption of sodium into the blood by the nephrons. The importance of aldosterone

in regulating sodium reuptake is difficult to overestimate: At high aldosterone levels, as little as 0.1 gram of sodium may be lost to the urine each
day; at low levels, as much as 40 grams may be excreted.

Aldosterone release, in large part, is controlled by the kidney itself as a
consequence of the renin-angiotensin system. **Renin** is an enzyme that is
released by the nephrons of the kidney in response to physiological factors
that are poorly understood. Once released into the bloodstream, renin acts
on the abundant supplies of **angiotensinogen**, which is the substrate for
angiotensin.

This system works in the following way. **Angiotensin I** is formed by
the action of renin on angiotensinogen. Angiotensin I is rapidly transformed into the biologically active **angiotensin II** by an unspecified angiotensin-converting enzyme. Angiotensin II has long been known to have
significant effects on blood pressure, a finding responsible for the name
of this peptide. It is angiotensin II that triggers the release of aldosterone
from the adrenal glands, which acts on the renin-releasing structures of
the nephron. Thus, there exists within the nephron a biochemical feedback loop by which its own function, with respect to sodium regulation,
may be controlled.

The reabsorption of water into the blood is driven by osmotic pressure resulting from the reabsorption of sodium; however, water reabsorption may be regulated independently of sodium reabsorption by factors
that affect the water permeability of the collecting tubules of the nephron.
Tubular permeability for water is governed in large part by the presence
of **antidiuretic hormone (ADH)** within the blood plasma. ADH acts to
increase the tubular permeability to water. Therefore, at low plasma ADH
levels, relatively little water is reabsorbed, and large volumes of urine are
produced. At high plasma ADH levels, a great deal of water is reabsorbed,
and, consequently, urine volume is small. Thus, ADH acts to retain water
within the body. In turn, plasma ADH concentrations are under neuronal
control.

The kidneys, responding to mechanical, neuronal, and hormonal factors, occupy a key position in regulating the water content of the body;
they act to conserve water when it is scarce and discharge water when it is
plentiful. For this reason, they are an important key to understanding the
sensation of thirst.

Water Regulation and Thirst

"**Thirst**," says one dictionary, is "a sensation, often referred to the mouth
and throat, associated with a craving for drink; ordinarily interpreted as a
desire for water."[1] Most commonly experienced as dryness in the mouth,
the sensation of thirst can be quite compelling. A very thirsty person will
abandon all else to search for water. Extreme thirst, like severe pain and
oxygen starvation, completely occupies the mind and dominates behavior
to achieve one goal, the elimination of the sensation. Considering the importance of proper fluid balance for the functioning of all bodily organs,
the compelling nature of thirst is not surprising. Walter Cannon, the great
American physiologist, stressed the mouth as the source of the sensation

---

[1]*Dorland's Illustrated Medical Dictionary*, 26th edition, 1981, p. 1362.

of thirst. In 1915, in his book *Bodily Changes in Pain, Hunger, Fear and Rage*, Cannon wrote,

> There is a general agreement that thirst is a sensation referred to the mucous lining of the mouth and pharynx, and especially to the root of the tongue and to the palate. McGee, an American geologist of large experience in desert regions, who made numerous observations on sufferers from extreme thirst, has distinguished five stages through which men pass on their way to death from lack of water. In the first stage there is a feeling of dryness in the mouth and throat, accompanied by a craving for liquid. This is the common experience of normal thirst. This condition may be alleviated, as everyday practice demonstrates, by a moderate quantity of water....In the second stage the saliva and mucus in the mouth and throat become scant and sticky. There is a feeling of dry deadness in the mucous membranes. The in-breathed air feels hot. The tongue clings to the teeth or cleaves to the roof of the mouth. A lump seems to rise in the throat, and starts endless swallowing motions to dislodge it. Water and wetness are then exalted as the end of all excellence. Even in this stage the distress can be alleviated by repeatedly sipping and sniffing a few drops of water at a time. "Many prospectors," McGee states, "become artists in mouth moistening, and carry canteens only for this purpose, depending on draughts in camp to supply the general needs of the system." The last three stages described by McGee, in which the eyelids stiffen over eyeballs set in a sightless stare, the tongue-tip hardens to a dull weight, and the wretched victim has illusions of lakes and running streams, are too pathological for our present interest. The fact I wish to emphasize is the persistent dryness of the mouth and throat in thirst. (Cannon, 1929, pp. 304-305)

The "Dry Mouth" Theory of Thirst There is little question that a dry mouth is associated with both dehydration and thirst; salivary output decreases as a nearly linear function of water deprivation. However, Cannon proposed a stronger theory—that dryness of the mouth is the primary cause of thirst and plays the critical role in regulating water intake. He reasoned that as dehydration occurs, the salivary glands reduce their secretions, which normally moisten the mouth, and that the resulting sensations from the mouth constitute the thirst stimulus that controls drinking.

This "dry mouth" theory of thirst, as it is often called, cannot be correct because continuous drinking occurs when water is made available to the mouth but prevented from reaching the stomach. This experiment was first performed in the 19th century by Claude Bernard (Bernard, 1856). Bernard surgically prepared a fistula, or opening, in the esophagus, the portion of the gastrointestinal tract that links the mouth and stomach. Figure 10.3 on the next page illustrates an esophageal fistula.

When the fistula was closed, the test animals drank normally, as would be expected. But when the fistula was opened, any water entering the mouth would empty through the fistula and fail to reach the stomach. Under these conditions, the mouth would never be dry, but no water would be absorbed by the body. An animal with an open esophageal fistula drinks continuously, as if it is very thirsty. Bernard's experiment has been repeated several times over the years, and the results are always the same.

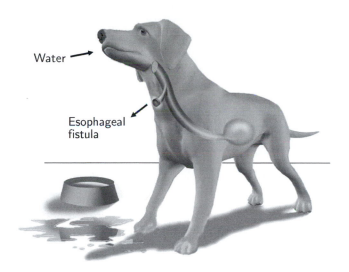

Figure 10.3. An Esophageal Fistula. Water ingested by the mouth does not reach the stomach when the fistula is opened, but water injected into the fistula does.

Similar results have been found in humans. For example, there is report of a man who attempted suicide by slitting his own throat; he succeeded in severing his esophagus, thus creating a fistula, but miraculously avoided cutting any of the arteries or veins of the neck. Over the course of his recovery, he became very thirsty and drank large amounts of water. But his thirst, like that of the fistulated animal, was not quenched, as water never reached his stomach. Water injected directly into the wound, however, emptied into the lower gastrointestinal tract and produced relief from thirst (Rolls & Rolls, 1982).

Thus, both experimental and clinical data agree that a dry mouth is associated with thirst, but it is not the primary cause of thirst. The mechanism by which thirst originates must involve more than just the sensory receptors of the mouth. The critical stimulus for thirst is not restricted to the mouth but rather is more general. It is now clear that thirst will occur when either the intracellular or extracellular body fluids are diminished.

Osmotic Thirst

Alfred Gilman provided the first clear demonstration that intracellular dehydration leads to thirst (Gilman, 1937). He elicited cellular dehydration in laboratory animals by administering concentrated or "hypertonic" solutions of sodium chloride. The animals rapidly became thirsty. Because the cell membrane is relatively impermeable to sodium, the effect of osmosis is to draw water from the intracellular fluid into the interstitial fluid and plasma, thereby reducing the concentration difference of sodium across the cell membrane. This osmotic movement of water dehydrates and shrinks the cells of the body. Thirst produced in this manner is often referred to as **osmometric thirst**.

Gilman obtained similar results with sucrose solutions. Sucrose is a sugar that cannot cross the cell membrane and therefore has osmotic effects like that of sodium chloride. However, the administration of concen-

Figure 10.4. The Anatomy of the Lateral Hypothalamus.

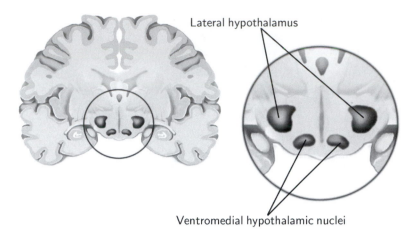

trated glucose solutions produced neither cellular dehydration nor thirst because glucose can cross the cell membrane by carrier transport and therefore is incapable of producing osmotic dehydration. Gilman's demonstration provided a clear indication that the depletion of intracellular fluid is a sufficient condition to produce profound thirst.

These and similar data suggest that some cells of the body must function as **osmoreceptors**, cells that signal osmotically induced changes in cell volume. Such osmoreceptors must provide the central nervous system with information concerning cellular hydration and dehydration. Although there is evidence for osmoreceptors in many tissues of the body, it appears that those within the brain are critical for the control of thirst.

A series of investigations by both Donald Novin and Alan Epstein provided convincing evidence that these osmoreceptors were located in the **lateral preoptic area (LPO)** of the diencephalon. Both laboratories independently demonstrated that small lesions of the LPO in animals selectively reduce the normal increase in drinking that follows intraperitoneal injection of hypertonic saline. However, these same animals do drink normally following fluid loss that does not affect the osmoreceptors. Such data indicate that the LPO contains mechanisms specific to osmometric thirst. Figure 10.4 shows the position of the LPO in relation to other structures in the vicinity of the hypothalamus.

Novin and his collaborators were able to identify the osmosensitive region of the brain by testing the idea that microapplications of either concentrated sodium chloride or sucrose solutions that should elicit drinking, but that concentrated urea should not (Peck & Novin, 1971). This argument follows from the fact that neurons are relatively impermeable to both sodium and sucrose, so these substances can produce osmotic effects. However, neurons are quite permeable to urea, so urea should not produce any osmotic effect, regardless of its concentration. More than 600 locations within the hypothalamus, amygdala, and septum were tested with microinjections of each of the three solutions. The only sites that produced drinking for both sodium chloride and sucrose, but not urea, were tightly bunched together in the LPO. This mapping of the osmoreceptive region of the brain fits perfectly with the mappings produced by microlesion studies and confirms the selective nature of osmoreceptors located in the region. The Epstein laboratory also demonstrated the osmoreceptive properties of LPO cells by showing that injections of plain water reduced drinking, a finding that follows naturally if some LPO cells are true osmoreceptors (Blass & Epstein, 1971).

Electrical recording from groups of cells within the LPO area shows that injections of either sodium chloride or sucrose into the brain blood supply increases the rate of firing of cells in this region (Rolls & Rolls, 1982). Furthermore, this response varies with the concentration of the injected solution. Finally, sodium chloride and sucrose are equally effective in eliciting this response when administered at equal concentrations.

Findings such as these provide convincing evidence of the existence of osmoreceptor cells within and probably confined to the LPO. It appears, therefore, that some cells within the LPO are capable of sensing osmotic changes in their microenvironment and so signal other brain regions to elicit an appropriate behavioral response: drinking of water to quench osmometric thirst.

Volumetric Thirst

Intracellular dehydration is not the only stimulus for drinking; the loss of extracellular fluid may produce profound thirst as well. Although the volume of the blood plasma and interstitial fluid is small in comparison to that of the intracellular fluid, a loss of blood plasma can lead to circulatory collapse and death. Drinking is one mechanism by which adequate levels of extracellular fluid are maintained. Thirst brought on by a loss of extracellular fluid is called **volumetric thirst** because it is a response to a decrease in the volume of blood plasma.

The simplest way in which the extracellular fluid may be depleted without affecting the intracellular fluid is by bleeding, or **hemorrhage**, in which blood plasma and all substances dissolved and suspended within it are lost from the body. Because both extracellular water and the substances dissolved within it are lost in equal proportion, there is no osmotic effect on the intracellular fluid. Hemorrhage results in a simple loss of extracellular fluid and blood cells.

Hemorrhage is accompanied by thirst, which appears to be mediated directly by the loss of extracellular fluid volume. This thirst disappears when the lost blood is replaced. Interestingly, injections of concentrated saline act to reduce the thirst produced by bleeding. Increasing the sodium content of the blood helps restore lost extracellular fluid by osmotically inducing the movement of intracellular water across the cell membrane into the extracellular fluid.

Extracellular fluid loss also may result from extremely low levels of dietary salt. The consequent sodium deficiency triggers an osmotic movement of water out of the extracellular fluid and into the cells of the body; as a result, the volume of the extracellular fluid is depleted. This leads to increased drinking in many species, including humans.

Finally, extracellular fluid loss may be experimentally produced by injection of colloids into the extracellular space (e.g., within the abdominal cavity). Colloids are gluey molecules that can trap large volumes of solutions (Rolls & Rolls, 1982). The injection of colloids effectively captures significant quantities of extracellular fluid, reducing the volume of extracellular fluids available for physiological purposes. Thus, a loss of extracellular fluid, whether produced by bleeding, salt deficiency, or the injection of colloids, results in thirst and drinking that cannot be mediated by the osmoreceptive system, which senses changes in cellular hydration.

Because the loss of extracellular fluid affects blood plasma volume directly, volumetric thirst is likely to be mediated by receptors located within the vascular system. Of the various sites within the vascular system that might be involved in sensing plasma volume and triggering thirst, the kidney appears to play the most important role. Restricting blood flow to the kidney by surgically constricting the renal (kidney) arteries does not affect either total blood volume or overall blood pressure, yet it produces profound thirst and excessive drinking. When blood pressure drops in the kidney, as is the case when blood plasma is lost, a strong volumetric thirst results.

The kidney responds to a decrease in renal blood pressure by releasing **renin**. Renin is the rate-limiting enzyme for the manufacture of angiotensin I and II; this means that the availability of renin controls the rate of angiotensin production. Angiotensin II has striking effects on thirst and drinking, as indicated by the effects of intravenous injections of that hormone. Laboratory animals will work very hard for water when injected with angiotensin II, pressing a lever as many as 64 times for a single small reward of 0.1 ml of water (Rolls, Jones, & Fallows, 1972). Food-deprived rats will stop eating to drink water if injected with angiotensin II. Angiotensin-produced thirst is evidently highly motivated.

Circulating angiotensin II probably has its effects within the central nervous system because injections of the hormone within the central nervous system are more than 1,000 times more effective in producing thirst than are peripheral injections. But there is confusion as to where it is within the central nervous system that angiotensin II exerts its effects. It was first suggested that the hormone may act within the preoptic area. This idea, however, faces the difficulty that angiotensin II is not believed to cross the blood-brain barrier. Thus, angiotensin II produced within the bloodstream should not be able to reach the presumed angiotensin II receptors located in the preoptic area or anywhere else within the central nervous system for that matter. However, the possibility has been raised that a seven-amino-acid segment of angiotensin II, called **angiotensin III**, may be both thirst producing and able to penetrate the blood-brain barrier. If this idea is correct, then the possibility of thirst-related angiotensin receptors within the central nervous system proper must be reconsidered.

But because of the apparent inability of angiotensin to cross the blood-brain barrier, attention has turned to the **circumventricular organs**, which are a series of structures located around the ventricles of the brain that might serve as receptors for circulating hormones. The circumventricular organs provide a bridge between the central nervous system and the other tissues of the body. Of the several circumventricular organs, the **subfornical organ (SFO)** and the **organum vasculosum of the lamina terminalis (OVLT)** are considered to be the most likely sites of the central angiotensin II receptors. These are illustrated in Figure 10.5 on the next page.

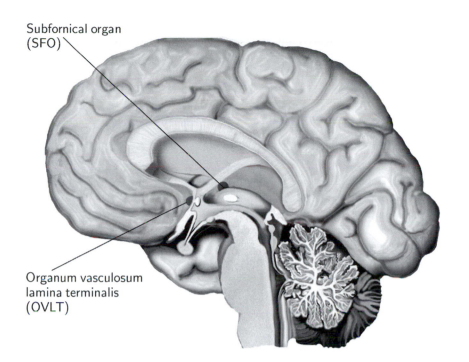

Subfornical organ
(SFO)

Organum vasculosum
lamina terminalis
(OVLT)

Figure 10.5. The Circumventricular
Organs. The circumventricular organs
are structures located around the
ventricles that provide the brain with
an opportunity to sense circulating
hormones.

Attention has focused primarily on the SFO as the structure mediating
the response of the brain to circulating angiotensin II. Laboratory rats normally drink substantially when angiotensin II is injected into the cerebral
ventricular system. However, lesions of the subfornical area completely
block this response in nearly all animals; lesions in neighboring brain regions have no such effect. This effect is restricted to volumetric thirst;
lesions of the SFO have no effects on drinking in response to cellular dehydration or water deprivation (Simpson & Routtenberg, 1973).

Electrophysiological recordings provide evidence for an important role
for the SFO in angiotensin II–induced thirst (Rolls & Rolls, 1982). About
one half of the individual cells in this region tested by microelectrode
recording increase their rate of responding with increasingly large microinjections of angiotensin II. Injections of saralasin—a specific competitive inhibitor of angiotensin II—prevented or reduced this cellular response. Such evidence argues strongly that the subfornical organ provides
the gateway by which circulating angiotensin II affects the central nervous
system.

There appears to be at least one other mechanism by which a loss of
blood volume produces thirst, in addition to the angiotensin II system.
Baroreceptors in the walls of the great blood vessels provide the nervous
system with an indication of levels of hydrostatic pressure within the cardiovascular system. These blood pressure receptors are known to send
messages to the brain through the vagus nerve that disinhibit the secretion of antidiuretic hormone, which in turn increases the reabsorption of
water by the kidneys and instigates a volumetric thirst. Decreases of blood
volume as small as 10% are sufficient to trigger this response. The maintenance of normal blood volume is of such critical biological importance

that it is regulated by a system of physiological mechanisms, including the renin-angiotensin system and the baroreceptors of the great vessels (Rolls & Rolls, 1982).

Thus, an extensive body of evidence has accumulated over the past several decades indicating that thirst arising from cellular dehydration and extracellular volume depletion is mediated by different brain mechanisms. In many natural circumstances, however, both factors participate in the production of thirst, a finding that is referred to as the double-depletion hypothesis. Both cellular dehydration and extracellular fluid loss are produced by water deprivation and by the sweating that forms a part of the body's defense against overheating. Yet the intracellular and extracellular aspects of thirst are independent and, in many circumstances, simply add together in determining thirst-provoked drinking. This summation of influences has been amply demonstrated in the laboratory rat, as well as in other animals. Thus, in most natural circumstances, both cellular dehydration and extracellular fluid depletion must be considered together in any consideration of thirst and drinking behavior.

HUNGER

Just as food is the partner of drink in our daily lives, hunger is the partner of thirst in the study of motivation. Because a continuous supply of nutrients is essential for the continued functioning of living organisms, it is not surprising to find that the control of feeding and digestive processes is complex, with both hormonal and neuronal factors playing important roles.

The study of **hunger**, the craving for food, and **satiety**, the gratification of hunger, has been an important problem in neurobiology, owing in part to the belief that hunger can serve as an experimental model for the biological study of motivation more generally. It has spawned an impressive amount of both experimental research and theoretical hypotheses. Many of the earlier theories proposed that a single crucial physiological variable—such as blood sugar level—might control eating in much the same way as a thermostat controls a furnace.

However, it now appears that no single variable is crucial. Moreover, remarkably few of the proposed biological bases of hunger can be confidently rejected either. It appears that none of these hypotheses is uniquely correct. Instead, each may represent a part of the total understanding of hunger and control of food intake.

Energy Balance   The control of eating—avoiding both inadequacy and excess—is of primary importance for both fitness and health. Most of us ingest just enough food to maintain an energy balance. **Energy balance** refers to the relationship between energy intake in the form of food and energy outflow or expenditure. If energy intake is greater than the body's energy needs, some of the extra energy-rich molecules are stored, often as fat tissue, and the individual gains weight. If energy intake is less than the body's needs, some of the stored energy reserves are used, and the person loses weight. It is only when energy intake equals energy output that the body weight remains stable.

In most adults, body weight does not change significantly for long periods of time, although energy requirements often vary sharply from day to day. These two facts indicate that food intake is regulated in some manner to achieve energy balance. Some understanding of the factors influencing energy balance may be obtained by experimentally varying either the nutritional density of the diet or the energy expended while measuring changes in the amount of food consumed.

Humans and other animals increase the amount of food consumed when the nutritional value of available food is diluted with either water or nonnutritive solids such as cellulose. This ensures an adequate supply of energy-rich substances. Several factors determine the precision with which energy balance is maintained in the face of dietary dilution. First, compensation is most exact when the composition of the food is only slightly diluted. Second, the longer the individual is on the diluted diet, the more precisely will energy balance be achieved. Third, the presence of fat stores lessens the necessity of increasing food consumption when the nutritional value of the diet is reduced; obese animals and people can tolerate dietary dilution without increasing food intake more easily than can lean individuals. Finally, there are also species differences in the precision with which energy balance is maintained in response to dietary dilution. For instance, dogs and cats show much less change in their eating habits than do rats, monkeys, and human beings.

Similarly, food intake increases during periods of exercise and is reduced when exercise is eliminated. There are many species differences in this effect, but humans are known to eat more when energy demands are increased. This is particularly true in lean individuals and is less apparent among the obese.

Energy balance is achieved by the regulation of bodily physiology and of behavior. The concept of **regulation** implies that at least one variable is monitored, and corrective adjustments are made when necessary. For example, in the familiar thermostatically controlled furnaces that heat our homes, room temperature is the monitored variable. A temperature-sensitive thermostat continuously measures the room's temperature. When that temperature drops below a previously determined set point, the furnace is activated. The furnace then begins heating the air until the desired temperature is once again achieved. In this example, the regulation of air temperature involves **negative feedback**, in which the action of the furnace corrects and reverses a naturally occurring decrease in air temperature to return the room's temperature to the desired level.

Understanding the regulation of food intake to achieve energy balance is a more difficult matter because it is not known which aspect or aspects of internal metabolism function as regulated variables. Is it energy use that is monitored? Or is it the total size of the fat store or the change in fat storage or body temperature that provides the key to understanding the regulation of food intake? These are critical issues in the study of hunger and satiety.

The Gastrointestinal Tract   The key structure in the process of digestion is the **gastrointestinal tract**, a long, bending tube that extends from the mouth through the stomach and intestines to the rectum. In addition to the gastrointestinal tract itself, two accessory structures have major importance for digestion: the liver and the pancreas. The organs of the digestive system are shown in Figure 10.6 on the facing page. In digestion, food is broken down into successively smaller molecules that can be absorbed through the walls of the tract. Only in this way can nutrients and other substances enter the body. The gastrointestinal tract forms a boundary between the body and the outside world. Thus, the contents of the stomach and intestines are outside rather than inside the body.

The mouth and throat constitute the initial portion of the gastrointestinal tract. Through the action of the teeth and the tongue, pieces of food are broken up and mixed together before being swallowed. This process is aided by secretions of the **salivary glands**, which can secrete between 1 and 2 liters of saliva each day. The composition of saliva varies, depending on circumstances. Saliva may contain mucins, which are proteins that give saliva a heavy, viscous characteristic that serves a lubricating function. Saliva also may contain salivary amylase, an enzyme that begins the process of splitting starch molecules into smaller fragments.

After swallowing, food reaches the **stomach**, an enlarged and specialized structure of the gastrointestinal tract. The stomach serves as an expandable reservoir that permits the controlled release of ingested food to the small intestine below. While being retained in the stomach, food substances are mixed with gastric secretions to begin the digestive process in earnest. Hydrochloric acid, secreted by specialized cells in the gastric glands, both aids the digestion of proteins and also kills many types of bacteria. Other cells of the gastric gland secrete pepsinogen. Pepsinogen is the precursor of the gastric enzyme pepsin, which facilitates the digestion of proteins by breaking peptide bonds for certain amino acids. The effect of both hydrochloric acid and pepsin within the stomach is to convert protein molecules into smaller peptide chains.

The contents of the stomach empty into the upper segment of the **small intestine**, which is the most important segment of the gastrointestinal tract for digestion and absorption of nutrients. The small intestine in humans is about 6 m in length and is divided into three regions that differ in the microscopic structure of the intestinal walls. The initial 25 cm of the small intestine is the **duodenum**, the next 2.5 m is called the **jejunum**, and the remaining 3.5 m forms the **ileum**. The contents of the ileum pass into the large intestine below it.

The food that enters the small intestine from the stomach is only incompletely digested and not yet ready for absorption. Some of the larger protein molecules have been broken into shorter polypeptide chains of amino acids, but digestion of fats has not even begun. Digestion is completed in the small intestine with the help of two fluids: pancreatic juice and bile.

The digestion and absorption of carbohydrates are rapid and are completed primarily within the duodenum. These plant starches and complex sugars are broken down into the simple sugars glucose, fructose, and galactose, which may be absorbed by the walls of the small intestine, where they enter the bloodstream. The digestion of proteins also occurs within the upper regions of the small intestine. These molecules are broken down into individual amino acids, which may be absorbed by the

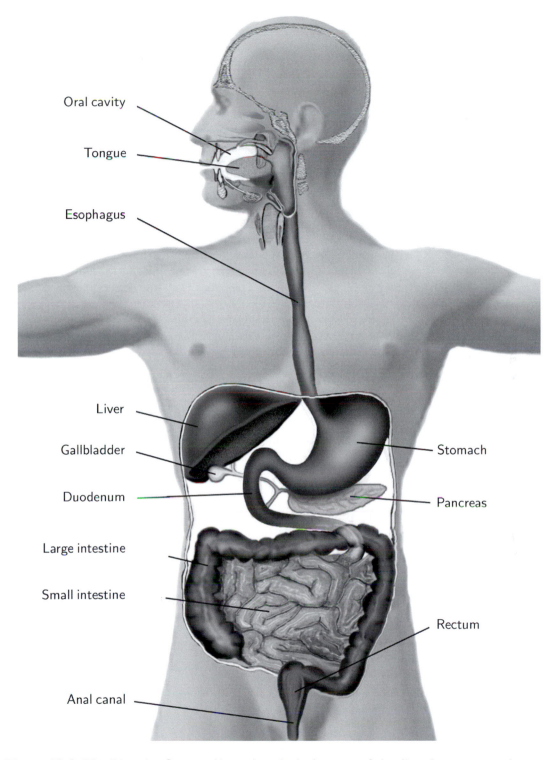

Figure 10.6. The Digestive System. Here, the principal organs of the digestive tract may be seen.

intestine. The enzymes of the pancreatic juice facilitate the digestion of both starch and protein.

The digestion of fats is more complex. It begins by breaking up or emulsifying large drops of fats into smaller droplets. Bile plays a major role in this process. These droplets are then digested by specific enzymes from the pancreatic fluid, which breaks the larger fat molecules down into free fatty acids and other molecules. However, some of the larger fat molecules are absorbed directly into the lymphatic system and are transported to the liver. There they are transformed into free fatty acids and glycerol.

The presence of a significant amount of fat in the duodenum triggers the release of the gut hormone **cholecystokinin (CCK)**. CCK facilitates the digestion of fats in two ways. First, it acts to contract the gallbladder, thereby increasing the flow of bile to the small intestine and speeding the emulsification of fat molecules. Second, CCK slows down the rate at which food is released into the duodenum by the stomach, giving the small intestine more time in which to digest fatty substances.

The digestion of carbohydrates, proteins, and fats is completed within the small intestine. The **large intestine**, which forms the final 1.5 m of the gastrointestinal tract, has rather little to do with digestion. The primary absorptive functions of the large intestine do not involve nutrients but rather are concerned with the uptake of sodium, chloride, and water in the formation of feces.

The Liver All of the molecules absorbed by the walls of the gastrointestinal tract enter the venous blood of the digestive tract. This oxygen-depleted and nutrient-rich blood is transported to the liver by the **hepatic portal system**. The **liver**, a large organ located on the right side of the diaphragm, performs a wide variety of metabolic functions, acting as an intermediary between the absorbed nutrients and the other organs of the body.

The liver is really a large collection of microscopic structures called the **liver lobules**. The liver lobules act as complex filters for the nutrient-rich venous blood leaving the digestive tract. Energy-rich molecules are captured by the liver and transformed as necessary to meet the metabolic needs of the body. Thus, the liver is in a position to store nutrients when they are plentiful and release them when required by the other bodily organs.

The liver's cells also cleanse the blood that passes through the liver by removing bacteria and other foreign material from the blood. A third function of the liver is the formation of bile. Bile leaves the liver lobule through microscopic bile ducts and is stored in the gallbladder until it is needed for digestion.

Metabolic States

Although some species feed almost continually, humans do not. We consume meals several times each day and fast between meals. This characteristic alternation of feeding and fasting has physiological consequences. The body alternates between two very different metabolic conditions, the absorptive and postabsorptive states (Friedman & Stricker, 1976).

The **absorptive state** occurs when nutrients are being absorbed from the digestive tract into the blood. During this period, the problem for the body is to store the newly digested molecules for future use. In the **postabsorptive state**, the problem is quite different. The digestive system is no longer supplying the necessary molecules to the other bodily organs, so molecules stored during the absorptive state must be used.

In the absorptive state, a number of adjustments are made in bodily metabolism to take full advantage of the abundance of nutrients available as the meal is digested: First, all tissues of the body are permitted to use glucose circulating in the blood as a source of energy. Second, the liver converts glucose either into the energy-rich insoluble carbohydrate **glycogen** or into fat, which is then stored for future use. Third, glucose is also converted to fat molecules in **adipose tissue**, where it is stored. Fourth, the liver releases fatty acids into blood that are absorbed and stored by adipose tissue. Fifth, muscles convert glucose to stored glycogen during the absorptive state. Muscle also uses the abundant amino acids in the circulating blood to build proteins and produce growth. Finally, the liver may metabolize excess amino acids as a source of energy during the absorptive state.

The Postabsorptive State   In contrast, the postabsorptive state, which is also called the "fasting state," is adapted for energy conservation. Because glucose from the digestive tract is no longer entering the bloodstream in large quantities, free fatty acids are employed by all bodily tissues except the brain as the primary source of energy. Fatty acids are released into the bloodstream by adipose tissue during the postabsorptive state. The liver either burns fatty acids for energy or converts them to **ketones**, molecules that may be used by any organ but the liver itself as a source of energy. The brain is permitted to consume blood glucose as well as ketones in the postabsorptive state. Glucose uptake is reduced in other tissues.

Blood glucose is produced by several sources in the postabsorptive state. First, the liver converts some of its glycogen stores into glucose, which it releases into the circulation for the brain's use. Second, adipose tissue converts some of its stored fats into **glycerol**, which it releases into the bloodstream. The liver then removes this glycerol and converts it to glucose. Finally, in extreme deprivation, muscle proteins are broken down into amino acids, which are released into the circulation and then transformed into glucose by the liver. In these three ways, the central nervous system is provided with glucose when the gastrointestinal tract is depleted of nutrients.

Regulation of Absorptive States   The change from the absorptive to the postabsorptive state is controlled primarily by the release of the pancreatic hormones **insulin** and **glucagon**. Insulin release induces most of the characteristics of the absorptive state. Insulin is required for the uptake of glucose by all cells except those of the central nervous system and the liver. Hence, insulin release is necessary for muscle and other organs to employ glucose as an energy source. Insulin also facilitates the storage of glucose as glycogen and as fat. Finally, insulin increases the uptake of amino acids by muscle and the absorption of circulating fats by adipose tissue. Thus, all major aspects of the absorptive state are attributed to the effects of increased insulin levels following the ingestion of a meal.

Diabetes mellitus results from an inability of the pancreas to produce normal amounts of insulin (Gilman, Goodman, Rall, & Murad, 1985). Thus, in diabetes, there is a high circulating level of blood glucose following a meal that cannot be used by the tissues of the body, as insulin is required for nonbrain cells to absorb glucose. Therefore, the body is required to depend strictly on fats and selected amino acids as sources of energy, with a number of unfortunate consequences.

The metabolic patterns of the postabsorptive state are induced in part by the absence of insulin. Energy storage is not facilitated, and glucose is reserved for the primary use of the central nervous system. The postabsorptive state also depends on an increase of pancreatic glucagon into the circulation. Glucagon facilitates the metabolism of fats and triggers the transformation of glycogen to glucose in the liver. Insulin and glucagon secretions are the primary mechanisms by which the absorptive and postabsorptive states are regulated.

What Does Hunger Signal?

The biochemical processes involved in energy production, regulation, and use must be intimately related to the internal feeling of hunger, which provides the motivating force for eating. It is, after all, the behavioral act of eating that ultimately provides the digestive system with energy-rich substances. However, human metabolism is complex, and any of a number of metabolic processes may serve as the trigger for hunger.

Over the years, a number of theories of hunger have been suggested. Many of these proposals concern glucose and its use, perhaps reflecting the central role of glucose in metabolism. Other theories have stressed the importance of fats (lipids) and energy use in the regulation of hunger. Although each proposal has certain merits, no single theory is yet capable of accounting for hunger in a completely satisfactory manner.

Glucostatic Hypotheses   One compelling idea is that hunger is somehow triggered by changes in glucose levels. After a meal, blood glucose levels are high, and no hunger is felt. After several hours, though, blood glucose levels begin to fall; at the same time, feelings of hunger occur. This suggests that hunger may be triggered by blood glucose levels.

The simplest **glucostatic hypothesis** is that hunger is related to variations in blood or interstitial glucose levels with respect to an optimal glucose level or **set point**. (The word **glucostat** implies a mechanism that regulates glucose levels about a set point much as a thermostat regulates a room's temperature about a preselected value.) Such a hypothesis seems reasonable, considering the overriding importance of glucose as a source of energy, particularly for the central nervous system. Evidence supporting this idea includes the fact that the injection of large amounts of insulin into normal humans reduces blood glucose levels (by increasing the glucose uptake of nonneural tissues) and also produces the sensation of hunger (Vijande, Lopez-Sela, & Brime, 1990).

However, this simple glucostatic hypothesis cannot be completely correct because it cannot account for the fact that large appetites, overeating, and even obesity occur in untreated diabetic patients. These individuals have high levels of circulating glucose, but—because of their insulin deficiency—are unable to use that glucose as a source of energy. Such people are chronically hungry despite the wealth of glucose within the circulation.

To account for this finding, Jean Mayer proposed that the critical variable in determining the presence or absence of hunger is *glucose utilization*, not glucose abundance (Mayer, 1955). Glucose utilization refers to the availability of circulating glucose for use as an energy source. One measure of glucose utilization is the difference in glucose concentrations between the arterial and venous blood (A-V difference). If both glucose and insulin are available, then large A-V differences result; under these circumstances, people report feeling sated. Hunger is associated with small A-V glucose differences. Small differences occur constantly in untreated diabetics because the lack of insulin precludes glucose uptake. In normal individuals, it occurs when blood glucose levels are low. Both conditions result in the perception of hunger.

Mayer proposed that certain neurons may function as **glucoreceptors**, or cells that signal the rate of glucose utilization within the body. Unlike other neurons, these cells should be insulin sensitive; that is, insulin should control their rates of glucose utilization. That such cells exist now seems quite certain, but much remains to be learned about their nature and detailed function. The sensing of glucose utilization undoubtedly plays one major role in the control of hunger and satiety, but other factors are of importance as well.

Lipostatic Hypotheses   The **lipostatic hypothesis** proposes that hunger is controlled by some aspect of lipid (fat) metabolism. Fat storage seems a plausible variable for the long-term regulation of body weight because in healthy individuals, nutrients that are not burned as energy sources are stored as lipid molecules in adipose tissue.

There is some direct evidence that the amount of fat tissue within the body is related to hunger and eating. For example, animals that are forced to overeat become obese by increasing their fat deposits, but once they are able to control their own diets, they eat less until these newly acquired fat deposits are metabolized and body weight returns to a normal level. More dramatic is the finding that a transplant of adipose tissue from one animal to another is usually rejected unless an equivalent amount of adipose tissue is simultaneously removed from the recipient animal. Such results suggest that the size of the body's fat store is regulated in a direct and powerful manner.

There is evidence from experimental studies of laboratory animals that the fat content of food can affect eating in a manner consistent with lipostatic regulation. For example, diabetic animals do not adjust their intake of carbohydrates to achieve an energy balance because of their difficulties with glucose metabolism. Nevertheless, they do adapt the amount of fats that they consume to meet their dietary needs. This provides evidence that lipid regulation of hunger may take place in the absence of carbohydrate regulation. Thus, glucostatic mechanisms cannot account for all facets of the control of hunger and food intake.

Aminostatic Hypotheses   The **aminostatic hypothesis** proposes that the availability of amino acids is the critically regulated variable in producing hunger and eating. This idea reflects the importance of obtaining amino acids for the syntheses of proteins in growth. Furthermore, a protein-rich diet is very satiating; a little bit of protein goes a long way in satisfying a hungry diner. Although a number of aminostatic theories have been put forward, few are seriously considered today to provide satisfactory explanations for the regulation of eating. Nonetheless, most researchers do believe that amino acid metabolism must make some contribution to the regulation of the energy supplies of the body.

Thermostatic Hypotheses   A fourth class of theories concerning the regulated variable proposes a **thermostatic hypothesis**, which argues that organisms eat to keep warm and stop eating to cool off. Such theories are based on the fact that body temperature increases with eating, as the metabolic activity of many bodily cells rises in the absorptive state. Interestingly, obese individuals exhibit little increase in heat production following a meal, a finding suggesting that obesity may in part be attributed to an abnormal pattern of energy use. The thermostatic hypothesis proposes that total body temperature provides an integrated index of general metabolic level. However, thermostatic theories of hunger are not widely supported today.

Where Do Hunger Signals Originate?

Just as there has been disagreement concerning which aspects of energy regulation trigger sensations of hunger, there also has been uncertainty as to where in the body these signals are detected. Three principal regions have been suggested: the stomach, the liver, and the brain.

Sensory Signals From the Stomach   The idea that hunger is associated with the stomach is well supported by common sense; after all, it is the stomach that feels empty when we are hungry and full when we are satiated. The great physiologist Walter Cannon provided some of the first experimental tests of the role of the stomach as the source of hunger sensations. In his classic book, *Bodily Changes in Pain, Hunger, Fear and Rage*, we get a feeling for the direct nature of early physiological research:

> In 1905, while observing in myself the rhythmic sounds produced by the activities of the alimentary tract, I had occasion to note that the sensation of hunger was not constant but recurrent, and that the moment of its disappearance was often associated with a rather loud gurgling sound as heard through the stethoscope. This and other evidence, indicative of a source of hunger sensations in the contractions of the digestive canal, I reported in 1911. That same year, with the help of one of my students, A.L. Washburn, I obtained final proof for this inference.... Almost every day for several weeks Washburn introduced as far as the stomach a small tube, to the lower end of

which was attached a soft-rubber balloon about 8 centimeters in diameter [to measure stomach contractions].... When Washburn stated
that he was hungry ... powerful contractions of the stomach were invariably being registered.... The record of Washburn's introspection
of his hunger pangs agreed closely with the record of his gastric contractions. (Cannon, 1929, pp. 268-290)

Cannon's theory was simple and straightforward; moreover, he provided experimental evidence to support it. But, like other theories of
hunger that were to follow it, the stomach contraction hypothesis could
not be the whole story. Most damaging for the theory was the finding that
surgical removal of the stomach does not abolish the sensation of hunger,
nor does it seriously disrupt the normal regulation of eating (except for the
fact that meals must be smaller and more frequent, as the ingested meal
proceeds directly to the small intestine).

This does not mean that the stomach plays no role in hunger and eating (Deutsch, 1990). More recent evidence has shown that the stomach
may be of major importance in regulating food intake. For example, when
the alimentary canal is temporarily blocked below the stomach, preventing the passage of food to the small intestine, animals nonetheless eat normal meals, stopping when their stomachs are full. Furthermore, if part
of the meal is experimentally removed from the stomach, animals begin
eating again until their stomachs are refilled. Clearly, receptors within the
stomach make a major contribution to the sensation of hunger and the
regulation of food intake, but other factors must also be important.

Sensory Signals From the Liver   More than two decades have passed
since Mauricio Russek first suggested that the liver may be the critical organ in regulating the appetite. Russek based this hypothesis on the finding
that glucose injected into the peritoneal cavity (the interior of the abdomen
within which the gastrointestinal tract and the liver are located) was far
more effective in inducing satiety than glucose injected directly into the
bloodstream (Russek, 1981). The logic behind this argument was that the
intraperitoneal glucose is selectively filtered through the liver, whereas the
circulating glucose only weakly acts on that organ.

There are also theoretical reasons to expect that the liver might play a
central role in regulating hunger and eating. The liver is the organ that
acts to stabilize blood glucose levels, storing away glucose in the absorptive state and releasing glucose into the circulation in the nutrient-depleted
postabsorptive state. Thus, the liver is the organ that is most directly involved in regulating the balances between freshly available energy sources
from the gastrointestinal tract, bodily energy demands, and stored energy
resources. Such an organ might well exert an influence in the control of
eating, which is the first step in energy acquisition and use.

Russek's (1981) hypothesis is plausible, but there are also problems
with the idea. For example, Russek argued that intraperitoneal injections
of glucose were swept up by the capillaries of the gut into the liver and
there stimulated liver glucoreceptors. If this idea is correct, then glucose
injected directly into the hepatic portal vein feeding the liver should be
even more effective. However, the empirical evidence on this point seems
to be mixed. Some investigations indicate that hepatic portal injections of

glucose produce satiety, but other experiments have found no noticeable effect of such injections on eating. How such conflicting evidence should be resolved remains uncertain. It may be that differences in the details of the experiments might explain matters, but for the moment, the issue remains controversial. Furthermore, the naturally occurring increases in portal glucose following ingestion of a meal are much smaller than the experimentally induced hepatic glucose levels that have a measurable effect on satiety in experimental animals.

Another difficulty of the theory is the fact that denervation of the liver has little effect on the feeding behavior of laboratory animals. The liver is known to have several types of sensory receptors that can register the presence or absence of various substances, including glucose, within the liver. Presumably, these receptors relay such information to the brain to control eating. However, there is confusion concerning the effectiveness of the surgeries that disconnect the nerves linking the liver to the central nervous system.

But despite such problems, there remains considerable interest in the neural signals that originate within the liver and are transmitted to the brain as messages that are of major importance in understanding hunger. But with respect to other single-organ theories of hunger, the case for the liver as the critical organ is not strong.

Sensory Signals From the Brain   Glucoreceptor cells also exist within the central nervous system, particularly in the region of the hypothalamus. Thus, chronically injected nutrients suppress eating when placed in either the ventricles or the ventromedial hypothalamus (see below); however, there are difficulties with any simple interpretation of these experiments. More compelling is the demonstration by Oomura (1976) of glucoreceptive properties of single hypothalamic neurons. Direct application of glucose excited about one third of all neurons in the ventromedial hypothalamus while tending to inhibit neurons in the lateral hypothalamus. These effects are dose dependent, as befitting a glucoreceptor cell. Furthermore, the response to glucose is enhanced by simultaneous administration of insulin.

However, the fact that glucoreceptors are present in the hypothalamic region does not necessarily mean that they operate in the normal appetite control system. That question remains to be resolved by experimental investigation.

Brain Mechanisms

Among physiological psychologists, a strong interest in hunger began in the 1950s, following John Brobeck's demonstration that bilateral lesions of the hypothalamus have profound effects on eating (Brobeck, 1955). These original investigations and a large number of experiments in the following years treated hunger and regulation of eating as a convenient program for the study of motivation more generally.

Two hypothalamic regions formed the focus of the early investigations, the region of the **ventromedial hypothalamic (VMH) nucleus** and the nearby **lateral hypothalamic area (LHA)**. Bilateral lesions in these two areas produced dramatic and opposite effects. Laboratory animals with bilateral LH lesions eat very little if anything. These aphagic animals rapidly lose weight and starve themselves to death unless given elaborate nursing care (**aphagic** means "not eating"; *phagia* is from the Greek word, meaning "one who eats"). In contrast, animals with VMH lesions overeat; such animals are said to be **hyperphagic**.

Effects of Lateral Hypothalamic Damage   The effects of lateral hypothalamic damage on feeding behavior have been observed in a wide variety of animal species, but no animal has been more extensively studied than the laboratory rat. Rats with extensive bilateral (both right- and left-sided) damage to the LH region drastically reduce the amount of food they eat and starve to death if left to their own devices. Intragastric tube feeding is required to maintain adequate nutrition during the period following surgery.

Recovery from LH damage generally is believed to be divided into four distinct stages. In the first, the animal neither eats nor drinks; food, when offered, is uniformly rejected. Neither food nor water seems appetizing to the rat. Not surprisingly, the animal's weight drops dramatically in the absence of intragastric feeding. In the second stage, the animal still refuses to drink but will eat very palatable food, although without any apparent appetite or enjoyment. In the third stage, the animal can regulate the amount of food that it eats but remains unwilling to drink water. (Some animals can be coaxed into drinking artificially sweetened water.) In the fourth stage, nearly normal patterns of both eating and drinking return. Unfortunately, not all animals enjoy full recovery from lateral hypothalamic damage.

The classical view of the lateral hypothalamic syndrome, which was first put forward by Philip Teitelbaum and Alan Epstein in the early 1960s (Teitelbaum & Epstein, 1962), has more recently been reconsidered. That early classification was extremely narrow in its focus, considering only the effects on feeding and eating while ignoring other aspects of the animal's behavior. For example, the first two stages following LH damage are also marked by profound sensory and motor disturbances. The animals show a very low level of activation. If placed in an unusual position, they fail to resume a normal posture. Unlike normal rats, they show no grooming behavior and appear to exist in a listless stupor. Interestingly, these animals will begin to eat and drink spontaneously if aroused by a painful stimulus, such as continuous pinching of the tail. Thus, to describe the initial phases of recovery from LH damage purely in terms of ingestive behavior is misleading at best; feeding disturbances are only a part of a general behavioral deficit (Wolgin & Teitelbaum, 1978).

Electrical stimulation of the lateral hypothalamus produces effects on feeding and eating that are the reverse of the effects of LH damage. Rats begin eating immediately when the LH is stimulated. They may even become obese if stimulation is repeatedly given. Such stimulation is also quite rewarding; even in the absence of food, animals work hard to obtain LH stimulation. Interestingly, this rewarding effect is linked to hunger and feeding. Animals will work harder for LH stimulation when they are deprived of food and work less when nutrients are placed within the stomach. These and other manipulations have similar effects on the apparent attractiveness of LH stimulation and on natural feeding behavior. Such results suggest the activity of brain mechanisms that reward the animal for eating.

Effects of Ventromedial Hypothalamic Damage   Bilateral lesions in the region of the ventromedial hypothalamus result in animals that eat large amounts of food and rapidly become obese. During the initial period following surgery, gastric secretion, insulin production, and other parasympathetic responses devoted to eating and storing nutrients all dramatically increase. However, after an initial period of substantial weight gain, the animal begins to regulate its eating; it consumes just enough food to maintain its weight at the new obese level. Further increases in body weight do not occur.

Electrical stimulation of the VMH region is not nearly as rewarding as stimulation to the LH. Sometimes, VMH stimulation is actually aversive. In many cases, whether stimulation of VMH will be rewarding or aversive depends on the animal's state of hunger. Stimulation that is mildly rewarding for a hungry animal will be aversive to a satiated animal.

The Dual-Center Hypothesis   The opposing effects of VMH and LH lesions on feeding led some psychologists to propose a **dual-center hypothesis** of the control of hunger, which is now known to be oversimplified.

The dual-center hypothesis suggested that LH and VMH are the two hypothalamic centers that together regulate feeding. LH was held to be the "hunger center." When activated, it would excite other regions of the nervous system, resulting in both hunger and eating. Furthermore, the LH hunger center was proposed to be under the inhibitory control of the VMH "satiety center." Furthermore, it was suggested that glucoreceptors within the hypothalamus respond to the presence of glucose in the circulating blood. The dual-center hypothesis held that glucoreceptors within the VMH actively inhibit cells in the LH hunger center. Thus, according to the theory, the LH is released from inhibition as blood glucose levels drop, and the animal becomes hungry and eats. As glucose enters the circulation, the VMH again becomes active, inhibiting the hunger center, rendering the organism satiated, and terminating the meal.

However, later evidence suggested that the dual-center interpretation of the LH and VMH lesion data may be substantially incorrect: The hypothalamic nuclei themselves—although certainly involved in the control of hunger and satiety—may not be responsible for the production of lesion-induced aphagia or hyperphagia. This conclusion, which strongly contradicts several decades of theory and research findings, is based on careful investigations using recently developed, highly precise experimental methods.

Specifically, the hypothalamus—like other regions of the diencephalon and brain stem—is a complexly organized and densely packed region that is filled with both intrinsic nuclei (collections of cell bodies) and fibers of passage (axons of cells located elsewhere that happen to pass through an area without making synaptic contact). Conventional lesioning techniques destroy considerable amounts of neural tissue, including both hypothalamic nuclei and fibers of passage. Thus, it is possible that the LH and VMH syndromes are not the consequence of damage to the hypothalamic nuclei but result from accidental destruction of fiber tracts that travel through this region of the brain.

It now appears that the LH syndrome is not produced solely by hypothalamic damage but may be produced by the destruction of neurons of the **nigrostriatal bundle**, which passes through the lateral hypothalamus. The nigrostriatal bundle is a collection of axons originating in the substantia nigra and projecting to the basal ganglia. Dopamine is the neurotransmitter employed by these cells.

When the nigrostriatal bundle is selectively lesioned by using careful surgical methods, the full LH syndrome appears (Marshall, Richardson, & Teitelbaum, 1974). Animals that have been subjected to this treatment exhibit both aphagia and **adipsia** (lack of drinking), as well as the listless stupor that is characteristic of large LH lesions. The same results occur regardless of whether the bundle is damaged within the lateral hypothalamus or elsewhere in its path to the basal ganglia. Furthermore, similar patterns of disrupted eating behavior occur following pharmacological depletion of central nervous system dopamine reserves.

Similarly, there is increasing evidence that the ventromedial hypothalamus does not serve as a satiety center, as has long been held. Again, more careful and advanced surgical procedures have been revealing. When surgery is carefully restricted to the VMH, no hyperphagia is present. However, if the lesion extends into a region slightly dorsal to the VMH proper, a profound hyperphagia is produced (Grossman, 1975). This area contains numerous bundles of fibers linking rostral and caudal portions of the central nervous system. Most important for the obesity effects appears to be a set of noradrenergic projections that terminate in the region of the pariventricular nuclei.

Is there a lateral hypothalamic "hunger center" or a ventromedial hypothalamic satiety center? Most neuroscientists now believe that these concepts are excessively simplified and are of little real use.

Does the hypothalamus play a role in hunger and the regulation of eating? Here the answer must be yes. Changes in the patterns of cellular firing are known to occur in the VMH following ingestion of a meal. In addition, electrical stimulation of the VMH and LH has significant effects on nutrient metabolism in the gastrointestinal tract and related organs. Thus, the LH and VMH appear to play a role in controlling hunger and satiety, but that role is more complex than was previously supposed.

Lepton and Neuropeptide Y

Mutant mice have made striking contributions to understanding both the genetics and pharmacology of hunger and eating, thanks to a powerful tool from new genetic engineering, the knockout mouse. Developed by molecular biologist Mario Capecchi and his colleagues, the idea behind the knockout mouse is simple (Travis, 1992). To study the roles that a particular protein plays in an organism, one must first disrupt the gene that produces that protein in a genetically engineered strain of mutants. Then, by examining the physiology and behavior of the genetically designed mutants, the functions that the protein normally performs may be made apparent.

A knockout mouse is a mouse—a species of convenience—in which foreign DNA is introduced at a particular place in the cell's chromosomes by homologous recombination, a naturally occurring cell process. This engineered mutation "knocks out" the selected gene and consequently the proteins that it produces. The practical advantage of the knockout mouse is that it eliminates the long and often unsuccessful search for naturally occurring mutations of the gene of interest. This little piece of biotechnology wizardry has resulted in a wide range of scientific breakthroughs, including the discovery of a potent biochemical system regulating feeding in mammals, the leptin/neuropeptide Y system. Here is what is currently known about this system.

Two strains of knockout mice are important here. One is the autosomal recessive diabetes mutation (db), which was first detected as a natural mutation in the 1960s. Db/db mice (having both copies of the recessive mutated gene) are severely obese, extremely insulin resistant, and very susceptible to diabetes. A second strain of mice shows exactly the same pattern of behavioral and physiological dysfunction but as the result of a different genetic mutation. The obese mutation (ob) is also recessive and expresses itself phenotypically in ob/ob mice.

In normal mice (and humans), adipose tissue secretes a hormone called leptin, which circulates in the blood in proportion to the fat content of the adipose tissue. Leptin is produced by the ob gene, a discovery made by Zhang and colleagues in 1994. **Leptin**, named from the Greek word *leptos*, meaning "thin," is a protein of about 150 amino acids.

Leptin is well positioned to function as a satiety signal from the body to the brain. In humans, leptin concentrations in both the blood plasma and cerebrospinal fluid are very closely related to fat concentration in the adipose tissue (Considine et al., 1996). In ob/ob mice, the adipose tissue cannot produce leptin, which in normal mice is related to body fat content. Thus, the brains of ob/ob mice have no indication that their bodies are becoming obese and continue to eat ravenously. But if leptin is injected into the bloodstream of obese ob/ob mice, the mice stop eating and begin to lose weight (Rohner-Jeanrenaud & Jenrenaud, 1996). This and similar evidence suggest that leptin, produced in adipose tissue, serves as a feedback signal to the normal brain that indicates the level of body fat of the animal. Ob/ob mice lack this signal and grow fat.

But for any feedback signal to be effective, it must be detected by a controlling mechanism. The receptor for leptin appears to be a neuronal membrane protein of the G-protein class that is encoded by the db gene. The mutant db/db mice lack this receptor protein and thus cannot detect even the extraordinarily high levels of leptin circulating in their cerebrospinal fluid (Chua et al., 1996). As a consequence, db/db mice become obese.

Recent evidence suggests that the db-encoded leptin receptor is concentrated on neurons within the paraventricular nucleus of the hypothalamus (Woods & Stock, 1996). The paraventricular region is an area where the blood-brain barrier is weak, a fact that helps explain how the very large leptin protein could gain access to molecular receptors within the central nervous system. Activation of these molecular receptors could provide other regions of the brain with critical information about body fat content to be used in regulating food intake.

The final link in this newly discovered molecular chain controlling hunger and food intake is provided by **neuropeptide Y (NPY)**, a peptide located almost exclusively within the central nervous system that functions as a neurotransmitter. NPY synthesis and release are inhibited by leptin binding to leptin receptors within the hypothalamus (Howlett, 1996). Unlike virtually any other substance, NPY induces voracious eating in a wide variety of animals when injected into the hypothalamus, producing obesity. Stanley and Gillard (1994) injected NPY into the hypothalamic paraventricular nucleus of female rats for a period of 10 days. By the 10th day, the body fat of the NPY-injected animals was three times that of control rats, which received no NPY. Thus, the effect of hypothalamically injected neuropeptide Y on feeding in otherwise normal animals is powerful and direct.

The effects of neuropeptide Y on hunger and feeding appear to result from the activity of a newly discovered NPY receptor subtype, called Y5, which has been cloned recently by Gerald and his collaborators (Gerald et al., 1996). This receptor appears both in the paraventricular nucleus and in the lateral hypothalamus, both regions that have been shown to play major roles in mammalian hunger regulation. The discovery of the NPY "feeding receptor" not only extends our knowledge of the neural systems regulating hunger in humans and other mammals, but it also provides the suggestion of new therapies for obesity through the development of selective Y5 agonists. The entire developing leptin-neuropeptide Y story appears to presage a new and exciting era of interaction between molecular genetics and behavioral neuroscience.

Eating Disorders

In most people, the control of food intake is well regulated and appropriate to the energy requirements of the individual, although it is not uncommon, particularly in later life, to lament a gradual increase in body fat. In some individuals, however, striking abnormalities in the normal patterns of food intake and weight regulation may be seen. Obesity, anorexia nervosa, and bulimia are the three most striking types of eating disorders reported in the medical literature.

Obesity **Obesity** is the gain of body weight above "normal" levels by the accumulation of fat in the body; consequently, obese people are simply overweight (Grinker, 1982). The distinction between normal and obese individuals depends in part on societal custom and aesthetic values. Standards of ideal weight have varied significantly between cultures and eras. The Rubenesque ideal woman of 17th-century Europe would be considered overweight in contemporary American society.

However, the concept of normal body weight also has physiological underpinnings. In normal human beings, about 15% of body weight is stored as fat in adipose tissue. This corresponds to a caloric supply for about 1 month. It appears that this concentration is actively defended, with energy expenditures being reduced when the fat store is threatened and food intake being reduced when target levels are exceeded. Nonetheless, obesity is usually defined medically in terms of excess weight rather than excess fat. A person is considered obese if his or her weight is more than 20% greater than that prescribed by normative weight tables.

One of the most striking findings about obesity is the profound difficulty of losing weight. Although reducing food intake for an extended period will inevitably lead to weight loss, it is surprisingly difficult for many individuals to sustain a reduced weight for any appreciable period of time. This rather disheartening finding suggests that for at least some individuals, it is the obese weight, rather than the normal weight, that is homeostatically defended.

Increasing interest has been paid to the adipose tissue itself in an attempt to understand the physiological basis of obesity. Normal individuals have about 25 billion adipose cells, each weighing about two thirds of a microgram. Not only do obese individuals have more adipose cells (about 65 billion), but each cell is considerably heavier (about 1 microgram).

Once an individual becomes obese, the increased number of adipose tissue cells appears to be an irreversible consequence of the weight gain. Dieting will reduce weight but only by decreasing cell weight; dieting does not reduce the number of adipose cells present in the body. Under most conditions, weight loss terminates when adipose cells have reached a normal size. Further shrinkage of these cells appears to be vigorously defended by internal homeostatic forces.

There is some evidence that obesity is linked to a feedback mechanism that uses signals from the adipose tissue itself. There is the suggestion that **brown adipose tissue** may play a special role in this process. Brown adipose tissue differs from the more abundant white adipose tissue in color. Its characteristic appearance results from the abundance of mitochondria within its cells, a histological sign of high-energy use.

Brown adipose tissue is known to play a major role in heat production. The weight of brown adipose tissue increases during maturation of the organism. This tissue, with its high metabolic rate, produces the temporary rise in body temperature, which follows ingestion of a meal.

Brown adipose tissue is richly supplied with blood vessels and is directly innervated by fibers of the sympathetic nervous system. In hibernating animals, this tissue is responsible for rewarming the organism before awakening. It also appears to serve as a mechanism for burning excess calories to prevent obesity in some species. Nonetheless, whether the brown adipose tissue is related to obesity and the long-term regulation of body weight in humans remains a matter of conjecture.

Anorexia Nervosa   **Anorexia nervosa** is a clinical disorder marked by a dramatic weight loss coupled with an intense fear of obesity (Halmi, 1987). It is also accompanied by a disturbance of body image, such that individuals "feel fat" even when their weight is markedly subnormal. Preoccupation with body size and appearance frequently occurs. Losses of more than 25% of original body weight are common, and the anorexic person soon takes on an emaciated appearance. Anorexia nervosa is primarily a disorder of young women: 95% of all anorexic patients are female, and the disorder appears most commonly between the ages of 12 and 18.

The weight loss of anorexia nervosa is the result of extreme changes in eating habits. There is a sharp reduction in food intake, particularly for high carbohydrate and fatty foods. Self-induced vomiting and laxatives may be employed to prevent the digestion of the meals that are eaten. Excessive exercise also may be undertaken as a further means of reducing body weight.

Such drastic alterations of normal eating patterns have profound physiological effects. One of the first consequences in young women is the cessation of menstruation. With further starvation, a number of metabolic and cardiac abnormalities occur, including a lowering of body temperature, blood pressure, and heart rate. Lanugo, a type of fine body hair found on neonates, may appear. Prolonged bouts of anorexia nervosa may result in death by starvation-induced circulatory or metabolic disturbances. The follow-up mortality rate for the disorder is between 15% and 20%. However, there is usually a single episode of self-induced starvation that is followed by complete recovery.

Bulimia   **Bulimia** is the third major type of eating disorder (Halmi, 1987). It is marked by episodes of binge eating, feelings that such binges are abnormal and wrong, and a fear of not being able to stop eating. Eating binges may be spontaneous or premeditated. The foods chosen are usually sweet, rich, and of a texture that may be rapidly consumed with little chewing. Once under way, the person continues to search for more and more food, until the binge is terminated by interruption, abdominal pain, sleep, or self-induced vomiting. A period of depression usually follows the eating binge. Bulimia typically occurs in females in adolescence or young adulthood. Although disturbing, bulimia does not have the disastrous physiological consequences that accompany anorexia nervosa. The biological basis of neither type of eating disorder is currently understood.

SEX

Hunger and thirst originate from nonneural bodily tissues and motivate us to seek food and water as needed. In each of these cases, something—either food or water—is lacking and becomes the object of our motivated behavior.

But sex is different: Sex is social. The determinants of sexual behavior, like hunger and thirst, are powerful and basic, but they are not rooted in simple individual deprivation but rather in a more complex matrix of individual and social factors that are just beginning to be understood. But one thing seems clear: Sex is deeply rooted in our neurobiology and is controlled by brain structures that share many similarities with those responsible for hunger and thirst.

Sex Chromosomes   Genetic sex is determined at the instant the union of the two **gametes**, the fertilization of the egg (or **ovum**) from the female by a **sperm** cell from the male. In that fusion, the 23 chromosomes of the human egg are linked with the 23 chromosomes of the human sperm cell, resulting in the full normal arrangement of 23 pairs of chromosomes. For both the ovum and the sperm, 22 of the 23 chromosomes are **autosomes**, chromosomes that have nothing to do with determining genetic sex. The remaining chromosome of the ovum is an X chromosome; the remaining chromosome of the sperm is either an X or Y chromosome. If the sperm contributes an X chromosome, the resulting cell becomes genetically XX and female. If the sperm contributes a Y chromosome, the cell becomes XY and male. These are the normal outcomes of fertilization.

The critical portion of the Y chromosome in determining sex lies in a particular region of the short arm of that chromosome, which constitutes a switch controlling biological differences between males and females. This set of genes is called the **testis-determining factor (TDF)**. It is the TDF that determines whether the primordial undifferentiated gonad of the fetus will develop into testes or ovaries.

Under some circumstances, genetic errors in sperm or the ovum occur. For example, occasionally the sperm will contain both an X and a Y chromosome. The resulting cell will then become XXY, a condition known as **Klinefelter's syndrome**. Rarer still are variants of the syndrome, including XXXY and XXXXY. The severity of the disorder increases with the number of extra X chromosomes. Such individuals develop a male body, but there are abnormalities and atrophies in the male reproductive ducts at adulthood. These children also have a low birth weight, poor physical development, and low IQ (Sheridan, Radlinski, & Kennedy, 1990).

A related abnormality occurs when one of the sperm or ovum contains two X chromosomes; the result will be a cell that is genetically XXX. Such individuals develop into otherwise normal genetic females.

A third chromosomal abnormality involves the donation of two Y chromosomes. The resulting XYY individual is genetically male. Although it was once thought that XYY males were hyperaggressive, and a proportionally larger number of them were in jails, subsequent research has indicated only that they are, on average, less intelligent.

Finally, in some instances, the sperm may simply fail to contribute either an X or Y chromosome. The result is an XO inheritance and a condition known as **Turner's syndrome**. In Turner's syndrome, the child has a female body, but the ovaries fail to develop. These children also have physical and cognitive impairments.

It has generally been believed that the Y chromosome determines maleness, as reflected in the development of the testes and the production of male hormones. Female development has been thought to be controlled either by the X chromosome, by some of the autosomes, or by the two in combination. As an example, at least one autosome in addition to the sex chromosomes is necessary for the development of normal ovaries in females.

However, recent analyses indicate that for males as well as females, the genetic mechanisms controlling sex are more complex than were previously suspected. For example, genes that are necessary for normal male development are not restricted to the Y chromosome alone but are found on the X chromosome as well. Thus, the specific chromosomal mechanisms by which genetic sex is determined are more complicated than any simple one-gene model.

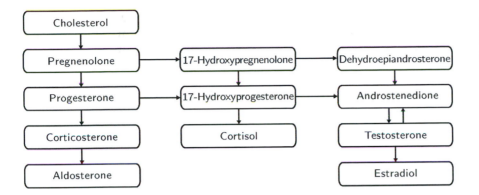

Figure 10.7. The Gonadal Steroid Hormones and Related Steroid Compounds.

Sex Hormones

Sexual development and behavior depend not only on sex chromosomes but on hormonal factors as well. **Hormones** are chemical substances that are secreted by a specific gland and carried in the blood to the site at which they produce a physiological effect. Hormones play extremely important organizational roles in the development of the sexual organs and certain central nervous system structures. Hormones have activating effects that influence the occurrence of sexual behaviors in the adult.

The **gonadal hormones** are produced by the testes and the ovaries. All known gonadal hormones are **steroids**, a family of chemically related lipid substances. These are shown in Figure 10.7. Two classes of steroids are produced by the ovaries: the **estrogens** and the **progestogens**. **Estradiol** is the most important of the estrogens; **progesterone** is the only type of progestogen that is known to be physiologically important in humans. Finally, the steroid hormones of the testes are the **androgens**, or masculinizing compounds. **Testosterone** is the most important of the androgens.

Related steroid hormones, such as cortisone, are manufactured by the adrenal cortex. The adrenal cortex also makes small amounts of androgens and estrogens in both men and women.

All of the gonadal hormones are closely related and appear to be produced by the same metabolic pathways in women and in men, as is shown in Figure 10.7. Cholesterol provides the common lipid substrate for these steroids. Progesterone, an ovarian hormone, serves as a common precursor for testosterone, the testicular hormone. Furthermore, testosterone is the immediate precursor of the principal ovarian estrogen, estradiol. This family of steroid hormones controls both the course of sexual development and the appearance of sexual behavior.

Hormonal Control of Gonadal Development   In humans, the development of the genital regions of embryos of both sexes proceeds indistinguishably through the first 5 weeks following conception. But in the 6th week, the testes of the male appear in a rapid period of growth and differentiation. During this period, the primordial genital tissue that will later form the female gonads continues to grow; it does not differentiate. This occurs at a later stage.

The further differentiation of the genital region is controlled both by genetic information from the chromosomes and by hormonal actions. Adjacent to the primordial tissue that develops into the testes or the ovaries lie the structures of the Müllerian and Wolffian systems. The **Müllerian system** is the precursor of the female internal organs, the uterus, the Fallopian tubes, and the upper vagina. The **Wolffian system** is the precursor of the male internal reproductive ducts, the seminal vesicles and the vas deferens. The differential development of these two systems begins at the end of the second month of pregnancy, following the differentiation of the primordial genitalia into the external sexual organs: the testes and penis in males and the ovaries, clitoris, and related structures in females.

In the male, the testes begin to produce **Müllerian-inhibiting substance**, a hormone that triggers the regression and disappearance of the Müllerian system. This causes the tissue that would have become the ovaries, vagina, and related structures to be reabsorbed by the body.

There is no corresponding hormone in the female. The primitive Wolffian system requires androgens to develop into the male genitalia; thus, in females, the primitive Wolffian structures remain in an undeveloped state in the normal female adult anatomy. In the absence of testosterone, the Müllerian system differentiates and grows into the adult female sexual organs. The development of the male and female genitalia is a clear example of **sexual dimorphism**, the appearance of two different forms of the same organ or structure in males and females.

The testes also produce androgens. Androgens play important roles in the development of sexual dimorphisms. For example, the androgens govern the development of the external genitalia. The undifferentiated tissue that will become the external genitalia develops in the male form only in the presence of androgens secreted by the testes. In the absence of circulating androgens, development of female genitalia occurs, regardless of the genetic sex of the fetus. In determining the structural anatomy of the developing fetus, the male testicular hormones exert an organizational effect, establishing a genital system that is organized along a male, not a female, pattern. These effects are more or less permanent. Later in life, sex hormones will produce transient activational effects, motivating particular sexual behaviors.

Later in development, other hormones also exert organizational effects on sexual growth. At puberty, the child's primary growth is ended, and the development of the secondary sexual characteristics is begun. The **secondary sexual characteristics** mark the difference between adult men and women and include such features as breast development in the female and the appearance of facial hair in the male. The onset of puberty is associated with the secretion of **gonadotropic-releasing hormones** by cells in the hypothalamus. These hormones do not act on the gonads directly but instead trigger the release of two **gonadotropic hormones** by the pituitary: **follicle-stimulating hormone (FSH)** and **luteinizing hormone (LH)**.

However, the effects of the gonadotropic hormones are quite different in the two sexes. In women, the effect is to stimulate the production of estrogens by the ovaries; in men, it triggers the production of testosterone by the testes. Estrogens induce the beginning of breast development and the maturation of the female genitalia. In males, testosterone facilitates the growth of facial and body hair, lowers the pitch of the male voice, stimulates the growth of skeletal muscles, and induces the maturation of the male genitalia.

Hormonal Abnormalities in Sexual Development

Circulating hormones play critical roles in the development of the fetus. In males, fetal testosterone levels are significantly enhanced from the 2nd through the 6th months of gestation. During this period, critical sexual differentiation of the male and female fetuses occurs. It therefore stands to reason that factors disrupting the normal pattern of fetal hormone function can have major consequences for the unborn child. Thus, endocrinological disorders of steroid production and function have profound effects on sexual development and behavior.

Congenital Adrenal Hyperplasia   One striking example of hormonally induced abnormal sexual development is **congenital adrenal hyperplasia (CAH)**—formerly called the **adrenogenital syndrome**—which results from 46, XX chromosomal abnormality. In CAH, the adrenal cortex— which normally plays no major role in sexual differentiation—produces extraordinary amounts of adrenal androgens. These steroids are capable of masculinizing the developing fetus. In genetic females, the result is extreme genital and behavioral masculinization. The clitoris is greatly enlarged, resembling the penis of the male. The labia of the vagina are also enlarged and may be fused, giving the appearance of a scrotum. Depending on the extent of the adrenal dysfunction, the effects can range from slight to complete masculinization of the genotypic female body. One example of complete masculinization is as follows:

> A 3-year-old child was brought to the Endocrine Clinic because of sexual precocity and a failure of the testicles to descend into the scrotum. Parents noticed appearance of pubic hair and increasing phallus size during the previous 6 months in this apparently male child. The stretched phallus length was then 6 cm (about 2.5 inches) and the scrotal sacs were well formed. The child was exceptionally tall for his age and had a bone age of 8 years. The child was raised as a male and believed himself to be a boy (male gender identity). The child's behavior and favorite activities were also those of a boy. However, chromosomal studies showed him to be a 46, XX genetic female. After the condition was explained to the parents, they preferred to continue his male identity. Hormone treatment was begun and the surgical removal of the uterus and ovaries was planned to prevent later medical complications. (Adapted from Harinarayan et al., 1992.)

In genetic males, CAH has no pronounced sexual effect because naturally occurring testosterone is already exerting a masculinizing influence; however, there are some reports of CAH in males inducing precocious sexual maturation.

Androgen Insensitivity Syndrome   Almost the converse of CAH is androgen insensitivity. In the **androgen insensitivity syndrome (AIS)**, there is an apparent lack of androgen receptors at the cellular level. Thus, these genetic and gonadally normal males produce testosterone, but that testosterone fails to masculinize the body. The testes also may produce estrogen. The result is an absence of the external male genitalia and the development of female secondary sexual characteristics. However, the internal female genitalia are also undeveloped because of the action of Müllerian-inhibiting substances released by the testes.

Individuals with complete AIS have a fully female body structure with normal deposits of female fat and normal or large breasts; scanty pubic hair; normal or somewhat underdeveloped female external genitalia, including a clitoris; and a vagina that is unconnected to the missing female internal organs (Morris, 1953). Such individuals are raised as females and are discovered to be genetic males only if tested extensively following a failure to menstruate at puberty. As adults, they experience normal female sexual activity. An example of a case of a completely feminized genetic male is the following:

> The patient was a 44-year-old housewife who was referred for gynecological examination following removal of an abdominal cancer; at that time it was discovered that she had a vagina of normal depth, but both the uterus and ovaries were absent. Her history revealed that she had developed apparently normally but had never menstruated. For this she had consulted a doctor on two occasions and was told there was nothing to do about it. She had been married for 20 years, with normal intercourse, sexual drive, and orgasm, but had no pregnancies. Her mother had three sisters, two of whom were married, that also had never menstruated, suggesting a family history of AIS.
>
> Physical examination revealed a typically female body, with well-developed breasts, little bodily hair, and a somewhat small clitoris. Her vagina ended in a blind pouch. (Adapted from Morris, 1953)

5-alpha Reductase Deficiency   Related to the androgen insensitivity syndrome is another disorder of the sex hormones, **5-alpha reductase deficiency**. 5-alpha reductase is a steroid that is responsible for converting testosterone produced by the testis into the biologically active steroid dihydrotestosterone in target cells. During gestation, the development of the internal sexual ducts in males—the Wolffian system—is controlled by testosterone and therefore is normal. During this same period, the differentiation of the external male genitalia—the scrotum and penis—is regulated by dihydrotestosterone, and they therefore fail to develop. As a result, the external appearance of the newborn male is that of a female baby. Such children are raised as females and consider themselves to be girls. They look forward to acquiring female sexual characteristics at puberty.

At puberty, unexpected developments take place. These little girls rapidly increase their muscle mass, grow larger bones, and gain deeper voices. An almost normally sized male penis and mature scrotum also appear. It appears that testosterone, not dihydrotestosterone, governs these secondary sexual characteristics at puberty. The role of dihydrotestosterone appears to be limited to the enlargement of the prostate, the growth of facial and bodily hair, and the appearance of acne. Thus, growth of the external genitalia in utero is regulated by dihydrotestosterone, whereas at puberty, this role is dominated by testosterone (Imperato-McGinley, Peterson, Gautier, & Sturla, 1979).

Perhaps the most striking change in these little girls is not physical but mental: They no longer regard themselves as females but easily and naturally adopt an unambiguous male gender identity. Gender identity appears to be determined by biology, not by pattern of rearing.

Circulating hormones in the mother may also affect the sexual development of the fetus. For example, diethylstilbestrol (DES) is a synthetic estrogen that was once widely used to prevent miscarriage during pregnancy. It is now believed (Hines, Alsum, & Roy, 1987) that this estrogen has masculinizing effects on the central nervous system and behavior of genetic females, although it does not alter the normal development of the external genitalia.

Hormones and Sexual Behavior

Hormones not only are critical in the development of the genitalia in the fetus but affect sexual activity and behavior in the adult as well. Some of these effects are rather straightforward, but others are much more subtle.

Sexual Functions In human males, the hormonal regulation of sexual functions is relatively simple. The pituitary gonadotropic-luteinizing hormone stimulates the rate of testosterone production by the testes, which in turn facilitates the production of sperm. Spermatogenesis is also fostered by secretions of follicle-stimulating hormones by the pituitary. However, psychological factors play a role in regulating blood levels of these hormones. For example, blood levels of luteinizing hormone increase up to 17-fold in a bull when it sees a cow; blood testosterone levels follow suit within 30 minutes.

Environmentally triggered variations in hormone levels also have been reported in human males. Thus, the male hormonal system governing sexual functions is not autonomous but may be modified by higher brain mechanisms.

The hormonal regulation of sexual functions in human females is more complicated (Bennett & Whitehead, 1983). Unlike males, who produce sperm more or less continuously, females produce a single mature egg once each 28 or so days. All phases of the menstrual cycle are hormonally regulated. In the initial week, increases in both follicle-stimulating hormone and luteinizing hormone stimulate the development of an **ovarian follicle**, the ovum and the cells surrounding it. Estrogen secretion is also stimulated. At midcycle, a marked increase in pituitary LH triggers the release of the mature ovum by the ovary. After ovulation, production of both LH and FSH declines. In this period, there is a sharp rise in both estrogen and progesterone. Progesterone acts to stimulate the lining of the uterus in preparation for receiving a fertilized ovum. In the absence of fertilization and implantation, the levels of both the pituitary and gonadal hormones decline preceding menstruation. It is this decline that initiates menstrual bleeding. Thus, in human females, hormones perform a complex and repetitive regulatory function in controlling the production and release of ova and in governing the events of the menstrual cycle.

Sexual Activity   In many species, gonadal hormones play an activating role in sexual behavior, but in humans, hormonal activating effects may be quite subtle.   Nonetheless, in males, castration—the removal of the testicles—results in the loss of the primary source of testosterone. The operation has been performed on farm animals for centuries to render them fatter and more docile. Castration of humans has been performed for a variety of reasons, including treating sex offenders and extending the useful years of the voices of boy sopranos in choirs.

In some nonhuman species, such as the laboratory rat, castration results in a rapid and complete decline of sexual drive; animals appear uninterested in copulating with previously desirable females following castration.   In humans, this suppression of drive is neither as complete nor as rapid, but it is nonetheless very real.   Within a year or two following loss of the testicles, many men lose both the ability and the desire to copulate, although others do not. The results of castration in humans are quite variable.

The decline in sexual drive following castration is mediated by testosterone, as evidenced by the effects of testosterone replacement therapy. For example, XXY males frequently show atrophy of the testicles accompanied by low levels of circulating testosterone. Impotence is a common consequence of this genetic abnormality. However, treatment with testosterone usually has the effect of curing the impotence and restoring normal sexual activity and interest. Similar results have been obtained with other conditions, resulting in extremely low testosterone levels.

The sexual behavior of human females is less dependent on circulating hormone levels. However, in species with estrus, or "heat" (such as dogs or cats), behavioral effects are striking. Such species alternate between periods of strong sexual receptivity and periods of sexual abstinence and uninterest. But in humans, despite the large fluctuations in both the estrogens and progesterone that accompany the human menstrual cycle, rather little difference in either sexual interest or sexual activity occurs during the cycle.

Additional evidence for the relative lack of female hormonal activating effects in women is seen in the sexual activity following menopause. After menopause, the ovaries effectively cease producing the ovarian hormones; in this sense, menopause is the endocrinological equivalent of castration in the male. Yet menopause usually has no significant effect on either sexual interest or sexual behavior. Occasionally, there may be a transient decrease in sexual drive in some individuals. But in others, the frequency of sexual activity may actually increase, perhaps resulting from a freedom from worry concerning unwanted pregnancy. A similar lack of effect is seen in young, otherwise healthy women following surgical removal of the ovaries. Thus, the gonadal sex hormones appear to have significant activational effects in men but much weaker activational effects in women.

Sexually Related Behavior   In addition to affecting overt sexual activity, gonadal hormones also influence a range of sex-linked behaviors, such as sexual orientation and the expression of aggression.

Sexual orientation refers to the preference of a male or a female as a sexual partner. In most cases, sexual orientation is heterosexual, men preferring women and women preferring men. However, this is not always the case; about 7% of all males prefer other males, and 3% of all females prefer other females as sexual partners (LeVay & Hamer, 1994).

These percentages change in individuals exposed to unusual levels of gonadal hormones during development (Hines, 1990). For example, CAH women—who have been exposed in utero to the masculinizing effects of adrenal steroids—are five times more likely than unexposed women to prefer women as a sexual partner. Similarly, women whose mothers took DES during pregnancy are more than four times more likely to have a homosexual or bisexual orientation than their unexposed sisters (Hines, 1990). DES exposure of male fetuses does not seem to have any effect on later sexual orientation (Kester, Green, & Ginch, 1980).

In addition to differences in sexual preference, other aspects of behavior show consistent sex differences. Men and women, for example, differ in the incidence of aggressive behavior that they express, although such differences are considerably less stable than other aspects of sexually related behavior. Men are more prone to physical violence than are women; men are much more likely to commit violent crimes than are women, as well as exhibiting other—less dramatic—evidence of aggressive behavior. Prenatal hormone exposure can alter this typical pattern of sex differences with respect to aggression. CAH females, for example, score higher on personality tests of aggression than do unexposed women (Resnick, 1982). Similarly, women who were exposed prenatally to androgens also exhibit enhanced physical aggression (Reinisch, 1981).

Finally, circulating gonadal hormones also may contribute to at least some of the documented difference in cognition or thinking between adult men and women (Collaer & Hines, 1995; Kimura & Hampson, 1994). On average, women tend to excel on tests of verbal fluency, perceptual speed, and fine motor skills. Conversely, men tend to score more highly than women on tests of visual-spatial skills, such as mental rotation of geometric objects, and mathematical reasoning.

In most people, the left hemisphere plays a particularly important role in producing and understanding language, a phenomenon known as language lateralization. When probed by special testing procedures, left cerebral dominance for language has been reported to be more pronounced in men than in women. Sex differences in other cognitive skills may also exist at the level of group-averaged performance; there is—as always—an enormous amount of overlap in the abilities of individual men and women. It must be stressed that the appearance of sexual differences in thinking in adulthood does not, in and of itself, address the question of the genetic, hormonal, or environmental determinants of these differential abilities.

However, just as hormones influence sexual behavior, there is now a substantial body of evidence that hormonal factors contribute to at least some of the cognitive differences between men and women (Hines & Green, 1991). For example, women masculinized by congenital adrenal hyperplasia show higher performance on tests of visual-spatial skills than do unexposed women (Resnick, Berebaum, & Gottesman, 1986). These CAH women exhibit cognitive skills more typical of males than females.

Conversely, men who experienced lower than normal levels of circulating androgens due to subnormal gonadal growth during development have been shown to have impaired visual-spatial abilities compared to unaffected males or males experiencing a reduction of androgens after puberty (Heir & Crowley, 1982).

Finally, women whose central nervous systems were masculinized by DES during fetal growth show increased language lateralization, the male pattern, when compared with their unexposed sisters (Hines & Shipley, 1984).

Hormonal Factors in CNS Development

Just as gonadal hormones affect the differential development of the male and female genitalia, they determine the relative growth of sexually dimorphic regions of the brain and spinal cord. This is a relatively recent finding, but there is little question that it is true. Gonadal hormones that are present in the circulation during critical periods of neural development establish at least some sexually related neuroanatomical differences between the male and female brain.

Hormones can exert their influence on the structural development of the nervous system by directly affecting the expression of genetic information contained within the DNA of the cell. Unlike neurotransmitters, which bind to specialized receptors on the surface of the cell membrane, gonadal steroids penetrate the cell body and bind to specialized receptors on the cell nucleus. Once bound, the hormone-receptor complex activates or deactivates specific genes, thereby altering the course of development of the cell (Kelly, 1991a, 1991b, 1991c).

A number of examples of sexually dimorphic structures within the central nervous system have been reported in such diverse species as rodents, birds, and humans. In some cases, these dimorphic neural structures are known to result directly from the action of gonadal hormones on the developing tissue.

The Spinal Nucleus of the Bulbocavernosus   One central nervous system structure that differs between males and females is the **spinal nucleus of the bulbocavernosus (SNB)**, a discrete nucleus of motor neurons in the lumbar spinal cord of the rat. In the male, it is a small nucleus composed of fairly large neurons. It innervates two perineal muscles that are attached exclusively to the penis of the male. The corresponding region of the female spinal cord contains about one third the number of cells found in the male, and these cells are much smaller. It is not clear what functions are served by these neurons in the female rat (Arnold & Jordon, 1988).

Cells of the SNB in adult males rapidly accumulate circulating testosterone but do not absorb either estrogen or estradiol. In the developing nervous system, it is testosterone that governs the growth of this sexually dimorphic nucleus. For this reason, the SNB is absent in male rats that are genetically androgen insensitive. These animals not only exhibit the feminine form of the SNB but also fail to develop the perineal muscles of the penis. Conversely, injections of testosterone into newborn female rat pups result in the development of a male SNB, which gradually atrophies unless maintained by continuing androgen treatments.

Hypothalamus and Preoptic Area The hypothalamus is a region of the brain concerned with many aspects of visceral function and emotion. In this region, there is a structure that was first discovered in rodents, the **sexually dimorphic nucleus of the preoptic area (SDN-POA)**, that shows specific differences in size between male and female brains. The SDN-POA is located in a region of the hypothalamus with known sexual functions, including the control of masculine sexual behavior and the release of gonadotropic substances producing ovulation. In rats (Gorski, Gordon, & Shryne, 1978; Hines, Davis, & Coquelin, 1985), the volume of the SDN-POA is between three and seven times larger in the male brain than in the female brain.

In rodents, the development of this region in the male is under the control of circulating androgens. Castration at birth reduces the size of the nucleus by 50%, but this effect can be prevented by administering testosterone on the following day. Similarly, testosterone administered to female rats at birth significantly increases the volume of the nucleus at adulthood.

There appears to be a critical period within which testosterone affects the development of a masculine SDN-POA in the rat. There is no anatomical dimorphism of the nucleus before birth, and androgens administered in adulthood have no effect on the size of the nucleus. However, in the 10 days following birth, the nucleus grows by a factor of five in the normal male. Thus, the sexual dimorphism of this region of the preoptic area develops in the first days and weeks of postnatal development.

Despite its location in a sexually relevant region of the hypothalamus, the functions performed by the SDN-POA remain elusive. Small lesions placed within the nucleus itself have no noticeable effect on the sexual behavior of the male rat, but similar lesions placed somewhat dorsally to the SDN-POA do disrupt male sexual behavior. Whatever the function may be, there can be little question that this nucleus is a region of the brain guided in its development by the presence of circulating hormones produced in the testes of the male.

In the human brain, the preoptic area is not clearly separated from the anterior hypothalamus but rather forms a section of its anterior border. This area, which shows regions of sexual dimorphism in other species, has been shown to contain sexual dimorphic nuclei in humans as well. Allen, Hines, Shryne, and Gorski (1989) searched this area microscopically in the brains of 22 neurologically normal cadavers. They discovered the existence of four nuclei in this region, which they termed the **interstitial nuclei of the anterior hypothalamus (INAH1-4)**, which are shown in Figure 10.8 on the next page. Two of them, INAH-1 and INAH-4, did not differ between the sexes, being of the same size in the male and female cadavers. However, the remaining nuclei exhibited marked sex differences. INAH-3 was nearly three times larger in the males, regardless of age. Similarly, INAH-2 was twice as large in the males.

Interestingly, the size of INAH-2 in the female brains appeared to vary

Figure 10.8. The Interstitial Nuclei of the Anterior Hypothalamus.

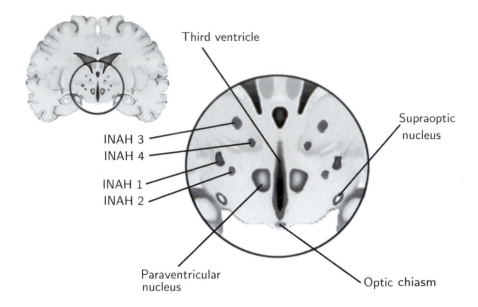

with circulating gonadal hormones. The size of this nucleus is nearly four times larger in women of childbearing age (presumably with circulating gonadal hormones) than in either prepubescent or postmenopausal females. This observation, however, requires independent confirmation because of the small number of cases in these two groups.

LeVay (1991) measured the size of the INAH in postmortem examinations of women, presumed homosexual men, and presumed heterosexual men. No differences were found in the size of INAH-1, -2, or -4. As Allen et al. (1989) had found, INAH-3 was more than twice as large in heterosexual men as in women. However, it was also more than twice as large in heterosexual men as in homosexual men. Thus, it appears that INAH-3 is dimorphic with sexual orientation rather than genetically determined sex. LeVay's findings have lent support to the idea that—in men—sexual orientation has a biological basis. For a full discussion of this issue, see the contrasting views presented by LeVay and Hamer (1994) and by Byne (1994).

Possible neuroanatomical bases of other aspects of human sexuality also have been recently discovered. Zhou, Hofman, Gooren, and Swaab (1995), for example, search sexually dimorphic regions of the human hypothalamus for structural differences related transsexuality. **Transsexuals** are people who have a strong feeling, often originating in childhood, that they have been born to the wrong sex. In these individuals, it is their core sexual identity that is discrepant with their genetic sex. Transsexuality is not an issue of sexual orientation, as some transsexuals prefer men as sexual partners, whereas others prefer women. Thus, an anatomical substrate for transsexuality should be related to cross-gender sexual identity but not sexual orientation.

The central bed nucleus of the stria terminalis (BSTc) in the hypothalamus meets these requirements. The BSTc is known to play a major role in masculine sexual behavior of rodents. It also is densely populated with estrogen and androgen receptors, indicating that it is involved in the sexual functioning of the organism. Moreover, sex differences in its size as the result of circulating gonadal hormones during development have been reported in other species. Finally, regions of the BST are known to be about 2.5 times larger in heterosexual men than in heterosexual women (Allen & Gorski, 1990).

Zhou et al. (1995) report that the volume of the BSTc in male to female transsexuals is similar to that of heterosexual females and significantly smaller than in either heterosexual or homosexual males. These results are shown in Figure 10.9. The presence of a female-appearing brain structure in genetically male transsexuals, along with other evidence, suggests that gender identity develops through the interaction of the growing brain and circulating sex hormones (Breedlove, 1995; Zhou, Hofman, Gooren, & Swaab, 1995).

SUMMARY

Much of our behavior is motivated by "basic drives," particularly by thirst, hunger, and sex. Thirst and hunger have served for decades as animal models for the study of motivated behavior because either can be easily induced in experimental animals.

A number of brain systems located within the region of the hypothalamus play particularly important roles in producing these motivated behaviors, but in all three cases, these neural systems have proven to be more complicated than investigators had originally hoped. Nonetheless, substantial progress has been made in understanding the neural systems by which biological drives are translated into human action.

SELECTED READINGS

- Stricker, E. M. (Ed.). (1990). *Handbook of behavioral neurobiology: Vol. 10. Neurobiology of food and fluid intake.* New York: Plenum. Although now a decade old, this volume still provides a comprehensive overview of the biological basis of hunger and thirst. J. T. Fitzimons's chapter, "Thirst and Sodium Appetite," gives a scholarly and thoroughly entertaining review of some highlights in history of thinking about thirst. Also treated are the issues of homeostasis, development of appetites, gastric and systemic factors, taste and feeding, comparative studies, clinical issues, and much more. This collection of first-rate articles is a must-read for anyone interested in the problems of hunger, thirst, and obesity.

- Kimura, D. (1992). Sex differences in the brain. *Scientific American, 267*(3), 118-125. Kimura, a leading researcher in neuropsychology, presents a clear and well-reasoned discussion of neural and cognitive differences between men and women.

- LeVay, S. (1993). *The sexual brain.* Cambridge: MIT Press. A provocative analysis of patterns of sexual differentiation in the brain and behavior by a leading neurobiologist.

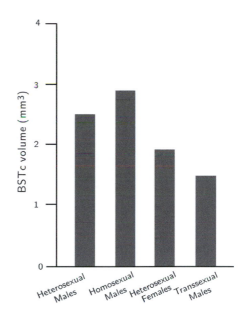

Figure 10.9. A Size Difference in a Sexually Dimorphic Nucleus of the Human Brain in Heterosexuals and Transsexuals. The volume of the central subdivision of the bed nucleus of the stria terminalis (BSTc) is significantly larger in heterosexual men than in heterosexual women. In male to female transsexuals, BSTc volume is significantly smaller than in heterosexual males and statistically equivalent to that of the heterosexual female brain. However, there is no relation between BSTc volume and sexual orientation.

KEY TERMS

absorptive state The state of the gastrointestinal tract after eating a meal, in which nutrients are made available to all organs and extra nutrients are stored for future use.

adipose tissue Fatty tissue.

adipsia A lack of drinking.

adrenal gland One of two endocrine glands, each located anterior to a kidney.

adrenogenital syndrome See *congenital adrenal hyperplasia*.

afferent arteriole The small-caliber artery bringing fresh blood into a nephron in the kidney.

aldosterone A hormone excreted by the cortex of the adrenal gland that acts to promote reabsorption of sodium and therefore of water in the nephron.

aminostatic hypothesis The proposition that hunger and eating are regulated by the availability of amino acids.

androgen A hormone with masculinizing properties (e.g., testosterone).

androgen insensitivity syndrome (AIS) A genetic disorder in which the activity of androgens is prevented from exerting a physiological effect, resulting in the feminization of genetic males.

angiotensin I A peptide composed of 10 amino acids that is produced by the action of renin on the substrate angiotensinogen in the blood.

angiotensin II A peptide composed of eight amino acids that is produced by the action of angiotensin-converting enzyme on angiotensin I; angiotensin II produces large increases in blood pressure, produces thirst, and promotes the release of aldosterone.

angiotensin III A peptide composed of seven amino acids that is produced by the action of aspartate amino peptidase on angiotensin II; angiotensin III produces smaller effects on the blood pressure than does angiotensin II but may cross the blood-brain barrier.

angiotensinogen A protein secreted by the liver into the blood plasma that is converted to angiotensin I by the action of renin.

anorexia nervosa A clinical eating disorder marked by a dramatic weight loss coupled with an intense fear of obesity.

antidiuretic hormone (ADH) A hormone secreted by the supraoptic nucleus of the hypothalamus and stored in the pituitary gland that stimulates the reabsorption of water in the kidney, resulting in reduced urine volume.

aphagic Refers to not eating.

autosome Any chromosome that is not a sex chromosome.

baroreceptor A sensory nerve ending in the walls of a blood vessel that is sensitive to changes in blood pressure.

blood plasma The extracellular fluid of the vasculature within which the cells of the blood are suspended.

brown adipose tissue The dark type of fat tissue, which is heavily vascularized and sympathetically innervated.

bulimia A clinical eating disorder marked by episodes of binge eating.

cholecystokinin (CCK) A peptide hormone secreted by the small intestine that stimulates the release of pancreatic enzymes and bile.

circumventricular organs A series of structures located around the ventricles of the brain that might serve as receptors for circulating hormones.

congenital adrenal hyperplasia (CAH) A condition in which the adrenal cortex produces large amounts of androgens, resulting in masculinization of the female child and precocious sexual development in the male.

diabetes mellitus A metabolic disorder marked by the failure of insulin secretion by the pancreas.

diffusion The movement of molecules from regions of high concentration to areas of lower concentration, accomplished by the probabilistic random movement of molecules driven by thermal energy.

dual-center hypothalamic hypothesis With respect to hunger, the idea that the lateral hypothalamus functions as a "hunger center" and the ventromedial hypothalamus as a "satiety center."

duodenum The initial segment of the small intestine.

efferent arteriole A small-caliber artery bringing blood out of a nephron.

egg See *ovum*.

energy balance The relation between ingested and expended energy.

estradiol A steroid sex hormone that is the major estrogen in humans.

estrogen A class of female sex hormones; hormones that induce estrus in certain species.

extracellular fluid The interstitial fluid and blood plasma, both being outside of cell bodies.

5-alpha reductase deficiency A condition in which a deficiency of the steroid 5-alpha reductase results in an in utero failure to masculinize the external genitalia, resulting in a phenotypically female child; at puberty, testosterone produced by the viable testes completes this masculization, turning the female child into a psychologically and physically male teenager.

follicle-stimulating hormone One of the gonadotropic hormones excreted by the pituitary.

gametes Haploid cells, sperm and ova.

gastrointestinal tract The stomach and the intestines. Also referred to as the alimentary canal.

glomerulus A cluster; with respect to the kidney, the tuft of blood vessels in a nephron.

glucagon A peptide hormone released by the pancreas in the postabsorptive state that facilitates the metabolism of fats and the production of glucose from stored energy sources.

glucoreceptor A cell that changes its rate of firing as a function of blood glucose levels.

glucostat A mechanism that regulates glucose levels about a set point.

glucostatic hypothesis The idea that blood glucose or glucose utilization is the regulated variable in the control of hunger and eating.

glycerol An intermediate product of fat metabolism, a trihydric sugar alcohol.

glycogen The principal carbohydrate storage molecule in animals, also referred to as animal starch.

gonadal hormones Hormones produced by the ovaries or testes.

gonadotropic hormones Pituitary hormones affecting gonadal function (for example, follicle-stimulating hormone and luteinizing hormone).

gonadotropic-releasing hormones Hypothalamic hormones that govern the release of two gonadotropic hormones by the pituitary.

hemorrhage Bleeding, the escape of blood from the vascular system.

hepatic portal system The vein bringing oxygen-depleted but nutrient-rich blood from the gastrointestinal tract to the liver.

hormone Chemical substances that are secreted by a specific structure and carried in the blood to the site at which they produce a physiological effect.

hunger The craving for food.

hyperphagic Refers to excessive eating.

ileum The lower portion of the small intestine.

insulin The major hormone regulating energy use in humans; released by the pancreas, it promotes storage of nutrients by liver, muscle, and fat tissue and enables nonneural tissue to metabolize glucose.

interstitial fluid That component of the extracellular fluid that surrounds cell bodies and lies outside the vasculature.

interstitial nuclei of the anterior hypothalamus (INAH 1-4) In humans, four hypothalamic nuclei in the vicinity of the preoptic area, two of which (INAH-2 and -3) are sexually dimorphic.

intracellular fluid The cytoplasm contained within a cell body.

jejunum The middle segment of the small intestine.

ketones An intermediate product of metabolism that is characterized by the presence of a carbonyl group.

kidney One of two large brown organs located at the back of the abdominal cavity that act to filter the blood and form urine, thereby playing a key role in water and salt regulation.

Klinefelter's syndrome The XXY chromosomal anomaly.

large intestine The final segment of the gastrointestinal tract.

lateral hypothalamus (LH) The region of the hypothalamus that is often hypothesized to serve as a "hunger center."

lateral preoptic area (LPA) The lateral regions of the periventricular gray matter surrounding the most rostral portion of the third ventricle in the diencephalon.

leptin A hormone encoded by the ob gene that is produced by adipose tissue in proportion to body fat content and circulates in the blood and cerebrospinal fluid.

lipostatic hypothesis The idea that fat metabolism or fat storage serves as the regulated variable in the control of hunger and eating.

liver The large gland in the upper abdomen that serves, in part, to filter blood, secrete bile, and store and release glucose as glucagon.

liver lobules The small functional units of the liver.

luteinizing hormone One of the gonadotropic hormones secreted by the pituitary.

Müllerian system The precursor of the female internal sexual organs.

Müllerian-inhibiting substance A hormone secreted by the testes that instigates the regression and atrophy of the Müllerian system.

negative feedback The response of a system to change in a regulated variable that acts to return that variable to its set point.

nephron The functional unit of the kidney.

neuropeptide Y A peptide neurotransmitter that triggers eating in mammals.

nigrostriatal bundle A set of dopaminergic fibers that originates in the substantia nigra and projects to the caudate nucleus and putamen (neostriatum).

obesity The gain of body weight above "normal" levels by the accumulation of fat in the body.

organum vasculosum of the lamina terminalis (OVLT) A small nucleus that constitutes one of the circumventricular organs, which may contain the angiotensin receptors that mediate volumetric thirst.

osmometric thirst Thirst produced by cellular dehydration.

osmoreceptor A neuron that signals osmotic pressure by responding to changes in the sodium concentration of the extracellular fluid or changes in cellular volume.

osmosis The movement of water or other solvent from a solution of lesser solute concentration to a solution of greater solute concentration across a membrane permitting the movement of solvent but not all solutes.

osmotic pressure At equilibrium, the force counteracting further net osmotic movement across a semipermeable membrane.

ovarian follicle The ovum and the cells that encase it.

ovum An egg, the female gamete.

postabsorptive state The metabolic state facilitating the release of stored energy sources.

progesterone A steroid excreted by the corpus luteum and other sites that prepares the uterus for the reception and development of a fertilized ovum.

progestogens Substances that have effects similar to those of progesterone.

regulation In physiology, the control of a variable to return it to a set point.

renin The enzyme secreted by the kidney that is the rate-limiting step in the synthesis of the angiotensins.

salivary glands The glands in the mouth that secrete saliva.

satiety The disappearance of hunger, the full gratification of appetite.

secondary sexual characteristics Sexual dimorphisms that appear at puberty under the control of gonadal hormones.

set point The desired value of a controlled variable in a homeostatic system.

sexual dimorphism The appearance of two different forms of organ or structure in males and females.

sexually dimorphic nucleus of the preoptic area (SDN-POA) A nucleus of the medial hypothalamus that is large in males and small in females, the size of which is controlled by circulating testosterone.

small intestine The portion of the gastrointestinal tract between the stomach and the large intestine.

sperm The gamete cells of the male.

spinal nucleus of the bulbocavernosus (SNB) A sexually dimorphic nucleus of the lumbar spinal cord that innervates the muscles of the male penis.

steroids A group of lipid compounds, including the gonadal hormones.

stomach The large segment of the gastrointestinal tract that serves as a temporary store of ingested food to be released to the small intestine.

subfornical organ (SFO) A circumventricular organ that may contain angiotensin receptors that mediate volumetric thirst.

testis-determining factor (TDF) A critical portion of the short arm of the Y chromosome that controls sexual dimorphism.

testosterone A steroid hormone produced by the testes.

thermostatic hypothesis The idea that body temperature serves as the regulated variable in the control of hunger and eating.

thirst A sensation, usually of dryness in the mouth, that is associated with the desire to drink liquids.

transsexual A person who has a strong feeling, often originating in childhood, that he or she has been born to the wrong sex.

tubule A small tube; in a nephron, containing the blood plasma entering from Bowman's capsule.

Turner's syndrome A disorder caused by the failure of the sperm to contribute a sex chromosome (e.g., XO).

ventromedial nucleus The hypothalamic nucleus that is postulated to serve as a "satiety center."

volumetric thirst Thirst produced by the loss of extracellular fluid.

Wolffian system Precursor of the male internal sexual organs.

Chapter 11

Language and Cognition

The year was 1861. The patient, a man named Leborgne, was then 51 years of age. He had spent the last 21 years of his life in a French hospital, the hospice of Bicêtre; his capacity for language was severely damaged. His physician, Paul Broca (see Figure 11.1 on the next page), described the situation in these words.

> When questioned... as to the origin of his disease, he replied only with the monosyllable "tan," repeated twice in succession and accompanied by a gesture of his left hand. I tried to find out more about the antecedents of this man, who had been at Bicêtre for twenty-one years.

Figure 11.1. Paul Broca. Broca was the first person to localize any function to a particular location of the human cerebral cortex. (Photograph courtesy of the History and Special Collections Division of the Louise M. Darling Biomedical Library, UCLA.)

I questioned his attendants, his comrades on the ward, and those of his relatives who came to see him, and here is the result of the inquiry...

When he arrived at Bicêtre, he had already been unable to speak for two or three months. He was then quite healthy and intelligent and differed from the normal person only in his loss of articulate language. He came and went in the hospice, where he was known by the name of "Tan." He understood all that was said to him. His hearing was actually very good, but whenever one questioned him, he always answered, "Tan, tan," accompanying his utterance with varied gestures by which he succeeded in expressing most of his ideas. If one did not understand his gestures, he was apt to get irate and added to his vocabulary a gross oath ("Sacre nom de Dieu!")...Tan was considered an egoist, vindictive and objectionable, and his associates, who detested him, even accused him of stealing. These defects could have been due largely to his cerebral lesion. They were not pronounced enough to be considered pathological, and although this patient was at Bicetre, no one ever thought of transferring him to the insane ward. On the contrary, he was considered to be completely responsible for his acts...

The state of Tan's intelligence could not be exactly determined. Certainly he understood almost all that was said to him, but, since he could express his ideas or desires only by movements of his left hand, this moribund patient could not make himself understood as well as he understood others. His numerical responses, made by opening or closing his fingers, were best...It cannot be doubted, therefore, that the man was intelligent, that he could think, that he had to a certain extent retained the memory of old habits. He could understand even quite complicated ideas...Nevertheless there were several questions to which he did not respond, questions that a man of ordinary intelligence would have managed to answer even with only one hand...Obviously he had much more intelligence than was necessary for him to talk. (Herrnstein & Boring, 1965, pp. 224-226)

Tan was to provide the first clue to the localization of language functions within the human brain. Paul Broca presented his case to the Société Anatomique de Paris in 1861 in an address that began the modern investigation of the biological basis of language. Tan's brain, in the same condition today as when Broca presented it to the University of Paris well over a century ago, is shown in Figure 11.2 on the following page.

HUMAN LANGUAGE

Tan could not speak, and—at least to that extent—his language was impaired. But human language is much more than speech; it is a system for representing knowledge that lies at the very core of human thought (Fromkin & Rodman, 1993). It is propositional in nature; that is, language is organized to say things about things. Even single-word utterances usually are understood as propositions. For example, if a child says "Candy," we take that to be the expression of a wish, "Give me candy." But we usually speak in sentences or sentence fragments that are full propositions in which information about things is sought or given. Linguists believe that propositions are the fundamental linguistic component of human language. Among the first to emphasize the propositional nature of speech was John Hughlings Jackson, the founder of British neurology.

Human language is a system of considerable power. Linguists say that language is **productive**, meaning that it can be used to convey new information, to state ideas that have never been previously expressed. New objects and ideas can be named, and one person can tell another exactly what that name means. This adaptability of language forms the basis of education, a process by which human beings transmit information between generations.

Language also has the capacity for **displaced reference**, meaning that one can refer to things that are not in the immediate environment. The referent, the thing being spoken of, may be displaced either in space (as when referring to a foreign city) or in time (as when referring to the past or future). This range of displacement frees language from the immediate present and gives language a tool to construct human culture.

Figure 11.2. Tan's Brain. Tan's brain—undoubtedly the most famous brain in neurology—resides in Musée Dupuytren, the anatomy museum of the École de Médicine of Paris. Although well over 100 years old, it remains perfectly preserved. The brain is resting on its occipital lobe, with the frontal cortex pointing upward. It is easy to see the extensive damage to the third frontal convolution of the left hemisphere, the region known today as Broca's area.

Hierarchical Structure of Language

Language derives its power from its **hierarchical organization**; that is, language is organized at several different levels. At each level, the rules, or grammar, of language are appropriate to the units being organized. Hierarchical organization eases the burden of building extremely complex systems because problems appropriate to each level can be dealt with at that level.

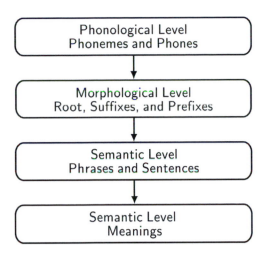

Figure 11.3. The Hierarchical Structure of Language.

As we will see, the first level of language is that of **phonemes**, the basic speech sounds of a language. Phonemes in turn are combined into **morphemes**, the smallest linguistic units that carry meaning. Morphemes can then be combined into words, and, finally, words may be combined into phrases and sentences. This structure is hierarchical because separate, relatively simple sets of rules control the functioning at each level. Figure 11.3 shows the hierarchical levels at which human language is organized.

This hierarchical structure, coupled with the rules by which elements of language may be combined, gives language its immense power. In English, for example, there are more than 40 phonemes that can be combined into morphemes that in turn can be organized into the hundreds of thousands of words in a standard English dictionary.

Language constitutes an open system that can be freely extended as a culture evolves. In contrast, a closed system—one that associates a meaning directly with a sound—cannot be easily extended. There are, after all, only so many different sounds that human beings can make. The richness of human language is possible only because of its hierarchical organization that—it now appears—is deeply embedded in the biological structure of the human brain.

Phonemes are speech sounds, the smallest units of a language that serve to distinguish one word from another (Fromkin & Rodman, 1993; Ladefoged, 1993). The word *dog* is composed of three phonemes, written as /d/, /o/, and /g/. These phonemes correspond to the three speech sounds that form that word. By changing any of these phonemes, a different word is produced, such as *fog*, *dig*, or *dot*. All words are composed of phonemes.

Different languages have different numbers of phonemes, which range from as few as 15 to well over 40 in languages such as English (Crystal, 1997). (Some of the letters of the English alphabet represent more than one phoneme, such as the hard and soft pronunciation of the letter "g.") Although different languages use different sets of phonemes, the total number of phonemes employed by all the world's human languages is no more than about 90. These consist of distinguishable speech sounds that can be made by the human respiratory apparatus. The phonemes that are used in any particular language are quite different from one another, ensuring that the listener understands easily and exactly which phonemes are spoken.

The production of phonemes is a product of the genetically determined brain language system. When all 6-month-old infants babble (babbling is an early stage of language acquisition) they produce all 90-some phonemes, including those used in languages that they have never heard. At that age, the babbling of infants is the same, regardless of the language that the child will later learn. This probably represents the emergence of the brain systems that will be subsequently used in actual speech production. By 9 months, this explosion of phonemes begins to be pruned. At this age, children produce only the phonemes of the language or languages to which they are exposed, the beginning step in learning a particular language.

The rules by which phonemes may be combined in any particular language are said to be the phonemic grammar of that language. The **phonemic grammar** specifies what sequences of phonemes are and are not permissible in the language.

In contrast to phonemes, morphemes are the smallest meaningful units of a language. Therefore, these units do not contain any meaningful subunits. The word *dog*, for example, is composed of a single morpheme. In contrast, *dogs* is composed of a pair of morphemes, the root word *dog* and the suffix *s*, which indicates that the word is plural. Morphemes may be root words, prefixes, or suffixes, all of which carry meaning. The rules by which morphemes may be joined to form words are the **morphemic grammar**.

In the English language, about 100,000 morphemes are currently defined. These may be combined to produce a total English vocabulary of more than 1 million words. The normal vocabulary of any individual is much smaller, ranging between 40,000 and 100,000 words.

Individual words are formed into phrases, clauses, and sentences according to the rules of the syntactic grammar. The basic sentence is composed of a verb and one or more noun phrases. Noun phrases have at least one noun, often an introductory article such as *a* or *the*, and sometimes one or more adjectives. *Harry, the dog*, and *the silver sports car* are all noun phrases. The **syntactic grammar** determines the combinations of words that are permitted in a given language.

The deepest level of language organization is that of *semantics*, which refers to the way in which language expresses meaning. Rather little is known about semantic units or the rules of semantic grammar except that the semantic system is thought to connect the language system to other stores of information within the brain.

The **semantic grammar** deals with what word meanings are and how word meanings combine to form phrase and sentence meanings. Even competent language speakers may not know the full or exact definition of the words that they use. Ordinary citizens may speak of atomic bombs and computers without being fully aware of the defining properties of such devices. Moreover, many words lack a precise definitional rule and instead are more like fuzzy concepts. Nonetheless, linguistic concepts of word meaning seem in the broadest sense to be like definitional rules of some sort.

If the problem of word meaning seems complex, the question of sentence meaning is much more difficult. Unlike word meaning, sentences can be true or false. Sentences make references to things and assertions about the things that are referenced. For this reason, sentences are said to have a truth value (true or untrue). Linguists often approach this problem by decomposing a sentence into the propositions about the world that it contains. However, in considering all but the simplest of sentences, propositional structures quickly become exceedingly complex. Yet the language system of the human brain allows even a child to correctly extract meaning from the complicated sentences and sentence fragments that we all use in our daily lives.

In normal speech, both the speaker and the listener are actively and simultaneously processing linguistic information. The speaker is automatically translating thoughts into words, phrases, and sentences. The listener is performing the reverse process of attempting to understand the speaker's meaning and intentions from the sentences that are spoken. Both processes occur unconsciously and without apparent effort. But the complexity of the neural mechanisms governing speech production and perception cannot be underestimated.

Speech Production Speech sounds are produced by the muscles of the respiratory system and of the mouth (Denes & Pinson, 1993). In everyday speech, most phonemes are voiced, or generated from a tone produced by forcing air from the lungs through the closed **vocal cords**. (Whispering is an example of unvoiced speech.) The vocal cords form a muscular valve that controls the flow of air from the lungs. When the vocal cords are firmly but not completely closed, the forced passage of air through this valve results in a complex sound wave.

The actual sound that is heard, however, depends on the position of the tongue, the lips, and other structures of the oral cavity. The movements of these structures alter the shape of the mouth and change the characteristics of the resulting sound, much as the shapes of different wind instruments give these instruments their characteristic sounds. The phonemes that are used in English as well as in other languages are the result of oral and respiratory muscle movements that yield distinguishable sounds. Each natural language has selected reliably and easily distinguished sounds from the range of all possible phonemes, the building blocks from which all other language functions are constructed.

Speech Perception Speech perception, in some sense, begins with the task of identifying the exact sequence of phonemes produced by a speaker, a process that we usually execute without thinking (Fromkin & Rodman, 1993). There is a fair amount of evidence that a special neural system functions in decoding speech sounds. Developmental studies indicate that it begins operating soon after birth. It functions to identify phonemes; information about auditory sounds that are not phonemes is quickly lost. This is termed **categorical perception**, meaning that the process simply decides which phoneme is presented and discards information concerning other physical properties of the acoustic stimulus. Categorical perception results in the ability to focus on the linguistic content of a speaker's message and ignore other acoustic features of the voice. The efficiency of categorical phoneme perception is indicated by the fact that we can process speech information at up to 30 phonemes per second; discrete nonspeech sounds cannot be comprehended nearly as quickly.

What is the next step in speech perception? It would seem reasonable to expect that the various grammars of human language might proceed in serial order. In such a view, phoneme perception would precede morpheme decoding, which would be followed by syntactic and finally semantic analysis.

There is strong evidence, however, that this is not the case. Instead, all levels of grammatical analysis appear to be operating more or less simultaneously. Furthermore, all levels of analysis seem to interact. For example, tentative judgments made by the semantic and syntactic grammars affect the ongoing analysis of the phoneme identification process. Entire phonemes may be experimentally deleted from tape-recorded natural speech, and such omissions are not perceived if the listener has any idea of what the speaker is saying (Ladefoged & Broadbent, 1960).

Animal Models of Language

Animal models have been particularly useful in the study of nervous system functions, providing basic information that can be applied to understanding the human nervous system. For this reason, a number of attempts have been made to find a species of animal in which language-like cognitive processes may be experimentally studied. Because of the similarities between human brains and those of other primates, much attention has been paid to the potential language-learning ability of those primates, particularly the chimpanzee. Unfortunately, most linguists and neuroscientists now believe that the attempts to teach chimpanzees and other primates language have not been successful.

Several different strategies have been used to teach language to nonhuman primates. William and Lorna Kellogg, for example, raised a chimpanzee at home along with their infant child. Perhaps not surprisingly, the child learned language, and the chimpanzee did not (Kellogg, 1968).

A somewhat more sophisticated approach was adopted by Allen and Beatrice Gardner, who reasoned that the chimps may simply have difficulty making speech sounds. So they raised a chimpanzee named Washoe using American Sign Language, which is not vocal but gestural. Their original report suggested that Washoe might have in fact learned ASL (Gardner & Gardner, 1969), but that report is now disputed.

Similarly, David Premack taught the chimpanzee Sarah to communicate using an artificial language based on plastic symbols of differing size, color, and shape (Premack, 1992). Although Sarah learned a great deal about manipulating plastic symbols, most people do not now believe that she learned the rules of language (Pinker, 1994).

The most recent attempts to demonstrate language in a nonhuman brain involve a pygmy chimp named Kanzi at the Yerkes Primate Research Center. Two psychologists who have studied Kanzi, Sue Savage-Rumbaugh and Patricia Greenfield, believe that this pygmy chimp can create sentences as grammatical as those of a 2-year-old child. Others, such as the theoretical linguist Noam Chomsky, are not convinced that any species would have the capacity for something as advantageous as language and not naturally use it. "It would be a biological miracle," says Chomsky, as "if humans had the capacity for flight and never thought of using it" (Gibbons, 1991, p. 1562). Nonetheless, Kanzi's accomplishments *are* impressive, and the debate as to Kanzi's acquisition of at least low level of language skills remains open at this time.

The issue is whether nonhumans can actually acquire the *grammars* of the language in a humanlike way, not that they can produce linguistically correct strings of symbols. One important difference between humans and other species is that humans do not have to be taught grammar at any level; that knowledge seems to be a genetically determined part of the human nervous system. Perhaps more accurate, the structure of human languages appears to have adapted itself to the properties of the human brain in a very exact fashion. Thus, any normal child will learn any language to which he or she is exposed. After all, if children had excessive difficulties learning a particular human language, that language would soon disappear from the face of the earth.

The conceptual question—whether true language can be learned by a nonhuman brain—may be clarified by considering the case of Clever Hans. Hans was a remarkable horse owned by a distinguished German, Baron von Osten. What made Hans remarkable was the fact that he could seemingly solve arithmetic problems posed to him by any individual.

When asked for the product two times three, Hans would stamp his foreleg six times. Hans was not a circus horse, trained to perform tricks. Rather, he appeared to be an equine prodigy. A blue ribbon commission, composed of a physiologist, a psychologist, the director of the Berlin Zoo, and others experienced in animal behavior, declared Hans to be authentic. In their opinion, Hans indeed knew mathematics, that is, had the rules of mathematics within his brain.

It remained for a more detailed analysis by Oscar Pfungst to explain matters (Pfungst, 1911). There was no question as to what Hans did; he was asked numerical problems, and he stamped out their solutions. The issue was how he found the solution. Pfungst discovered that when people asked a question of Hans, they would bend forward to observe Hans's feet. At that cue, Hans would begin tapping. People would also lean back when the "correct" answer was given; at that point, Hans would stop tapping. Hans did not know mathematics; he was instead a keen observer of human behavior.

The lesson from Hans applies as well to the question of primate models of language. Although today's researchers studying Kanzi are much more sophisticated that those who studied Hans nearly a century ago, the question still remains: Is there sufficient evidence to conclude that nonhumans have acquired the rules—the grammars—of the languages being taught? Most, but not all, neuroscientists remain somewhat skeptical about claims of primate language acquisition.

Cerebral Dominance

The neural structures that control language within the human brain have developed in a most curious way, at least from the perspective of evolution. Throughout the vertebrates, bilateral symmetry of neural function has long been thought to be the rule. The term **bilateral symmetry** means that the two sides of the brain are very much alike, both anatomically and functionally. This is true for many functions of the human brain as well, but it is not true for language.

In most individuals, it is the left hemisphere that contains the neural mechanisms that control language; the corresponding tissue of the right cerebral hemisphere appears to serve other, nonlanguage functions. This asymmetry of control of language function is commonly termed **cerebral dominance**, with an implicit reference to language, although other types of cerebral dominance certainly exist. For example, the right cerebral hemisphere is usually dominant for spatial perception.

The initial indication of the special linguistic roles played by the left hemisphere came from the common clinical observation that damage to the left hemisphere frequently results in **aphasia**, the loss of language function, whereas corresponding damage in the right hemisphere disrupts language much less frequently. These asymmetrical effects of brain damage on language are more pronounced in right-handed than in left-handed individuals.

The clinical observations have been substantiated in recent years by more systematic assessments of cerebral dominance. The **Wada test** is one such method (Milner, 1974). This procedure was developed in the late 1940s by Juan Wada to determine cerebral dominance for language in patients awaiting brain surgery. Knowledge of cerebral dominance in a particular patient helps guide the surgeon away from the language areas of the patient's brain, thereby avoiding an accidental aphasia as a consequence of the surgery.

Wada's test is conceptually straightforward, making use of the fact that the right and left carotid arteries bring blood from the heart to the right and left cerebral hemispheres, respectively. Injecting a short-acting barbiturate (sodium amytal) into one of the two arteries may anesthetize one half of the brain, resulting in a selective loss of function in one of the cerebral hemispheres. The effect of the hemianesthesia is verified by testing bilateral motor function; there should be a temporary paralysis of the contralateral side of the body with normal control of the ipsilateral musculature.

If the injection is on the side of the dominant hemisphere, a total and sudden aphasia results; if the injection is on the nondominant side, language function continues to be more or less normal during the 5 to 10 minutes of anesthesia. In some people, however, language is not severely impaired no matter which hemisphere is anesthetized. This indicates that both hemispheres contain neuronal circuitry that is sufficient to produce language. Such people are said to have **mixed dominance**.

The results from the Wada test indicate that the distribution of cerebral dominance is somewhat different in right- and left-handed individuals (see Figure 11.4 on the facing page). Among the right-handed, 96% show the normal pattern of left-hemisphere dominance for language, whereas

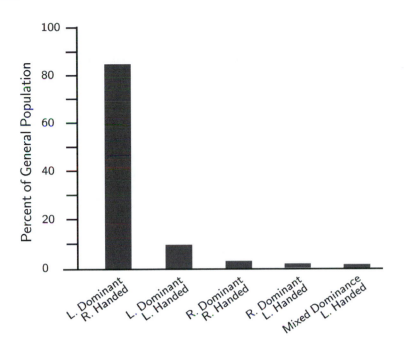

Figure 11.4. The Distribution of Both Handedness and Cerebral Dominance for Language. Notice how infrequently cases of right dominance occur. For this reason, very little is known about the organization of language within the right hemisphere of right-dominant individuals.

4% exhibit the reverse pattern of right-hemisphere dominance (Milner, 1974). Virtually no cases of mixed dominance exist in right-handed people.

These percentages change somewhat in the population of left-handers. In this group, 70% have left-hemisphere dominance, 15% have right-hemisphere dominance, and 15% exhibit mixed dominance. Considering that about 90% of all people are right-handed, more than 90% of people in general have left-hemisphere cerebral dominance.

Human language is not just spoken language but includes gesturally signed languages as well. The left hemisphere appears to be dominant for the comprehension and production of American Sign Language (ASL), which is significant because ASL differs from spoken language in some fundamental ways. Like spoken language, ASL has a complex organizational structure with a hierarchical grammatical system, but it is not derived from spoken English. ASL relies on spatial movements and contrasts to express syntax. The grammatical functions of spoken language that are transmitted by the linear ordering of phonemes, morphemes, words, and phrases are performed in ASL by essentially visual and spatial mechanisms. Because, in most individuals, the right hemisphere has some specialization for processing spatial information, the question of cerebral dominance for ASL is a matter of some interest.

Damasio and his colleagues report the case of a 27-year-old, right-handed, English-speaking woman who learned ASL at age 18 (Damasio, Bellugi, Damasio, Poizner, & Gilder, 1986). By profession, she worked as an interpreter and counselor for deaf people and is a skilled signer. Her cerebral dominance was tested in preparation for surgical removal of the right temporal lobe for the treatment of epilepsy. Wada's test revealed an interesting pattern of results. When the left hemisphere was anesthetized, there was aphasia for both English and ASL. The signing aphasia included word substitutions, loss of grammar, and the production of nonsense word signs. She could speak and sign simultaneously, making frequent mismatches between spoken words and signs, with English often correct but ASL mistakes in both meaning and grammar.

After removal of the right temporal lobe, her use of ASL was unaffected, despite the spatial nature of the ASL language. This neurological case clearly suggests that the left cerebral hemisphere is normally dominant for language, no matter whether that language is spoken or gestural in its nature. But case studies are by definition examinations of single individuals and therefore cannot provide strong statistical support for any general hypothesis.

Statistical confirmation that the left hemisphere is usually dominant for both spoken and sign languages has been provided by Hickok, Bellugi, and Klima (1996). They studied the effects of unilateral brain damage in a group of 23 ASL users, of which 13 had left-hemisphere lesions and 10 had damage to the right hemisphere. All were tested using a version of the Boston Diagnostic Aphasia Examination that had been adapted for American Sign Language. This examination tests various aspects of language use, such as production, comprehension, naming, and repetition. On all these measures, persons with left-hemisphere damage performed significantly more poorly than individuals with right-hemisphere damage. Left-hemisphere damage consistently produced aphasia in ASL, whereas right-hemisphere damage did not. ASL, like spoken language, shows left-hemispheric dominance.

Furthermore, the observed ASL deficits were not a consequence of the fact that ASL is based on visual-spatial symbols made by hand movements instead of the rapidly changing auditory signals used in spoken language. Four left-hemisphere damaged individuals were markedly aphasic in ASL but retained normal visual-spatial skills, whereas four of the right-hemisphere damaged patients were not aphasic in ASL but showed a substantial loss of visual-spatial comprehension. Thus, the loss of language in these ASL users cannot reflect a simple loss of the abilities to produce and interpret visual and spatial information but must indicate a loss of a higher-order brain system that regulates this system at the level of language, not at the level of the physical signals that language uses.

DISORDERS OF LANGUAGE

As useful as the Wada test may be in determining *which* cerebral hemisphere is dominant for language, it reveals nothing about the anatomical or functional organization of the language system *within* the dominant hemisphere. Evidence concerning the intrahemispheric systems controlling language has come from the careful examination of neurological patients with restricted brain damage. By far, the most useful information is obtained from individuals who have suffered cerebral strokes, a disorder of the blood supply to the brain that may produce extensive neuronal damage within a confined brain area and no damage elsewhere.

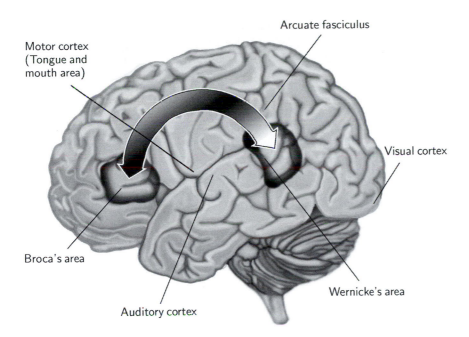

Figure 11.5. The Anatomical Structure of the Language System of the Left Hemisphere.

Broca's Aphasia

Broca's patient Tan may have been a stroke victim.

On April 17, 1861, Tan died, following additional neurological complications. Broca performed the autopsy, removing Tan's diseased brain, storing it in alcohol, and transporting it to the Société d'Anthropologie for detailed examination. Broca's task was to identify the portion of the brain that was likely to have been the cause of the original aphasia, which had been present for more than two decades. Broca reached the conclusion that Tan's language difficulties, now known as **Broca's aphasia**, resulted from damage to the third convolution of the frontal lobe of the left cerebral hemisphere. This region, called **Broca's area**, is shown in Figure 11.5.

A modern case study of an individual with Broca's aphasia following a stroke much like Tan might have suffered was reported by Howard Gardner, a neuropsychologist, in his classic book *The Shattered Mind*. The man with whom Gardner spoke was a 39-year-old Coast Guard radio operator named David Ford. Gardner asked him about his work before entering the hospital. This was the conversation:

"I'm a sig...no...man...uh, well,...again."

"Let me help you," I interjected. "You were a signal..."

"A sig-nal man...right," Ford completed my phrase triumphantly.

"Were you in the Coast Guard?"

"No, er, yes, yes...ship...Massach...chusetts...Coastguard...years." He raised his hands twice, indicating the number "nineteen."

"Oh, you were in the Coast Guard for nineteen years?"

"Oh...boy...right...right," he replied.

"Why are you in the hospital, Mr. Ford?" Ford looked at me a bit strangely, as if to say, Isn't it patently obvious? He pointed to his paralyzed arm and said,

"Arm no good," then to his mouth and said, "Speech... can't say... talk, you see."

"What happened to make you lose your speech?"

"Head, fall, Jesus Christ, me no good, str, str... oh Jesus... stroke."

"I see. Could you tell me, Mr. Ford, what you've been doing in the hospital?"

"Yes, sure. Me go, er, uh, P. T. nine o'cot, speech... two times... read... wr... ripe, er, rike, er, write... practice... get-ting better."

"And have you been home on the weekends?"

"Why, yes... Thursday, er, er er, no, er, Friday... Bar-ba-ra... wife... and, oh, car... drive... purnpike... you know... rest and... tee-vee."

"Are you able to understand everything on television?"

"Oh, yes, yes... well... al-most." (Gardner, 1976, pp. 60-61)

In Broca's aphasia, the patient says very little. Speech is obviously effortful and very slow; articulation—the correct formation of phonemes—is poor. Broca's area aphasics have substantial difficulties with language at the phonemic level. There may be right-side paralysis, as in the case of Mr. Ford, if the region of the stroke extends into the nearby motor cortex. Right-side paralysis is not an uncommon accompaniment of Broca's aphasia.

Aside from phonemic problems, Ford's speech is also syntactically incorrect; he does not speak in sentences. Linguists distinguish between two general categories of words. The **open-class words** are the content words of the language, consisting of nouns, verbs, adverbs, and adjectives. The number of such words is limitless, and the class of such words is constantly growing. In contrast, the list of **closed-class words** is fixed in number. It consists primarily of function words, such as pronouns, prepositions, and conjunctions (Fromkin & Rodman, 1993). Only rarely does a new function word enter a language.

Notice that Ford's spoken vocabulary consists nearly entirely of open-class words; closed-class words are virtually absent. For this reason, the speech of a Broca's area aphasic is said to be **telegraphic**, omitting the grammatical words that change strings of nouns into sentences. When asked what day it is, the patient might reply appropriately, "Monday." However, when urged to form a sentence, the best that can be done is something like "Day... Monday." To say "The day is Monday" requires the use of closed-class words and is not easy for patients with Broca's aphasia.

The problems are not simple failures of the motor system; after all, Broca's area lies immediately anterior to the portion of the motor strip controlling the organs of speech. Could it be possible that a lack of motor control is the problem in these patients? The answer to this question must be *no* because the same problems that occur in speech also appear in writing. Broca's area aphasics write telegraphically, with abundant phonemic errors. Furthermore, many patients are able to sing old, well-learned songs without difficulty but nonetheless are unable to generate new grammatically correct sentences. The difficulty is with the spontaneous use of language, not with the control of the vocal motor system.

The relative lack of closed-class words and the telegraphic nature of speech in Broca's aphasia do give rise to comprehension difficulties for sentences with complex syntactic construction. Broca's area aphasics can easily comprehend conjoined sentences, such as, "The woman was carrying a book and the woman sat down at her desk," but not embedded sentences carrying the same information, such as, "The woman, who was carrying a book, sat down at her desk" (Nass & Gazzaniga, 1987). Furthermore, they can understand sentences in the active voice (e.g., "The boy is chasing the girl") but not in the passive voice, as in "The girl is chased by the boy." Clauses that modify the subject of a sentence are correctly interpreted; there is no problem with sentences such as, "The boy that is chasing the girl is fast." But problems arise when it is the object that is being modified, as in "The boy that the girl is chasing is fast" (Cornell, Fromkin, & Mauner, 1993).

Despite these difficulties, in ordinary circumstances, Broca's area aphasics show evidence of satisfactory if not exemplary comprehension of both spoken and written language. They may correctly answer questions, perform mental calculations, and carry out commands that are either spoken or written. Because such responses are appropriate, they constitute evidence that these patients can process the meaning or semantic content of spoken and written language (Kertesz, 1979).

Wernicke's Aphasia

Broca's aphasia is not the only type of aphasia that may occur following brain damage. This point was made clear in 1874 when Carl Wernicke (see Figure 11.6 on the following page), then a 26-year-old neurologist, not only described a type of aphasia that today carries his name but also outlined the basic features of the language system of the left hemisphere (Wernicke, 1874).

Wernicke's aphasia results from damage to the superior surface of the anterior left temporal lobe. **Wernicke's area**, as this region is known, is immediately adjacent to the cortical auditory area and very near a number of cortical and subcortical regions that are implicated in human memory (see Figure 11.5 on page 375). It is not surprising that damage in such a region produces different effects on language than does damage in Broca's area.

In contrast to patients with Broca's aphasia, patients with Wernicke's aphasia speak rapidly and effortlessly. Their speech may be even faster than normal, but it contains all the normal inflections and rhythms. Speech in Wernicke's aphasia sounds very good; the problem is that it contains little or no meaning.

Unlike the speech of Broca's area aphasics, the speech of Wernicke's area aphasics is dominated by grammatical connectives, pronouns, and abstract nouns having very general referents. Here is one example, again from Gardner. The patient is a 72-year-old retired butcher named Gorgan.

"What brings you to the Hospital?"

Figure 11.6. Carl Wernicke. Wernicke not only discovered the language area of the temporal lobe but also developed a general theory of the organization of language areas within the dominant left hemisphere. (Photograph courtesy of the History and Special Collections Division of the Louise M. Darling Biomedical Library, UCLA.)

"Boy, I'm sweating, I'm awful nervous, you know, once in a while I get caught up, I can't mention the tarripoi, a month ago, quite a little, I've done a lot well, I impose a lot, while, on the other hand, you know what I mean, I have to run around, look it over, trebbin and all that sort of stuff."

I attempted several times to break in, but was unable to do so against this relentless steady and rapid outflow. Finally, I put up my hand, rested it on Gorgan's shoulder, and was able to gain a moment's reprieve. "Thank you, Mr. Gorgan. I want to ask a few..."

"Oh sure, go ahead, any old think you want. If I could I would. Oh, I'm taking the word the wrong way to say, all of the barbers here whenever they stop you it's going around and around, if you known what I mean, that is typing and tying for repucer, repuceration, well we were trying the best that we could while another time it was with the beds over the same thing..." (Gardner, 1976, p. 68)

Gorgan's speech, like that of other Wernicke's aphasics, is full of words, is grammatically correct, but is remarkably devoid of meaning. Wernicke's aphasics express themselves similarly in writing. Curiously, these patients seem unaware of their failures to communicate with others.

Just as their speech means very little, they extract very little meaning from the speech of others; thus, Wernicke's aphasia is marked by a profound comprehension deficit. A simple command may sometimes be executed, but more complicated commands are usually not understood. Similar difficulties exist for the written language. Although retaining both phonemic and syntactic capabilities, the extraction of meaning at the level of semantics is severely compromised. For this reason, Wernicke's aphasics cannot function as social creatures; they are deprived of meaningful linguistic communication with any other person.

Global Aphasia

Global aphasia is the most debilitating form of aphasia (Kertesz, 1979). The syndrome of **global aphasia** results from massive damage to the language system of the dominant hemisphere. Although a variety of causes may produce global aphasia, the most common is a stroke or blockage of the middle cerebral artery of the left hemisphere, which provides blood to the language areas. All aspects of language function are lost. Such patients cannot speak or write; at most, they may produce a few meaningless words. They cannot read, nor can they comprehend spoken language.

Anomic Aphasia

As the name suggests, **anomic aphasia** is characterized only by difficulties in finding the appropriate word in speech. Here, Gardner is talking with Mr. MacArthur, an anomic aphasic.

> I asked Mr. MacArthur to name some common objects around the room. When I pointed to a clock, he responded, "Of course, I know that. It's the thing you use for counting, for telling time, you know, one of those, its a..."
>
> "But doesn't it have a specific name?"
>
> "Why, of course it does. I just can't think of it."
>
> When I indicated his elbow and asked him to name it, he responded, "That's the part of my body where, my hands and shoulders, no that's not it." At this point he grasped his elbow and rubbed it back and forth as if to evoke the name by some kind of magic. "No, Doctor, I just can't get it, isn't that terrible?" When I told him that the part of his body in question was an elbow, he repeated the word over and over again, saying, "It could be an elbow, I've heard that word before, but I just don't know." (Gardner, 1976, p. 76)

Anomic aphasia is the most common of all aphasic syndromes. Often, this word-finding difficulty results in speech that is excessively "wordy" with numerous connectives or grammatical words. Attempts at word substitution are frequent. Unlike Wernicke's aphasia, comprehension is relatively preserved. Unlike Broca's area aphasia, open-class content words are only sparsely present. This gives the speech of an anomic aphasic a characteristically vacuous quality. Similar difficulties also appear frequently in writing.

Anomic aphasia most often results from damage to the supramarginal or angular gyrus; it also may arise from other causes. Anomia is a common residual deficit following partial recovery from many more severe types of aphasia. In fact, anomic aphasia may be produced by damage to almost any part of the cortical language system and a number of other cortical areas as well (Kertesz, 1979).

Disconnection Syndromes

The four types of aphasia described above—Broca's aphasia, Wernicke's aphasia, global aphasia, and anomic aphasia—all result from the destruction of cortical tissue. But other types of aphasia also occur. In these aphasias, cortical tissue is not damaged. Rather, the fiber pathways linking different cortical regions are destroyed.

Such aphasias are termed **disconnection syndromes** because necessary connecting pathways are no longer present (Geschwind, 1970). A number of specific disconnection syndromes were predicted by Wernicke and have subsequently been demonstrated. One major disconnection syndrome is conduction aphasia.

Conduction Aphasia Wernicke reasoned that the language areas of the temporal lobe (Wernicke's area) and the frontal lobe (Broca's area) should be connected and that disruption of this connection should lead to a definite and predictable pattern of aphasia. Wernicke's conjecture has proved to be quite correct. The **arcuate fasciculus** is the band of association fibers in the white matter that links Wernicke's area with Broca's area. Disruption of this pathway results in conduction aphasia.

In patients with **conduction aphasia**, speech remains fluent and rhythmic because Broca's area is preserved. Similarly, these patients have little difficulty comprehending either the spoken or the written word because Wernicke's area remains intact. One problem in conduction aphasia is in producing meaningful speech; conduction aphasics make many errors of word usage.

In contrast to Wernicke's aphasic speech, errors are comprehended by the patient, who may stop and begin laboriously searching for the correct word. Such errors are most likely to occur for the meaningful words of the sentence, being less pronounced for filler words. This deficit is easily seen when patients are asked to repeat words that are spoken to them, a task at which they consistently fail.

Conduction aphasics behave as if they have lost the principal, high-speed, reliable pathway from Wernicke's to Broca's area. Instead, they must depend on slower, less reliable routes through the brain to transfer information between the language areas of the left cerebral hemisphere. The symptoms of conduction aphasia follow naturally from such a neurophysiological hypothesis.

Pure Word Blindness A second disconnection syndrome described by Wernicke is **pure word blindness**, a rare disorder in which patients cannot read or point to letters or words on command (Geschwind, 1970). Nevertheless, they speak normally, can understand what is said to them, and can repeat what is said. Although they can write from dictation, they cannot read what they have written.

Wernicke predicted that such a syndrome would occur if the language system were isolated from the visual cortex. That is, in fact, the case in pure word blindness. Most typically, the lesion destroys the left visual cortex and extends forward into the posterior region of the corpus callosum. It is the damage to the corpus callosum that prevents visual information originating in the intact right visual cortex from crossing into the left hemisphere and entering the language system. In other cases, the lesion is located deep in the white matter of the left parieto-occipital area. This lesion prevents information from either visual cortex from gaining access to the language cortex.

Pure Word Deafness   Pure word deafness is another disconnection syndrome predicted by Wernicke (Geschwind, 1970). In **pure word deafness**, there is a deficit of auditory comprehension and consequently an inability to repeat what is heard or to follow spoken commands. Patients with pure word deafness speak, read, and write normally. They often say that they cannot hear, but shouting does not help, and their hearing of nonlinguistic material is normal. The lesion in these patients is bilateral and occurs between the primary auditory cortex and the language system.

Transcortical Aphasia   Perhaps the most extreme of the disconnection syndromes is **transcortical aphasia** (Benson, 1985). Resulting from a lack of oxygen—often from carbon monoxide poisoning—transcortical aphasia is characterized by extensive destruction of the areas bordering the anterior, middle, and posterior cerebral arteries. Such damage isolates the language system, including Broca's area, Wernicke's area, and the arcuate fasciculus, together with the auditory and motor areas, from the remainder of the brain. Thus, the language system remains intact but unable to communicate with the rest of the brain.

These patients have fluent speech but have nothing to say. They cannot comprehend either spoken or written language. Their speech is empty and devoid of information; they cannot use language to convey thoughts and desires originating outside the language system. Patients with transcortical aphasia frequently echo word phrases or songs that they hear, much like a parrot that learns sounds without learning meaning.

Two milder types of transcortical aphasia are also well known (Benson, 1985). In **transcortical motor aphasia**, comprehension, in addition to repetition, is well preserved. However, verbal output is completely abolished, except when repeating. Correspondingly, reading may be normal, but writing skills will be severely disrupted. A patient with transcortical motor aphasia differs from a Broca's area aphasic primarily in the perfection with which repetition tests are performed. Typically, the disorder results from damage to the frontal lobe anterior or superior to Broca's area. As with mixed transcortical aphasia, the disorder is often the result of a cerebral stroke. Transcortical motor aphasia is much more common than aphasia of the mixed type.

Less common are cases of **transcortical sensory aphasia**. In transcortical sensory aphasia, patients show excellent repetition and fluent speech but with very limited comprehension of either spoken or written language. It is the presence of unimpaired repetition that distinguishes transcortical sensory aphasia from aphasia of the Wernicke's type. It has been suggested that this relatively rare aphasia results from lesions of the parietal-occipital junction within the dominant left hemisphere.

Recovery From Aphasia

Although aphasia can result from a number of very different causes, stroke and head trauma are the most common aphasia-producing disorders. Both stroke and head trauma trigger edema, cellular infiltration, and increased intracranial pressure. Such general disruptive consequences typically disappear in the first 2 or 3 weeks, resulting in a significant improvement in the aphasia.

After the general, nonspecific effects of the incident have dissipated, there exists a longer period of further recovery. Recovery is most accelerated in the initial few months, after which the rate of improvement lessens. After a year has passed, very little improvement is seen. Often, comprehension seems to recover more fully than fluency. The mechanisms mediating this return of language are unknown (Kertesz, 1979).

The amount of language function that will eventually return is related to both the type of aphasia and to its initial severity. Figure 11.7 on the facing page presents final outcome as a function of type of aphasia. Global and Wernicke's aphasics fare most poorly. Broca's aphasics recover significantly more satisfactorily than do Wernicke's patients. Those with disconnection syndromes and anomia have even better outcomes. As one might expect, within each category, the more severely aphasic individuals are more impaired in their language functions after recovery.

The question of how the brain reorganizes itself to allow language to return is an issue of fundamental importance. One possibility is that the undamaged nondominant cerebral hemisphere takes over for the damaged cortex. In those unusual instances when the entire dominant left hemisphere is removed, in a procedure called **hemispherectomy**, the right hemisphere must be the hemisphere in which language is relearned.

But the much more common case, when damage is limited to a portion of the dominant hemisphere, is for the dominant left hemisphere to reorganize itself. This may be demonstrated by use of the Wada test following recovery (Rasmussen & Milner, 1977).

Aphasia and Intelligence

The relationship between language and thought has been a longstanding problem for philosophers. Some, such as Plato, have argued that thought and language are inseparable, though being only "a conversation which the soul has with itself" (Kertesz, 1979). Others, such as George Berkeley, believed that thought is quite independent of language. Although a philosophical discussion is unlikely to be settled to a philosopher's satisfaction by scientific observation, a biologist may help clarify the role that language plays in thinking by examining the remaining cognitive processes in aphasic patients.

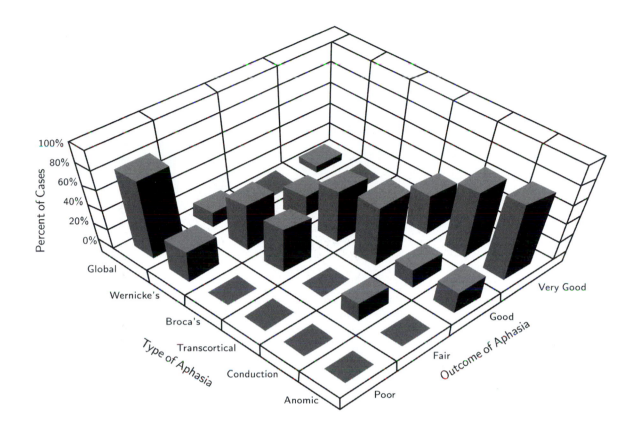

In many aphasics, such as Tan, there are ample indications of a continued intelligence accompanying the loss of language. The problem, however, is in measuring that intelligence because most intelligence tests are verbal tests. Any verbal measure of intellectual functioning would obviously be depressed in aphasic patients and therefore be an inaccurate indication of the patient's remaining intellectual abilities. For this reason, nonverbal intelligence tests provide the best hope of measuring cognitive function in aphasics.

One of the most widely used nonverbal tests of intelligence is *Raven's Colored Progressive Matrices (RCPM)*. RCPM is a test of logical reasoning and visual-spatial ability that requires no verbal skills for its performance. Most important, it correlates very well with standard measures of intelligence in non-brain-damaged individuals. One version of the test was designed to be administered to children and is exceptionally simple and straightforward, an advantage in testing brain-damaged patients.

Andrew Kertesz (1979) and his colleagues used the RCPM to evaluate the cognitive abilities of a large sample of aphasic patients. Their results are shown in Figure 11.8 on the next page. Global aphasics, not unexpectedly, performed most poorly on the test. Similarly, both transcortical

Figure 11.7. Final Outcome of Aphasia as a Function of Type.

Figure 11.8. Percentage of Normal Intelligence as Measured by Raven's Colored Progressive Matrices in Different Types of Aphasia.

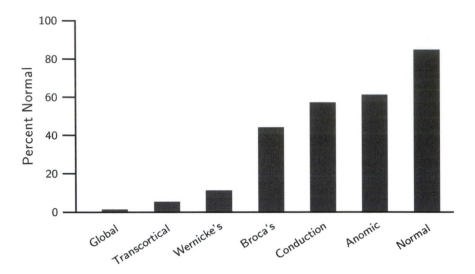

aphasics and Wernicke's aphasics also showed a severe impairment of intellectual function. All of these types of aphasia are characterized by a loss of comprehension of spoken and written language. Perhaps, then, it is not surprising that their performance on a nonverbal test of intelligence is compromised as well.

In contrast, patients with Broca's or conduction aphasia showed substantially improved performances. These scores are similar to those of control groups who had some brain damage but no aphasia; they are also nearer the mean performance of age-matched, non-brain-damaged individuals. Thus, in aphasics who have retained the capacity of language comprehension, the decline of intelligence, as measured by Raven's Colored Progressive Matrices, is far less severe.

Developmental Dyslexia

Aphasia is an *acquired* disorder, specifically a loss of language functions that had been normal. In contrast, *developmental* disorders—including developmental disorders of language—are abnormalities in the original acquisition of an ability or capacity.

Neuropsychologists use the term **developmental dyslexia** in reference to a wide range of disorders in which the normal process of learning to read is severely disrupted. (Pure word blindness may be considered an *acquired* dyslexia.) In developmental dyslexia, only reading is impaired; other cognitive functions are normal (Galaburda, 1993).

Dyslexic children usually exhibit a characteristic pattern of reading difficulties. They seem to have unusual problems in processing language at a phonemic level. These children have great difficulty in relating the characters of the written language with the speech sounds that the characters represent. Without such symbol-sound correspondences, reading becomes all but impossible. Interestingly, dyslexics have little trouble relating nonlinguistic symbols with the concepts that such symbols represent.

Such children also frequently show evidence of left-right confusion.

For example, they may begin writing an English sentence from the right, rather than the left, side of the page. Furthermore, characters that are distinguished only by left-right orientation, such as *d* or *b* or *p* or *q*, are often confused by these children.

Dyslexia is much more prevalent in boys than in girls; more than 80% of all dyslexic children are males. Furthermore, left-handed children are more prone to dyslexic difficulties than are right-handers.

The late Norman Geschwind, a neurologist who pioneered much of the modern study of brain lateralization and language, looked at the distribution of dyslexia and other disorders in a population of 1,400 individuals, of whom 500 were strongly left-handed and 900 were strongly right-handed (Geschwind & Behan, 1984). In this group, dyslexia and other developmental learning problems were 10 times more prevalent in left-handed than in right-handed individuals. Interestingly, there was also a marked increase in autoimmune diseases. These differences were much more common among males than females.

The fact that dyslexia is both sex linked and related to anomalous lateralization, as indicated by left-handedness, led Geschwind to suggest that both the handedness and the dyslexia might be dependent on a male neuroendocrinological factor, possibly testosterone, acting during the development of the nervous system.

There are also indications of cortical abnormalities in some dyslexic individuals. In an autopsy examination of the brains of five dyslexics, Galaburda reported striking abnormalities in the cellular architecture of the left hemisphere in the vicinity of the Sylvian fissure and the classical language areas of the left hemisphere. Specifically, Layer I (the molecular layer of the cortex), which usually contains few neurons and a mass of processes originating in deeper cortical layers, is marred by the presence of collections of inappropriately located nerve cells. There are also major distortions of the normal pattern of cell distribution in the deeper cortical layers. These malformations in the structure of the language cortex could result from injury occurring in the last stages of neural migration during the development of the cortex in about the 6th month of gestation. These abnormalities may provide a neuroanatomical basis for at least some types of developmental dyslexia (Galaburda, 1993).

Stuttering

Another type of language dysfunction is **stuttering**. Stuttering is a disorder in the motor control of the respiratory and facial muscles that results in abnormal pauses and repetitions in the production of speech (Adams, Victor, & Ropper, 1997). The result makes vocal expression choppy and sometimes very difficult.

A **stutter**—the prolonged repetition of a phoneme—typically occurs at the beginning rather than at the end of a word. For example, in attempting to pronounce the word *soup*, a stutterer might say "s– s– s– soup" instead. Although it might seem that the problem is one of terminating the production of the phonemes, it is now believed that the difficulty is actually in the production of the remaining phonemes. The repetition of the stuttered phoneme may simply reflect an attempt to maintain speech until the rest of the word can be produced.

About 1 of every 100 hundred people stutter. Although much remains to be learned about the factors governing this speech difficulty, stuttering does appear to be partially genetically determined and sex linked. A genetic factor is indicated by the observation that stuttering is more common among identical twins of stutterers than among fraternal twins. A sex-linked component may be involved because stuttering, like dyslexia, is more common in males than in females.

It has been suggested that stuttering results from a failure to develop normal language dominance. As a result, both hemispheres might simultaneously issue conflicting commands to the vocal musculature, resulting in stuttering (Bloodstone, 1995). It also has been proposed that stuttering is the consequence of motor hyperactivity, either in the premotor cortex or the basal ganglia (Caruso, 1991).

Finally, there are indications that at least some forms of stuttering may result from abnormalities of the auditory system. First, normal individuals will stutter when listening to their own speech if it is slightly delayed electronically. This indicates that abnormal auditory input is sufficient to induce stuttering. Second, stutterers frequently are able to speak normally when the sound of their voice is masked by loud broadband noise or when chorus reading (reading aloud with a group). This evidence argues that auditory factors must be considered in any understanding of the biological basis of stuttering.

New insight into the neurobiology of stuttering has come from functional brain imaging to assess differences in the patterns of brain activation produced in normal and stuttered speech that lends some support to each of these diverse hypotheses. Fox and his collaborators (Fox et al., 1996) used positron-emission tomography (PET) scanning to measure local cerebral blood flow in a group of 10 men who were chronic stutterers and 10 linguistically normal right-handed men, who served as controls. Fox compared chorus reading and reading aloud alone in the stutterers. Chorus reading induced fluency in the stutterers; not 1 of the 10 stutterers stuttered once in three periods of chorus reading in which brain activity was measured. In contrast, all stutterers stuttered in solo reading. No one in the normal control group stuttered while reading aloud.

The normal controls showed a pattern of brain activation similar to that occurring in single-word reading. With the exception of the visual areas and the cerebellum, which showed bilateral involvement, all brain regions activated by reading aloud were lateralized to the left hemisphere. These regions included the primary motor cortex for the mouth, the supplementary motor area, Broca's area, and the anterior secondary auditory cortex of the temporal lobe.

In sharp contrast, the stutterers showed a distinctly abnormal pattern of brain activation when reading alone. Compared with the normal controls, activation of the primary motor cortex was right, not left, lateralized. Furthermore, the supplementary motor area was far more activated in the stutterers reading alone than it was in the controls. This region also showed right-hemisphere enhancement. Finally, a number of other motor regions, such as the superior premotor cortex and parts of the basal ganglia, were also hyperactive during stuttering.

Deactivations, relative to either baseline or the controls, also occurred in stuttering. These included cortex in the vicinity of both Broca's and Wernicke's areas of the dominant left hemisphere, regions that have been proposed to constitute a system for monitoring verbal fluency in the normal human brain (Friston, Frith, Liddle, & Frackowiak, 1991).

Chorus reading markedly reduced all these abnormal patterns of brain activation, with the exception of the abnormal lateralized response of both the primary motor cortex and also the supplemental motor area.

This pattern of results indicates a widespread pattern of cerebral dysfunction in producing stuttered speech. There is clear evidence of abnormal hemispheric lateralization, as well as hyperactivation of the forebrain motor systems and deactivation of the normal left-hemisphere verbal fluency system. Stuttering, therefore, must be the result of large-scale alterations in the organization of the cerebral neural systems that produce normal human speech with such apparent ease.

HEMISPHERIC ASYMMETRIES

Examination of an extraordinary group of neurological patients not only has confirmed the specialized role that the left hemisphere plays in language but has offered some insights concerning the specialized functions of the right hemisphere as well. These are the so-called *split-brain* patients, a small number of individuals suffering from intractable epilepsy in whom the right and the left cerebral hemispheres were surgically disconnected from each other, a procedure known as **commissurotomy**.

The most widely studied commissurotomies were those performed by Joseph Bogen in Los Angeles. In this procedure, the corpus callosum, the anterior commissure, the hippocampal commissure, and the massa intermedia were all lesioned. The **corpus callosum** is the massive bridge of reciprocal pathways, composed of more than 200 million fibers, that links corresponding regions of the two cerebral hemispheres. The **anterior commissure** is a smaller bundle of fibers linking portions of the right and left temporal lobes. The **hippocampal commissure** is an even smaller pathway joining the two hippocampi. Finally, the **massa intermedia** is a collection of cell bodies in the medial thalamus that is only occasionally present in humans. These structures constitute all possible pathways by which the two cerebral hemispheres may communicate directly with each other.

In the 1960s, Bogen performed commissurotomies on 16 epileptic individuals, all of whom were reported to have benefited from the surgery. In most of this group, preexisting asymmetric brain damage and other complications made a detailed examination of the separate functions of the two hemispheres impossible. However, studies of a few of these patients by Roger Sperry and his students have provided important clues concerning cerebral cognitive asymmetries. Sperry received the Nobel Prize in 1981 for this and other work.

Effects of Commissurotomy   The most striking observation about commissurotomy patients is that, superficially, they appear to be unaffected by the surgery (Gazzaniga, 1970; Sperry, 1974). It is often said that after a year's recovery in the absence of complications, a person may easily go through a routine medical checkup without revealing that anything was particularly wrong; speech, verbal intelligence and reasoning, calculation, motor control, temperament, and personality are all retained, despite the absence of interhemispheric connections.

However, a closer analysis reveals the true effects of the surgery. Such analyses require that each hemisphere be tested separately, which is possible because of the lateralized organization of vision, touch, and motor control. This is shown in Figure 11.9 on the facing page.

Because the fibers of the temporal and nasal portions of the retina cross and project to opposite sides of the brain, any object that is present in the left visual field is relayed to the right cerebral hemisphere, and any object that is present in the right visual field is relayed to the left cerebral hemisphere. The right and left **visual fields** are those portions of the visual world to the right and left of the point of fixation. Normally, information from the two visual fields is integrated by fibers of the corpus callosum, but in split-brain patients, such integration is impossible. Each hemisphere receives information from the contralateral, but not the ipsilateral, visual field.

Similarly, each hemisphere receives touch information from the contralateral half of the body and controls the movements of the contralateral arm and leg. Restricting information to one visual field and requiring a response from each hand separately allows the cognitive capacities of each isolated cerebral hemisphere to be measured.

In the months following surgery, both of the hemispheres showed evidence of cognitive processes. Either hemisphere could point to an object shown in the appropriate visual field, using the hand that it controls, for example. Thus, each hemisphere could recognize objects that were visually presented to it.

The left hemisphere, which in all patients was dominant for language prior to surgery, retained its linguistic competence. Following surgery, the left hemisphere was easily able to name any object that was presented in the right visual field, for example. All significant linguistic functions performed by these patients were mediated by the left-hemisphere language system.

The question of right-hemisphere language is more complicated. In most of the patients, the right hemisphere appeared to completely fail any verbal test, but a few patients showed some evidence of right-hemisphere language processing. For example, some were able to use the left hand to follow simple verbal commands. This provides evidence of minimal linguistic processing within the right cerebral hemisphere because it is the right hemisphere alone that controls the movements of the left hand. Furthermore, a few patients were able to use the left hand to pick out objects that were verbally described, again an indication of right-brain language. Finally, in some cases, the right hemisphere was able to read the names of objects that were presented to the left visual field and use that information to direct the left hand to the appropriate object.

However, such evidence of right-hemisphere language function must be taken with caution. All of the split-brain patients have had a long history of cerebral epileptic pathology, a situation that may well have led to an abnormal reorganization of language functions within the cerebral

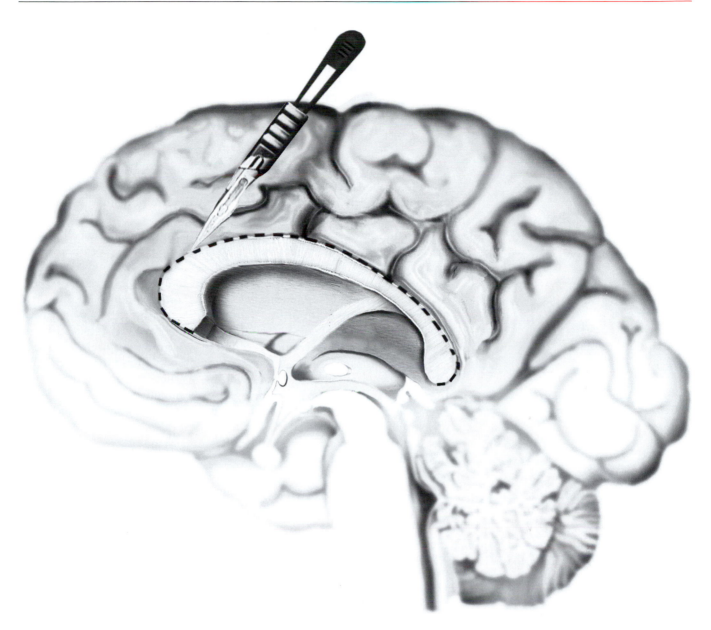

hemispheres. Furthermore, it should be emphasized that even within this small and variable group of patients, only a few individuals showed any evidence whatsoever of right-hemisphere language. Therefore, these results may not be relevant to understanding the language functions of the right hemisphere in normal individuals.

Although the right hemisphere may be deficient in its linguistic capabilities, it demonstrates clear superiority in other areas, particularly in visual-spatial skills. For example, it is the left hand, not the right, that is superior in drawing or copying figures after commissurotomy. Furthermore, in solving jigsawlike puzzles, the left hand (right brain) is generally

Figure 11.9. Commissurotomy Separates the Two Cerebral Hemispheres. In commissurotomized individuals, it is possible to obtain a unique glimpse of the behavioral capacities of each hemisphere in relative isolation.

quick and accurate, whereas the right hand (left brain) is slow and confused. The right hemisphere is also generally superior to the left in tasks requiring mental translations between two- and three-dimensional representations of simple geometric objects. This and other evidence gives rise to the idea that the right hemisphere is specialized for some type of visual-spatial information processing, but the exact nature of such right-hemisphere functions remains a mystery.

Cerebral Asymmetry   The functional specialization of the human cerebral hemispheres, particularly the specialization of the left hemisphere for language, appears to result from genetically determined anatomical asymmetries in the structure of the cerebral hemispheres.

The first clear evidence of significant anatomical difference between the hemispheres that might provide the physical basis of cerebral dominance was reported by Geschwind and Levitsky in 1968, who dissected and measured portions of the left and right temporal lobes from 100 human brains. Their results indicated that the anterior portions of the two temporal lobes are more or less symmetrical, but the region posterior to the primary auditory cortex (Heschl's gyrus) showed a statistical hemispheric asymmetry. This region is called the **planum temporale** and forms a part of Wernicke's area. Geschwind and Levitsky found that the planum temporale was usually larger in the left hemisphere (65 brains) than in the right (11 brains, the remainder being approximately equal in size). However, Geschwind and Levitsky had to rely on dissections to make their measurements, a procedure that may seem to be exact and precise but in fact is difficult and error prone when it comes to making estimates of cortical volumes.

Today, quantitative estimates of the sizes of structures may be made much more easily and precisely using three-dimensional magnetic resonance imaging. For example, in a recent study, Foundas and her collaborators (1994) used three-dimensional magnetic resonance imaging (MRI) to measure the volume of the planum temporale in 12 people (11 right-handers and 1 person with mixed handedness), whose cerebral lateralization for language had been previously established by the Wada test. The 11 right-handed people were all left-dominant by the Wada test. In these left-dominant people, the planum temporale was uniformly larger in the left hemisphere than in the right. In the lone non-right-hander, language was lateralized to the right hemisphere. In that person, the right planum temporale was in fact larger than its counterpart in the left hemisphere.

The findings of both Geschwind and Foundas provide strong evidence for the existence of an anatomical asymmetry in Wernicke's area that corresponds with the functional phenomenon of cerebral dominance for language.

Foundas then measured a portion of Broca's area, using these same 12 people (Foundas, Leonard, Gilmore, Fennell, & Heilman, 1996). The **pars triangularis** is a region of Broca's area in the frontal lobe of the left cerebral hemisphere that is bounded by three easily identifiable cortical structures: the inferior frontal sulcus, the anterior horizontal ramus (a small sulcus), and the anterior ascending ramus. Because of its sharp anatomical demarcation, the pars triangularis makes an excellent target for quantitative neuroanatomical measurement.

As with the planum temporale, the 11 people who had left-language dominance also had a larger pars triangularis in the left hemisphere than in the right. The one right-dominant individual showed the reversed pattern of pars triangularis size, being larger in the right than in the left.

Thus, there are at least subportions of both Wernicke's and Broca's area that show anatomical asymmetries that match precisely the behavioral language dominance of the individual. Although it is conceivable that such anatomical differences could be acquired through patterns of learned language usage, it seems more likely that they instead represent a predisposing anatomical factor for the establishment of functional cerebral laterality during human language development.

BRAIN ACTIVATION IN COGNITION

More direct approaches relating cognitive and linguistic function to the anatomy of the human brain are now becoming available by using either PET or functional MRI. These technologies are capable of measuring various aspects of local or regional cerebral blood flow (rCBF) with a high degree of anatomical and temporal resolution.

The reason that the rate of regional cerebral blood flow is of interest is that cerebral blood flow is directly regulated by the rate of information-processing activity of cortical neurons. By measuring rCBF, it is possible to discover which populations of neurons are activated by a particular cognitive task. This is because when neurons process information, they increase their firing rate and rate of neurotransmitter release, which places increased demands on the metabolic activity of the cell. In turn, increased metabolic activity increases the cellular production of carbon dioxide and heightens the cells' demand for oxygen. Both factors act directly to increase local cerebral blood flow to meet the needs of the activated cells.

At present, most PET measurements of rCBF are obtained by injecting ^{15}O-labeled water to be mapped by the PET system. By this method, the state of regional cortical activation for a period of some tens of seconds can be measured. Recently developed functional magnetic resonance imaging (fMRI) methods for measuring rCBF provide much finer temporal resolution if cortical activation changes.

Processing Single Words

Cognitive neuroscientists have used these advanced methods to chart the landscape of language and thought across the human cerebral cortex. In one of the very first studies, Petersen, Fox, Posner, Mintun, and Raichle (1988) measured rCBF to study the processing of singly presented words in the human brain. Needless to say, the processing of words must activate the brain at many levels. An auditorily presented word will activate not only components of the language system but also the relevant portions of the auditory system. Similarly, visually presented words will activate both the visual and language systems. If the words are to be spoken, the motor systems of the brain also will be activated.

To cut through the complexity of these multiple functions that must overlap in time, an experimental approach called the *subtractive method* is employed. In the subtractive method, each person is tested in a series of experimental conditions, which differ from each other by the presence or absence of a particular step of mental processing. If the conditions are chosen correctly, it is possible to isolate the cortical regions that contribute to the mental processes of interest.

The Petersen experiment provides a clear example of the use of the subtractive method to localize specific regions of the cerebral cortex activated during both auditory and visual language processing.

1. In the control state, subjects simply stared at a fixation point in the distance, providing an estimate of *brain activation under unstimulated conditions*.

2. Then, single words were presented either auditorily or visually, but the subject was not required to make any response. This condition added the factors of *sensory input* and *involuntary word processing* to the baseline condition.

3. Next, the person was required to speak, reading visually presented words or repeating auditorily presented words. This level added *output coding* and *speech production* to the demands of the previous level.

4. Finally, the person was required to speak each of the presented words. These conditions required *semantic processing* of the presented information.

When the baseline conditions were subtracted from the passive auditory and visual word presentation conditions, only the primary and secondary sensory regions were activated. These areas were completely separate for the two modalities. Visual presentation activated the primary visual cortex and a small number of higher-level visual areas with the occipital lobe. During auditory presentation, the primary auditory cortex was activated bilaterally, as were the temporoparietal, anterior superior temporal, and inferior anterior cingulate cortex of the left (dominant) hemisphere. Lesions in these areas have been associated with phonological deficits.

When speaking the presented word is required, cortical regions involved in articulatory coding and motor output are also activated. Unlike the passive presentation conditions, in which completely different cortical regions were activated for auditory and visual presentation, the addition of speech activated similar cortical regions for both sensory modalities. These regions were the primary sensory-motor cortex controlling the respiratory apparatus and mouth, the premotor cortex and supplementary motor area, and regions near Broca's area. Regions corresponding to Broca's area of the right cerebral hemisphere also increased in rCBF. However, this bilateral activation also occurred when subjects were instructed to simply move their mouths and tongues, an indication that the bilateral involvement was not specifically related to language processing.

When required to give a use for the presented words, two regions showed increased rCBF in both auditory and visual presentation. One was the left inferior frontal cortex. The second region was the anterior cingulate gyrus, an area known to be involved in attentional selection of action. Additional lines of evidence suggested that only the left frontal cortex was involved in semantic processing of the presented words (Petersen, Fox, Posner, Mintun, & Raichle, 1988).

These results have interesting implications. One finding is that none of the visually presented words activated the cortex in the vicinity of Wernicke's area. This suggests that in reading, the visual system has direct access to the phonemic output system of the left frontal cortex. A second finding of importance is that semantic processing activates the left frontal, rather than left temporal, cortex. These results add a new dimension of insight into the theories of language representation in the brain based on the study of brain-damaged patients.

Processing Words in Two Languages

Most children learn a single language, that spoken by others in the environment in which they are raised. It is reasonable to assume that our brains are crafted by evolutionary processes to learn the one language quickly and completely.

But what happens when circumstances permit the learning of multiple languages? Various possibilities exist. There may be a single language system within the brain that is used by all languages that an individual may know, as was suggested by Wilder Penfield, among others (Penfield & Roberts, 1966). Another possibility is that different languages may be processed by partially unique but partially overlapping regions of the cortical regions (Ojemann, 1983). Finally, it could be the case that any second languages uses fundamentally different brain regions than are used to speak the first language. Obviously, these three hypotheses cannot all be correct, but it has been difficult to choose between these alternatives on the basis of solid experimental evidence.

Functional brain imaging studies have provided new insights into the neurobiology of bilingualism. Klein and his coworkers at McGill University in Montreal studied volunteers who were bilingual, with English as their first language (Klein, Zatorre, Milner, Meyer, & Evans, 1994; Klein, Milner, Zatorre, Meyer, & Evans, 1995). They all learned their second language, French, after age 5, an age at which their primary language acquisition was firmly established.

In the first experiment (Klein, Zatorre, Milner, Meyer, & Evans, 1994), the bilingual volunteers were asked to repeat words presented in either their first or their second language, as local brain blood flow was measured with positron-emission tomography. In the second experiment (Klein, Milner, Zatorre, Meyer, & Evans, 1995), subjects were required either to provide a synonym for the word in the language in which it was presented or to translate a word from one language to the other.

The same pattern of cortical activation was observed under all conditions for both first and second languages. Klein found that processing auditorily presented words activated a number of structures in the frontal, parietal, and temporal areas of the dominant left hemisphere, primarily in Broca's area, Wernicke's area, and surrounding cortical regions. The activity of cortical areas in the right hemisphere was not affected. These results were in full accord with Petersen's previous findings (Petersen, Fox, Posner, Mintun, & Raichle, 1988).

Most important, Klein found that both first and second languages invoked the identical set of cortical structures when repeating words, giving synonyms, or producing translations. This result provides strong evidence favoring the idea that a single cortical language system is employed, no matter what specific language is being used. All of the world's languages, therefore, appear to share a common neural substrate.

There was, however, one significant difference in subcortical activation between speaking in the first and second languages. The second language always activated the left putamen, a part of the basal ganglia that plays a major role in the execution of complex movements. Thus, the systematic activation of the left putamen in second-language speech seems to indicate that extra motor control is required when speaking in a language learned later in life, a fact that is easily appreciated by anyone learning to communicate in a language that is not one's mother tongue.

Interestingly, lesions limited to the putamen have been reported to produce a disruption of the normal articulation of spoken language (Blumstein, Alexander, Ryalls, Katz, & Sworetzky, 1995; Gurd, Bessell, Bladon, & Bamford, 1988). The result is that speech in the native tongue no longer sounds as if it were produced by a native speaker but rather by a person who has acquired the language later in life. This condition, called **foreign accent syndrome**, suggests that the putamen plays an important role in automatically generating speech in an individual's native language.

Phonetic and Pitch Discrimination

Zatorre and his colleagues (Zatorre, Evans, Meyer, & Gjedde, 1992) used a similar approach to study the cortical regions involved when different types of judgments are to be made about the same auditory stimuli. Here the question is whether different brain regions will be activated when stimuli need to be classified on the basis of linguistic and nonlinguistic features. The critical stimuli were consonant-vowel-consonant real speech syllables. For each pair, the center vowels were always different. In half of the pairs, the final consonants were the same (e.g., *bag-big*), and in half they were different (e.g., *fat-tid*). In addition, the second syllable was higher in pitch than the first in half the trials and lower in the remainder. Thus, the second syllable could be the same as or different from the first in its final consonant and higher or lower than the first in pitch.

There is some evidence from the study of brain lesions that phonetic and pitch discrimination judgments rely on different neural mechanisms. To test this proposition and to map those cortical mechanisms, regional cerebral blood flow was measured in 10 volunteers using ^{15}O-labeled water under five experimental conditions. In the control state, rCBF was measured as the subject sat in a silent room. In the second condition, the subject listened to paired noise bursts and depressed a key for every other pair of noises. This condition was designed to activate the primary auditory cortex and the neural systems controlling motor responses. A third condition tested passive speech perception. Here, syllable pairs were presented,

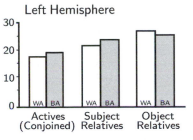

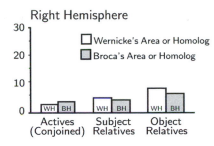

Mean Number of Voxels Activated

Figure 11.10. Brain Activation in Processing Sentences of Differing Complexity. Voxels are small 3-dimensional cubes that form a volume brain image. By counting the number of voxels activated in a particular condition, one can estimate the extent of brain activation that resulted.

and the subject was required to depress a key for every other syllable pair.

The two critical conditions were the judgment tasks. In the *phonetic judgment condition*, the subject depressed the key whenever both members of a syllable pair ended with the same consonant. In the *pitch discrimination condition*, the subject depressed the key whenever the second syllable was higher in pitch than the first.

In comparing the noise with the silence condition, bilateral activation of the primary auditory cortex was observed. There was also activation of the hand area of the left sensory-motor cortex and the right cerebellum, both patterns that are consistent with right-hand key pressing.

In subtracting the noise condition from passive speech, higher auditory regions of the superior temporal gyrus of both hemispheres were observed. This may well reflect the increased complexity of the three-phoneme syllables as compared with noise bursts. In addition, there were unilateral left-hemisphere peaks of activation in both the temporal lobe and the inferior frontal lobe, regions that were previously associated with linguistic processing.

When passive speech was subtracted from the phonetic judgment condition, activation was largely limited to the left hemisphere. Increased blood flow was seen in Broca's area, the superior left parietal cortex, and the left cingulate gyrus. In contrast, when passive speech was subtracted from the pitch discrimination condition, two large regions of activation were seen in the right prefrontal cortex. Because the stimuli presented in the phonetic and pitch discrimination conditions were identical, the differences observed in these conditions must reflect fundamental differences in the neural mechanisms that are used to make phonemic and acoustic judgments. This pattern of findings indicates that different cortical mechanisms mediate phonetic and pitch discrimination.

Comprehending Sentences

Understanding human language requires more than phonemic processing. Phoneme sequences are concatenated into morphemes and words, which in turn are joined by the syntactic grammar into phrases, clauses, and sentences. The sentences that result vary in the complexity of their syntactic structures and, as a result, impose differing work loads on the nervous system as they are spoken or comprehended (Just & Carpenter, 1992, 1993).

To examine the effects of syntactic complexity on cortical activation during sentence processing, Just, Carpenter, Keller, Eddy, and Thulborn (1996) presented subjects with three types of nine-word sentences that differ from each other only in syntactic complexity. The simplest of these were active conjoined sentences containing no embedded clause (e.g., *The reporter attacked the senator and admitted the error*). Next most difficult were sentences containing a subject-relative clause, such as, *The reported that attacked the senator admitted the error*. Most difficult were sentences with an object-relative clause, such as, *The reporter that the senator attacked admitted the error*. These seemingly simple manipulations of syntactic structure that increase sentence complexity result in both systematic increases in comprehension errors as well as increases in autonomic measures of demands for attentional processes (Beatty, 1982). Brain activation was measured using functional magnetic resonance imaging as sentences of each type were presented. The particular method employed provided excellent resolution of both the left and right lateral surfaces of the brain, including Wernicke's and Broca's areas in the left hemisphere and the corresponding cortical tissue in the right.

To assess comprehension, subjects were required to make simple judgments to statements about these sentences (e.g., *The reporter attacked the senator, true or false?*). Both error and reaction time analyses confirmed the expected effects of syntactic complexity on sentence comprehension.

The functional mapping data indicated clearly the sentence comprehensive task. Figure 11.10 on the page before shows the extent of cortical activation produced by the three different types of sentences in Broca's area, Wernicke's area, and the two corresponding regions of the right hemisphere. Not unexpectedly, Broca's and Wernicke's areas were both activated by the sentence comprehension task. What is striking is the finding that the extent of this activation increases with increasing syntactic complexity of the sentence structure.

In the right hemisphere, activation is very much less pronounced, but the homologous right-hemisphere structures do exhibit increased neuronal activity during sentence processing. Furthermore, the amount of right-hemispheric involvement also grows as syntactic complexity increases. This may reflect the recruitment of additional cortical resources when the language system of the left cerebral hemisphere is required to process more complicated linguistic material.

Locating the Lexicon

To most of us, a lexicon is just another word for a dictionary, but to a linguist, the word has a special, technical meaning. The **lexicon** of a person is the total stock of morphemes available to that individual.

Where and how those morphemes are stored are a matter of some interest in cognitive neuroscience. Over the past decade, there has been increasing evidence in the neuropsychological literature of brain damage producing selective impairments in specific categories of semantic knowledge. For example, Warrington and McCarthy (1987) presented the case of a patient suffering from a global aphasic disorder, who had much more difficulty in naming foods or living things than in naming manmade objects. Even within the category of objects, there were differences in lexical access. She had much more difficulty naming small objects than large ones. She also was much better at naming proper nouns with a unique referent than common proper nouns (see also McCarthy & Warrington, 1994). This sort of pattern of selective memory deficit leads to the perhaps surprising idea that our brain's lexicon may be categorized in ways that are not completely obvious to us.

A new pair of experimental studies has been presented recently by Damasio and her colleagues (Damasio, Grabowski, Tranel, Hichwa, & Damasio, 1996) that clarify our understanding of the distributed neural representation of the human semantic lexicon. In these two studies, Damasio examined both the patterns of lexical memory impairment shown by patients with restricted cortical lesions and the patterns of brain activation shown by normal individuals in accessing different types of lexical items. Words representing three distinct conceptual categories—unique persons, nonunique animals, and nonunique tools—were tested.

In the first study, 127 patients with single, focal brain lesions were tested. These lesions were located in all regions of both hemispheres of the cerebral cortex. The site of these lesions was mapped in three dimensions using either magnetic resonance or computerized tomography scans.

Each subject was shown a series of 327 pictures that they were requested to name. One third of these depicted well-known people, whom the patients were to uniquely name. The remaining photographs were divided evenly between pictures of animals and pictures of common tools. The patients were requested to give a nonunique common noun name for these photographs.

Most of these patients named all the photographs as well as did a group of normal controls. But of the 30 who showed naming error, 29 had damage within the left cerebral hemisphere. These individuals were then separated into groups reflecting the kinds of items that they had difficulty in recalling. The brain scans for individuals in each group were then combined, as shown in Figure 11.11 on the following page. Difficulty with recalling the names of individual persons was correlated with damage to the left temporal pole, the most anterior portion of the left temporal lobe. Difficulty with naming animals resulted from more posterior lesions of the anterior inferotemporal cortex. Finally, tool-naming deficits were associated with damage to the posterolateral inferotemporal cortex, near the junction of the temporal, occipital, and parietal lobes. None of the subjects who showed normal recall had lesions in any of these regions. Each of these regions in which damage produced deficits in lexical access is located in the cortex adjacent to the classically defined language areas of the dominant left cerebral hemisphere.

Damassio's second study differed radically in its approach but reached the very same conclusions concerning the distributed localization of the lexicon within the dominant left hemisphere. She presented the same three tasks to normal volunteers and used positron-emission tomography to measure the patterns of brain activation elicited by the three types of pictures. Taken together, the brain lesion and the imaging data provide strong support that the neural systems serving word memory are segregated into reasonably distinct regions within the dominant left hemisphere

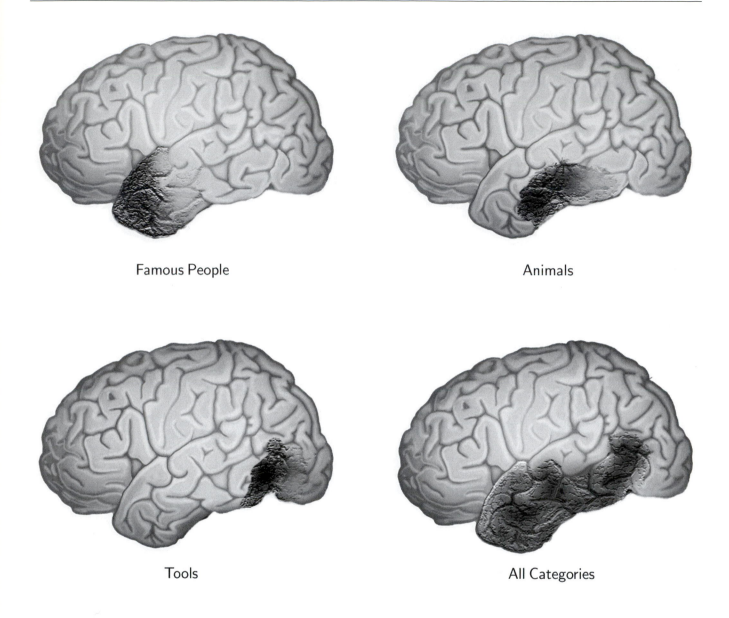

Figure 11.11. Brain Regions Damaged in Individuals With Selective Word Memory Losses.

of the human brain. Our neural lexicons appear to be sorted and stored by category.

Impact of Neuroimaging on Cognitive Neuroscience   All of these results are exciting because they extend the analysis of the functional neuroanatomy of a wide variety of higher-level mental functions far beyond the information that can be gleaned from the analysis of brain-damaged patients. These experiments—and others yet to be performed—will form the basis of a much more detailed and sophisticated view of human cognition.

SUMMARY

Language is a hierarchically organized system of communication that permits humans to exchange complex information. It is propositional in character and well suited to refer to events that are displaced in both space and time. There are four levels of language organization: the phonemic, morphological, syntactic, and semantic systems, each with its own set of units and rules or grammars.

In most individuals, the left cerebral hemisphere is dominant for language. Within the left hemisphere, two regions—Broca's and Wernicke's areas—are particularly important for language. Damage to Broca's area produces a disruption of both phonemic and syntactic processing. Damage of Wernicke's area disrupts semantic processing and results in severe deficits of comprehension. Disconnection syndromes result from damage to the pathways linking Broca's and Wernicke's areas with each other and with the auditory and visual systems.

The classical picture of the cortical organization of language and cognitive processing is based on correlational studies of brain damage and behavior in neurological patients. Recently, functional imaging techniques such as positron-emission tomography and functional magnetic resonance imaging permit the detailed study of the pattern of cortical activation in normal individuals performing complex cognitive tasks. These higher functions include processing single words, bilingual speech, phonemic and nonphonemic discrimination, sentence comprehension, and lexical access. Such investigations open new and exciting opportunities in the study of brain, language, and cognition.

SELECTED READINGS

- Crystal, D. (1997). *The Cambridge encyclopedia of language* (2nd ed.). Cambridge, UK: Cambridge University Press. A lucid and comprehensive treatment of all aspects of human language.

- Pinker, S. (1994). *The language instinct: How the mind creates language.* New York: Morrow. An influential and highly readable analysis of human language from the perspective of Chomskian linguistics and contemporary neurobiology.

- Springer, S. P., & Deutsch, G. (1998). *Left brain, right brain* (5th ed.). New York: Freeman. The current edition of what is now the standard text on hemispheric differences in human cognition.

KEY TERMS

anomic aphasia An aphasic disorder marked only by difficulties in finding the appropriate word in speech or writing.

anterior commissure A commissural pathway linking portions of the right and left temporal lobes.

aphasia A loss of language function.

arcuate fasciculus A fiber pathway within the left hemisphere that connects Wernicke's and Broca's areas.

bilateral symmetry In anatomy, the similar appearance of corresponding structures on the right and the left; in physiology, the similar function of corresponding structures on the right and the left.

Broca's aphasia An aphasia resulting from damage to Broca's area that is characterized by both phonemic and syntactic difficulties.

Broca's area The region of the inferior third convolution of the left frontal lobe.

categorical perception With respect to language, the conscious perception of the spoken phoneme rather than the acoustical properties of the spoken phone.

cerebral dominance With respect to language, the hemisphere containing the neuronal circuitry necessary for language function.

closed-class words The function words in a language, such as pronouns, prepositions, and conjunctions, which are not continually expanded by speakers of the language.

commissurotomy The surgical destruction of the commissural pathways linking the left and right cerebral hemispheres.

conduction aphasia An aphasia resulting from damage to the arcuate fasciculus that is characterized in part by an inability to repeat spoken material.

corpus callosum The arched mass of transverse commissural fibers connecting most regions of the right and left cerebral hemispheres.

developmental dyslexia A family of disorders that disrupts the normal process of learning to read.

disconnection syndrome With respect to language, an aphasia resulting from damage to pathways connecting Wernicke's and Broca's areas with each other or with other regions of the cortex.

displaced reference A reference to things that are not in the immediate environment.

foreign accent syndrome A rare neuropsychological syndrome in which aspects of fine motor control of speech output are disrupted, resulting in speech of a native language that is like that of a nonfluent foreign speaker.

global aphasia A severe aphasia in which little or no language function is preserved.

hemispherectomy The removal of one cerebral hemisphere.

hierarchical organization Having a multilevel organization of control.

hippocampal commissure A bundle of fibers connecting the right and left hippocampi.

lexicon The total stock of morphemes available to an individual.

massa intermedia A midline thalamic structure that is sometimes present in humans.

mixed dominance With respect to language, the situation in which each hemisphere contains the neuronal machinery necessary for language function.

morphemes The smallest meaningful units of speech: root words, prefixes, and suffixes.

morphemic grammar The rules of language pertaining to morphemes.

open-class words The content words of the language, consisting of nouns, verbs, adverbs, and adjectives, which are limitless and constantly growing.

pars triangularis A portion of Broca's area.

phonemes The smallest unit of speech used to distinguish different utterances in a particular language.

phonemic grammar The rules of language pertaining to phonemes.

planum temporale The region of the superior surface of the temporal lobe that is immediately posterior to Heschl's gyrus; a portion of Wernicke's area.

productive With respect to language, capable of conveying new information that has never been previously expressed.

pure word blindness A disconnection syndrome resulting in the selective inability to read.

pure word deafness A disconnection syndrome resulting in the selective inability to comprehend spoken language.

semantic grammar The rules of language pertaining to meaning.

stutter The prolonged repetition of a phoneme.

stuttering A disorder of motor control of the respiratory and facial muscles that results in abnormal pauses and repetitions in the production of speech.

syntactic grammar The rules of language pertaining to the construction of phrases and sentences.

telegraphic With respect to speech, omitting the grammatical words that change strings of nouns into sentences.

transcortical aphasia A disconnection syndrome in which the language areas of the left hemisphere, together with the auditory and motor cortex, are separated from the rest of the brain.

transcortical motor aphasia An aphasic disorder in which both comprehension and repetition are preserved in the absence of spontaneous speech or writing.

transcortical sensory aphasia An aphasic disorder in which repetition and fluent spontaneous speech and writing are preserved in the almost complete absence of comprehension.

visual fields The portion of the environment that may be seen without altering fixation; often divided into left and right visual fields.

vocal cords The muscular valve of the larynx that is responsible for voiced speech.

Wada test A procedure for determining cerebral dominance involving the injection of sodium amytal into the right or left carotid artery.

Wernicke's aphasia An aphasia produced by damage to Wernicke's area that is characterized by a loss of comprehension of both spoken and written language.

Wernicke's area The region of the superior temporal cortex of the left hemisphere posterior to the auditory cortex.

Chapter 12

Learning, Memory, and Brain Plasticity

All organisms—including humans—prosper by adapting to their environments. We change our behavior as a result of our experience. With new experiences, we learn; that is, changes take place within our nervous systems as a function of our experiences.

By common definition, **learning** is the storage of information as a function of experience, resulting in a relatively permanent change in behavior (at some level). The faithful partner of learning is **memory**, the stored information produced by learning. Finally, **encoding** is the placing of new information into memory, whereas **retrieval** is the accessing of that information at some later time. These are terms familiar to every psychologist and behavioral neuroscientist.

Physiologists and functional anatomists often use the term **plasticity** in describing these and similar phenomena, often at the cellular level. Thus, people talk about *cortical plasticity* when describing the effects of altered experience on physiologically measured cortical cell properties or *synaptic plasticity* when studying the efficacy of particular synapses as a function of physiological manipulations.

TYPES OF MEMORY

Learning, memory, and neuronal plasticity are broad terms that are useful in the general discussion of biological adaptation. But it would be a mistake to believe that each of these terms refers to a single biological entity because they do not. Each day of our lives, we depend on a number of different types of memories with very different properties. Children riding bicycles, for example, need spatial memory to find their way, motor skill memory to control the bicycles, verbal memory to converse with each other, and, of course, very much more. Two points are clear: Virtually every aspect of our everyday lives involves memories of some sort, and these different kinds of memory differ qualitatively from each other. But of all these differences, one of the most fundamental distinctions is between short-term and long-term memories.

Short-Term and Long-Term Memory

It is **short-term memory (STM)**, also called **working memory**, that stores a limited amount of information for short periods of time, usually no more than a few seconds. Short-term memory defines the time of the conscious present because material retained in working memory seems to be a part of the present and not part of the past. It is this working, short-term memory that provides the continuity of our mental life. It enables us to envision the future and recall the past.

Thus, short-term memory temporarily holds information for use in such basic cognitive activities as comprehending, reasoning, and problem solving (Eichenbaum et al., 1999). People have proposed that this system is composed of three elements. The first is a limited-capacity workspace or executive controller, which is supported by two subsystems. This first is the **phonological loop**, which holds verbal information for short periods that may be extended by rehearsal or conscious repetition.

The capacity of the phonological loop is severely restricted, limited to about six or seven items under most conditions. Although information usually disappears from working memory within a few seconds, some items may be retained for extended periods by active rehearsal. We all do this from time to time, for example, when trying to retain a telephone number while dialing.

The second is the **visuospatial sketchpad**, which holds visually encoded spatial information in an analogous manner. Other subsystems may well exist, but these two are certainly of major importance and have formed the twin foci of research in working memory for the past few decades.

In contrast, **long-term memory (LTM)** is the memory of the past. Unlike short-term memory, LTM appears to have no limit to its capacity. Everything that is remembered and everything that could possibly be remembered must be stored in LTM. LTM is very robust; memories of the past survive despite periods of unconsciousness, anesthesia, or coma. For this reason, LTM is probably produced by structural changes within the nervous system and does not depend on dynamic patterns of interactions being actively maintained by a group of neurons. Since structural changes are likely to involve the construction of new proteins, protein synthesis and the processes that control it must provide the chemical basis of LTM. The physical trace that stores memory information is referred to as the **engram**; **consolidation** is the process of constructing an engram. The distinction between working short-term memory and long-term memory has been useful in the biological study of memory processes. Factors that influence LTM appear to be relatively independent of those affecting working memory.

Declarative and Nondeclarative Memory

Another important distinction between types of human memory is that between declarative and nondeclarative memory. The term **declarative memory** (or **explicit memory**) refers to those things that one can bring to mind and declare (describe in words). In contrast, **nondeclarative memory** (or **implicit memory**) is the type of memory we use for things that cannot be declared or explained in any straightforward fashion, such as the skill of bicycle riding.

Declarative memories themselves may be divided into two subtypes. The first is **semantic declarative memory**, which is meaning related. Thus, semantic declarative memory is the memory of general facts, concepts, and knowledge: the fact that the Eiffel Tower is in Paris, the knowledge that Parisians speak French, not English, and so on, are all examples of semantic memories. Semantic memory is not linked to any particular time or place but instead constitutes a body of *general* knowledge. Semantic memory is the memory of *knowing*.

The second type of declarative memory is **episodic memory**, which is the personal memory for events in one's past: what one had for breakfast this morning, last year's birthday party, and so on. Thus, episodic memory is infused with the sense of self, which it defines as a personal history. Episodic memory is the memory of *remembering*.

But whether concerned with general knowledge or personal history, the essence of declarative memory is that of knowing *what*. In this sense, all declarative memories seem to form a biological meaningful class and are probably produced by a single complex brain system (Squire, 1994).

Psychologists use the term **nondeclarative memory** to refer to everything else, that is, all memories that are *not* declarative memories. As we might expect, nondeclarative memories are not all of the same sort, nor are they even all products of a single brain system (Squire & Kandel, 1999). There are many different types of nondeclarative human memory, none of which can be described in words.

One familiar type of nondeclarative memory results from skill learning, that is, learning *how* rather than learning *what*. It is a common experience that attempting to verbalize a learned skill is often not only difficult, but it also may actually impair skilled performance. Skills may be primarily motoric (as in riding a bicycle), perceptual (as in acquiring perfect pitch), or cognitive (as in learning how to memorize lists).

TYPES OF LEARNING

Sensitization, habituation, and conditioning are other types of nondeclarative memory that may be studied in a wide variety of species. Habituation is the simplest form of **nonassociative** nondeclarative learning. (If learning a relation between two stimuli or between a stimulus and behavior is required, learning is said to be *associative*; if only a single stimulus—or environmental event—is involved, the learning is considered *nonassociative learning*.)

Nonassociative Learning

Habituation   In **habituation**, an organism learns over repeated presentations to ignore a weak or nonnoxious stimulus that is neither rewarded nor punished. Habituation results in a decrease in the vigor or probability of the naturally occurring behavioral response to that stimulus. We all experience this form of nonassociative learning when frequently occurring nonnoxious stimuli—such as household noises—cease to attract attention. As a general rule, weaker stimuli habituate more rapidly than stronger stimuli. But if any habituated stimulus has not been presented for a sufficiently long time, habituation will dissipate, and the response will return with its initial strength.

Sensitization   Sensitization is another form of nonassociative nondeclarative or implicit learning. In **sensitization**, an organism learns to increase the vigor of a response after exposure to a noxious or threatening stimulus. A truly noxious stimulus, such as an earthquake, sensitizes us to any weak environmental vibration or noise, as Californians can attest. In general, the stronger the stimulus, the more pronounced its sensitizing effects will be. Sensitization can completely reverse habituation, a phenomenon known as **dishabituation**. After the earthquake, even occasional household noise elicits a startle, even though such noise is unrelated to the sensitizing event.

Associative Learning

Associative learning provides animals with a means of learning about regularities, which are indicative of causal relationships in the world in which they live (Rescorla, 1988). Humans—like other species—appear to construct some kind of mental representation of the world's causal structure that guides our behavior. These representations appear to be continually adjusted on the basis of experience in a never-ending series of refinements (Beggs et al., 1999). Thus, associative learning provides the basis for behavioral adaptation by providing increasingly accurate internal representations of causal relationships in the external environment. Classical and instrumental conditioning are two simple forms of associative learning.

Classical Conditioning   Unlike habituation and sensitization, **classical conditioning** involves learning specific relations between environmental stimuli and thus is associative. As in sensitization, the response of one sensory-motor pathway is increased by activity in another; unlike sensitization, that enhancement is not widespread but rather is selectively limited to responses with which it is temporally paired.

Classical conditioning was originally used as an experimental procedure by Ivan Pavlov. Pavlov, who studied the digestive system, noticed that his experimental dogs began to salivate at the sight of a food dish and had the insight to ask whether they might give a similar response to any other stimulus that was systematically associated with feeding. He answered this question by ringing a bell just before feeding his animals and discovered that they quickly learned to salivate whenever the bell rang. The once-meaningless bell had become a dinner bell for Pavlov's dogs.

Thus, classical conditioning involves the pairing of an initially innocuous stimulus—the *conditioned stimulus* (CS)—with a second stimulus—the *unconditioned stimulus* (UCS)—that elicits a natural response from the animal, the *unconditioned response* (UCR). After training, the CS is able to elicit a *conditioned response* (CR) that is similar in many respects to the UCR.

In the well-known example of Pavlov's dogs (Pavlov, 1960), the conditioned stimulus was a bell, a stimulus that elicited no obvious behavioral responses before conditioning. The unconditioned stimulus was chosen for precisely the opposite reason: It always evoked a behavioral response, perhaps innately. When food was presented as a UCS, the dog would salivate, in which case salivation was the unconditioned response. When that UCS was systematically preceded by the innocuous CS, the CS would begin to elicit salivation by itself, an example of a conditioned response.

A critical aspect of classical conditioning is that human subjects, like Pavlov's dogs, cannot control the occurrence of either the conditioned or the unconditioned stimulus, which is completely determined by the experimenter. It is the experimenter, not the subject, who establishes the relationship between the two stimuli (Beggs et al., 1999).

Operant Conditioning   In contrast, **operant conditioning** is a form of nondeclarative associative learning in which the strength or probability of a particular response depends on the effect of that response on the environment. The learned relation is between the motor act and its consequences. Perhaps the best-known example of operant conditioning is the laboratory rat that presses a response lever to receive food pellets in its cage. Operant conditioning, also called **instrumental conditioning**, has been a very powerful tool in the study of brain reinforcement systems.

MEMORY LOSS

Simply put, **amnesia** is the loss of long-term declarative memory. Often a consequence of brain damage, amnesia may be just one component in a general pattern of disturbed mental functions. However, amnesia sometimes occurs in relatively pure forms—a loss of memory of past events with little evidence of other cognitive impairment. Although many amnestic individuals have difficulties with permanent or long-term memory, their short-term memory may be normal. Such amnestic patients can retain information for extended periods only by continuous attention and verbal rehearsal, but once attention is diverted, the contents of the short-term memory appear to be completely and irretrievably lost.

Amnesia may be present for events either preceding or following brain trauma. In **anterograde amnesia**, the patient is unable to recall events occurring after the onset of the brain damage, but memory for earlier events is preserved. In **retrograde amnesia**, memories are lost for events that occurred before the onset of the amnestic episode, but recall for subsequent experiences may be relatively undisturbed. However, in many actual cases of amnesia, both anterograde and retrograde disturbances are present.

Amnesia may result from a variety of causes. Head trauma with concussion is perhaps the most frequent source of amnesia, often resulting in a transient memory disturbance. Brain lesions may also produce amnesia, and, in some cases, studies of patients with specific restricted lesions have revealed much concerning the neuroanatomy of normal memory. Amnesia also is a distinguishing feature of **Korsakoff's syndrome**, which is described below.

Amnestic patients with restricted brain lesions provide a unique opportunity to study the biological basis of human memory because rather small lesions in particular regions of the brain are sufficient to produce a profound loss of memory. Much larger lesions elsewhere have little effect on memory. Thus, critical elements of the human memory system appear to be anatomically restricted.

Amnesia: The Case of H. M.

The first clear evidence linking human memory to neural structures in the region of the temporal lobes came from the study of patients in whom temporal lobe structures had been surgically removed. The most famous such case was H. M., an assembly-line worker suffering from intractable epilepsy.

H. M. entered the Montreal Neurological Institute in 1953, a patient of the neurosurgeon William Scoville (Milner, Corkin, & Teuber, 1968). To relieve his condition, the mesial portions of both the right and left temporal lobes were surgically removed. Figure 12.1 on the next page illustrates the extent of this operation. The operation involved the anterior 8 cm of the temporal lobes, bilaterally destroying two thirds of the hippocampus and all of the amygdala; only the lateral portions of the temporal lobes were spared. This procedure had a markedly beneficial effect on H. M.'s seizures. However, it had a disastrous effect on H. M.'s memory, resulting in both a mild retrograde amnesia and a profound and continuous antero-

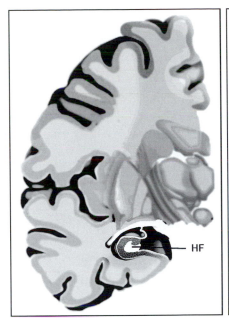

Figure 12.1. The Area Surgically Removed in Patient H. M. The left panel shows a drawing of a coronal section of one normal human brain for purposes of illustration; HF indicates the position of the normal hippocampal formation. The right panel shows the corresponding section (mirror image) through H. M.'s brain, with the hippocampus and adjacent structures removed. Since H. M.'s lesion was bilateral, the hippocampus was removed from *both* hemispheres.

grade amnesia lasting three decades, from which H. M. has never recovered. From that time on, H. M. has been unable to form new memories, although he can recall events preceding the surgery with ease.

With the striking exception of his amnesia, H. M. shows no intellectual impairment. He has retained an above-normal level of intelligence and a fully adequate working memory. Furthermore, nondeclarative learning—such as acquiring new motor skills—was not impaired: He was able to learn a mirror-tracing task over a 3-day period, although each day he reported never having tried the task before. But because of his inability to form permanent declarative memories, H. M. lives in a ceaseless present, devoid of any past. This absence of personal history remains troublesome for H. M. He expresses his problem this way:

> Right now, I'm wondering. Have I done or said anything amiss? You see, at this moment everything looks clear to me, but what happened just before? That's what worries me. It's like waking from a dream; I just don't remember. (Milner, 1970, p. 37)

Since H. M.'s unfortunate surgery, much attention has been paid to the question of which particular structures within the temporal region are responsible for temporal lobe amnesia. One potential candidate is the hippocampus, a long, winding ridge of primitive cortical neural tissue lying along the floor of the lateral ventricle. The word *hippocampus* means *seahorse*, which it physically resembles (see Figure 12.2 on the following page).

The hippocampus does appear to play a major role in establishing declarative memories. This conclusion rests not only on the study of memory loss in nonhuman primates but also on the study of very special cases of amnesia in humans.

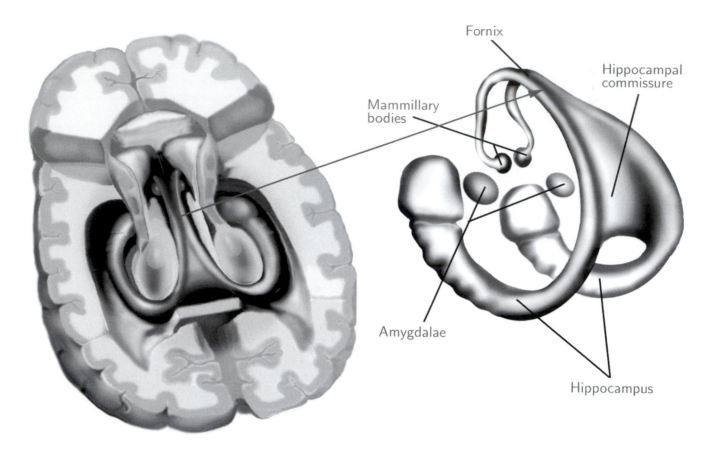

Figure 12.2. The Hippocampus and Surrounding Structures.

Squire and his colleagues report the case of R. B., who developed amnesia in 1978 as the result of cortical blood insufficiency following open-heart surgery (Squire, 1992; Zola-Morgan, Squire, & Amaral, 1986). The result of this reduction of blood supply to the brain was the complete destruction of both the right and the left hippocampus, as confirmed by autopsy in 1983. Similar findings have been obtained with four other patients using magnetic resonance imaging to determine the extent of the lesion. The most important finding from all of these cases is that the amnesia that was observed, although profound, was not nearly as massive as that displayed by H. M., whose amnesia resulted from the loss not only of the hippocampus but of other temporal lobe structures as well. There is now considerable evidence that these secondary structures are regions of the temporal cortex that are connected to the hippocampus, such as the entorhinal, perirhinal, and parahippocampal cortex (Squire, 1992, 1994).

The study of neurological patients such as H. M. has made it clear that permanent memory does not reside in the hippocampus and related structures. Rather, these regions serve as a temporary repository for newly learned information that will later be stored in other cortical regions. The hippocampus and its adjacent tissues hold information during the process of memory consolidation elsewhere.

Korsakoff's Syndrome

Structures in the diencephalon beneath the cerebral hemispheres are a second anatomical focus in the study of amnesia. The importance of diencephalic areas for memory was first made clear to clinical neurologists in examining patients with Korsakoff's syndrome.

Korsakoff's syndrome is a disorder found in severely alcoholic patients as a consequence of secondary nutritional deficiencies. However, other precipitating factors, such as head trauma, can elicit the syndrome. The syndrome is marked by both anterograde and retrograde amnesia; patients with Korsakoff's syndrome can neither recall information that was well learned before the onset of the amnesia nor learn new information. However, cognitive functions that place only minor demands on memory show little impairment. Korsakoff patients understand both written and spoken language and are capable of solving problems that can be held within STM. However, Korsakoff patients appear to be rather dull, showing little initiative and spontaneity in their behavior, and often fabricate complex and improbable stories in response to questioning, perhaps in an attempt to deal with a lost memory.

An example of a conversation between a Korsakoff patient named John O'Donnell and a neuropsychologist, Howard Gardner, which took place some years ago, reveals the essence of this disorder:

> "How are you?" I asked the pleasant-looking, forty-five-year-old man who was seated quietly in the corridor, thumbing through a magazine.
>
> "Can't complain, Doctor," he retorted immediately...
>
> "Tell me, have you seen me before?" (I had been talking with him nearly every day for two months.)
>
> "Sure, I've seen you around. Not sure where, though..."
>
> "How's your memory been?"
>
> "*Comme ci, comme ça*," he said. "O.K. for a man of my age, I guess."
>
> "How old are you?"
>
> "I was born in 1927."
>
> "Which makes you?"
>
> "Let's see, Doctor, how I always forget, the year is ..."
>
> "The year is what?"
>
> "Oh, I must be thirty-four, thirty-five, what's the difference..." He grinned sheepishly.
>
> "You'll soon be forty-six, Mr. O'Donnell, the year is 1973."
>
> Mr. O'Donnell looked momentarily surprised, started to protest, and said, "Sure, you must be right, Doctor. How silly of me. I'm forty-five, that's right, I guess." (Gardner, 1976, pp. 177-178)

In contrast to the loss of long-term declarative memory, nondeclarative memory is relatively unaffected in Korsakoff's syndrome. Korsakoff patients can learn to perform a motor pursuit task as easily as normal individuals. The motor pursuit task is a commonly used measure of nondeclarative learning. It involves tracking a moving target with a pointer and requires that hand-eye coordination appropriate to that test be learned.

Anatomically, Korsakoff's syndrome in alcoholic patients is accompanied by symmetrical brain lesions of the walls of the third and fourth ventricles, destruction to regions of the cerebellum, and some cortical atrophy or shrinkage. However, the most critical damage with respect to the amnesia of Korsakoff's syndrome appears to be in the dorsal medial thalamus and/or mammillary bodies, both structures that are associated with amnesia in other types of patients. In alcoholic patients, these lesions are the consequence of a prolonged Vitamin B1 (thiamine) deficiency.

Traditionally, attention has been paid to the diencephalon because the mammillary bodies are often damaged in patients with Korsakoff's syndrome. However, the damage to the diencephalon in Korsakoff's syndrome is normally not restricted to the mammillary bodies but rather is widespread. Furthermore, the diencephalic amnesia can occur in cases in which the mammillary bodies remain intact (Squire, 1987).

Thalamic Amnesia: Patient N. A.

Our knowledge of diencephalic memory has been expanded substantially by the study of one patient, N. A., in whom a discrete diencephalic lesion produced profound amnesia. N. A. was a 22-year-old U.S. airman in 1960, when he was injured in a fencing accident. In a mock duel with another airman, a miniature foil entered his right nostril in a leftward direction and punctured the base of his brain (Squire, 1987). Figure 12.3 on the next page shows the resulting brain lesion. The only significant brain damage revealed in this computerized X ray is limited to the left dorsomedial nucleus of the thalamus. The temporal lobes and hippocampus were unaffected by the accident.

As a result of this injury, N. A. shows an incapacitating anterograde amnesia, which is most severe for verbally presented material. Memory for visual images is less impaired. This selective loss of linguistic memory is not too surprising because in most individuals, it is the left hemisphere and left thalamus that play particularly important roles in language perception and production. N. A.'s marked lack of verbal memory stands in sharp contrast to his otherwise superior intelligence; his most recent overall score on a standard IQ test was 124, for example. The case of N. A. is particularly interesting because the size of the brain lesion is very small, yet its selective effect on memory is very large.

For N. A., learning new declarative information is difficult, but not impossible, as it is for H. M. However, once new information has been learned, N. A. does not forget the new learning any more quickly than do normal individuals. This pattern of impaired learning with normal forgetting also is seen in patients with Korsakoff's syndrome and in N. A. Such results indicate that the dorsomedial thalamus contributes in some manner to the encoding of declarative memories but is not an essential component for their retrieval.

In sharp contrast to the loss of long-term declarative memory in diencephalic amnesia, long-term nondeclarative memory is unaffected. For example, N. A. was able to learn to read words that are mirror reversed, an example of a learned nondeclarative perceptual skill. His performance improved with each day of practice, and this newly learned skill was retained

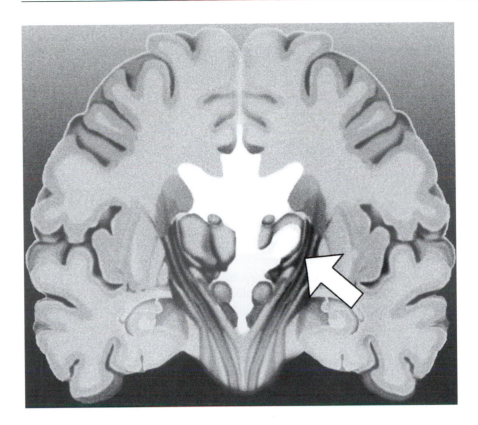

Figure 12.3. N. A.'s Lesion. The lesion, produced by a toy sword, is indicated by the arrow.

at normal levels for at least 3 months. Despite acquiring this perceptual skill through long hours of practice, N. A. had no declarative memory of any of the words that he read session after session.

Nondeclarative Memory Loss

Cases such as H. M. and N. A., in which declarative memory is virtually destroyed while nondeclarative memory is preserved, argue that declarative and nondeclarative memories depend on different brain systems. However, other explanations could also account for such findings. For example, it may simply be the case that nondeclarative memory is simpler and more robust than declarative memory and thus is less affected by damage to the hypothetical brain memory system. However, if it could be shown that lesions in a different region of the brain selectively impair only nondeclarative memory and spare declarative memory, the idea that the two types of human memory have different biological bases would be strengthened substantially. Such a finding is called a *double dissociation* and is important evidence for disentangling the neural basis of human cognition (Shallice, 1988; Teuber, 1955).

Double dissociation for human declarative and nondeclarative memory has been reported by Knowlton, Mangels, and Squire (1996). Knowlton and her colleagues used an ingenious probability learning task as a measure of one kind of human nondeclarative learning. Subjects were required to learn associations between a set of four visual cues and two pos-

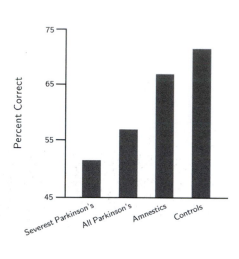

Figure 12.4. Nondeclarative Learning in the Weather Prediction Test.

sible outcomes, presented as a game in which the subject learns to predict the weather, which every weatherman knows is an exercise in probabilities and guessing.

Subjects were shown one, two, or three of the cards on each trial and asked to make a prediction of rain or shine based on what they had seen. Each card was more predictive of one outcome (sunshine or rain) than the other, but these relations were only probabilistic. Thus, there was no simple deterministic relation between cues and outcomes that the subjects could memorize. Instead, they had to learn to estimate the probabilities associated with each of the cards if they were to improve their guessing accuracy. People did learn to make increasingly accurate predictions from these fallible cues.

Because subjects are not aware of the specific information that they were learning, this task is by definition a type of nondeclarative learning, more like learning a habit than learning a fact.

Subjects also were questioned about details of the experiment after the probability learning task was completed. Performance on this test of factual knowledge provided a measure of declarative memory in these same subjects.

Using these procedures, Knowlton et al. (1996) tested two different groups of neurological patients that were chosen on the basis of previous studies of memory in laboratory animals. These animal studies had demonstrated that the hippocampus and related structures are involved in spatial learning in rodents—which is similar in many ways to declarative learning in humans—but that habit learning—which is like human nondeclarative learning—is not affected by hippocampal lesions in these animals. Instead, habit learning is affected by lesions of the dorsal striatum, the structure formed by the caudate nucleus and the putamen (Graybiel, 1995).

With these laboratory findings as a guide, Knowlton compared declarative and nondeclarative memory in amnestic patients (with hippocampal, temporal, or diencephalic lesions) and in patients with Parkinson's disease (which produces a profound disruption of neostriatal functioning). In Parkinson's disease, there is neuronal degeneration of the substantia nigra that disrupts the caudate and putamen by eliminating one of the major inputs to these neostriatal structures.

Knowlton results were striking. Both the amnestic patients and a group of matched normal controls learned the task equally well. By the end of 50 training trials, both groups were making predictions with about 70% accuracy. (Chance performance is 50% accuracy in this task because the outcomes of sun and rain were equally likely.) In sharp contrast, the parkinsonian patients learned very little, as is shown in Figure 12.4. In fact, a subgroup of these patients with the most advanced parkinsonism learned nothing whatsoever in the probability task. These findings form the first part of a double dissociation between human declarative and nondeclarative memory.

The second part of the dissociation is given by the performance of these patients on the declarative memory task, their answers to questions about the weather prediction test after training was completed. These data are shown in Figure 12.5 on the next page. All patients with Parkinson's disease remembered just as much about the conditioning procedure as did the normal controls despite the fact that the controls learned the task and the parkinsonians did not. In contrast, the amnestic patients recalled virtually nothing about the conditioning procedure, despite the fact that they learned to predict sunshine or rain every bit as well as the neurologically normal control subjects.

This double dissociation is strong evidence of the separation of declarative and at least one type of nondeclarative memory in the human central nervous system. It indicates that the limbic-diencephalic regions and the neostriatum support separate and parallel learning systems that are used by human beings in acquiring different kinds of knowledge about the world in which we live.

Thus, it seems clear that different forms of human memory depend on different sets of brain regions. For declarative human memory, the primary structures involved lie within the limbic and diencephalic areas of the brain. In contrast, a number of different brain areas support the various forms of nondeclarative memory.

All available evidence suggests that the physical changes in neurons that maintain memory occur in the region of the synapse. For short-term memories, synaptic alterations may be fleeting, but for permanent memory, such changes must be extraordinarily stable and robust.

Long-term alterations in neuronal structures without doubt arise from protein synthesis. It is likely that the proteins responsible for long-term memory arise from gene expression and protein synthesis at synapses. It is very unlikely that information can be retained for prolonged periods by sustained neural activity, that is, by actively repeating patterns of neural discharge. Rather, long-term memory must result from alterations in neuronal structure that can withstand such insults as coma and seizure. After all, neither surgical anesthesia nor epileptic convulsion erases our permanent memory of facts, events, or learned skills.

One approach to studying the basis of memory at the level of the cell is to examine simple nervous systems in which individual neurons or groups of neurons can be identified and examined. The study of simple nervous systems has proved to be a fruitful approach to learning about the synaptic events that underlie neural plasticity and memory.

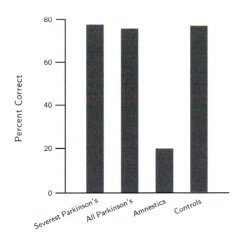

Figure 12.5. Declarative Recall of the Weather Prediction Test.

CELLULAR BASIS OF SIMPLE LEARNING

Striking advances in understanding the biological basis of learning and memory have been made in the past few years by examining the simpler nervous systems of invertebrates. Not only are the nervous systems of these organisms composed of fewer neurons than are vertebrate nervous systems (something on the order of 10,000 to 100,000 cells in contrast to 1,000,000,000,000 for large vertebrates), but the neurons of invertebrates are much larger as well. These two facts combine to make it possible to identify corresponding individual large neurons from animal to animal. Thus, neuronal circuit analysis may be undertaken, permitting a true cellular understanding of the way in which specific neuronal events are involved in controlling specific behaviors of the animal. Furthermore, advanced invertebrates are capable of several forms of learning. These find-

Figure 12.6. The Gill and Siphon Withdrawal Reflex of Aplysia.

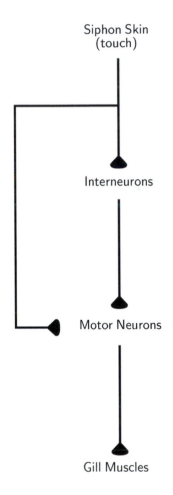

Figure 12.7. The Neuronal Circuits Mediating the Gill Withdrawal Reflex. There are about two dozen sensory receptors in the siphon, but only one is shown here. These cells project to about half a dozen motor cells that control the gill. The sensory neurons also provide excitatory input to the interneurons, which in turn innervate the motor neurons.

ings permit both electrophysiological and biochemical investigations of the cellular basis of learning and memory. One interesting example of this approach may be found in the work of Eric Kandel and his colleagues (Kandel, 1991a).

Aplysia is the Latin name for the sea slug, or sea hare, an invertebrate that has been the subject of extensive neurophysiological investigation. Its nervous system contains about 20,000 nerve cells. This marine mollusk has a large exposed gill and siphon, which are reflexively controlled. The gill is used for obtaining oxygen from the water, as is the gill of a fish. The siphon is a small spout above the gill that is used to eject seawater and waste. If the siphon or the mantle shelf that covers it is lightly touched, the animal defensively retracts both the gill and the siphon, protecting these delicate organs from harm. This unconditioned reflex is illustrated in Figure 12.6.

The neuronal circuitry mediating the defensive gill response is now almost completely understood. The controlling circuit consists of 13 central motor cells and 30 peripheral motor cells. These peripheral motor neurons project directly to the muscles that produce the reflex movement. The central motor neurons receive input from about 48 sensory neurons located in the gill and siphon. In addition to the sensory and motor cells, there are several interneurons, which modulate the reflex. Excitatory input from the sensory neurons to both the motor neurons and the interneurons initiates the reflex. Some of these interneurons are excitatory, and others are inhibitory. Figure 12.7 gives the circuit diagram for this system.

The strength of the defensive response may be modified by three types of nonassociative learning: habituation, sensitization, and classical conditioning. In this neural system, it is possible to investigate each element of the circuit to determine where learned changes are effected.

Habituation

In Aplysia, habituation of the gill response may be seen when the siphon is repeatedly touched; the initially vigorous reflex habituates and becomes weaker and weaker. This habituation has been shown to result from a reduction in the amount of neurotransmitter released at the synapses between the siphon sensory neurons and the motor neurons of the gill and siphon, as well as the interneurons. The habituation of the gill reflex is shown in Figure 12.8 on the facing page.

The depression of synaptic output from the sensory neurons, in turn, appears to be mediated by a decrease in calcium influx at the end-feet of

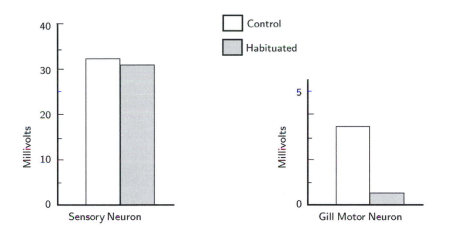

Figure 12.8. Habituation of the Gill Withdrawal Reflex. In an untrained (control) animal (left), stimulation elicits a response from the sensory neuron and a vigorous response from the gill motor neurons. After habituation (right), the sensory neuron response remains as strong, but the gill motor neuron response has nearly disappeared.

the sensory neurons that normally occurs with each action potential. In Aplysia, as in other systems, calcium modulates the release of neurotransmitters. Lowering the level of intracellular calcium reduces the number of packets of transmitter that are released by an action potential, whereas increasing intracellular calcium has the opposite effect.

The duration of habituation depends on the amount of stimulation provided. The effects of a single short (10 stimulations) training period lasts for several minutes before the reflex returns to its normal vigor. However, with multiple training sessions, habituation may be observed for several weeks.

Sensitization

In Aplysia, sensitization may be demonstrated after presenting a noxious sensitizing stimulus to the tail of the animal; after such a stimulus, defensive gill reflexes are enhanced, as are a range of other defensive responses in the animal's behavioral repertoire. Following presentation of several noxious stimuli, this increased responsiveness may continue for a period of hours. However, if many stimuli are presented, sensitization may be observed for many days.

The neuronal mechanism mediating sensitization of the gill reflex, like the site of habituation, is at the synapses between the sensory neurons and their target cells. Sensitization results from an increased release of neurotransmitter at these synapses that is produced by a complex series of cellular events. Noxious stimulation of the tail activates a group of facilitator neurons that synapse on the end-feet of the sensory neurons and act to increase the amount of neurotransmitter released by these end-feet through a process of presynaptic facilitation (see Figure 12.9 on the next page). One of the transmitters released by the facilitator neurons and taken up by the end-feet of the sensory neurons is serotonin.

The uptake of serotonin within the end-feet of the sensory cells initiates a series of molecular events within those end-feet that result in increased neurotransmitter release in the circuit mediating the gill reflex. Serotonin probably activates the enzyme adenylate cyclase in the end-feet of the sen-

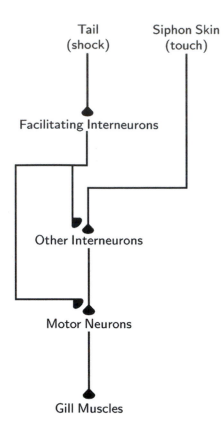

Figure 12.9. Neural Mechanisms Mediating Sensitization of the Gill Withdrawal Reflex. When a noxious stimulus is applied to the tail, sensory neurons there are activated that synapse on facilitating interneurons. These facilitators release serotonin on presynaptic end-feet at both the interneurons and motor neurons, which enhances the release of excitatory neurotransmitter by these neurons.

sory neurons. Adenylate cyclase increases the level of free cyclic adenosine monophosphate (cAMP) within the end-feet. Elevation of cAMP, in turn, activates a second enzyme, a protein kinase. This kinase appears to close a number of potassium channels within the membrane of the end-foot by means of protein phosphorylation.

The closure of some potassium channels reduces the number of channels that may be opened in the recovery phase of an action potential and thereby elongates subsequent action potentials arriving at that end-foot of the sensory neuron. These elongated action potentials permit increased amounts of calcium to enter the neuron during the period of the action potential. By increasing intracellular calcium, the release of neurotransmitter by the end-foot is facilitated. Thus, through a cascade of molecular events within the end-foot of a sensory neuron, the release of serotonin by a facilitator neuron results in sensitization of the gill reflex.

Classical Conditioning

In Aplysia, classical conditioning may be demonstrated by applying a strong shock to the tail (the unconditioned stimulus) about one half second following a weak stimulus to the siphon (the conditioned stimulus). To obtain conditioning, the CS must precede delivery of the UCS. Before such pairing, the CS alone elicits a weak defensive response; following conditioning, the response to the CS is vigorous. That this learned response is selective may be demonstrated by testing the effects of two CSs, one a weak shock to the siphon and the other a similar shock to the mantle shelf. When one of these CSs is paired with a UCS and the other is not, the response to the paired stimulus is much more vigorous than the response to the unpaired stimulus. This demonstration constitutes evidence for classical conditioning.

The cellular basis for classical conditioning in Aplysia is an elaboration of the mechanism of sensitization, presynaptic facilitation at the sensory neuron end-foot (see Figure 12.10 on the facing page). In some way, the temporal pairing of the UCS with the CS produces facilitation that is selective to that pathway. One possibility is that the discharge of serotonin by the facilitator cells affects the release of cyclic AMP by adenylate cyclase, resulting in an increase in the amount of intracellular calcium available during the action potential of the sensory neuron. However, this hypothesis has yet to be experimentally verified.

Studies of both associative and nonassociative learning in Aplysia have a number of implications for understanding the biological basis of learning and memory more generally. They suggest that learning is not the product of a diffuse brain system but rather results from alterations of membrane properties and synaptic activities in specific nerve cells. Modulation of the amount of neurotransmitter released by individual end-feet may be an important mechanism in other types of learning and in a variety of species. Similarly, molecular mechanisms involving cyclic nucleotides as second messengers and the modulation of specific ion channels may provide the fundamental basis of behavioral plasticity in general.

It seems likely that the short-term changes observed in the sensitization of the Aplysia's withdrawal reflex flow naturally into long-term changes.

A single sensitizing trial produces a memory lasting several hours; 16 such trials spaced over 4 days result in a memory lasting several weeks, a finding that suggests long-term learning in the sea slug. Furthermore, these behavioral alterations are accompanied by microscopic structural changes at the modified synapses, the number of presynaptic release sites nearly doubling after repeated sensitization. It is possible that serotonin might also have a long-term effect in controlling the molecular structures that regulate the activity of the protein kinase, but definite information concerning the development of long-term memory in the Aplysia is not yet available.

CELLULAR BASIS OF COMPLEX LEARNING

Driven by clinical cases such as patient H. M., the search for the brain mechanisms responsible for declarative memory has concentrated on the hippocampus and related forebrain structures. Lacking a hippocampus, H. M. is unable to establish new declarative memories, although he shows no impairment in nondeclarative forms of learning. For this reason, any evidence of cellular plasticity of neurons within the hippocampal formation may be of major importance for understanding declarative memory at the level of cellular systems.

Long-term potentiation and long-term depression are umbrella terms for two distinct kinds of change in neuronal synaptic efficiency that may well underlie some types of human memory.

Long-term potentiation (LTP) is the strengthening of the effect of a presynaptic input in a postsynaptic cell as a consequence of using that synapse in particular ways. **Long-term depression (LTD)** is the mirror image of LTP and results in a reduction of synaptic efficiency. The general rules of synaptic usage that govern LTP and LTD production have not yet been discovered, but a number of particular manipulations are known to elicit LTP and LTD reliably at specific synapses (Stevens, 1996). A number of recent studies strongly argue that LTP in mammalian hippocampal neurons is responsible for some important aspects of declarative or explicit learning.

Hippocampal Structure and Pathways   The hippocampus is located on the medial aspect of the cerebral hemispheres and is a part of the allocortex, the structurally simpler and evolutionary older portion of the forebrain (Duvernoy, 1988). The hippocampus has a strikingly curved form and is composed of two enfolded tissues, the hippocampus proper and the dentate gyrus.

The hippocampus proper is also called Ammon's horn, or *cornu Ammonis* in Latin. (Ammon was an ancient Egyptian deity represented in Greek mythology by the horns of a ram, which curl in a manner similar to the structure of the hippocampus proper.) It is divided into four separate regions, designated as CA1, CA2, CA3, and CA4, where CA signifies *cornu Ammonis*. The pyramidal cells of CA1 region are particularly important in the study of LTP and learning in the hippocampus. The hippocampus proper is continuous with both the subicular complex and the entorhinal

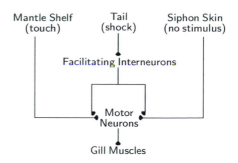

Figure 12.10. Neural Mechanisms Mediating Classical Conditioning of the Gill Withdrawal Reflex. Here the conditioned stimulus is given to the mantle paired in time with the unconditioned stimulus of a noxious shock to the tail. As a control, the siphon skin is stimulated but never in conjunction with the tail shock. When stimulation of the mantle shelf precedes tail shock, the mantle sensory neurons are primed to respond more strongly to the facilitator neurons on the US pathway. Such an increase in responsiveness does not occur for the siphon skin.

Figure 12.11. The Intrinsic Circuits of the Hippocampal Formation. Here the CA1 and CA3 fields may be seen, along with the dentate gyrus. The three principal intrinsic pathways of the hippocampal formation are the perforant pathway, the mossy fiber pathway, and the Schaffer collateral pathway.

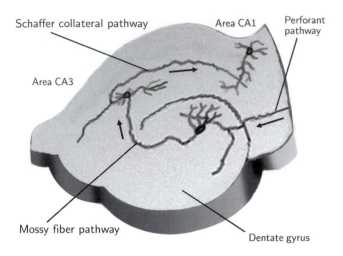

cortex, which in turn is adjacent to the neocortex of the cerebral hemispheres.

Information pathways through the hippocampal formation are well organized (Kennedy & Marder, 1992). Input to the hippocampus originates in the adjacent entorhinal cortex, as may be seen in Figure 12.11. The entorhinal cortex itself receives information from many cortical association areas and thus provides the hippocampal formation with a rich source of data from which to construct memory. The entorhinal cortex relays information to the granule cells of the dentate gyrus through projections called the perforant pathway.

In turn, the granule cells of the dentate gyrus project to the CA3 field of the hippocampus proper. Axons of the granule cells are called the mossy fibers, and together they form the mossy fiber pathway.

The pyramidal cells of area CA3 have axons that bifurcate or branch in two directions. One branch stays within the hippocampus and synapses on the pyramidal cells in area CA1; these axons form the Schaffer collateral pathway. The remaining branch of the CA3 axons leaves the hippocampus and terminates elsewhere.

Finally, the axons of the CA1 pyramidal cells project back to the entorhinal cortex by way of a neighboring structure, the subiculum. This completes the circuit of information flow within the hippocampal formation. All neurons in the hippocampal formation except those of the dentate gyrus send axons to other regions of the cerebral cortex. Thus, the hippocampus is positioned to contribute to memory function in widespread regions of the brain.

LTP in CA1 Pyramidal Cells

Long-term potentiation—first discovered in 1973 by Timothy Bliss and Terje Lømo—can be produced by applying a brief train of high-frequency electrical stimulation to any of the three hippocampal pathways: the **perforant pathway**, the **mossy fiber pathway**, or the **Schaffer collateral pathway**. In each case, the excitatory synaptic response of the hippocampal neurons is markedly increased. Because this facilitating effect persists for considerable periods of time—often weeks—the name *long-term potentiation* is appropriate.

Despite apparent similarity of LTP within the hippocampal formation, there are important differences in both the characteristics and molecular mechanisms of LTP at different hippocampal sites. At present, LTP at CA1 pyramidal cells seems by far the most interesting because of the real possibility that it might be the mechanism by which at least some types of declarative memory are formed.

In the CA1 region, LTP can be produced at synapses between Schaffer collaterals and CA1 pyramidal cells, either in hippocampal brain slices or in the intact animal. A bundle of Schaffer collaterals that provides input to the cell are used for stimulation. The cell is tested periodically with brief shocks to these inputs, and the size of the excitatory postsynaptic potential is measured. Without specific stimulation to produce LTP, the response of the CA1 pyramidal cell does not change.

LTP can be induced by stimulating the Schaffer collateral fibers at a high frequency, such as 100 stimuli in a 1-second period. (High-frequency electrical stimulation is called *tetanus*.) It is important to note that the high rate of stimulation artificially achieved in tetanus can be produced by neurons within the brain without artificial input. Thus, tetanus is representative of some naturally occurring physiological phenomena.

The effect of tetanus is to produce a profound depolarization of the CA1 pyramidal cell that—in turn—induces LTP to change the cell's response to future input from the stimulated fibers. In the future, nontetanic activation of these same Schaffer collaterals will produce a larger excitatory postsynaptic potential, making a response of the CA1 cell more likely. Furthermore, the size of the CA1 cell's response to other inputs not active during the tetanus is unaffected. For this reason, LTP in CA1 hippocampal pyramidal cells is said to be selective.

LTP in the CA1 pyramidal cells is also associative, meaning that it can establish a relationship between two of its inputs. Specifically, other inputs to the CA1 pyramidal cells that were activated during tetanus are also potentiated. LTP affects both the tetanic input and any simultaneously active nontetanic inputs. Thus, LTP provides a cellular mechanism in which two simultaneously activated inputs to the cell are associated, which is essential for associative learning.

Associative LTP in CA1 Pyramidal Cells

Most excitatory synapses within the hippocampal formation—as in the brain more generally—use the amino acid glutamate as a neurotransmitter. This single neurotransmitter can have markedly different effects at different synapses, however, depending on the properties of the postsynaptic receptor system with which it binds. These postsynaptic receptors are categorized by the agonists with which they bind. The principal distinction for glutamate receptors is between the **N-methyl-D-aspartate (NMDA) receptors** that bind with NMDA and those that do not.

At non-NMDA receptors, glutamate functions as an ordinary excitatory neurotransmitter, controlling a simple transmitter-gated ion channel.

At these synapses, glutamate produces an excitatory postsynaptic potential that can lead to firing of the postsynaptic cell. Such non-NMDA glutamate receptors are responsible for all excitatory activity within the CA1 region; when they are blocked, all excitatory postsynaptic potentials disappear. In contrast, selective blocking of the NMDA receptors has minimal effect on postsynaptic excitation.

However, the binding of glutamate with NMDA receptors on the CA1 pyramidal cells is responsible for associative long-term potentiation. When CA1 NMDA receptors are blocked, all traces of associative LTP in CA1 disappear.

The NMDA glutamate receptor, which controls the entry of Ca^+ to the cell, is well suited for producing associative learning because it is doubly gated. Its activation requires that both neurochemical and membrane potential criteria must be met simultaneously. The neurochemical requirement is that glutamate is bound to the NMDA receptors; thus, the NMDA receptor is a neurotransmitter-gated ion channel. The membrane potential criterion is that the postsynaptic cell is substantially depolarized; for this reason, the NMDA receptor is also a voltage-gated ion channel. Both criteria must be fulfilled at the same time for the NMDA channel to open. For this reason, the NMDA receptor responds only to contiguously associated events.

LTP, then, is triggered by the opening of NMDA-calcium channels and the consequent increase in intracellular calcium levels. Increasing intracellular calcium activates two related protein kinases. (A protein kinase is an enzyme that phosphoralates a specific amino acid of its target protein, thereby altering the function of the protein.) These two activated enzymes are protein kinase C and calcium-calmodulin-dependent protein kinase II (or CaMKII). Both kinases are essential for LTP. If either is blocked, LTP cannot be produced.

The ways in which these protein kinases act is now beginning to be understood. One major mechanism involves increasing the effectiveness of the postsynaptic non-NMDA glutamate receptors that are activated simultaneously with the NMDA receptors (see Figure 12.12 on the facing page). When glutamate binds to the NMDA receptor, calcium enters the postsynaptic cell. Calcium ions switch CaMKII to its active form, which unleashes a biochemical cascade that permanently increases the responsiveness of non-NMDA glutamate receptors to the neurotransmitter. By structurally altering the non-NMDA glutamate receptors, future inputs at these associated non-NMDA synapses will be enhanced.

There is also evidence of a presynaptic contribution to LTP. Protein kinases activated in the postsynaptic cell appear to release a retrograde messenger back into the synaptic cleft, which travels back to the presynaptic neuron. There, the retrograde messenger induces the presynaptic neuron to release more neurotransmitter when that cell is activated in the future. One substance that may serve as the retrograde messenger is the gas, nitric oxide, which has neuroactive effects and can pass freely through the membranes of both the pre- and postsynaptic neurons.

Thus, LTP in the CA1 pyramidal cells of the mammalian hippocampus is selective and associative. It is regulated by doubly gated NMDA receptors and initiated by synaptically produced increases of intracellular

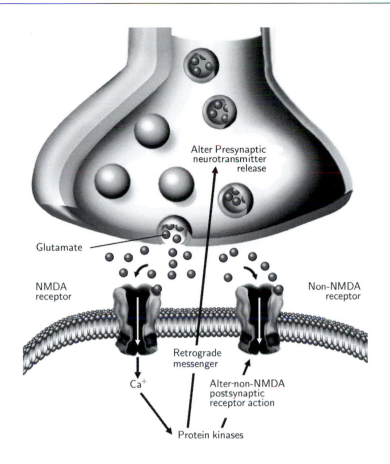

Figure 12.12. Molecular Mechanisms Responsible for LTP. Long-term potentiation is initiated by the influx of calcium through an activated NMDA receptor, which activates protein kinases. The activated protein kinases can exert two effects. First, they can produce a permanent increase in the responsiveness of non-NMDA glutamate receptors so that they will respond more vigorously to input in the future. Second, they can release a retrograde transmitter or messenger, such as nitric oxide, that alters the response of the presynaptic cell, inducing it to release more neurotransmitter for each action potential that it receives in the future. Thus, the NMDA-protein-kinase system can produce long-lasting changes both presynaptically and postsynaptically as a function of its experience.

calcium in the postsynaptic cell. LTP requires that both protein kinase C and CaMKII be activated. Finally, LTP may result in both the postsynaptic modification of non-NMDA glutamate receptors and presynaptic changes in factors governing glutamate release at the modified synapse.

Evidence of long-term potentiation also has been found in a number of other brain tissues, including the cerebral cortex (see below), but LTP in the hippocampus remains the best understood example of this apparently widespread neural process underlying many forms of learning and plasticity.

Insights From Transgenic Animals

The study of memory at the level of the cell recently has been advanced by the creation of transgenic animals in which gene expression is manipulated with striking specificity. This breakthrough in molecular genetics already has shed light on the cellular biochemistry of LTP in the CA1 pyramidal cells of the rodent hippocampus.

A **transgenic animal** is an animal that has incorporated one or more genes from another cell or organism into its genome and can pass the altered gene on to its offspring. Transgenic animals can be used to study the effects that a particular protein plays in any biological process of interest by creating animals in which that protein has been genetically altered.

Transgenic animals are made in the following way. First, the protein of interest is selected. (For studying LTP, the protein CaMKII is a reasonable choice.)

Next, the gene coding of the protein must be identified and its nucleotides sequenced. (A gene is simply a region of the chromosomal DNA that specifies an inheritable characteristic, most often the structure of a specific protein.)

Third, the true sequence is altered, so that the mutant gene will create an altered protein when the gene is later expressed. Finally, the mutant gene is transferred to a fertilized egg, where it is entered into the genome using recombinant genetic methods.

In this way, the organism that has acquired the gene will manufacture the genetically altered protein whenever that gene is expressed. The altered gene becomes a permanent part of the organism's genome and can be inherited by its offspring.

Using this strategy, entire strains of organisms with specifically altered genetic structures can be created. Such transgenic animals are often called "knockout animals" because one specific gene has been removed from the genome and its associated protein eliminated from the organism.

Such transgenic knockout animals have been used for a number of years in studying a wide range of biological phenomena, including the neurobiology of memory. Although this pursuit has been extraordinarily fruitful, it has one major drawback—namely, that gene expression is altered throughout the entire body. As a result, the mutant organisms often show severe developmental defects and early death (Joyner, 1994). Moreover, in surviving organisms, there are often difficulties in ascribing the effects of the gene alteration to any particular cell type or tissue (Tsien et al., 1996).

Very recently, such problems have been solved by the development of technologies that permit a specific gene to be deleted only in a specific cell type in a specific tissue (Roush, 1997). It is almost certain that this new tissue- and cell-type-specific method will be applied widely to a variety of problems. But the initial application of these methods was to examine spatial learning and the molecular biology of LTP in the CA1 pyramidal cells of the mouse hippocampus.

Disruption of Spatial Memory in Transgenic Mice   Spatial learning is an important part of the behavioral repertoire of rodents. In these foraging animals, spatial information is stored by a form of explicit, fact-based learning that is similar to declarative learning in humans. Rats excel in spatial learning and quickly develop a cognitive map of their surroundings.

The hippocampus is important in establishing spatial maps in rodents. When the hippocampus is bilaterally removed, rats and mice can no longer learn tasks that depend on spatial maps, such as the Morris water maze (Morris, Garrud, Rowlins, & O'Keefe, 1982).

The Morris water maze has proven to be a useful measure of spatial learning in rodents. The maze consists of a small tub filled with milk-colored water, which prevents the animal from seeing beneath its surface.

Distant visual cues are placed around the pool to allow the animal to orient itself in space. Rodents are trained to find a hidden platform beneath the surface of the milky water, using only the spatial information provided by the distal cues. Normal rodents learn such a maze without difficulty.

Nonspatial learning ability can be tested in this same apparatus in the so-called "landmark task" in which the platform is moved on every block of trials, but the platform's position is indicated by a clearly visible marker placed on the pool wall near the platform (Kolb, Buhrmann, McDonald, & Sutherland, 1994).

Several years ago, reports by Silva and Tonegawa provided evidence suggesting that both spatial learning and CA1 LTP in mice were dependent on CaMKII (Silva, Paylor, Wehner, & Tonegawa, 1992; Silva, Stevens, Tonegawa, & Wang, 1992). They used traditional knockout methods to delete the alpha subunit of CaMKII in a genetically engineered strain of mice. Although apparently normal in most respects, these transgenic mice showed no evidence of LTP in CA1 pyramidal cells. Furthermore, they also were impaired in spatial learning, as measured by the Morris water maze. Such behavioral evidence is consistent with the argument that hippocampal long-term potentiation is necessary for spatial memory in rodents.

But because CaMKII was missing in every cell of the organism, other explanations of both the observed learning deficit and the lack of LTP cannot be dismissed. Thus, the causal arguments relating the NMDR receptor, CA1 long-term potentiation, and rodent spatial learning have been enhanced greatly by a set of new experiments using tissue- and cell-specific knockout methods to reexamine the neural mechanisms that underlie rodent spatial learning.

Tsien and his coworkers, in the laboratory of Susumu Tonegawa, created strains of mice in which the NMDA R(eceptor) 1 gene was eliminated (knocked out) only in the pyramidal cells of the CA1 region hippocampus. As a result, the CA1 pyramidal cells in this strain of adult mice lack functioning NMDA receptors. Tsien calls this strain NMDAR1 CA1-KO or simply CA1-KO mice.

Furthermore, the tissue-specific deletion of the NMDAR1 gene does not begin until 3 weeks after birth, at which time the normal synaptic structure of the hippocampus is firmly in place (Roush, 1997). Because of this spatial and temporal specificity, any deficits of either spatial learning or CA1 LTP observed in these mice can be directly ascribed to alterations of the hippocampal CA1 pyramidal cells, the only cells in which the NMDA receptor was selectively deleted.

The CA1-KO mice differed both behaviorally and electrophysiologically. First and foremost, the CA1-KO mice were seemingly unable to learn the spatial water maze task (Tsien, Huerta, & Tonegawa, 1996). Both CA1-KO mice and a number of different groups of control mice were given 12 blocks of training in the Morris water maze. At the end of this training, all animals were given a transfer test, in which the platform was removed from the pool. If the animals had formed a spatial map of the test apparatus, they should spend most of their time swimming in the portion of the pool where the platform had been located. This is precisely what the control mice did. In contrast, the CA1-KO mice navigated throughout the

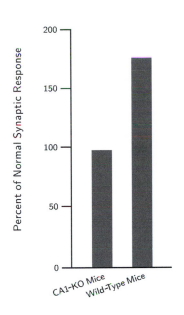

Figure 12.13. Lack of LTP in Transgenic CA1-KO Mice. After long-term potentiation conditioning, the synaptic response of CA1 pyramidal cells to the standard stimulus is enhanced (potentiated) in the wild-type control mice but unchanged in the CA1-KO mice (based on Tsien, Huerta, & Tonegawa, 1996).

pool, indicating they lacked a spatial map of the platform's location.

Second, the CA1-KO mice showed no evidence of LTP in the CA1 region of the hippocampus when tested electrophysiologically. In response to intense stimulation (100 stimuli in 1 second) of Schaffer collateral fibers, the CA1 pyramidal cells of the CA1-KO mice showed no evidence of long-term potentiation, whereas the response of the CA1 pyramidal cells in all control animals was potentiated as expected. These results are shown in Figure 12.13 on the page before.

Third, CA1-KO mice were not impaired in other, nonspatial forms of learning. Although they learned somewhat more slowly than control mice, they were able to master the nonspatial, landmark version of the Morris water maze and equaled performance of the control mice by the end of training.

Tsien's findings give strong support to the theory that long-term hippocampal memory in rodents is produced—at least in part—by associative learning in the pyramidal cells of the CA1 region of the hippocampus. Spatial learning requires functioning NMDA receptors in those cells and is likely to be mediated by the same cellular processes that give rise to CA1 long-term potentiation.

This one elegant experiment provides insights into the biology of memory at the levels of genetics, molecular biology, cell function, and behavior, a most impressive accomplishment. The expanded and innovative use of tissue-specific and cell-type-specific genetic knockout methods is likely to provide new and fundamental insights into the molecular basis of mammalian memory.

Short-Term Memory

Short-term memory has been called the "blackboard of the mind" because we depend on it to store pieces of information from moment to moment in our mental lives. Human short-term memory depends heavily on neural systems within the prefrontal regions in the cerebral cortex. This conclusion rests on several lines of experimental evidence.

Short-term memory is usually evaluated by using delayed-response tests, which evaluate the organism's capacity to act on the basis of temporarily stored information, rather than immediate sensory cues or long-term knowledge. In such tests, a cue is first given indicating where the animal is to respond. That cue is then removed or hidden. After a several-second delay, a response signal is presented. The animal is to choose the response or location indicated by the first cue. If the animal chooses correctly, a reward is given. Typically, the correct response changes from trial to trial. Such delayed-response tests probe short-term memory because the animal must rely on short-term memory to pick the correct response.

These tests are similar to the object permanence task used with children by Jean Piaget, a noted developmental psychologist (Goldman-Rakic, 1992). In that task, a toy is placed into one of two boxes while the child watches. The boxes are then closed. Some time later, the child is asked to find the toy. Performance on this task is closely related to the maturation of the prefrontal cortex. In humans, the prefrontal cortex is not functional until about 8 months of age. Children younger than this perform poorly on the object permanence task, as do monkeys with lesions in the prefrontal areas. As in humans, the normal monkey's ability to perform this task first appears as the prefrontal cortex becomes functional, at about 2 to 4 months after birth.

If recordings are made of individual neurons in the prefrontal cortex during the delayed-response test, several different patterns of responding may be seen. Some units discharge exclusively during cue presentation, and others discharge during responding (Fuster, 1989). However, a third group of cells seems to be related to short-term memory: They respond only during the interval between cue and response. Moreover, in a spatial memory task, Goldman-Rakic (1992) reports that individual cells respond selectively for individual locations where the target may be located. Such cells provide sufficient information to completely account for spatial delayed-response performance in the primate.

CORTICAL PLASTICITY

A final and very powerful approach to the study of learning and memory exploits the tendency of the cerebral cortex to form topographic maps of the information that it processes. A **topographic map** is a representation that preserves the surface structure and the relations between its elements, at least to some extent. Thus, a visual cortical area contains a *retinotopic map* that preserves the spatial relations among retinal photoreceptors at the level of the cortex. Similarly, the primary and secondary somatosensory areas of the cortex are marked by *somatotopic maps* that preserve the local spatial relations among somatosensory receptors in their cortical representations.

In primates, both types of maps show large-scale distortions in their topographic mappings. In primate vision, the extreme variations in photoreceptor density between fovea and periphery necessitate a near-logarithmic global transformation between the retinal and cortical maps.

In somatosensation, global discontinuities between the skin surface and the cortex necessarily result from the fact that the skin enclosing the body is a three-dimensional structure, whereas the cortical area containing the somatosensory map is a two-dimensional surface. But in both cases, *local* spatial relations are maintained in the cortex despite the presence of these *global* transformations.

Cortical maps provide an excellent means for studying learning because these maps are *plastic*, that is, capable of changing as the result of experience. There are now numerous examples of the effects of experience on cortical maps that increasingly point to the conclusion that change and adaptation are the rule in the human cerebral cortex, rather than the exception.

Deafferentation Studies   Monkeys, like humans and other species, have an orderly somatopic map in the primary somatosensory cortex (Brodmann's area 3b) that devotes considerable cortical space to the sensitive and dexterous digits of the hand. This mapping may be demonstrated by recording from a large number of cortical cells using many closely spaced microelectrode penetrations and determining the receptive field of each

Figure 12.14. Mapping the Somatopic Organization of Somatosensory Cortex in the Monkey after Amputation. Left: An outline of the monkey's hand. Middle: The map of the hand region in a normal monkey. Right: The map of the hand area following amputation of the third digit.

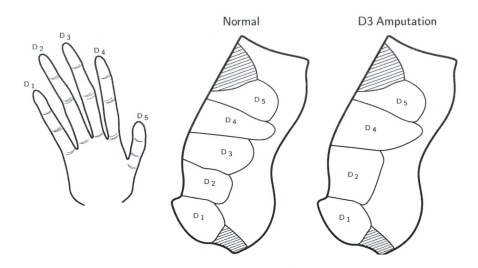

cell encountered. The typical results for the hand region of a normal monkey are shown in the first panel of Figure 12.14. Notice the orderly representation of the digits in the cortical map.

These somatotopic maps are so consistent from animal to animal that it is tempting to think of them as genetically determined and unlikely to be changed as the result of experience, but—surprisingly—this is not at all the case. Instead, the somatotopic map appears to be dynamically maintained and subject to substantial reorganization as determined by somatosensory experience. Consider an early experiment by Morris Merzenich and his students.

Merzenich et al. (1984) examined the effects of amputation (or **deafferentation**, the elimination of sensory input) of the third (middle) finger on the normal somatopic representation of the hand in area 3b. They mapped the hand area before amputation of the finger and again several months afterwards. Their results were striking: The monkey's cortex had reorganized itself so that cortical neurons in the region that once corresponded to the missing finger now responded to input from the adjacent unamputated digits. The new map is orderly but four-fingered, as shown in the second panel of Figure 12.14.

Web-Fingered Monkeys   The receptive fields of neurons in the finger areas of the primate somatotopic map are characteristically small and are contained entirely within a single-digit pad. Thus, the information processed by such cortical neurons arises within a discrete, well-defined, continuous region of the skin. Such a finding seems to be dictated by the hardwired connections of the peripheral nervous system, but this apparently straightforward conclusion seems now to be in error. Consider the following simple experiment by Allard, Clark, Jenkins, and Merzenich (1991).

The monkey hand—like that of a human—is a dexterous and flexible structure, with the separate fingers normally moving independently of each other. Thus, the sensory input to the individual fingers is usually uncorrelated. But what would happen if two fingers were temporarily su-

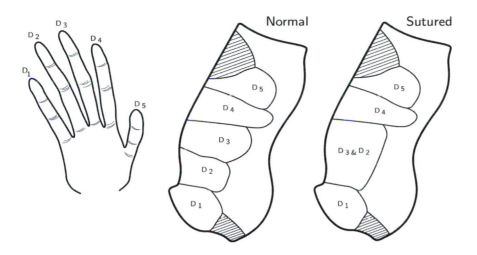

Figure 12.15. Mapping the Somatopic Organization after Suturing. Left: An outline of the monkey's hand. Middle: The map of the hand region in a normal monkey. Right: The map after suturing together the second and third fingers of the monkey's hand, in which the cortical representation of the two affected fingers has merged into a single zone, in which individual cells have receptive fields spanning both fingers.

tured together, so that they were constrained mechanically to always move in unison?

Under such conditions, the hand area of the cortex reorganizes itself in the region of the two sutured fingers (see Figure 12.15). The receptive fields of individual cells grow larger and extend from one finger to the other. Such multidigit receptive fields are virtually never seen in normal animals but are characteristic of animals with sutured fingers. There seems to be no other explanation for this powerful finding other then that sensory receptors in both fingers experience highly correlated patterns of temporal input after being joined into a single mechanical structure. From the perspective of the monkey's cerebral cortex, there is really no difference in the messages being sent from touch receptors in the two fingers joined together by surgical thread (Allard, Clark, Jenkins, & Merzenich, 1991).

Cortical Changes in Motor Skill Learning   But both amputation and surgical suturing of the fingers are in some ways extreme intrusions into the life of the monkey. Do much more ordinary changes in the sensory experiences of the fingers induce plastic change of the cerebral cortex as well? Recent evidence by Xerrie and his colleagues, again in Merzenich's laboratory, indicates that the answer to this question is emphatically *yes:* Cerebral cortex is continuously remodeled by our experiences (Xerri, Merzenich, Jenkins, & Santucci, 1999).

Xerri et al. (1999) provided his monkeys a very simple opportunity to learn a little bit of fine motor coordination: They could enjoy banana pellet hors d'oeuvres each day before mealtime, but these tidbits were served in five "cups" of varying size, the smallest of which required that the monkeys make careful finger movements to extract the pellets from their containers. This task was, in fact, a variant of the Klüver Board, a device used for assessing fine motor skills in humans.

Each of the nine monkeys was given the opportunity to snack on 100 pellets distributed among the various cups on 3 days a week preceding their normal feeding time for a total of between 24 and 42 practice sessions. Training was ended for each monkey when it was able to retrieve a food

Figure 12.16. Changes in the Monkey Hand Map With Practice. Practice in skilled movement decreases the receptive field size and increases the cortical magnification factor for the digits involved.

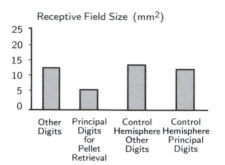

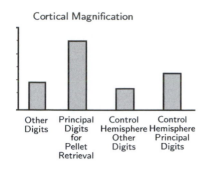

pellet from any of the cups on its first attempt.

Following training, the area 3b hand-maps for each monkey were measured, and the results are shown in Figure 12.16. The left-hand panel of this figure shows the cortical magnification of various fingertips. **Cortical magnification** is the ratio of the cortical area to receptor surface area; here, it is the ratio of the size of the cortical region devoted to each fingertip to the skin surface area of that fingertip. Xerri et al.'s (1999) results were striking: The cortical magnifications of the fingertips used by each individual monkey to remove banana pellets from the containers were more than twice as large as those on the untrained fingers.

Underlying this increase in cortical magnification was the shrinkage of receptive field size in the digits used for pellet retrieval. These results are shown in the right-hand panel of Figure 12.16. These animals appear to have reorganized their cortex in a way that provided them with a larger number of cortical cells each with smaller receptive fields, thereby increasing the precision of the somatosensory information available to the animal from those fingertips. Other studies corroborate this finding, including the results of functional neuroimaging studies in humans (Elbert, Pantev, Wienbruch, Rockstroh, & Taub, 1995).

Such results are important because they indicate that cortical plasticity is not a rare phenomenon that appears only in response to amputation and other drastic insults to the integrity of the organism. Rather, plasticity is a normal property of ordinary life. Even banana-flavored hors d'oeuvres can alter the cortical landscape if they provide the animal with the opportunity for new learning.

LEARNING: NEW SYNAPSES AND NEW CELLS

These studies of rapid and extensive reorganization of primate cerebral cortex in response to apparently modest changes in patterned sensory stimulation suggest that the cerebral cortex is much more amenable to change than has been previously realized. But exactly *how* such change is implemented at the cellular level is far from clear.

Until very recently, there appeared to be only two possibilities: (a) either the effectiveness of existing synapses between cortical cells could change with learning, or (b) new synapses might be formed among existing cortical neurons. The third possibility, that new neurons might be created to support new memory, was long believed to be impossible. However, recent evidence suggests that all three mechanisms might provide a physical basis for learning within the primate brain.

Strengthening Existing Connections   There are numerous mechanisms by which the effectiveness of an existing synapse between cells may be altered. Altered synaptic strength has been demonstrated at a number of different synapses under a wide range of experimental conditions. Changes that alter the efficacy of neurotransmitter release, the speed at which reuptake processes operate to remove neurotransmitter from the synaptic cleft, and mechanisms that alter either binding or its expression in the postsynaptic cell all can alter synaptic efficiency. Such processes have been widely documented in a number of neuronal systems.

Creating New Connections   Much less is known about the formation of new synapses as the result of learning, but recent findings suggest that learning may produce new synaptic growth that strengthens connections between neurons in the hippocampal long-term potentiation paradigm (Toni, Buchs, Nikonenko, Bron, & Muller, 1999).

Over the years, many investigators have suggested that learning may proceed by both by the remodeling of existing synapses and the formation of new synapses between neurons showing LTP. Recently, Toni et al. (1999) tested this idea by (a) using electron microscopy to examine the structure of synapses between neurons before and after the induction of LTP in a hippocampal slice preparation and (b) identifying the specific neurons actually involved in LTP within the slice by staining the cells for accumulated calcium (a telltale sign of LTP) within the dendritic spines of synapses within the slice.

Using this sophisticated method, Toni et al. (1999) found that within an hour following the induction of LTP, there was a marked increase in the number of postsynaptic neurons within the hippocampal slice showing double-spine synapses, that is, synapses in which two, rather than one, dendritic spines extended from the postsynaptic cell to make contact with the axon terminal of the presynaptic neuron. This arrangement only occurred at synapses involved in LTP, as marked by heightened Ca^+ levels within the postsynaptic dentritic spines. An example of both single and doubled dendritic spines is shown in Figure 12.17.

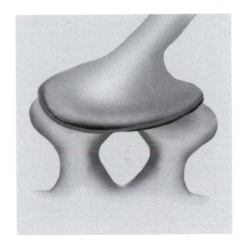

Thus, Toni et al. (1999) demonstrated anatomically new synaptic growth between neurons activated by a physiological process, LTP, that is believed to be responsible for at least some forms of learning within the primate brain. LTP also might produce new connections between other neurons in which none had previously existed, but such synapses would not be detected by the particular methods used in Toni et al.'s study. Thus, the long-lasting changes in synaptic efficiency produced by LTP are likely to be the result of new synaptic spines increasing the connectivity between an activated axon terminal and its target cell. This finding would help explain the numerous reports of the increased number of synapses observed in animals subjected to learning experiences and enriched environmental stimuli.

Figure 12.17. Doubled Dendritic Spines Produced by Long-term Potentiation (LTP). The top panel shows a single dendritic spine observed at a synapse not participating in LTP, as indicated by normal levels of Ca^+ within the spine itself. In contrast, the bottom panel shows a doubled spine at a synapse changed by LTP.

Creating New Neurons   Nerve cells are the substance of the brain, and when the brain learns, something must change. For many years, neuroscientists believed that existing nerve cells may change their connections or properties as the brain learns, but—for a number of reasons—it was thought that new nerve cells were never created in the adult brain. But that widely held belief appears to be wrong. There is new, very strong evidence that the primate brain *does* manufacture new nerve cells in adulthood in precisely those brain regions that are likely to store newly learned information (Gould, Reeves, Graziano, & Gross, 1999).

Gould et al. (1999) examined the brains of 12 adult macaque monkeys using a variety of cell-staining methods, including bromodexyuridine (BrdU), which marks cells as they are forming and any other cells that are formed from the originally marked cells. Thus, BrdU staining differentiates between newly created and preexisting neurons. Gould et al. found clear evidence of new neurons in the prefrontal, inferior temporal, and parietal cortex of animals as early as a week following BrdU injection. These regions are all classical "cortical association areas" that are believed to play major roles in complex learned behavior.

Gould et al.'s (1999) finding is particularly important in that it opens up many new ways of thinking about the anatomical basis of learning in the primate and human brain. The idea that neurogenesis (the creation of nerve cells) may provide a continuing anatomical basis for the storage of newly learned information within the brain is an exciting and unexplored possibility.

The Ubiquity of Plasticity   As all of these wide-ranging studies of learning have demonstrated, there is now strong evidence that human memory is not a single entity. Rather, memory is distributed among a diverse set of brain structures that are responsible for various types of qualitatively different behavior. However, studies of plasticity at the molecular and cellular levels also suggest that there may be a rather limited number of molecular processes that are used by nerve cells to express memory. Thus, the various different types of human memory may be the product of the same restricted set of cellular events.

SUMMARY

Learning and memory are characteristic features of the nervous systems of adaptive organisms. In humans, as in other species, memory takes a variety of formats. All learning involves synaptic change. The changes that produce short-term memory may depend on short-lasting physiological processes, but long-term memory requires a more permanent representation, accomplished by protein synthesis in behavioral-specific regions of the nervous system.

In the Aplysia, for example, sensitization and habituation of the defensive gill retraction reflex are produced by increasing or decreasing the presynaptic facilitation controlled by a population of interneurons at the primary synapse between the sensory and motor neurons. Classical conditioning appears to result from a modification of the cellular events producing sensitization, but the exact nature of this modification is unknown.

Memory produced by the hippocampal formation may depend on the physiological phenomenon of long-term potentiation. In long-term potentiation, high-frequency electrical stimulation of any of the three intrinsic pathways of the hippocampal formation—the perforant path, the mossy fiber pathway, or the Schaffer collaterals—markedly increases the excitatory synaptic response of hippocampal cells. LTP may be either associative or nonassociative, depending on which pathway is stimulated. LTP is mediated by the NMDA glutamate receptors that gate the flow of calcium in the postsynaptic neuron. Transgenic animals with highly restricted spatial regions of altered gene expression are beginning to provide firm confirmation of the roles played by the NMDA system and its related protein kinases producing both LTP and behavioral learning.

The biological basis of learning also has been extended by studies of cortical plasticity, which demonstrate large-scale alterations within topographic cortical maps in response to changes in patterned sensory stimulation. Recent studies indicate that learning within the central nervous system may result from changes in synaptic efficiency, new synaptic growth, or perhaps even the generation of new cortical neurons.

SELECTED READINGS

- Schachter, D. L. (1996). *Searching for memory: The brain, the mind, and the past.* New York: Basic Books. A knowledgeable and readable survey of the memory and the brain that incorporates findings from clinical neuropsychology, functional imaging, and other experimental methods, including a discussion of the controversial concept of "recovered" early memories, by a leading expert in the field.

- Squire, L. R., & Kandel, E. R. (1999). *Memory: From mind to molecules.* New York: Scientific American Library. A clearly written and authoritative introduction to the memory systems of the brain, written by a leading neuropsychologist and neurophysiologist who have made distinguished contributions to the study of learning.

KEY TERMS

amnesia The loss of memory for past experiences.

anterograde amnesia The loss of memory for events occurring after the onset of the amnesia.

Aplysia An invertebrate otherwise known as a sea hare or sea slug.

classical conditioning A type of training that pairs the presentation of a neutral stimulus (conditioned stimulus) with another stimulus (unconditioned stimulus) that elicits a natural response (unconditioned response); after training, the formerly neutral stimulus presented alone elicits a response (conditioned response) that is similar to the unconditioned response.

consolidation The formation of long-term memory.

cortical magnification The ratio of cortical area to receptor surface area.

deafferentation The removal of sensory input by disrupting sensory neurons.

declarative memory The memory for knowledge of facts or events that can be overtly verbally expressed or declared; knowing *what*.

dishabituation The reversal of habituation by a sensitizing stimulus.

encoding The establishment of new information in memory.

engram The physical representation of long-term memory.

episodic memory Memory for personally experienced events.

explicit memory See *declarative memory*.

habituation A simple form of learning in which the response to a weak repetitive stimulus is reduced.

implicit memory See *nondeclarative memory*.

instrumental conditioning See *operant conditioning*.

Korsakoff's syndrome A severe form of amnesia with the preservation of other cognitive functions in some chronic alcoholics.

learning The storage of information as a function of experience, resulting in a relatively permanent change in behavior.

long-term depression (LTD) A long-lasting decrease of the effect of a particular synapse on a postsynaptic neuron when the synapse is used in particular specifiable ways.

long-term memory (LTM) The relatively permanent memory of past learning.

long-term potentiation (LTP) A long-lasting increase of the effect of a particular synapse on a postsynaptic neuron when the synapse is used in particular specifiable ways.

memory The stored information produced by learning.

mossy fiber pathway The projections of the axons of the granule cells of the dentate gyrus to area CA3 of the hippocampus.

N-methyl-D-aspartate (NMDA) receptors A class of glutamate receptors to which NMDA binds; they are thought to form the basis of LTP.

nonassociative learning Learning involving a single stimulus.

nondeclarative memory Memory that cannot be declared or explained (e.g., skill learning).

operant conditioning A form of associative learning in which the persistence of a response depends on the effect of the response on the environment.

perforant pathway The fibers projecting from the entorhinal cortex to the granule cells of the dentate gyrus.

phonological loop A system that holds verbal information for short periods, which may be extended by rehearsal or conscious repetition.

plasticity The change of neural structure or function as the result of experience.

retrieval The extraction and use of information stored in memory.

retrograde amnesia The loss of memory for events that occurred before the onset of the amnesia.

Schaffer collateral pathway The axons of the pyramidal cells of area CA3 of the hippocampus that project to the pyramidal cells of area CA1.

semantic declarative memory The memory of facts.

sensitization A simple form of learning resulting in an increased response to a repetitive stimulus.

short-term memory A limited-capacity system storing information from all senses, usually for no more than a few seconds.

topographic map A representation that to some extent preserves the surface structure and the relations between its elements.

transgenic animal An animal that has incorporated one or more genes from another cell or organism into its genome and can pass the altered gene on to its offspring.

visuospatial sketchpad A system that holds visually encoded spatial information for short periods of time.

working memory See *short-term memory*.

Chapter 13

Disorders of the Nervous System

When faced with some types of nervous system disorders, identifying the disorder and determining its cause—**diagnosis**—are straightforward, but other cases may be much more difficult. Determining the nature of a disorder rests on **signs** and **symptoms**. Symptoms are what the patient reports. Signs are what the examiner observes, whether directly (e.g., a slowness of gait) or by the use of special tests (e.g., an abnormality in a magnetic resonance image). Progress in clinically understanding a disorder or set of disorders depends on the identification of a **syndrome**, a pattern of signs and symptoms that cluster together in a particular group of patients.

The validity of a syndrome rests on one or more of three types of independent measures (Kandel, 1991b; Kaufman, 1995). The first is *natural history*. By natural history is meant the way in which the disorder changes over time. Dementia, for example, is marked by a progressive deterioration of the individual, whereas epilepsy is often episodic, marked periods of intermittent activity.

A second consideration in defining a syndrome is the *response* of patients to specific treatments. For example, manic depression—but no other central nervous system (CNS) disorder—may be controlled by lithium. This suggests that manic depression constitutes a unique CNS disorder or family of disorders that differ in an important way from other types of neurological problems.

But the most compelling method of confirming the validity of a syndrome is to determine its *cause*, perhaps a specific anatomic, molecular, or genetic defect. The existence of demonstrable specific pathology is the criterion by which a syndrome may be shown to result from a single, particular disease. As we will see, not all types of mental disorders—that is, syndromes—result from a single cause. Epilepsy provides a clear example of a clinical syndrome that may be produced by an extensive range of specific mechanisms.

The possibility that multiple causal factors can result in a single clinical syndrome must always be kept in mind in studying nervous system dysfunction. Indeed, the major types of mental illness affecting society today—schizophrenia and depression—have traditionally been considered to be **functional disorders**, meaning a syndrome for which strong evidence of causal mechanism is lacking.

Many neurological disorders are defined specifically by their underlying causes or etiology. Cerebral trauma, vascular disorders, tumors, and infections are some of the major types of etiologically defined neurological disorders.

CEREBRAL TRAUMA

One of the most common types of nervous system disorder is **cerebral trauma**, or brain injury. There are two general types of cerebral trauma: **penetrating wounds** and **blunt head injuries**. Most penetrating cerebral wounds in both military and civilian life are the results of bullets fired from rifles or handguns that enter the brain. (But other causes exist; remember the case of N. B. in Chapter 12, who was injured by a fencing foil.)

If the bullet enters the brain stem, the patient dies immediately as the result of loss of respiratory and cardiac functions, which are controlled in this region. If the bullet passes completely through the brain, there is only about a 20% chance of survival. Epilepsy frequently occurs in those who survive.

Blunt head injuries result from a blow to the head in which the skull is not penetrated by a foreign object. If internal bleeding, called **hemorrhage**, results, the injury is said to be a **contusion**, or bruising without breaking. Within the brain there is a very small amount of bleeding, which frequently produces scar tissue. The effects of contusion may be severe and lasting, particularly if consciousness is lost for a prolonged period.

If there is no clear evidence of hemorrhage, the injury is considered to be a **concussion**, a reversible traumatic disruption of neurological function. Concussion often produces a loss of consciousness (for less than half an hour), failure of spinal reflexes causing a standing person to fall, and temporary blockage of respiration. The effects of concussion may last for only a few seconds or remain for several hours. Even though the skull is not penetrated, blunt head injuries often cause major brain damage. This results from the sudden impact of the soft brain tissue floating in cerebrospinal fluid against the rigid and bony skull. The recovery of nervous functions following concussion occurs in stages, beginning with the most primitive and proceeding to higher-level processes.

People with a history of repeated blunt head injuries, particularly boxers, show the cumulative effects of their injuries. This condition is referred to in the profession as being "punch drunk"; neurologists call it **dementia pugilistica** (Stern, 1991). Dementia pugilistica occurs most often in boxers who are small in stature, are alcoholic, or have lost many fights (Kaufman, 1995). Unfortunately, the disorder progresses even after retirement. A similar syndrome is sometimes seen in battered women.

In dementia pugilistica, movements become increasingly slow and uncertain, much as they do in Parkinson's disease (see Chapter 7). There is a slowing and disruption of speech, increased forgetfulness, and difficulty of thinking. Reflexes also may be impaired. The ventricles are frequently enlarged, indicating a loss of brain tissue. MRIs show small focal contusions, white matter abnormalities, and cerebral atrophy, among other changes. Autopsy reveals a proliferation of neurofibrillary tangles and plaques that are like those found in Alzheimer's dementia, which is discussed below (Kaufman, 1995). There is often no sign of any single large contusion or episode of cerebral hemorrhage. Instead, the boxer must have sustained a series of small concussions, each of which causes minor brain damage. The idea—common in some sports—that concussions are not harmful is not correct.

Primary Brain Injury   The primary effects of head trauma appear immediately. They include both neuronal and vascular damage. Bleeding is common, often into the subdural space. Diffuse axonal injury is also frequent as axons are cut by the mechanical shearing action of sudden mechanical impact. Axonal flow may be blocked in other neurons. There, axons begin to balloon as axoplasmic fluid accumulates, causing the axon to burst some hours later. Finally, ischemia may be produced if the damaged vascular is not functional, thereby leading to further neuronal cell death.

Secondary Brain Injury   The effects of cerebral trauma do not stop here. Instead, the initial trauma begins a cascade of events that continue to damage not only the brain tissue injured in the original trauma but additional tissue as well (Grafman & Salazar, 1996). As dead neurons are metabolized, a number of biologically active and potentially neurotoxic substances are formed. These include prostaglandins, oxygen-free radicals, and excitotoxins such as agonists of NMDA glutamate receptors, which, when present in large quantities, are known to produce cell death.

Because the secondary effects of traumatic head injury are so serious, the prime objective in treating traumatic injuries of the brain is the prevention of further damage by secondary mechanisms.

CEREBROVASCULAR DISORDERS

Abnormalities of the blood vessels of the brain are called **cerebrovascular disorders** by neurologists and account for about half of the neurological problems of all adults. They include the blocking and rupture of blood vessels, which disrupt the flow of blood to the regions of the brain that they serve, a condition termed **ischemia**. More than any other type of cell, the neuron requires continuous access to fresh blood to survive. When the human heart stops pumping, unconsciousness results within 10 seconds. A lack of blood supply to the brain for more than 3 minutes results in irreversible brain damage.

Cerebrovascular Accidents

A **cerebrovascular accident (CVA)**, commonly called a **stroke**, is a blockage of brain blood flow that results in cell death. The area of cell death produced by a sudden insufficiency of the arterial or venous blood supply is called an **infarction** or **infarct**.

All CVAs have a characteristic time course that differs from most other neurological disorders. Strokes have an extremely rapid onset, measured often in seconds or minutes, depending on their underlying causes. The extent of the resulting deficit may be of minor consequence or may be devastating, depending on the extent and location of the ischemic region.

Sometimes an examiner can determine the location and extent of a stroke by studying the patient to determine the neural functions that have been lost. The function patterns of deficits seen in CVAs are as diverse as the brain itself.

CVAs in the anterior cerebral artery often result in a weakening or paralysis of the contralateral leg and loss of speech. Middle cerebral artery CVAs may produce contralateral weakness and contralateral loss of somatic sensations, as well as aphasia. A stroke occurring in the posterior cerebral artery may be marked by visual impairments (Kaufman, 1995). Thus, analysis of behavioral symptoms can indicate which portion of the cerebral vasculature has sustained damage. The study of stroke victims provided the initial evidence leading to the discovery of the language system of the brain.

Age is the greatest risk factor for CVAs, with the incidence increasing almost exponentially with age after 65 (Kaufman, 1995). Hypertension is another major risk factor for stroke, particularly in middle-aged people. CVAs are also produced by cocaine, particularly by "crack" cocaine.

Transient Ischemic Attacks

A **transient ischemic attack (TIA)** is a temporary interruption of the blood supply of the brain that causes short-lasting functional disruptions. TIAs typically last from a few seconds to a few minutes. They are like CVAs, except that they quickly reverse themselves. Usually, TIAs are produced by an embolus—or blood clot—that temporarily blocks a portion of an artery and produces a short-lasting ischemia. As with a CVA, the effects produced by a TIA depend on the portion of the brain that is affected. Common symptoms include seizure, confusion, headache, paralysis, blindness, numbness, tingling, amnesia, and aphasia.

One particularly striking form of TIA occurs when the basilar artery is involved. The basilar artery supplies portions of the temporal lobe, the hippocampus, and various limbic system structures. A transient ischemic attack in the basilar artery can produce the extraordinary syndrome of **transient global amnesia** that is marked by a profound but temporary impairment of memory, which is sometimes accompanied by changes of personality. During the attack, the person shows a profound amnesia, usually being unable to recall information learned during the preceding several days, and is unable to memorize new information. If such patients are taken to an emergency room, they will not understand where they are or how they got there. They often cannot maintain an ordinary conversation, having quickly forgotten what was previously spoken. They must be reintroduced repeatedly to the person with whom they are speaking. There is usually no aphasia, and the motor systems are unaffected. Episodes of transient global amnesia may last for up to a day before they resolve themselves (Kaufman, 1995).

Arteriovenous Malformations

A quite different type of cerebrovascular disorder is the arteriovenous malformation. An **arteriovenous malformation (AVM)** is a congenital disorder in which blood is shunted directly from the arterial to the venous system through a series of tangled large vessels, bypassing the capillary system entirely in the vicinity of the AVM. Because of the lack of blood carrying oxygen and nutrients, neurons never develop in the region of the AVM. For this reason, the developing brain reorganizes itself to make up for its deviant anatomical form.

At birth, there are usually no symptoms, and the child develops normally. Then, often between the ages of 10 and 30 years, the person experiences the first overt symptoms; sometimes it is a seizure, but hemorrhages and headaches are also common. Such symptoms result from the gradual expansion of the malformed vessels with age, compromising the function of the otherwise healthy brain regions. Figure 13.1 on the following page shows one example of an AVM in a 27-year-old man who had just experienced his first epileptic seizure (Martin et al., 1993).

Arteriovenous malformations are more common in men than they are in women. Because they are congenital, they tend to run in families. Usually, AVMs are surgically removed to prevent a later fatal stroke from the weakening tangle of abnormal vessels.

Figure 13.1. An Arteriovenous Malformation (AVM). The large tangle of arteries and veins, indicated by the arrow, are characteristic of an arteriovenous malformation. The direct shunting of blood from the arterial to the venous system and the absence of capillaries prevent the development of normal brain tissue in the region of the AVM.

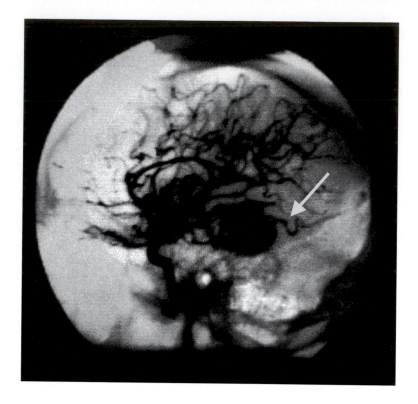

TUMORS

A **tumor**—also called a **neoplasm**—is new growth of tissue that is uncontrolled and progressive. Tumors may occur in any organ system, including the brain. About 10% of all human malignant neoplasms are within the central nervous system (Mendelow, 1993). Many types of tumors may arise within various regions of the brain. Figure 13.2 on the next page shows a large tumor of the frontal lobe.

Brain tumors usually destroy the tissues in which they are located. Thus, the immediate behavioral consequences of a brain tumor directly reflect the functions of the neural systems in the vicinity of the tumor.

Because tumors increasingly occupy space as they grow within the confines of the skull, they progressively displace healthy tissue. These space-occupying lesions can exert any of several effects. Initially, they frequently induce dysfunctions in the normal tissue that lies adjacent to the growing tumor. Epileptic discharge and seizure may be triggered by a growing tumor in the tissue that it abuts. As it grows, the activity in increasingly distant brain regions is altered.

Furthermore, many tumors are situated in such a way as to exert force on nearby tissues. These local distorting forces may result in lesions of otherwise healthy tissue where that tissue makes contact with bony intracranial structures of the skull. The result is often herniation of the brain.

Tumors located within the frontal lobes often produce behavioral effects in early stages of their development, before they result in increased intracranial pressure. Some early signs of frontal tumors are reduced emo-

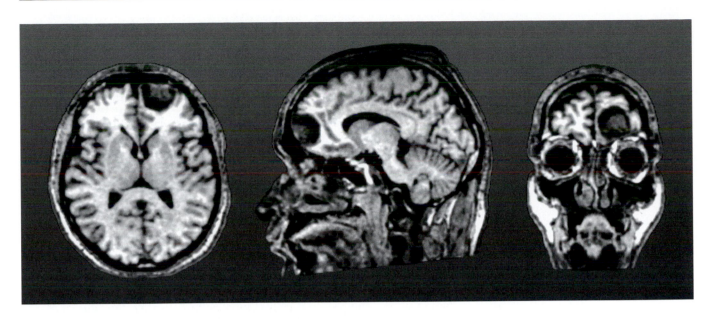

Figure 13.2. A Cerebral Tumor. This large tumor within the frontal lobe is shown in the horizontal plane (left), sagittal plane (center), and coronal plane (right). (Image courtesy of Professor Tyrone Cannon, UCLA.)

tionality, the loss of initiative, and an inability to deal with complex problems (Kaufman, 1995).

Finally, increases of intracranial pressure often occur. In the initial stages of tumor growth, compensation for the increasing size of the tumor is made by small reductions in cerebrospinal fluid volume. This is necessary because the intracranial cavity is rigidly bounded by the bony, unyielding skull. But if growth is prolonged or rapid, such compensations will fail, and intracranial pressure will increase.

Increased intracranial pressure also results when the tumor blocks the normal flow of cerebrospinal fluid through the ventricular system, most frequently in the narrow fourth ventricle. The result is a condition called **obstructive hydrocephalus**.

Heightened intracranial pressure has a variety of consequences, none of which are desirable. First, the cerebral circulation is compromised. The profusion pressure of the circulation, which is simply the arterial pressure of the blood entering the skull minus the intracranial pressure within the skull, is of necessity reduced because the pumping heart now faces a larger resistance. Thus, the blood supply to the brain is less effective. Moreover, the risk of infarction or hemorrhage also is increased.

Chronic increases in intracranial pressure result in headache, vomiting, and disturbances of consciousness (Mendelow, 1993). The headache results from compression of both the dura mater and of the blood vessels, which have pain receptors within their walls. Vomiting occurs as a consequence of pressure placed on the autonomic regulatory nuclei within the medulla. Respiratory problems, changes of reflexes, and impairment in consciousness, including coma, are also the result of pressure applied to brain stem nuclei.

CNS INFECTIONS

Brain infections constitute another major etiological category of neurological disorders. The medical term for infection of the brain is **encephalitis**. The term is derived from the Greek word *enkephalos*, which means "brain," and the suffix *-itis*, indicating inflammation. Infections are multiplications of parasitic organisms with the body. Infections of the brain can arise from a number of sources, including worms, fungi, and protozoa. But the major sources of encephalitis are bacteria, viruses, and prions, a newly discovered class of infectious agents.

Bacterial Infections

Many brain infections are transmitted by bacteria, the simplest of biological organisms. Bacteria are single living cells. The bilipid cell membrane of the bacterium is often encrusted with a hard protective coating, or cell wall. DNA, RNA, proteins, and many small molecules are contained within the bacterial cell membrane but—unlike the cells of plants and animals—lack internal subcellular structures. Bacteria replicate by division and can do so with extreme rapidity when in a favorable environment. Bacterial **encephalitis**—infection of the brain—occurs when bacteria enter the brain of the host and multiply profusely. When bacteria infect the meninges that cover and protect the brain, the resulting infection is **meningitis**.

The disease **neurosyphilis** is perhaps the most notorious variety of the bacterial encephalitis, an infection produced by the spirochete *Treponema pallidum*, a bacterial organism discovered in 1909 by Schaudinn and Hoffmann. Syphilitic infection proceeds in stages (Wiles, 1993).

Within a few weeks following the invasion of the spirochete into its host, a syphilitic chancre (pronounced *shang-ker*) or sore first appears as a hard, red spot on the skin. It then develops into an ulcer that heals itself in a month or so. This is the primary syphilitic infection. In the second stage, the organism infiltrates the body, the blood, and reaches the nervous system. A period of bacterial latency follows. Between 5 and 10 years later, the tertiary stage of syphilis may develop, an infection of the nervous system or neurosyphilis. Symptoms vary widely, but they often include severe headache, cognitive confusion, memory impairment, apathy, and dementia. Aphasia may become evident. Sphincter control is often lost. Convulsions may occur. If untreated, the patient will pass into a semistuporous state. Fortunately, the ravages of neurosyphilis have been largely eliminated by the introduction and widespread use of effective antibiotic agents.

Another form of bacterial CNS infection is **Lyme disease**, named after the village of Lyme, Connecticut, where an outbreak of the disease occurred in the 1970s. The organism that produces the disease, named *Borrelia burgdorferi*, was first discovered in 1982 and is another spirochete (Burgdorfer, Barbour, & Hayes, 1982). Larval ticks feed off infected animals and in so doing acquire the bacterium. When the larva develops into an adult, it infects the organisms on which it feeds, including humans walking in rural areas. Symptoms can include impaired memory, seizures, and movement difficulties. Like other bacterial infections, Lyme disease responds to antibiotic treatment.

Viral Infections

Other infections are produced by viruses. A **virus** is a mobile piece of genetic material that is protected by a coating permitting it to travel from cell to cell. There are many types of viruses with very diverse properties. Viruses differ from each other in the type of protective coating that they employ, the way in which they infiltrate a host cell, the manner in which they replicate, and the type of genetic material that they contain. A virus may be composed of either RNA or DNA. Some viruses have protein molecules attached to their surface.

Viruses can replicate themselves only when within a host cell because the virus needs access to the host's genetic mechanisms, which it subverts for its own reproduction. Different viruses accomplish this stealthy feat in different ways, but all require a host to replicate.

Often, viral replication is so rapid within the host that the sheer volume of new viral particles bursts the cell membrane of the host, thus killing the host cell. The viral progeny then spill onto neighboring cells, which then become infected, starting the cycle of viral replication anew. Common cold sores are produced by the *herpes simplex* virus in exactly this way.

Viruses may enter the human body in several ways, including through the lungs (e.g., mumps and measles), through the mouth (e.g., polio), by genital contact (herpes simplex and HIV), or through skin puncture (e.g., rabies). Once inside the body, the virus multiplies and often causes achiness, tiredness, and fever.

Most neuroactive viruses enter the central nervous system through the bloodstream. Usually, protective mechanisms in the blood keep the circulating viruses under control and the CNS virus free. But if such mechanisms fail, viruses may enter the brain through the cerebral capillaries.

Other viruses, such as the rabies virus, the *herpes simplex encephalitis-producing* virus, and the *herpes zoster* virus (which gives rise to shingles) enter the central nervous system through the peripheral nerve and then migrate backward up the axon into the spinal cord. These viruses enter the axons of peripheral nerve cells and ascend to the cell body of the peripheral neuron, where they replicate. They progress further into the central nervous system by crossing the synapses onto the peripheral neuron cell bodies and thereby successively infect adjacent neurons.

Viral encephalitis rarely occurs as a complication of common viral infections; only a special group of specifically neuroactive viruses are able to enter the nervous system. The general features of the encephalitis produced by all of these viruses are similar.

The disease begins with fever and malaise. With the start of the encephalitis comes headache, disorientation, alterations of consciousness, seizures, and other symptoms, depending on the particular brain regions affected. Very few of these viruses are amenable to drug treatment, but—nonetheless—the prognosis for recovery is generally good, with the exception of rabies, which is fatal, and herpes simplex, which produces profound neural wasting (Anderson, 1993).

Prion Diseases

A handful of unusual but very similar neurological diseases has posed a major puzzle for modern neurobiology because none of these diseases behaves like any others known to science and medicine. These diseases are now known to form a group called the **transmissible spongiform encephalopathies (TSE)**. They are all rapidly progressive, devastating CNS disorders with wide-ranging symptoms, including diverse cognitive, sensory, and motor dysfunctions (Goldfarb & Brown, 1995). They are also called **spongiform encephalopathies** because they produce neuronal loss and the development of vacuoles, or small empty spaces, in the infected tissue. Thus, the disease gives the brain a spongelike appearance.

Perhaps the most exotic of the TSE disorders is **kuru**. Kuru was first described in Western medicine by Gajdusek and Zigas in 1957, in a special article in the *New England Journal of Medicine*. They reported 114 cases of an unusual neurological disease among the Fore highlanders of Papua, New Guinea, which the inhabitants called *kuru*, a word meaning "to be afraid" or "to shiver" in the native Fore language.

The disease begins with motor slowing, weakness, and loss of coordination. Gradually, speech becomes blurred and intelligence diminishes. The face of the kuru victim becomes immobile as the deterioration continues. Incontinence develops, and swallowing becomes impossible. The patient quickly dies from some combination of starvation, ulcers, and pneumonia. This entire progression occurs within a year, and no person has been known to recover.

Among the Fore in general, about 1% of the population had active cases of kuru at the time of the initial report, and about 1% of the population had died yearly from kuru in the recent past. But in certain Fore clans and tribes, rates of infection as high as 10% were observed. These original observers could find no apparent cause of this widespread and unusual neurological wasting disorder (Gajdusek & Zigas, 1957). But later, it was discovered that kuru is transmitted by ritual cannibalism traditionally practiced by the Fore aboriginals, who ceremonially ate the brains of deceased clan members as a gesture of respect. Following this discovery, the Fore ceased their cannibalistic custom, and kuru was virtually abolished (Anderson, 1993).

In the West, **Cruezfeldt-Jakob disease (CJD)** produces an identical set of symptoms and runs an identical course to that produced by kuru among the Fore. Cannibalism is not the mechanism of CJD infection in the West; instead, most known cases of CJD transmission have arisen from errors of medical practice.

The first descriptions of medically transmitted CJD were of a patient in the United States who received a corneal graft from a person who was later discovered to have died from CJD and of two Swiss epileptic patients, who had depth electrodes implanted that had been previously used with a patient later discovered to have had CJD. Subsequently, a number of other similar cases have been uncovered. The most common source of medically transmitted CJD involves contaminated human growth hormone, which was made from human pituitaries accidentally obtained from patients dying of CJD. Fifty-eight such cases are now known in the United States, Europe, New Zealand, and Brazil (Goldfarb & Brown, 1995).

TSEs are not limited to the human species. Sheep farmers have long been aware of the devastating disease **scrapie**, a TSE of sheep. The spread of TSE to cattle has been of major concern in Great Britain, with the advent of *mad cow disease* or **bovine spongiform encephalopathy**. It is believed that the outbreak of TSE in cattle is the result of English cattle farmers enriching their cattle's feed with ground sheep meat that, unfortunately, included tissue from sheep with scrapie. A number of TSEs have now been demonstrated to produce infection across species (DeArmond & Prusiner, 1995).

W. J. Hadlow was the first to recognize the similarity between the human disease kuru and the veterinary disease of scrapie in domestic sheep (Hadlow, 1959). It is from his observation that the current concept of transmissible spongiform encephalopathies as a group of closely related diseases has arisen. All diseases in this group show similar neuropathology, in which the brain is marked by neuronal loss, vacuolation, **gliosis** (a proliferation of astrocytes), and the deposition of **amyloid plaques** throughout the tissue. The amyloid (starchlike) plaques are now known to be formed from a substance called *prion protein*.

For many years, the TSEs were thought to be produced by very unusual viruses with extremely long incubation periods, which were called *slow viruses*. However, there were a number of problems in attributing these infections to a virus, slow or otherwise. For example, sterilization methods that are effective for all known viruses were not effective against the TSE agent, whatever it might be. This belated finding provided the explanation for some of the spread of CJD through surgical procedures.

It slowly became clear, in large part due to the work of Stanley Prusiner, that the agent responsible for the TSEs did not contain nucleic acid of any type and therefore could not be a virus. Rather, the agent seemed to be a rogue protein of some sort. Prusiner—almost single-handedly—defied conventional wisdom in his pursuit of these aberrant proteins. These lethal proteins are now called **prions** (Prusiner, 1995), and for their discovery, Prusiner was awarded the Nobel Prize in 1997.

Prions (the name signifies *proteinaceous infectious particles*) are abnormally folded versions of normal cellular proteins. In the TSEs, the prion is an incorrectly folded molecule of prion protein (PrP), which is a normal part of the cell membrane. This protein is highly conserved in evolution and widely dispersed among species and tissues. Despite its ubiquity, its normal functions are unknown (Anderson, 1993).

PrP^C is the designation of the normal form of the prion protein, where the superscripted C signifies cellular. It differs only in its spatial configuration from the lethal prions that produce Cruezfeldt-Jakob Disease, PrP^{CJD}, and scrapie, PrP^{Sc}.

The differences between PrP^C and PrP^{Sc} are several. The normal version of the protein is completely digested by *proteinase K* (an enzyme that degrades this protein). However, the scrapie version of the protein is only partially degraded by proteinase K. During infection, PrP^{Sc} accumulates in large quantities, forming the amyloid bodies characteristic of the TSEs. Furthermore, there are different strains of the scrapie prions, which produce different incubation times and patterns of spongiform degeneration, with or without amyloid plaques (DeArmond & Prusiner, 1995).

It now seems clear that scrapie PrP is produced from normal cellular PrP (DeArmond & Prusiner, 1995; Mestel, 1996). Prions are thought to replicate by recruiting normal PrP and shaping it into the prion PrP^{Sc} form. The way in which a prion guides the refolding of normal PrP^{C} molecules is not known at this time. Nonetheless, refolded PrP^{C} molecules become full-fledged PrP^{Sc} molecules, which go on to infect PrP^{C} molecules in other cells, other individuals, and—often—other species as well.

This view of prion infection receives strong support from experiments with transgenic mice. Strains of transgenic (knockout) mice in which the gene for normal PrP protein has been removed should not be susceptible to scrapie if prions act by converting normal PrP^{C} molecules to the lethal PrP^{Sc} form. In fact, such mice are immune to scrapie. Even more striking evidence that scrapie propagates itself by corrupting normal membrane protein was provided by Brander et al. (1996). Brander grafted neural tissue that overexpresses PrP^{C} into the brains of PrP^{C}-deficient knockout mice. The mice were then inoculated intracerebrally with scrapie prions. Neurons within the grafted normal brain tissue immediately accumulated high levels of PrP^{Sc} and developed severe spongiform pathology, but the PrP^{C}-deficient tissue of the host developed no such pathology, even 16 months after infection. Thus, brain tissue in which the PrP^{C} gene has been genetically removed is not only resistant to the foreign scrapie prions, but it is also resistant to prions produced by PrP^{Sc} produced within its own body.

The ultimate proof that the TSE originate and are maintained by prion infection would be to construct scrapie prions *de novo* in the laboratory directly from raw amino acids and not from any biological tissue or molecules originating in a TSE-infected animal. Such a demonstration would silence even the staunchest critics of the prion hypothesis, but—to date—this piece of biomolecular wizardry has not been accomplished (Mestel, 1996).

AIDS-RELATED NEUROLOGICAL DISORDERS

The **acquired immunodeficiency syndrome (AIDS)** is caused by the **human immunodeficiency virus (HIV)**, which weakens the immune system, attacks the brain, and renders the individual vulnerable to a wide range of opportunistic infections and tumors.

The human immunodeficiency virus contains RNA. When the virus enters a host cell, the RNA is converted to DNA by the reverse transcriptase enzyme. That DNA is then incorporated into the genome of the host cell's chromosomes. The virus replicates in the circulating blood very rapidly during the first month of infection. During this period, the virus enters both the brain and the lymphoid tissues. Following this initial period of prolific replication, the host's immune system may drastically lower viral replication rates and viral abundance. Between 6 and 8 years later, the AIDS syndrome appears, with both primary infections and secondary, opportunistic infections. Death usually follows within 4 years (Heyes, 1995).

HIV replicates in both immune system T cells, which freely enter the brain, and macrophages, or microglia, which reside within the brain and serve immunological functions for the CNS. HIV not only enters the brain,

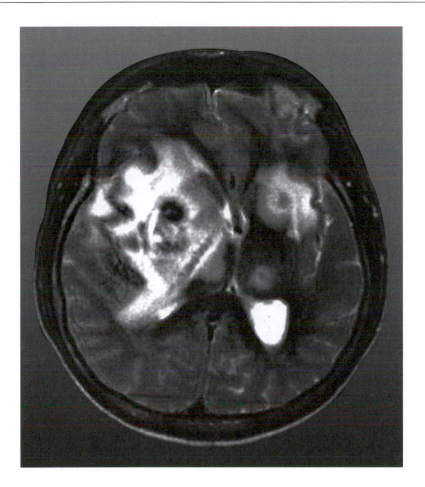

Figure 13.3. An AIDS-devastated Brain. A wide variety of opportunistic disorders can occur in the brain once the immune system is compromised.

but it is also **neurotropic**; that is, it enters and replicates in neurons (Dubois-Dalcq, Altmeyer, Chiron, & Wilt, 1995).

HIV is an infectious neurovirus that produces both direct and indirect neurotoxic effects within the human brain. Its direct effect is a viral attack on brain neurons. HIV encephalitis kills nerve cells by several mechanisms, including elevating levels of intracellular free calcium and extracellular excitatory neurotoxins. HIV, by weakening the immune system, allows other opportunistic disease processes to infect the brain as well (Stern, Perkins, & Evans, 1995).

The most prevalent neural syndrome in AIDS is subacute encephalitis, which is also called AIDS-related dementia. It is marked by losses of memory and concentration, apathy, and movement difficulties, such as weakness and imbalance. Acute psychosis also has been reported. The emotional consequences include withdrawal and depression.

HIV-1-Associated Dementia Complex   From the very beginning of the AIDS epidemic, a wide range of progressive neurocognitive symptoms was reported. This constellation of progressively severe symptoms and their associated neurological signs constitute the HIV-1-associated dementia complex (Janssen, 1991). The HIV-1-associated dementia complex is the first diagnosable AIDS-related disorder in about 25% of all AIDS patients; in another 15% of patients, it appears concurrently with another AIDS illness (Stern, Perkins, & Evans, 1995). The complex is produced by both direct and indirect effects of HIV infection.

MULTIPLE SCLEROSIS

Multiple sclerosis (MS) is a demyelinating disease, that is, one that primarily attacks the myelin coating on the axons of nerve cells while sparing the nerve cells themselves (Adams, Victor, & Ropper, 1997). In its wake, the disease leaves lesions of the myelin up to several centimeters in size, although most are very much smaller. These lesions are called plaques. They disrupt the normal functioning of the affected nerve cells.

The resulting symptoms vary quite naturally with the location of the lesions. Common symptoms include muscular weakness and coordination failure, disturbances in speaking, tingling of the hands and feet, a loss of vision and the control of eye movements, and difficulties of autonomic control. Interestingly, the cognitive processes are spared, at least until the terminal phase of the illness.

The period between the onset of the disease and the appearance of the first symptoms is about two decades. At first, only symptoms related to the primary white matter lesion are apparent. Later, more regions of the nervous system are affected, confirming the presence of MS.

Quite surprisingly, the incidence of multiple sclerosis is related to geographical location (Ebers & Sadovnick, 1993). At the equator, fewer than 1 person in 100,000 will develop MS. In the south of the United States and Europe, that number grows to 10. In the northern United States, Canada, and northern Europe, the incidence jumps to between 30 and 80 per 100,000 people. Moreover, this effect seems to be operating during youth. When people move between climates, they retain the incidence rates of their childhood.

There is also a racial difference in susceptibility to multiple sclerosis. Blacks have a lower incidence of MS than do Caucasians, but both groups show the same north-to-south differences in the prevalence of the disorder. Why this dramatic effect occurs remains an unsolved mystery.

Finally, there is probably a genetic factor involved as well because close relatives of MS patients are about 10 times more likely to develop the disease than is the general population.

DEMENTIA

Dementia is a progressive pathological decline in cognitive function, in memory, and in learned cognitive skills. It is not simply the result of aging; in healthy individuals, a high level of cognitive functioning may be preserved throughout the life span.

Dementia is diagnosed when a number of criteria are met: (a) The patient exhibits impaired memory as well as deficits in at least one other area of cognitive function (or a change in personality), (b) the impairment interferes with work or social relations, (c) the patient is not delirious, (d) and the decline cannot be attributed to any nonorganic mental disorder (Wells & Whitehouse, 1996). Thus, dementia itself is not a disease; rather, it is a syndrome of cognitive decline that results from any of several different underlying causes.

The most common cause of dementia is Alzheimer's disease, which accounts for two thirds of all dementia in the United States (about 4 million people). In another sixth of the cases of dementia, the underlying cause is vascular in nature, with multi-infarct dementia being a frequent clinical occurrence. The HIV-1-associated dementia complex, unfortunately, is increasingly common. The remaining cases of dementia have diverse neuropathologies, including Huntington's chorea and Parkinson's disease.

Alzheimer's Disease

Alzheimer's disease (AD) was named for Alois Alzheimer, a 19th-century German neurologist and neuroanatomist who first described the brain histology that characterizes AD. Auguste D. was the 51-year-old demented patient on which Alzheimer based his original description of this devastating neurological disorder. A recently discovered photograph of her is shown in Figure 13.4 on the following page.

Alzheimer's disease usually appears in the fifth or sixth decade of life. It is a relentlessly progressive and fatal dementia. Twenty percent of all patients in psychiatric institutions are hospitalized for Alzheimer's disease. There is now clear evidence that some types of AD are inherited; the presence of a first-degree relative with AD significantly increases risk for acquiring the disorder. However, inherited Alzheimer's disease is autosomal and not sex linked; it occurs equally often in men and in women. However, most patients with AD do not show clear evidence of inheriting the disorder (Lendon & Goate, 1995).

The disease itself is tragic in its consequences. It begins almost imperceptibly, with occasional lapses of memory. Names may be forgotten, the same questions may be asked repeatedly, appointments are missed, and there may be periods of confusion. But the situation quickly worsens. Major gaps in memory appear. Speech becomes labored as the patient searches for lost words.

With time, the dementia becomes profound. Sentences are not completed, as the patient forgets the intent of the sentence as it is being spoken. Visual orientation and skilled behavior also fail. The patient cannot use common objects, has difficulty dressing, and frequently becomes lost. All evidence of common manners and social courtesy vanishes. Sexual indiscretions often occur. The patient may become both paranoid and deluded. Finally, even the basic reflexes that aid in movement and regulate autonomic functions begin to fail; the Alzheimer's patient becomes both bedridden and incontinent. The dementia is then complete. Death usually occurs a decade following the first symptoms of the AD; most frequently, opportunistic infections are the cause of death (Lendon & Goate, 1995).

Neuronal loss and cerebral **atrophy**, or shrinkage, are constant features of AD. These general effects are widespread. The gyri of the cerebral cortex become smaller, and the sulci between them widen. The ventricles of the brain then expand to fill the void left by deteriorating brain tis-

Figure 13.4. Alois Alzheimer's Patient Auguste D. Auguste D. was a 51-year-old woman with dementia who became one of Alzheimer's patients in 1901. Auguste was demented and remained under Alzheimer's care in a Frankfurt hospital for the remaining 5 years of her life. An autopsy of her brain, performed in 1906, revealed an abundance of neurofibrillary tangles and plaques that uniquely identify Alzheimer's disease. Alzheimer based his description of the disorder on her case, but her case file had been lost for nearly a century. But in December 1995, the file was found in the hospital's archive. It was in pristine form and included this photograph of Auguste, looking worried and helpless. (By permission of Prof. Dr. K. Maurer, Goethe–Universität, Frankfurt am Main. This image was first published in *Lancet*, 1997, 249: 1546-1549.)

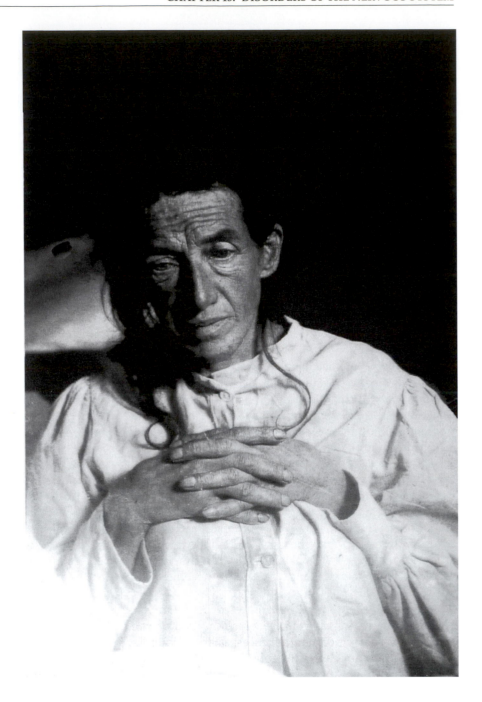

sue. Often, the atrophy of the brain is most extensive in the frontal and temporal cortex, but there is considerable variation in the gross pattern of pathology among patients. Yet all patients with Alzheimer's disease show a profound memory loss.

The cortical atrophy associated with Alzheimer's disease results from a combination of two factors. The first is *neuron death*; postmortem cell counts in patients with dementia reveal that fewer neurons are present in the cortex of Alzheimer's patients. The second cause of cerebral atrophy is *dendritic shrinkage*; the remaining cells lose much of their extensively branched dendritic trees, which are characteristic of principal neurons of the cerebral cortex.

In addition to cell loss and shrinkage, Alzheimer's disease is marked by the degeneration of the cholinergic innervation of the forebrain by neurons in the nucleus basalis. The loss of these cholinergic projections in the cerebral cortex is a critical factor in Alzheimer's disease. It is the first sign to appear, and the magnitude of the cholinergic loss is an excellent predictor of clinical deterioration. This suggests a primary relation between the forebrain cholinergic system and the cognitive decline that marks AD.

There is also preliminary evidence that stimulating cholinergic neurons in the basal forebrain with nerve growth factor may preserve these cholinergic neurons and retard the progression of the dementia (Wells & Whitehouse, 1996). Noncholinergic neural systems appear to become damaged later in the disease process, suggesting that they may play only secondary roles in producing the symptoms of AD. There is documented cell loss in both the serotonergic raphe nuclei and the noradrenergic cells of the locus ceruleus, although cell loss in these regions is less consistent than that reported for forebrain cholinergic neurons (Larson, Kukull, & Katzman, 1992; Wells & Whitehouse, 1996).

Alzheimer's primary contribution to the study of the dementia that now bears his name was in describing the unique and defining histological features that today define this disorder. It was Alois Alzheimer who first called attention to the intracellular neurofibrillary tangles and the extracellular senile plaques that distinguish AD from other forms of dementia.

Neurofibrillary tangles are pathological webs of neurofilaments that develop within the nerve cell. The twisted neurofilaments are not normal cellular proteins but may in fact be derived from them.

Neurofibrillary tangles are present in patients with Alzheimer's disease but are rare in healthy individuals. They are most prominent in the large neurons of the forebrain, including hippocampal and cortical pyramidal cells. Tangles are also seen in a number of other CNS disorders, including Down's syndrome, Parkinson's disease, and dementia pugilistica.

Senile plaques are microscopic extracellular agglomerations with an amyloid (starchlike) core composed of amyloid β protein. The core is surrounded by deformed neural processes and glial cells, forming a plaque. Senile plaques appear as irregular, spherelike structures ranging up to a few hundred micrometers in diameter. They are concentrated in the gray matter of the cerebral cortex, the hippocampus, and the amygdala structures.

Amyloid protein is a segment of a much larger protein called the amyloid precursor protein (APP). Mutations in the APP gene, which is located on chromosome 21, can cause certain types of Alzheimer's disease (Wells & Whitehouse, 1996). This is the same chromosome that also is responsible for Down's syndrome, a dementing disorder of childhood.

Little is known about the functional significance of the senile plaques, except that they are abundant in the brains of Alzheimer's patients. Few such plaques are seen in the brains of normally functioning aged individuals. However, recent studies using cultured brain tissue indicate that introducing strings of amyloid β protein both damages neurons and activates microglia, two indications that these protein strings are themselves neurotoxic (Selkoe, 1997).

There are now four different mutations, including the mutation of chromosome 21 mentioned above, that have been shown to underlie different strains of inherited AD. All these mutations act to increase either the production or the deposition of amyloid β protein. These findings, together with recent results from transgenic mice, indicate that amyloid β protein accumulation by cortical neurons occurs early and invariably in the development of AD (Selkoe, 1997). Other aspects of AD pathology only appear at later stages of the disease pathology. The ongoing familial and genetic studies of Alzheimer's disease may well provide clues at the molecular level, leading to new methods for pharmacological treatment for this pervasive, debilitating, and ultimately fatal disorder.

Multi-Infarct Dementia

Multi-infarct dementia (MID) is a syndrome of stepwise cognitive deterioration produced by multiple, often individually small strokes. In populations characterized by hypertension, including African American men, MID may be more frequent than AD as a source of cognitive decline (Geldmalcher & Whitehouse, 1995).

MID can be distinguished unequivocally from other causes of dementia by magnetic resonance imaging. Small, focal infarcts produce lacunae that are visible in MRIs. A CNS **lacuna** (from the Latin diminutive of *lacus*, meaning "lake") is a small cavity that appears in brain tissue. Lacunae are normally less than 2 cm in diameter. They are closely associated with hypertension.

Other types of neuropathology are also present in MID. Tissues showing lacunae also display evidence of axonal demyelination and axonal lesions. Breaks in the blood-brain barrier are also evident. These kinds of neuropathology are constant features of MID and may lie at the heart of the cognitive decline associated with numerous small cerebral strokes.

EPILEPSY

The disease of epilepsy was best defined nearly 150 years ago by John Hughlings Jackson, based on his clinical judgments and scientific acumen. Jackson said simply that "epilepsy is the name for occasional sudden, excessive, rapid and local discharges of the gray matter" (Taylor, 1958). The name "epilepsy" derives from the Greek word *epilesia*, meaning "to seize as with one's hand." The incidence of epilepsy is high. Following stroke, it is the second most prevalent neurological disorder in the United States, affecting more than 1 million people.

Epilepsy is a syndrome characterized by a cluster of signs and symptoms that occur together. It is not a disease because the epileptic syndrome may be produced by a diverse assortment of underlying causes, including congenital abnormalities, cerebral trauma, tumors, stroke, and toxic poisoning, among other etiologies (Trimble, Ring, & Schmitz, 1995).

The symptoms that accompany an epileptic attack or seizure in different individuals depend on the site at which the disturbance originates within the brain and the extent and pattern of the disruption. Analysis of the seizure itself can reveal much concerning its site of origin. For example, if the seizure characteristically begins with spasms of the left foot, the foot area of the contralateral precentral gyrus is very likely to be near the origin of the epileptic discharge. Although an epileptic seizure may spread to any region of the brain, its site of origin usually is restricted to the forebrain, specifically the cerebral cortex, hippocampus, amygdala, and related areas (Avoli & Gloor, 1987).

Seizures may be classified in different ways. Perhaps the most useful distinction is between **generalized seizures** and **partial seizures** (Laidlaw & Richards, 1993). All **generalized seizures** have two primary characteristics: (a) They do not have a localized onset, although they may be preceded by an aura indicating the originating site, and (b) similar abnormal epileptic electrical activity may be recorded on either side of the head throughout the seizure. The two most common types of generalized seizures are **grand mal seizure** and **petit mal seizure**. In contrast, partial seizures do have a clear point of origin, and electrical activity recorded during the seizure reflects its restricted scope. Partial seizures may be categorized as *simple* or *complex*.

Grand mal seizures, also known as **generalized convulsive seizures**, are marked by convulsion followed by coma. The seizure may or may not be preceded by an **aura**, which is taken as a warning sign of the impending seizure but is in fact the beginning of the seizure itself. Typical auras include a sinking feeling in the stomach, a movement (often an involuntary turning of the head of the body), and peculiar sensations arising somewhere in the body. The nature of the aura, when present, provides information about the originating source of the generalized seizure, although by the time consciousness is lost, all forebrain regions are involved.

The convulsion itself begins with the **tonic phase**, in which there is a violent contraction of the muscles of the body. The muscles controlling respiration are paralyzed in spasm. Consciousness is lost. The body, deprived of oxygen, turns blue. The tonic phase of the seizure lasts for about 10 seconds. It is followed by the **clonic phase**, in which violent spasms of contraction rhythmically distort the entire body of the unconscious person. This clonic phase lasts about a minute. The strength of these convulsions is often sufficient to break bones or cause other bodily injury.

After the clonic phase subsides, the person enters a coma in which the muscles are relaxed and breathing is normal. This lasts 5 or 10 minutes, after which the person either awakens dazed and confused or passes into normal sleep.

Petit mal seizures stand in marked contrast to the violence of a grand mal attack. In petit mal, the entire seizure is characterized simply by a sudden loss of consciousness, which lasts several seconds, after which the person resumes normal activity as if uninterrupted. For this reason, the petit mal seizure is often termed an *absence attack*.

During the period of the petit mal seizure, there may be gentle automatic movements of the fingers or lips, but the person does not fall and continues to perform automatic actions such as walking. The electroen-

Figure 13.5. A Petit Mal or Absence Seizure. Petit mal is marked by a characteristic three-per-second spike and wave electroencephalographic pattern.

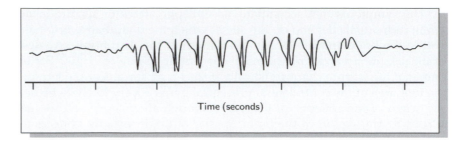

Time (seconds)

cephalogram shows a unique three-per-second spike and wave pattern, which is shown in Figure 13.5.

Partial seizures differ from generalized seizures in that the entire cortex is not involved, making the point of origin much clearer. **Complex partial seizures** normally originate in the temporal lobe or related tissue and are marked by an aura that is a complex hallucination or perceptual disturbance. Also, unlike in a generalized seizure, the person does not completely lose control of behavior but rather acts in a confused manner. There may be feelings of intense familiarity (*déjà vu*), that is, the sense that the person is actually reliving a past experience, or intense strangeness (*jamais vu*), in which the environment momentarily becomes alien.

Simple partial seizures lack these cognitive changes and instead are the product of focal discharge in sensory or motor regions. The person may experience sparks of light or feel tingling in some portion of the body. If the focus is on the motor cortex, there will be contraction of the muscles controlled by the region of the focus. If the seizure spreads along the motor cortex, the muscles of the body will be activated in the order in which they are represented on the motor cortex. This sequence is known as the **Jacksonian march**, in honor of its discoverer, John Hughlings Jackson.

The study of epileptic phenomena has provided a rich source of knowledge about human neurobiology in the many years following Jackson's seminal work. Electrical recordings made from preoperative epileptic patients have provided a unique opportunity to record the activity neurons in awake and cognizant human brains. Electrical stimulation using the same electrodes has helped neuroscientists to understand some things about the effects of neuronal activity on human behavior. In various ways over many years, epilepsy has truly given neuroscience a rare opportunity to observe the neurobiology of human thought.

SCHIZOPHRENIA

"Why do you think people believe in God?"

"Uh, let's, I don't know why, let's see, balloon travel. He holds it up for you, the balloon. He don't let you fall out, your little legs sticking down through the clouds. He's down to the smoke stack, looking through the smoke trying to get the balloon gassed up you know. Way they're flying on top that way, legs sticking out, I don't know, looking down on the ground, heck, that'd make you so dizzy you just stay and sleep you know. I used to sleep out doors, you know, sleep out doors instead of going home. He's had a home but he's not tell where it's at you know." (Chapman & Chapman, 1973, p. 3)

This strange answer to a rather thought-provoking question was given by a person suffering from **schizophrenia**, a form of psychosis and perhaps the most bizarre of all psychiatric disorders.

Unlike the disruptions of mental tranquility that disturb everyone from time to time, schizophrenic episodes represent a severe departure from normal mental functioning. The disorder has a distinctly biological character, suggesting that its fierce psychotic episodes reflect physiological alterations in normal brain function.

Psychotic Symptoms of Schizophrenia Schizophrenia is the diagnostic term for a family of severe mental disorders that involve both psychotic features—a loss of contact with reality—and a widespread deterioration of the level of mental functioning. Schizophrenic disorders are relatively longstanding; brief, isolated psychotic episodes are not classified as schizophrenic. Schizophrenia has a worldwide lifetime prevalence of approximately 1 in 100; it is equally common in men and women (Jacobson & Jacobson, 1995). The disease usually appears in adolescence or young adulthood. Schizophrenia always involves delusions, hallucinations, or similar disturbances of thought.

A **delusion** is an aberration in the content of thought—specifically, false beliefs about reality that are not shared with others and that persist despite firm contradictory evidence. Schizophrenic delusions are often persecutory, as in the belief that a television newscaster is making fun of the viewing individual. Other typical delusions are more bizarre: The individual may believe that his or her thoughts are being broadcast so that everyone nearby can hear them or that other people are inserting thoughts into his or her head. Also common is the conviction that one's thoughts and behavior are controlled by others, perhaps by radio waves. Such delusional beliefs represent a marked failure in assessing reality.

Characteristic abnormalities in the form of thought also frequently occur. Most common is a loosening of associations, in which ideas shift from one topic to another in an apparently unrelated manner. When this is severe, speech becomes incoherent.

Also common are **hallucinations**, perception without external stimulation of the sensory systems. Most hallucinations are auditory, involving voices that may make insulting statements or provide a continuing critical commentary on the individual's behavior. Tactile and somatic hallucinations, such as the perception of snakes crawling inside the abdomen, also occur. Visual hallucinations are rare.

The emotions of the schizophrenic patient are usually flattened or inappropriate. "Flattened" means a loss of emotional intensity; the patient speaks in a monotone, the face is expressionless, and the patient reports that normal feelings are no longer experienced. At other times, emotion may be present but is inappropriate to the circumstance. Disorganization is widespread in schizophrenic speech and behavior. There is also a lack of initiative, an unwillingness to speak or act.

These symptoms lead to a gross distortion of the person's interactions with the real world. There is a deterioration in social functioning, resulting in part from a preoccupation with internal thoughts and fantasies. In many cases, the acute active phase of florid schizophrenic symptoms persists for a prolonged period. While there may be a relative remission of symptoms, a complete return to normal functioning is very unusual. In fact, such a recovery calls into question the diagnosis of schizophrenia.

Cognitive Impairment in Schizophrenia   Finally, cognitive impairment is evident in schizophrenic individuals (Gold & Weinberger, 1995; Jeste, Galasko, Corey-Bloom, Walens, & Granholm, 1996). Unlike the florid psychotic symptoms that come and go throughout a schizophrenic's life, the cognitive impairment is now known to be persistent and enduring. Cognitive abilities neither lessen as psychotic symptoms appear nor improve when a psychotic episode remits. Pharmacological treatments may ameliorate psychotic symptoms, but the ongoing cognitive deterioration is unaffected (Cassens, Inglis, Appelbaum, & Gutheil, 1990; Goldberg et al., 1990).

In recent years, increasing attention has been paid to these cognitive deficits in schizophrenic patients. Although the psychotic symptoms initially captured the attention of researchers, many now believe that the less ostentatious cognitive deficits of schizophrenia may be the essential and defining core of schizophrenic disease (Gold & Weinberger, 1995; Jeste, Galasko, Corey-Bloom, Walens, & Granholm, 1996).

The pervasiveness of the cognitive deficit in schizophrenics was made clear in a recent study by Goldberg (Goldberg, Greenberg, & Griffin, 1993; Goldberg & Gold, 1995). Goldberg compared the cognitive abilities of monozygotic (identical) twins that were discordant for schizophrenia. Each twin was given standard cognitive tests that assessed memory, attention, vigilance, verbal fluency, response speed, abstraction, and IQ. On all of these tests, the unaffected twin nearly always performed at a higher level than the schizophrenic twin. Thus, when tested against age-matched, gene-matched, and socioeconomically matched controls (the unaffected twins), schizophrenics consistently were impaired. This suggests that cognitive deficit is a consistent core feature of the schizophrenic syndrome.

Genetics of Schizophrenia   One approach to studying the biology of a disease is to examine its inheritance. For schizophrenia, there seems to be an inheritable predisposition or susceptibility to the disorder, as shown in Figure 13.6 on the facing page. In the general population, the risk of schizophrenia is less than 1%.

However, this risk is much greater for relatives of schizophrenics. The parents of a schizophrenic child have about a 5% risk of schizophrenia, the siblings of a schizophrenic have about an 8% risk, and the children of a schizophrenic parent have about a 14% chance of developing the disorder. If both parents are schizophrenic, the child has a risk factor of about 25%.

The incidence of schizophrenia in monozygotic (identical) twins—when one twin is schizophrenic—is approximately 50%, which is much lower than would be expected of a purely genetic trait transmitted by a single gene. Polygenetic inheritance is suggested by these data to describe the genetic factors that predispose an individual to schizophrenic disorders (Crowe, 1995). Acquired factors must also be operating.

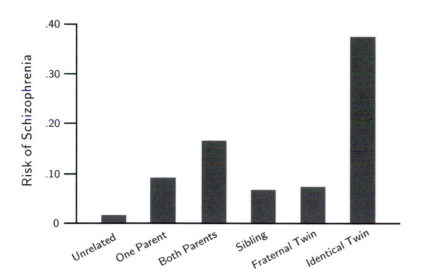

Figure 13.6. Concordance in Schizophrenia.

Further evidence of a genetic component in schizophrenia comes from studies of the children of schizophrenic patients who were separated from their parents at birth. Although reared in a normal environment, these children grow up developing schizophrenia at the same rate as offspring reared by schizophrenic parents. Such results appear to rule out explanations of schizophrenia in terms of purely environmental factors.

Early Indications of Schizophrenia   Although the psychotic symptoms of schizophrenia do not appear until many years after birth, evidence of abnormality is present very early in life.

Recent studies have shown that clear signs of cognitive and behavioral impairment are evident at a very early age and thus precede the onset of any schizophrenic symptomatology by many years. Walker and Lewine (1990), for example, demonstrated the pervasiveness of early childhood behavioral and cognitive deficits in preschizophrenic infants using home movies of schizophrenic patients and their siblings that were taken in infancy and young childhood, years before the first clinical evidence of schizophrenia appeared. Blind viewers of the films could reliably discriminate between the children who would become schizophrenic and those who would not.

Using the same method, which they call *archival observation*, Walker, Savoie, and Davis (1994) found evidence of early neuromotor dysfunction in the preschizophrenic children, as compared with their healthy siblings, with the healthy siblings of parents with affective disorders, and with children from families without mental illness. The preschizophrenic motor abnormalities were similar to the motor patterns and hand postures that commonly occur in adult schizophrenia patients. Strikingly, they were most evident when the children were photographed between infancy and 2 years of age. This is strong evidence that the abnormalities underlying adulthood schizophrenia are established very early in life and are probably present at birth.

Preschizophrenic children also have been shown to be delayed in motor development in comparison with a carefully matched sample of normal children. Jones, Rodgers, Murray, and Marmot (1994) used a cohort of 5,362 English children born in the week of March 3 to 9, 1946, in a prospective population study of child development. Thirty of these children developed schizophrenia as adults. As children, they showed evidence of neuromotor impairment. Compared with the normal children, they were delayed in walking by about 5 weeks and were later in attaining other motor milestones as well. Furthermore, the preschizophrenic children also showed more speech problems as children than did their matched controls (Jones, Rodgers, Murray, & Marmot, 1994).

Developmental Cortical Neuropathology   Anatomical studies have provided strong support for behavioral indications that schizophrenia begins early, rather than later, in life. In addition, both imaging and histological studies suggest the nature of the neural deficits that underlie schizophrenic illness.

At the level of gross anatomy, there have been repeated demonstrations of small differences in the cerebral cortices of schizophrenic patients. It was established quite some time ago that the schizophrenic brain has larger ventricles and cortical sulci, which is indicative of reduced cortical volume (Shelton & Weinberger, 1987). At the microscopic level, reduced cell counts in schizophrenics also have been reported consistently for selected cortical and periventricular regions (Weinberger, 1995).

But perhaps most compelling is the growing evidence of an error in the prenatal development of the cerebral cortex of schizophrenic patients, which may be inferred from cytoarchitectural (cell structural) analysis of the brain at autopsy.

In humans, corticogenesis (the creation of the cerebral cortex) begins in the 6th embryonic week and continues through the 17th week of fetal life (Rakic, 1995). Cortical neurons are manufactured by special cells, called progenitor cells, that are located on the ventricular surface in the center of the developing cerebral hemispheres. Special radial glial cells form long stringlike bridges between the ventricular surface and the pial surface, where the neurons forming the cortex are to be deposited.

As each neuron is formed at the ventricular surface, it attaches itself to the base of a radial glial cell and then migrates along the glial string until it reaches the pial surface, where it is deposited to form a part of the developing cerebral cortex. This region of developing cortex is called the cortical plate. As each new neuron migrates to its cortical destination, it passes through its predecessors in the developing cortical plate before depositing itself on the plate's outer surface. Thus, the cortex is constructed from the inside out. The first neurons to arrive form the innermost cortical layer, and the last to arrive form the outermost layer.

With this outline of corticogenesis in mind, the implications of some recent histological studies of the cerebral cortex in schizophrenia are clear (Jones, 1995). In one of the earliest of these cytoarchitectural studies, Jakob demonstrated that the dorsal lateral frontal cortex of schizophrenic patients contained fewer than the expected number of cells in the most superficial cortical layers but an excess of the same type of cell in a deeper layer (Jakob & Beckman, 1986). Such a finding is strong evidence of a disruption of migration late in corticogenesis, resulting in erroneous cortical wiring.

Akbarian, Bunney, et al. (1993) used a similar approach to look for the final location of a special group of neurons that are created early in corticogenesis and form a temporary structure called the *subplate*, which is located immediately beneath the developing cortex. At the end of corticogenesis, many of the subplate neurons are eliminated by programmed cell death, but some are spared and either migrate into the cortex proper or remain in place in the white matter immediately beneath the gray matter of the cerebral cortex.

Using a stain for these specific subplate neurons, Akbarian found that in the frontal cortex of normal individuals, the vestigial subplate neurons are concentrated, as they should be, at the top of the white matter abutting the deepest layer of cerebral cortex, a remnant of the transitory subplate (Akbarian, Bunney, et al., 1993). But in schizophrenics, these same cells are dispersed within the white matter instead. The same group also has reported similar findings for the temporal region of the brain (Akbarian, Vinuela, et al., 1993).

These findings have two clear implications. The first is that the subplate itself may have been misplaced at the beginning of corticogenesis in schizophrenics, and, as a result, the cerebral cortex would be formed erroneously. This would explain the presence of subplate-type cells deep in the white matter of the brain.

Second, there also must have been errors in the orderly migration of neurons into the developing cortex to explain the relative lack of subplate-type neurons in the upper white matter and the cortex itself. Improper migration also would have serious consequences for subsequent cortical function.

A similar pattern of results has recently been reported by the same research group in a study of the gene expression for NMDA receptor subunits in the schizophrenic cerebral cortex. Akbarian (Akbarian et al., 1996) found significant alterations of the normal pattern of NMDA receptor subtypes that was confined to the prefrontal regions of the cerebral cortex in schizophrenics, another indication of erroneous wiring in the schizophrenic brain. This result is even more interesting because NMDA antagonists can produce schizophrenic-like psychosis in normal individuals.

One important aspect of these findings is that they help define a timetable that specifies when pathological changes must have occurred in producing the cortical abnormalities observed in schizophrenic brains. The cytoarchitectural abnormalities just described must occur during the period of corticogenesis, that is, between the 42nd and 120th postconceptual day. Thus, whatever the pathological process may be that produces the observed cortical abnormalities must begin sometime within the period of corticogenesis.

There is also suggestive evidence that the pathological process may not continue into the third trimester of pregnancy because no signs of gliosis are seen in schizophrenia (Jeste, Galasko, Corey-Bloom, Walens, & Granholm, 1996). After birth, the brain responds to a wide variety of events that produce cell damage by triggering a glial response, a proliferation of glial cells called gliosis. The mechanisms that trigger gliosis become operative in the third trimester of pregnancy. Thus, any injury occurring at birth or any postnatal infection would leave behind the telltale signs of cortical gliosis. But no such signs are present reliably in the brains of schizophrenic patients. The most likely conclusion is that the disruptive event had occurred prenatally after the onset of corticogenesis and before the onset of the gliosis response.

These and similar results (Arnold, Hyman, Van Hoesen, & Damasio, 1991; Benes, McSparren, Bird, San Giovanni, & Vincent, 1991) suggest the presence of pervasive, diffuse neurodevelopmental abnormalities occurring long before the first appearance of overt schizophrenic symptoms. The documented deficits appear as aberrations of cortical development that must occur principally in the second trimester of pregnancy. The most appealing conclusion is that these structural abnormalities produce functional deficits in high brain functions that, in certain predisposed individuals, are expressed in young adulthood as schizophrenia (Weinberger, 1995).

Viral Insult and Schizophrenia   One interesting hypothesis is that the cortical abnormalities seen in schizophrenia may result from viral infection in the mother during the second trimester of pregnancy. This idea was proposed by Mednick, who analyzed records of hospital admissions in Helsinki, Finland (Mednick, Machon, Huttunen, & Bonett, 1988). Mednick reported that a disproportionate number of schizophrenia cases were found among individuals who were in the second trimester in utero at the time of the 1957 influenza A-2 epidemic. The idea is that the viral infection in some way disrupted brain development, resulting in schizophrenia in genetically predisposed individuals. However, there is considerable controversy over Mednick's hypothesis, which has stimulated a series of similar studies that so far have been inconclusive (Weinberger, 1995).

Biochemical Theories of Schizophrenia   Despite two decades of impressive advances in the fields of neurochemistry and neuropharmacology, little progress has been made in understanding the biochemical changes that produce the schizophrenic psychoses. There is evidence of abnormalities in a variety of brain neurotransmitter systems, but many empirical findings are controversial and do not as yet combine to provide a coherent explanation of this complex disorder. But some key features of the neurochemistry of schizophrenia are summarized below.

Dopamine   There is some evidence that abnormalities of the central nervous system dopamine system produce schizophrenia. The dopamine abnormality hypothesis of schizophrenia was stimulated by two major discoveries (Jeste, Galasko, Corey-Bloom, Walens, & Granholm, 1996). First, drugs that either reduce dopamine release or block dopamine receptors have powerful antipsychotic effects. Furthermore, the clinical efficiency of the antipsychotic drugs is nearly perfectly correlated with the degree to which these drugs block dopamine (D2) receptor sites. Second, psychotic symptoms are worsened in schizophrenics by administration of drugs that increase brain dopamine levels, block reuptake, or increase dopamine release.

One implication of the dopamine hypothesis is that there should be indications of increased dopaminergic activity in the brains of schizophrenic patients. This is in fact the case. Examinations of the brains of untreated schizophrenics and normal individuals have demonstrated a greater number of dopamine receptors—particularly D2 receptors—in schizophrenics (Wong, Wagner, & Tune, 1986). Such findings have convinced many investigators that abnormalities of the central dopamine system play key roles in the biology of psychosis.

However, it has become increasingly apparent over the past decade that the dopamine hypothesis is insufficient as a full description of schizophrenia (Kahn & Davis, 1995). Schizophrenia researchers are now convinced that one of the core features of schizophrenia is chronic cognitive impairment, a feature that is not addressed by the dopamine hypothesis. Furthermore, our understanding of the very nature of the dopamine system itself has become increasingly detailed, differentiated, and sophisticated as more is learned about the differing properties of various receptor subtypes. There is now a serious attempt to understand the roles that dopaminergic neurons play in different regions of the brain, particularly the interactions between the prefrontal cortex and subcortical portions of the dopamine system.

Serotonin There is also evidence that alterations of serotonergic neurons are present in schizophrenia and that these neurons interact with cells of the dopamine systems (Roth & Meltzer, 1995).

The idea that serotonin may play a role in schizophrenia is not new. It has been nearly 50 years since Wooley and Shaw (1954) suggested the possibility that the **psychotomimetic drugs** (compounds that produce psychoticlike effects) might provide a key to understanding the naturally occurring illness. A number of compounds are psychotomimetic.

Mescaline, for example, produces both visual and auditory hallucinations, as well as delusional thought. Mescaline is obtained from the flowering heads of the Mexican peyote cactus. **Psilocybin** is another hallucinogenic compound, which is derived from the desert teonanacatl mushroom. Because these hallucinogenic compounds mimic several aspects of psychotic disorder, it was argued that they might provide the needed key to understanding schizophrenia.

The chemical structures of these and other psychotomimetic agents are closely related to the brain catecholamines and to serotonin. In fact, both the catecholamines and serotonin can be transformed into substances with psychotomimetic properties by the relatively simple biochemical process of **transmethylation**, the transfer of a methyl group from one molecule to another. However, there is very little evidence to support the idea that the brain manufactures endogenous psychotomimetic substances in schizophrenia and quite a bit to refute it. There is no evidence, for example, of increased levels of transmethylated amines in the brains of schizophrenics. Large-scale studies attempting to affect transmethylation biochemically also have failed to support this early psychotomimetic model of schizophrenia (Ban, 1975).

Nonetheless, it is certain that presynaptic and postsynaptic changes in serotonergic neuronal activity in schizophrenia affect activity in other neurotransmitter systems as well (Roth & Meltzer, 1995). These interactions include the norepinephrine system, the cholinergic system, and the glutamate system of the brain (Bunney, Bunney, & Carlsson, 1995).

AFFECTIVE DISORDERS: DEPRESSION AND MANIA

Just as dementia is a disorder of the intellect, depression and mania are disorders of emotion or—more specifically—disorders of affect or mood, a sustained and enduring emotional state. Disorders of mood are termed **affective disorders** (Cummings & Benson, 1988; Depue & Iacono, 1989). **Depression** is the most common affective disorder, accounting for about 50% of all psychiatric hospital admissions. It is also responsible for another 10% of regular medical admissions, in which the patient's depression masquerades as a variety of physical complaints, including headache, anemia, and chronic pain syndromes.

The primary characteristic of depression is a prevailing mood of dejection, sadness, hopelessness, or despair. There is a loss of interest in people and things. Activities that previously had been pleasurable no longer seem attractive. Depressed individuals often withdraw from family and friends.

Appetite disturbances frequently occur. Usually, a normal interest in food disappears, and the person begins to lose weight. However, some depressed individuals experience a pronounced increase in appetite, which results in weight gain. Disturbances of sleep are also common.

Although some depressed people become agitated, continually moving, or restless, most experience a slowing and depression of motor activity. Speech becomes less rapid and less energetic. The depressed individual moves more slowly and accomplishes less. Even simple tasks may seem hopelessly difficult and demanding. Thinking is also slowed, and there is usually difficulty in concentration. Ruminating thoughts of death and suicide are common.

Some depressed individuals experience psychotic delusions. These delusions are congruent with a depression of mood, centering on such themes as disease and destruction. However, psychotic delusions are not a necessary feature of profound depression.

There is no typical age for the onset of depression; it occurs with approximately equal frequency at any age from childhood to old age. About 20% of all females and 10% of all males experience at least one major depressive episode during their lifetimes. The incidence of depressive episodes requiring hospitalization is about 6% for women and 3% for men.

A distinction must be made between depression and **grief**, or uncomplicated bereavement. The death of a loved one often provokes a full depressive syndrome, either immediately or within the first few months following the death. Such a reaction is normal and dissipates by itself with time. The sadness of bereavement differs from that of depression in that it is not unrelenting and all-pervasive.

Some depressed people also experience periods of mania. In a number of aspects, **mania** is the mirror image of depression. A manic episode is marked by an elevated, often euphoric mood. There is a continual and uncritical enthusiasm for interacting with people and doing things. In some people, however, mania results in irritability rather than exuberance.

Manic individuals make endless plans and engage in ceaseless activities. Often, their behavior is domineering and demanding. The unrealistic optimism and lack of judgment may result in careless behavior, such as extensive shopping sprees, unwise business activities, or uncharacteristic sexual adventures.

Unlike the depressed patient, the manic individual has apparently limitless energy. Speech is rapid and loud, sometimes reflecting loose associations and a flight of ideas. Concentration is impaired by distractibility. Sleep may be reduced; sometimes, individuals will go for days without sleeping at the height of a manic episode. If delusions are present, their content is in keeping with the euphoric manic mood.

The initial manic episode nearly always occurs before the age of 30. Some individuals experience isolated manic episodes that are separated by many years of normal functioning; in others, periods of mania occur in clusters. The incidence of mania is less than 1% and is equally prevalent in men and women.

In nearly all manic individuals, manic episodes alternate with periods of depression. This syndrome is termed **bipolar depression**, reflecting the characteristic alternation between these two polar extremes of mood; **unipolar depression** is depression in the absence of mania.

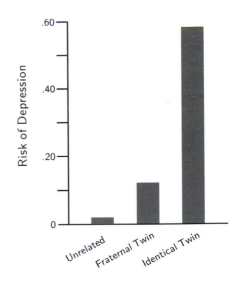

Figure 13.7. Concordance in Bipolar Depression.

Genetic Factors in Depression and Mania Although all people may become depressed in response to life's adversities, certain individuals are more likely to enter a profound depression than are others. There is little question that this tendency may be inherited. Relatives of depressed individuals have an increased vulnerability to depression. For example, the incidence of bipolar depression in the general population is on the order of 1%. However, this figure rises to between 10% and 25% for relatives of manic-depressive patients.

Perhaps the most striking evidence of genetic factors in bipolar depression comes from the study of twins, as shown in Figure 13.7. The probability that a dizygotic (fraternal) twin of a manic-depressive patient will incur this unlikely disorder is about 15%. For monozygotic (identical) twins, who develop from the same genetic material, the probability is more than 70%.

These rates differ from those reported for unipolar depression. The probability that a dizygotic twin of a person with unipolar depression will also exhibit the disorder is about 15%; for monozygotic twins, the probability is about 40%.

The difference in inheritance probabilities of unipolar and bipolar depression suggests that unipolar and bipolar disorders have different genetic bases. Furthermore, the inheritance patterns for neither disorder follow any simple genetic model. Multiple genes must be responsible for the predisposition to either unipolar or bipolar depression.

Biochemical Factors in Depression The ancient Greeks had a biochemical theory of depression. They held that depression resulted from the failure of the liver to remove toxic substances from food. The accumulation of black bile was thought to produce depression. Today, we use the word

Figure 13.8. The Serotonin Projection
System of the Human Brain.

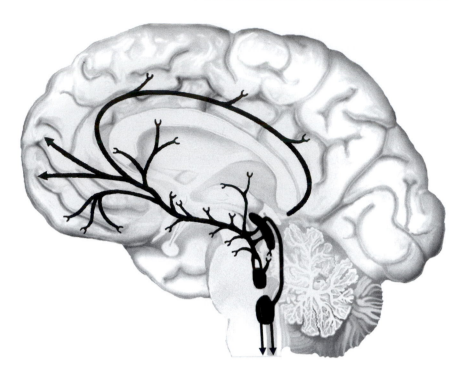

melancholy to refer to sadness; some psychiatrists term extreme depression *melancholia*. (In Greek, *melan* means "black," and *chole* means "bile.") Modern biochemical theories of depression are not concerned with bile of any sort but rather with the accumulation and depletion of brain neurotransmitters. There is no complete biochemical theory of depression, but a number of significant advances in understanding the biological basis of depression have been made.

Contemporary biochemical theories of depression have focused on two of the monoamines: norepinephrine and serotonin. The major serotonergic neurons are located in the raphe nuclei of the brain stem, as shown in Figure 13.8. These cells project diffusely throughout the nervous system,

Similarly, the noradrenergic system also projects widely from cell bodies located in the locus ceruleus (see Figure 13.9 on the next page). This system plays a major role in maintaining arousal and alertness in the normal brain (Aston-Jones, 1985).

Several lines of converging evidence seem to implicate these two neurotransmitters in affective disorders (Hardman & Limbird, 1996). The first finding concerns reserpine. **Reserpine** is an alkaloid derived from the Indian medicinal herb *Rauwolfia serpentina*, which has been used on the Indian subcontinent to treat illness for hundreds of years. Reserpine was introduced to Western medicine in the 1950s as a treatment for schizophrenia but was soon found to elicit depressive symptoms in schizophrenic patients. Pharmacologically, reserpine acts to deplete presynaptic supplies of the catecholamines within the CNS. These facts suggested that depression might result from the depletion of one or more of the biogenic amines.

The second line of evidence linking the monoamines and depression comes from the fact that monoamine oxidase inhibitors provide an effec-

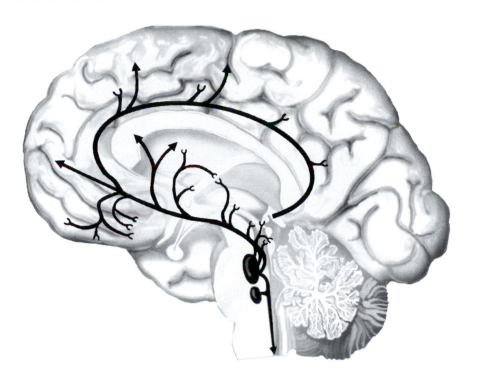

Figure 13.9. The Noradrenergic Projection System of the Human Brain.

tive treatment in many cases of depression. Monoamine oxidase inhibitors block the central action of the enzyme monoamine oxidase. **Monoamine oxidase (MAO)** is the enzyme that inactivates norepinephrine, dopamine, and serotonin, converting these molecules into biologically inactive compounds. Thus, the MAO inhibitors both clinically relieve depression and pharmacologically slow the destruction of brain monoamines. This lends support to the idea that depression results from a depletion of monoamines within the CNS.

A third line of converging evidence is supplied by the tricyclic antidepressants. The **tricyclic antidepressants** are a family of compounds that are derived from phenothiazine, a potent antipsychotic agent. Tricyclic antidepressants are thought to relieve depression by blocking the reuptake of the monoamines by the presynaptic element. In this way, more of the neurotransmitter substance remains within the synaptic cleft, where it may exert its effect.

These three findings form much of the biochemical basis linking the monoamines and depression, but there are difficulties with the monoamine hypothesis. One problem is that reserpine may not, in fact, produce depression but may simply mimic the motor slowing that is common in depressed patients. This motor slowing is attributable to the depletion of dopamine and may be reversed by administering the dopamine precursor L-DOPA. Unfortunately, L-DOPA has no effect as an antidepressant.

A second problem concerns the antidepressant effects of the MAO inhibitors. Although these drugs are potent therapies for depression, it is not clear that they produce their benefits by blocking monoamine oxidase. In particular, these compounds also reduce the reuptake of the catecholamines at the presynaptic synapse and therefore may function in the same manner as the tricyclic antidepressants. Such a result would still be congruent with the monoamine hypothesis. However, until the mechanism of action of the MAO is established, the question remains open.

There are also problems with the reuptake hypothesis of understanding the antidepressant effects of the tricyclics. If blocking monoamine reuptake is the critical factor by which the tricyclics exert their effects, then any agent that blocks reuptake should be an effective antidepressant. However, cocaine is a potent inhibitor of monoamine reuptake within the CNS, yet this drug is without effect in treating depression. Such findings are confusing and prevent any clear acceptance of the monoamine hypothesis of depression, at least for the moment.

Biochemical Factors in Mania   Closely related to depression is mania. Rather little is known about the biochemistry of mania, except for one significant fact: Mania may be effectively and specifically controlled by **lithium**. Lithium is one of the elements, a simple atom that forms a white metal. Lithium was first introduced into medical practice in the 1800s in the form of a salt for the treatment of gout. However, for a variety of reasons, this practice was abandoned, and lithium virtually disappeared from medical practice.

In 1949, John Cade, an Australian, discovered that lithium has a marked effect in treating mania (Cade, 1982). Lithium is neither a tranquilizer nor a sedative; it does not render the patient sluggish or sleepy. Rather, lithium appears to normalize the mood of a manic patient, both taming the bouts of mania and moderating the periods of depression. Interestingly, lithium has little effect on nonmanic individuals. Because of this specificity, lithium may hold a key to understanding the biochemistry of manic disorders.

The biochemical effects of lithium within the body are widespread. Lithium is immediately absorbed by the gastrointestinal tract and transported to virtually every tissue of the body. It remains within the tissues for about 1 day before being excreted by the kidneys. Lithium alters the body concentrations of sodium and potassium as well as the excretion rates for both these basic biological ions. Lithium also affects the hormones that control body electrolyte balance, such as aldosterone. Such far-reaching and fundamental biological effects may be responsible for lithium's antimanic properties.

Furthermore, lithium alters the regulation of the monoamines within the CNS. For example, lithium has profound effects on serotonergic function. Lithium results in an increased brain uptake of tryptophan, the substrate from which serotonin is produced. However, lithium also induces a decrease in the activity of tryptophan hydroxylase, the initial enzyme involved in the synthesis of serotonin. The net effect is that serotonin levels remain unchanged. It is suspected that the change in the dynamics of serotonin synthesis may stabilize serotonergic function and thereby stabilize the mood of manic patients.

Lithium also affects brain catecholamines; it increases the efficiency of norepinephrine reuptake by the presynaptic membrane and thereby decreases the availability of norepinephrine at the postsynaptic neuron. Together, the effects of lithium on both catecholaminergic and serotonergic activity further implicate these monoamines in affective disorders.

Serotonin Reuptake Blockers   Striking advances in the clinical treatment of depression have followed the introduction of highly selective serotonin blockers, specifically fluoxetine (Prozac) (Grilly, 1998; Montgomery, 1995). Fluoxetine does not produce the unwanted side effects that are induced by other antidepressants, such as anxiety, insomnia, and nausea. It is highly effective in treating depression and is now widely prescribed.

The success of fluoxetine also has generated a new and perhaps deeper understanding of the role of monoamines in affective disorders. At low serotonin levels, norepinephrine may drive affect, such that low norepinephrine results in depression and high norepinephrine produces mania. Increasing serotonin appears to stabilize the system, accounting for the effectiveness of fluoxetine as an antidepressive agent. Interestingly, one of the long-term effects of lithium is to stabilize serotonin synthesis (Grilly, 1998; Montgomery, 1995).

GENE THERAPY FOR BRAIN DISORDERS

Molecular biology has not only fundamentally deepened our understanding of the human brain and its dysfunctions, but it is also beginning to suggest powerful new approaches to the treatment of neurological disorders. In the past, molecular biology and genetics have served medicine well both by providing molecular characterizations for a number of disease processes and by creating new pharmaceuticals with which diseases may be treated.

But the idea of gene therapy is something much more radical. By **gene therapy** is meant the introduction of functional genetic material into specific bodily cells for the treatment of disease. In gene therapy, genetic material provides the treatment. Such therapy for diseased brains, an idea that once seemed impossible, is now the subject of active investigation and may someday offer new hope for patients with neurological diseases (Mullitan, 1993).

Gene therapies are being considered for several types of neurological disorders (Karpati, Hochmüller, Nalbantoglu, & Durham, 1996). The first is genetic diseases, such as Huntington's chorea, which was described in Chapter 7. Here, the underlying defect is a genetic mutation. For diseases in which the mutant gene is recessive, a direct gene replacement therapy for cells expressing the gene may be effective. For diseases resulting from the expression of a dominant mutant gene, more complex strategies may be required (Karpati, Hochmüller, Nalbantoglu, & Durham, 1996).

For genetic diseases of unknown origin and nongenetic neurological disorders, other strategies of gene therapy may be possible. One is the insertion of genes that encode neuroprotective molecules and would reduce cell death and destruction in cells affected by the disease. It may also be desirable to insert genes that encode neurotrophic substances to counteract specific effects of certain disorders. Genes that express neurotransmitter molecules, receptor proteins, and other functionally important components of the neuronal environment are other potential tools for gene therapy. Such treatments may someday prevent, or at least slow, the loss of specific neuronal populations that are attacked by disease processes.

Gene-therapeutic strategies also have been suggested for treating tumors of the central nervous system. It may be possible to genetically remove malignant CNS tumors by introducing so-called "suicide genes" or vascularization inhibitory factors that would target tumor cells growing within the brain. All of these prospects are tantalizing possibilities for applying the new genetic technologies to the fight against neurological dysfunction.

But the questions dominating discussions of gene therapy for the nervous system are concerned primarily with how to apply these developing technologies to neurological medicine safely and effectively. Here the issue of vectors is of major concern.

A **vector** is an agent that inserts genetic material into an organism or a cell. Vectors are usually either a virus (a segment of DNA or RNA enclosed in a protein coat that replicates within a host cell) or a **plasmid** (a small circular piece of DNA that replicates independently of the genome). Both viruses and plasmids are widely used as vectors in molecular biology.

At present, two of the most promising vectors for gene therapy experiments are *replication-incompetent herpes simplex virus* and various *adenovirus* preparations. Herpes simplex vectors have been used in vitro to introduce functioning transgenes into cultured neurons from the rodent spinal cord, cerebellum, basal ganglia, thalamus, hippocampus, and neocortex. In vivo, herpes simplex–based vectors have successfully targeted primary injection sites in the caudate, dentate gyrus, and cerebellar cortex of the rat. Adenoviral recombinant vectors also have been used to target a variety of cell types within the rodent central nervous system (Karpati, Hochmüller, Nalbantoglu, & Durham, 1996).

Vectors containing therapeutic genes might be directed at their targets in several ways. Small targets might be inoculated by using stereotaxically guided syringes for direct injection into the target tissue. Other cell populations could be targeted indirectly, taking advantage of the retrograde axonal-transport affinities of certain viral vectors. Such an indirect procedure has been proposed for applications of gene therapy involving spinal or brain stem motor neurons.

One indication of the possible efficacy of gene therapy for human neurological disorders was provided by Choi-Lundberg and his coworkers (Choi-Lundberg et al., 1997). They studied the effects of glial cell line-derived neurotrophic factor (GDNF) on dopaminergic neurons in the substantia nigra, using a rodent model of human Parkinson's disease. GDNF is a neurotropic factor that protects dopaminergic neurons in both primate and rodent models of Parkinson's disease. It must be continuously available to the affected neurons to be effective. This is not practical using conventional methods for administering drugs to the human brain stem.

Choi-Lundberg et al. (1997) circumvented this problem by using an adenoviral vector to deliver human GDNF to the substantia nigra of rats that had been given 6-hyrdroxydopamine (6-OHDA) progressive lesion, a well-studied rodent model for human Parkinson's disease. They injected a viral vector with human GDNF (or an impotent mutant of GDNF) unilaterally into a site immediately dorsal to the substantia nigra.

The results were clear. The vectored GDNF provided significant protection against cell death for dopaminergic neurons in the substantia nigra on the injected side of the brain. Mutant GDNF provided no protection against the Parkinson's-like lesions produced by 6-OHDA. Furthermore, synthesis of GDNF protein produced by the gene vector continued in therapeutically meaningful amounts for at least 3 weeks following gene treatment. Such findings indicate that true gene therapy for neurological diseases may indeed be possible.

Although today's visions of new gene-therapeutic procedures for treating the age-old diseases of the brain will undoubtedly be proven wrong in many details, both molecular biologists and neuroscientists are convinced that the broad outlines of our present dreams of neurological gene therapy will be proven by time to be correct and that safe, practical, and effective gene therapies will eventually be developed. That is an exciting possibility.

SUMMARY

Dysfunctions of the central nervous system may arise from many different causes and produce effects of minor or major consequence. Cerebral trauma—penetrating wounds, contusion, and concussion—are among the most common causes of CNS dysfunction. Cerebrovascular accidents or strokes result in brain lesions, as neural tissue is deprived of fresh blood. Transient ischemic attacks are similar but short lasting. Congenital ateriovenous malformations shunt blood away from the capillary system and prevent neuronal development in that brain region. Space-occupying tumors first disrupt activity in their immediate vicinity, but, as intracranial pressure increases, widespread neural dysfunctions may result.

Infections can produce catastrophic effects, as is evident in a number of disorders, including AIDS-related dementia. Multiple sclerosis, a disease that attacks the myelin sheath of axons, and the epilepsies, syndromes marked by uncontrolled neural discharge, are other types of neurological disorders.

Alzheimer's disease is a progressive and debilitating dementia, a progressive decline in cognitive function. Similar cognitive decline is produced in multi-infarct dementia.

Epilepsy is the sudden synchronous discharge of neurons within a region of the brain. It may be produced by a wide variety of underlying disease processes. Seizures may be either partial or generalized.

Schizophrenia is a debilitating psychotic disorder that is characterized by loose associative thought, delusions, hallucinations, flattened or inappropriate emotion, and withdrawal from the environment. A predisposition to schizophrenia is inherited, but the genetics of that inheritance are not simple. Preschizophrenic children manifest behavioral abnormalities long before the onset of the first psychotic symptoms. There are also multiple indications of early developmental abnormalities in the formation of the cerebral cortex of schizophrenic patients.

Mania and depression are forms of affective disorder. Depression is marked by a dejection of mood and a slowing of thought and behavior and may be accompanied by delusions. In bipolar depression, periods of depression alternate with episodes of mania. The tendency toward depression is inheritable. The most common biochemical theories of depression postulate abnormalities in one or more of the brain monoamine projection systems, but no convincing evidence for any biochemical theory of affective disorder is yet available.

Gene therapies, which will involve the introduction of functional genetic material into the human brain, are being developed for the treatment of a number of neurological disorders. They represent an entirely new and potentially very powerful tool for neurological treatment in the not too distant future.

SELECTED READINGS

- Ogden, J. A. (1996). *Fractured minds: A case-study approach to clinical neuropsychology*. New York: Oxford University Press. An extraordinarily readable introduction to neuropsychology through the artful presentations of individual patients. Accurate and insightful, Ogden's book is recommended reading for anyone concerned about neural dysfunctions.

- Kaufman, D. M. (1995). *Clinical neurology for psychiatrists* (4th ed.). Philadelphia, PA: Saunders. A clearly written textbook of neurological disorders. Although aimed at physicians, many others will find this a rewarding book to read. Numerous questions with concise answers aid even a casual reader in mastering neurological information.

- Fogel, B. S., & Schiffer, R. B. (1996). *Neuropsychiatry*. Baltimore, MD: Williams & Wilkins. This large scholarly collection of authoritative essays provides up-to-date summaries of the most important topics in contemporary neuropsychiatric research. It is an excellent starting point for anyone wishing a deeper understanding of psychiatric disorders and their neurobiological underpinnings.

- Jacobson, J. L., & Jacobson, A. M. (1995). *Psychiatric secrets*. Philadelphia, PA: Hanley and Belfus. This immensely readable book is a part of a larger series of books that provide practical guidance to medical students and other health care professionals. Written in question-and-answer format, its "secrets" are useful to anyone concerned with psychiatric disorders and their treatment.

KEY TERMS

acquired immunodeficiency syndrome (AIDS) A disorder of the immune system caused by the HIV virus that renders the person vulnerable to a wide range of opportunistic infections and tumors.

affective disorders A class of psychiatric disorders marked by a disturbance of mood or emotion.

Alzheimer's disease (AD) A progressive dementia resulting from cerebral atrophy.

amyloid plaques Starchlike deposits formed from prion protein.

arteriovenous malformation (AVM) A congenital disorder in which blood is shunted directly from the arterial to the venous system through a series of large vessels that bypass the capillary system.

atrophy Shrinking.

aura The consciously perceived onset of a seizure, the content of which varies between individuals depending primarily upon seizure locus.

bipolar depression An affective disorder in which depression alternates with episodes of mania.

blunt head injury An injury caused by a blow to the head in which the skull is not penetrated by a foreign object.

bovine spongiform encephalopathy A transmissible spongiform encephalopathy of cattle, commonly referred to as *mad cow disease*.

cerebral trauma Brain injury.

cerebrovascular accident (CVA) A blockage of cerebral blood flow resulting in cell death.

cerebrovascular disorders Abnormalities of the blood vessels of the brain.

clonic phase The second period of a grand mal seizure, marked by violent convulsions.

complex partial seizures Seizures marked by an aura that is a complex hallucination or perceptual disturbance.

concussion Cerebral trauma without evidence of hemorrhage.

contusion Cerebral trauma with evidence of hemorrhage.

Cruezfeldt-Jakob disease (CJD) A spongiform encephalopathy marked by dementia and other neurological manifestations that rapidly proceeds to coma and death.

delusion An aberration in the content of thought—specifically, false beliefs about reality that are not shared with others and that persist despite firm contradictory evidence.

dementia The loss of intellectual function produced by brain damage.

dementia pugilistica A dementia resulting from repeated cerebral trauma, usually concussion; punch drunk.

depression A dejection of mood, to be distinguished from grief.

diagnosis The determination of cause; identifying a disease from its signs and symptoms.

encephalitis An inflammation of the brain.

epilepsy An intermittent derangement of the brain produced by a sudden, intense, uncontrolled discharge of cerebral neurons.

functional disorder A syndrome lacking strong evidence of a causal mechanism.

gene therapy The introduction of functional genetic material into specific bodily cells for the treatment of disease.

generalized seizure A seizure without localized onset in which similar electrical activity can be recorded from either side of the head during the seizure.

gliosis A proliferation of astrocytes.

grand mal seizure A generalized convulsive seizure.

grief A naturally occurring emotional response to the loss of a loved one; to be distinguished from depression.

hallucinations Perception without external stimulation of the sensory systems.

hemorrhage Bleedding, the escape of blood from the vascular system.

human immunodeficiency virus (HIV) The virus that gives rise to the acquired immunodeficiency syndrome (AIDS).

infarct An infarction.

infarction An area of cell death resulting from a sudden insufficiency of the arterial or venous blood supply.

ischemia A disruption of the flow of blood.

Jacksonian march A focal seizure involving the motor cortex in which the sequence of convulsive movements represents the somatotopic mapping of the prefrontal gyrus.

kuru A fatal prion infection transmitted by cannibalistic rituals among the Fore people of New Guinea.

lacuna A small cavity in a tissue.

lithium A white metal element that is useful in treating mania.

Lyme disease A bacterial CNS infection.

mania An affective disorder that is characterized by elation and heightened activity; the opposite of depression.

meningitis An infection of the meninges.

mescaline A hallucinogenic alkaloid derived from a desert cactus.

monoamine oxidase (MAO) The brain enzyme that inactivates the monoamines norepinephrine, dopamine, and serotonin.

multi-infract dementia (MID) A syndrome of stepwise cognitive deterioration produced by multiple, often individually small strokes that is often linked with hypertension.

multiple sclerosis (MS) A demyelinating disease of the nervous system.

neoplasm See *tumor.*

neurofibrillary tangles Pathological webs of neurofilaments within the nerve cell, a characteristic of Alzheimer's disease.

neurosyphilis A bacterial encephalitis, an infection produced by the spirochete *Treponema pallidum*.

neurotropic With respect to a virus, one that enters neurons and replicates there.

obstructive hydrocephalus The blockage of normal cerebrospinal fluid flow resulting in increased intracranial pressure.

partial seizure An epileptic seizure that does not involve the entire cortex.

penetrating head wounds An injury caused when the skull is penetrated by a foreign object.

petit mal seizure An epileptic seizure marked by a loss of consciousness lasting several seconds without convulsions and marked by a characteristic three-per-second spike and wave pattern in the encephalogram.

plasmid A small circular piece of DNA that replicates independently of the genome.

prion (proteinaceous infectious particle) A malfolded version of a normal cellular protein.

psilocybin A hallucinogenic crystalline substance obtained from a desert mushroom.

psychotomimetic drug A compound that produces psychoticlike symptoms.

reserpine A compound derived from the Indian medicinal herb *Rauvolfia serpentina*, once used extensively in the treatment of schizophrenia, that may produce side effects resembling depression.

schizophrenia A type of psychosis characterized by loose associations, delusions, hallucinations, inappropriate emotion, and withdrawal.

scrapie A form of transmissible spongiform encephalopathy found in sheep.

senile plaques Abnormal deposits seen on neurons of patients with Alzheimer's disease.

sign Any objective evidence of a disease or syndrome.

simple partial seizures Focal seizures lacking an elaborate aura.

spongiform encephalopathies A class of neurological diseases that produce neuronal loss and the development of vacuoles, or small empty spaces, in the infected tissue, giving the brain a spongelike appearance

stroke See *cerebrovascular accident*.

symptom Any subjective evidence of a disease, as perceived by a patient.

syndrome A pattern of signs and symptoms that occur together in a particular group of patients.

tonic phase The initial phase of a grand mal seizure marked by continuous tension of the muscles.

transient global amnesia A profound but temporary impairment of memory produced by transient ischemic attack within the basilar artery.

transient ischemic attack (TIA) A temporary interruption of the brain's blood supply that causes short-lasting functional disruption of the brain through ischemia.

transmethylation The transfer of a methyl group from one type of molecule to another.

transmissible spongiform encephalopathy (TSE) A rapidly progressive, devastating CNS disorder with wide-ranging symptoms that produce neuronal loss and the development of vacuoles, or small empty spaces, in the infected tissue, giving it a spongelike appearance.

tricyclic antidepressants A family of antidepressant agents derived from phenothiazine that are thought to achieve their effect by blocking the reuptake of the monoamines.

tumor A new, uncontrolled, and progressive growth of tissue.

unipolar depression Depression without mania.

vector An agent that inserts genetic material into an organism or a cell.

virus A segment of DNA or RNA enclosed in a protein coat that replicates within a host cell.

References

Adams, R. D., Victor, M., & Ropper, A. H. (1997). *Principles of neurology* (6th ed.). New York: McGraw-Hill.

Ader, R., Madden, K., Felten, D. L., Bellinger, D. L., & Schiffer, R. B. (1996). Psychoneuroimmunology: Interactions between the brain and the immune system. In B. S. Fogel & R. B. Schiffer (Eds.), *Neuropsychiatry* (p. 193-221). Baltimore, MD: Williams & Wilkins.

Adolphs, R., Tranel, D., Damasio, H., & Damasio, A. (1994). Impaired recognition of emotion in facial expressions following bilateral damage to the human amygdala. *Nature, 372,* 669-672.

Adolphs, R., Tranel, D., Damasio, H., & Damasio, A. (1995). Fear and the human amygdala. *Journal of Neuroscience, 15(9),* 697-706.

Akbarian, S., Bunney, W. E. J., Potkin, S. G., Wigal, S. B., Hagman, J. O., Sandman, C. A., & Jones, E. G. (1993). Altered distribution of nicotiamide-adenine dinucleotide phosphate-diaphorase cells in frontal lobe of schizophrenics implies disturbances of cortical development. *Archives of General Psychiatry, 50,* 169-177.

Akbarian, S., Sucher, N. J., Bradley, D., Tafazzoli, A., Trinh, D., Hetrick, W. P., Potkin, S. G., Sandman, C. A., Bunney, W. E. J., & Jones, E. G. (1996). Selective alterations in gene expression for NMDA receptor subunits in prefrontal cortex of schizophrenics. *Journal of Neuroscience, 16,* 19-30.

Akbarian, S., Vinuela, A., Kim, J. J., Potkin, S. G., Bunney, W. E. J., & Jones, E. G. (1993). Distorted distribution of nicotiamide-adenine dinucleotide phosphate-diaphorase neurons in temporal lobe of schizophrenics implies anomalous cortical development. *Archives of General Psychiatry, 50,* 178-187.

Akil, H. A., & Morano, M. I. (1996). Stress. In B. S. Fogel & R. B. Schiffer (Eds.), *Neuropsychiatry* (p. 773-785). Baltimore, MD: Williams & Wilkins.

Alberts, B., Bray, D., Lewis, J., Raff, M., Roberts, K., & Watson, J. D. (1994). *Molecular biology of the cell* (3rd ed.). New York: Garland.

Aldrich, M. S. (1992). Narcolepsy. *Neurology, 42 (Suppl. 6).*

Allard, T., Clark, S. A., Jenkins, W. M., & Merzenich, M. M. (1991). Reorganization of somatosensory area 3b representations in adult owl monkeys after digital syndactyly. *Journal of Neurophysiology, 66,* 1048-1058.

Allen, L. S., & Gorski, R. A. (1990). Sex difference in the bed nucleus of the stria terminalis of the human brain. *Journal of Comparative Neurology, 302,* 669-672.

Allen, L. S., Hines, M., Shryne, J. E., & Gorski, R. (1989). Two sexually dimorphic cell groups in the human brain. *Journal of Neuroscience, 9,* 497-506.

Allman, J., & Brothers, L. (1994). Faces, fear and the amygdala. *Nature, 372,* 613-614.

American Psychiatric Association (APA). (1994). *Diagnostic and statistical manual of mental disorders: DSM-IV.* Washington, D.C.: American Psychiatric Association.

Anderson, M. (1993). Virus infections of the nervous system. In J. Walton (Ed.), *Brain's diseases of the nervous system* (10th ed., p. 317-350). Oxford, UK: Oxford University Press.

Anholt, R. R. (1993). Molecular neurobiology of olfaction. *Critical Reviews in Neurobiology, 7,* 1-22.

Arnold, A. P., & Jordon, C. L. (1988). Hormonal organization of neural circuits. *Frontiers in Neuroendocrinology, 10,* 185-214.

Arnold, S. E., Hyman, B. T., Van Hoesen, G. W., & Damasio, A. R. (1991). Some cytoarchitectural abnormalities of the entorhinal cortex in schizophrenia. *Archives of General Psychiatry, 48,* 625-632.

Asanuma, H. (1989). *The motor cortex.* New York: Raven.

Aston-Jones, G. (1985). Behavioral functions of locus coeruleus derived from cellular attributes. *Physiological Psychology, 13,* 118-126.

Avoli, M., & Gloor, P. (1987). Epilepsy. In G. Adelman (Ed.), *Encyclopedia of neuroscience* (p. 400-403). Boston: Birkhäuser.

Ban, T. A. (1975). Nicotinic acid in the treatment of schizophrenias: Practical and theoretical considerations. *Neuropsychobiology, 1,* 133-145.

Baylor, D. (1996). How photons start vision. *Proceedings of the National Academy of Science of the USA, 93,* 560-565.

Beatty, J. (1982). Task-evoked pupillary responses, processing load, and the structure of processing resources. *Psychological Bulletin, 91,* 167-172.

Beatty, J., Barth, D. S., Richer, F., & Johnson, R. A. (1986). Neuromagnetometry. In M. G. H. Coles, E. Donchin, & S. W. Porges (Eds.), *Handbook of psychophysiology* (p. 26-42). New York: Guilford.

Beggs, J. M., Brown, T. H., Byrne, J. H., Crow, T., LeDoux, J. E., LeBar, K., & Thompson, R. F. (1999). Learning and memory: Basic mechanisms. In M. J. Zigmond, F. E. Bloom, S. Landis, J. L. Roberts, & L. R. Squire (Eds.), *Fundamental neuroscience* (p. 1411-1454). San Diego, CA: Academic Press.

Békésy, G. von. (1956). Current status of theories of hearing. *Science, 123,* 779-783.

Békésy, G. von. (1960). *Experiments in hearing.* New York: McGraw-Hill.

Benes, P. M., McSparren, J., Bird, E. T., San Giovanni, J. P., & Vincent, S. L. (1991). Deficits in small interneurons in prefrontal and cingulate cortices of schizophrenic and schizoaffective patients. *Archives of General Psychiatry, 48,* 996-1001.

Bennett, G. W., & Whitehead, S. A. (1983). *Mammalian neuroendocrinology.* New York: Oxford University Press.

Benson, D. F. (1985). Aphasia. In K. M. Heilman & E. Valenstein (Eds.), *Clinical neuropsychology.* New York: Oxford University Press.

Bergeijk, W. A. van. (1967). The evolution of vertebrate hearing. In W. Neff (Ed.), *Contributions to sensory physiology* (Vol. 2). New York: Academic Press.

Bernard, C. (1856). *Leçons de physiologie expérimentale appliquée à la medicine faites au college de france* (Vol. II). Paris: Bailliere.

Bernstein, J. (1979). Investigations on the thermodynamics of biolelectric currents, translated from the original: *Pflüger Arch.,* 521-562, 1902. In G. R. Kepner (Ed.), *Cell membrane permeability and transport* (p. 184-210). Straudsburg, PA: Dowden, Hutchinson, and Ross.

Betz, A. L., Goldstein, G. W., & Katzman, R. (1994). The blood-brain-cerebrospinal fluid barriers. In G. J. Siegel & B. W. Agranoff (Eds.), *Basic neurochemistry: Molecular, cellular, and medical aspects* (5th ed., p. 681-699). New York: Raven.

Blasdel, G. G., Obermayer, K., & Kiorpes, L. (1995). Organization of ocular dominance and orientation columns in neonatal macaque monkeys. *Visual Neuroscience, 12,* 589-603.

Blasdel, G. G., & Salama, G. (1986). Voltage-sensitive dyes reveal a modular organization in the monkey striate cortex. *Nature, 321,* 579-585.

Blass, E. M., & Epstein, A. N. (1971). A lateral preoptic osmosensitive zone for thirst. *Journal of Comparative and Physiological Psychology, 76,* 378-394.

Bliss, T. V. P., & Lømo, T. (1973). Long-lasting potentiation of synaptic transmission in the dentate area of the anaesthetized rabbit following stimulation of the perforant path. *Journal of Physiology (London), 232,* 331-356.

Bloodstone, O. A. (1995). *Handbook of stuttering.* San Diego, CA: Singular Group.

Blumstein, S. E., Alexander, M. P., Ryalls, J. H., Katz, W., & Sworetzky, B. (1995). On the nature of the foreign accent syndrome: A case study. *Brain and Language, 31,* 215-244.

Bowden, D. M., & Martin, R. F. (1995). NeuroNames brain hierarchy. *Neuroimage, 2,* 6383.

Bozarth, M. A., & Wise, R. A. (1986). Involvement of the ventral tegmental dopamine system in opioid and psychomotor stimulant reinforcement. *NIDA Research Monograph, 67,* 190-196.

Brandner, S., Isenmann, S., Raeber, A., Fischer, M., Sailer, A., Kabayashi, Y., Marino, S., Weissmann, C., & Aguzzi, A. (1996). Normal host prion protein necessary for scrapie-induced neurotoxicity. *Nature, 379,* 339-343.

Brazier, M. A. B. (1960). *The electrical activity of the nervous system.* New York: Macmillan.

Breedlove, S. M. (1995). Another important organ. *Nature, 378,* 15-16.

Bremer, F. (1977). Cerebral hypnogogic centers. *Annals of Neurology, 2,* 1-6.

Bremner, J. D., Randall, P., Scott, T. M., Bronen, R. A., Seibyl, J. P., Southwick, S. M., Delaney, R. C., McCarthy, G., Charney, D. S., & Innis, R. B. (1995). MRI-based measurement of hippocampal volume in patients with combat-related posttraumatic stress disorder. *American Journal of Psychiatry, 152,* 973-981.

Brobeck, J. R. (1955). Neural regulation of food intake. *Annals of the New York Academy of Science, 63,* 44-55.

Brodal, A. (1981). *Neurological anatomy in relation to clinical medicine* (3rd ed.). New York: Oxford University Press.

Brownstein, M. J. (1994). Neuropeptides. In G. J. Siegel, B. W. Agranoff, R. W. Albers, & P. B. Moninoff (Eds.), *Basic neurochemistry: Molecular, cellular, and medical aspects* (5th ed., p. 341-365). New York: Raven.

Bunney, B. G., Bunney, W. E. J., & Carlsson, A. (1995). Schizophrenia and glutamate. In F. E. Bloom & D. J. Kupfer (Eds.), *Psychopharmacology: The fourth generation of progress* (p. 1205-1214). New York: Raven.

Burgdorfer, W., Barbour, A. G., & Hayes, S. F. (1982). Lyme disease: A tick borne spirochaetosis. *Science, 216,* 1317-1319.

Burke, R. E. (1978). Motor units: Physiological, histochemical profiles, neural connectivity, and functional specialization. *American Zoologist, 18,* 127-134.

Byne, W. (1994). The biological evidence challenged. *Scientific American, 270,* 50-55.

Cade, J. F. (1982). Lithium salts in the treatment of psychotic excitement. *Australia and New Zealand Journal of Psychiatry, 16,* 128-133.

Cannon, W. B. (Ed.). (1929). *Bodily changes in pain, hunger, fear, and rage* (2nd ed.). New York: Harper & Row.

Caruso, A. J. (1991). Neuromotor processes underlying stuttering. In H. F. M. Peters, W. Hulstijn, & C. W. Starkweather (Eds.), *Speech motor control and stuttering* (p. 101-116). Amsterdam: Exerpta Medica.

Cassens, G., Inglis, A., Appelbaum, P., & Gutheil, T. (1990). Neuroleptics: Effects on neuropscholigical function in chronic schizophrenic patients. *Schizophrenia Bulletin, 16,* 477-499.

Chapman, L. J., & Chapman, J. P. (1973). *Disordered thought in schizophrenia.* New York: Appleton-Century-Crofts.

Chase, M., & Weitzman, E. D. (1983). *Sleep disorders: Basic and clinical research.* New York: SP Medical and Scientific Books.

Choi-Lundberg, D. L., Lin, Q., Chang, Y. N., Chiang, Y. L., Hay, C. M., Mohajeri, H., Davidson, B. L., & Bohn, M. C. (1997). Dopaminergic neurons protected from degeneration by GDNF gene therapy. *Science, 275,* 838-841.

Chua, S. C. J., Chung, W. K., Wu-Peng, S., Zhang, Y., Liu, S. M., Tartaglia, L., & Leibel, R. L. (1996). Phenotypes of mouse diabetes and rat fatty due to mutations in the OB (leptin) receptor. *Science, 271,* 994-996.

Coghill, R. C., Talbot, J. D., Evans, A. C., Meyer, E., Gjedde, A., Bushnell, M. C., & Duncan, G. H. (1994). Distributed processing of pain and vibration by the human brain. *Journal of Neuroscience, 14,* 4095-4108.

Coleman, R. M. (1986). *Awake at 3:00 A. M.: By choice or by chance.* New York: Freeman.

Collaer, M. L., & Hines, M. (1995). Human behavioral sex differences: A role for gonadal hormones during early development? *Psychological Bulletin, 118,* 55-107.

Considine, R. V., Sinha, M. K., Heiman, M. L., Kriauciunas, A., Stephens, T. W., Nyce, M. R., Ohannesian, J. P., Marco, C. C., McKee, L. J., Bauer, T. L., & Caro, J. F. (1996). Serum immunoreactive-leptin concentrations in normal-weight and obese humans. *New England Journal of Medicine, 354,* 292-295.

Cooper, J. R., Bloom, F. E., & Roth, R. H. (1996). *The biochemical basis of neuropharmacology* (7th ed.). New York: Oxford University Press.

Corbett, D., & Wise, R. A. (1980). Intracranial self-stimulation in relation to the ascending dopaminergic systems of the midbrain: A moveable electrode mapping study. *Brain Research, 185,* 1-15.

Cornell, T. L., Fromkin, V. A., & Mauner, G. (1993). A linguistic approach to language processing in Broca's aphasia: A paradox resolved. *Current Directions in Psychological Science, 2,* 47-52.

Crane, T. (1999). The mind-body problem. In R. A. Wilson & F. C. Keil (Eds.), *The MIT encyclopedia of the cognitive sciences* (p. 546-548). Cambridge: MIT Press.

Critchley, M. (1986). *The citadel of the senses and other essays.* New York: Raven.

Crowe, R. R. (1995). Genetics. In F. E. Bloom & D. J. Kupfer (Eds.), *Psychopharmacology: The fourth generation of progress* (p. 1821-1833). New York: Raven.

Crystal, D. (1997). *The Cambridge encyclopedia of language* (2nd ed.). Cambridge, UK: Cambridge University Press.

Cummings, J. L., & Benson, F. (1988). Psychological dysfunction accompanying subcortical dementias. *Annual Review of Medicine, 39,* 53-61.

Cuvier, G. (1805). *Lecons d'anatomie comparee.* Paris: Crochard et Cie.

Dale, H. H. (1953). *Adventures in physiology.* London: Pergamon.

Dalessio, D. J., & Silberstein, S. D. (1993). *Wolff's headache and other head pain.* New York: Oxford University Press.

Damasio, A. R., Bellugi, U., Damasio, H., Poizner, H., & Gilder, J. V. (1986). Sign language aphasia during left-hemisphere amytal injection. *Nature, 322,* 363-365.

Damasio, H., & Damasio, A. R. (1969). *Lesion analysis in neuropsychology.* New York: Oxford University Press.

Damasio, H., Grabowski, T. J., Frank, R., Galaburda, A. M., & Damasio, A. R. (1994). The return of Phineas Gage: Clues about the brain from the skull of a famous patient. *Science, 264,* 1102-1105.

Damasio, H., Grabowski, T. J., Tranel, D., Hichwa, R. D., & Damasio, A. R. (1996). A neural basis for lexical retrieval. *Nature, 380,* 499-505.

Darwin, C. (1859). *The origin of species by means of natural selection, or the preservation of favoured races in the struggle for life* (1st ed.). London: John Murray.

Darwin, C. (1872). *The expression of emotion in man and animals.* London: John Murray.

Davis, B. J. (1991). The ascending gustatory pathway: A Golgi analysis of the medial and lateral parabrachial complex in the adult hamster. *Brain Research Bulletin, 27,* 63-73.

DeArmond, S. J., & Prusiner, S. B. (1995). Prion diseases. In F. E. Bloom & D. J. Kupfer (Eds.), *Psychopharmacology: The fourth generation of progress* (p. 1521-1530). New York: Raven.

DeLorey, T. M., & Olsen, R. W. (1994). GABA and glycine. In G. J. Siegel, B. W. Agranoff, R. W. Albers, & P. B. Moninoff (Eds.), *Basic neurochemistry: Molecular, cellular, and medical aspects* (5th ed., p. 389-399). New York: Raven.

Dement, W. C. (1974). *Some must watch while some must sleep.* San Francisco: Freeman.

DeMoranville, B. M., & Jackson, I. M. D. (1996). Neuropsychiatry. In B. S. Fogel & R. B. Schiffer (Eds.), *Neuropsychiatry* (p. 173-192). Baltimore, MD: Williams & Wilkins.

Denes, P. B., & Pinson, E. N. (Eds.). (1993). *The speech chain: The physics and biology of spoken language.* New York: Freeman.

Depue, R. A., & Iacono, W. G. (1989). Neurobehavioral aspects of affective disorders. *Annual Review of Psychology, 40,* 457-492.

Descartes, R. (1835). *Œuvres philosophiques de Descartes, publièes d'apreès les textes originaux, avec notices, sommaires et èclaircissements par Adolphe Garnier.* Paris: L. Hachette.

Deutsch, J. A. (1990). Food intake: Gastric factors. In E. M. Stricker (Ed.), *Neurobiology of food and fluid intake: Handbook of behavioral biology* (Vol. 10, p. 151-182). New York: Plenum.

DiChiara, G., & Imperato, A. (1987). Perferential stimulation of dopamine release in the nucleus accumbens by opiates, alcohol, and barbiturates: Studies with transcerebral dialysis in freely moving rats. *Annals of the New York Academy of Science, 473,* 367-381.

Ding, J. M., Chen, D., Weber, E. T., Faiman, L. E., Rea, M. A., & Gillette, M. U. (1994). Resetting the biological clock: Mediation of nocturnal circadian shifts by glutamate and NO. *Science, 266,* 1713-1717.

Dingledine, R., & McBain, C. J. (1994). Excitatory amino acid transmitters. In G. J. Siegel, B. W. Agranoff, R. W. Albers, & P. B. Moninoff (Eds.), *Basic neurochemistry: Molecular, cellular, and medical aspects* (5th ed., p. 367-388). New York: Raven.

Dowling, J. E. (1987). *The retina: An approachable part of the brain.* Cambridge, MA: Harvard University Press.

Dubois-Dalcq, M., Altmeyer, R., Chiron, M., & Wilt, S. (1995). HIV interactions with cells of the nervous system. *Current Opinion in Neurobiology, 5,* 647-655.

Duman, R. S., & Nestler, E. J. (1995). Signal transduction pathways for catecholamine receptors. In F. E. Bloom & D. J. Kupfer (Eds.), *Psychopharmacology: The fourth generation of progress* (p. 303-320). New York: Raven.

Duvernoy, H. M. (1988). *The human hippocampus.* Munich: J. F. Bergmann Verlag.

Ebers, G. D., & Sadovnick, A. D. (1993). The geographic distribution of multiple sclerosis: A review. *Neuroepidemiology, 12,* 1-5.

Eccles, J. C., & Gibson, W. C. (1979). *Sherrington: His life and thought.* Berlin: Springer-Verlag.

Eichenbaum, H. B., Cahil, L. F., Gluck, M. A., Hasselmo, M. E., Keil, F. C., Martin, A. J., McGaugh, J. L., Murre, J., Myers, C., Petrides, M., Roozendaal, B., Schacter, D. L., Simons, D. J., Smith, W. C., & Williams, C. L. (1999). Learning and memory: Systems analysis. In M. I. Zigmond, F. E. Bloom, S. C. Landis, J. L. Roberts, & L. R. Squire (Eds.), *Fundamental neuroscience* (p. 1455-1486). San Diego, CA: Academic Press.

Ekman, P. (Ed.). (1982). *Emotion in the human face.* Cambridge, UK: Cambridge University Press.

Elbert, T., Pantev, C., Wienbruch, C., Rockstroh, B., & Taub, E. (1995). Increased cortical representation of the fingers of the left hand of string players. *Science, 270,* 305-307.

Essen, D. C. van, Anderson, C. H., & Felleman, D. J. (1992). Information processing in the primate visual system: An integrated systems perspective. *Science, 255,* 419-423.

Fain, G. L. (1999). *Molecular and cellular physiology of neurons.* Cambridge, MA: Harvard University Press.

Fawcett, D. W. (1981). *The cell* (2nd ed.). Philadelphia, PA: W. B. Saunders.

Felleman, D. J., & Essen, D. C. van. (1991). Distributed hierarchical processing in the primate cerebral cortex. *Cerebral Cortex, 1,* 1-47.

Fibiger, H. C., Le Piane, F. G., Jakubovic, A., & Phillips, A. G. (1987). The role of dopamine in intracranial self-stimulation of the ventral tegmental area. *Journal of Neuroscience, 7,* 3888-3896.

Fischman, M. W. (1984). The behavioral pharmacology of cocaine in humans. In J. Grabowski (Ed.), *Cocaine: Pharmacology, effects, and treatment of abuse* (p. 73-92). Washington, DC: Government Printing Office.

Foundas, A. L., Leonard, C. M., Gilmore, R. L., Fennell, E. B., & Heilman, K. M. (1994). Planum temporale asymmetry and language dominance. *Neuropsychologia, 32,* 1225-1231.

Foundas, A. L., Leonard, C. M., Gilmore, R. L., Fennell, E. B., & Heilman, K. M. (1996). Pars triangularis asymmetry and language dominance. *Proceedings of the National Academy of Science of the USA, 93,* 719-722.

Fox, P. T., Ingham, R. J., Ingham, J. C., Hirsch, T. B., Downs, J. H., Martin, C., Jerabek, P., Glass, T., & Lancaster, J. L. (1996). A PET study of the neural systems of stuttering. *Nature, 382,* 158-162.

Frazer, A., & Hensler, J. G. (1994). Serotonin. In G. J. Siegel, B. W. Agranoff, R. W. Albers, & P. B. Moninoff (Eds.), *Basic neurochemistry: Molecular, cellular, and medical aspects* (5th ed., p. 283-308). New York: Raven.

Friedman, M. I., & Stricker, E. M. (1976). The physiology of hunger: A physiological perspective. *Psychological Review, 83,* 409-431.

Friston, K. J., Frith, C. D., Liddle, P. F., & Frackowiak, R. S. J. (1991). Investigating a network model of word generation with positron emission tomography. *Proceedings of the Royal Society of London, Series B, 244,* 101-106.

Fromkin, V., & Rodman, R. (Eds.). (1993). *An introduction to language* (5th ed.). Fort Worth, TX: Harcourt Brace.

Fuster, J. M. (1989). *The prefrontal cortex: Anatomy, physiology, and neuropsychology of the frontal lobe.* New York: Raven.

Gajdusek, D. C., & Zigas, V. (1957). Degenerative disease of the central nervous system in New Guinea: The endemic occurrence of kuru in the native population. *New England Journal of Medicine, 257,* 974-978.

Galaburda, A. M. (1993). Neurology of developmental dyslexia. *Current Opinion in Neurobiology, 3,* 237-242.

Garcia, J., & Rusiniak, K. W. (1977). Visceral feedback and the taste signal. In J. Beatty & H. Legewie (Eds.), *Biofeedback and behavior* (p. 59-71). New York: Plenum.

Gardner, H. (1976). *The shattered mind: The person after brain damage.* New York: Knopf.

Gardner, R. A., & Gardner, B. (1969). Teaching sign language to a chimpanzee. *Science, 165,* 664-672.

Gazzaniga, M. S. (1970). *The bisected brain.* New York: Appleton-Century-Crofts.

Geldmalcher, D. S., & Whitehouse, P. J. (1995). Multi-infarct dementia. In F. E. Bloom & D. J. Kupfer (Eds.), *Psychopharmacology: The fourth generation of progress* (p. 1513-1520). New York: Raven.

Gelineau, J. B. E. (1977). De la narcolepsie. In D. A. Rottenberg & F. H. Hochberg (Eds.), *Neurological classics in modern translation* (p. 283-285). New York: Hafner. (Original work published 1880)

Gerald, C., Walker, M. W., Criscione, L., Gustafson, E. L., Batzl-Hartmann, C., Smith, K. E., Vaysse, P., Durkin, M. M., Laz, T. M., Linemeyer, D. L., Schaffhauser, A. O., Whitebreat, S., Hofbauer, K. G., Taber, R. I., Branchek, T. A., & Weinshank, R. L. (1996). A receptor subtype involved in neuropeptide-Y-induced food intake. *Nature, 382,* 168-171.

Geschwind, N. (1970). The organization of language and the brain. *Science, 170,* 940-944.

Geschwind, N., & Behan, P. O. (1984). Laterality, hormones, and immunity. In N. Geschwind & A. M. Galaburda (Eds.), *Cerebral dominance: The biological foundation* (p. 211-224). Cambridge, MA: Harvard University Press.

Geschwind, N., & Levitsky, W. (1968). Human brain: Left-right asymmetries in temporal speech region. *Science, 161,* 186-187.

Geyer, S., Ledberg, A., Schieicher, A., Kinomura, S., Schormann, T., Burgel, U., Klingberg, T., Larsson, J., Zilles, K., & Roland, P. E. (1996). Two different areas within the primary motor cortex of man. *Nature, 382,* 805-807.

Gibbons, A. (1991). Deja vu all over again: Chimp-language wars. *Science, 251,* 1561-1562.

Gilman, A. G. (1937). The relation between blood osmotic pressure, fluid distribution, and voluntary water intake. *American Journal of Physiology, 120,* 323-328.

Gilman, A. G., Goodman, L. S., Rall, T. W., & Murad, F. (1985). *The pharmacological basis of therapeutics* (7th ed.). New York: Macmillan.

Gloor, P. (1969). *Hans Berger on the electroencephalogram of man.* Amsterdam: Elsevier.

Goa, J. H., Parsons, L. M., Bower, J. M., Xiong, J., Li, J., & Fox, P. T. (1996). Cerebellum implicated in sensory acquisition and discrimination rather than motor control. *Science, 272,* 545-547.

Gold, J. M., & Weinberger, D. (1995). Cognitive deficits and the neurobiology of schizophrenia. *Current Opinion in Neurobiology, 5,* 225-230.

Goldberg, T. E., & Gold, J. M. (1995). Neurocognitive functioning in patients with schizophrenia. In F. E. Bloom & D. J. Kupfer (Eds.), *Psychopharmacology: The fourth generation of progress* (p. 1245-1257). New York: Raven.

Goldberg, T. E., Greenberg, R., & Griffin, S. (1993). The impact of clozapine on cognition and psychiatric symptoms in patients with schizophrenia. *British Journal of Psychiatry, 162,* 43-48.

Goldberg, T. E., Ragland, D. R., Gold, J., Bigelow, L. B., Torrey, E. F., & Weinberger, D. R. (1990). Neuropsychological assessment of monozygotic twins discordant for schizophrenia. *Archives of General Psychiatry, 47,* 1066-1072.

Goldfarb, L. G., & Brown, P. (1995). The transmissible spongiform encephalopathies. *Annual Review of Medicine, 46,* 57-65.

Goldman-Rakic, P. S. (1992). Working memory and the mind. *Scientific American, 267,* 110-117.

Gorski, R. A., Gordon, J. H., & Shryne, J. E. (1978). Evidence for a morphological sex difference within the medial preoptic area of the rat brain. *Brain Research, 148,* 333-346.

Gould, E., Reeves, A. J., Graziano, M. S. A., & Gross, C. G. (1999). Neurogenesis in the neocortex of adult primates. *Science, 628,* 548-552.

Grafman, J., & Salazar, A. (1996). Traumatic brain injury. In B. S. Fogel & R. B. Schiffer (Eds.), *Neuropsychiatry* (p. 935-945). Baltimore, MD: Williams & Wilkins.

Graybiel, A. M. (1995). Building action repertoires: Memory and learning functions of the basal ganglia. *Current Opinion in Neurobiology, 5,* 733-741.

Grilly, D. M. (1998). *Drugs and human behavior* (3rd ed.). Boston: Allyn & Bacon.

Grinker, J. A. (1982). Physiological basis of human obesity. In D. W. Pfaff (Ed.), *The physiological mechanisms of motivation* (p. 145-163). New York: Springer-Verlag.

Grossman, S. P. (1975). Role of the hypothalamus in the regulation of food and water intake. *Psychological Review, 82,* 200-224.

Gurd, J. M., Bessell, N. J., Bladon, R. A., & Bamford, J. M. (1988). A case of foreign accent syndrome, with follow-up clinical, neuropsychological and phonetic descriptions. *Neuropsychologia, 25,* 237-251.

Guyton, A. C. (1991). *Textbook of medical physiology* (8th ed.). Philadelphia, PA: W. B. Saunders.

Hadlow, W. J. (1959). Scrapie and kuru. *Lancet, 2, 289.*

Hall, Z. W. (1992). *Introduction to molecular neurobiology.* Sunderland, MA: Sinauer and Associates.

Halmi, K. A. (1987). Anorexia nervosa and bulimia. *Annual Review of Medicine, 38,* 373-380.

Hardman, J. G., & Limbird, L. E. (Eds.). (1996). *Goodman and Gilman's the pharmacological basis of threapeutics* (9th ed.). New York: McGraw-Hill.

Harinarayan, C. V., Ammini, A. C., Karmarkar, B. G., Prakash, V., Gupta, R., Taneja, N., Mohapatra, I., Kucheria, K., & Ahuja, M. M. S. (1992). Congenital adrenal hyperplasia and complete masculinization masquerading as sexual precocity and cryptoorchidism. *Indian Pediatrics, 29,* 103-106.

Heath, R. (1964). *The role of pleasure in behavior.* New York: Harper & Row.

Heilman, K. M., & Satz, P. (Eds.). (1983). *Neuropsychlogy of human emotion.* New York: Guilford.

Heir, D., & Crowley, W. (1982). Spatial ability in androgen deficient men. *New England Journal of Medicine, 306,* 1202-1205.

Hellemans, A., & Bunch, B. (1988). *The timetables of science: A chronology of the most important people and events in the history of science.* New York: Simon & Schuster.

Herbert, T. B., & Cohen, S. (1993). Depression and immunity: A meta-analytic review. *Psychological Bulletin, 113,* 472-486.

Herrnstein, R. J., & Boring, E. G. (Eds.). (1965). *A source book in the history of psychology.* Cambridge, MA: Harvard University Press.

Heyes, M. P. (1995). Potential mechanisms of neurologic disease in hiv infection. In F. E. Bloom & D. J. Kupfer (Eds.), *Psychopharmacology: The fourth generation of progress* (p. 1559-1566). New York: Raven.

Hickok, G., Bellugi, U., & Klima, E. S. (1996). The neurobiology of sign language and its implications for the neural basis of language. *Nature, 381,* 699-702.

Hille, B. (1992). *Ionic channels of excitable membranes* (2nd ed.). Sunderland, MA: Sinauer Associates.

Hille, B., & Catterall, W. A. (1994). Electrical excitability and ion channels. In G. J. Siegel, B. W. Agranoff, R. W. Albers, & P. B. Molinoff (Eds.), *Basic neurochemistry: Molecular, cellular, and medical aspects* (5th ed.). New York: Raven.

Hines, M. (1990). Gonadal hormones and human cognitive development. In J. Balthazart (Ed.), *Hormones, brain, and behavior in vertebrates: 1. Sexual differentiation, neuroanatomical aspects, neurotransmitters, and neuropeptides* (Vol. 8, p. 51-63). Basel: Karger.

Hines, M., Alsum, P., & Roy, M. (1987). Estrogenic contributions to sexual differentiation in the female guinea pig: Influences of diethylstilbestrol and tamoxifen on neural, behavioral, and ovarian development. *Hormones and Behavior, 21,* 402-412.

Hines, M., Davis, F. C., & Coquelin, A. (1985). Sexually dimoprhic regions in the medial preoptic area and the bed nucleus of the stria terminalis of the guinea pig brain: A description and and investigation of their relationship to gonadal steroids in adulthood. *Journal of Neuroscience, 5,* 40-47.

Hines, M., & Green, R. (1991). Human hormonal and neural correlates of sex-typed behaviors. *Review of Psychiatry, 10,* 536-555.

Hines, M., & Shipley, C. (1984). Prenatal exposure to tiethylstilbestrol and development of sexually dimorphic cognitive abilities and cerebral lateralization. *Developmental Review of Psychiatry, 20,* 81-94.

Hobson, J. A. (1985). The neurobiology and pathophysiology of sleep and dreaming. *Discussions in the Neurosciences, 2,* 1-50.

Hobson, J. A. (1987). Functional theories of sleep. In G. Edelman (Ed.), *Encyclopedia of neuroscience* (Vol. 1, p. 1100-1101). Boston: Birkhäuser.

Hobson, J. A. (1995). *Sleep.* New York: Scientific American Library.

Hodgkin, A. L. (1964). *The conduction of the nervous impulse.* Liverpool, UK: Liverpool University Press.

Hodgkin, A. L., & Katz, B. (1949). The effect of sodium ions on the electrical activity of the squid. *Journal of Physiology, 108,* 37-77.

Howard, I. P. (1986). The vestibular system. In K. R. Boff, L. Kaufman, & J. P. Thomas (Eds.), *Handbook of perception and performance* (Vol. 2). New York: John Wiley.

Howlett, R. (1996). Prime time for neuropeptide Y. *Nature, 382,* 113.

Hubel, D. H. (1982). Explorations of the primary visual cortex: 1955–1978. *Nature, 299,* 515-524.

Hubel, D. H. (1995). *Eye, brain, and vision* (2nd ed.). New York: Scientific American Library.

Hubel, D. H., & Livingstone, M. S. (1987). Segregation of form, color, and stereopsis in primate area 18. *Journal of Neuroscience, 7,* 3378-3415.

Hubel, D. H., & Wiesel, T. N. (1961). Integrative action in the cat's lateral geniculate body. *Journal of Physiology, 155,* 385-398.

Hubel, D. H., & Wiesel, T. N. (1962). Receptive fields, binocular interaction, and functional architecture in the cat's visual cortex. *Journal of Physiology, 160,* 106-154.

Imperato-McGinley, J., Peterson, R. E., Gautier, T., & Sturla, E. (1979). Male pseudohermaphroditism secondary to 5-alpha-reductase deficiency: A model for the role of androgens in both the development of the male phenotype and the evolution of male gender identity. *Journal of Steroid Biochemistry, 11,* 637-645.

International Anatomical Nomenclature Committee. (1983). *Nomina Anatomica* (5th ed.). Baltimore, MD: Williams & Wilkins.

Jacobson, J. L., & Jacobson, A. M. (1995). *Psychiatric secrets.* Philadelphia, PA: Hanley and Belfus.

Jakob, H., & Beckman, H. (1986). Prenatal developmental disturbances in the limbic allocortex in schizophrenics. *Journal of Neural Transmission, 65,* 303-326.

James, W. (1890). *Principles of psychology* (Vol. II). New York: Dover.

Jansen, A. S. P., Nguyen, X. V., Karpitskiy, V., Mettenleiter, T. C., & Loewy, A. D. (1995). Central command neurons of the sympathetic nervous system: Basis of the fight-or-flight response. *Science, 270,* 644-646.

Janssen, R. S. (1991). Nomenclature and research case definitions for neurological manifestations of human immunodeficiency virus-type 1 (HIV-1) infection: Report of a working group of the American Academy of Neurology AIDS Task Force. *Neurology, 41,* 778-785.

Jarvilehto, T., Hamalainen, H., & Soininen, K. (1981). Peripheral neural basis of tactile sensations in man: 2. Characteristics of human mechanoreceptors in the hair skin and correlations of their activity with tactile sensation. *Brain Research, 219,* 13-27.

Jeste, D. V., Galasko, D., Corey-Bloom, J., Walens, S., & Granholm, E. (1996). Acute treatment of schizophrenia. In B. S. Fogel & R. B. Schiffer (Eds.), *Neuropsychiatry* (p. 325-344). Baltimore, MD: Williams & Wilkins.

Jones, B. E. (1991). *The role of noradrenergic locus coeruleus neurons and neighboring cholinergic neurons of the pontomesencephalic tegmentum in sleep-waking states.*

Jones, E. G. (1995). Cortical development and neuropathology in schizophrenia. *Ciba Foundation Symposium, 193,* 277-295.

Jones, P., Rodgers, B., Murray, R., & Marmot, M. (1994). Child development risk factors for adult schizophrenia in the British 1946 birth cohort. *Lancet, 344,* 1398-1402.

Joyner, A. L. (1994). Gene targeting and development of the nervous system. *Current Opinion in Neurobiology, 4,* 37-42.

Just, M. A., & Carpenter, A. (1992). A capacity theory of comprehension: Individual differences in working memory. *Psychological Review, 99,* 122-149.

Just, M. A., & Carpenter, A. (1993). The intensity dimension of thought: Pupillometric indices of sentence processing. *Canadian Journal of Experimental Psychology, 47,* 310-339.

Just, M. A., Carpenter, P. A., Keller, T. A., Eddy, W. F., & Thulborn, K. R. (1996). Brain activation modulated by sentence comprehension. *Science, 274,* 114-116.

Kachalsky, S. G., Jensen, B. S., Barchan, D., & Fuchs, S. (1995). Two subsites in the binding comain of the acetylcholine receptor: An aromatic subsite and a proline subsite. *Proceedings of the National Academy of Science of the USA, 92,* 10801-10805.

Kahn, R. S., & Davis, K. L. (1995). New developments in dopamine and schizophrenia. In F. E. Bloom & D. J. Kupfer (Eds.), *Psychopharmacology: The fourth generation of progress* (p. 1193-1203). New York: Raven.

Kandel, E. R. (1991a). Cellular mechanisms of learning and the biological basis of individuality. In R. R. Kandel, J. H. Schwartz, & T. M. Jessell (Eds.), *Principles of neural science* (3rd ed.). New York: Elsevier.

Kandel, E. R. (1991b). Disorders of thought: Schizophrenia. In R. R. Kandel, J. H. Schwartz, & T. M. Jessell (Eds.), *Principles of neural science* (3rd ed.). New York: Elsevier.

Karni, A., Tanne, D., Rubenstein, B. S., Askenasy, J. J. M., & Sagi, D. (1994). Dependence on REM sleep of overnight improvement of a perceptual skill. *Science, 263,* 679-682.

Karpati, G., Hochmüller, H., Nalbantoglu, J., & Durham, H. (1996). The principles of gene therapy for the nervous system. *Trends in Neurosciences, 19,* 49-54.

Katz, B. (Ed.). (1966). *Nerve, muscle, and synapse.* New York: McGraw-Hill.

Kaufman, D. M. (Ed.). (1995). *Clinical neurology for psychiatrists* (4th ed.). New York: Oxford University Press.

Kaupp, U. B., & Koch, K. W. (1992). Role of cGMP and Ca^2 in vertebrate photoreceptor excitation and adaptation. *Annual Review of Physiology, 54,* 153-176.

Kean, D., & Smith, M. (Eds.). (1986). *Magnetic resonance imaging: Principles and applications.* Baltimore, MD: Williams & Wilkins.

Kellogg, W. N. (1968). Communication and language in home-raised chimpanzee. *Science, 162,* 423-427.

Kelly, D. D. (1991a). Disorders of sleep and consciousness. In E. R. Kandel, J. H. Schwartz, & T. M. Jessell (Eds.), *Principles of neural science* (3rd ed., p. 805-819). New York: Elsevier.

Kelly, D. D. (1991b). Sexual differentiation of the nervous system. In E. R. Kandel, J. H. Schwartz, & T. M. Jessell (Eds.), *Principles of neural science* (3rd ed., p. 959-973). New York: Elsevier.

Kelly, D. D. (1991c). Sleeping and dreaming. In E. R. Kandel, J. H. Schwartz, & T. M. Jessell (Eds.), *Principles of neural science* (3rd ed., p. 792-804). New York: Elsevier.

Kennedy, M. B., & Marder, E. (1992). Cellular and molecular mechanisms of neuronal plasticity. In Z. W. Hall (Ed.), *Introduction to molecular neurobiology.* Sunderland, MA: Sinauer Associates.

Kertesz, A. (Ed.). (1979). *Aphasia and associated disorders: Taxonomy, localization, and recovery.* New York: Grune and Stratton.

Kester, P., Green, R., & Ginch, S. (1980). Prenatal "female hormone" administration and psychosexual development in human males. *Psychoneuroendocrinology, 2,* 269-285.

Ketter, T. A., Andreason, P. J., George, M. S., & Lee, C. (1996). Anterior paralimbic mediation of procaine-induced emotional and psychosensory experiences. *Archives of General Psychiatry, 53,* 59-69.

Kimura, D., & Hampson, E. (1994). Cognitive pattern in men and women is influenced by fluctuations in sex hormones. *Current Directions in Psychological Science, 3,* 57-61.

Kinnamon, S. C., & Cummings, T. A. (1992). Chemosensory transduction mechanisms in taste. *Annual Review of Physiology, 54,* 715-731.

Kinomura, S., Larsson, J., Gulyas, B., & Roland, P. E. (1996). Activation by attention of the human reticular formation and thalamic intralaminar nuclei. *Science, 271,* 512-515.

Klein, D., Milner, B., Zatorre, R. J., Meyer, E., & Evans, A. C. (1995). The neural substrates underlying word generation: A bilingual functional-imaging study. *Proceedings of the National Academy of Science of the USA, 92,* 2899-2903.

Klein, D., Zatorre, R. J., Milner, B., Meyer, E., & Evans, A. C. (1994). Left putaminal activation when speaking a second language: Evidence from PET. *NeuroReport, 5,* 2295-2297.

Klein, D. C., Moore, R. Y., & Reppert, S. M. (1992). *Superchiasmatic nucleus: The mind's clock.* New York: Oxford University Press.

Knowlton, B. J., Mangels, J. A., & Squire, L. R. (1996). A neostriatal habit learning system in humans. *Science, 273,* 1399-1402.

Koelle, G. B. (1965). Neuromuscular blocking agents. In L. S. Goodman (Ed.), *The pharmacological basis of therapeutics.* New York: Macmillan.

Kolb, B., Buhrmann, K., McDonald, R., & Sutherland, R. (1994). Dissociation of the medial prefrontal, posterior parietal, and posterior temporal cortex for spatial navigation and recognition memory in the rat. *Cerebral Cortex, 4,* 664-680.

Krantz, D. S., Kop, W. J., Santiago, H. T., & Gottdiener, J. S. (1996). Mental stress as a trigger of myocardial ischemia and infarction. *Cardiology Clinics, 14,* 271-287.

Kuch, K., & Cox, B. J. (1992). Symptoms of PTSC in 124 survivors of the holocaust. *American Journal of Psychiatry, 149,* 337-340.

Kuffler, S. (1953). Discharge patterns and functional organization of the mammalian retina. *Journal of Neurophysiology, 16,* 37-68.

Ladefoged, P. (1993). *A course in phonetics.* Fort Worth, TX: Harcourt Brace.

Ladefoged, P., & Broadbent, D. (1960). Perception of seequence in auditory events. *Quarterly Journal of Experimental Psychology, 12,* 162-170.

Laidlaw, J., & Richards, J. A. (Eds.). (1993). *A textbook of epilepsy.* Edinburgh, UK: Churchill-Livingstone.

Larson, E. B., Kukull, W. A., & Katzman, R. L. (1992). Cognitive impairment: Dementia and Alzheimer's disease. *Annual Review of Public Health, 13,* 431-449.

Lashley, K. S. (1941). Patterns of cerebral integration indicated by the scotomas of migraine. *Archives of Neurology and Psychiatry, 46,* 331-339.

LeDoux, J. E., & Hirst, W. (1986). *Mind and brain: Dialogs in cognitive neuroscience.* Cambridge, UK: Cambridge University Press.

Lema, M. J. (1995). Local anesthetic agents. In C. M. Smith & A. M. Reynard (Eds.), *Essentials of pharmacology.* Philadelphia, PA: W. B. Saunders.

Lendon, C. L., & Goate, A. M. (1995). Towards and understanding of the genetics of Alzheimer's disease. In F. E. Bloom & D. J. Kupfer (Eds.), *Psychopharmacology: The fourth generation of progress* (p. 1361-1369). New York: Raven.

Leor, J., & Kloner, R. A. (1995). The January 17, 1994 Los Angeles earthquake as a trigger for acute myocardial infarction (abstract). *Journal of the American College of Cardiology, 25 (Suppl. A),* 105A.

LeVay, S. (1991). *The sexual brain.* Cambridge: MIT Press.

LeVay, S., & Hamer, D. H. (1994). Evidence for a biological influence in male homosexuality. *Scientific American, 270,* 44-49.

Levinson, R. W. (1992). Autonomic nervous system differences among emotions. *Psychological Science, 3,* 23-27.

Levitan, I. B., & Kaczmarek, L. K. (1991). *The neuron: Cell and molecular biology.* New York: Oxford University Press.

Li, W., & Graur, D. (1991). *Fundamentals of molecular evolution.* Sunderland, MA: Sinauer Associates.

Linnaeus, C. (1735). *Systema Naturae.* Stockholm: Laurentii Salvii.

Livingstone, M. S., & Hubel, D. H. (1987a). Connections between layer 4B of area 17 and the thick cytochrome oxidase strips of area 18 in the squirrel monkey. *Journal of Neuroscience, 7,* 3371-3377.

Livingstone, M. S., & Hubel, D. H. (1987b). Psychophysical evidence for separate channels for the perception of form, color, movement, and depth. *Journal of Neuroscience, 7,* 3416-3468.

Livingstone, M. S., & Hubel, D. H. (1988). Segregation of form, color, movement, and depth: Anatomy, physiology, and perception. *Science, 240,* 740-749.

London, E. D., Grant, S. J., Morgan, M. J., & Zukin, S. R. (1996). Autism and pervasive developmental disorders. In B. S. Fogel & R. B. Schiffer (Eds.), *Neuropsychiatry* (p. 635-678). Baltimore, MD: Williams & Wilkins.

Lyell, C. (1830). *Principles of geology: Being an attempt to explain the former changes of the earth's surface by references to causes now in operation.* London: John Murray.

MacLean, P. D. (1949). Psychosomatic disease and the "visceral brain": Recent developments bearing on the Papez theory of emotion. *Psychosomatic Medicine, 11,* 338-353.

Madsen, P. L., & Vorstrup, S. (1991). Cerebral blood flow and metabolism during sleep. *Cerebrovascular and Brain Metabolism Reviews, 3,* 281-286.

Mahowald, M. W., & Schenck, C. H. (1992). Dissociated states of wakefulness and sleep. *Neurology, 42 (Suppl. 6),* 44-52.

Malthus, T. R. (1826). *An essay on the principle of population* (6th ed.). London: Johnson.

Manquet, P., Peters, J. M., Aerts, J., Delfiore, G., Degueldre, C., Luxen, A., & Franck, G. (1996). Functional neuroanatomy of human rapid-eye-movement sleep and dreaming. *Nature, 383,* 163-166.

Marr, D. (1982). *Vision.* New York: Freeman.

Marshall, J. F., Richardson, J. S., & Teitelbaum, P. (1974). Nigrostriatal bundle damage and the lateral hypothalamic syndrome. *Journal of Comparative and Physiological Psychology, 87,* 808-830.

Martin, N. A., Beatty, J., Johnson, R., Collaer, M. L., Vinuela, F., Becker, D. P., & Nuwer, M. R. (1993). Magnetoencephalographic localization of a language processing cortical area adjacent to a cerebral arteriovenous malformation: Case report. *Journal of Neurosurgery, 79,* 584-588.

Maunsell, J. H. R., & Newsome, W. T. (1987). Visual processing in monkey extrastriate cortex. *Annual Review of Neuroscience, 10,* 363-401.

Mayer, J. (1955). Regulation of energy intake and body weight: The glucostatic theory and the lipostatic hypothesis. *Annals of the New York Academy of Science, 63,* 15-43.

McCarthy, R. A., & Warrington, E. K. (1994). Disorders of semantic memory. *Philosophical Transactions of the Royal Society of London. Series B: Biological Sciences, 346,* 89-96.

McEwen, B. S., & Sapolsky, R. M. (1995). Stress and cognitive function. *Current Opinion in Neurobiology, 5,* 205-216.

McHenry, L. C. J. (1969). *Garrison's history of neurology.* Springfield, IL: Charles C Thomas.

Mednick, S. A., Machon, R. A., Huttunen, M. O., & Bonett, D. (1988). Adult schizophrenia following prenatal exposure to an influenza epidemic. *Archives of General Psychiatry, 45,* 189-192.

Meister, M. (1996). Multineuronal codes in retinal signaling. *Proceedings of the National Academy of Science of the USA, 93,* 609-614.

Meister, M., Lagnado, L., & Baylor, D. A. (1995). Concerted signaling by retinal ganglion cells. *Science, 270,* 1207-1210.

Mendelow, A. D. (1993). Raised intracranial pressure, cerebral oedema, hydrocephalus, and intracranial tumour. In J. Walton (Ed.), *Brain's diseases of the nervous system* (10th ed., p. 144-183). Oxford, UK: Oxford University Press.

Mendelson, W. B. (1993). Insomnia and related sleep disorders. *Psychiatric Clinics of North America, 16,* 841-851.

Merzenich, M. M., Nelson, R. J., Stryker, M. P., Cynader, M. S., Schoppmann, A., & Zook, J. M. (1984). Somatosensory cortical map changes following digit amputation in adult monkeys. *Journal of Comparative Neurology, 224,* 591-605.

Mestel, R. (1996). Putting prions to the test. *Science, 273,* 184-189.

Miller, N. E. (1985). The value of behavioral research on animals. *American Psychologist, 40,* 423-440.

Milner, B. (1970). Memory and the medial temporal regions of the brain. In K. H. Pribram & D. E. Broadbent (Eds.), *Biology of memory.* New York: Academic Press.

Milner, B. (1974). Hemispheric specialization: Scope and limitations. In F. O. Schmitt & F. G. Worden (Eds.), *The neurosciences: Third study program.* Cambridge: MIT Press.

Milner, B. (1976). Hemispheric asymmetry of the control of gesture sequences. In *Proceedings of the XXI international congres of psychology*. Paris.

Milner, B., Corkin, S., & Teuber, H. L. (1968). Further analysis of the hippocampal amnestic syndrome: 14-year follow up study of H. M. *Neuropsychologia, 6*, 215-234.

Montgomery, S. A. (1995). Selective serotonin reuptake inhibitors in the acute treatment of depression. In F. E. Bloom & D. J. Kupfer (Eds.), *Psychopharmacology: The fourth generation of progress* (p. 1043-1051). New York: Raven.

Moore-Ede, M. C., Sulzman, F. M., & Fuller, C. A. (1982). *The clocks that time us*. Cambridge, MA: Harvard University Press.

Morris, J. M. (1953). The syndrome of testicular feminization in male pseudohermaphrodites. *American Journal of Obstetric Gynecology, 65*, 1192-1211.

Morris, J. S., Frith, C. D., Perrett, D. I., Rowland, D., Young, A. W., Calder, A. J., & Dolan, R. J. (1996). A differential neural response in the human amygdala to fearful and happy facial expressions. *Nature, 383*, 812-814.

Morris, R. G. M., Garrud, P., Rowlins, J. P., & O'Keefe, J. (1982). Place navigation impaired in rats with hippocampal lesions. *Nature, 297*, 681-683.

Moruzzi, G., & Magoun, H. W. (1949). Brain stem reticular formation and activation of the EEG. *Electroencephalography and Clinical Neurophysiology, 1*, 455-473.

Mullitan, R. C. (1993). The basic science of gene therapy. *Science, 260*, 926-932.

Nass, R. D., & Gazzaniga, M. S. (1987). Cerebral lateralization and specialization in the human central nervous system. In J. R. Pattenheimer (Ed.), *Handbook of physiology, section 1: The nervous system, volume 5: Higher functions of the brain, part 2* (p. 701-761). Bethesda, MD: American Physiological Society.

Neidermeyer, E., & Lopes da Silva, E. (1982). *Electroencephalography: Basic principles, clinical applications, and related fields*. Baltimore, MD: Urban and Schwartzberg.

Newsome, W. T., Britten, K. H., & Movshon, J. A. (1989). Neural correlates of a perceptual decision. *Nature, 341*, 52-54.

Noback, C. R., Strominger, N. L., & Demarest, R. J. (1996). *The human nervous system: Structure and function* (5th ed.). Baltimore, MD: Williams & Wilkins.

Nunez, P. L. (1995). *Neocortical dynamics and human EEG rhythms*. New York: Oxford University Press.

Ojemann, G. A. (1983). Brain organization for language from the perspective of electrical stimulation mapping. *Behavioral and Brain Science, 6*, 189-230.

Oldendorf, W. H. (Ed.). (1980). *The quest for an image of the brain*. New York: Raven.

Oldendorf, W. H., & Oldendorf, W. H. J. (Eds.). (1988). *Basics of magnetic resonance imaging*. New York: Martinius Nijhoff.

Olds, J., & Milner, P. (1954). Positive reinforcement produced by electrical stimulation of septal area and other regions of the rat brain. *Journal of Comparative and Physiological Psychology, 47*, 419-427.

Olds, M. E., & Olds, J. (1963). Approach-avoidance analysis of rat diencephalon. *Journal of Comparative and Physiological Psychology, 120*, 259-295.

Olshausen, B. A., & Field, D. J. (1996). Emergence of simple-cell receptive field properties by learning a sparse code for natural images. *Nature, 381*, 607-609.

Olzak, L. A., & Thomas, J. P. (1986). Seeing spatial patterns. In K. R. Boff, L. Kaufman, & J. P. Thomas (Eds.), *Handbook of perception and human performance, volume 1: Sensory processes and perception* (p. 7.1-7.56). New York: John Wiley.

Oomura, Y. (1976). Significance of glucose, insulin and free fatty acid on the hypothalamic feeding and satiety neurons. In D. Novin, W. Wyrwicka, & G. Bray (Eds.), *Hunger: Basic mechanisms and clinical implications*. New York: Raven.

Ortells, M. O., & Lunt, G. G. (1995). Evolutionary history of the ligand-gated ion-channel superfamily of receptors. *Trends in Neuroscience, 18*, 121-127.

Palmer, S. E. (1999). *Vision science: Photons to phenomenology*. Cambridge: MIT Press.

Papez, J. W. (1937). A proposed mechanism of emotion. *Archives of Neurology and Psychiatry, 38*, 725-744.

Parent, A. (1996). *Carpenter's human neuroanatomy* (9th ed.). Baltimore, MD: Williams & Wilkins.

Parkes, C. M., Benjamin, B., & Fitzgerald, R. G. (1969). Broken heart: A statistical study of increased mortality among widowers. *British Medical Journal, 1*, 740-743.

Parkes, J. D. (1993). ABCs of sleep disorders: Daytime sleepiness. *British Medical Journal, 306*, 772-775.

Parkinson, J. (1817). *An essay on the shaking palsy*. London: Printed by Whittingham and Rowland for Sherwood, Neely, and Jones.

Pavlov, I. P. (1960). *Conditioned reflexes: An investigation of the physiological activity of the cerebral cortex* (W. H. Gantt, Trans.). New York: Liveright.

Peck, J. W., & Novin, D. (1971). Evidence that osmoreceptors mediating drinking in rabbits are in the lateral preoptic area. *Journal of Comparative and Physiological Psychology, 74*, 134-147.

Penfield, W., & Rasmussen, T. (1950). *The cerebral cortex of man: A clinical study of localization of function*. New York: Macmillan.

Penfield, W., & Roberts, L. (1966). *Speech and brain-mechanisms*. New York: Atheneum.

Penn, A. S., & Rowland, L. P. (1984). Myesthenia gravis. In L. P. Rowland (Ed.), *Merritts' textbook of neurology* (7th ed., p. 561-565). Philadelphia, PA: Lea and Febiger.

Peters, A., Palay, S. L., & Webster, H. (1991). *The fine structure of the nervous system: Neurons and their supporting cells* (3rd ed.). New York: Oxford University Press.

Petersen, S. E., Fox, P. T., Posner, M. I., Mintun, M., & Raichle, M. E. (1988). Positron emission tomographic studies of the cortical anatomy of single-word processing. *Nature, 331*, 585-589.

Pfungst, O. (1911). *Clever Hans (the horse of Mr. Von Osten): A contribution to experimental animal and human psychology*. New York: Holt, Rinehart, & Winston.

Phillips, A. G., & Fibiger, H. C. (1989). Neuroanatomical bases of intracranial self-stimulation: Untangling the Gordian knot. In J. M. Leibman & S. J. Cooper (Eds.), *The neuropharmacological basis of reward* (p. 66-105). Oxford UK: Clarendon.

Pinker, S. (1994). *The language instinct*. New York: William Morrow.

Plata-Salaman, C. R., & Scott, T. R. (1992). Taste neurons in the cortex of the alert cynomolgus monkey. *Brain Research Bulletin, 28*, 333-336.

Posner, M. I., & Raichle, M. E. (1994). *Images of mind*. New York: Scientific American Library.

Premack, D. (1992). Language in chimpanzee? *Science, 172*, 808-822.

Prusiner, S. B. (1995). The prion diseases. *Scientific American, 272*, 48-57.

Rakic, P. (1995). A small step for the cell, a giant leap for mankind: A hypothesis of neocortical expansion during evolution. *Trends in Neurosciences, 9*, 383-388.

Ramon y Cajal, S. (1909). *Histologie du systeme nerveux de l'homme et des vertebres* (L. Azoulay, Trans.). Paris: A. Maloine.

Rasmussen, T., & Milner, B. (1977). The role of early left brain damage in determining the lateralization of cerebral speech functions. In S. Dimond & D. Blizard (Eds.), *Evolution and lateralization in the brain* (Vol. 299, p. 355-369). New York: New York Academy of Science.

Rauschecker, J. P., Tian, B., & Hauser, M. (1995). Processing of complex sounds in the macaque nonprimary auditory cortex. *Science, 268*, 111-114.

Ray, J. (1660). *Catalogus Plantarum circa Cantabrium Nascentium*. Cambridge, UK: J. Field.

Reinisch, J. M. (1981). Prenatal exposure to synthetic progestin increases potential for aggression in humans. *Science, 211*, 1171-1173.

Reis, D. J., & LeDoux, J. E. (1987). Some central neural mechanisms governing resting and behaviorally coupled control of blood pressure. *Circulation, 76(1, Pt. 2)*, I2-9.

Rescorla, R. A. (1988). Behavioral studies of Pavlovian conditioning. *Annual Review of Neuroscience, 11*, 329-352.

Resnick, S. M. (1982). *Psychological functioning in individuals with congenital adrenal hyperplasia: Early hormonal influences on cognition and personality*. Unpublished doctoral dissertation, University of Minnesota.

Resnick, S. M., Berebaum, S. A., & Gottesman, I. I. (1986). Early hormonal influences on cognitive functioning in congenital adrenal hyperplasia. *Developmental Psychology, 22*, 191-198.

Richter, C. P. (1965). *Biologicval clocks in medicine and psychiatry*. Springfield, IL: Charles C Thomas.

Rinn, W. E. (1984). The neuropsychology of facial expression: A review of the neurological and psychological mechanisms for producing facial expressions. *Psychological Bulletin, 95*, 52-77.

Risner, M. E., & Jones, B. E. (1980). Intravenous self-administration of cocaine and norcocaine by dogs. *Psychopharmacology, 71*, 83-89.

Rodieck, R. W. (1998). *The first steps in seeing*. Sunderland, MA: Sinauer Associates.

Rohner-Jeanrenaud, F., & Jenrenaud, B. (1996). Obesity leptin, and the brain. *Science, 334*, 324-325.

Roland, L. P. (1984). *Merritt's textbook of neurology* (7th ed.). Philadelphia, PA: Lea and Febiger.

Roland, P. E. (1985). Cortical organization of voluntary behavior in man. *Human Neurobiology, 4*, 144-167.

Rolls, B. J., Jones, B. P., & Fallows, D. J. (1972). A comparison of the motivational properties of thirst induced by intracranial angiotensin and water deprivation. *Physiology and Behavior, 9*, 777-782.

Rolls, B. J., & Rolls, E. T. (1982). *Thirst*. Cambridge, UK: Cambridge University Press.

Roper, S. D. (1992). The microphysiology of peripheral taste organs. *Journal of Neuroscience, 12*, 1127-1134.

Roth, B. L., & Meltzer, H. Y. (1995). The role of serotonin in schizophrenia. In F. E. Bloom & D. J. Kupfer (Eds.), *Psychopharmacology: The fourth generation of progress* (p. 1215-1227). New York: Raven.

Roush, W. (1997). New knockout mice point to molecular basis of memory. *Science, 275*, 32-33.

Russek, M. (1981). Current status of the hepatostatic theory of food intake control. *Appetite, 2*, 137-143.

Sack, W. H., Clarke, G., & Him, C. (1993). A 6-year follow-up study of cambodian refugee adolescents traumatized as children. *Journal of the American Academy of Child and Adolescent Psychiatry, 32*, 431-437.

Salzman, C. D., Britten, K. H., & Newsome, W. T. (1990). Cortical microstimulation influences perceptual judgments of motion direction. *Nature, 346*, 174-177.

Sanes, J. N., Donoghue, J. P., Thangaraj, V., Edelman, R. R., & Warach, S. (1995). Shared neural substrates controlling hand movements in human motor cortex. *Science, 268*, 1775-1777.

Sapolsky, R. M. (1996). Why stress is bad for your brain. *Science, 273*, 749-750.

Sato, M. (1986). Acute excerbation of methamphetamine psychosis and lasting dopaminergic supersensitivity: A clinical survey. *Psychopharmacology Bulletin, 22*, 751-756.

Saver, J. L., Salloway, S. P., Devinsky, O., & Bear, D. M. (1996). Neuropsychiatry of aggression. In B. S. Fogel & R. B. Schiffer (Eds.), *Neuropsychiatry* (p. 423-548). Baltimore, MD: Williams & Wilkins.

Scheibel, A. B. (1988). In memoriam: Alf Brodal, M.D. *Journal of Comparative Neurology, 273*, 1-2.

Schiller, P. H., & Logothetis, N. K. (1990). The color-opponent and broadband channels of the primate visual system. *Trends in Neuroscience, 13*, 392-398.

Schneeweis, D. M., & Schnapf, J. L. (1995). Photovoltage of rods and cones in the macaque retina. *Science, 268*, 1053-1056.

Schwartz, G. E. (1986). Emotion and psychophysiological organization: A systems approach. In M. G. H. Coles, E. Donchin, & S. W. Porges (Eds.), *Psychophysiology: Systems, processes, and applications* (p. 354-377). New York: Guilford.

Schwartz, S. H. (1994). *Visual preception: A clinical orientation*. Norwalk, CT: Appleton and Lange.

Selkoe, D. J. (1997). Alzheimer's disease: Genotypes, phenotype, and treatments. *Science, 275*, 630-631.

Shallice, T. (1988). *From neuropsychology to mental structure*. Cambridge, UK: Cambridge University Press.

Shaver, P., Schwartz, J., Kirson, D., & O'Connor, C. (1987). Emotion knowledge: Further exploration of a prototype approach. *Journal of Personality and Social Psychology, 52*, 1061-1086.

Sheline, Y. I., Wang, P. W., Gado, M. H., Csernansky, J. G., & Vannier, M. W. (1996). Hippocampal strophy in recurrent major depression. *Proceedings of the National Academy of Sciences of the USA, 93*, 3908-3913.

Shelton, R., & Weinberger, D. R. (1987). Brain morphology in schizophrenia. In H. Meltzer, J. C. W. Bunney, K. David, R. Schuster, R. Shader, & G. Simpson (Eds.), *Psychopharmacology: The third generation of progress* (p. 772-781). New York: Raven.

Shepherd, G. H., & Greer, C. A. (1994). Olfactory bulb. In G. M. Shepherd (Ed.), *The synaptic organization of the brain* (3rd ed.). New York: Oxford University Press.

Shepherd, G. M. (Ed.). (1990). *The synaptic organization of the brain* (3rd ed.). New York: Oxford University Press.

Shepherd, G. M. (Ed.). (1991). *The foundations of the Neuron Doctrine*. New York: Oxford University Press.

Sheridan, M. K., Radlinski, S. S., & Kennedy, M. D. (1990). Developmental outcome in 49,xxxxy klinefelter syndrome. *Developmental Medicine and Child Neurology, 32*, 528-546.

Sherrington, C. S. (Ed.). (1906). *The integrative action of the nervous system*. New Haven, CT: Yale University Press.

Shizgaal, P., & Murray, B. (1989). Neuronal basis of intracranial self-stimulation. In J. M. Leibman & S. J. Cooper (Eds.), *The neuropharmacological basis of reward* (p. 106-163). Oxford, UK: Clarendon.

Silva, A. J., Paylor, R., Wehner, J. M., & Tonegawa, S. (1992). Impaired spatial learning in a-calcium-calmodulin kinase mutant mice. *Science, 257*, 206-211.

Silva, A. J., Stevens, C. E., Tonegawa, S., & Wang, Y. (1992). Deficient hippocampal long-term potentiation in a-calcium-calmodulin kinase mutant mice. *Science, 257*, 201-205.

Simon, M. I., Strathmann, M. P., & Gautam, N. (1991). Diversity of G proteins in signal transduction. *Science, 252*, 802-808.

Simpson, J. B., & Routtenberg, A. (1973). Subfornical organ: Site of drinking elicitation by angiotensin II. *Science, 105*, 1772-1775.

Snyder, S. H. (1980). *Biological aspects of mental disorder*. New York: Oxford University Press.

Snyder, S. H., & Dawson, T. M. (1995). Nitric oxide and related substances as neural messengers. In F. E. Bloom & D. J. Kupfer (Eds.), *Psychopharmacology: The fourth generation of progress* (p. 609-618). New York: Raven.

Society for Neuroscience. (1993). *Guidelines for the use of animals in neuroscience research*. Washington, DC: Society for Neuroscience.

Southwick, S. M., Bremner, D., Krystal, J. H., & Charney, D. S. (1994). Psychobiologic research in post-traumatic stress disorder. *Psychiatric Clinics of North America, 17*, 251-264.

Sperry, R. W. (1974). Lateral specialization in the surgically separated hemispheres. In F. O. Schmitt & F. G. Worden (Eds.), *The neurosciences: Third study program* (p. 5-20). Cambridge: MIT Press.

Springer, S. P., & Deutsch, G. (1998). *Left brain, right brain* (5th ed.). New York: Freeman.

Squire, L. R. (1987). *Memory and brain*. New York: Oxford University Press.

Squire, L. R. (1992). Memory and the hippocampus: A synthesis from findings with rats, monkeys, and humans. *Psychological Review, 99*, 195-231.

Squire, L. R. (1994). Declarative and nondeclarative memory: Multiple brain systems supporting learning and memory. In D. L. Schachter & E. Tulving (Eds.), *Memory systems 1994* (p. 203-231). Cambridge: MIT Press.

Squire, L. R., & Kandel, E. R. (1999). *Memory: From mind to molecules*. New York: Scientific American Library.

Stanley, B. G., & Gillard, E. R. (1994). Hypothalamic neuropeptide Y and the regulation of eating behavior and body weight. *Current Directions in Psychological Science, 3*, 9-15.

Starkman, M. N., Gebarski, S. S., Berent, S., & Schteingart, D. E. (1992). Hippocampal formation volume, memory dysfunction, and cortisol levels in patients with Cushing's syndrome. *Biological Psychiatry, 32*, 756-765.

Stein-Behrens, B., Mattson, M. P., Chang, I., Yeh, M., & Sapolsky, R. (1994). Stress exacerbates neuron loss and cytoskeletal pathology in the hippocampus. *Journal of Neuroscience, 14*, 5373-5380.

Stellar, J. R., Kelley, A. E., & Corbett, D. (1983). Effects of peripheral and central dopamine blockage on lateral hypothalamic self-stimulation: Evidence for both reward and motor deficits. *Pharmacology, Biochemistry, and Behavior, 18*, 433-442.

Steriade, M. (1992). Basic mechanisms of sleep generation. *Neurology, 42 (Suppl. 6)*, 9-18.

Steriade, M. (1996). Arousal: Revisiting the reticular activating system. *Science, 271*, 225-226.

Stern, M. B. (1991). Head trauma as a risk factor for Parkinson's disease. *Movement Disorders, 6*, 95-97.

Stern, R. A., Perkins, D. O., & Evans, D. L. (1995). Neuropsychiatric manifestations of HIV-1 infection and AIDS. In F. Bloom & D. Kupfer (Eds.), *Psychopharmacology: The fourth generation of progress* (p. 1545-1558). New York: Raven.

Stevens, C. F. (1996). Spatial learning and memory: The beginning of a dream. *Cell, 87*, 1147-1148.

Stuss, D. T., & Benson, D. F. (1983). Emotional concomitants of psychosurgery. In K. M. Heilman & P. Satz (Eds.), *Neuropsychology of human emotion*. New York: Guilford.

Sutker, P. B., Winstead, D. K., & Galina, Z. H. (1991). Cognitive deficits and psychophthology among former prisoners of war and combat veterans of the Korean conflict. *American Journal of Psychiatry, 148*, 67-72.

Taylor, J. (1958). *Selected writings of John Hughlings Jackson*. New York: Basic Books.

Taylor, P., & Brown, J. H. (1994). Acetylcholine. In G. J. Siegel, B. W. Agranoff, R. W. Albers, & P. B. Moninoff (Eds.), *Basic neurochemistry: Molecular, cellular, and medical aspects* (5th ed., p. 231-260). New York: Raven.

Teitelbaum, P., & Epstein, A. N. (1962). The lateral hypothalamic syndrome: Recovery of feeding and drinking after lateral hypothalamic lesions. *Psychological Review, 69*, 74-90.

Teuber, H. L. (1955). Physiological psychology. *Annual Review of Psychology, 6*, 267-296.

Tomb, D. A. (1994). The phenomenology of post-traumatic stress disorder. *Psychiatric Clinics of North America, 17*, 237-250.

Toni, N., Buchs, P. A., Nikonenko, I., Bron, C. R., & Muller, D. (1999). LPT promotes formation of multiple spine synapses between a single axon terminal and a dendrite. *Nature, 402*, 421-425.

Travis, J. (1992). Scoring a technical knockout in mice. *Science, 256*, 1392-1394.

Trichopoulos, D., Katsouyanni, K., & Zavitsanos, X. (1983). Psychological stress and fatal heart attack: The Athens (1981) earthquake natural experiment. *Lancet, 1(8322)*, 441-443.

Trimble, M. R., Ring, H. A., & Schmitz, B. (1995). Neuropsychiatric aspects of epilepsy. In F. E. Bloom & D. J. Kupfer (Eds.), *Psychopharmacology: The fourth generation of progress* (p. 771-803). New York: Raven.

Tsagarakis, S., & Grossman, A. (1995). Corticotropin-releasing hormone: Interactions with the immune system. *Neuroimmunomodulation, 1,* 329-334.

Tsien, J. Z., Chen, D. F., Gerber, D., Tom, C., H., M. E., Anderson, D. J., Mayford, M., Kandel, E. R., & Tonegawa, S. (1996). Subregion- and cell type-restricted gene knockout in mouse brain. *Cell, 877,* 1317-1326.

Tsien, J. Z., Huerta, P. T., & Tonegawa, S. (1996). The essential role of hippocampal CA1 NMDA receptor-dependent synaptic plasticity in spatial memory. *Cell, 877,* 1327-1336.

Ur, E., & Grossman, A. (1994). Corticotropin releasing hormone in health and disease: An update. *Acta Endocrinologica, 127,* 193-199.

Van De Graaff, K. M., & Fox, S. I. (1992). *Concepts of human anatomy and physiology.* Dubuque, IA: William C. Brown.

Van Hoesen, G. W., Morecraft, R. J., & Semendeferi, K. (1996). Functional neuroanatomy of the limbic system and prefrontal cortex. In B. S. Fogel & R. B. Schiffer (Eds.), *Neuropsychiatry* (p. 113-143). Baltimore, MD: Williams & Wilkins.

Vijande, M., Lopez-Sela, P., & Brime, J. I. (1990). Insulin stimulation of water intake in humans. *Appetite, 15,* 81-87.

Vries, M. J. de, Cardozo, B. N., Want, J. van der, Wolf, A. de, & Meijer, J. H. (1993). Glutamate immunoreactivity in terminals of the retinohypothalamic tract of the brown Norwegian rat. *Brain Research, 612,* 231-237.

Walker, E., & Lewine, R. J. (1990). Prediction of adult onset schizophrenia from childhood nome movies of the patients. *American Journal of Psychiatry, 147,* 1052-1056.

Walker, E. F., Savoie, T., & Davis, D. (1994). Neuromotor precursors of schizophrenia. *Schizophrenia Bulletin, 20,* 441-451.

Wandell, B. (1995). *Foundations of vision.* Sunderland, MA: Sinauer.

Warrington, E. K., & McCarthy, R. A. (1987). Categories of knowledge. further fractionations and an attempted integration. *Brain, 110,* 1273-1296.

Watson, S., & Girdlestone, D. (1995). TiPS on nomenclature. *Trends in Pharmacological Sciences, 6,* 15-16.

Weinberger, D. (1995). Neurodevelopmental perspectives on schizophrenia. In F. E. Bloom & D. J. Kupfer (Eds.), *Psychopharmacology: The fourth generation of progress* (p. 1171-1183). New York: Raven.

Weiner, N., & Molinoff, P. B. (1994). Catecholamines. In G. J. Siegel, B. W. Agranoff, R. W. Albers, & P. B. Moninoff (Eds.), *Basic neurochemistry: Molecular, cellular, and medical aspects* (5th ed., p. 261-281). New York: Raven.

Weiss, L., & Greep, G. (1977). *Histology.* New York: McGraw-Hill.

Wells, C. E., & Whitehouse, P. J. (1996). Cortical dementia. In B. S. Fogel & R. B. Schiffer (Eds.), *Neuropsychiatry* (p. 871-893). Baltimore, MD: Williams & Wilkins.

Wernicke, C. (1874). *Der aphasische symptomenkomplex.* Bresau: Cohn and Weigart.

Wiles, C. M. (1993). Spirochaetal diseases, some other specific infections and intoxications, and their neurological complications. In J. Walton (Ed.), *Brain's diseases of the nervous system* (p. 289-316). Oxford, UK: Oxford University Press.

Williams, P. L., & Warwick, R. (1980). *Gray's anatomy* (36th British ed.). Philadelphia, PA: W. B. Saunders.

Wise, R. A., & Bozarth, M. A. (1987). A psychomotor stimulant theory of addiction. *Psychological Review, 94,* 469-492.

Wolgin, D. L., & Teitelbaum, P. (1978). Role of activation and sensory stimuli in recovery from lateral hypothalamic damage in the cat. *Journal of Comparative and Physiological Psychology, 92,* 474-500.

Wong, D. E., Wagner, H. N. J., & Tune, L. E. (1986). Positron emission tomography reveals elevated D2 dopamine receptors in drug-naive schizophrenics. *Science, 234,* 1558-1563.

Wong, G. T., Gannon, K. S., & Margolskee, R. F. (1996). Transduction of bitter and sweet taste by gustducin. *Nature, 381,* 796-800.

Woods, A. J., & Stock, M. J. (1996). Leptin activation in hypothalamus. *Nature, 381,* 745.

Wooley, D. W., & Shaw, E. (1954). A biochemical and pharmacological suggestion about certain mental disorders. *Proceedings of the National Academy of Science of the USA, 40,* 228-231.

Xerri, C., Merzenich, M. M., Jenkins, W., & Santucci, S. (1999). Representational plasticity in cortical area 3b paralleling tactual-motor skill acquisition in adult monkeys. *Cerebral Cortex, 9,* 264-276.

Young, D. (1992). *The discovery of evolution.* London: Cambridge University Press.

Young, J. Z. (1936). The giant nerve fibres and epistellar body of cephalopods. *Quarterly Journal of Microscopical Science, 78,* 367-386.

Young, J. Z. (1987). *Philosophy and the brain.* Oxford, UK: Oxford University Press.

Zatorre, R. J., Evans, A. C., Meyer, E., & Gjedde, A. (1992). Lateralization of phonetic and pitch discrimination in speech processing. *Science, 256,* 846-849.

Zecevic, D. (1996). Multiple spike-initiation zones in single neurons revealed by voltage-sensitive dyes. *Nature, 381,* 322-325.

Zeffiro, T. A. (1990). Motor cortex. In G. Paxinos (Ed.), *The human nervous system* (p. 803-810). San Diego, CA: Academic Press.

Zhou, J. N., Hofman, M. A., Gooren, L. J. G., & Swaab, D. F. (1995). A sex difference in the human brain and its relation to transsexuality. *Nature, 378,* 68-70.

Zito, K. A., Vickers, G., & Roberts, D. S. C. (1985). Disruption of cocaine and heroin self-administration following kainic acid lesions of the nucleus accumbens. *Pharmacology, Biochemistry, and Behavior, 23,* 1029-1036.

Zola-Morgan, S., Squire, L. R., & Amaral, D. G. (1986). Human amnesia and the medial temporal regions: Enduring memory impairment following a bilateral lesion limited to field CA1 of the hippocampus. *Journal of Neuroscience, 6,* 2950-2967.

Name Index

Subject Index

About the Author

Jackson Beatty, Ph.D., is Professor of Psychology and Neuroscience at UCLA. He is the author of nearly one hundred scientific publications, including ten articles in the prestigious interdisciplinary journal *Science.* His current research in neuroinformatics seeks a greater understanding of the neural organization of the cerebral cortex that underlies human cognition.

In addition to his experience as a research scientist, he is Vice Chair of the UCLA Department of Psychology with responsibilities for undergraduate education, and Director of the Psychology Honors Program. He regularly teaches Introduction to Psychobiology, which is a general education course introducing human brain research to 300-plus undergraduate students from all of the university's diverse majors. He also teaches an upper-division course called Cortex and Cognition, which explores the most recent research in the rapidly developing field of cognitive neuroscience.